# California Topics

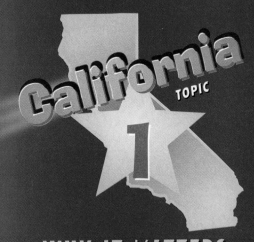

## WHY IT MATTERS

**The Ancient Bristlecone Pine Forest in Inyo National Park has the oldest living trees in the world.**

## SCIENCE WORDS

**rain shadow** an area that gets little precipitation because storms are blocked by a mountain range

**precipitation** any form of water particles that falls from the atmosphere and reaches the ground

**tree line** the line on a mountain that trees will not grow above

**conifer** any of a group of gymnosperms that produce seeds in cones and have needlelike leaves

**tissue** a group of similar cells that work together at the same job

**dendrochronology** dating past events or climatic changes by comparing them to growth rings on trees

# The Ancient Bristlecone Pine Forest

**A** 20-square-kilometer (7.7-square-mile) area near Bishop, California, has been set aside as the White Mountain Scientific Area. It is the home of bristlecone pine trees that are more than 4,000 years old. The trees have been studied by *biologists, botanists,* and *ecologists.* Biologists study living things. Botanists study plants. Ecologists study the environment.

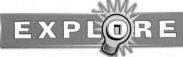

**EXPLORE**

**HYPOTHESIZE How can scientists tell how old a tree is? What can studying trees tell us about history? Write a hypothesis in your *Science Journal.* How can you test your ideas?**

# What Is the Weather in the White Mountains?

The Ancient Bristlecone Pine Forest is part of the Inyo National Forest in the White Mountains, east of the Sierra Nevada mountain range. The trees live at 2,700 to 3,400 meters (9,000 to 11,000 feet) above sea level. The White Mountains are some of the tallest mountains in North America.

The White Mountains are in the **rain shadow** of the Sierra Nevada. They are located a few miles west, across the deep Owens Valley. Rain shadow areas get little **precipitation** (pri sip'i tā'shən) because storms that could bring rain, snow, sleet, or hail are blocked by a mountain range.

As Pacific storms move eastward, most of the precipitation falls on the Sierra Nevada. This leaves the White Mountains with strong, dry winds and less than 30 centimeters (12 inches) of precipitation a year. Most of it arrives as snow in winter. In the summer the White Mountains have a low amount of moisture in the air.

Weather in the White Mountains is cold and dry. At the base of the mountains, the temperature can range from 3°C to 21°C (37°F to 70°F). Where the bristlecone pines grow, the temperature ranges from –32°C to 2°C (–26°F to 36°F). Because there is little snow and the temperatures are cold, the environment near the **tree line** is very harsh. The tree line is the line on a mountain that trees will not grow above.

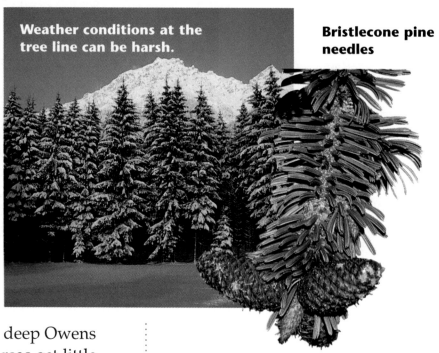

Weather conditions at the tree line can be harsh.

**Bristlecone pine needles**

## The Bristlecone Pine Tree

Bristlecone pine trees live under these very extreme conditions. The strong winds can blow the small amount of snow that falls down the mountain. This leaves little water for the pine trees when the snow melts in the spring.

The soil in which the bristlecone pines grow is very poor. It holds little water, and much of the soil is swept away by the wind.

The bristlecone pine is a **conifer**. Conifers are any of a group of gymnosperms that produce seeds in cones and have needlelike leaves. Wind can take moisture away from trees through their leaves. The needles of conifers have a waxlike coating that keeps the wind from taking moisture.

# How Old Is the Oldest Tree?

The oldest living tree in the world grows in the Ancient Bristlecone Pine Forest at 3,000 meters (10,000 feet) above sea level. It is called Methuselah. In 1957 Methuselah was found to be 4,723 years old. How old is it today?

This tree has lived a millennium longer than any other tree. A millennium is 1,000 years. When Methuselah was a seedling, the ancient pyramids in Egypt were being built. You can walk along the Methuselah Trail in the Inyo National Park, but you may not see Methuselah. No one knows which tree is Methuselah except for park rangers. They are keeping its identity a secret to protect it.

There are many bristlecone pine trees that are between 3,000 and 4,000 years old. Even though they are the oldest living trees, they are not the biggest. The trees grow very slowly, adding only $\frac{1}{100}$ of an inch to the diameter of their trunks every year. They grow slowly to conserve energy. Conserving energy helps them to survive the harsh winters.

## Dating Bristlecone Pine Trees

Since bristlecone pine trees grow slowly, they develop thick bark. This helps to protect them from the cold winds and temperatures on the mountains. The trees also have an amazing

Many bristlecone pine trees are over 3,000 years old.

Scientists count the growth rings of a tree to tell its age.

ability to let their own **tissue** die back when it is damaged by fire or drought. Tissue is a group of similar cells that work together at the same job. When this happens the tree keeps a small portion of its bark alive and keeps growing.

Many people study the bristlecone pine trees. **Dendrochronology** (den′drō krə nol′ə jē) is dating past events or climatic changes by comparing them to growth rings on trees. Trees add one growth ring to their trunks every year. You can tell how old a tree is by counting its growth rings. By studying the rings, dendrochronologists can tell if a tree went through floods, droughts, or fires and when they occurred. This helps us to know what the weather and climate was like thousands of years ago.

# REVIEW

**Choose the letter of the best answer. Mark your answer on a separate sheet of paper.**

1. What do botanists study?
   - **A** climates
   - **B** plants
   - **C** animals
   - **D** environments

2. How old is the oldest living tree?
   - **A** close to 10,000 years
   - **B** approximately 3,500 years
   - **C** over 5,000 years
   - **D** over 4,700 years

3. Which part of the tree has a wax-like coating that helps keep the wind from taking moisture?
   - **A** the trunk
   - **B** the roots
   - **C** the needles
   - **D** the bark

4. One of the ways the bristlecone pine tree has adapted to harsh weather is
   - **A** letting some of its tissue die
   - **B** growing quickly
   - **C** using a lot of energy
   - **D** having thin bark

5. How old are the trees in the Ancient Bristlecone Pine Forest?
   - **A** 500 to 1,000 years
   - **B** 3,500 to 5,500 years
   - **C** 2,000 to 2,500 years
   - **D** 3,000 to 4,000 years

6. Bristlecone pine trees are
   - **A** angiosperms
   - **B** ferns
   - **C** deciduous
   - **D** conifers

7. Look at the tree rings on page CA26. Which year was there the least amount of precipitation?
   - **A** 1954
   - **B** 1955
   - **C** 1956
   - **D** 1957

8. According to the information on page CA26, what probably happened in 1956?
   - **A** a flood
   - **B** a drought
   - **C** a tornado
   - **D** a fire

9. Areas in the rain shadow of a mountain range get little
   - **A** fire
   - **B** rain
   - **C** wind
   - **D** light

**Write the answer to the question below on your piece of paper.**

10. Explain how a dendrochronologist knows when a tree has lived through fire, flood, or drought.

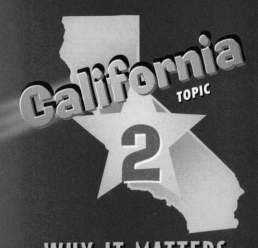

## California TOPIC 2

## WHY IT MATTERS

Many of the weather patterns in California are controlled by the "rain shadow effect."

### SCIENCE WORDS

**weather** what the lower atmosphere is like at any given place and time

**climate** the average weather pattern of a region

**condensation** the changing of a gas into a liquid

**humidity** the amount of water vapor in the air

**evaporation** the changing from a liquid into a gas

**rain shadow effect** the lack of rain on the leeward side of a mountain

# California's Climate

**W**here do you live in California? What is it like where you live? Is it windy, rainy, dry, hot, or cold? Do you think other regions of the state are the same?

California is a very large state. It has mountains, a coastline, and even deserts. Conditions can be very different from place to place, but they can form for the same reasons. Let's explore what these are!

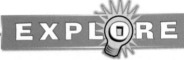

## EXPLORE

**HYPOTHESIZE** Which city in California receives the most rainfall? Which city receives the most snow? Write a hypothesis in your *Science Journal.* How would you test your ideas?

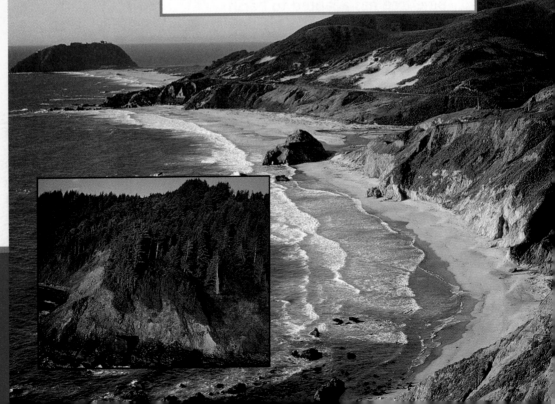

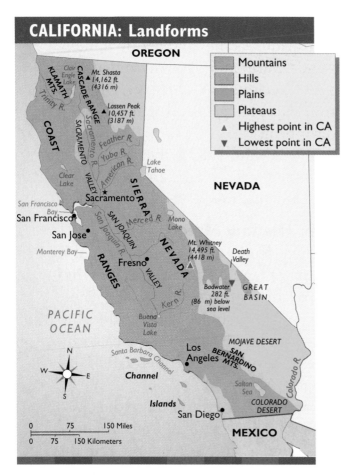

## CALIFORNIA: Landforms

OREGON

| | |
|---|---|
| | Mountains |
| | Hills |
| | Plains |
| | Plateaus |
| ▲ | Highest point in CA |
| ▼ | Lowest point in CA |

KLAMATH MTS.
Clair Engle Lake
Trinity R.
CASCADE RANGE
Mt. Shasta ▲ 14,162 ft. (4316 m)
Lassen Peak ▲ 10,457 ft. (3187 m)
COAST
SACRAMENTO
Sacramento R.
Feather R.
Yuba R.
American R.
Clear Lake
Lake Tahoe
NEVADA
San Francisco Bay
San Francisco
Sacramento ★
SIERRA
Merced R.
Mono Lake
San Jose
SAN JOAQUIN
San Joaquin R.
NEVADA
Mt. Whitney 14,495 ft. (4418 m)
Death Valley
Monterey Bay
Fresno
VALLEY
RANGES
Kern R.
Badwater ▼ 282 ft. (86 m) below sea level
GREAT BASIN
PACIFIC OCEAN
Buena Vista Lake
Los Angeles
SAN BERNARDINO MTS.
MOJAVE DESERT
Santa Barbara Channel
Channel
Salton Sea
Colorado R.
COLORADO DESERT
Islands
San Diego
N W E S
0   75   150 Miles
0   75   150 Kilometers
MEXICO

**There are several mountain ranges in California.**

# What Is the Climate of California?

**Weather** (we<u>th</u>′ər) is what the lower atmosphere is like at any given place and time. **Climate** (klī′mit) is the average weather pattern of a region. The climate in most areas of California is hot, dry summers and cool, wet winters. Northern California tends to have colder winters and milder summers than southern California.

Most of California has two main seasons—rainy and dry. Some areas, like the Mojave Desert, are dry year round. The rainy season in northern California lasts from October to April. In the south it lasts from November to March.

The northern coast of California has the rainiest season. Areas near Eureka, California, can receive more than 200 centimeters (79 inches) of rain a year.

## Winds in California

The western boundary of California borders the Pacific Ocean. Winds called *westerlies* blow off the ocean onto California. They blow from west to east across much of the United States and southern Canada.

These winds bring warm, moist air to the west coast. Moisture in these winds can fall as rain, snow, or other precipitation. Along the coastline in California, it is usually in the form of rain.

As you move eastward, the amount of precipitation decreases. This is especially true if you cross a mountain range. How many California mountain ranges can you find on the map on the left?

**Winds called *westerlies* blow from west to east across California.**

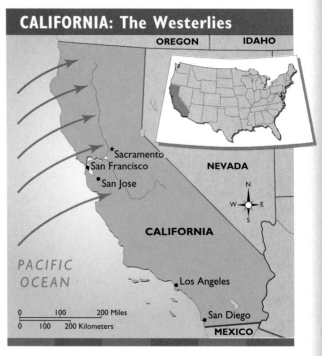

## CALIFORNIA: The Westerlies

OREGON    IDAHO

Sacramento ★
San Francisco
San Jose
NEVADA
N W E S
CALIFORNIA
PACIFIC OCEAN
Los Angeles
San Diego
0   100   200 Miles
0   100   200 Kilometers
MEXICO

# How Do Mountains Alter Rain Patterns?

A mountain has a *windward* side. This is the side that is exposed to wind. Since westerlies blow from west to east, the western side of a California mountain is the windward side.

The other side of a mountain is called the *leeward* side. This side is not exposed to wind. The eastern side of a California mountain is the leeward side.

The windward sides of mountains are often the wettest regions in the world. The leeward sides are typically dry. Why do you think this is true?

When warm, moist winds reach the Cascade Mountains, they blow up the windward side. The air cools as it rises to higher altitudes.

When the air cools enough, the water in the air **condenses**. It changes from a gas into a liquid. When enough water condenses, it falls as precipitation onto the windward side of the Cascades.

When the winds reach the top of the Cascades, they have lost a large amount of their **humidity**, or mois-

ture. These winds blow down the leeward side. As they move down, the winds warm and dry. Any remaining water in clouds **evaporates**, changes from liquid to gas, and rain clouds disappear.

The leeward side of the Cascades is usually dry. This lack of rain is called the **rain shadow effect**.

## Rain Shadow Effect

There seems to be a "shadow," or a region of land, behind the rainy windward side that receives no rain. These dry areas can stretch for hundreds of miles! Valleys located on the eastern sides of larger ranges often fall in the ranges' "shadows."

Rain shadow effects cause the climates in many parts of California. Western regions receive more rain than eastern regions. Leeward sides of mountains and ranges are often dry.

The rain shadow effect even played a role in developing the Mojave Desert. The warm, dry air traveling down the leeward side of the mountains to the east of the desert continues to support desertlike conditions there.

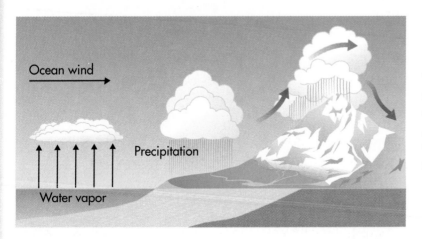

Ocean wind

Precipitation

Water vapor

**Winds are cooled as they move up the windward side of a mountain. Air is warmed and dried as it moves down the leeward side of a mountain.**

# REVIEW

**Choose the letter of the best answer. Mark your answer on a separate sheet of paper.**

1. Which is *not* a fact about California weather?

   A California has many climates.

   B Most areas have a rainy season and a dry season.

   C There are some common weather conditions in California.

   D All areas of California receive a great deal of rain.

2. In this topic the word *windward* is defined as

   A a type of climate

   B the side of a mountain that the wind blows on

   C the dry side of a mountain

   D the eastern side of a mountain

3. According to this topic, westerlies

   A blow onto California from the Pacific Ocean

   B blow from east to west

   C carry cold, dry air up the windward sides of mountains

   D are the sides of mountains that the winds blow on

4. The rainy season

   A is longer in southern California

   B is longest in the Mojave Desert

   C spans from October to April in northern California

   D spans from November to March in all of California

5. Look at the graphs on page CA27. Which month is the coolest in both cities?

   A November

   B May

   C January

   D March

6. Using the graphs on page CA27, the temperature in August is

   A the same in both cities

   B less than 10 degrees warmer in San Francisco than Los Angeles

   C less than 10 degrees warmer in Los Angeles than San Francisco

   D more than 10 degrees warmer in Los Angeles

7. According to the graphs on page CA27, the temperature range in Los Angeles is

   A 25°F

   B 19°F

   C 14°F

   D 10°F

8. According to the graphs on page CA27 and the maps found in this lesson, which is true?

   A Los Angeles has warmer seasons because it is farther south.

   B San Francisco has warmer seasons because it is farther south.

   C Los Angeles and San Francisco share the same temperatures because they are on the coast.

   D San Francisco has cooler temperatures because it is shadowed by a mountain range.

**Write the answer to the question below on your piece of paper.**

9. Describe the rain shadow effect of mountain ranges.

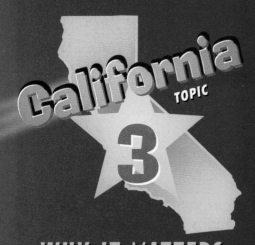

## WHY IT MATTERS

**Chuck Yeager's flight from Edwards Air Force Base led the way to supersonic flight and space exploration.**

## SCIENCE WORDS

**supersonic** travel above the speed of sound

**sonic boom** a loud noise caused when an aircraft moves at supersonic speed

**vibration** a back-and-forth motion

**sound wave** a vibration that spreads away from a vibrating object

# Breaking the Sound Barrier

**W**hen Chuck Yeager climbed into his bright orange Bell X-1 aircraft, he knew he was taking a risk. He was trying to break the "sound barrier." He was attempting to fly faster than the speed of sound. Some scientists thought that such a flight was impossible. They believed that the forces at such speeds would tear an aircraft apart.

## EXPLORE

**HYPOTHESIZE** Are airplanes the only things that can break the sound barrier? What everyday things travel faster than the speed of sound? Write a hypothesis in your *Science Journal.* How could you test your ideas?

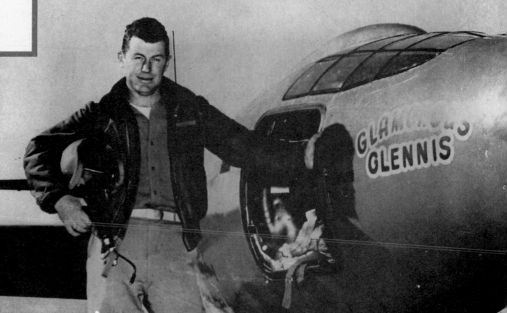

# What Happened at Supersonic Speed?

On October 14, 1947, Chuck Yeager sat in the Bell X-1 waiting for the flight to begin. The plane was powered by rockets but could not take off on its own. It was carried by a B-29 bomber and dropped into the air when the bomber reached about 7,600 meters (25,000 feet) in altitude.

When the X-1 was freed from the bomber, Captain Yeager began to fire the rockets. From earlier flights he knew that as he approached the speed of sound, the plane would begin to shake. Controlling the plane would be difficult. What would happen if he went even faster? Would the plane shake apart? Would it be impossible to control?

He turned on the third rocket. Soon he was flying at **supersonic** (sü′pər son′ik) speed! *Supersonic* means "travel above the speed of sound."

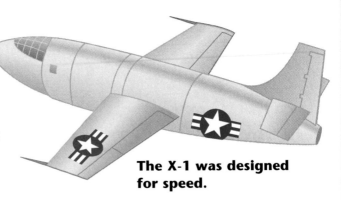

**The X-1 was designed for speed.**

Chuck Yeager was amazed by how smooth the ride felt. The plane did not shake to pieces; in fact it was calmer than at slower speeds.

The ground crew heard a huge noise and were afraid that the plane had exploded. What they had really heard was a **sonic boom**. A sonic boom is a loud noise caused when a plane travels at supersonic speed. The plane breaks through the waves of air that had been piling up in front of it. These waves now trail behind the plane. You'll see the plane pass overhead, but you won't hear it until those waves hit the ground.

Chuck Yeager's flight paved the way for other historic flights from Edwards Air Force Base, including the first supersonic flight by a woman, in 1953, and tests of the space shuttle during the 1970s.

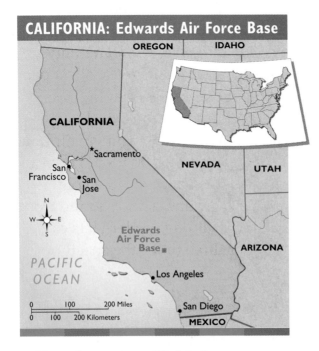

**Many important flights began at Edwards Air Force Base.**

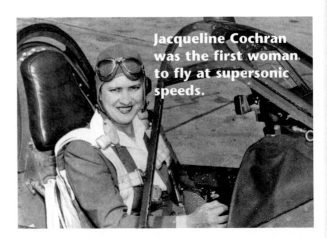

**Jacqueline Cochran was the first woman to fly at supersonic speeds.**

# What Is Sound?

Sound is made by the **vibration** of materials. A vibration is a back-and-forth motion. If you put your hand on your throat as you hum, you can feel the vibration of your vocal cords. Once the vibration is made, whether by humming, blowing a tuba, or knocking on a door, it spreads away from the vibrating object. This moving vibration is called a **sound wave**.

We usually hear sound waves that have come through the air, but sound waves can also move through other materials, such as water or iron.

## The Speed of Sound

Sound waves move more easily through some materials than through others, so the speed of sound is not always the same. Sound travels through water about 4 times faster than through air and through iron about 15 times faster than through air.

The speed of sound also depends on other things, like temperature. Sound travels faster in warm air than in cold air. At 0°C (32°F), sound travels at

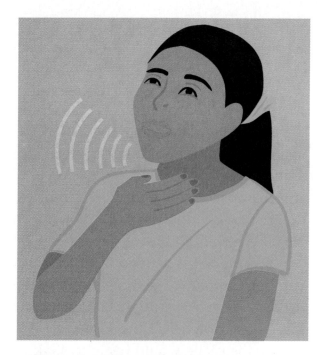

You can feel the vibration of your vocal cords when you sing. The sound waves you produce spread away from your mouth.

about 1,194 kilometers (742 miles) per hour. At 20°C (68°F), it travels at about 1,239 kilometers (770 miles) per hour.

When Chuck Yeager broke the sound barrier, the speed of sound at ground level was 1,223 kilometers (760 miles) per hour. Yet he was traveling only about 1,062 kilometers (660 miles) per hour. How can we say that he was moving at the speed of sound?

The Bell X-1 was flying at an altitude of 12,200 meters (40,000 feet). The temperature of the air was much colder than on the ground, so sound moved more slowly. Today modern jets can travel over three times the speed of sound.

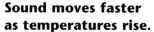

Sound moves faster as temperatures rise.

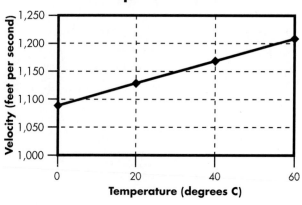

**Choose the letter of the best answer. Mark your answer on a separate sheet of paper.**

1. Which is a fact about the speed of sound?
   A The speed of sound is always the same.
   B Sound travels faster in cold air than in warm air.
   C Sound travels faster through water than through air.
   D The speed of sound is unknown.

2. Look at the chart on page CA28. Through which of the following materials does sound pass most quickly?
   A air
   B salt solution
   C oak
   D iron

3. The Bell X-1 was bullet-shaped so it could
   A weigh less
   B slip through the air easily
   C look better
   D make less sound

4. Look at the chart on page CA28. Traveling through hydrogen, about how many miles would sound travel in ten seconds?
   A 12 miles
   B 3 miles
   C 9 miles
   D 8 miles

5. How many years after Chuck Yeager's first supersonic flight did Jaqueline Cochran fly at supersonic speeds?
   A 8 years
   B 6 years
   C 2 years
   D 5 years

6. According to the topic, the Bell X-1 could not
   A break the sound barrier
   B carry more than three passengers
   C take off by itself
   D land by itself

7. When he reached supersonic speed, Chuck Yeager was surprised by
   A his altitude
   B how nervous he felt
   C the loud sonic boom he heard
   D how smooth the ride felt

8. When Chuck Yeager broke the sound barrier, he was flying at about
   A 660 miles per hour
   B 760 miles per hour
   C 580 miles per hour
   D 700 miles per hour

**Write the answer to the question below on your piece of paper.**

9. Explain why you do not hear a sonic boom until a plane traveling at supersonic speed has passed over you.

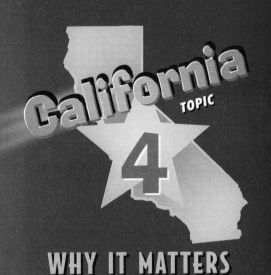

## California TOPIC 4

### WHY IT MATTERS

California has many landforms that continue to change because of volcanoes and movements in Earth's crust.

### SCIENCE WORDS

**core** the center of Earth, lying below the mantle

**mantle** the layer beneath Earth's crust

**crust** the rocky surface that makes up the top of the lithosphere and includes the continents and the ocean floor

**fault** a crack in the crust whose sides show evidence of motion

**magma** hot, molten rock deep below Earth's surface

**igneous rock** a rock formed when melted rock material cools and hardens

**extrusive rock** igneous rock that forms above ground and cools very quickly

**lava** magma that reaches Earth's surface

**intrusive rock** igneous rock that forms underground and cools very slowly

# Landforms in California

Imagine walking through this great lava tube found at Lava Beds National Monument in California. It was formed millions of years ago when the outer lava flow cooled around hot, flowing lava. Lava Beds National Monument also features lava beds, craters, and cinder cones. In fact California has many awesome sights such as these.

Let's explore how volcanoes and movements in Earth's crust are responsible for many landforms found in California.

### EXPLORE

**HYPOTHESIZE** What other landforms have you seen near your area? How do you think they were formed? Write a hypothesis in your *Science Journal.* How could you test your ideas?

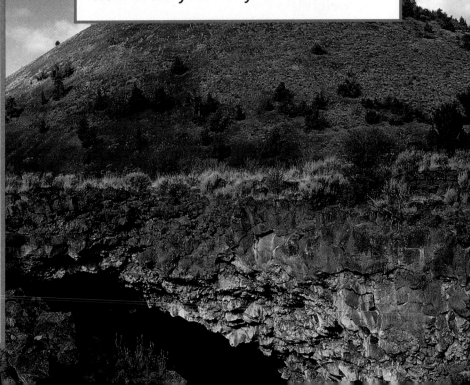

# What Is the Ring of Fire?

The Ring of Fire is an imaginary circle that surrounds the Pacific Ocean. Many volcanoes have erupted along this ring, causing fiery blasts. Earthquakes are also very common.

Earth is made up of layers—the solid inner **core** (kôr), the liquid outer core, the **mantle** (man′tǝl), and the **crust** (krust). Deep in the mantle, high pressures and temperatures cause rocks to flow.

The crust floats on the flowing mantle. The crust is broken into several pieces called *plates*. These plates cover Earth like jigsaw puzzle pieces. As the mantle flows, it drags the plates with it. As they move and collide, *tension*, or stress,

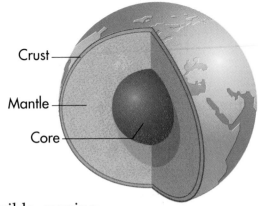

builds, causing volcanoes and earthquakes throughout the Ring of Fire.

California is in an area where plates meet, causing a great deal of tension. The earthquakes and volcanoes caused by this tension have created many of the landforms in California.

**California borders one part of the Ring of Fire.**

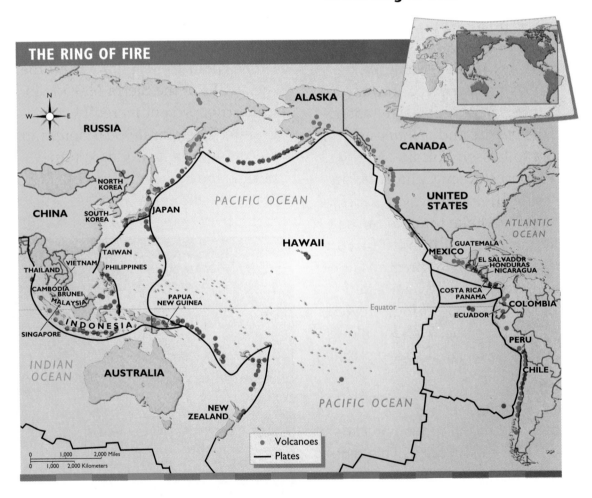

THE RING OF FIRE

• Volcanoes
— Plates

# How Are Igneous Rocks Formed?

As the tension builds along plate lines in California, **faults** (fôlts), or cracks in the crust, appear. Hot, molten rock called **magma** (mag′mə) rises through these cracks. Sometimes it flows slowly onto the surface. Other times it erupts violently, spraying high into the air. As the hot magma cools, it forms two kinds of **igneous** (ig′nē əs) **rocks**.

## Extrusive Rock

The first kind of igneous rock is **extrusive** (ek strü′siv) **rock**. This rock cools quickly as the molten magma, now called **lava** (lä′və), flows on the surface. Examples of this type of rock are *obsidian* (əb sid′ē ən), which looks like glass, and *basalt* (bə sôlt′), which looks like dark rivers of lava. When lava that has been spewed into the air cools, it forms other extrusive materials such as *pumice* and *volcanic ash*.

Visitors to Lassen Volcanic National Park or Mono Lake in California can view wonderful examples of extrusive rocks. At Mono Lake tourists can see breathtaking views of tufa (tü′fə) towers. These towers are a direct result of the strange reaction between lake water and freshwater springs created by volcanic eruptions. Walking along the shores, people can also see pumice and obsidian chips.

## Intrusive Rock

The second kind of igneous rock is **intrusive** (in trü′siv) **rock**. This rock cools very slowly as it moves under-

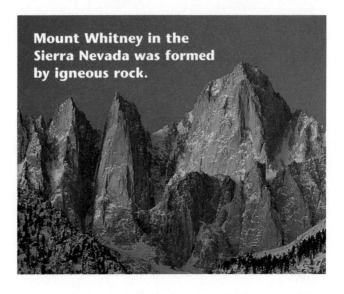

Mount Whitney in the Sierra Nevada was formed by igneous rock.

ground. Examples of this kind of rock are *granite* (gran′it) and *gabbro* (gab′rō). Usually intrusive rocks can be seen only if the rock found above them wears away or is pushed up. Often intrusive rocks are pushed above the surface when the plates in Earth's crust shift and collide, forming mountains.

The Klamath Mountains and the rock walls of the Sierra Nevada in California present incredible cliffs of granite. One granite peak found in the Sierra Nevada is Mount Whitney. This peak is the highest point in the United States, excluding Alaska.

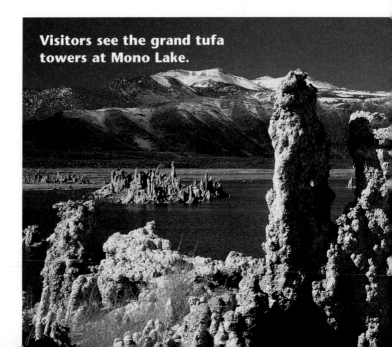

Visitors see the grand tufa towers at Mono Lake.

Choose the letter of the best answer. Mark your answer on a separate sheet of paper.

1. According to this topic, what have formed many of the landforms in California?
   A volcanoes and earthquakes
   B fire and ice
   C lakes and mountains
   D tufa and gabbro

2. In this topic the word *magma* means
   A rock that cools slowly
   B liquid that rapidly explodes
   C hot, molten rock deep below Earth's surface
   D a cluster of mountains found in the Ring of Fire

3. Which is a fact about igneous rock?
   A There are two kinds of igneous rocks.
   B The texture of igneous rock is always smooth.
   C Igneous rocks erupt from earthquakes.
   D Igneous rock is never found on the surface.

4. According to the topic, what is the Ring of Fire?
   A a circle of flames that surrounds an island
   B an imaginary ring surrounding the Pacific Ocean
   C the top part of a volcano's dome
   D the edge of California that faces the ocean

5. Obsidian, pumice, and ash are examples of
   A volcanoes
   B intrusive rock
   C extrusive rock
   D mountain ranges

6. According to the map on page CA29, in how many regions can extrusive rock be found?
   A six
   B three
   C five
   D four

7. Look at the map on page CA29. Which region is closest to the state of Oregon?
   A Los Angeles Ranges
   B Klamath Mountains
   C Central Valley
   D Sierra Nevada

8. Look at the map on page CA29. You can tell by the names of the regions that California is covered by many
   A faults
   B lakes
   C deserts
   D mountains

Write the answer to the question below on your piece of paper.

9. Explain the difference between intrusive and extrusive rock. Give an example of each.

TEST-TAKING SKILLS

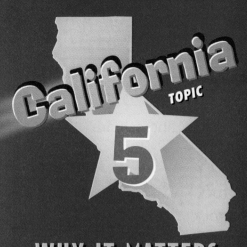

# California TOPIC 5

## WHY IT MATTERS

Smog is very common in southern California and is harmful to people's health.

### SCIENCE WORDS

**smog** a mixture of smoke and fog

**pollution** any harmful substances added to Earth's land, water, or air

**ozone layer** a layer of ozone gas in the atmosphere that screens out much of the Sun's UV rays

# Smog in California

**S**mog, a mixture of smoke and fog, is a problem in many parts of southern California. Brownish gray smog can often be seen in the air. It blocks views of hills, buildings, and mountains. It makes eyes itch and causes many other problems.

Many people have taken steps to help get rid of smog.

## EXPLORE

**HYPOTHESIZE** How can cities be planned to reduce smog? What factors in cities lead to the most smog? Write a hypothesis in your *Science Journal*. How would you test your ideas?

# Where Does Smog Come From?

During the summer months, warm winds blow off the Pacific Ocean and over an area called the South Coast Air Basin. This warm air acts as a lid. It traps the air below it in the basin. This air quickly becomes **polluted** (pə lüt′əd) by traffic exhaust and industrial smoke. Pollution is any harmful substances added to Earth's land, water, or air.

The trapped air is exposed to sunlight and heat. Sunlight and heat cause the pollutants to chemically change into smog. People living in these areas breathe the air and so breathe the smog.

Breathing smog can cause health problems. Smog affects millions of people. It limits what they can do safely outside.

Thousands of southern California residents suffer health effects from breathing the smog. Exposure to high levels of smog for a short time can cause nose and throat irritation, painful breathing, and coughing and can lower the lungs' ability to work.

Long-term exposure to smog can age the lungs quickly. They can lose their ability to function correctly and fight disease and can suffer permanent damage.

It is estimated that smog causes 1,600 premature deaths a year of people living in southern California. People with lung diseases such as asthma and bronchitis are at most risk. Who else is at risk?

The smog affects several areas in this region more than others. Most of Los Angeles County, all of Orange County, parts of Riverside County, western San

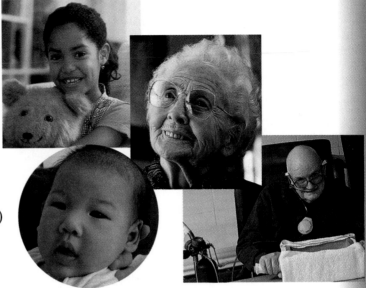

**Many people are at risk of health problems caused by smog.**

Diego County, and parts of San Bernardino County are California's smoggiest counties. What cities also suffer from high smog levels?

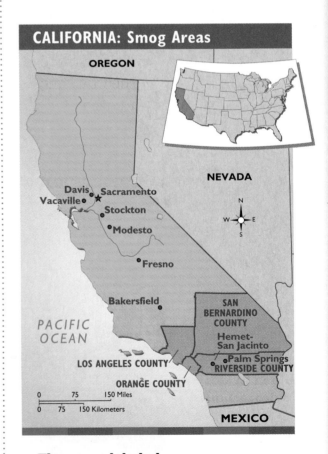

**CALIFORNIA: Smog Areas**

OREGON

NEVADA

Davis
Vacaville
Sacramento
Stockton
Modesto
Fresno
Bakersfield
SAN BERNARDINO COUNTY
Hemet-San Jacinto
PACIFIC OCEAN
LOS ANGELES COUNTY
Palm Springs
RIVERSIDE COUNTY
ORANGE COUNTY

0    75    150 Miles
0    75    150 Kilometers

MEXICO

**The areas labeled are California's smoggiest.**

# What Is Smog?

Smog is a chemical mixture of several gases. These gases react to form a brownish-colored haze. It affects urban areas more than rural areas. This is because urban areas have more traffic and industry.

When chemicals called hydrocarbons mix with nitrogen oxide compounds in the presence of heat and sunlight, they react and produce many chemical compounds. One of these is the gas ozone.

Ozone also occurs naturally. High up in the atmosphere, the **ozone layer** protects Earth from ultraviolet, or UV, radiation. However, at ground level this gas can make people sick.

Common products contain these compounds. Gasoline, paint, and even cleaning-product fumes contain hydrocarbons. Nitrogen oxides are produced when fossil fuels are burned by cars, electric power plants, and other devices. Fingernail polish remover and lighter fluid also produce nitrogen oxide. Check the circle graph on page CA31 to see where the air pollution in California comes from.

## How to Fight Smog

Since burning gasoline is the leading cause of smog in California, all cars are tested each year. If a car gives off too much exhaust or its exhaust is too dirty, the owner must fix the problem or stop driving the car.

California officials encourage people to use public transportation. This reduces traffic, which reduces exhaust, which reduces smog.

Tests also monitor industries in California. Any wastes they produce must not be high in hydrocarbons or nitrogen oxide compounds.

Alternative sources of energy, such as solar power and wind power, are being used in some areas. Electric cars are on the roads today.

**Nitrogen Oxides + Hydrocarbons + Sunlight** 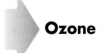 **Ozone**  **Smog**

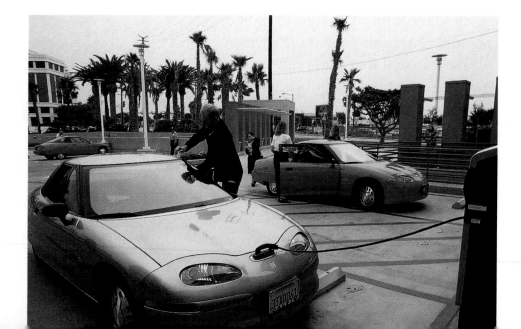

**Electric cars do not burn fossil fuels. They do not produce nitrogen oxides or hydrocarbons. They help reduce air pollution.**

# REVIEW

Choose the letter of the best answer. Mark your answer on a separate sheet of paper.

1. Which is true about smog in California?

   A Northern California suffers from more smog than southern California.

   B Smog is trapped in the South Coast Basin Area.

   C People in California do not breathe smog.

   D Smog affects only a few hundred people.

2. According to this topic, smog can cause all of the following *except*

   A muscle cramps

   B loss of lung function

   C itchy eyes

   D painful breathing and coughing

3. Smog-causing chemicals are produced by

   A solar power

   B electric cars

   C wind and rain

   D gasoline and paint fumes

4. According to this topic, *smog*

   A is produced only in the summer months

   B is caused only by burning gasoline

   C is worse in urban areas

   D doesn't need heat or light in order to form

5. According to the graph on page CA30, the number of days with unhealthy air has

   A gradually decreased since 1976

   B rapidly decreased since 1976

   C gradually increased since 1976

   D not changed since 1976

6. Look at the graph on page CA30. Which year had the most days of unhealthy air?

   A 1995

   B 1988

   C 1987

   D 1980

7. Look at the circle graph on page CA31. Gasoline fumes cause what percentage (%) of air pollution in California?

   A 0%

   B 25%

   C 50%

   D 100%

8. According to the circle graph on page CA31, which cause the least amount of smog in California?

   A airplanes and trains

   B gasoline-fueled vehicles

   C methods of waste disposal

   D diesel-fueled vehicles

**Write the answer to the question below on your piece of paper.**

9. Describe how people in California can reduce smog.

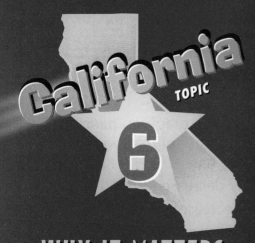

## WHY IT MATTERS

The Mojave Desert is a fragile ecosystem in southeastern California.

### SCIENCE WORDS

**ecosystem** all the living and nonliving things in an area interacting with each other

**biome** one of Earth's large ecosystems, with its own kind of climate, soil, plants, and animals

**desert** a sandy or rocky biome, with little precipitation and little plant life

**adaptation** a characteristic that enables a living thing to survive in its environment

**abiotic factor** a nonliving part of an ecosystem

**biotic factor** a living part of an ecosystem

# The Mojave Desert

The Mojave (mō hä′vē) Desert spreads across four states. It is located in southeastern California and parts of Utah, Nevada, and Arizona. It is larger than 65,000 square kilometers (25,000 square miles). About 39,000 square kilometers (15,000 square miles) are in California.

Plants and animals that live there have adapted to its harsh environment.

## EXPLORE

**HYPOTHESIZE Do all desert plants have the same adaptations? What types of adaptations do you think they have? Write a hypothesis in your *Science Journal*. How would you test your ideas?**

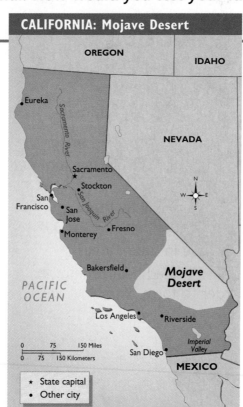

CALIFORNIA: Mojave Desert

# What Is a Desert?

An **ecosystem** (ek'ō sis'təm) is all the living and nonliving things in an area interacting with each other. A **biome** (bī'ōm) is one of Earth's large ecosystems, with its own kind of climate, soil, plants, and animals. A **desert** (dez'ərt) is a sandy or rocky biome with little precipitation and little plant life.

The Mojave Desert receives less than 13 centimeters (5 inches) of precipitation each year. The temperature changes a great deal daily. Days are hot, and nights are cold. Animals and plants of the desert must have special characteristics, or **adaptations** (ad'əp tā'shənz), that help them survive.

Winter is the rainy season in the Mojave Desert. Summers are windy, hot, and dry. Temperatures on a summer day can reach above 38°C (100°F). Winters can have freezing temperatures. The soil is mostly sand and gravel. These **abiotic factors** (ā'bī ot'ik fak'tərz), or nonliving parts of this ecosystem, make living there difficult.

Despite these conditions, deserts do have life, or **biotic factors** (bī ot'ik fak'tərz).

## Animals of the Mojave Desert

Over 300 species of animals live in the Mojave Desert. Coyotes, mule deer, bighorn sheep, rabbits, desert tortoises, and burros are common. These animals often seek shelter from the Sun's hot rays under shrubs and in canyons. Rather than drinking water, some of these animals get water from the plants they eat.

Nearly 200 species of birds live in the Mojave Desert. Large golden eagles and hawks fly over the desert's flatlands in search of prey. Smaller birds such as mourning doves and quail live in canyons, where there is usually more water, food, and shelter. These birds feed on seeds and insects, which are plentiful in this ecosystem.

Spiders and scorpions also live there, as well as smaller animals such as rats and snakes. Many larger animals depend on them as food.

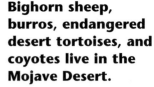

**Bighorn sheep, burros, endangered desert tortoises, and coyotes live in the Mojave Desert.**

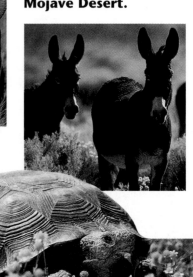

# Plants in the Desert?

In an arid, or dry, environment, little water is available. Wind and high temperatures cause water to evaporate very quickly. Desert plants have adapted to these conditions.

When water is available, plants must absorb as much as possible and store it for later use. The extensive root system of the creosote bush is one adaptation that helps it compete with other plants for scarce water supplies.

Structures such as small leaves with less surface area help to lower the rate of evaporation. Waxy coverings on leaves also prevent water loss due to evaporation. Creosote leaves have a sticky coating to help prevent water loss. Plants can also lose their water supplies to thirsty desert animals. Adaptations such as the thorns on cacti can prevent animals from biting. Creosote leaves do not have thorns, but they do have a bad flavor. Most animals will not feed on the distasteful leaves of this bush.

While plant life is scattered in the Mojave Desert, the desert contains about 200 native species of plants. Besides cacti there are a number of types of shrubs. Only one type of tree grows in this desert. It is the Joshua tree. Plants grow in the flat areas, in canyons, and on the hillsides. Shrubs grow in most areas of the desert. A few of these are the creosote bush, big sagebrush, and bursage. On hillsides Mojave yuccas, desert Spanish bayonets, and Joshua trees grow.

Animals depend on these desert plants. They feed on their seeds, bark, leaves, and fruits. They use the plants as shelter. They also get much of their water from eating plants.

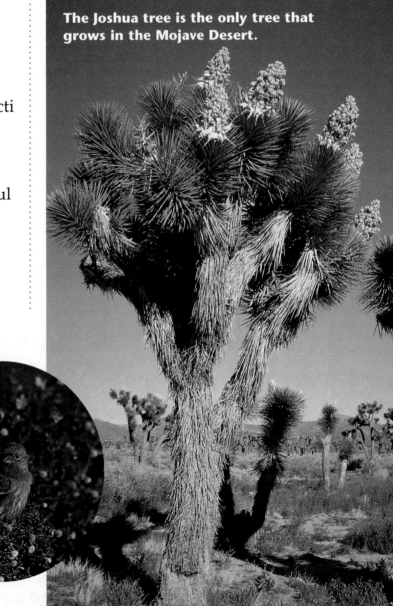

The Joshua tree is the only tree that grows in the Mojave Desert.

The leaves and roots of the creosote bush are well adapted to desert life.

**Choose the letter of the best answer. Mark your answer on a separate sheet of paper.**

1. According to this topic, the Mojave receives in a year
   A less than 10 inches of rain
   B more than 10 inches of rain
   C less than 5 inches of rain
   D no rain

2. According to this topic, how much of the Mojave Desert is *not* located in California?
   A 65,000 square kilometers
   B 39,000 square kilometers
   C 26,000 square kilometers
   D all of it

3. Which is a fact about animals in the Mojave Desert?
   A All eat plants.
   B All live in canyons.
   C All are adapted to the hot, dry climate.
   D No birds live in the desert.

4. Which is a fact about plants in the Mojave Desert?
   A They need adaptations for storing water.
   B They all have short roots.
   C They do not have to protect their water supplies from animals.
   D They all have thorns.

5. According to page CA32, how many main biomes are there in California?
   A two
   B four
   C one
   D three

6. According to the map on page CA32, the desert
   A is located in the north
   B is located in the south
   C is located in the middle region
   D is not located in the state

7. Which statement is true according to the table on page CA32?
   A An area that gets 12 inches of rain is a desert.
   B An area that gets 47 inches of rain is a temperate coniferous forest.
   C An area that gets less than 2 inches of rain is a chaparral.
   D An area that gets 66 inches of rain is a temperate coniferous forest.

8. According to the table on page CA32, which is an example of an organism found in the desert and in the chaparral?
   A black bear
   B mule deer
   C chipmunk
   D coyote

**Write the answer to the question below on your piece of paper.**

9. Describe how plants have adapted to life in the Mojave Desert.

# CALIFORNIA DATA BANK

## Topic 1

# Dendrochronology

In Topic 1 you learned about dendrochronology, the reading of tree rings to find out what the climate was like in the past. Bristlecone pine trees grow faster if there is more moisture. If they grow faster, they get bigger growth rings. They grow more slowly if there is less moisture. The following is an example of a small cross section of a bristlecone pine tree.

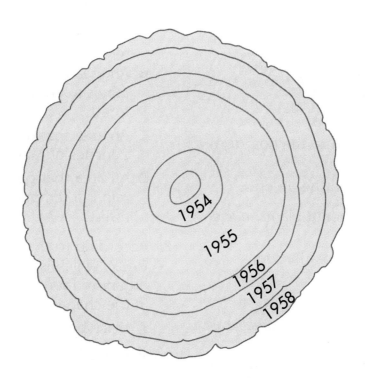

1954
1955
1956
1957
1958

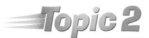

# California Weather

## AVERAGE MONTHLY HIGH TEMPERATURES IN LOS ANGELES

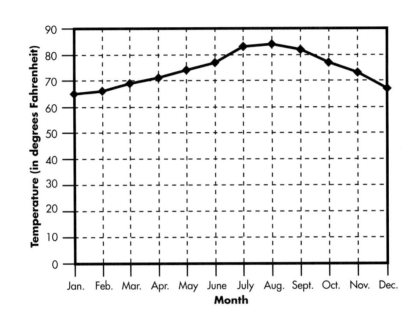

## AVERAGE MONTHLY HIGH TEMPERATURES IN SAN FRANCISCO

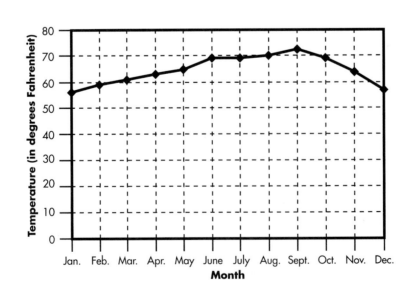

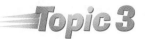

# Speed of Sound

Sound moves at different speeds, depending on the material through which it is passing. The chart below shows the speed of sound passing through a variety of gases, liquids, and solids.

| State of Material (gas, liquid, or solid) | Material | Speed of Sound (feet per second) |
| --- | --- | --- |
| Gas | air | 1,092 |
| Gas | hydrogen | 4,164 |
| Liquid | salt solution | 5,132 |
| Liquid | rubbing alcohol | 4,218 |
| Solid | gold | 51,717 |
| Solid | iron | 16,822 |
| Solid | oak | 12,662 |

Through which material does sound pass most quickly? Least quickly?

Traveling through gold, how many feet would sound travel in an hour? How many miles? (1 mile = 5,280 feet)

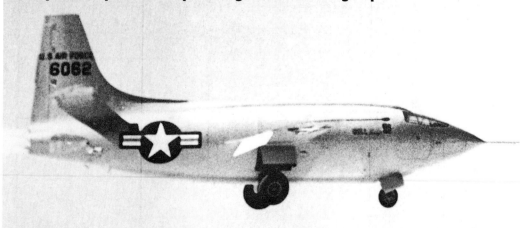

As any plane flies, it has to push aside the air it is flying through. The faster the plane goes, the harder this becomes. The X-1's bulletlike shape allowed it to cut through the air. Its wings were very thin and bladelike. These properties helped the plane to slip through the air at high speed.

CALIFORNIA DATA BANK

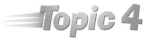

# California's Land Regions

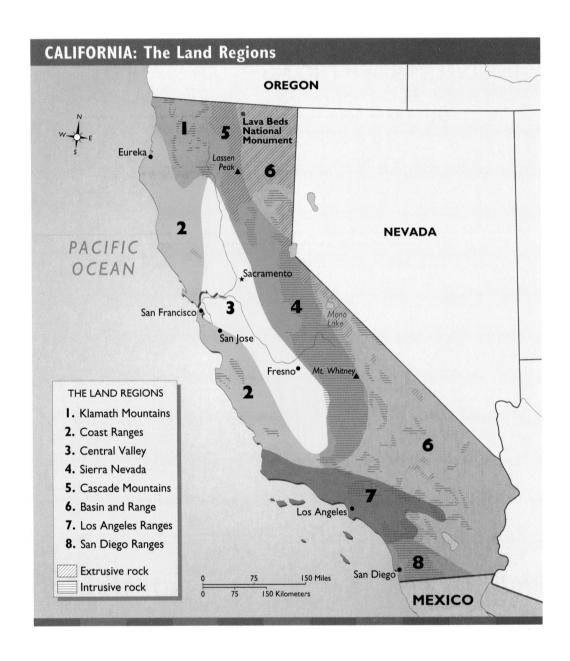

CALIFORNIA: The Land Regions

THE LAND REGIONS
1. Klamath Mountains
2. Coast Ranges
3. Central Valley
4. Sierra Nevada
5. Cascade Mountains
6. Basin and Range
7. Los Angeles Ranges
8. San Diego Ranges

Extrusive rock
Intrusive rock

# California Smog

## NUMBER OF CALIFORNIA DAYS WITH OZONE LEVELS ABOVE THE ACCEPTED STATE LEVEL

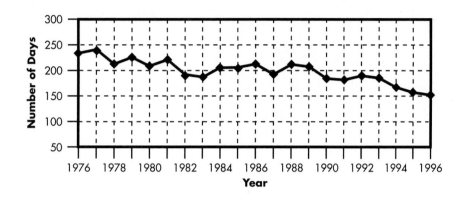

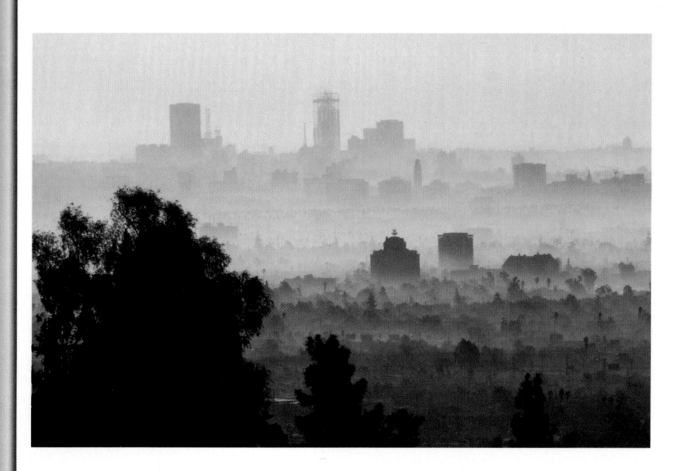

# THE POLLUTION IN CALIFORNIA

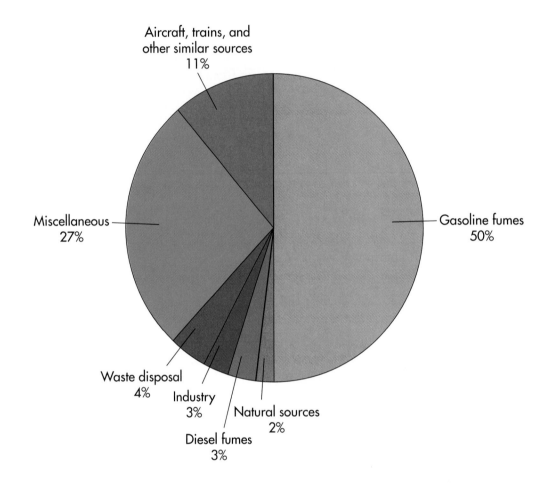

Aircraft, trains, and
other similar sources
11%

Miscellaneous
27%

Gasoline fumes
50%

Waste disposal
4%

Industry
3%

Natural sources
2%

Diesel fumes
3%

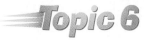

## California Biomes

There are three main biomes in California. They are *temperate coniferous forest*, *desert*, and *chaparral* or *scrub forest*. Look at the map to see where they are located. The types of animals and plants differ from ecosystem to ecosystem. The weather is also different.

| Biome | Yearly Precipitation | Major Plants | Major Animals |
|---|---|---|---|
| Temperate coniferous forest | 30–50 inches | coniferous evergreen trees, including redwood, sequoia, cedar, hemlock, and pine | black bears, elk, mountain lions, wolves, insects, small mammals |
| Desert | less than 10 inches | cacti, yucca plants, and sage plants | snakes, lizards, insects, birds, mule deer, coyotes |
| Chaparral or scrub forest | often summer droughts | scrub oak trees and grasses | rabbits, chipmunks, coyotes, small birds, lizards, snakes, insects |

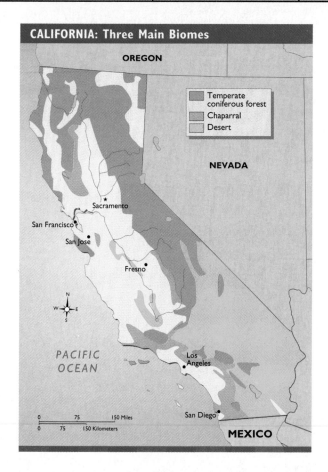

CALIFORNIA: Three Main Biomes

# McGRAW-HILL
# SCIENCE

## MACMILLAN/McGRAW-HILL EDITION

**RICHARD MOYER** ■ **LUCY DANIEL** ■ **JAY HACKETT**
**PRENTICE BAPTISTE** ■ **PAMELA STRYKER** ■ **JOANNE VASQUEZ**

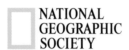

NATIONAL
GEOGRAPHIC
SOCIETY

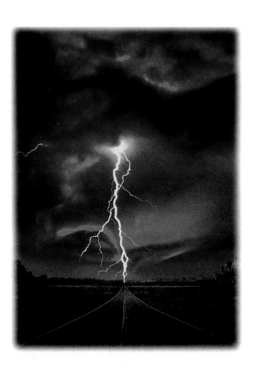

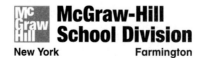

**McGraw-Hill
School Division**

New York          Farmington

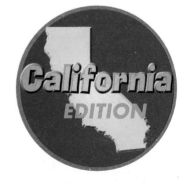

California
EDITION

# PROGRAM AUTHORS

**Dr. Lucy H. Daniel**
*Teacher, Consultant
Rutherford County Schools,
North Carolina*

**Dr. Jay Hackett**
*Emeritus Professor of Earth
Sciences
University of Northern
Colorado*

**Dr. Richard H. Moyer**
*Professor of Science
Education
University of Michigan-
Dearborn*

**Dr. H. Prentice Baptiste**
*Professor of Curriculum and
Instruction
New Mexico State
University*

**Pamela Stryker, M.Ed.**
*Elementary Educator and
Science Consultant
Eanes Independent School
District
Austin, Texas*

**JoAnne Vasquez, M.Ed.**
*Elementary Science
Education Specialist
Mesa Public Schools,
Arizona
NSTA President 1996–1997*

NATIONAL
GEOGRAPHIC
SOCIETY

*Washington, D.C.*

## CONTRIBUTING AUTHORS

**Dr. Thomas Custer**
**Dr. James Flood**
**Dr. Diane Lapp**
**Doug Llewellyn**
**Dorothy Reid**
**Dr. Donald M. Silver**

## CONSULTANTS

Dr. Danny J. Ballard
Dr. Carol Baskin
Dr. Bonnie Buratti
Dr. Suellen Cabe
Dr. Shawn Carlson
Dr. Thomas A. Davies
Dr. Marie DiBerardino
Dr. R. E. Duhrkopf
Dr. Ed Geary
Dr. Susan C. Giarratano-Russell
Dr. Karen Kwitter
Dr. Donna Lloyd-Kolkin
Ericka Lochner, RN
Donna Harrell Lubcker
Dr. Dennis L. Nelson
Dr. Fred S. Sack
Dr. Martin VanDyke
Dr. E. Peter Volpe
Dr. Josephine Davis Wallace
Dr. Joe Yelderman

## *McGraw-Hill School Division*

*A Division of The McGraw·Hill Companies*

McGraw-Hill School Division
Two Penn Plaza
New York, New York 10121

Printed in the United States of America

ISBN 0-02-279932-X / 5

9 10 11 12 027/046 09 08 07

# CONTENTS

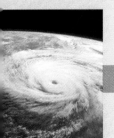

# UNIT 2 WEATHER AND CLIMATE
## EARTH SCIENCES

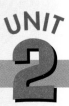

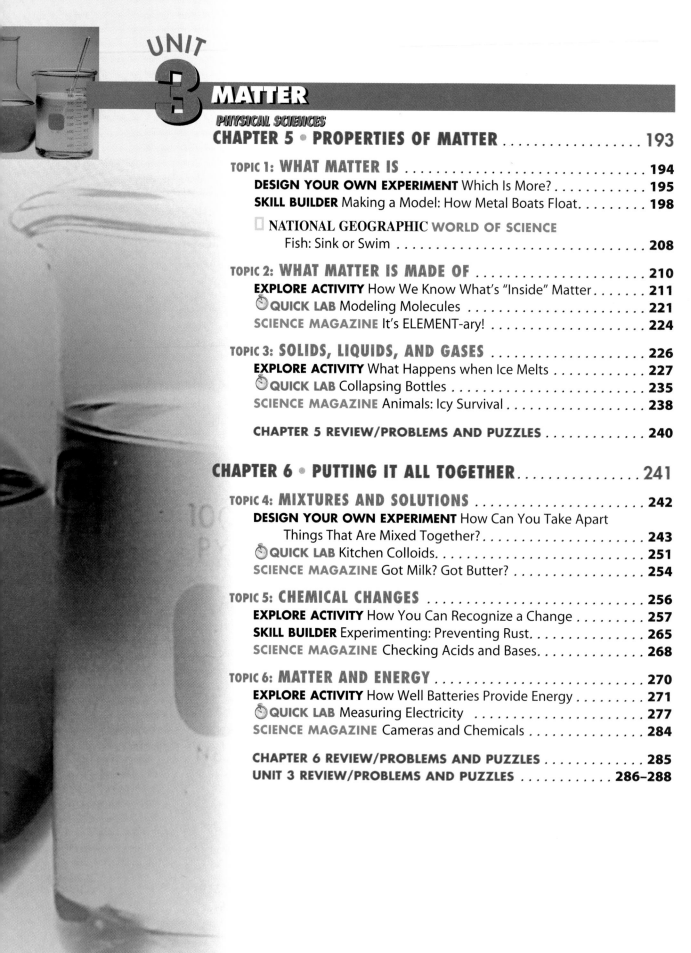

# UNIT 3

# MATTER

*PHYSICAL SCIENCES*

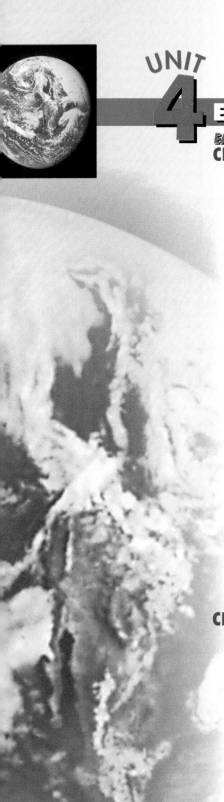

# UNIT 4 EARTH AND ITS RESOURCES

*EARTH SCIENCES*

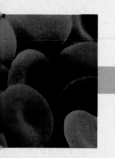

# YOUR TEXTBOOK at a Glance

Begin each topic with an **Explore** question. Investigate further by doing an **Explore Activity**.

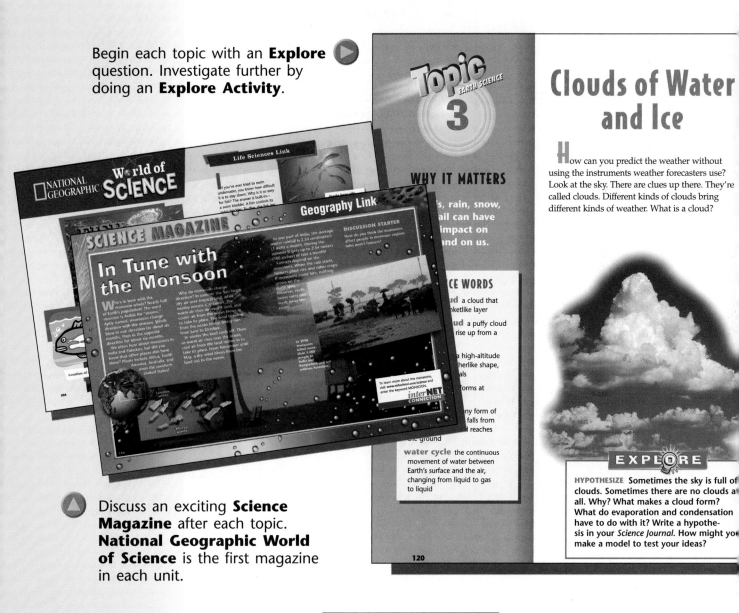

**Life Sciences Link**

**NATIONAL GEOGRAPHIC World of SCIENCE**

SCIENCE MAGAZINE

**In Tune with the Monsoon**

**Geography Link**

DISCUSSION STARTER

To learn more about the monsoons, visit www.mhschool.com/science and enter the keyword MONSOON.
interNET CONNECTION

## Topic EARTH SCIENCE 3

### WHY IT MATTERS

...s, rain, snow, ...ail can have ...impact on ...and on us.

...CE WORDS

...ud a cloud that ...nketlike layer

...ud a puffy cloud ...rise up from a

...a high-altitude ...herlike shape,

...forms at

...ny form of ...falls from ...reaches ...ground

**water cycle** the continuous movement of water between Earth's surface and the air, changing from liquid to gas to liquid

120

## Clouds of Water and Ice

How can you predict the weather without using the instruments weather forecasters use? Look at the sky. There are clues up there. They're called clouds. Different kinds of clouds bring different kinds of weather. What is a cloud?

### EXPLORE

**HYPOTHESIZE** Sometimes the sky is full of clouds. Sometimes there are no clouds at all. Why? What makes a cloud form? What do evaporation and condensation have to do with it? Write a hypothesis in your *Science Journal*. How might you make a model to test your ideas?

Discuss an exciting **Science Magazine** after each topic. **National Geographic World of Science** is the first magazine in each unit.

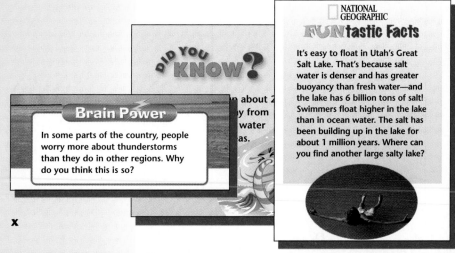

**DID YOU KNOW?**

**Brain Power**

In some parts of the country, people worry more about thunderstorms than they do in other regions. Why do you think this is so?

...n about 2... ...y from ...water ...as.

**NATIONAL GEOGRAPHIC**
**FUNtastic Facts**

It's easy to float in Utah's Great Salt Lake. That's because salt water is denser and has greater buoyancy than fresh water—and the lake has 6 billion tons of salt! Swimmers float higher in the lake than in ocean water. The salt has been building up in the lake for about 1 million years. Where can you find another large salty lake?

Flex your brain with questions about real-world facts.

# EXPLORE ACTIVITY

## Investigate Why Clouds Form

Watch what can happen when you cool off some air.

### PROCEDURES

**SAFETY** Be careful handling the hot water. Use the handle to hold the mug. Do not burn yourself.

1. Chill container 1 by putting it in a refrigerator or on ice for about ten minutes.

2. Fill a mug with hot tap water.

3. **MAKE A MODEL** Fill container 2 with hot water. Place empty cold container 1 upside down on top of container 2 with the water. Fit the mouths together carefully. Place the ice cubes on top of container 1.

4. **OBSERVE** Write your observations in your *Science Journal*.

### MATERIALS

- hot tap water
- 2 identical clear containers
- mug
- 3 ice cubes
- food coloring
- refrigerator or freezer
- *Science Journal*

### CONCLUDE AND APPLY

1. **COMMUNICATE** What did you observe?

2. **COMMUNICATE** Where did this take place?

3. **COMMUNICATE** Where did the water come from?

4. **INFER** Explain what made it happen.

### GO FURTHER: Apply

5. **DRAW CONCLUSIONS** Where would you expect to find more clouds— over the ocean or over a desert? Why?

6. **INFER** Why don't all clouds look the same?

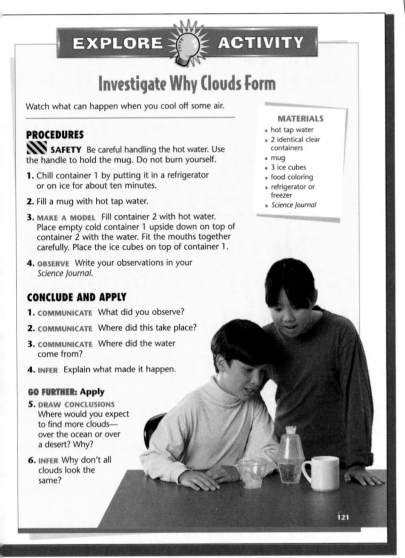

121

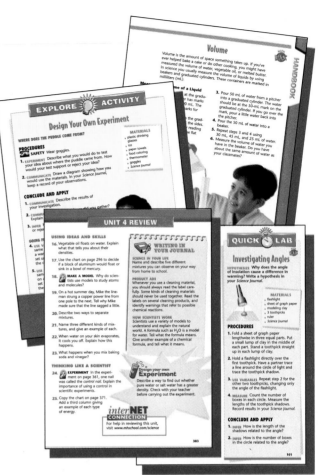

**Design Your Own Experiments**, do **Quick Labs**, use **Internet Connections**, and try **Writing in Your Journal**. Use the **Handbook** for help.

**Reading Graphs, Diagrams, Maps**, and **Charts** help you learn by using what you see.

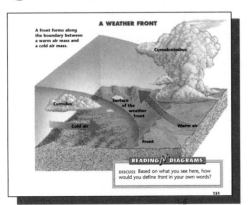

A WEATHER FRONT

A front forms along the boundary between a warm air mass and a cold air mass.

Cumulonimbus

Cumulus

Surface of the weather front

Cold air

Warm air

Front

**READING ✓ DIAGRAMS**

DISCUSS Based on what you see here, how would you define *front* in your own words?

151

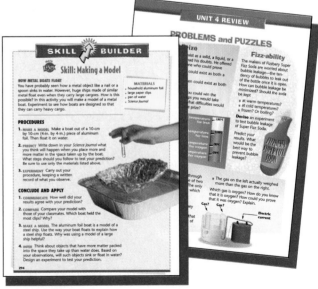

Build your skills with **Skill Builders** and **Problems and Puzzles**.

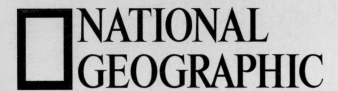

## INVITATION TO
# SCIENCE

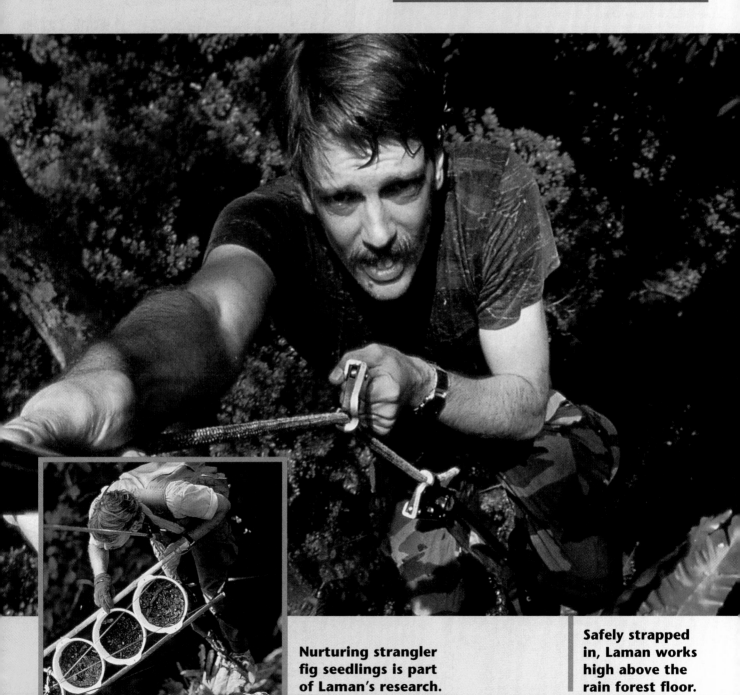

**Nurturing strangler fig seedlings is part of Laman's research.**

**Safely strapped in, Laman works high above the rain forest floor.**

# Tim Laman

Tim Laman's research takes him up into the sky-high rain forest canopy of Indonesia's Gunung Palung National Park. The Harvard University biologist climbs trees in the rain forest to study strangler figs. The figs sprout high in the trees and send their roots snaking down to the ground. Eventually the roots circle the host tree, cutting off growth.

Laman is a careful observer. Sometimes an observation pays off dramatically. One day when he was collecting samples high in a tree, Laman noticed tiny ants carrying fig seeds. "As I followed the trail of ants to their tree-crotch nest site, I realized I had discovered a new player in the strangler fig's seed dispersal."

Laman had already discovered that birds play a major role in spreading strangler fig seeds. Birds eat the figs and then scatter the seeds throughout the rain forest. The seeds most likely to sprout are the ones that fall in decayed leaves high in the clefts of tree branches.

Measuring the growth of strangler fig seedlings is another part of Laman's work. High above the forest floor, he has planted more than 6,000 strangler fig seeds in the crowns of 45 trees.

Laman calls the pristine Indonesian rain forest a "biological frontier where there is much to discover."

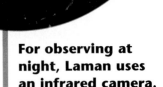

**For observing at night, Laman uses an infrared camera.**

**Birds like this rhinoceros hornbill help spread the fig seeds through the rain forest.**

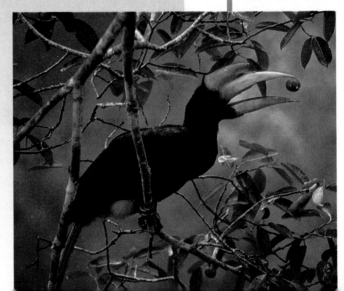

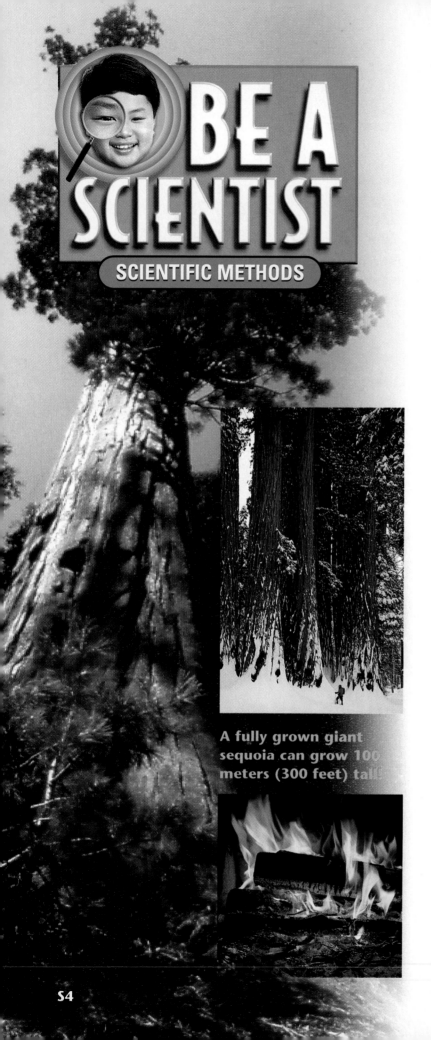

# BE A SCIENTIST

## SCIENTIFIC METHODS

A fully grown giant sequoia can grow 100 meters (300 feet) tall.

Have you ever watched a tree grow from a tiny seed? Trees can grow taller than any other living things. Giant sequoias can grow taller than a 20-story sky-scraper and weigh about 13 times more than the heaviest dinosaur that ever lived! **Mass** (mas) is what scientists use to measure the amount of matter in an object. Giant sequoias started as small seeds. How did they gain so much mass?

Think of a heavy log burning in a fireplace. After several hours there is nothing left but a few ounces of ash. What happened to the rest of the log?

## EXPLORE

Where do plants get their mass? Write some possible explanations in your *Science Journal*. How might you test your explanations?

# Investigate Where Plants Get Their Mass

Where do you think the extra mass comes from as a plant grows?

*Think of a hypothesis about this question. A hypothesis is a statement in answer to a question. You must be able to test the statement in an experiment.*

### MATERIALS

- package of lima bean seeds
- 4 paper cups
- soil
- balance
- ruler
- water
- *Science Journal*

## PROCEDURES

1. Fill the paper cups with a premeasured amount of soil. Use the same amount for each cup. Record the mass of the soil and the date in your *Science Journal.*

2. Find the mass of the seed. Record it and the date. Plant one lima bean seed in each cup.

3. Place the cups where they will get sunlight. Water the soil the same amount each week.

4. **OBSERVE** After three months, measure the plant height with the ruler and record your findings. Carefully remove the plant and root from the soil. Find the mass of the plant, and record it. Find the mass of the soil again, and record it.

5. **INTERPRET DATA** Compare the mass of the plant and soil now to the start of the experiment.

**Sample data**

|  | September | December |
|---|---|---|
| Plant height | 7.6 cm (3 in.) | 25.4 cm (10 in.) |
| Mass of plant | 2 g | 68 g |
| Mass of soil | 225 g | 223 g |

## CONCLUDE AND APPLY

1. **DRAW CONCLUSIONS** How much mass did the plant gain in three months?

2. Do you think the added mass of the plant came from the soil? Why? Do you think it came from the water you added? Explain.

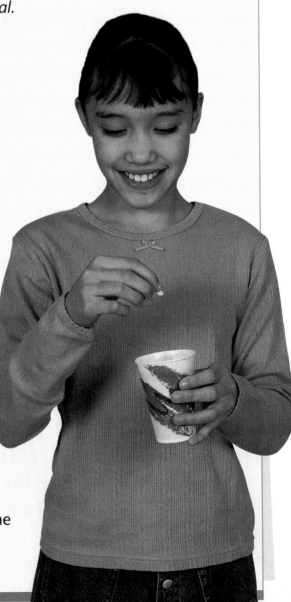

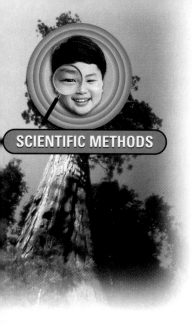

# Where Do Plants Get Their Mass?

All around us things are changing their properties due to chemical changes. A **chemical change** is a change of matter that occurs when atoms link together in a new way, creating a new substance different from the original substances.

The Explore Activity showed that a chemical change took place when the seed was planted in the soil. Plants use energy from the Sun, water, nutrients from the soil, and air to make their own food and grow. The food-making process in green plants that uses sunlight is called **photosynthesis**.

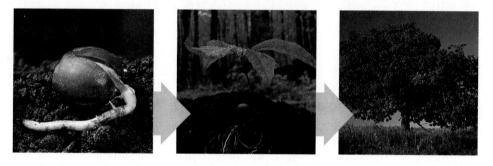

There are many types of chemical changes. Fire (1) causes a chemical change in burning wood. As the wood burns, the chemical energy stored in it is changed to light and heat. Some of the chemicals in the wood produce gas as they burn. Smoke is formed when the gas mixes with tiny particles of the burnt wood. The only solid material left behind is the ash, which has much less mass than the log.

Vinegar and baking soda (2) combine to form a gas. The gas is so light it rises into the air. Metals (3) turn to rust after being exposed to air for a long time.

**1**

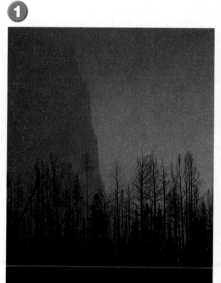

**2**

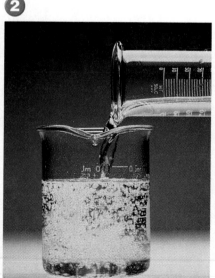

**3**

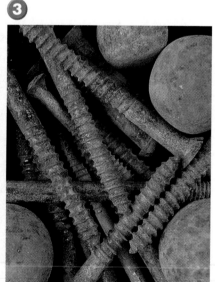

## How Do Scientists Begin?

For hundreds of years, scientists have studied the chemical changes that make green plants grow. At one time it seemed reasonable to think that plants got their food by absorbing soil through their roots. A scientist named Jan Baptista van Helmont helped change that view over 300 years ago.

Scientists are curious about the world around them. This curiosity causes them to ask questions about things they don't understand. Sometimes they question the explanations accepted by others. This was the case with Helmont. He wondered whether plants really absorbed soil as others thought. He wondered whether anyone had ever actually tested the idea. He thought about how he could test this idea himself.

Does the mass of a tree come from absorbing the soil it grows in? He concluded that if a tree uses up soil to get its food, then the soil around it should get lighter. Helmont conducted an experiment to test his hypothesis. His findings changed the way scientists thought about how green plants grow.

Scientists need to think of ways to control as many parts of an experiment as they can. This helps determine what is or what isn't causing the change they are investigating. To investigate whether plants were absorbing the soil around them for food, Helmont decided to measure it.

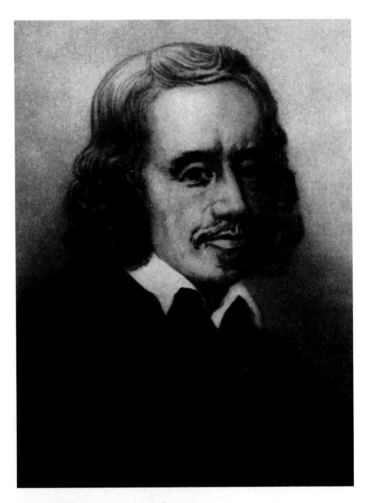

**Jan Baptista van Helmont was a doctor and chemist.**

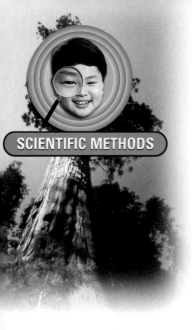

# How Do Scientists Learn from the Work of Others?

Helmont planted a young willow tree that weighed 5 pounds in a tub that contained 200 pounds of soil. Then he carefully studied the tree and the soil for five years, recording all the changes that occurred. During this period his measurements showed that the tree grew to a weight of 169 pounds. In all that time, the soil lost only 2 ounces! The evidence showed that the tree had not gained all its mass directly from the soil. In fact it gained very little of its added mass from the soil!

The experiment answered one question, but it raised another question! How did the tree increase its mass?

After his experiment Helmont guessed that water provided everything a plant needed to grow. Now we know he was only partly right. Plants do need water to increase their mass, but most of all, green plants need sunlight. Thanks to the work of many scientists since Helmont's day, we know that few organisms can survive without receiving energy directly or indirectly from the Sun. Green plants use photosynthesis to mix energy from the Sun with water, air, and soil nutrients to make a kind of sugar. The sugar is used by the plant to grow its stems, its roots, its seeds, and all its other parts.

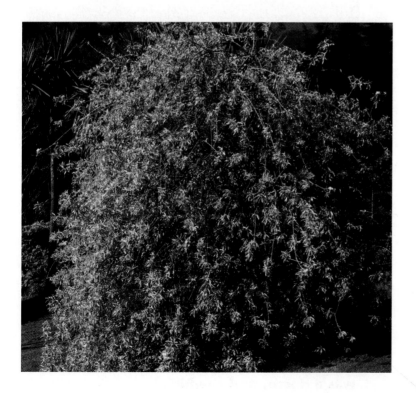

**Helmont studied the growth of a willow tree to explore where plants get their mass.**

## How Do Scientists Know What Questions to Ask?

Scientists today understand much about photosynthesis, but not everything. They still can't make it happen in a laboratory experiment. We *have* learned that the relationship between plants and soil is much more complicated than what was believed in Helmont's time.

One scientist who studies the way trees grow is Roy Renkin. Renkin is a **biologist** (bī ol′ə jist) who works for the National Park Service at Yellowstone National Park in Wyoming. A biologist is a scientist who studies plant and animal life. Thanks to the work of Helmont, Renkin learned that the trees he studies don't absorb much soil to increase their mass. When scientists answer one question, it often leads to more questions. Renkin had two questions. What makes forests grow? When a forest dies, how does it grow back?

In August 1988 a huge forest fire raged at Yellowstone National Park. Winds tore through the park at 112 kilometers (70 miles) per hour. Flames soared 110 meters (360 feet) into the sky. When it was over, more square miles of Yellowstone Park had burned during one

**Roy Renkin is a biologist for Yellowstone National Park.**

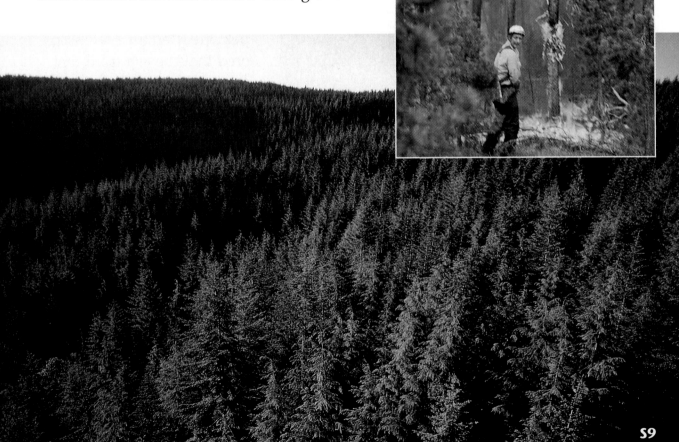

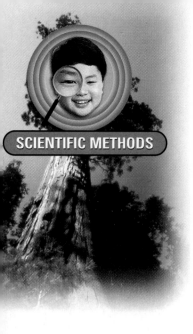

week than during any ten-year period since 1872! The fire burned nearly 1 million acres of forest, an area larger than the entire state of Rhode Island!

The fire seemed to be a great tragedy, but for Roy Renkin it was also the chance of a lifetime. It gave him the chance to investigate the questions he had about how forests begin to grow.

Scientists once believed that intense forest fires destroyed the roots and soil nutrients that plants need to grow. The Yellowstone fire helped show that that was not true.

Some trees use a forest fire to help them reproduce. Some of the pine cones dropped by a lodgepole pine evergreen tree open to release their seeds only after they have been burned! After the Yellowstone fire, Renkin and other scientists found as many as one million or more lodgepole pine seeds per acre. Renkin also discovered that the ash from the fire made the soil's nutrient levels increase for the first year or two after the fire. Within five years after the fire, he found the forest ground was covered with new growth.

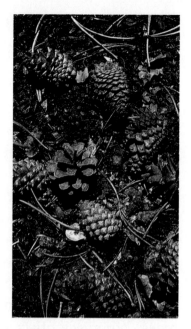

**Some lodgepole pine cones open only after a fire.**

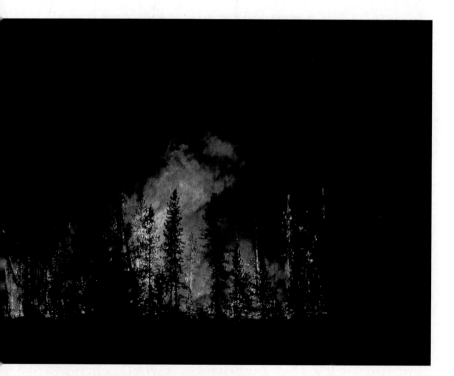

**The 1988 Yellowstone fire destroyed nearly 1 million acres of forest!**

Renkin also investigated the park's aspen trees after the fire and made an important discovery. He discovered that a forest fire is one the best things that can happen to aspens.

Aspens grow mostly in the western areas of North America. Scientists know that groups of aspens are connected underground through a large root system. Scientists used to think that new aspen trees grew only as shoots from the underground root system of the older aspens. After the Yellowstone fire, Renkin discovered aspens growing from seedlings. He also discovered they were growing from seeds because the fire changed the forest soil. The change in the soil's nutrients and moisture content because of the fire created the conditions in which the aspen seedlings could grow on their own!

Renkin has helped us understand that fire can be a natural process

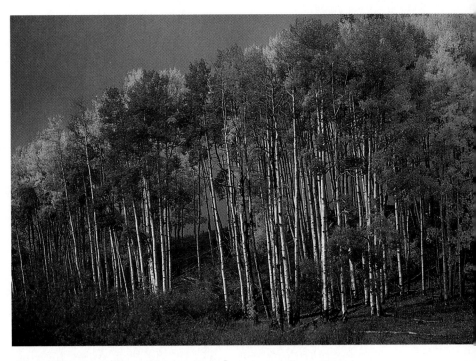

**Aspen trees often share one huge root system.**

that helps a forest. As forests age, dead timber builds up on the ground. Fires become more likely. Careless people cause many forest fires, but lightning can also start one. Lightning striking a new forest may have little effect, but if it strikes the downed, dry timber of an old forest, it can spark a widespread fire. Some trees, like the lodgepole pine and the aspen, have developed ways to use the new conditions to their benefit.

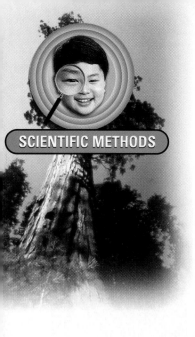

# How Can I Be Like a Scientist?

Scientists start with curiosity! They **look carefully** at things around them and **ask questions**. How can trees grow so tall? How can heavy, burning logs turn into lightweight ashes? Do forest fires prevent new young trees from growing, or do they help them? You may have observed things around you that made you wonder.

Thinking like a scientist means trying to find answers to questions like these. Sometimes it means not believing the explanations of others. Helmont conducted his experiment because he did not believe the conclusions of the scientists before him.

Try picking a favorite tree and learning what you can by observing it over the course of a year. See if your observations lead to another hypothesis you might be able to test.

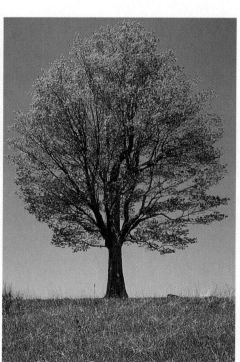 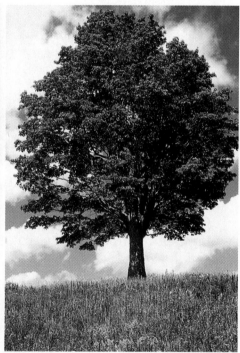 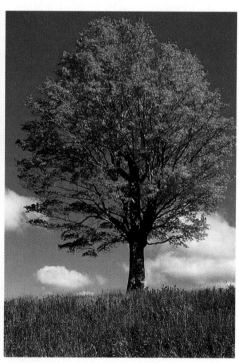

**A deciduous tree changes with the seasons.**

Now let's go back and look at how you thought like a scientist when you did the Explore Activity on the increase in mass during plant growth.

## YOU ASKED YOURSELF QUESTIONS

To be a scientist means asking questions about the world around you.

When you thought about tall trees growing from tiny seeds, you wondered where their mass came from. You asked yourself: How can I test my ideas to answer my questions?

## YOU SET UP AN INVESTIGATION

At the beginning of the Explore Activity, you thought about a **hypothesis**. It was an idea or a guess about what would happen that you could test. You then **planned your experiment** and planted your seeds.

You **measured** the materials and **started your observations**. You **recorded** and **organized** the information to help you understand it better. You **shared your observations** with others in the class. Just as later scientists learned from Helmont, you learned by looking at the data of the other students.

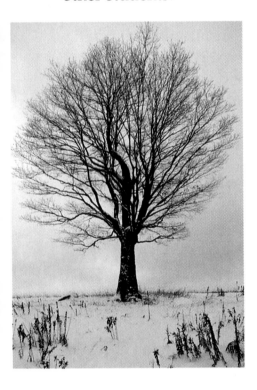

## YOU USED THE RESULTS OF YOUR INVESTIGATION TO ANSWER QUESTIONS

To be a scientist, you need to observe the process of your experiment closely. You also need to **analyze the results** and **draw conclusions**. After you studied the measurements of the experiment, it was clear the gain

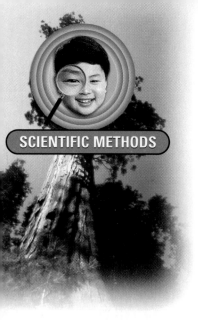

in mass by the plant did not come from the soil. From this you learned whether or not your hypothesis was correct.

Scientists **share the findings** of their experiments. During the Explore Activity, you shared your analysis of the data with your partner. You also recorded your explanations in your *Science Journal*. The data table you put together made the information easier to understand.

Sharing the results of an experiment helps scientists decide how strong or weak their hypothesis is. They can **compare their results** with the results of other scientists doing the same experiment. To be even more certain, scientists often **repeat their experiment**.

Just as Renkin learned from Helmont's experiment, you learned from the experiments of other students. The results of the experiment did show that the mass of the plant did not come from the soil. The results did not tell you where the added plant mass did come from.

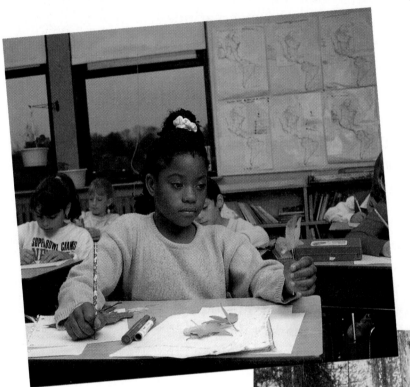

How might you improve on the experiment conducted by Helmont? Using what you now know, what other questions about growing plants does your experiment raise? For example: Does water account for all the increase in the mass of the plant? How could you find out?

For scientists a successful experiment often raises more questions than it answers. What are some of the new questions you have about chemical changes that are occurring around you? Can you think of ways to test these questions to learn more about them?

In this book you will be doing many Explore Activities. Complete all the steps you just learned each time. It's called a scientific method. It's what makes you a real scientist! Answers are important. In science it's also important *how* you found the answers.

## WHY IT MATTERS

The Smokey Bear campaign changed our ideas about forest fires. It has been telling us for years that we need to prevent forest fires. The campaign has been a success because it's a good message. The carelessness of humans still results in the destruction of too many acres of valuable forest.

**Local fire departments warn people about how likely fires can be in their areas.**

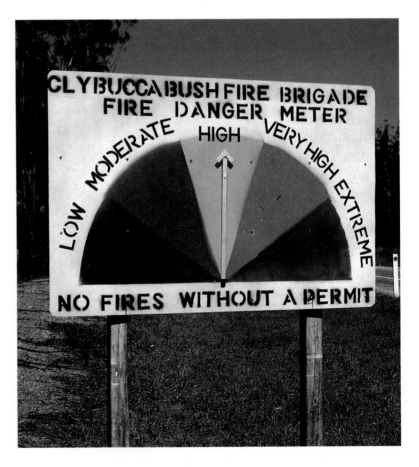

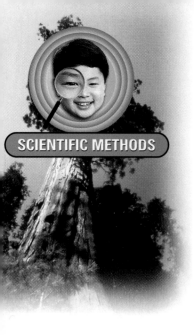
The work of scientists like Roy Renkin has also changed our ideas about forest fires. It is only recently that we have begun to realize the benefits of burning to some forests. As the Yellowstone fire showed, fire allows old forests to be replaced by young ones more quickly. The fire gave the soil more nutrients for new plants to grow in. After the fire there were also clear, open areas where more rain and sunlight could reach the new growth.

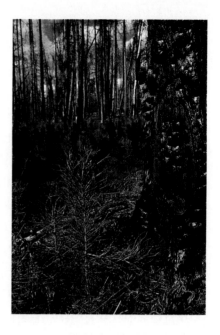

From the work of scientists, we've also learned how beneficial trees are to us. Trees are actually large air conditioners! They cool the air by absorbing water from the ground and releasing moisture through their leaves. A single large tree has the cooling power of five air conditioners. Scientists have also shown that tree leaves filter air pollution. This can be very helpful because a large tree may have 200,000 leaves.

Using this information scientists in Dayton, Ohio, discovered that the temperature in an urban area ecosystem can be reduced by 2°C (4°F) by planting enough trees in the area.

In 1987, 13 eight-year-olds in El Segundo, California, used the information scientists have gathered about trees to help their community. It is an urban environment with very few trees. When the students learned how beneficial trees can be, they decided to start a new organization.

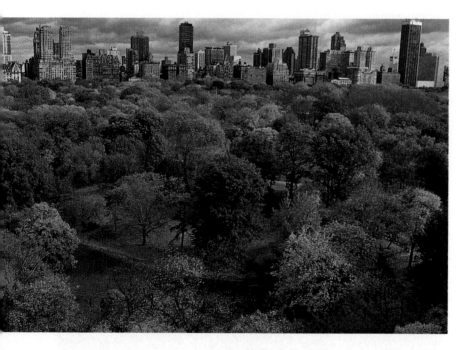

El Segundo is near Los Angeles. It has a huge oil refinery on one side and the enormous Los Angeles Airport on the other. Both the refinery and the airport produce a lot of pollution. Calling themselves the Tree Musketeers, the group decided to try to plant enough trees to create a "pollution barrier" around their town.

By 1993 the Tree Musketeers had planted more than 700 trees in their community. They have also inspired other young people around the United States to plant thousands more trees.

The Tree Musketeers group is run entirely by kids. The county of Los Angeles and the state government of California both gave awards to the group. Several years ago the Tree Musketeers even received the President's Volunteer Action Award in a special White House ceremony!

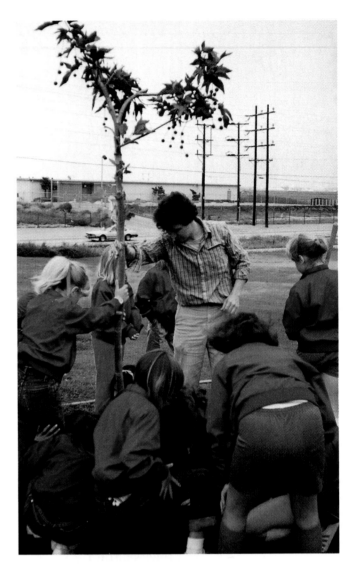

**Tree Musketeers planting a tree.**

## REVIEW

1. Where do plants get their mass?

2. How do scientists study trees and plants?

3. What discoveries did Roy Renkin make about forest fires?

4. Why do you think the lodgepole pine has cones that open only after a fire?

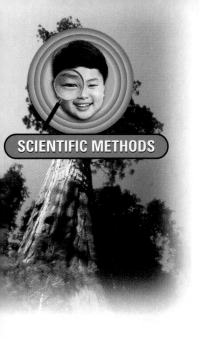

# BE A SCIENTIST Glossary

*These are skill words that you will see printed in red in the Explore Activities, Skill Builders, and Quick Labs throughout this book.*

## A

**analyze**  separate anything into its parts to find out what it is made of and how it is put together

## C

**cause and effect**  something (cause) that brings about a change in something else (effect)

**classify**  place materials that share properties together in groups

**collect data**  put together all useful information

**communicate**  share information

**compare and contrast**  find out how things are the same (compare) and how they are different (contrast)

## D

**define**  put together a description that is based on observations and experience

**draw conclusions**  put together in a statement all the facts you have learned

## E

**evaluate**  find out the value or amount of something

**evidence**  clues used to solve a problem

**experiment**  a test that is used to discover or prove something

## H

**hypothesis**  a statement in answer to a question; you must be able to test the statement

## I

**identify**  name or recognize

**identify patterns**  find a group of facts that repeat or do not change

**infer**  form an idea from facts or observations

**interpret data**  use the information that has been gathered to answer questions or solve a problem

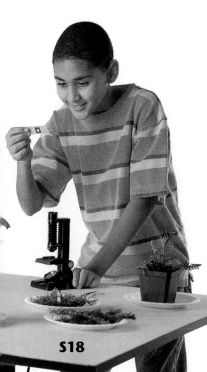

# M

**make decisions** make up your mind from many choices

**measure** find the size, volume, area, mass, weight, or temperature of an object or how long an event occurs

**model** something that represents an object or event

# O

**observe** use one or more of the senses to identify or learn about an object or event

# P

**plan** think out ahead of time how something is to be done or made, including methods and materials

**predict** state possible results of an event or experiment

# R

**reproduce results** repeat an experiment to verify findings

**revise** examine and improve

# S

**sequence** a series of things that are related in some way

# T

**test** the examination of a substance or event to see what it is or why it happens

**theory** an explanation based on observation and reasoning

# U

**use numbers** ordering, counting, adding, subtracting, multiplying, and dividing to explain data

# V

**variable** a thing in an experiment that can be changed or controlled

*These are new science words that you learned in Be a Scientist. You will see and learn more Science Words printed in blue as you read this book.*

**biologist** a scientist who studies plant and animal life

**chemical change** a change of matter that occurs when atoms link together in a new way, creating a new substance different from the original substances

**mass** a measure of the amount of matter in an object

**photosynthesis** the food-making process in green plants that uses sunlight

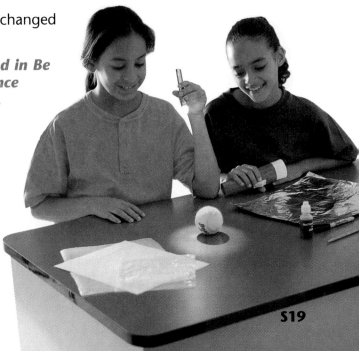

# METHODS OF SCIENCE

Here is a chart that shows the steps to follow when solving a problem in science.

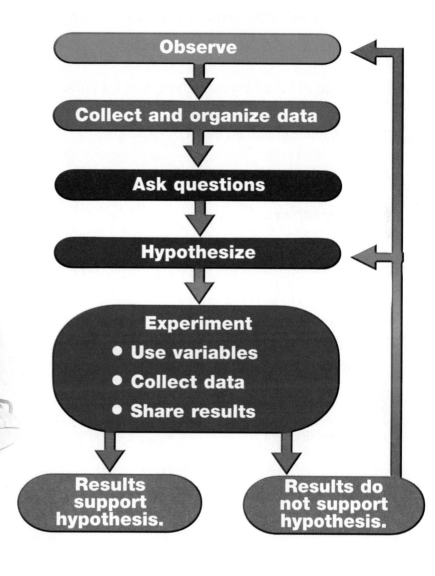

```
            Observe
               ↓
    Collect and organize data
               ↓
        Ask questions
               ↓
         Hypothesize
               ↓
         Experiment
         • Use variables
         • Collect data
         • Share results
          ↓              ↓
    Results         Results do
    support         not support
    hypothesis.     hypothesis.
```

READING 📊 CHARTS

**WRITE** How would you solve a problem in science? Write a paragraph based on the chart.

# UNIT 1

# PLANTS

## CHAPTER 1

# THE IMPORTANCE OF PLANTS

Plants give us shade and protect our soil. They give us food, such as fruits and vegetables. They also provide food for animals that people eat.

Plants also give us beautiful flowers we use as gifts and for decoration.

In Chapter 1 you will draw conclusions about things. Drawing conclusions means making reasoned judgments. You will draw conclusions from facts—things you can see and measure.

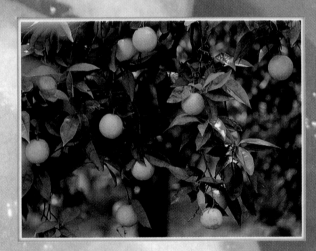

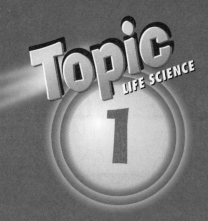

## WHY IT MATTERS

**There are many different kinds of plants, and they are used in many different ways.**

## SCIENCE WORDS

**chlorophyll** a green chemical in plant cells that allows plants to use the Sun's energy for making food

**vascular** plants that contain tissue through which water moves up and food moves down

**nonvascular** plants that do not have tissue through which water and food move

**fungus** a member of a kingdom that contains one-celled and many-celled living things that absorb food from their environment

**protist** a member of a kingdom that contains one-celled and many-celled living things, some that make food and some that hunt for food

**bacterium** a member of either of two kingdoms of one-celled living things that have no nucleus, or center, in their cell body

# The Plant Kingdom

**W**hat things in a ballpark come from plants? What things that you use every day come from plants? Wood products, cotton clothes, many medicines and foods are from plants. Plants make oxygen! Meats that you eat come from animals that eat plants or from animals that eat animals that eat plants.

Trees, shrubs, grasses, and flowers are familiar and easy to identify as plants. Others may not be so familiar. Are mushrooms plants? Is seaweed a plant?

## EXPLORE

**HYPOTHESIZE** Most plants live on land, but some live in water. Some are tiny, and others grow very large. Do all plants have common traits? Write a hypothesis in your *Science Journal*. Then test your ideas.

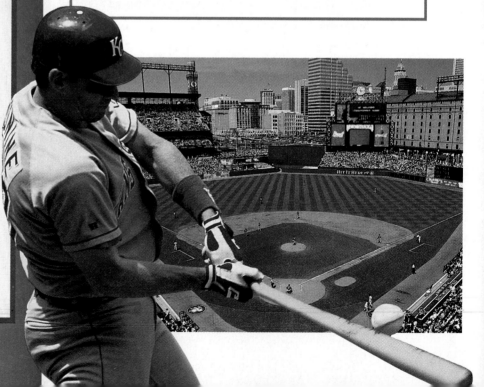

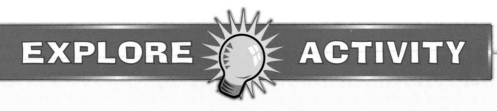
# Investigate What Plants Have in Common

Define what a plant is by observing four plants and comparing their characteristics.

## MATERIALS

- *Elodea* plant
- moss plant
- fern plant
- geranium (or other flowering plant)
- microscope
- microscope slide
- coverslip
- dropper
- water
- *Science Journal*

## PROCEDURES

1. **OBSERVE**  Your group will need to get four plants from your teacher. Observe each of the plants.

2. **COMMUNICATE**  As you observe each plant, draw the plant and describe the plant in your *Science Journal*.

3. Make a wet-mount slide of an *Elodea* leaf by placing the leaf in a drop of water in the center of the slide and carefully putting a coverslip on top.

4. **OBSERVE**  View the slide under low power.

5. **COMMUNICATE**  In your *Science Journal*, draw what you see under low power.

## CONCLUDE AND APPLY

1. **COMMUNICATE**  What plant traits can you observe without using the microscope?

2. **COMMUNICATE**  What other plant traits can you observe with the microscope?

3. **DEFINE**  Based on what you observed, come up with your own definition of a plant.

### GOING FURTHER: Problem Solving

4. **HYPOTHESIZE**  Examine some other kinds of plants with the microscope. Do all the plants seem to have the same traits, or do some plants look quite different from the others? Do plants that look similar under the microscope have the same traits? How would you set up an experiment to find out?

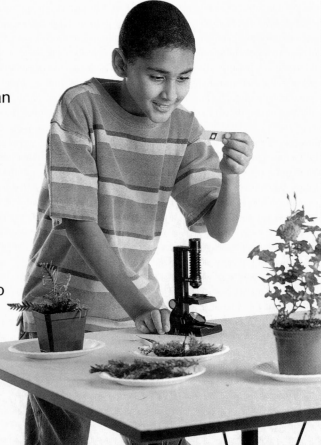

# What Do Plants Have in Common?

You don't need a microscope to discover that all of the plants in the Explore Activity are green. That's because their cells contain a green chemical called **chlorophyll** (klôr'ə fil'). It allows plants to use the Sun's energy to make their own food. The other things plants need to make food are water and minerals from the soil and carbon dioxide from the air.

## What Are Plants Made Of?

If you looked at the *Elodea* leaf under a microscope, you would see what looked like little boxes. These are the cells, or basic building blocks, of the *Elodea*. All living things are made up of cells. Plants are made up of many different kinds of cells. All plant cells have certain things in common that help plants live and grow.

Let's look at a tree to find out how its cells help it survive. A tree rises up from the ground. Its rigid trunk supports all its weight. Its roots anchor it into the soil. It doesn't walk, run, or swim. In order to live and grow, the tree must be made of rigid building blocks—rigid cells that support it.

What did you discover when you looked at *Elodea* cells under the microscope? You found cells that looked like

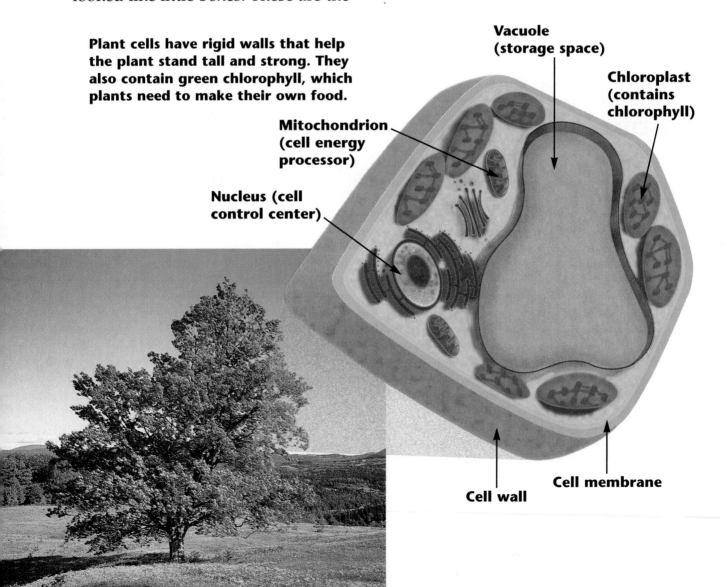

Plant cells have rigid walls that help the plant stand tall and strong. They also contain green chlorophyll, which plants need to make their own food.

**Vacuole (storage space)**

**Chloroplast (contains chlorophyll)**

**Mitochondrion (cell energy processor)**

**Nucleus (cell control center)**

**Cell wall**

**Cell membrane**

boxes. What is one characteristic of boxes? They have walls, which keep them from collapsing into a heap. All plant cells have walls. That's why an oak tree can stand tall and strong.

## How Do Cells Work Together?

The cells of all plants work together to keep the plants alive. Different kinds of cells do different kinds of jobs. Each job contributes to the health and survival of the plant. For example, in a tree, cells in leaves make the plant's food. Cells in stems, branches, roots, and the trunk form tubes through which the food or water is moved, or *transported* (trans pōrt'əd). Other cells may form flowers, fruits, and seeds that allow the tree to reproduce.

Cells are organized into *tissues* (tish´üz). The "strings" in celery stalks and the flesh of fruits are examples of plant tissues. Some tissues carry water and minerals to various parts of the plant. Some tissues support the plant.

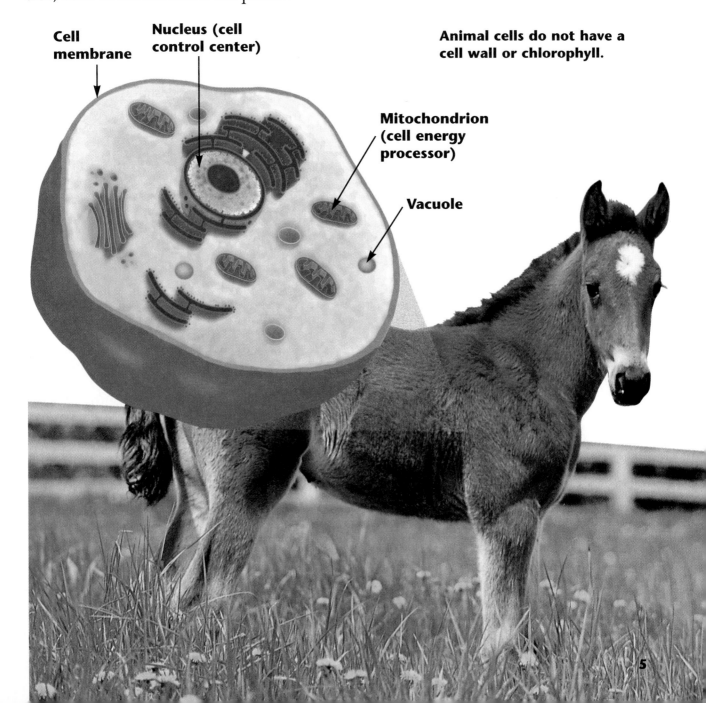

**Cell membrane**

**Nucleus (cell control center)**

**Animal cells do not have a cell wall or chlorophyll.**

**Mitochondrion (cell energy processor)**

**Vacuole**

# How Can Plants Be Grouped?

People have always tried to make sense of their surroundings. One way to do this is to look for patterns. Finding such patterns among plants can help answer very important questions, such as: What plants are good to eat? What plants are poisonous? What plants contain valuable medicines? What plants produce wood that is strong and hard?

The science of finding patterns among living things is called *classification* (klas´ə fi kā´shən). Ancient scientists came up with very simple classification systems for plants. These were based on characteristics that anyone could see. Remember, there were no microscopes or other complex instruments in those days. In 350 B.C. the Greek scientist Aristotle classified plants into three large groups—herbs (little plants), shrubs (bigger plants), and trees (the biggest plants). Aristotle's classification system was based on size.

This made sense at the time. However, as scientists learned more about plants, they realized that size was not a sensible way to classify them.

For example, today we know that a tiny blade of grass is more like a bamboo that is as tall as a ten-story building than it is like a moss that grows close to the ground.

**The chart shows the two largest groups in the plant kingdom and examples of each.**

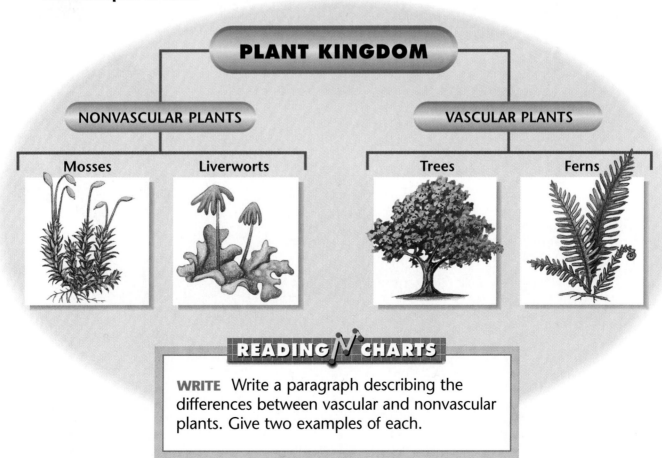

**PLANT KINGDOM**

**NONVASCULAR PLANTS**

Mosses    Liverworts

**VASCULAR PLANTS**

Trees    Ferns

**READING** **CHARTS**

**WRITE** Write a paragraph describing the differences between vascular and nonvascular plants. Give two examples of each.

## What Are Two Major Plant Groups?

By getting a look at what goes on inside plants—not what they look like on the outside—scientists have been able to divide them into two large groups. So let's take a close look inside plants to see what scientists found; something that separates one large group from the other.

First, look inside the stem of a moss. What do you see? You see lots of cells packed together like pieces in a jigsaw puzzle. The cells look very much like one another. Water from outside is passing directly into the cells.

Now, do the same thing with the stem of a corn plant. You see something very different here. Lengths of tubelike cells tunnel up and down the stem. Water taken in by the plant's roots is moving up one set of tubes toward the plant's leaves, flowers, and other parts. At the same time, foods made in the leaves are moving down the other set of tubes, which lead to all of the plant's parts. These tubes are called *vascular tissue*.

Scientists call plants that have this kind of tissue—such as trees and flowering plants—**vascular** (vas′kyə lər) plants. *Vascular* means "composed of or containing vessels," like the veins and arteries in your body. Scientists call plants that don't have this kind of tissue—such as mosses and other simple plants—**nonvascular** plants. All plants fall into one of these two groups.

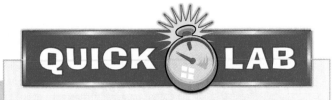

# QUICK LAB

## Tubelike Plant Parts

**HYPOTHESIZE** How does water get to different parts of a plant? Write a hypothesis in your *Science Journal.* Then test your ideas.

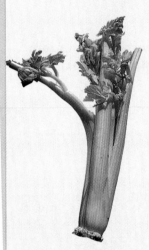

### MATERIALS
- celery stalk
- bit of moss
- lettuce leaf
- oak or maple leaf
- water
- food coloring
- narrow-mouthed bottle
- hand lens
- knife
- *Science Journal*

## PROCEDURES

1. **OBSERVE/COMMUNICATE** Use the hand lens to examine the plant parts. Describe in your *Science Journal* the structures you see.

2. **HYPOTHESIZE** Make a guess about the function of each structure.

3. Add water to the bottle so the water is about an inch deep. Add a few drops of food coloring to the water.

4. Try putting different plant pieces in the colored water. Observe them after a few minutes. Record your observations in your *Science Journal.*

## CONCLUDE AND APPLY

1. **INTERPRET DATA** Write an explanation. Include a statement about why your observations support or don't support your guess.

## How Are Plant Groups Divided?

As you've discovered, all plants have certain characteristics in common. Every living thing that has these characteristics belongs to the plant kingdom. A kingdom is the largest subdivision of living things.

While all plants have certain characteristics in common, they have their differences, too. As you have seen, plants may be vascular or nonvascular. However, the plants within each of these two groups are far from identical. This observation prompted scientists to divide nonvascular plants into smaller and smaller

**The divisions of the plant kingdom and the kinds of plants in each**

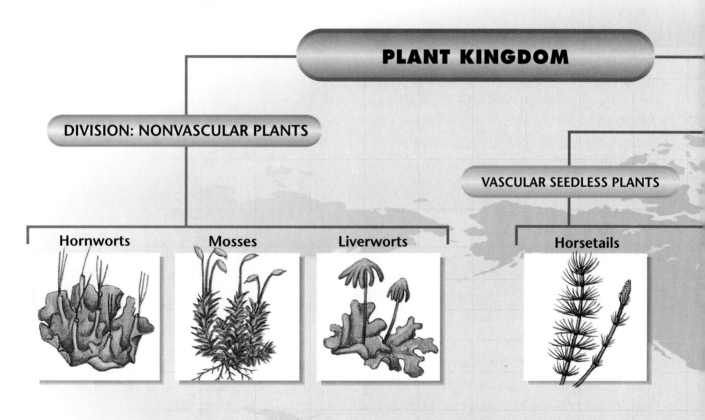

PLANT KINGDOM

DIVISION: NONVASCULAR PLANTS

VASCULAR SEEDLESS PLANTS

Hornworts     Mosses     Liverworts     Horsetails

## READING N CHARTS

1. **DISCUSS** Name two plants you are familiar with and the division you think each belongs to.
2. **WRITE** Pick two plant divisions from the chart. List two ways they are alike. List two ways they are different.

groups. The scientists did the same for vascular plants.

The smallest groups would have plants most like one another. The larger groups would have plants least like one another. This meant that the smaller the group, the more closely related were its members.

The chart on these two pages shows the plants divided into groups called *divisions*. These divisions make up the plant kingdom. You will discover the other kingdoms of living things on the following four pages.

**Brain Power**

What division of plant is most common where you live? Are there any plants from the other division there?

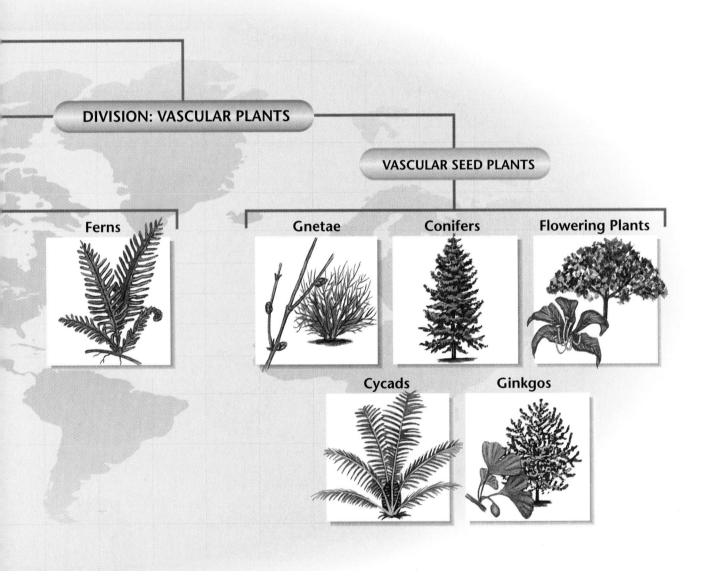

DIVISION: VASCULAR PLANTS

VASCULAR SEED PLANTS

Ferns

Gnetae

Conifers

Flowering Plants

Cycads

Ginkgos

# What Makes Animals Different from Plants?

Unlike plants, animals cannot make their own food. Animals also differ from plants because animals can move from one place to another during some parts of their lives.

All animals are grouped into one kingdom, known as the animal kingdom. The animal kingdom is divided into smaller and smaller groups. The chart on this page shows two of these groups. The first level contains groups called *phyla* (fī´lə) (singular, *phylum*). Some are shown on the left. The next level contains groups called *classes*. Some examples of animals in these groups are shown on the right.

**The phyla in the animal kingdom are like the divisions in the plant kingdom. Not all the phyla are shown in the chart.**

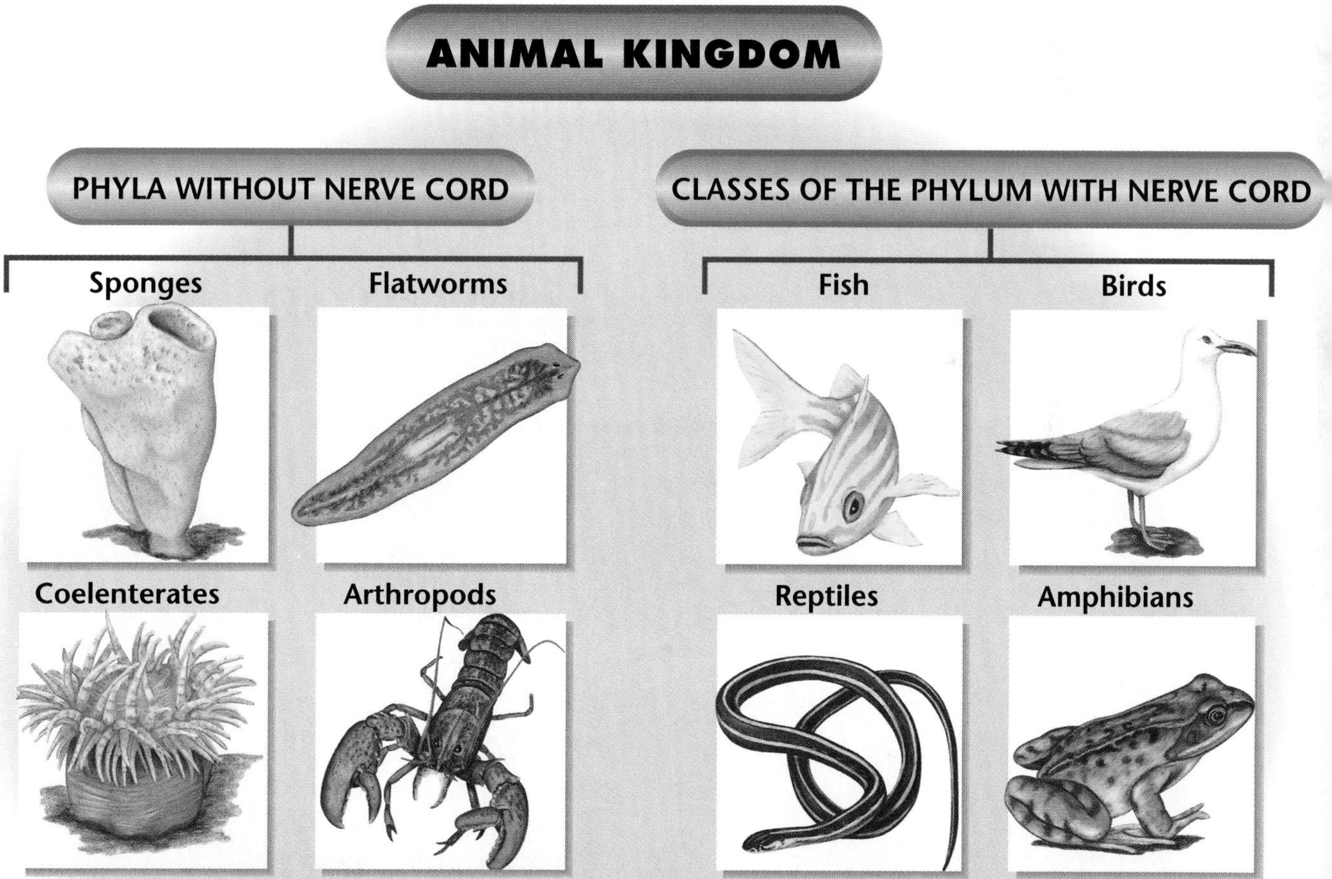

## ANIMAL KINGDOM

### PHYLA WITHOUT NERVE CORD

Sponges

Flatworms

Coelenterates

Arthropods

### CLASSES OF THE PHYLUM WITH NERVE CORD

Fish

Birds

Reptiles

Amphibians

Mammals

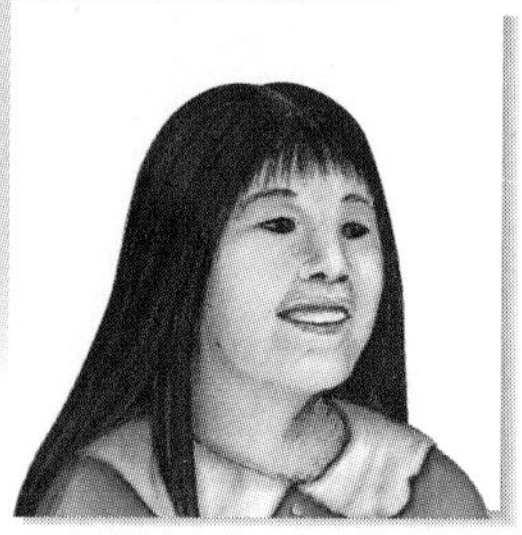

## READING N CHARTS

1. **DISCUSS**  Name five animals you are familiar with and the phylum or class you think each belongs to.
2. **WRITE**  Pick two animal phyla or classes. List two ways they are alike. List two ways they are different.

# What Is a Fungus?

It may be one celled or many celled. It doesn't make its own food as plants do or take in food as animals do. Instead it simply absorbs (takes in) food from decaying dead organisms and wastes in its environment. What is it? It's a **fungus** (fung′gəs).

*Fungi* (fun′jī)—the plural of fungus—can be very useful living things. Some of them have great flavors. Others contain chemicals that fight diseases. Still others put the bubbles in your favorite loaf of bread or turn cheeses sharp and tangy. Fungi in soil break down decaying plants and animals so that their chemicals can be used by living things. So you might say that such fungi clean up our environment.

Unfortunately, the fungus kingdom also contains organisms that cause problems for people. Some fungi are poisonous. Some fungi give people itchy diseases, like athlete's foot. Some fungi turn foods bad and ugly. Some fungi coat bathroom tiles and basement walls with smelly black or white fuzz. In the autumn of 1997, one kind of fungus was even responsible for the closing of a library in Staten Island, a part of New York City. The fungus, which grows in damp places like the library's basement, caused people to cough and sneeze as if they had the flu.

The chart on this page shows the groups of the fungus kingdom.

## FUNGUS KINGDOM

**Yeasts, Morels, Mildews**

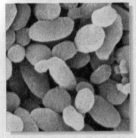

**Molds**

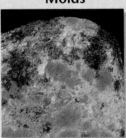

**Mushrooms, Smuts, Rusts**

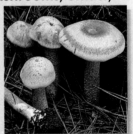

## READING ✓ CHARTS

1. **DISCUSS** Which fungus can cause problems in your shower?
2. **REPRESENT** Make a chart listing useful fungi. Draw a picture of the fungi. Label each kind of fungus with its name. Write a sentence about how the fungus is used.

# What Is a Protist?

What do you see when you look into a lake, pond, river, or ocean? Sometimes it looks like clear water. Yet that "clear" water is home to millions of microscopic living things that belong to the **protist** (prō´tist) kingdom. This kingdom isn't made up of just microscopic living things. It also includes living things you can see without a microscope, such as seaweed and green pond scum. Although most protists live in water, some inhabit the land.

Some protists are single cells that swim in the water in search of smaller living things to eat. Others, like seaweeds, are made up of groups of the same cells that are linked together. Called algae, these protists don't have to hunt for food. They contain chloro-phyll. All they have to do is float on water in the Sun, soak up the Sun's rays, and make their own food. Still other kinds of protists are one celled, swim around, and contain chlorophyll.

Members of the protist kingdom certainly seem very different. Yet if scientists put them in the same kingdom, they must have something in common. You would discover that "something" if you peered at the cells of protists under a microscope. You'd notice a dense, dark structure, called a *nucleus* (nü´klē əs) inside each cell. If you looked very carefully, you'd see that the nucleus was surrounded by a thin envelope. Scientists call this envelope a *membrane* (mem´brān). The nucleus of the *Elodea* plant could also have been seen in the Explore Activity.

**The chart shows some of the groups of the protist kingdom.**

## PROTIST KINGDOM

Slime molds

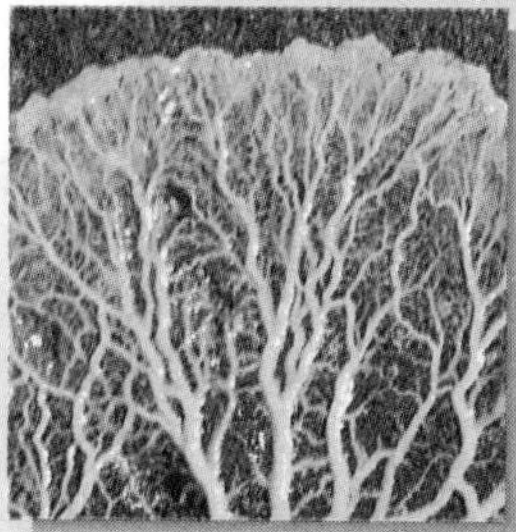

Diatoms

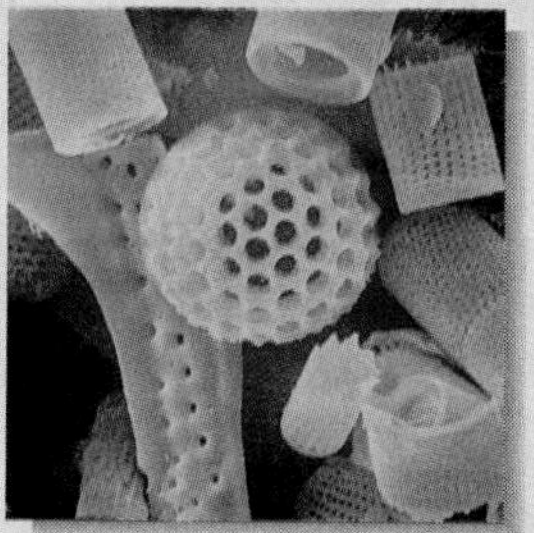

Dinoflagellates

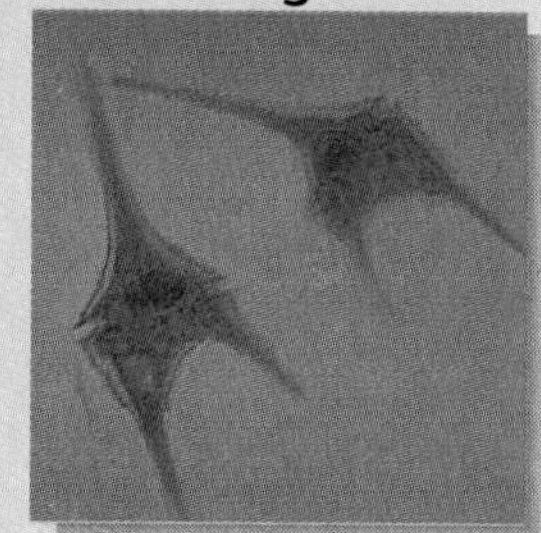

Euglenas

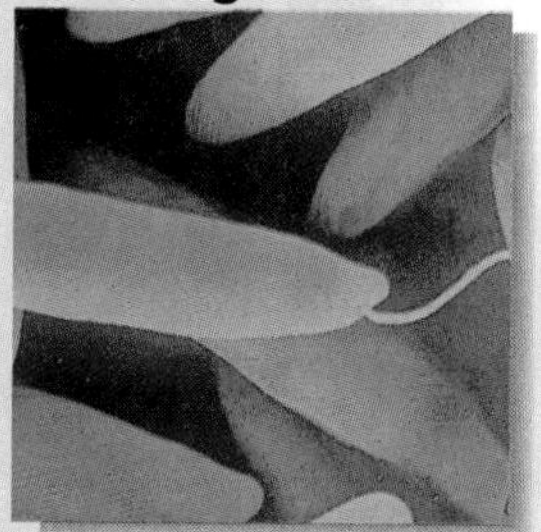

Green algae

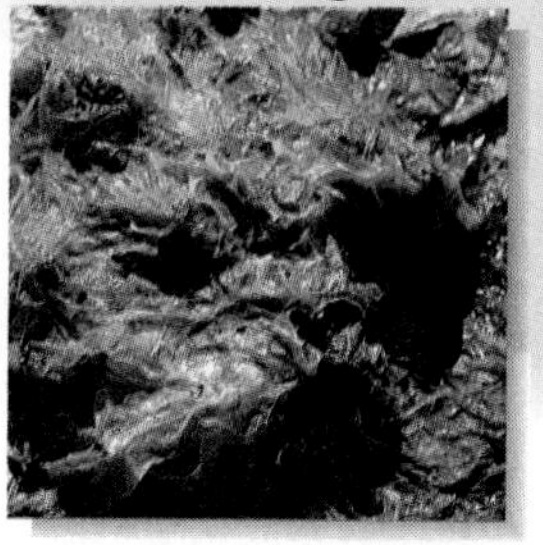

## READING CHARTS

1. **DISCUSS** What are some of the ways some protists are like animals?
2. **WRITE** What are some of the ways some protists are like plants?

# What Are the Tiniest Living Things?

**Bacteria** (bak tîr′ē ə) are both tiny and very simple. Some can cause a great deal of trouble, like infections. Others are necessary for animals and plants to survive.

Some kinds of bacteria group together in clusters or chains. Other kinds don't. You can only see bacteria under a microscope. Each *bacterium* (bak tîr′ē əm) is a single cell without a nucleus.

The "ancient" bacteria kingdom includes some fascinating organisms. One type lives in the digestive system of cows. It helps the cow by digesting cellulose, the main substance in grass, which the cow eats but can't digest. Still another kind of "ancient" bac-terium lives deep in the ocean, where lava seeps through cracks in the ocean floor. The red-hot lava heats the water up to 105°C. That's hotter than the temperature of boiling water!

The true bacteria kingdom also contains some unusual members. Have you ever seen a blue-green spot in a polar bear's white fur? If so, you detected *cyanobacteria* (sī′ə nō bak tîr′ē ə). The prefix *cyano-* means "blue."

Some true bacteria cause diseases in plants and animals. A "strep" throat is caused by a true bacterium. If your stomach aches after eating spoiled food, the culprit's likely to be another true bacterium. More serious diseases like tuberculosis and certain kinds of pneumonia are also caused by true bacteria.

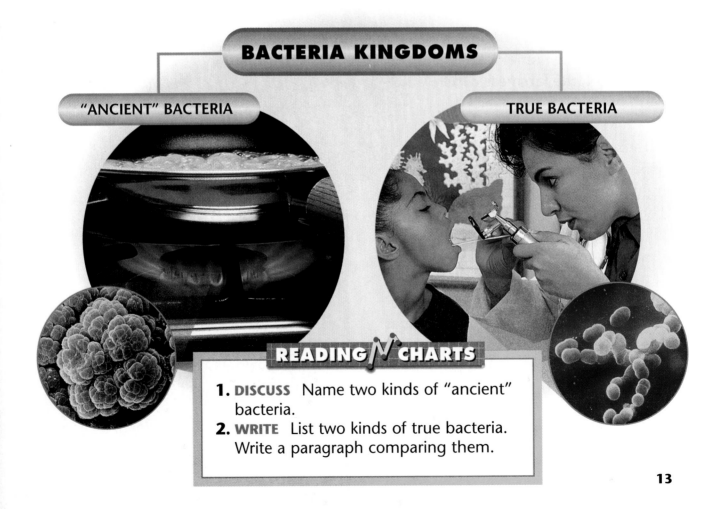

**BACTERIA KINGDOMS**

**"ANCIENT" BACTERIA**

**TRUE BACTERIA**

**READING N CHARTS**

1. **DISCUSS** Name two kinds of "ancient" bacteria.
2. **WRITE** List two kinds of true bacteria. Write a paragraph comparing them.

13

# What Was the Vine That Ate the South?

The year was 1876. People all over the United States were celebrating the nation's 100th birthday. In Philadelphia the celebration focused on the exhibits of the Philadelphia Centennial Exposition. Many countries showed off their prized possessions there. The Japanese were known for their fine gardens, and there were many unusual plants at the Japanese exhibit.

One plant undoubtedly caught the eye of many passersby. It was a woody vine. Little hairs sprang from the edges of its 10-centimeter-wide (4-inch-wide) green leaves. However, what stopped viewers in their tracks were the plant's purple flowers. Although each was only $1\frac{1}{4}$ centimeters ($\frac{1}{2}$ inch) long, they hung in long clusters. The flowers also gave off a powerful aroma. When asked the name of the wonderful plant, the Japanese caretaker simply replied, "Kudzu."

Today people in America's southern states call it other things: "Mile-a-Minute Vine," "Foot-a-Night Vine," and more frighteningly, "The Vine That Ate the South."

There is more than some truth in all of these names. "Mile-a-Minute Vine" is an exaggeration, but "Foot-a-Night Vine" is not. The plant can grow that much each day. It can spread out over 60 feet in a single summer and choke the life out of other weaker plants.

How did kudzu escape from Philadelphia? Why does it now cover seven million acres of America's southland? It was pretty. In the late 1800s, American homeowners used it to decorate gardens and homes. It was tasty to animals. In the 1920s American farmers grew it to feed cows, sheep, and other farm animals. Its huge 2-meter-long (6-foot-long) roots grew to be 18 centimeters (7 inches) in diameter and weighed up to 182 kilograms (400 pounds). Those roots hung on to soil in a tight grip. In the 1940s American conservation workers planted it all over the South to prevent soil from being washed away by heavy rains.

What nobody counted on was the hardiness of the plant. It grew best

**The purple flowers of the kudzu are very beautiful. They smell good, too. Lots of people bought the plants to decorate their properties.**

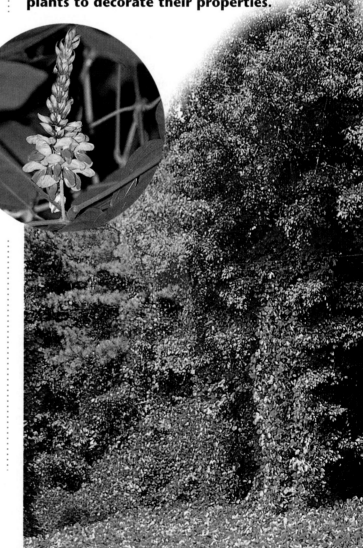

where temperatures rose above 27°C (80°F) and where 102 centimeters (40 inches) or more of rain fell. It found an ideal home in the South. There was something else that promoted its rapid growth. Something kept it in check in Japan but not in America—its natural enemies. These were insect pests that lived in Japan but not in the American South.

Today kudzu is labeled a weed by the United States Department of Agriculture. Many people are trying to find ways to control it. Will they succeed, or will the vine continue to gobble up huge chunks of the South? The answer is anyone's guess.

There are many different kinds of plants, but they are all very important. Without plants, life would be impossible on Earth. Almost everything you eat comes from plants, or from animals that eat plants.

**Kudzu is a very fast growing plant. It can spread 60 feet in a single summer.**

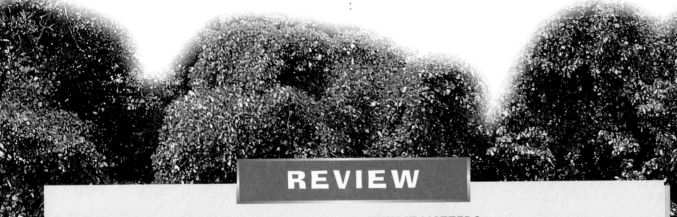

## REVIEW

**1.** What do plants have in common?

**2.** How are plants similar to animals, protists, fungi, and bacteria? How are plants different?

**3.** How are vascular plants different from nonvascular plants?

**4. COMMUNICATE** Describe three characteristics of plants.

**5. CRITICAL THINKING** *Analyze* How can plants that are imported from other parts of the world become pests here?

**WHY IT MATTERS** THINK ABOUT IT
How are plants important to your survival?

**WHY IT MATTERS** WRITE ABOUT IT
Write a paragraph explaining what plants are important in your life.

**READING SKILL**
Write a paragraph to describe any conclusions you can draw about plants after reading this lesson.

# Analyzing ALGAE

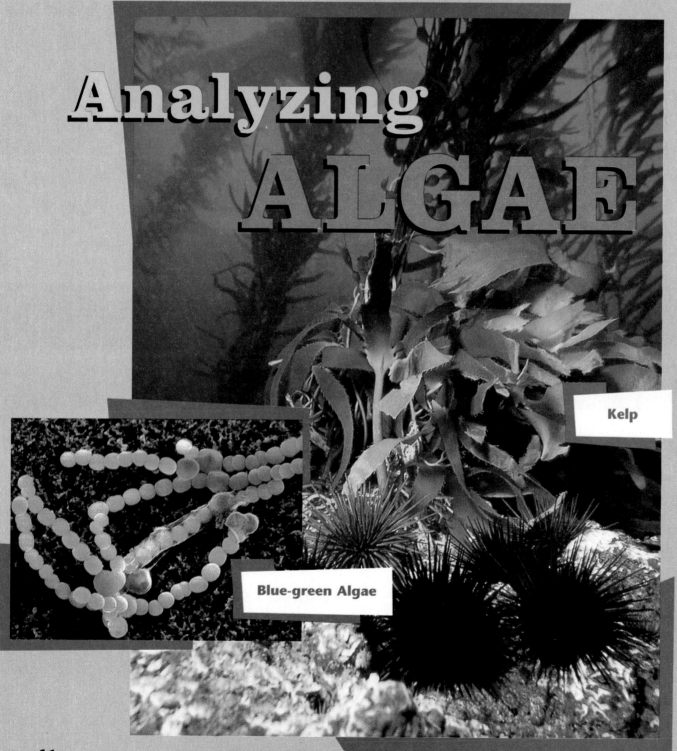

Kelp

Blue-green Algae

# History of Science

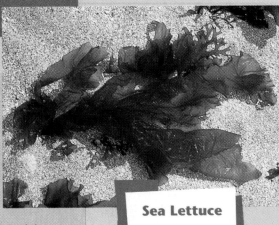

**Sea Lettuce**

**A**ristotle was the first to divide all living things into two kingdoms—plants and animals. He put algae in the plant kingdom because many algae looked like plants, made their own food, and didn't seem able to move on their own.

With the development of microscopes, scientists could examine algae more closely. They discovered that some, such as the tiny green algae in pond water, had just one cell. Other algae had many cells and looked like tiny palm trees, mushrooms, lettuce, or moss. One kind of algae, kelp, can grow to be 61 meters (200 feet) long!

Even the largest algae are still simple organisms. They're collections of nearly identical cells. Algae with many cells have no root, leaf, or seed tissue. Lettuce-shaped algae are just sheets of cells, two cells thick.

Today scientists place most algae in the protist kingdom because of their simple structures. Blue-green algae have no nucleus in their cells, so some scientists place them in the bacteria kingdom.

Most scientists believe that green algae are the ancestors of plants. All algae contain chlorophyll, even brown and red algae. Green algae have cell walls and store starch as food. They're so much like plants that they probably were Earth's first plants!

Scientists today group living things into six different kingdoms, with protists making up their own kingdom, Protista.  Scientists continue to study algae. They want to know for sure whether algae are plants, protists, or members of a whole new kingdom of their own!

## Discussion Starter

**1** Why do you think scientists had trouble placing algae in a kingdom?

**2** In what kingdom or kingdoms would you place algae? Why?

*inter***NET** CONNECTION To learn more about algae, visit *www.mhschool.com/science* and enter the keyword **ALGAE.**

17

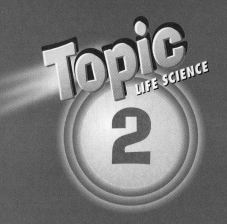

# Topic 2
## LIFE SCIENCE

## WHY IT MATTERS

**Every part of a plant helps it and us to survive.**

### SCIENCE WORDS

**root cap** a thin covering made up of cells that protect the root tip as it grows into the soil

**epidermis** an outermost layer of parts of a plant, such as roots and leaves

**cortex** a layer just inside the epidermis of roots and stems

**xylem** tissue through which water and minerals move up through a plant

**phloem** tissue through which food from the leaves moves down through a plant

**cambium** a layer that separates xylem from phloem

**chloroplast** a part of a plant cell containing chlorophyll, the green substance that enables the plant to produce food

**transpiration** the loss of water through a plant's leaves, as water rises up through the plant replacing the lost water

# Plant Survival

**W**hat do you have in common with a plant? Would you believe that you and a plant have similar needs? However, there is a big difference. You can move around to get things. You can change things around you—like your room temperature. Plants stay in one place. However, different kinds of plants can survive in very different places. How?

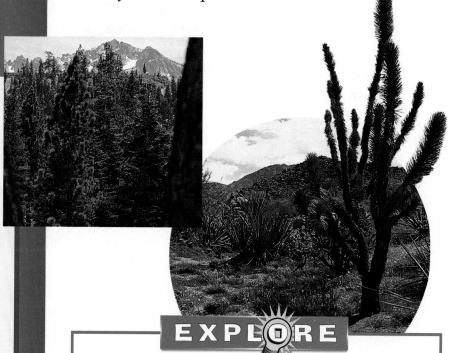

## EXPLORE

**HYPOTHESIZE** How may plants from different places differ from each other? How do the differences help the plants survive in their surroundings? Write a hypothesis in your *Science Journal*. Then test your ideas.

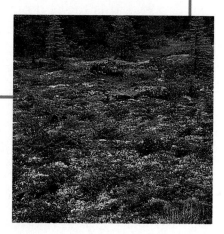

# EXPLORE ACTIVITY

# Investigate How a Plant's Parts Help It Survive

Observe differences in plants that come from different environments.

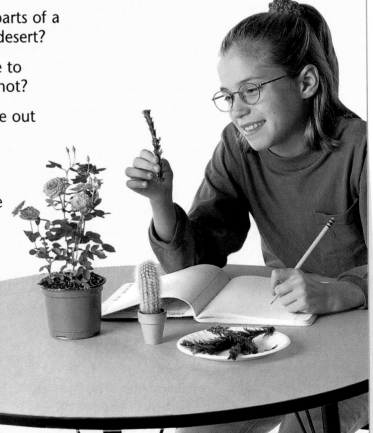

## MATERIALS

- cactus
- water plant, such as an *Elodea* or a duckweed
- flowering plant, such as a geranium
- *Science Journal*

## PROCEDURE

1. **OBSERVE** Look at the physical properties of the leaves of each plant. Note the color, size, and shape of the leaves in your *Science Journal.*

2. **ANALYZE** List any other plant parts that you see.

3. **COMMUNICATE** Observe the physical properties of these parts and record your observations in your *Science Journal.*

4. Record any other physical properties that you observe.

## CONCLUDE AND APPLY

1. **DRAW CONCLUSIONS** How do the parts of a cactus help it survive in a hot, dry desert?

2. **INFER** Would the geranium be able to survive in the desert? Why or why not?

3. **INFER** Could the water plant survive out of water? Why or why not?

### GOING FURTHER: Problem Solving

4. **PREDICT** Could these plants survive outside where you live? Why or why not? For each plant what conditions would you have to change so that the plant could survive outside where you live?

# How Do a Plant's Parts Help It Survive?

Some plant roots help you survive. That's because they are foods. Beets, carrots, sweet potatoes, radishes, and turnips are the roots of different plants. As the Explore Activity showed, plant parts help plants survive. How do roots help a plant survive?

Most plants have roots that hold them in the ground. Some plants, like mosses, don't have true roots. Still, mosses have rootlike structures that anchor them. Roots help keep plants from getting swept away by wind and running water. Roots draw up water and minerals from the soil. Plants must have water and minerals to make their own food. Roots also store food for the plant. That's especially true of sweet potato, sugar beet, and carrot plants.

A root gets its start early in the life of a plant. If you were to look at a lima bean as it sprouted, you would see a tiny piece of the young plant growing straight downward. This is the plant's first root.

This root bores deeper and deeper into the soil. Why don't the rough particles of soil rub away and harm the young root? The tip of the root is protected by a layer of tough cells called the **root cap**.

Soon more roots branch out from the sides of the original root. *Taproots* have

## PARTS OF A ROOT

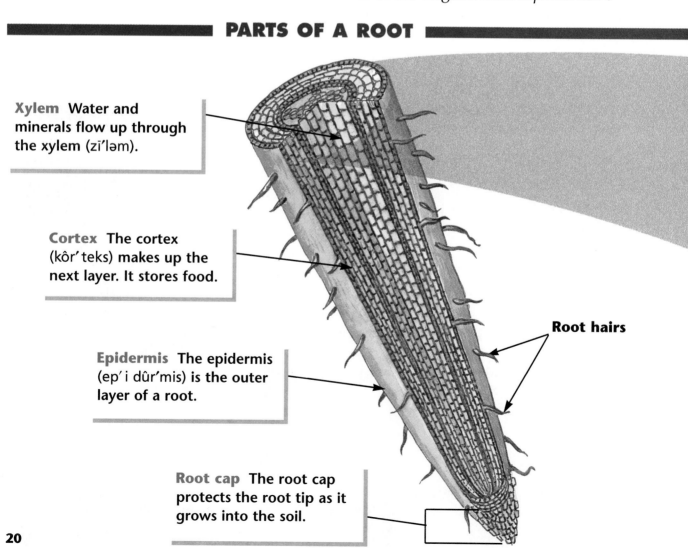

**Xylem** Water and minerals flow up through the xylem (zī′ləm).

**Cortex** The cortex (kôr′ teks) makes up the next layer. It stores food.

**Epidermis** The epidermis (ep′ i dûr′mis) is the outer layer of a root.

**Root hairs**

**Root cap** The root cap protects the root tip as it grows into the soil.

20

one large root with a few hairy branching roots. They look like a carrot or a beet. Other roots, like those of grass or rye plants, are made up of only thin hairy branching roots called *fibrous roots*.

Taproots tend to grow deep into the ground and reach water deep down. Fibrous roots spread out near the soil's surface. They collect water where there is little rain that only soaks into the very top layer of soil.

Fibrous roots can make huge networks. The total surface area of the root system of a single rye plant was 639 square meters (almost 7,000 square feet)!

Some plants like orchids, that grow high in the branches of rain forest trees, have *aerial roots*. These roots never touch the ground. They take in moisture from the air. *Prop roots*, like those of a corn plant, grow like fingers out of the bottom of the stem. These roots help prop up the plant.

## How Do Roots Work?

The structure of a root helps it absorb water and minerals and send them to other parts of the plant. These drawings show how this happens.

### READING N DIAGRAMS

**REPRESENT** Organize the information in this diagram into a table or map.

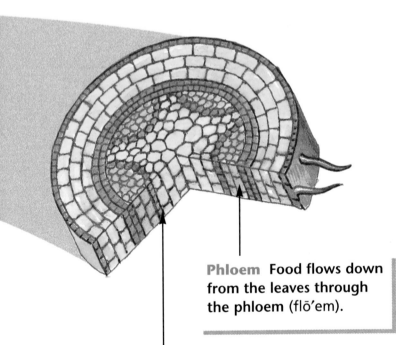

**Phloem** Food flows down from the leaves through the phloem (flō'em).

**Cambium** The cambium (kam'bē əm) separates the xylem from the phloem. The cambium is where new xylem and phloem grow.

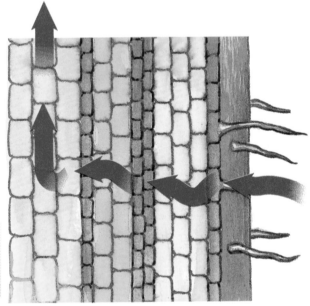

Water and minerals enter the root hairs. They pass through the root's cortex to the xylem. They then move up the xylem, into the plant's stem, and to all parts of the plant.

# How Are Stems Similar?

Some stems are soft and delicate, like those of a young corn plant. Others are hard and tough, like those of a giant redwood tree. No matter what they look like, all stems have certain things in common.

All stems support leaves. Some also support flowers. Stems help leaves reach open places, where the leaves can be bathed in sunlight.

Stems also hold the transportation system for plants. This system lets water and minerals move from the roots to all parts of the plant, especially its leaves. It moves foods made in leaves to all other parts of the plant.

The *xylem* makes up the part of the transportation system that moves water and minerals up from the roots. The *phloem* moves food from the plant's leaves to its other parts. Many stems also have a *cambium*—a layer of cells—that separates the two. In addition woody stems are protected by a tough outer layer of tissue, called bark.

## READING /V DIAGRAMS

**WRITE** How are the xylem, phloem, and cambium arranged differently in a woody stem and in a soft stem?

## PARTS OF A STEM

Soft and woody stems have the same basic parts for transporting water, minerals, and food to all parts of a plant.

**WOODY STEM**

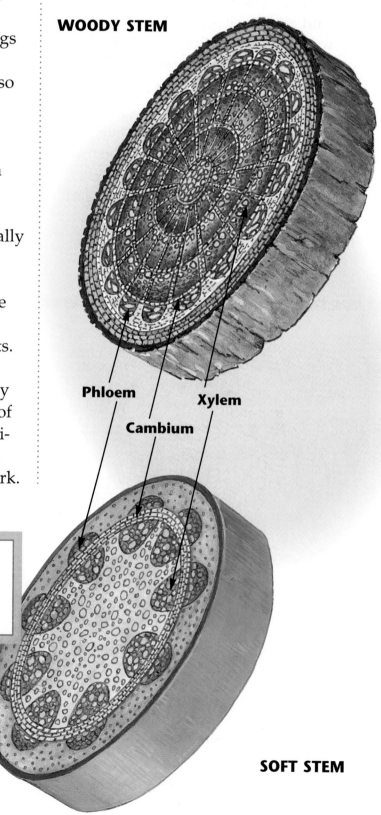

Phloem

Xylem

Cambium

**SOFT STEM**

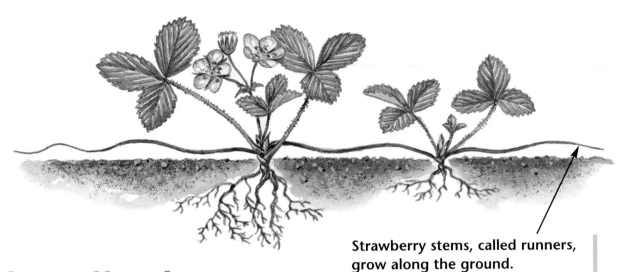

Strawberry stems, called runners, grow along the ground.

## Stems: How Are They Different?

Some stems do more than support a plant and give it a transportation system. For example, the stems of plants like potatoes and sugarcane store food for the plants to use later. The potatoes and sugarcane you eat actually are stems. The stems of cactus plants store water, which the plants use during long dry periods in the desert. Still other stems, like those of asparagus, help make the plant's food.

Not all stems grow up into the air. Those of strawberries grow along the ground. That's how a strawberry patch spreads and grows.

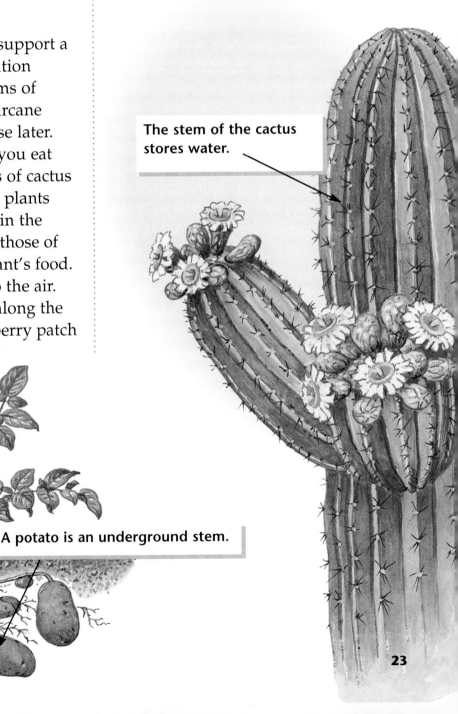

The stem of the cactus stores water.

A potato is an underground stem.

23

# PARTS OF LEAVES

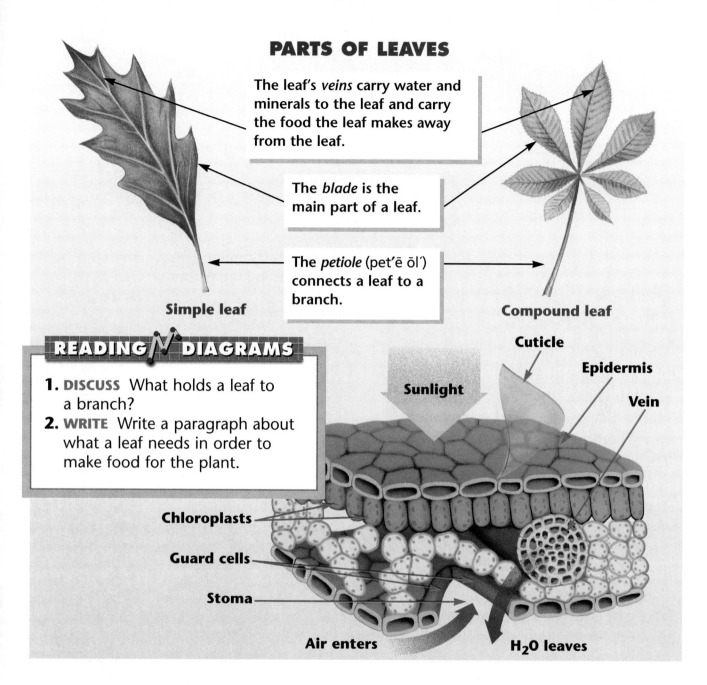

The leaf's *veins* carry water and minerals to the leaf and carry the food the leaf makes away from the leaf.

The *blade* is the main part of a leaf.

The *petiole* (pet′ē ōl′) connects a leaf to a branch.

**Simple leaf**

**Compound leaf**

Cuticle

Epidermis

Sunlight

Vein

Chloroplasts

Guard cells

Stoma

Air enters

H₂O leaves

## READING ✍ DIAGRAMS

1. **DISCUSS** What holds a leaf to a branch?
2. **WRITE** Write a paragraph about what a leaf needs in order to make food for the plant.

## What Are Leaves?

Leaves come in all shapes and sizes. Most of the leaves you see hang from their plants as single leaves or in groups. Maple and oak trees have single leaves. They're called *simple* leaves.

Horse chestnut and locust leaves come in clusters. These are called *compound* leaves.

The parts of a leaf work together to help keep the plant alive.

The outermost layer of a leaf is its *epidermis*. Cells of the epidermis secrete a waxy coating, called a *cuticle* (kū′ti kəl). The cuticle helps keep water from leaving the leaf.

The leaf makes food in cells between the layers of the epidermis. These cells contain **chloroplasts** (klôr′ə plasts′), the green food factories of plants. In addition to sunlight, these factories need water, minerals, and the carbon dioxide in air to make food.

The air comes through tiny pores in the bottom of the leaves called *stomata* (stō′mə tə) (singular, *stoma*). When the stomata are open to let in air, water can also evaporate from the leaf. The job of opening and closing each stoma is performed by two *guard cells* that surround it.

When the plant has plenty of water, the guard cells swell and pull open the stoma. When the plant has too little water, the guard cells shrink and close the stoma.

### How Leaf Shapes Differ

Many leaves have green, broad, flat surfaces that help "capture" the sunlight the plant needs to make its food. Other leaves have different shapes for different purposes. The spines on a cactus protect the plant. The needles of a pine tree are covered with a wax that keeps the tree from losing too much water. The crunchy layers of an onion store food. The leaves of the garden pea plant wind around objects to give the plant added support.

The leaves of the Venus's-flytrap are colorful insect traps. They snap shut when an insect flies inside.

### Leaves Help Roots Get Water

Leaves are often far from roots, yet they help roots take in water from soil. When water evaporates from the leaves, more water moves up through the plant to replace the lost water. This process is called **transpiration** (tran′spə rā′shən).

### Leaves as Food

People eat all parts of plants, including leaves such as lettuce, cabbage, parsley, and spinach. Why are leaves important to you?

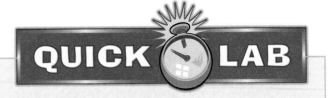

# QUICK LAB

## Leaves

**HYPOTHESIZE** In what ways are the leaves that are important to you alike? In what ways are they different? Write a hypothesis in your *Science Journal.*

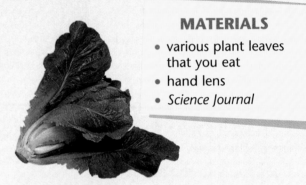

### MATERIALS
- various plant leaves that you eat
- hand lens
- *Science Journal*

## PROCEDURES

1. Collect a variety of different leaves that you eat as food.

2. **OBSERVE** Examine them with a hand lens. Record your observations in your *Science Journal.*

3. **COMPARE** What do the leaves you brought have in common?

4. **COMPARE** In what ways are they different from each other?

## CONCLUDE AND APPLY

1. **COMMUNICATE** Write how the leaves you examined are similar and how they are different.

2. **COMPARE AND CONTRAST** Compare the leaves you examined with the leaves your classmates looked at. In what ways are your leaves similar to theirs? In what ways are they different?

**Dangling their roots in the air, these orchids cling to trees high in the canopy of a tropical rain forest. Their aerial roots soak up water that trickles along tree trunks and branches.**

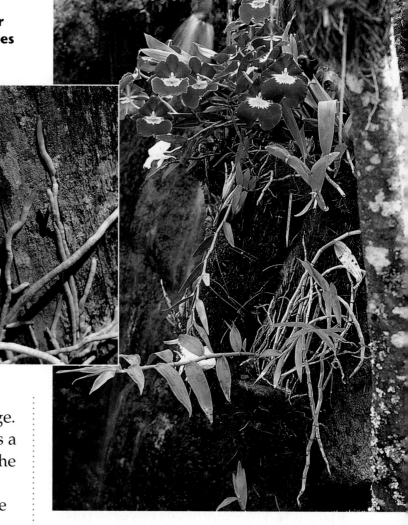

## Rooted Firmly in . . . the Air?

Many kinds of orchids are rooted in the ground. However, in tropical rain forests, certain orchids grow high up in the trees, dangling their roots in the air. The orchids' colors "paint" the trees with flashes of red, purple, pink, and orange.

One kind of orchid looks and smells a lot like a certain kind of female bee. The orchid attracts male bees. As the bees go from flower to flower, they help the orchids reproduce.

A sudden shower drenches the tree where the orchid lives. Tiny streams of water trickle down the tree's bark. The orchid's exposed roots soak up some of the water that washes off the tree trunk and branches above. Along with the water come minerals the orchid needs.

The roots of a nearby orchid are very strange. They are flat, as long as you are tall, and wrapped around the branches of a tree like a huge flat worm. In fact the scientific name of the orchid means "tapeworm leaf."

You might think that this is a strange name for a root. However, in a way, it makes sense. The roots of this plant are green, like leaves! Scientists have discovered that these roots do two jobs for the orchid. They absorb water and minerals that pass by, and like leaves, they make food for the orchid. This orchid needs no leaves, although it has some very little ones covering its stem.

Orchids are expensive and beautiful. If you have an older sister, you may know that orchids do more than cling to rain forest trees. That's because orchids are the favorite flowers for girls to wear to a prom.

Since plants are needed by all living things, it is important to know how they survive. Part of a plant's ability to survive depends on how well its parts work together to move water and minerals in one direction and food in the other direction. The parts that do this are roots, stems, and leaves.

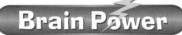

### Brain Power

What parts of plants do you use most often? Explain your answer.

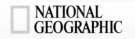

## FUNtastic Facts

The giant leaves of the royal water lily are strong enough to bear the weight of a small child. A network of air-filled ribs keeps the 2.5-meter-wide (8-foot) leaves floating on the surface of the water. Royal water lilies grow in sluggish streams in the Amazon basin of South America. How do the leaves of the royal water lily help the plant survive?

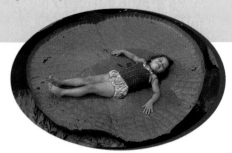

# REVIEW

1. List three things plants need in order to live and grow.

2. **COMPARE AND CONTRAST** Describe two or more different kinds of roots. Explain how they are different and how they are similar. Do the same for stems and leaves.

3. How do roots, stems, and leaves help a plant survive?

4. How can rain forest orchids live high up in the trees?

5. **CRITICAL THINKING** *Analyze* How do you think that having flowers that look like bees can help a plant survive?

**WHY IT MATTERS** THINK ABOUT IT
What plant parts are especially important to you? Can you think of some plants whose leaves are important to you? Can you think of some plants whose stems are important to you? Can you think of some plants whose roots are important to you?

**WHY IT MATTERS** WRITE ABOUT IT
Write a paragraph about a plant that is important to you because of its stems, roots, or leaves. Can you think of a plant that is important to you because you use several of its parts? Write about the things you use that plant for.

# Plant Power: MEDICINES

**W**hat good are plant parts? Bitter or poisonous chemicals in some plant parts protect them from predators. The chemicals have powerful effects on animals that eat them. They might also be useful in medicines for humans!

## Fever Powder of Peru

Missionaries to Peru in the 1600s found natives making a bitter powder. It was ground-up bark from the cinchona, a rare jungle tree. The powder cured the fever of malaria!

Suddenly there was a demand for cinchona bark, and the quinine in it. Most cinchonas were cut down.

Doctors now use artificial quinine and other drugs to treat malaria. However, the parasite that causes malaria is becoming resistant to the drugs. Only cinchona bark still works when modern medicine fails!

## Poison to Kill Cancer?

Humans have used yews for thousands of years. Spears and bows were made from the wood. The bark yielded a poison.

In the 1960s the National Cancer Institute began looking for plant chemicals that might kill cancer cells. In 1963 they found such a chemical, taxol, in the bark of the Pacific yew.

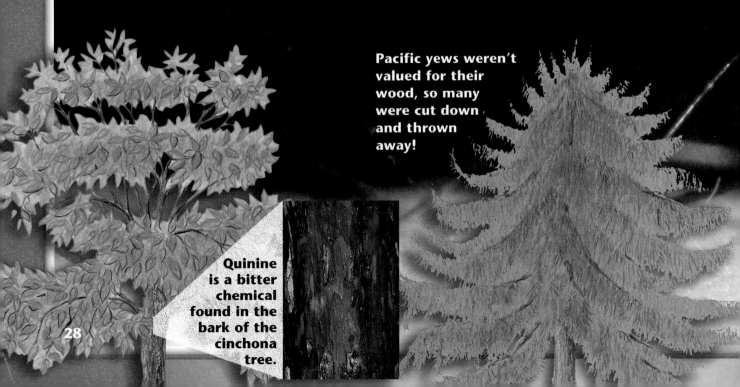

Pacific yews weren't valued for their wood, so many were cut down and thrown away!

Quinine is a bitter chemical found in the bark of the cinchona tree.

# Science, Technology, and Society

By the time cancer scientists proved that taxol works against cancer, the Pacific yew was rapidly disappearing. Today scientists make taxol from needles and twigs of all kinds of yews, not just the bark of the Pacific yew.

Many plants may be in danger of extinction. People are destroying Earth's rain forests. If plants die off before they're found, we'll never know if their chemicals could have cured diseases.

## MEDICINES FROM PLANTS
### Here are a few medicines made from plant parts.

| PLANT | PARTS | MEDICINE | USED FOR |
|---|---|---|---|
| Belladonna | leaves/roots | atropine | breathing problems |
| Foxglove | leaves | digitalis | heart problems |
| Periwinkle | leaves | vinblastine | leukemia |
| Rauwolfia | roots | reserpine | high blood pressure |
| Willow | bark | aspirin | reducing pain and fever |
| Wild Mexican yam | tuberous roots | cortisone | curbing inflammation |

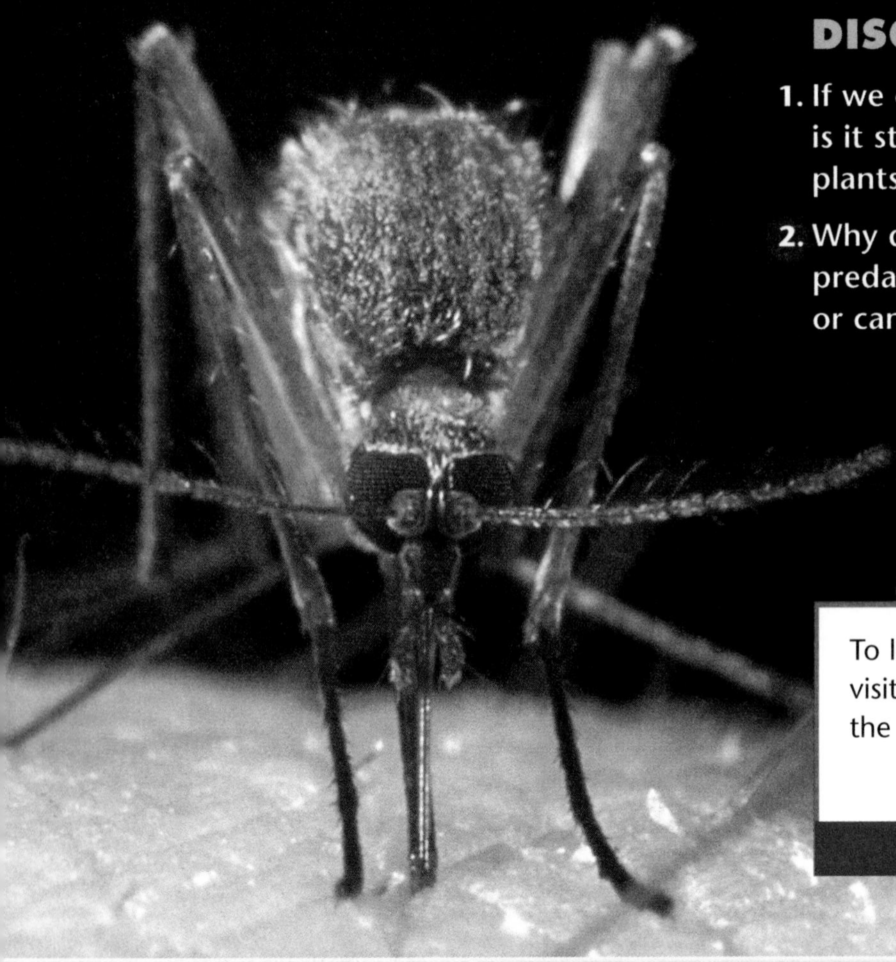

## DISCUSSION STARTER

1. If we can make imitation chemicals, is it still important to protect wild plants? Why or why not?

2. Why do plant chemicals that stop predators also kill malaria parasites or cancer cells?

To learn more about medicines from plants, visit *www.mhschool.com/science* and enter the keyword MEDICINE.

*inter*NET
CONNECTION

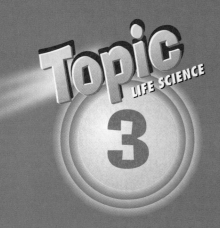

# Topic 3
## LIFE SCIENCE

## WHY IT MATTERS

**Plants and animals need each other to survive.**

### SCIENCE WORDS

**photosynthesis** a food-making process that uses sunlight

**respiration** the release of energy from food (sugar)

# Making Food

**D**id you ever wonder why crops are planted in open fields, not in the shade? Do plants need light? If so, why? What happens to plants that are kept in a dark corner of the room? Do they do as well as plants that get more light?

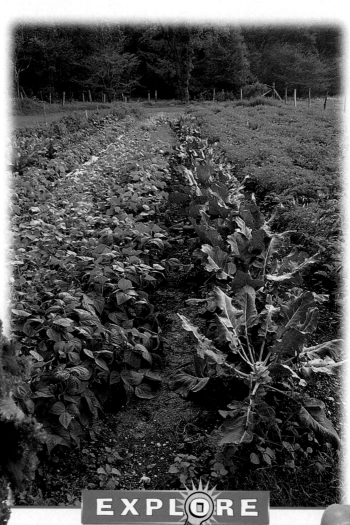

# EXPLORE

**HYPOTHESIZE** How will a plant change if it does not get sunlight for several days? Why does it change? Write a hypothesis in your *Science Journal.* Then test your ideas.

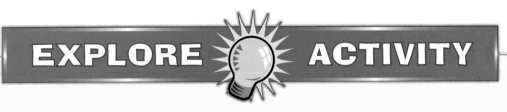
# Investigate What Light Does for a Plant

Observe how plant leaves are affected when they don't get light.

## MATERIALS

- growing plant (window plants from home or plants from an aquarium)
- opaque paper or aluminum foil
- *Science Journal*

## PROCEDURES

**SAFETY** Be sure to wash your hands after handling plants.

1. Cover part of a leaf of a growing plant.

2. **USE VARIABLES** Cover at least four different leaves of the plant in the same way.

3. Place the whole plant in a window that gets lots of light.

4. **COLLECT DATA** Remove the foil from one leaf after one class period. How is that leaf different from the uncovered leaves? Record your observations in your *Science Journal*. Then cover the leaf again.

5. **COLLECT DATA** Continue your observations. Remove the foil from another leaf after one day, another after two days, and another after a week. Record your observations in your *Science Journal*. Replace the foil each time.

## CONCLUDE AND APPLY

1. **OBSERVE** After one class period, how was the leaf you had just uncovered different from the uncovered leaves?

2. **IDENTIFY PATTERNS** How did the difference you noticed change after a day, two days, and a week?

3. **DRAW CONCLUSIONS** How do light and darkness affect the growth of leaves?

### GOING FURTHER: Problem Solving

4. **USE VARIABLES** Remove the coverings from the four leaves, and observe them for another week. How do they respond to being uncovered? Do their differences from the other leaves remain or disappear?

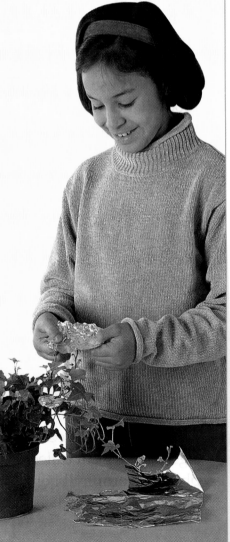

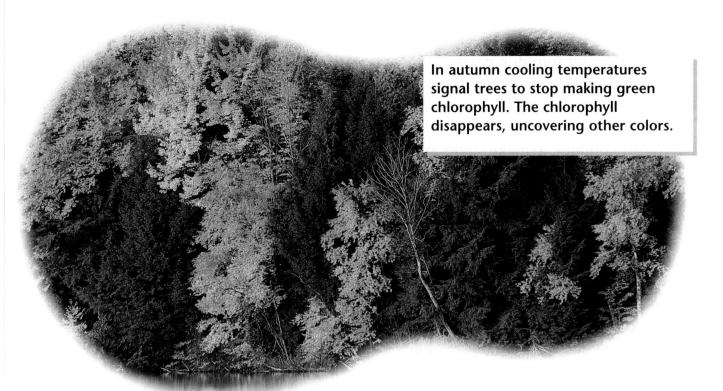

In autumn cooling temperatures signal trees to stop making green chlorophyll. The chlorophyll disappears, uncovering other colors.

## How Do Leaves Change Color?

Do you live in an area where the leaves change color in the autumn? If so, you may have noticed that the leaves of all plants, except evergreens, change color in the fall. You wake up one morning in September or October and the trees near where you live are speckled with flashes of yellow, orange, and maybe red.

All the yellows and oranges were inside the leaves ever since summer. However, you couldn't see them because there was too much green chlorophyll there.

It's as if you put some yellow and orange objects in the bottom of a bucket of green paint. The yellow and orange objects would be in there. Yet all you would see is green.

However, if you could take out all the green paint, what would you see? The answer is what you see in the fall.

But how is the greenness taken out of leaves in the fall?

As temperatures begin to drop, the leaves of trees other than evergreens stop making chlorophyll. Slowly the chlorophyll that remains begins to break down and vanishes. Now you can see the yellow and orange colors. If the weather is especially cool and the sky is clear most of the time, you may see another color—red. This color wasn't in the leaves to begin with. It's made by them in places where the fall climate is cool and clear. Where the climate is warmer and the sky is cloudy a lot of the time, the colors will be mostly yellows and oranges.

### Brain Power

Let's say you thought the amount of rainfall was the reason leaves changed color. Make a set of drawings showing an experiment that would test this hypothesis.

# Skill: Experimenting

## WHY DO LEAVES CHANGE COLOR?

To find an answer to this question, the first thing you might do is figure out what changes occur in the fall that *might* cause leaves to change color. Scientists call such changes *variables.* You might identify two of these variables as the amount of daylight and the temperature, both of which go down in the fall.

Next you would make a guess that *seems* to make sense about which variable causes leaves to change color. This guess is called a *hypothesis.* It is often made in the form of an *if ...then...*statement. For example, "*If* the plant doesn't get water, *then* it won't grow." To see if your hypothesis is a good idea, you would perform an experiment. That experiment has to be set up so that it gives a clear answer.

**MATERIALS**
- *Science Journal*

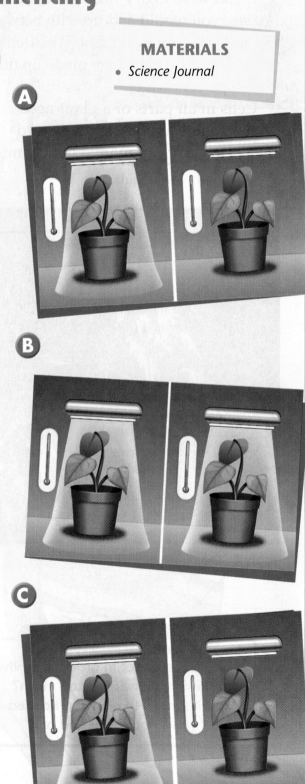

## PROCEDURES

1. Look at the drawings. They show three experiments—A, B, C. Study the setups.

2. **OBSERVE** What variable or variables are being tested in the first experiment? Write your answer in your *Science Journal.* What variable or variables are being tested in the other two experiments?

## CONCLUDE AND APPLY

1. **INFER** Which experiment is testing to see whether light causes leaves to change color? Explain why in your *Science Journal.*

2. **INFER** Which experiment is testing to see whether temperature causes leaves to change color? Explain why.

3. **INFER** Which experiment will not give a clear answer? Explain why not.

# Air to Breathe

Where do we get the oxygen we breathe? Much of it comes from plants, trees, and other organisms that give off oxygen during photosynthesis.

Among the earliest living things on Earth were cyanobacteria that lived in the oceans. They gave off oxygen during photosynthesis, and some of it got into the air. Finally, there was enough oxygen for animals to survive.

Did you know that 90 percent of all photosynthesis still takes place in the oceans? Simple, one-celled algae still live there. Some blue-green algae fossils are 3.4 billion years old!

Some ocean algae aren't green, but they still contain chlorophyll. Algae may be golden brown, red, or even pink-orange.

Most algae live in water. That green scum you see on ponds is floating algae! Some algae live on dry land. They also get their energy through photosynthesis.

About 600 million years ago, the atmosphere was only 1 percent oxygen. Today, thanks mostly to photosynthetic organisms, the air we breathe is about 21 percent oxygen!

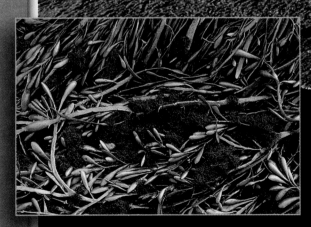

Red and green algae

# Earth Science Link

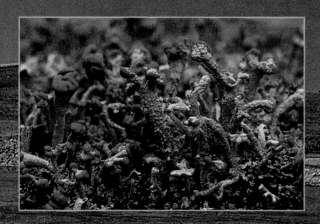

Some green algae live with fungi to form lichens (lī'kənz). Fungi cells enter the algae and absorb food made by photosynthesis.

## DISCUSSION STARTER

1. Why are organisms such as algae, which are not plants, able to produce oxygen?

2. How did algae help animals on Earth develop?

Euglena (ū glē'nə) can produce its own food, but it can also move by whipping a tail-like form. Therefore, it's a transition between plantlike and animal-like organisms.

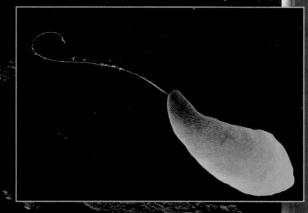

To learn more about oxygen, visit *www.mhschool.com/science* and enter the keyword OXYGEN.

*inter*NET
CONNECTION

# CHAPTER 1 REVIEW

## SCIENCE WORDS

| | |
|---|---|
| cambium p.21 | nonvascular p.7 |
| chlorophyll p.4 | phloem p.21 |
| chloroplast p.24 | photosynthesis p.32 |
| cortex p.20 | respiration p.33 |
| epidermis p.20 | root cap p.20 |
| fungus p.11 | xylem p.20 |

## USING SCIENCE WORDS

**Number a paper from 1 to 10. Fill in 1 to 5 with words from the list above.**

1. The outer layer of a root is the ___?___.

2. Water and minerals flow up through the ___?___.

3. Foods flow down from the leaves through the ___?___.

4. Water and minerals then pass through the root's ___?___ to the xylem.

5. A green chemical called ___?___ allows plants to use the Sun's energy to make their own foods.

6–10. **Pick five words from the list above that were not used in 1 to 5 and use each in a sentence.**

## UNDERSTANDING SCIENCE IDEAS

11. What is the difference between the way plants make food and the way plants use food?

12. Discuss why vascular plants can be taller than nonvascular plants.

13. Discuss how food travels through a plant.

14. Discuss how water travels through a plant.

15. Describe the "food factory" inside a plant.

## USING IDEAS AND SKILLS

16. **READING SKILL: DRAW CONCLUSIONS** What is there about ferns that allows them to grow taller than mosses?

17. How does photosynthesis contribute to the life of animals?

18. **EXPERIMENT** Design an experiment to determine how much mosses, ferns, and grasses depend on water for survival. Write how you would set up the experiment. Write down your hypothesis. Tell what variables you would test.

19. **THINKING LIKE A SCIENTIST** You dig in the ground and find a fossil of a fern. You then dig deeper and find a fossil of a club moss. What reasoning might let you conclude that club mosses evolved earlier than ferns?

## PROBLEMS and PUZZLES

**Why Is It Green?** Why do plants look green? Hold a sheet of green paper about 10 cm above a sheet of white paper. Aim a flashlight up to hit the underside of the green paper. What do you see on the white paper? Repeat with other colors of paper. Explain what is happening.

# CHAPTER 2
# PLANT
# REPRODUCTION
# AND
# RESPONSE

There are plants that have seeds and plants that don't have seeds. How do all these different kinds of plants produce new plants?

Flowers aren't just nice to look at. Flowers serve a purpose for a plant. What role do flowers play in plants' lives?

How do plants respond to changes in their world?

In Chapter 2 you will compare and contrast ways different kinds of plants produce new plants. To compare means to find ways two things are alike. To contrast means to find ways two things are different.

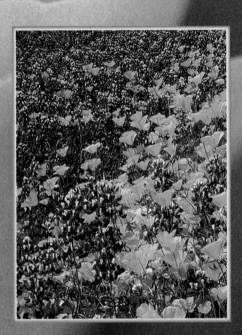

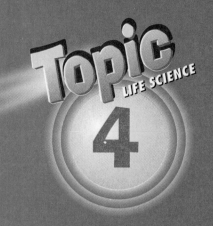
## WHY IT MATTERS

**Mosses help make the soil needed by other plants.**

### SCIENCE WORDS

**rhizoid** hairlike fiber that anchors a moss to the soil and takes in water from the soil

**spore** cell in seedless plant that grows into new organism

**frond** the leaf of a fern

**rhizome** the underground stem of a fern

**asexual reproduction** the production of a new organism from only one cell

**fertilization** the joining of a female sex cell and a male sex cell into one cell, a fertilized egg

**sexual reproduction** the production of a new organism from a female sex cell and a male sex cell

# Plants Without Seeds

**H**ave you ever seen plants like these? If so, probably there were none as tall as these. You are looking at ferns in Costa Rica's Monteverde rain forest, one of Earth's dampest places. This fern grows taller than a six-story building. Its leaves are more than three times longer than you are tall.

You may have seen mosses growing on trees, on rocks, or on damp ground. Mosses and ferns grow best in warm, wet places. Why do you think this is so?

## EXPLORE

**HYPOTHESIZE** Why do ferns grow tall while mosses grow only very close to the ground? How do the parts of mosses help them live where they do? Write a hypothesis in your *Science Journal*. Test your ideas.

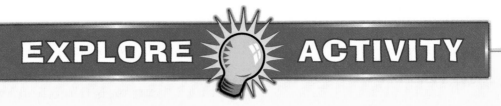

# EXPLORE ACTIVITY

# Investigate How Mosses Get Water

Examine a moss plant to find out how its parts allow the plant to live where it does.

## PROCEDURES

1. **OBSERVE** Place a moss on a paper towel. Examine it with a hand lens. Find its rootlike cells. Use the hand lens to view the stemlike and leaflike parts. Record your observations in your *Science Journal*.

2. **MEASURE** Use the forceps to remove a leaflike part. Make a wet-mount slide of the part. Observe its cells using the microscope on low power. Determine how thick the leaflike part is by moving the focus up and down.

3. **OBSERVE** Find a capsule-shaped object at the end of the brownish stalk. Observe it with the hand lens. Place the capsule on a slide. Add a drop of water. Place a second slide on top of the capsule. Press down on the top slide with your thumb, and crush the capsule. Carefully remove the top slide and place a coverslip over the crushed capsule.

4. **OBSERVE** Examine the released structures under low power. Draw what you see.

## CONCLUDE AND APPLY

1. **OBSERVE** Which parts of the moss are green? Explain why they are green.

2. **OBSERVE** How many cell layers make up the leaflike structure?

3. **INTERPRET DATA** What structures anchor the moss plant? What was the capsule?

### GOING FURTHER: Problem Solving

4. **PREDICT** What do you think the objects inside the capsule do? How would you set up an experiment to test your prediction?

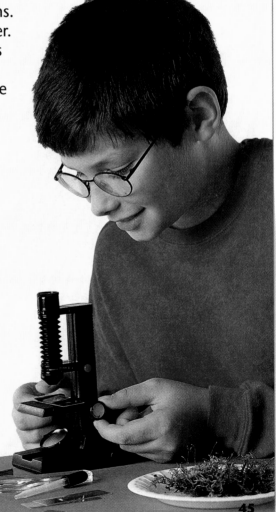

# How Do Mosses Get Water?

Mosses and their close relatives the liverworts are nonvascular plants. They don't have the long tubelike structures vascular plants have. They cling to damp soil, sheltered rocks, and the shady side of trees. Mosses and liverworts are tiny plants, only 2 to 5 centimeters tall. Mosses' leaves are only one or two cells thick.

Mosses and liverworts don't have roots. However, they stay anchored in one place. That's because they have hairlike fibers that do a job much like roots. The fibers are called **rhizoids** (rī′zoidz). Rhizoids, like other parts of mosses and liverworts, can take in water from their surroundings. The water then travels directly from one cell to the next.

Most of the plants you see every day grow from seeds. However, mosses and liverworts are seedless plants. They grow from **spores**. Spores are cells that can develop into new organisms. Those tiny structures inside the capsule on the moss were spores. The capsule seen in the Explore Activity is called a *spore capsule*.

Many mosses look like green, fuzzy pillows. Many liverworts look more like flat leaves. Ancient people thought that the shape of these plants resembled a liver. That's how they got their name.

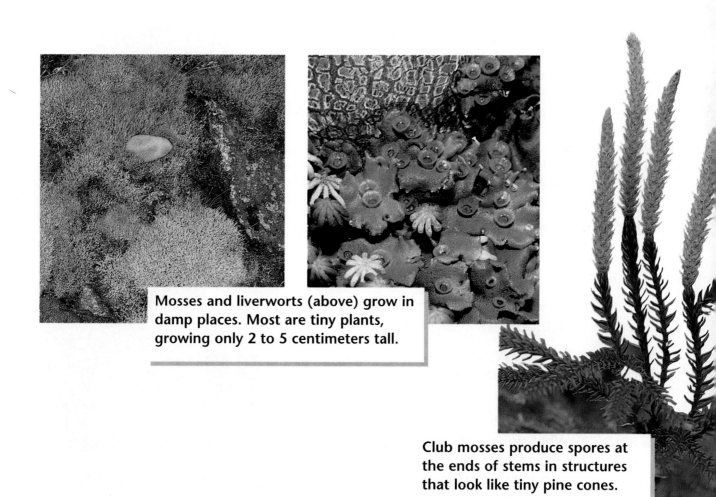

Mosses and liverworts (above) grow in damp places. Most are tiny plants, growing only 2 to 5 centimeters tall.

Club mosses produce spores at the ends of stems in structures that look like tiny pine cones.

## Seedless Vascular Plants

True mosses and liverworts are seedless plants. So are their more distant relatives club mosses, spike mosses, horsetails, and ferns. All of them use spores to reproduce. However, mosses and liverworts are different from the other four in a very important way. Mosses and liverworts don't have a vascular system. Club mosses, spike mosses, horsetails, and ferns do.

The vascular tissue in these plants is made up of long tubelike cells. These cells let water and food move easily over long distances. That is why vascular plants can grow very tall and thick. That is also why nonvascular plants like true mosses and liverworts are so short and delicate. The trunks of the largest ferns can be as thick as your body.

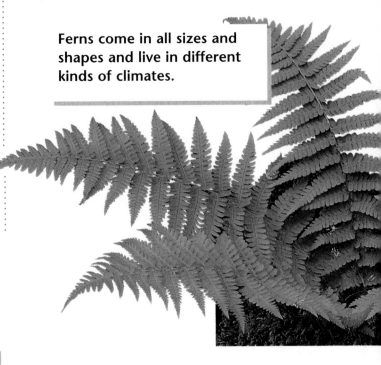

Ferns come in all sizes and shapes and live in different kinds of climates.

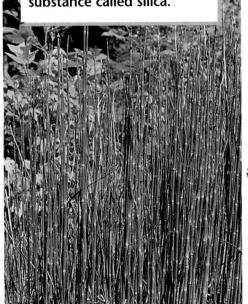

The stems of horsetails are hollow, have a ring of vascular tissue and joints, and contain a gritty, sandy substance called silica.

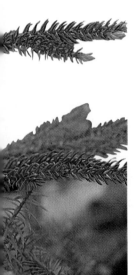

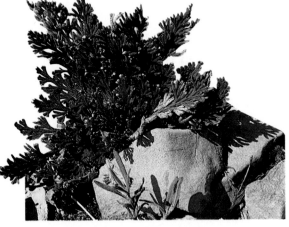

Spike mosses, such as this "resurrection plant," live in the desert. Resurrection plants can dry out when there is no rain, but they do not die. They revive when water becomes available again.

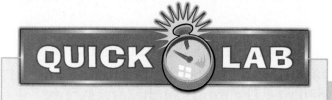

# Ferns

**HYPOTHESIZE** In what ways are ferns and mosses alike and different? Write a hypothesis in your *Science Journal*. Then examine a fern, and compare the results with those from the Explore Activity.

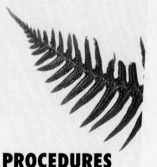

### MATERIALS
- fern plant
- fern leaf with spore cases
- microscope
- microscope slide
- toothpick
- water
- *Science Journal*

## PROCEDURES

**1. OBSERVE**
Carefully examine the whole fern plant. Look at the stem. Observe how the leaves grow from the stem. Find the veins in the leaves. Record your observations in your *Science Journal*.

**2. OBSERVE** Find a leaf whose bottom is covered with brownish spots. These are spore cases.

**3. EXPERIMENT** Place a drop of water on a clean slide. Use a toothpick to scrape one of the spore cases into the drop of water. Observe the spore case under the low power of a microscope.

## CONCLUDE AND APPLY

**1. OBSERVE** What do the spore cases contain?

**2. INFER** What do ferns and mosses have in common?

# What Are Ferns?

Ferns once formed huge forests on Earth. You can still find them today in many wooded areas. Many people also grow ferns at home. What are ferns like?

**①**

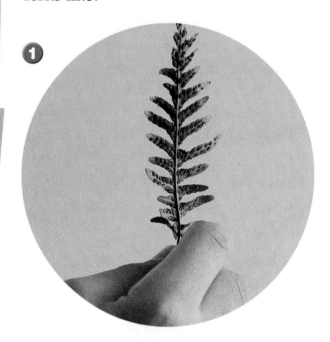

**Finding spore cases on the bottom of a fern leaf**

**②**

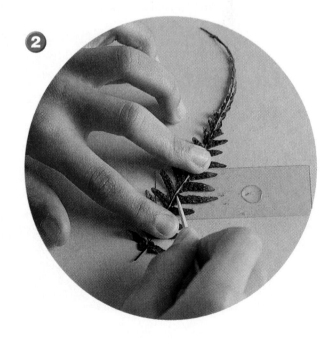

**Preparing a slide for viewing one spore case**

## More About Ferns

The whole fern plant you examined in the activity is at the stage of its life cycle when it forms spores. As you'll soon discover, there are other stages in the life cycle of a fern.

The leaves you saw are called **fronds** (frondz). They grow above the ground from an underground stem called a **rhizome** (rī'zōm). Roots, which anchor the plant to the soil or to a tree, branch out from the rhizome.

As you found out, the bottom sides of some fronds are covered with rows of brownish or rust-colored spore cases that contain spores. Under the right conditions, the spore cases pop open and spray spores as far away as a few meters. If the spores land in a place where conditions are right for fern growth, the spores will develop into the first stage in a new fern's life cycle.

Spore cases arranged on the bottom of a fern frond will pop open, spraying spores all around. If conditions are right where the spores fall, the spores will produce new fern plants.

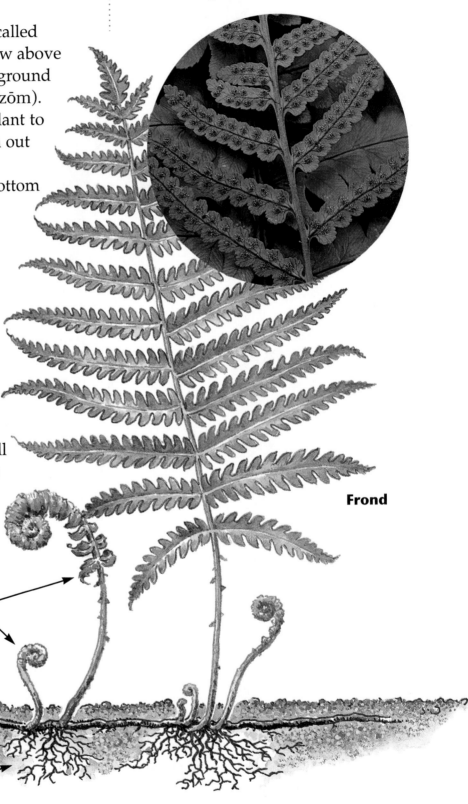

**Frond**

**Young ferns (fiddleheads)**

**Rhizome**

**Roots**

49

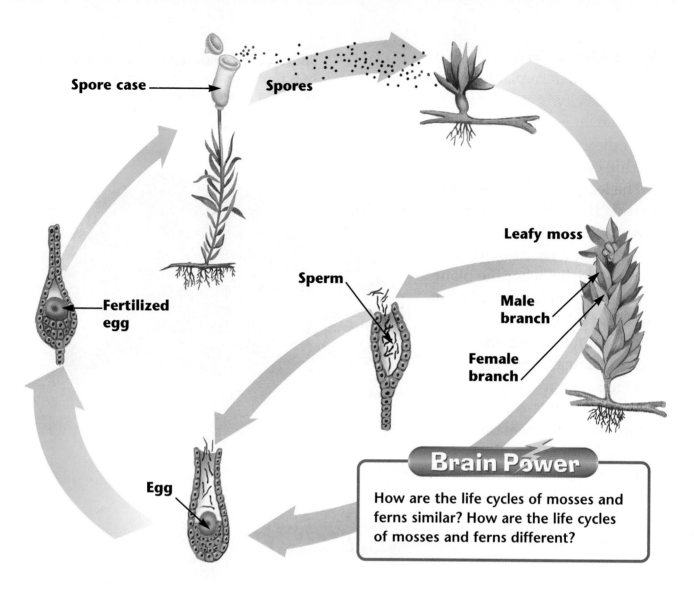

Spore case —— Spores

Leafy moss

Sperm

Male branch

Female branch

Fertilized egg

Egg

**Brain Power**

How are the life cycles of mosses and ferns similar? How are the life cycles of mosses and ferns different?

# How Do the Life Cycles of Mosses and Ferns Differ?

Since mosses and ferns use spores to reproduce, you might guess that their life cycles are similar. That guess would be correct. But there are differences, too.

Look at the drawings on these two pages as you read on. They will help you compare and contrast the life cycles of mosses and ferns.

## The Life Cycle of a Moss

Both mosses and ferns have two separate stages to their life cycles. One stage is when they produce spores.

This stage in the life cycle is called **asexual reproduction** (ā sek′shü əl rē′prə duk′shən). That's because the plant needs only one type of cell— the spore—in order to *reproduce* (rē′prə düs′).

Moss spores grow into leafy moss plants that have male branches and female branches. The male branches produce *sperm*—male sex cells. The female branches produce eggs—female sex cells. When a male sex cell meets a female sex cell, the two may join together. When this happens, the egg is **fertilized** (fûr′tə līzd′).

50

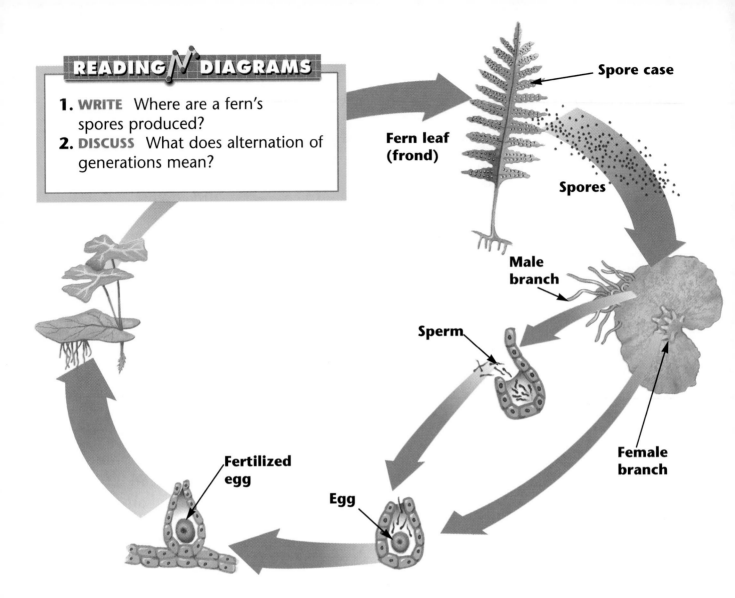

**READING ✓ DIAGRAMS**

1. **WRITE** Where are a fern's spores produced?
2. **DISCUSS** What does alternation of generations mean?

Spore case

Fern leaf (frond)

Spores

Male branch

Sperm

Female branch

Fertilized egg

Egg

This stage in the cycle is called **sexual reproduction** (sek′shü əl rē′prə duk′shən). That's because the plant needs both male sex cells and female sex cells in order to reproduce.

The fertilized egg eventually becomes a thin stalk with a spore case on top. When the spore case opens, the spores are released. Spores that land on damp ground may grow into new moss plants, and the cycle begins again.

This process of going from sexual reproduction to asexual reproduction to sexual reproduction again is called *alternation of generations* (ôl′tər nā′shən uv jen′ə rā′shənz).

## The Life Cycle of a Fern

Ferns also reproduce by alternation of generations. Leafy fern plants produce spores on the undersides of their fronds.

Spores landing in shady, moist soil are most likely to grow. The spores grow into small, heart-shaped plants. These plants produce male and female sex cells.

If a male sex cell fertilizes a female sex cell, the fertilized egg starts to form a new plant. The new plant develops into a leafy fern plant. Spore cases on the fern's fronds produce spores, and the cycle begins again.

**Angiosperms**   **Gymnosperms**   **Ferns**   **Mosses**

**310 million years ago**

**130 million years ago**

**275 million years ago**

**420 million years ago**

**Green algae**

# What Were the Ancestors of Plants?

The first land plants developed from living things that lived in the water. Which living things were the ancestors of land plants?

Scientists searched for clues linking organisms that lived in water to those that first grew on land. A good place to start was with photosynthetic organisms. These were living things that made their own food.

To narrow the search, the scientific detectives compared the chlorophyll of various simple organisms living today with that of plants. They found the closest match was with green algae.

Scientists found other clues. The cell walls of both green algae and plants contain cellulose. Cellulose can help plants survive on land, since a strong cell wall helps plants stay upright.

There was another clue. Both green algae and plants store food as starch.

Next, scientists hunted for fossils—the preserved remains of living things. Fossils are found mostly in rocks. Scientists have ways of finding out how old different rocks are. If you know the age of a rock, you also know the age of the fossil in it.

Putting all the pieces of this puzzle together, scientists concluded that the first land plants to evolve, or develop, from algae were probably similar to mosses. Recall that mosses and their close relatives, the liverworts, are nonvascular plants. These early land plants first appeared about 420 million years ago. Vascular plants appeared more recently. The earliest vascular plants, the ferns, were seedless.

The first plants with seeds were gymnosperms, such as conifers, followed by angiosperms, or flowering plants.

**This fernlike plant was found in rock that is over 340 million years old.**

# How Do Mosses Help the Environment?

After a forest fire or the eruption of a volcano, the land can be stripped of all plants. Nothing may remain except ashes. As time passes, plants return. The first ones are often mosses, which prepare the way for other plants.

Mosses do this in three important ways. First, their rhizoids grasp rocks and break off tiny pieces of them. These pieces contain minerals that all plants need to stay healthy.

Mosses also soak up water during rain showers and help keep the soil moist. In addition, their clinging rhizoids hold the top, most fertile layer of soil from being washed away. When the wind blows a seed of a shrub or tree onto the soil, the seed finds good conditions for it to sprout. Soon the mosses find themselves sharing the land with all sorts of plants.

## WHY IT MATTERS

Mosses and ferns were among the first plants to live on land. Today mosses are often the first plants to return to an area where plant life has been destroyed. Mosses help break down rocks into soil. Mosses also help hold on to the soil, making it easier for other plants to survive in the area. Without mosses, perhaps your favorite plants would never have had a chance to grow where they do.

**A volcanic eruption or forest fire leaves the land empty of plants. The first to return are often mosses, which create the conditions for other plants to grow.**

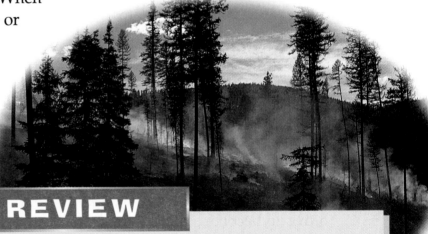

## REVIEW

1. Why do mosses grow close to the ground?

2. **INFER** Why do people sometimes add moss to a garden?

3. How do mosses change rocky areas so other plants can grow?

4. List two differences between mosses and ferns.

5. **CRITICAL THINKING** *Analyze* How do cell walls help plants survive on land?

**WHY IT MATTERS** THINK ABOUT IT
Think about your lawn or a park you have gone to. What might it be like if the rocks had never been turned into soil?

**WHY IT MATTERS** WRITE ABOUT IT
Write a paragraph about why what mosses do for the soil is important to you.

# ANIMAL LIFE CYCLES

**W**hat if you saw a tadpole but had never seen a frog? Would people have a hard time convincing you a frog was a grown-up tadpole?

When you see seedlings, you can predict that the fully grown plants will be on stems and have leaves. However, some baby animals look nothing like the adults. They change shape by going through metamorphosis.

Frogs lay eggs in ponds and lakes. The eggs hatch into tadpoles. They must live in water because they have gills, like fish, not lungs.

The tadpoles begin to change. They grow legs. Their tails disappear. They develop lungs and lose their gills. Now they can live on land and in the water!

Insects have two kinds of metamorphosis—complete and incomplete. In complete metamorphosis an egg hatches into a wormlike larva. It eats a lot and grows to become a pupa. This is a resting phase. Many body changes take place. Some larvae spin protective cocoons. Finally, the adult winged insect emerges.

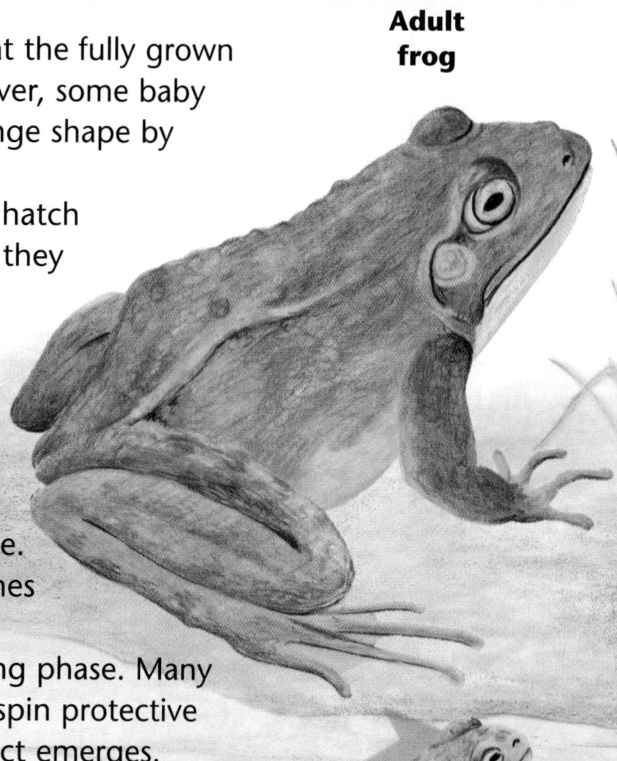

**Adult frog**

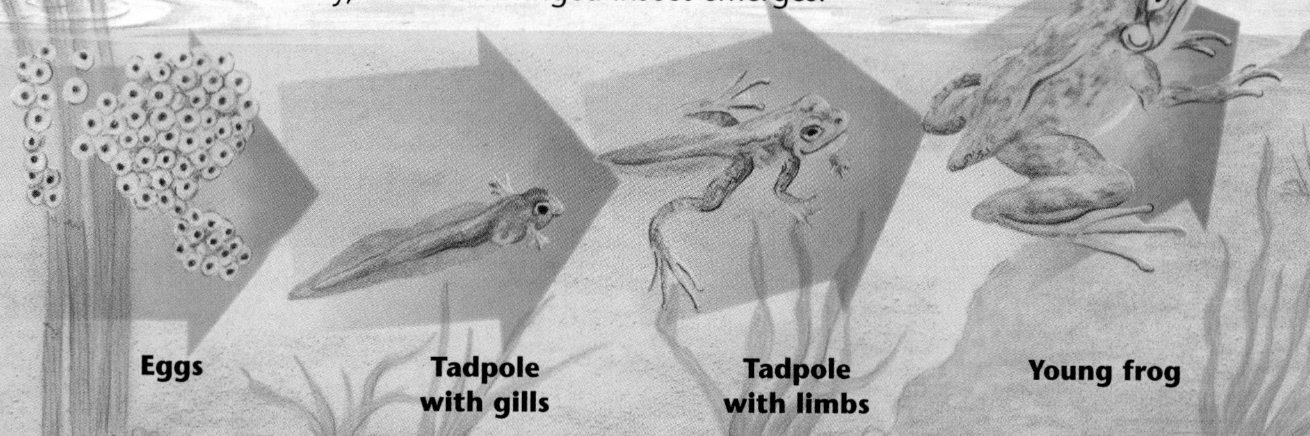

**Eggs**

**Tadpole with gills**

**Tadpole with limbs**

**Young frog**

54

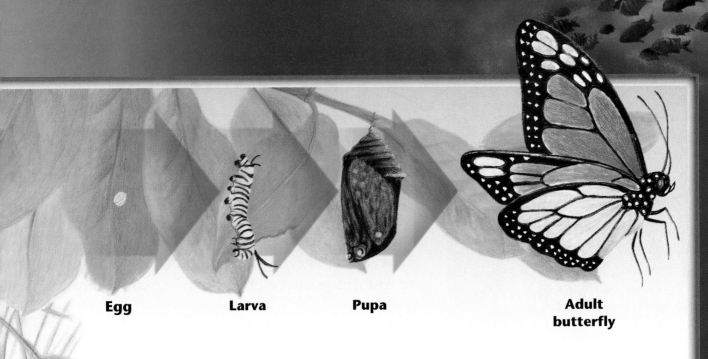

**Egg**  **Larva**  **Pupa**  **Adult butterfly**

During incomplete metamorphosis the insect changes shape gradually as it grows. An egg hatches into a nymph. It looks like a small adult, but without wings. As a nymph the insect grows and slowly changes. Finally, it grows wings and becomes an adult.

Changes in metamorphosis allow animals to move and get food in different ways. For example, a caterpillar has jaws to help it eat plants. A butterfly, however, has no teeth. Instead it has a long, hollow tongue that helps it suck nectar from flowers.

**Egg**  **Nymph**  **Adult grasshopper**

## DISCUSSION STARTER

1. Compare complete and incomplete metamorphosis.

2. What advantages do you think animals that go through metamorphosis have?

To learn more about metamorphosis, visit *www.mhschool.com/science* and enter the keyword CHANGING.

*inter***NET**
**CONNECTION**

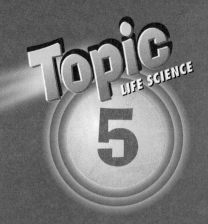

## WHY IT MATTERS

Seed plants are used for food, clothing, and many other important things.

## SCIENCE WORDS

**seed** an undeveloped plant with stored food sealed in a protective covering

**angiosperm** a seed plant that produces flowers

**gymnosperm** a seed plant that does not produce flowers

**conifer** any of a group of gymnosperms that produce seeds in cones and have needle-like leaves

**cotyledon** a tiny leaflike structure inside a seed of an angiosperm

**monocot** an angiosperm with one cotyledon in each seed

**dicot** an angiosperm with two cotyledons in each seed

# Plants with Seeds

How many plants do you munch on? When you munch on an apple, a watermelon, a grape, an orange, a peanut, or a banana, you are munching on a member of one main group of plants.

Have you ever picked up a pine cone? If so, you were holding a part of a plant from another main plant group.

Just about all the plants you are most familiar with can be grouped together with one or the other of the plants shown here. How are the two plants here different? How are they alike? One way they are alike is they produce seeds. They are seed plants.

## EXPLORE

**HYPOTHESIZE** Have you ever noticed the differences in plant leaves? Are some leaves larger than others? How do these differences help the plant survive? Write a hypothesis in your *Science Journal*. How would you test your ideas?

# Investigate How Seed Plants Differ

Compare the leaves of three kinds of plants to find how they enable each plant to survive in its environment.

## MATERIALS

- small pine seedling or other conifer
- grass plant
- garden plant or houseplant, such as a geranium
- hand lens
- microscope slide
- coverslip
- microscope
- *Science Journal*

## PROCEDURES

1. **OBSERVE** Examine each plant. Use the hand lens to examine a leaf from each one. In your *Science Journal*, draw each leaf and label it with the name of the plant it came from.

2. **OBSERVE** Remove a part of the lower epidermis from the grass leaf. Make a wet-mount slide. Examine the slide under low power.

3. **COMMUNICATE** In your *Science Journal*, draw what you observe.

4. **OBSERVE** Repeat step 2 with a pine needle and a houseplant leaf (such as a geranium). In your *Science Journal*, draw what you observe.

## CONCLUDE AND APPLY

1. **COMPARE AND CONTRAST** How are the leaves of the three plants alike? How are the leaves of the three plants different from one another?

2. **INFER** Which one of the plants do you think is least like the other two? Explain your reasoning in your *Science Journal*.

### GOING FURTHER: Problem Solving

3. **EXPERIMENT** Predict which of the plants you examined could survive best in a dry environment. How do you think the plant's leaves would help it do this? Design an experiment that would test your prediction.

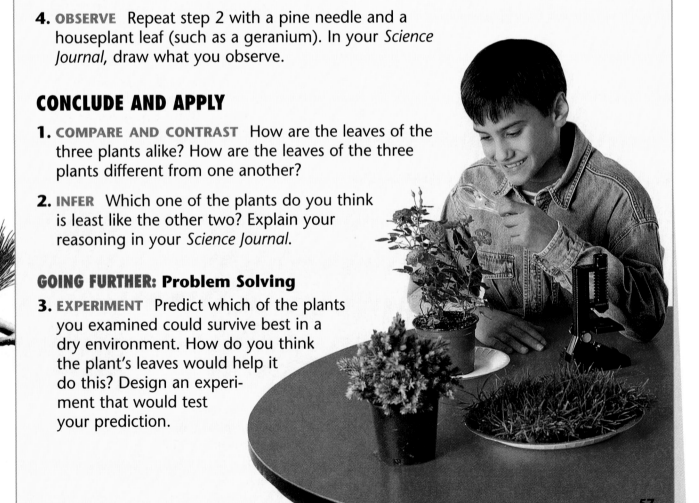

57

# How Do Seed Plants Differ?

The Explore Activity showed the leaves of three seed plants. Two leaves came from one major group of seed plants, while the other came from a different group.

Both groups are vascular plants. Both groups reproduce from **seeds**. A seed contains an undeveloped plant and stored food for the young plant.

Most of the plants that you see every day are seed plants. They include grasses, trees, shrubs, and bushes. They all have roots, stems, and leaves. Some, called **angiosperms** (an′jē ə spûrmz′), produce flowers. The others, called **gymnosperms** (jim′nə spûrmz′), do not produce flowers. These are the two major groups of seed plants.

The gymnosperms are the oldest seed plants. They include such evergreen trees as pine, fir, cedar, juniper, yew, larch, and spruce.

Gymnosperms first appeared on Earth about 250 million years ago. One hundred million years would pass before the first angiosperms appeared.

The fruits, vegetables, grains, and almost all of the nuts you eat are produced by angiosperms. However, one tasty nut—the pine nut, or pignoli—is a gymnosperm seed. It is the seed of certain pine trees.

## What Kinds of Gymnosperms Are There?

The gymnosperms are divided into four divisions. They are the **conifers** (kon′ə fərz), *cycads* (sī′kadz), *ginkgoes* (ging′kōz), and *gnetophytes* (ne′tō fits′).

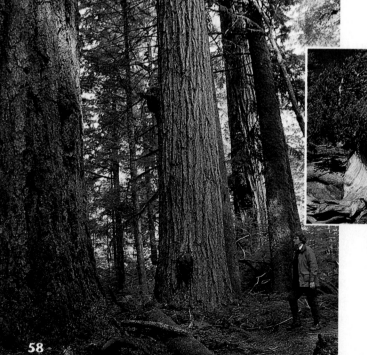

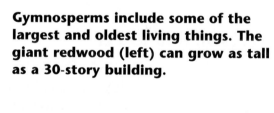

**Gymnosperms include some of the largest and oldest living things. The giant redwood (left) can grow as tall as a 30-story building.**

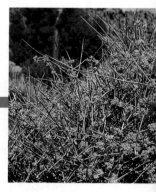

**The seed for this bristlecone pine (above) sprouted about 5,000 years ago.**

Look at the photographs on this page. You'll notice that these plants look different. Yet they all have certain things in common.

Their seeds are produced on the scales of female cones. The seeds are not surrounded by a fruit. The leaves of most gymnosperms look like needles or scales. Most gymnosperms are *evergreens*. Evergreens lose only a few leaves at a time and constantly replace the leaves they have lost.

Some conifers, such as the larch, dawn redwood, and bald cypress, lose their leaves each fall. Plants that do this are called *deciduous* (di sij′ü əs).

When gymnosperms evolved, most of Earth was cold and dry. These plants are well adapted to cold, dry climates. For example, the needles of conifers have a very small surface area and are covered with a thicker cuticle. They lose less water than the wider leaves of flowering plants.

## Brain Power

How do gymnosperms and angiosperms differ from mosses and ferns?

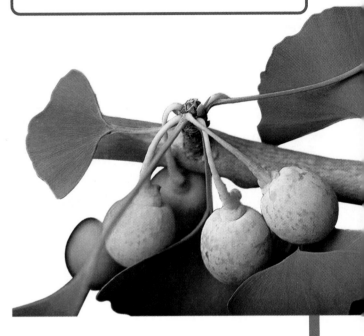

The maidenhair tree is the only member of the ginkgo division. It lives where the climate is neither too hot nor too cold.

Cycads live in warm climates. The red strawberry-shaped structures are not fruits but female cones.

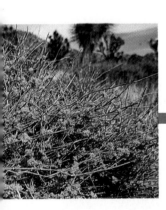

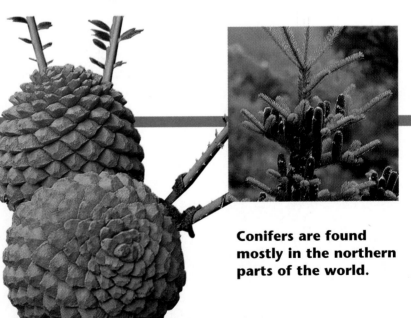

Gnetophytes are more closely related to flowering plants than any other gymnosperm.

Conifers are found mostly in the northern parts of the world.

# What Kinds of Angiosperms Are There?

Angiosperms are the most recently evolved and best-adapted division of seed plants. There are about 235,000 different kinds of angiosperms, which makes them the largest division in the plant kingdom.

Some, like duckweed, float on water and are about the size of a large bee's eye. Duckweed is the smallest flowering plant. The largest flowering plant is the giant eucalyptus tree, which can be 100 meters tall and 20 meters in circumference.

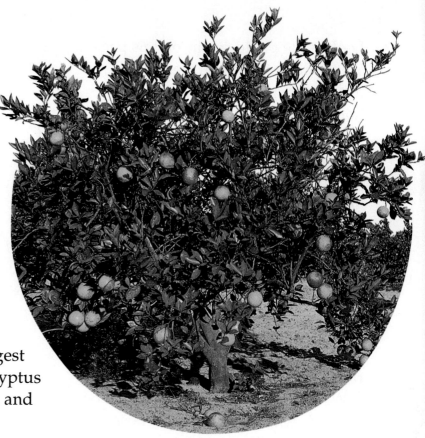

Flowering trees (top) produce the fruits you eat. Wheat (bottom), an angiosperm, is a grass that produces one of the world's most important food crops.

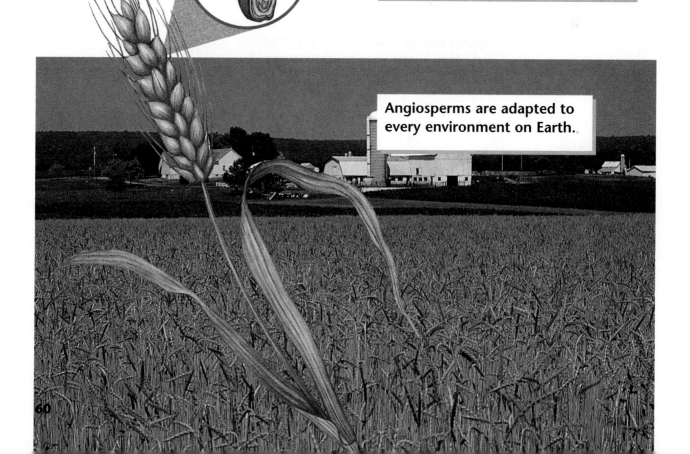

Angiosperms are adapted to every environment on Earth.

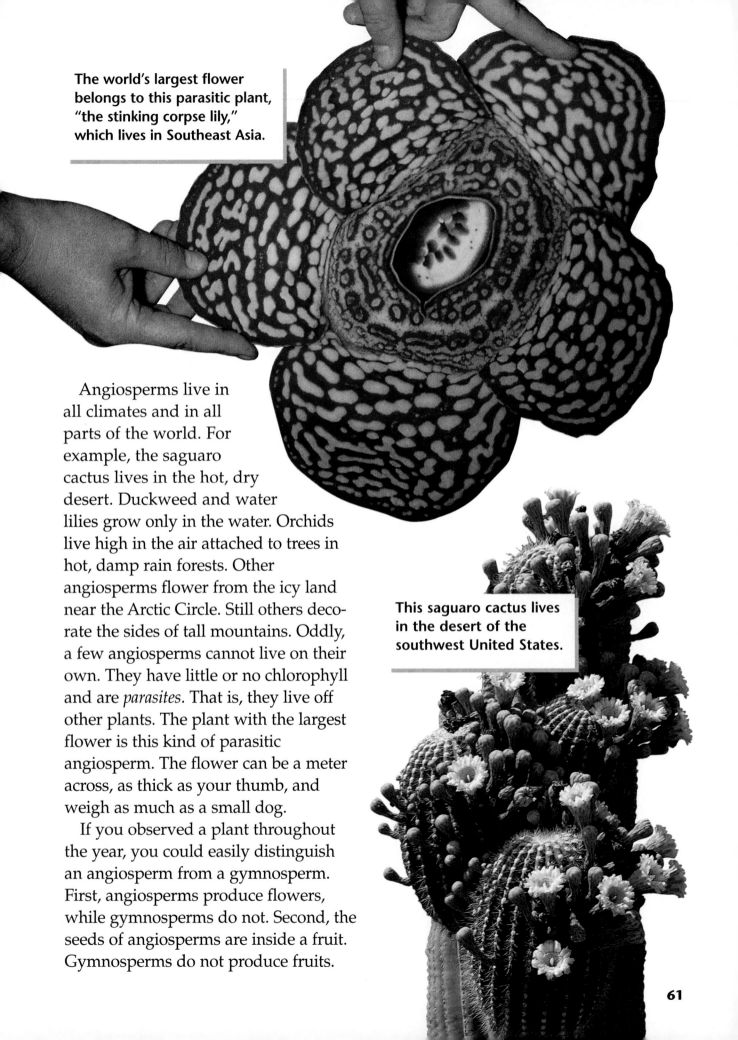

Angiosperms live in all climates and in all parts of the world. For example, the saguaro cactus lives in the hot, dry desert. Duckweed and water lilies grow only in the water. Orchids live high in the air attached to trees in hot, damp rain forests. Other angiosperms flower from the icy land near the Arctic Circle. Still others decorate the sides of tall mountains. Oddly, a few angiosperms cannot live on their own. They have little or no chlorophyll and are *parasites*. That is, they live off other plants. The plant with the largest flower is this kind of parasitic angiosperm. The flower can be a meter across, as thick as your thumb, and weigh as much as a small dog.

If you observed a plant throughout the year, you could easily distinguish an angiosperm from a gymnosperm. First, angiosperms produce flowers, while gymnosperms do not. Second, the seeds of angiosperms are inside a fruit. Gymnosperms do not produce fruits.

This saguaro cactus lives in the desert of the southwest United States.

**61**

# How Many Leaves Are Inside a Seed?

Scientists divide the angiosperms into two classes. As you might guess, scientists are able to do this because of some particular characteristic that sets the two classes apart. That characteristic turns out to be the number of an angiosperm's **cotyledons** (kot´ə lē´dənz). A cotyledon is a tiny leaflike structure inside a seed.

Some angiosperm seeds contain only one cotyledon. Plants whose seeds contain only one cotyledon are called *monocotyledons*, or **monocots** (mon´ə kots´) for short. (The prefix *mono-* comes from a Greek word meaning "one.") There are over 60,000 different kinds of monocots.

Angiosperms whose seeds contain two cotyledons are called *dicotyledons*, or **dicots** (dī´kots) for short. (The prefix *di-* comes from a Greek word meaning "two.") There are over 170,000 kinds of dicots. Corn, rice, wheat, grasses, orchids, and coconut palms are examples of monocots. Bean plants, maple trees, rose plants, and cactuses are some of the dicots.

## READING CHARTS

**DISCUSS** Describe three differences between monocots and dicots.

MATH LINK

## Main Differences Between Monocots and Dicots

| Characteristics | Monocots | Dicots |
|---|---|---|
| Cotyledons | 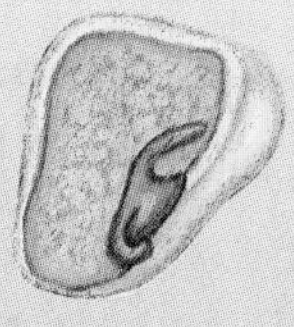 One | Two 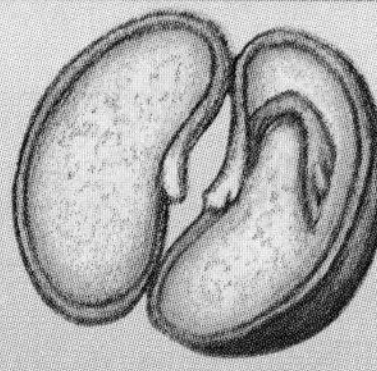 |
| Leaf veins | Parallel 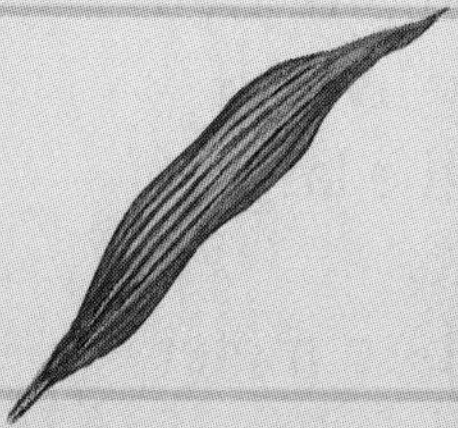 | 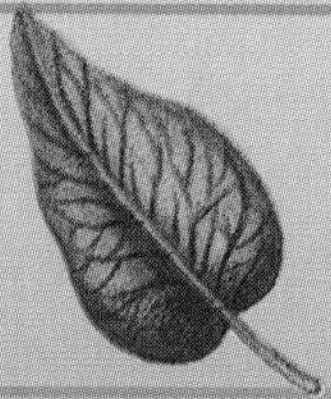 Branched |
| Flower parts | 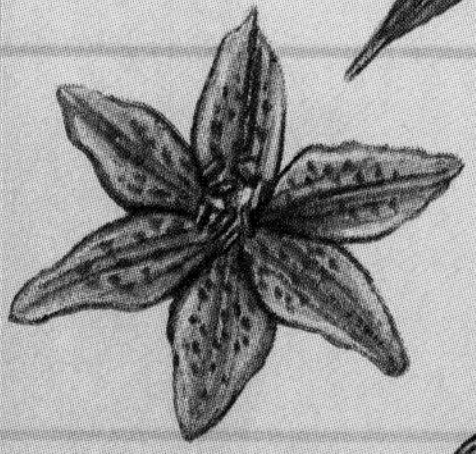 Multiples of three | Multiples of four or five 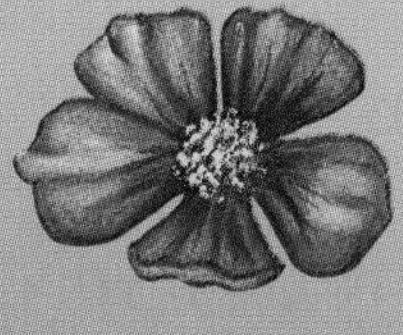 |
| Vascular system | Scattered in bundles 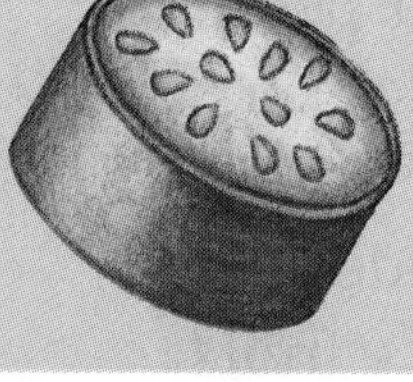 | 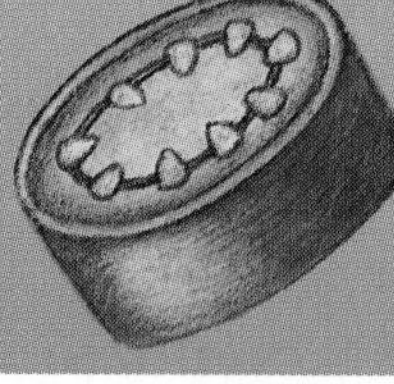 In rings |

62

# SKILL ↑ BUILDER

## Skill: Classifying

### FLOWERING PLANTS

In this activity you will classify flowering plants. That is, you will examine several plants and try to determine whether each is a monocot or a dicot. As you examine each plant sample, refer to the chart on page 62 to help you classify each sample.

**MATERIALS**

- sample leaves and flowers from various angiosperms
- *Science Journal*

### PROCEDURES

**1. OBSERVE** Get together with a few of your classmates and go on a leaf- and flower-collecting field trip. (Make sure to avoid poison ivy, poison oak, and poison sumac leaves. Your teacher can tell you how to spot them.)

**2. OBSERVE** Find a number of different angiosperms. Try to get a sample of a leaf and flower from each plant. If you can't get a flower, a leaf will do.

**3. INTERPRET DATA** Look at the chart of Main Differences Between Monocots and Dicots. It will give you clues on how to tell if the sample leaves and flowers you chose are monocots or dicots.

### CONCLUDE AND APPLY

**1. OBSERVE** Examine the plant parts you have chosen. For each sample leaf, describe how the leaf veins look. For each sample flower, tell how many parts each flower has. Record your answers in your *Science Journal*.

**2. CLASSIFY** Mount the leaves and flowers on a heavy sheet of cardboard, and indicate whether each came from a monocot or a dicot.

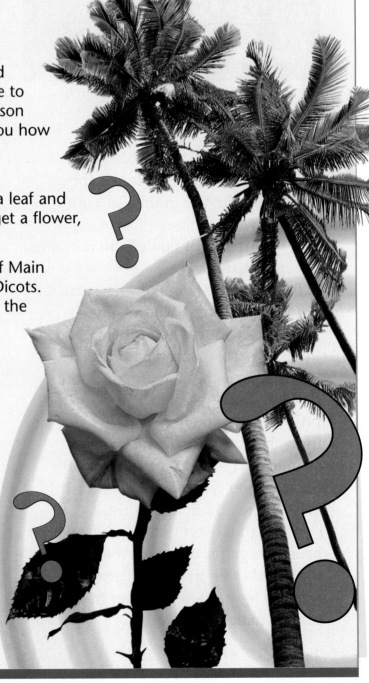

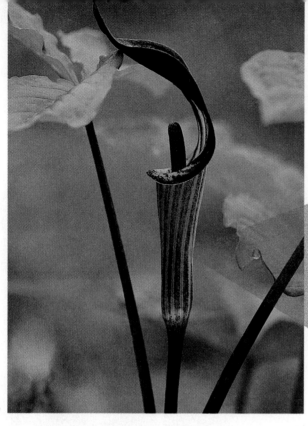

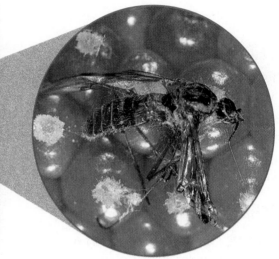

**The awful-smelling jack-in-the-pulpit flower attracts insects that help the plant reproduce.**

## Why Do Flowers Have Aromas?

The characteristics of living things help them survive in their environment. It would make sense to expect that the aromas of flowers do the same for their plants.

To your nose some of these aromas are very pleasing. That's why chemicals that produce the aromas of such flowers as roses and jasmines are used in perfumes. However, some flowers, like those of the jack-in-the-pulpit plant, smell awful. Yet, surprisingly, both beautiful and awful aromas serve the same purpose for these plants. They attract insects! What's the advantage of this?

When the insect enters the flower, it brushes against a part of the flower that holds tiny grains of dust, called *pollen*. These grains contain the plant's male sex cells.

The pollen sticks to the insect. As the insect moves around the flower—or moves to another flower on the plant—some of the pollen rubs off on parts of the flower that hold female sex cells. The two sex cells join, and the reproduction of a new plant has begun.

However, why should the awful smell of a plant attract insects? First, many plants attract one particular kind of insect. In the case of the awful-smelling jack-in-the-pulpit, the insects are dung beetles and flies. These insects generally feed on dead or decaying animals or animal wastes, which smell awful. The insects mistake the aroma of the plant for that of a good meal.

Once inside the flower, the insects discover that its sides are so smooth that they can't climb out. But they try. As they rush around the inside of the flower, they keep transferring pollen to the part of the flower that holds female sex cells.

After about 24 hours, something strange happens. The inside of the flower changes from smooth to wrinkled. Their job done, the insects can now get a foothold and escape. They will live to make the same "mistake" again and give a new life to the awful-smelling jack-in-the-pulpit.

Almost all of the food you eat that comes from plants is produced by flowering plants. Flowering plants also decorate the landscape and homes with beautiful colors. Some produce chemicals that are used in perfumes and other cosmetics. Others, such as plants used as spices, flavor the foods you eat. Like all plants, flowering plants help keep the balance of gases in the air by using up carbon dioxide and producing oxygen.

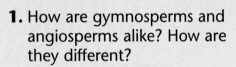

# REVIEW

1. How are gymnosperms and angiosperms alike? How are they different?

2. How are flowers important to a plant?

3. **CLASSIFY** List five plants that are angiosperms and five plants that are gymnosperms. Explain what characteristics helped you determine which was which.

4. What are the differences between monocots and dicots?

5. **CRITICAL THINKING** *Apply* How have seed plants become adapted to the environment?

**WHY IT MATTERS** THINK ABOUT IT
Think about the flowering and nonflowering plants you are familiar with. Which ones are most important in your life?

**WHY IT MATTERS** WRITE ABOUT IT
Write a paragraph about a day in your life and all the plants that are important to you. Classify the plants as angiosperms or gymnosperms and as monocots or dicots.

**READING SKILL**
Write a paragraph to compare and contrast some of the plants you read about in this lesson.

# A Wildflower Crusade

Growing up in the woods of east Texas, Lady Bird Johnson loved wildflowers. When Lady Bird was young, most people didn't think about the environment. Years later, as the wife of President Lyndon B. Johnson, Lady Bird helped to change that!

As First Lady, Lady Bird promoted the nation's parks. She worked to ban billboards along America's roads. The Highway Beautification Act of 1965 that banned billboards on rural highways was called Lady Bird's Bill.

In 1969 Lady Bird and her husband left the White House. In 1982 she founded the National Wildflower Research Center, now known as the Lady Bird Johnson Wildflower Center, in Austin, Texas. The center tells people about plants unique to different parts of our country.

One of Lady Bird's goals was to "provide a sense of place: California would look like California, Pennsylvania like Pennsylvania, and Texas like Texas."

Lady Bird Johnson helped to make people aware of the beauty and importance of wildflowers.

# Making a Difference

To do that the center gave people information about plants native to different areas. It told people how to get them and how to grow them.

Lady Bird pointed out many good reasons to grow native plants. They have adapted to the land. They need less watering. They use less fertilizer. They use fewer pesticides. They do well with what nature provides!

Another reason to grow them is one that Lady Bird called "dear to my heart." They bring "beauty, regionalism, and seasonal color."

Interest in the center has grown. It now has one of the largest collections of information about North America's native plants. Like her wildflowers Lady Bird's idea has taken root and done well!

## DISCUSSION STARTER

1. How would having a wildflower center help maintain the diversity of plant life in this country?

2. Why would people use less water, fewer pesticides, and less fertilizer if they planted native plants?

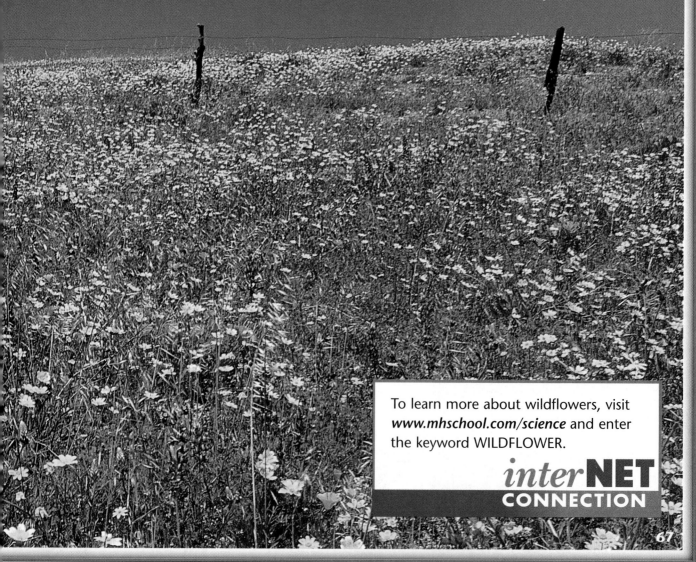

To learn more about wildflowers, visit *www.mhschool.com/science* and enter the keyword WILDFLOWER.

*inter*NET
CONNECTION

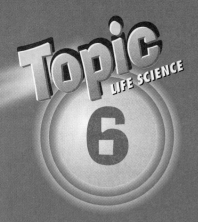

# Topic 6

## LIFE SCIENCE

## WHY IT MATTERS

**People eat all of the parts of flowering plants.**

### SCIENCE WORDS

**ovary** a structure containing egg cells

**pollination** the transfer of a pollen grain to the egg-producing part of a plant

**embryo** the immature plant inside a seed

**seed coat** the outer covering of a seed

**fruit** the ripened ovary of a flowering seed plant

# From Plant to Seed to Plant

**W**hat do people use flowers for? What do bees use them for? Have you ever seen bees buzzing around? Don't disturb them if you ever do see them. From a distance you might watch as a bee goes from flower to flower, as if it is collecting or giving out something. What do you think it is doing?

Not just bees, but other insects—and other animals—hover around flowers as well. A hummingbird is one example. What do you think the hummingbird is doing?

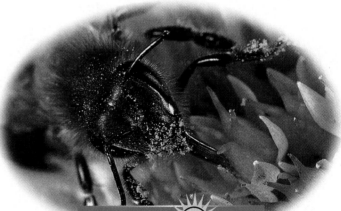

### EXPL**O**RE

**HYPOTHESIZE** Are all flowers alike? If not, how are flowers different? How are they alike? What do you think plants use their flowers for? Write your ideas in your *Science Journal*. Test your ideas.

68

# Design Your Own Experiment

## HOW DO FLOWERS DIFFER?

## PROCEDURES

**1. PLAN** Decide on how you will compare the flowers you look at. You may choose to look for parts that they seem to have in common. Describe what the parts are and how they differ from plant to plant.

**2.** Begin by removing the outer leaflike parts. Examine them. Draw what they look like in your *Science Journal.*

**3.** Remove the petals. Examine them. Draw what they look like in your *Science Journal.*

**4. OBSERVE** Examine the rest of the flower as you decide.

**5. COMMUNICATE** In your *Science Journal,* draw the parts you examined.

### MATERIALS

- several large flowers from different plants
- hand lens
- forceps
- dropper
- toothpick
- black paper
- *Science Journal*

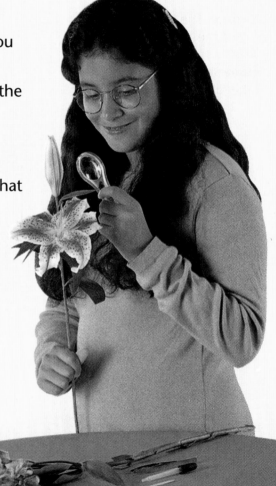

## CONCLUDE AND APPLY

**1. COMMUNICATE** What color is each flower? What do you think the job of the petals is? How would you design an experiment to find out?

**2. INFER** What do you think the various parts of each flower are for? Do you think the same parts of different flowers do the same kinds of jobs for their plants?

### GOING FURTHER: Apply

**3. INFER** Why do you think a plant has flowers? Make a hypothesis. Design an experiment to test your ideas.

# How Do Flowers Differ?

Not all flowers are alike. Some flowers, like the one in the Explore Activity, are *complete flowers*. Complete flowers have sepals, petals, stamens, and pistils. *Incomplete flowers* are missing one of these parts. Some flowers are called perfect. *Perfect flowers* have both female and male parts, that is, both pistils (female parts) and stamens (male parts).

Imperfect flowers have either pistils or stamens but not both. You might think of these flowers as "female" or "male." Some plants, like corn and oak trees, have separate male and female flowers on the same plant. Other plants, like willow trees and holly trees, have only male flowers or female flowers.

## PARTS OF A FLOWER

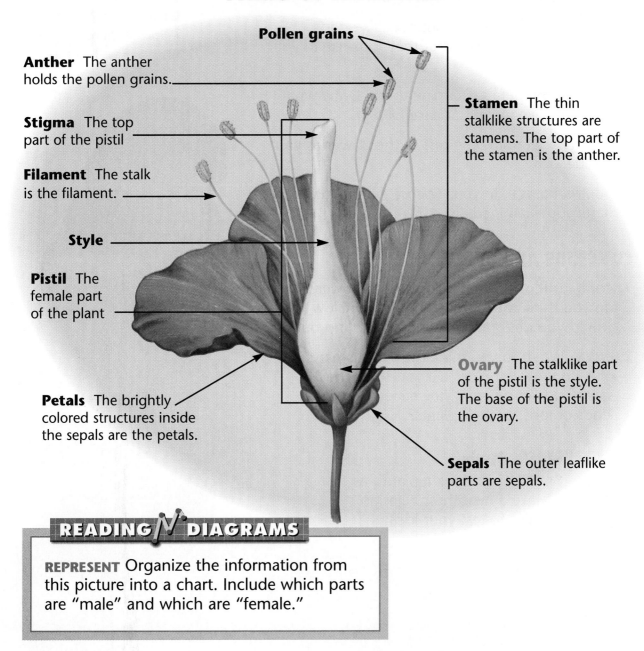

**Pollen grains**

**Anther** The anther holds the pollen grains.

**Stigma** The top part of the pistil

**Filament** The stalk is the filament.

**Style**

**Pistil** The female part of the plant

**Petals** The brightly colored structures inside the sepals are the petals.

**Stamen** The thin stalklike structures are stamens. The top part of the stamen is the anther.

**Ovary** The stalklike part of the pistil is the style. The base of the pistil is the ovary.

**Sepals** The outer leaflike parts are sepals.

## READING *N* DIAGRAMS

**REPRESENT** Organize the information from this picture into a chart. Include which parts are "male" and which are "female."

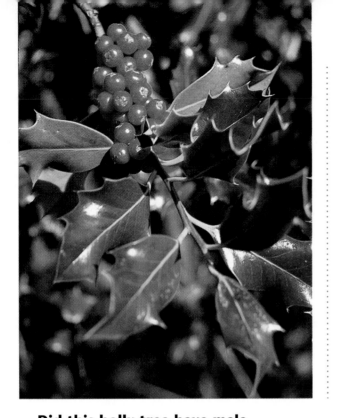

The red holly berries that you see on holly trees in the late fall appear only on holly trees with female flowers. In order to produce the berries (the holly's fruit), the tree with female flowers needs to be fertilized by pollen from a holly tree with male flowers.

## Brain Power

A fruit will only develop if male and female sex cells join. Based on this information, suggest why a person who wants to grow fruit may be advised to buy at least two trees.

**Did this holly tree have male flowers or female flowers? How can you tell?**

**An oak tree has both male and female flowers on the same tree.**

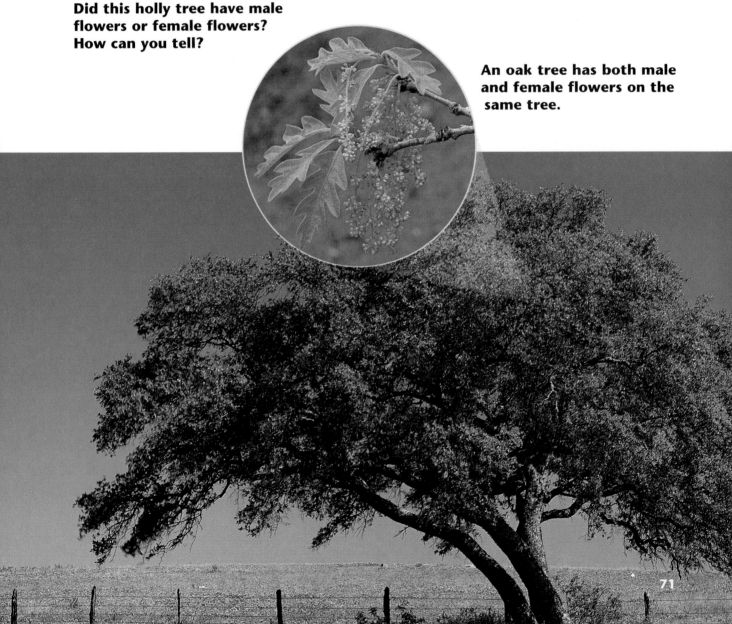

## How Do Seeds Develop?

Some seeds are very tiny, while others are really large. The largest is produced by the double-coconut tree, whose seeds can be about half your weight. Some of the smallest seeds belong to orchid plants. You could put thousands of them in a teaspoon.

But no matter how large or small, all seeds develop the same way. As you read on, pause every now and then to look at the drawings on this page. They will help you follow what you are reading.

First, a pollen grain must be transferred from a flower's anther to its stigma, or to another flower's stigma. Pollen grains contain sperm, which are male sex cells. This transfer is called **pollination** (pol´ə nā′shən).

## ▰ POLLINATION ▰

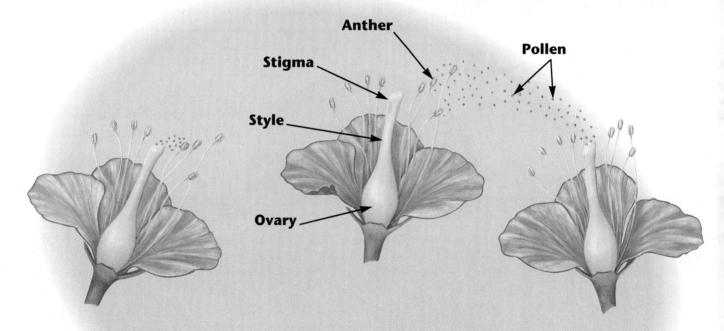

**SELF-POLLINATION**
Pollination occurs when a pollen grain from an anther reaches the stigma. This flower is pollinating itself because its own pollen is reaching its own stigma.

**CROSS-POLLINATION**
Pollination can occur between two or more flowers on separate plants. Here the pollen of one flower reaches the stigma of another.

### READING♪DIAGRAMS

1. **DISCUSS** How are self-pollination and cross-pollination alike? How are they different?
2. **WRITE** Write a paragraph describing the steps in fertilization.

If the pollen is transferred from an anther to a stigma in the same flower, the process is called *self-pollination*. If the transfer is from one flower to the flower of another plant, the process is called *cross-pollination*.

On the stigma a tube forms from the pollen grain. The tube grows down the style and into the flower's ovary. Sperm travel down the tube, through the style, and into the ovary. There a sperm cell combines with, or fertilizes, an egg cell. This combining is called *fertilization* (fûr′tə lə zā′shən).

A seed develops from a fertilized egg cell. Under the right conditions, a new plant will develop from the seed. The process of making a new plant from the joining of a sperm and an egg cell is called *sexual reproduction*.

# AND FERTILIZATION

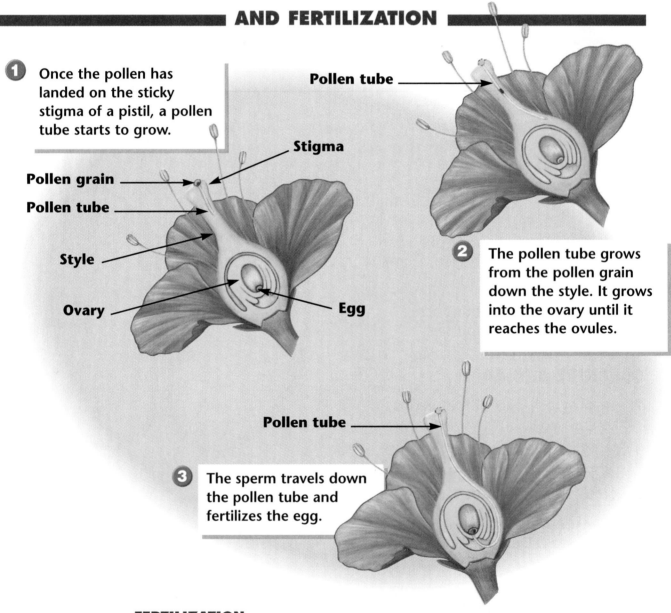

**1** Once the pollen has landed on the sticky stigma of a pistil, a pollen tube starts to grow.

Pollen tube

Stigma

Pollen grain

Pollen tube

Style

Ovary

Egg

**2** The pollen tube grows from the pollen grain down the style. It grows into the ovary until it reaches the ovules.

Pollen tube

**3** The sperm travels down the pollen tube and fertilizes the egg.

**FERTILIZATION**
**Fertilization occurs when a sperm from a pollen grain travels down the style and combines with an egg in the ovary.**

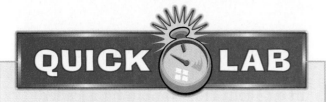

# QUICK LAB

## Inside a Seed

**HYPOTHESIZE** What does a seed do? Where does it store its food? How do different seeds compare? Write a hypothesis in your *Science Journal*.

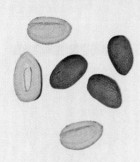

### MATERIALS
- bean seed (such as a lima bean)
- corn seed
- water
- hand lens
- *Science Journal*

## PROCEDURES

1. Soak the bean seed in water overnight.

2. **OBSERVE** Then carefully pull apart the two halves of the seed. Examine the halves with a hand lens.

3. **COMMUNICATE** In your *Science Journal*, draw what you see.

## CONCLUDE AND APPLY

1. **INFER** Which part of the seed is the embryo?

2. **IDENTIFY** On your drawing, label the seed coat and the place where you think food is stored.

3. **COMPARE AND CONTRAST** Look at a corn seed. Describe how its parts are similar to or different from a bean seed.

4. **COMMUNICATE** Explain why you think one is the seed of a dicot and the other is the seed of a monocot. Which is which?

# What's in a Seed?

A seed is made up of three main parts. One part is an **embryo** (em′brē ō′). An embryo is an immature plant. Another part is where food is stored in the form of starch. The third part is the **seed coat**. The seed coat encases the whole seed in a tough, protective covering.

## PARTS OF A SEED

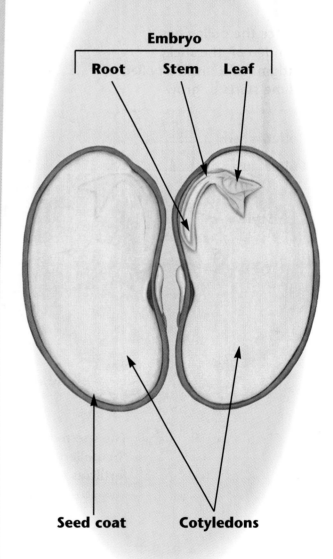

Embryo
Root    Stem    Leaf

Seed coat    Cotyledons

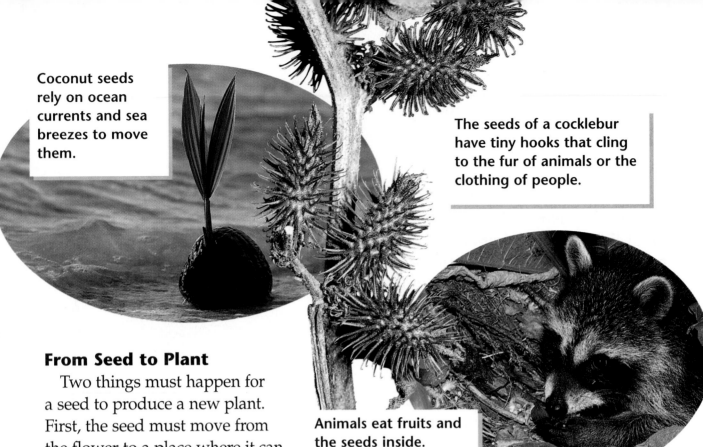

Coconut seeds rely on ocean currents and sea breezes to move them.

The seeds of a cocklebur have tiny hooks that cling to the fur of animals or the clothing of people.

Animals eat fruits and the seeds inside.

## From Seed to Plant

Two things must happen for a seed to produce a new plant. First, the seed must move from the flower to a place where it can sprout. This is called *seed dispersal* (sēd di spûr′səl). Second, the place must provide everything that is needed for sprouting, which is called *germination* (jûr′mə nā′shən). A warm temperature and water are the two most important needs for germination. Food is not needed because the seed has its own supply of stored food.

Usually the seed must move a relatively long distance from its parent plant. Why? Competition from its parent, and plants like it, may make the development of a new plant difficult. For example, nearby plants may block sunlight from reaching the young plant. They may soak up the water or minerals from the soil that the new plant needs.

Seeds have evolved all sorts of adaptations for dispersal. For example, dandelion fruits and cottonwood seeds have feathery "parachutes." These parachutes can be blown great

distances by the wind. Animals also help move plant seeds.

Animals eat **fruits**. A fruit is a mature ripened ovary of a plant. The animals digest the soft parts of the fruits but not the hard seeds inside. As the animals move from place to place, they deposit the seeds in their wastes.

Scientists have discovered that animals tend to eat only ripe fruits. Only the seeds of ripe fruits are ready for dispersal. How do the fruits reveal that they are ripe? They change color and flavor. For example, a Macintosh apple will turn from green to red. Its flesh will turn from sour to sweet. Both of these changes signal animals that the fruit is ready to eat. These changes help ensure that the apple tree will have successful offspring.

# How Do Seeds Travel?

Some seeds, like those of the witch hazel and the dwarf mistletoe, explode from their fruits under special conditions. In the witch hazel, when its fruits dry out, they split open with great force. Their seeds are propelled up to 45 meters (148 feet). In the dwarf mistletoe, fluids build up in the fruits. When the pressure gets too great, the fruits burst, sending their seeds flying at 100 kilometers (62 miles) an hour.

## How Gymnosperms Spread Their Seeds

Gymnosperms don't produce fruits. They disperse their seeds in other ways. For example, the cones of the balsam fir tree shatter. When they do this, they release winglike seeds that ride on the wind. Animals move cones from place to place. Heavy rains, floods, and streams can disperse them also.

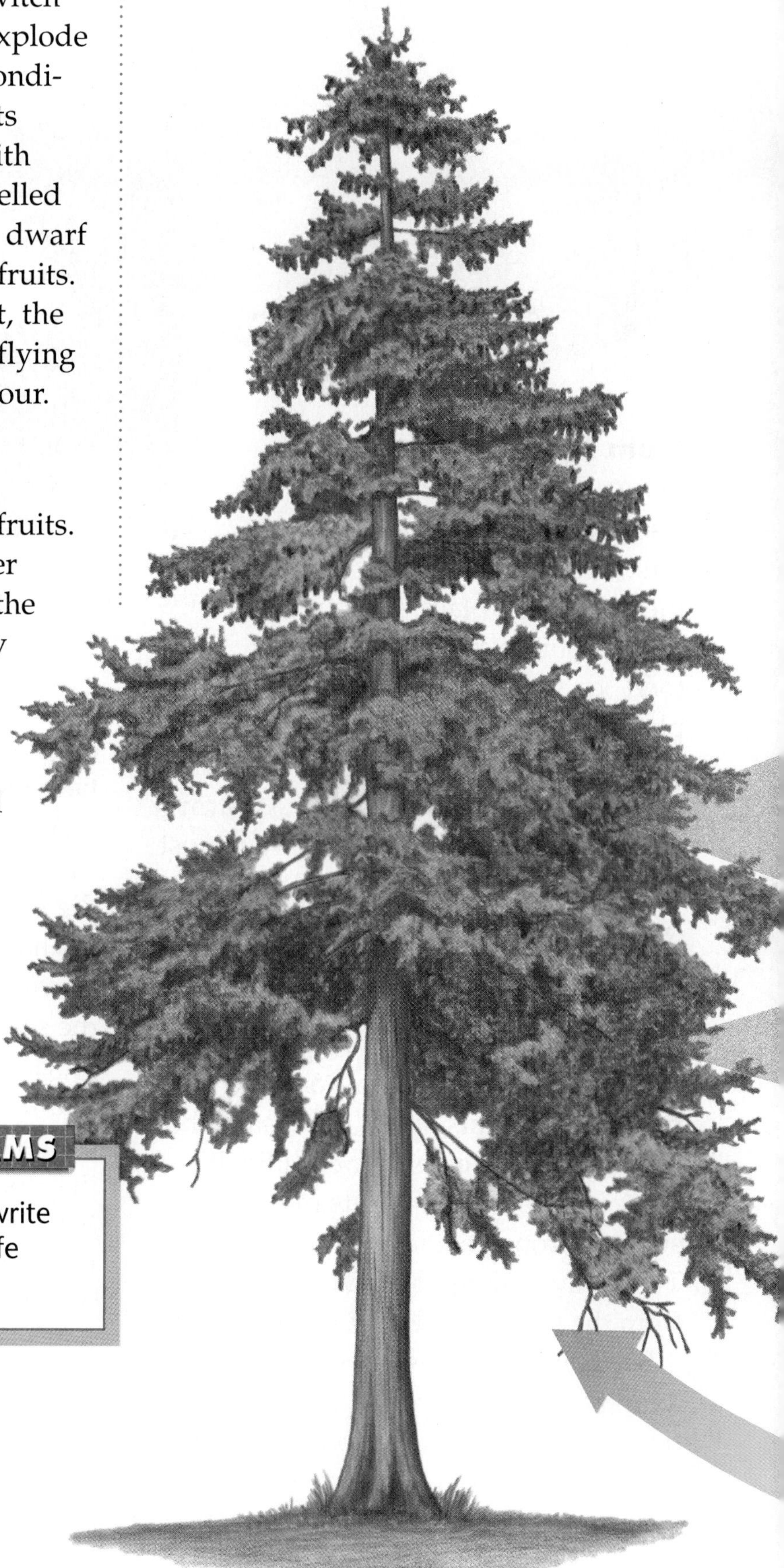

**Mature tree**

## READING **N** DIAGRAMS

**REPRESENT** Use the picture to write an outline of the steps in the life cycle of a conifer.

## Life Cycle of a Conifer

Since gymnosperms don't produce flowers or fruits, their life cycle is not the same as angiosperms. However, there are similarities. As you read on and look at the drawings on this page, make a list of the similarities and differences.

Let's examine the life cycle of a pine tree. A pine tree belongs to a group of gymnosperms called conifers. Pines produce male and female cones on a mature tree. The scales that form the cones carry spore cases that produce the plant's sperm and egg cells. Male cones produce pollen grains, which contain sperm cells.

When pollen grains fall away from a male cone, the wind carries them through the air. If a pollen grain happens to land on a female cone, a sperm cell from the pollen may fertilize an egg cell in the female cone.

The fertilized cell eventually becomes a seed. As autumn and winter come, the female pine cones fall from the trees. Their seeds scatter on the ground. Sometimes wind or water will carry the seeds far from the tree. If they end up in a place where conditions are right for germination, the seeds will sprout, and a new pine tree will start growing.

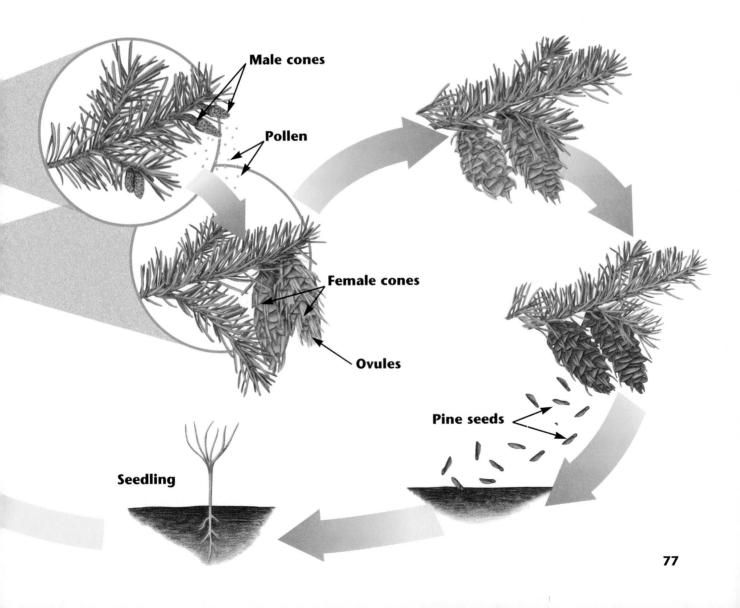

Male cones

Pollen

Female cones

Ovules

Pine seeds

Seedling

**Breakfast cereals are made from the seeds of plants such as rice, wheat, corn, and oats.**

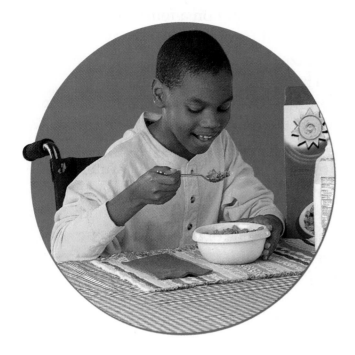

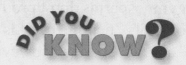

After seeds are produced, most stay dormant for a time. Dormant means "inactive." They do not sprout without the correct temperature, a large amount of water, and enough oxygen. Seeds of many vegetables may remain dormant several years (such as pumpkin, for four years). After that they no longer sprout. How can dormant seeds help plants survive?

## Which Seeds Do We Eat?

Although you eat seeds and their products every day, your life may not depend on eating such things. However, your health does. That's because certain seeds and things made from them make up one of the major food groups—grains. For many people on Earth, seeds and their products *are* a matter of life or death. That's because a large part of these people's diets is made up of seed products. For example, rice—which is a seed—is the main food of many people who live in Asia.

Bread also makes up a large part of some people's diets. Bread is made from flour, which is made mostly from ground up seeds of wheat plants. Flour is also made from corn, rye, and other seeds. Altogether the countries of the world produce an amazing 1.8 billion metric tons of rice, wheat, and corn. (A metric ton equals 1,000 kilograms, or 2,205 pounds.) This figure does not include other seeds people eat, like oats, peanuts, beans, and peas.

Every time you eat a breakfast cereal, you eat the seeds of plants such as rye, barley, rice, oat, corn, and wheat. When you spread margarine on a slice of bread, you are putting the product of seeds—the margarine—on another product of seeds—bread. Margarine is made from the oils of seeds. What's more, the bread may be dotted with sesame, poppy, or caraway seeds to give it more flavor.

Do you like salad oil, or do your parents use cooking oils to prepare certain foods? Many of these oils come from seeds like sunflower, soybean, corn, and sesame.

## Can You Start New Plants Without Seeds?

Some plants can be grown from pieces of the plant—such as stems, leaves, and roots—rather than from seeds. This is called *vegetative propagation*. It is also called *asexual reproduction* because it happens without sperm and egg cells joining. For example, strawberry plants send shoots into the soil from stems that grow along the ground. Each shoot will make a new strawberry plant.

Flowering plants produce almost all of the plants you eat. People eat all of the parts of these plants. The parts include the flowers themselves, fruits, seeds, leaves, stems, and roots. Flowering plants are also eaten by animals that we, in turn, eat.

**New African violet plants can be grown from a cutting of a leaf that has a small bit of stem attached to it.**

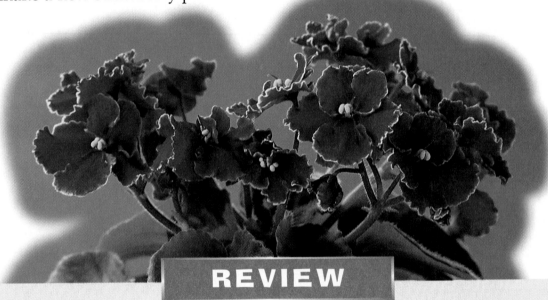

## REVIEW

**1.** Identify the different parts of a flower and tell what each part does.

**2.** Explain how seeds are produced.

**3.** Give at least three examples of how seeds are dispersed.

**4. COMPARE AND CONTRAST** Describe the difference between fertilization and germination.

**5. CRITICAL THINKING** *Analyze* How do you think trees that produce seedless oranges are grown? Write down your prediction. Then do library research to see if your prediction was correct.

**WHY IT MATTERS** THINK ABOUT IT
Flowers, fruits, seeds, leaves, stems, and roots all play important roles in your life. Which plant parts do you use most often?

**WHY IT MATTERS** WRITE ABOUT IT
Write a paragraph that describes the plants and plant parts that are most important to you. Be sure to explain why they are important.

# Timing Trees

How do you know a tree's age? Look at its rings! Not the kind you wear on your fingers, but the kind you see in the cross section of a log!

A tree forms a layer of wood each year. In spring large thin-walled cells form below the bark. As summer ends, new cells become smaller, and the walls are thicker. In winter growth stops.

This process continues for as long as the tree lives. You can see the layers in a cross section from a tree. Scientists use those layers, or rings, to tell the age of a tree.

Rings not only tell a tree's age, they give clues about weather in the area. A year with warm temperatures and lots of rain produces a thick ring. A year with cold temperatures and little rain produces a thin ring. Trees in the same area have similar ring patterns.

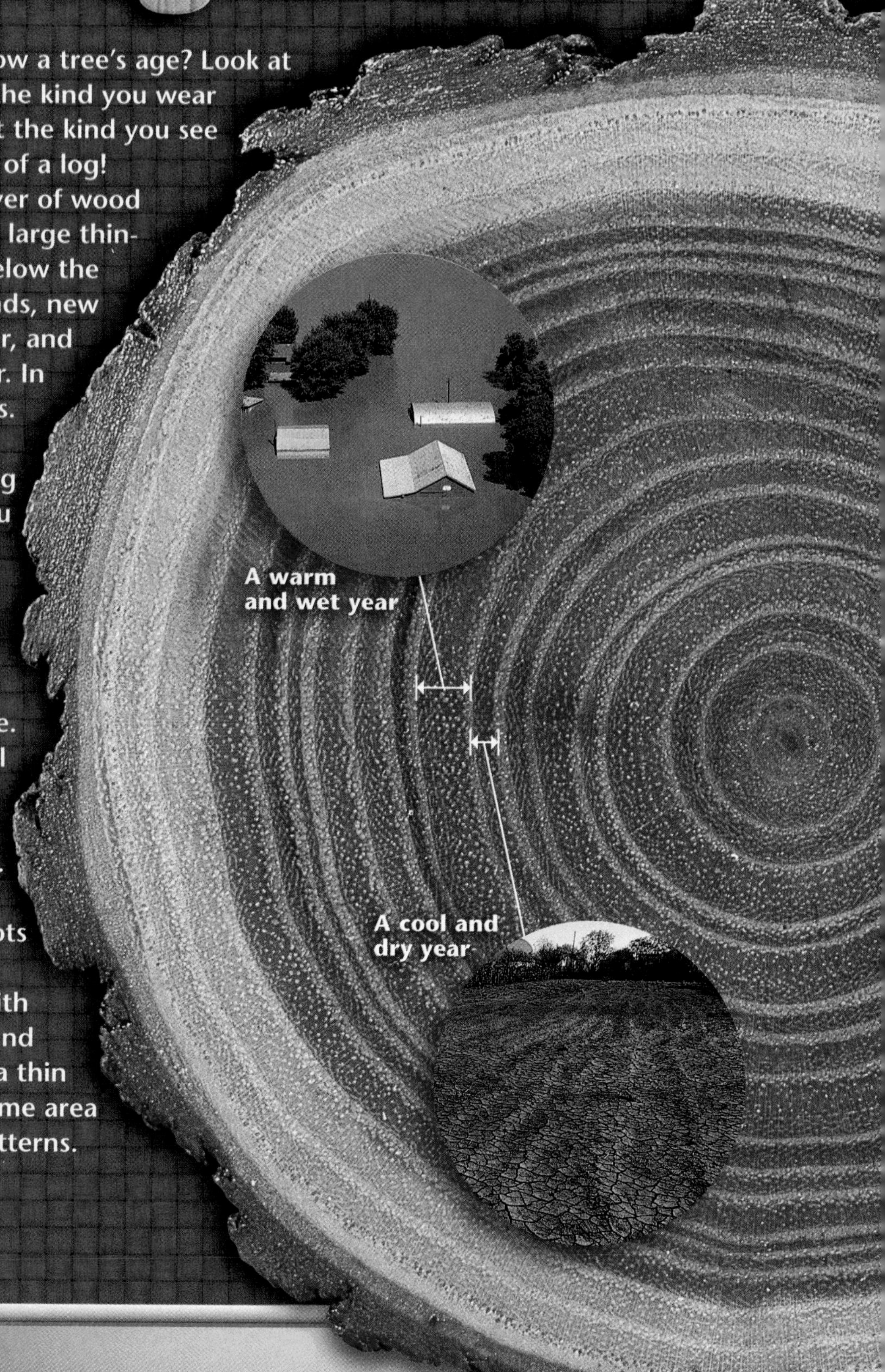

**A warm and wet year**

**A cool and dry year**

# Math Link

Because of this, tree rings help scientists date wood found in ancient ruins. They find a cross section from a living tree nearby. Then they compare its rings to the wood from the ruins. This has been very helpful in the southwestern United States, where the dry climate helps to preserve trees.

In ancient Native American villages there, scientists found wooden beams used to hold up roofs centuries ago. Some beams were so old, they showed the marks of stone axes!

The beams were compared with wood from many sources. Using wood cut on a known date, scientists dated beams with similar ring patterns. The scientists were able to date Native American villages 1,500 years old. The people who lived there left no written records, but the trees they cut told their story for them!

## DISCUSSION STARTER

1. Explain why the pattern of a tree's cross section looks the way it does.

2. What was the weather like if a tree ring for that year is thin?

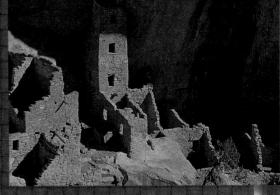

**Mesa Verde, a Native American village, is about 1,500 years old!**

To learn more about tree rings, visit *www.mhschool.com/science* and enter the keyword TIMING.

*inter*NET
CONNECTION

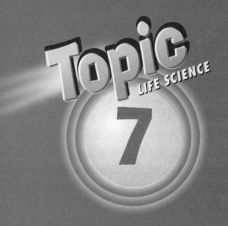

## WHY IT MATTERS

**Some behaviors are inherited. Others have to be learned.**

### SCIENCE WORDS

**response** what a living thing does as a result of a stimulus

**stimulus** something in the environment (such as light or heat) that causes a living thing to react

**tropism** a growth response of a plant toward or away from a stimulus

**adaptation** a characteristic that enables a living thing to survive in its environment

# Plant Responses

**W**hat happens when you jump up? What happens to skateboard jumpers when they reach the top of the slope? Why don't they just fly up and away from Earth's surface?

There is a pull between Earth and everything on it. This pull is called gravity. It never stops. How does gravity affect what you do?

How do you think gravity affects what a plant does—for example, how it grows? Gravity pulls things downward. However, as plants grow, do their parts—roots, stems, and leaves—grow downward?

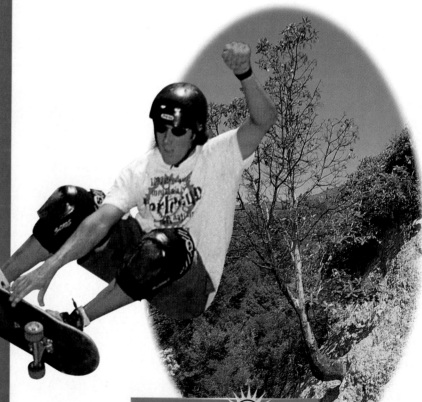

## EXPLORE

**HYPOTHESIZE** Do roots always grow "down" no matter how you plant a seed? Write a hypothesis in your *Science Journal.* Then test your ideas.

# Investigate How Roots Grow

Place seeds in many positions to observe how roots grow from them.

## MATERIALS

- petri dish (plastic)
- 2 paper towels
- marking pen
- tape
- 4 bean seeds that have been soaked in water overnight
- *Science Journal*

## PROCEDURES

1. Soak two paper towels. Wrinkle the paper towels and place them in the bottom half of the petri dish.

2. Place the four seeds on top of the wet paper towels as shown in diagram 1. Place the seeds so that the curved part is turned toward the center of the dish.

3. Place the top on the petri dish. The top will hold the seeds in the wet paper towels. Seal the top with transparent tape. Draw an arrow on the petri dish with the glass-marking pen as shown in diagram 2. This will show which direction is down. Write the number or name of your group on the petri dish.

4. In a place your teacher provides, stand the petri dish on its edge so the arrow is pointing downward. Tape the petri dish so that it will remain standing. Do not lay the dish down flat.

5. **PREDICT** In your *Science Journal*, make a prediction about the direction you think the roots will grow.

6. **COMMUNICATE** Examine the seeds for the next four days. Record the direction of root growth.

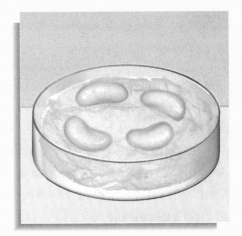

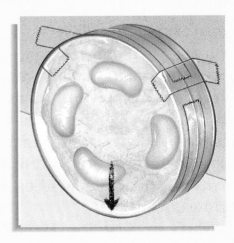

## CONCLUDE AND APPLY

1. **OBSERVE** In what direction were the roots growing on day 1? On day 4?

2. **INFER** Is your prediction supported by your data?

### GOING FURTHER: Problem Solving

3. **PREDICT** What would happen if a seedling were not able to grow its roots down into the soil? Design an experiment to test your prediction.

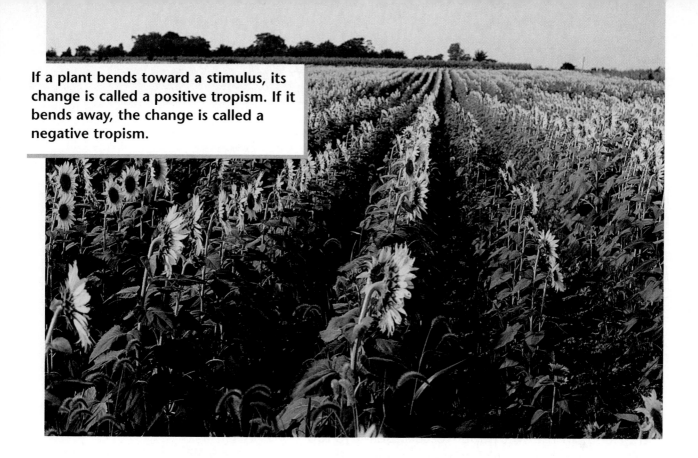

If a plant bends toward a stimulus, its change is called a positive tropism. If it bends away, the change is called a negative tropism.

## How Do Roots Grow?

If the flash of a camera goes off near your eyes, you are likely to respond to the bright light by blinking. The flash of light stimulated your blinking. Anything in the environment—light, heat, gravity, and more—that produces such a **response** is called a **stimulus** (stim′yə ləs).

Plants also respond to a stimulus, but they tend to respond more slowly than animals do. Plants slowly bend or curve toward or away from a stimulus. Scientists call this kind of response a **tropism** (trō′piz əm). Tropisms help a plant survive in its environment. The Explore Activity showed that as seeds sprout, their roots grow downward. Why do you think the seeds' roots grow downward?

There are several major kinds of tropisms. You already explored one of

these—gravitropism. The plant's roots were responding to a stimulus. That stimulus was gravity.

The roots of a plant show positive gravitropism. No matter how the plant is tilted, its roots will always grow downward into the soil. The roots grow in the direction Earth's gravity is pulling them. Stems show negative gravitropism. They grow away from the force of gravity. They grow into the air, where their leaves can get the most sunlight.

Light, of course, is very important to plants' survival. Plants respond to changes in light. These responses are called *phototropisms*. (*Photo* comes from a Greek word meaning "light.") If a plant is exposed to light coming from only one direction, its stem will bend in that direction. That is positive phototropism.

# What Makes a Plant's Parts Move?

If you examine the roots of a willow tree growing near a stream, you will discover *hydrotropism. Hydro* means "water." The willow's roots show positive hydrotropism. They grow toward a source of water.

Some plants, like squash and grape plants, show a response to touch. Grape vines grow around posts farmers stick in the ground. The vines send out threadlike tendrils. The tendrils coil toward whatever they touch.

People long knew about plant tropisms. Yet they didn't always know the process inside a plant that made a plant's parts move. The first clue was discovered by Charles Darwin and his son Francis in the 1870s. Charles Darwin cut off the tips of some very young plant shoots. He left other plants alone. The plants with tips bent toward light. The plants without tips did not. Darwin concluded that something in the tips was causing the bending, but what?

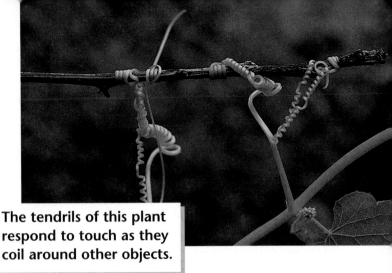

The tendrils of this plant respond to touch as they coil around other objects.

The second clue was found in the 1920s by Dutch scientist Frits Went. Went guessed that a chemical made only in the shoot's tip was responsible for the bending. He separated many chemicals from shoot tips. One by one he placed them on the cutoff tops of plant shoots. Finally, he found the chemical that let the cut shoots bend toward light.

The chemical is called an *auxin.* Auxins are chemicals that stimulate plant growth. Auxins work on stems, roots, tendrils, and all other parts of the plant. Auxins cause tropisms of all kinds. How do auxins cause plant parts to bend? When one side of a stem is exposed to light, for example, auxins move to the other side and down. Auxins cause more cells to grow— and some to grow more in length—on the dark side, but not on the side facing the light. This unequal growth causes the stem to bend toward the light.

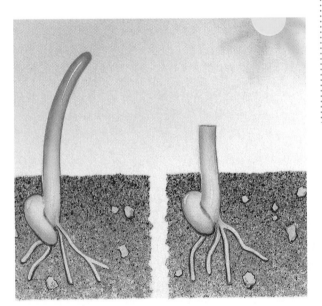

Charles Darwin showed that when the tip of a plant shoot is cut off, the plant will not bend toward light.

# How Do Plants Survive?

Plants survive in deserts, rain forests, and the arctic. They survive in all these places because they have adapted to their environment. An **adaptation** (ad´əp tā'shən) helps an organism survive in its environment.

## Water Shortages

Desert plants have adaptations for collecting, storing, and saving water. Cactus plants have roots that absorb water very quickly. The water is stored in the center of the plant. A thick, waterproof, waxy coating helps stop water loss. Finally, the plant's stomata only open at night, when temperatures are cooler. Less water is lost through transpiration.

Carnivorous (meat-eating) plants can't get enough nutrients from the soil. These plants trap and digest insects to get some of the nutrients they need.

## Changes in Light

Plants like spinach, lettuce, and wheat bloom in late spring and early summer. They are called *long-day* plants. That's because when they bloom, there is much more daylight than darkness. By contrast, *short-day* plants, like strawberries, soybeans, and ragweed, bloom in early spring or in the fall. Short-day plants bloom when there is more darkness and less daylight. This flowering response is called *photoperiodism*.

## SHORT-DAY, LONG-DAY PLANTS

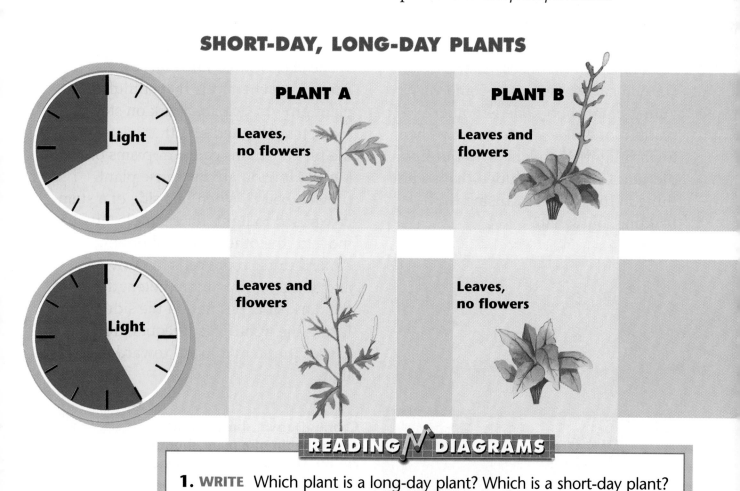

PLANT A

Light

Leaves, no flowers

PLANT B

Leaves and flowers

Leaves and flowers

Light

Leaves, no flowers

## READING DIAGRAMS

1. **WRITE** Which plant is a long-day plant? Which is a short-day plant?
2. **DISCUSS** In what season would plant A bloom?

## Why Do Plants Compete?

Like all organisms, plants compete with one another for what they need to survive and grow—sunlight, water, and nutrients.

Each plant has its own strategy for winning its battle with other plants. Vines, like ivy and honeysuckle, climb the trunks of trees to get a greater share of sunlight. The trees themselves rise to great heights. They spread their branches to form leafy canopies above the forest. That's why in a forest, trees like oaks and maples have more leaves at their tops.

Have you ever been in a forest full of giant redwoods or other conifers? If so, you probably felt as if you were in a huge building filled with soaring columns. Only when you look high up do you see branches covered with green needles. Trees like these also preserve the nutrients and water in the soil for themselves. They do this by blocking sunlight from reaching the ground. Without sunlight few plants can grow in the soil and soak up nutrients and water near great trees.

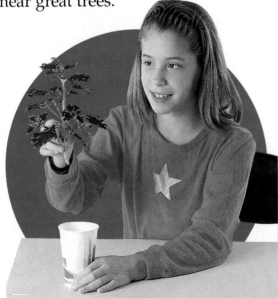

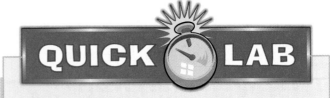

# QUICK LAB

# Plants Compete for Light

**HYPOTHESIZE** Do some plants need more light than others? Can some plants survive in shady areas? Write a hypothesis in your *Science Journal.*

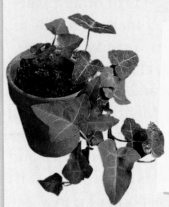

### MATERIALS
- grass seed
- ivy plant
- various houseplants
- paper cup
- soil
- camera (optional)
- *Science Journal*

## PROCEDURES

1. Collect samples of various house-plants that grow to different widths and heights.

2. Plant them, with some grass seed, in your cup. Record in your *Science Journal* the types of plants you used.

3. **OBSERVE** Examine your plants over the next few days. You may wish to take pictures to help you answer the following questions.

## CONCLUDE AND APPLY

1. **OBSERVE** Which plants are being shaded by others? Are the plants in the shade doing as well as the plants that are getting more light?

2. **HYPOTHESIZE** How would you design an experiment to test which plants need more light to grow? How could you determine if these plants have anything else in common?

## How Else Do Plants Fight for Survival?

Some plants use another strategy for keeping other plants at a distance. They produce chemicals that are poisons to other plants. Creosote bushes, which live in dry areas, release such a poison from their roots. The poison keeps the seeds of other plants from germinating. It may even kill other plants that are already growing.

Plants also make chemicals that discourage insects and animals from feeding on or infecting them. The most powerful insect-fighting plant chemical is made by the neem tree of Africa and Asia. This chemical is so strong that if you dissolved a teaspoon of it in a medium-sized swimming pool and sprayed the water on a plant, insects would not feed on it. Some plants, like the hemlock, even make poisons that can kill a person.

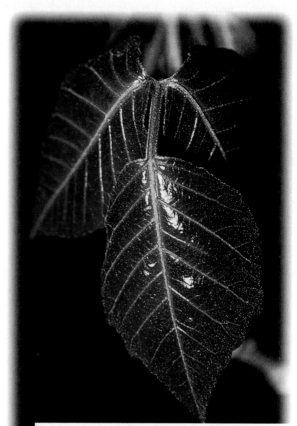

Unlike the plant below, which is being eaten by an insect, other plants such as the poison ivy above, produce chemicals that keep insects away or make them sick.

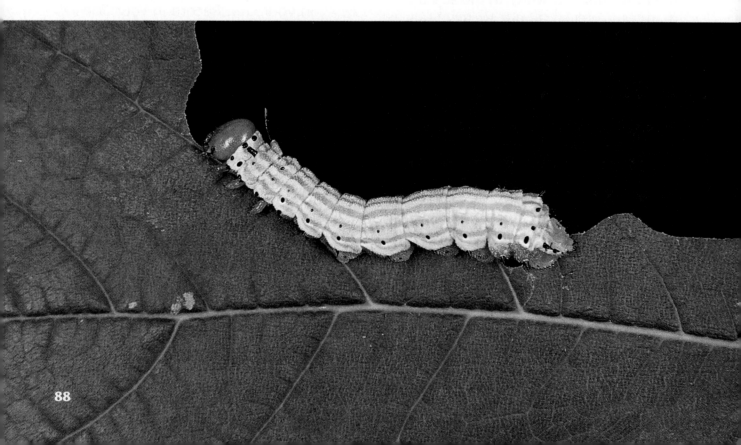

# How Do Animals Adapt?

If you've ever smelled the spray of a skunk, you unpleasantly discovered an adaptation of animals. It's one that protects an animal from harm.

Animals have many adaptations that help them survive in their environment. Some are able to run or swim fast to escape from a predator. Others have sharp claws or teeth to hunt or fight with. Plants rely mostly on adaptations like color, aroma, poisonous chemicals, and structures like thorns.

## How Does Looking Like Something Else Protect an Animal?

Looking like something else—especially something unpleasant—is called *mimicry*. Mimicry can be a powerful protector. For example, the viceroy butterfly tastes good to birds. Yet birds tend to avoid eating viceroys. Why? Viceroys look like the bad-tasting monarch. Predators also avoid some perfectly harmless flies and bugs because they look like stinging wasps or bees.

Some animals mimic plants or their parts. For example, the *kallima* butterfly of Asia looks just like a dead leaf. It also has markings that look very much like the fungus that grows on dead leaves. A stick insect looks just like the twig of a plant on which it is resting.

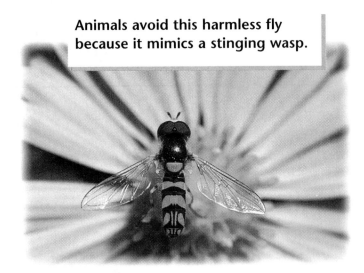

Animals avoid this harmless fly because it mimics a stinging wasp.

Leaf butterflies look so much like leaves that a bird looking for a meal will fly right by.

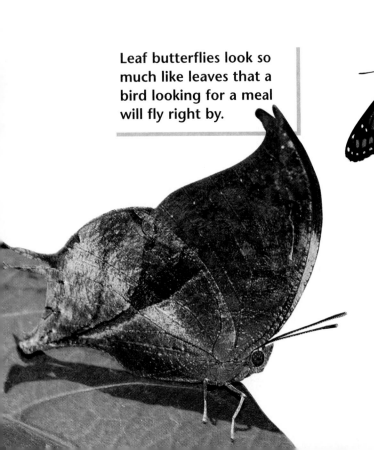

The good-tasting viceroy butterfly (top) mimics the bad-tasting monarch butterfly (bottom). Birds leave the viceroy alone because they've learned that insects with the same color patterns taste bad.

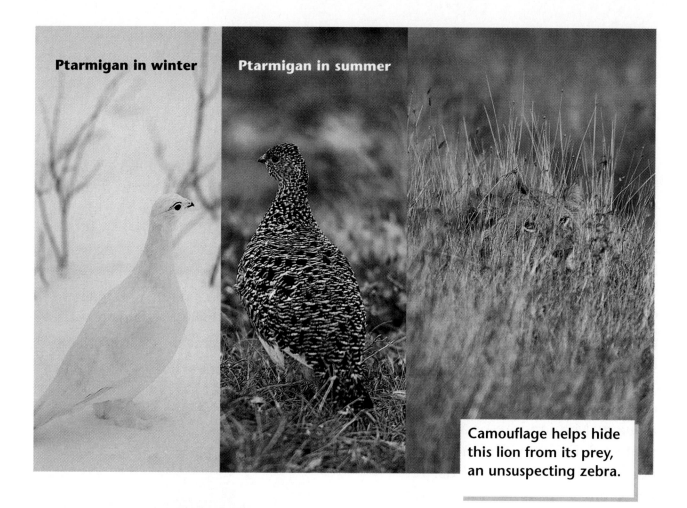

Ptarmigan in winter

Ptarmigan in summer

Camouflage helps hide this lion from its prey, an unsuspecting zebra.

## How Does Camouflage Help Animals?

An animal that does not move, or moves very, very slowly, and looks like its surroundings is *camouflaged*. In this way a tan-colored lion poised on a sandy African plain can surprise a zebra. However, if the zebra is standing in a thicket of bushes, its stripes may blend in with the pattern of twigs and branches. This hides the zebra from the lion. This kind of camouflage is called *protective coloration*.

Some animals—like chameleons, which are lizards—change color to match the background. Chameleons don't decide to do this. It happens automatically. Other animals change color with the seasons. This is true of an arctic bird known as the *ptarmigan* (tär′mi gən). The ptarmigan's feathers are white in winter, when the arctic is covered with snow. In summer, when many plants paint the landscape all sorts of colors, the ptarmigan's feathers turn brown.

### Brain Power

When do people camouflage themselves? Why?

# Inherited or Learned?

What behaviors do you inherit? What behaviors do you learn? Many traits animals have are automatic responses. These are inherited from their parents. However, some animal behaviors are learned. Birds that avoid eating viceroy butterflies have learned butterflies that look like viceroys taste awful. Your cat may come to the kitchen every time she hears you opening a can. She has learned that the sound could mean dinner is coming.

Some things you do are automatic responses. You pull your hand away from a hot stove before you have a chance to think about what you are doing. You avoid moving cars when you cross the street. Other things you do are learned. You learn how to cook a good meal. You learn to safely cross a street by waiting for the light to turn green.

All living things respond to changes in their environment. They do these things in order to survive. Many of their behaviors are traits inherited from their parents. However, some behaviors are learned. Your pet learns to come when you call. You learn important skills at home and in school that will help you now and in the future.

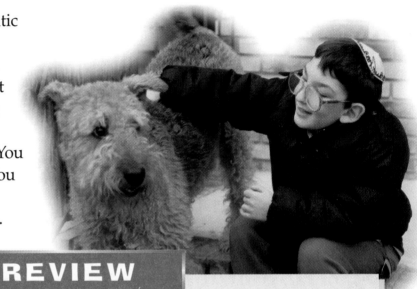

# REVIEW

1. What are tropisms? Give an example of one.

2. Where does a cactus store water?

3. How do auxins help plants grow toward the light?

4. **COMPARE AND CONTRAST** In what ways are plant behaviors like certain animal behaviors? In what ways are some animal behaviors different from plant behaviors?

5. **CRITICAL THINKING** *Analyze* What do you think might happen if all the plants bloomed at the same time?

**WHY IT MATTERS** THINK ABOUT IT
Think about your favorite animal. What are some of its inherited responses? What are some of its learned behaviors?

**WHY IT MATTERS** WRITE ABOUT IT
Write a paragraph about some of your favorite animal's behaviors. Which of its behaviors are automatic? Which of its behaviors are learned? Write another paragraph about some of your automatic responses. Compare them to some of the things you have learned to do.

# Cut Trees, Save Forests?

In Greece 2,000 years ago, people told of a "Golden Age" when hills were covered with trees. Then the forests were gone, and the Greeks discovered that when trees go, soil washes away. Greece has never recovered from the loss of its trees.

Lots of rainfall west of the Rocky Mountains helps trees grow larger than anywhere in the world. Lumber companies built roads into the forests. All the trees were cut down, but only the biggest logs were used. That's called clear cutting, and it leaves large bare patches. Forest animals lose their homes. Soil washes into streams, and the fishes' environment is changed!

Today helicopters fly in workers and tools. A tree is cut and lifted away. The other trees, the animals, and the soil all remain in the forest.

## DISCUSSION STARTER

1. Where does soil go if it washes away?

2. Write or act out a scene in which people who fish for a living and a home builder discuss clear cutting. How might their views differ?

To learn more about saving forests, visit *www.mhschool.com/science* and enter the keyword FORESTS.

*inter*NET
CONNECTION

## SCIENCE WORDS

adaptation p.86    fruit p.75

angiosperm p.58    gymnosperm p.58

cotyledon p.62    pollination p.72

dicot p.62    seed p.58

embryo p.74    spore p.46

fertilization p.50    stimulus p.84

frond p.49    tropism p.84

## USING SCIENCE WORDS

**Number a paper from 1 to 10. Fill in 1 to 5 with words from the list above.**

1. A seed plant that does not produce fruits is a(n) __?__.

2. A new moss plant is produced by a(n) __?__.

3. The leaflike structure of a fern is a(n) __?__.

4 A tiny leaflike structure inside a seed is a(n) __?__.

5. Something in the environment that produces a response in an organism is a(n) __?__.

6–10. **Pick five words from the list above that were not used in 1 to 5, and use each in a sentence.**

## UNDERSTANDING SCIENCE IDEAS

11. What causes sunflowers to bend toward the sunlight?

12. When a bee travels from flower to flower, how does it help the plants produce seeds?

13. Give an example of asexual reproduction.

14. Describe how fruits help plants spread their seeds.

15. Describe the part of the seed that protects the embryo.

## USING IDEAS AND SKILLS

16. **READING SKILL: COMPARE AND CONTRAST** What is the difference between a monocot and a dicot?

17. What would happen if a tree sprouted from the side of a cliff?

18. Describe two ways that adaptations can help plants survive.

19.  **CLASSIFY** Tell which of these plants are angiosperms and which are gymnosperms—bristlecone pine, rose, wheat, oat, fir, cedar, lily, juniper, yew, larch, violet, tomato, spruce, giant redwood tree.

20. **THINKING LIKE A SCIENTIST** If you were lost in the woods in the United States, had no compass, and could not see the sky, how might plants help you infer direction?

## PROBLEMS and PUZZLES

**Turning Food into Plants** Place a sweet potato at the top of a glass of water, so that water is soaking into the sweet potato. However, it should not sink in the water.

Observe what happens over time. Keep the water level the same.

## SCIENCE WORDS

adaptation p.86    fungus p.11

angiosperm p.58    photosynthesis p.32

chlorophyll p.4    spore p.46

embryo p.74        tropism p.84

epidermis p.20     xylem p.20

## USING SCIENCE WORDS

**Number a paper from 1 to 10. Beside each number write the word or words that best completes the sentence.**

1. The chemical that makes plant leaves green is __?__.

2. Yeast and mushrooms are members of the __?__ kingdom.

3. The outer layer of a root is the __?__.

4. Water moves up the part of a root or stem called the __?__.

5. Plants make food by a process called __?__.

6. Ferns do not reproduce with seeds, but with __?__.

7. Plants with flowers are members of the __?__ division of the plant kingdom.

8. The immature plant within a seed is called a(n) __?__.

9. The movement of a leaf toward light is an example of a(n) __?__.

10. A cactus's special features that allow it to live in a desert are examples of __?__.

## UNDERSTANDING SCIENCE IDEAS

**Write 11–15. For each number write the letter for the best answer. You may wish to use the hints provided.**

11. Which of the following is a fungus?
    a. mold
    b. moss
    c. fern
    d. conifer
    *(Hint: Read page 11.)*

12. In the process of making food, plants give off
    a. sugar
    b. carbon dioxide
    c. oxygen
    d. chloroplasts
    *(Hint: Read pages 32–33.)*

13. What kinds of plants do very well in hot, damp climates?
    a. apple trees
    b. ferns
    c. fir trees
    d. grains
    *(Hint: Read page 44.)*

14. Which of the following are gymnosperms?
    a. apple trees
    b. ferns
    c. fir trees
    d. grains
    *(Hint: Read page 58.)*

15. Tropism is the process of
    a. movement of a plant toward or away from a stimulus
    b. making sugar from sunlight
    c. transporting water along a stem
    d. adaptation to a hot climate
    *(Hint: Read page 84.)*

## USING IDEAS AND SKILLS

16. Describe what makes plants different from fungi and algae.

17. Make a simple diagram that shows how water moves from the ground to a leaf in a plant.

18. Explain why having a needle-shaped leaf is important to a pine tree's survival.

19. 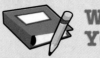 **EXPERIMENT** Bo grew two tomato plants. One grew well but the other barely grew at all. Write three questions that you would ask Bo to find out why they grew so differently.

20. Diagram the life cycle of a fern. Use labels as appropriate.

21. How are monocot and dicot seeds different from each other?

22. Is this leaf from a monocot or a dicot? Explain how you can tell.

23. Explain why bees are important to many farmers.

## THINKING LIKE A SCIENTIST

24. **CLASSIFY** Classify angiosperms according to how we use them. See how many categories you can think of.

25. Explain how a gardener helps vegetable plants compete with each other and with weeds.

## WRITING IN YOUR JOURNAL

### SCIENCE IN YOUR LIFE
Describe how people use wood. List what kinds of plants produce wood, and explain what parts of those plants the wood comes from. Present some of your information in a chart.

### PRODUCT ADS
Look at the ingredients listed on boxes of breakfast foods. What kinds of plants are most commonly used to make breakfast foods? Explain why.

### HOW SCIENTISTS WORK
Classifying is one of the most valuable methods of studying living things. Give two different examples from this unit that show how scientists have classified living things to understand them better.

## Design your own Experiment

Plan a method to determine how the amount of water a bean seed gets affects how fast it produces sprouts. Review your experiment with your teacher before trying it out.

## interNET CONNECTION

For help in reviewing this unit, visit *www.mhschool.com/science*

# PROBLEMS and PUZZLES

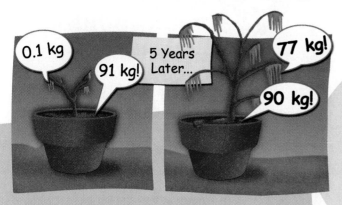

0.1 kg

91 kg!

5 Years Later...

77 kg!

90 kg!

## Van Helmont's Experiment

A 17th-century Belgian doctor named Jan Baptista van Helmont planted a tiny seedling in a large pot. The pot contained 91 kilograms of soil. Van Helmont watered the plant for five years. During that time he did not add or take away soil from the pot. After five years had passed, van Helmont found that the plant weighed 77 kilograms.

How do you explain van Helmont's results? How did the plant gain so much weight? What materials did it use to gain this weight?

## Planet Hollyhocks

Which of these planets would be best for growing plants? Choose one of the three planets shown. Support your choice with a list of reasons.

| Planet | Muton-4 | Vungus-A | Yerth |
|---|---|---|---|
| Atmosphere | 100% oxygen | carbon dioxide, oxygen | hydrogen, oxygen, sulfur |
| Sunlight | strong | low | medium |
| Water | lakes, rivers, oceans | puddles | oceans |
| Soil | mineral-rich | some minerals | mineral-rich |

## Bright Green Thumb Top Ten

Scientists for the Bright Green Thumb Plant Company made a list of experimental future projects. Rank the projects shown from 1 to 10. Which project do you think has the greatest chance of success? Which project would be the most useful to people?

- Rootless plants
- Plants with square fruits
- Leafless plants
- Plants that move
- Plants that grow in complete darkness
- Seedless flowering plants
- Soilless plants
- Nongreen plants
- Waterless plants
- Talking plants

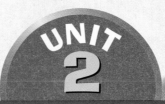

# UNIT 2

# WEATHER AND CLIMATE

## CHAPTER 3

# WEATHER

Weather is all around you. It affects you every day. Weather can affect how you feel. It can also affect the plans you've made.

In Chapter 3 you'll explore what makes up the weather. For example, why do some clouds give us rain or snow, while others just float overhead? Why do clouds form?

 In Chapter 3 you will read to find the main idea and details that support the main idea.

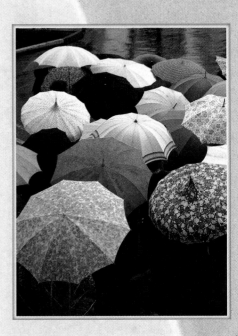

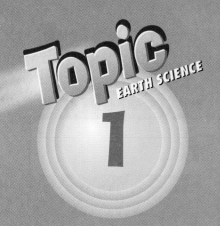

# Topic
### EARTH SCIENCE
# 1

## WHY IT MATTERS

**Many things affect how hot it can get.**

### SCIENCE WORDS

**insolation** the amount of the Sun's energy that reaches Earth at a given time and place

**atmosphere** the blanket of gases that surrounds Earth

**troposphere** the layer of the atmosphere closest to Earth's surface

**air pressure** the force put on a given area by the weight of the air above it

**weather** what the lower atmosphere is like at any given place and time

**barometer** a device for measuring air pressure

# Atmosphere and Air Temperature

Is it always hot everywhere in summer? Vacationers in the heart of Africa on a July day might see lions snoozing in the afternoon heat. On the same day, tourists huddled on a cruise ship in Alaska might be watching seals play near icy glaciers. How can two places on Earth have such different temperatures?

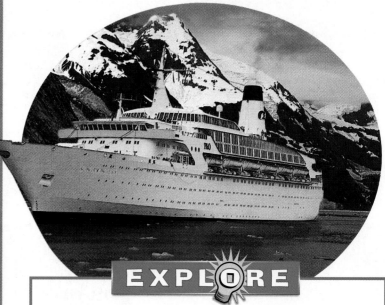

## EXPLORE

**HYPOTHESIZE** How does the angle at which the Sun's energy hits Earth affect the warming of Earth? Write a hypothesis in your *Science Journal*. Set up an experiment to test your ideas.

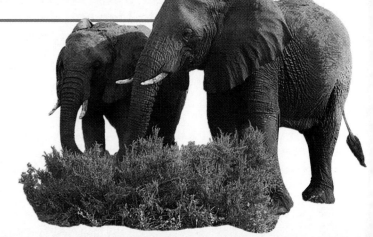

# Investigate if the Sun's Angle Matters

Test what factors might affect how warm an area gets.

## PROCEDURES

**SAFETY** Do not look into the lamplight. Prop up a foam bowl, using a plate or clay, to shield your eyes from the light.

1. Place a thermometer onto each of the three blocks, as shown. Cover each with black paper. Put blocks 20 cm from the bulb, level with its filament (curly wire).

2. **OBSERVE** Measure the starting temperature at each block. Record the temperatures in your *Science Journal*.

3. **PREDICT** What will happen when the lamp is turned on? Turn the lamp on. Record the temperature at each block every two minutes, for ten minutes.

4. **COMMUNICATE** Make a line graph showing the change in temperature at each block over time.

5. **USE VARIABLES** Repeat the activity with white paper.

### MATERIALS
- 3 thermometers
- triangular blocks
- black paper
- white paper
- centimeter ruler
- scissors
- tape
- 150-W clear bulb lamp
- stopwatch
- foam bowl
- clay
- *Science Journal*

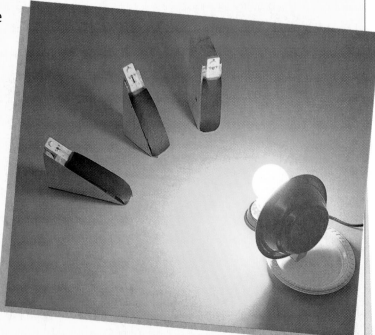

## CONCLUDE AND APPLY

1. **COMMUNICATE** Which block's surface was warmed most by the lamplight? Which block's surface was warmed the least?

2. **INFER** How does the angle at which light hits a surface affect how much the surface is heated? How does the surface color affect how much it is heated?

## GOING FURTHER: Problem Solving

3. **EXPERIMENT** What other factors might affect how much a surface is warmed by sunlight? How would you test your ideas?

## Does the Angle Matter?

Where do you think you might find warm temperatures all year long? Where would you find very cold weather? As the Explore Activity shows, angles make a difference in how much the Sun warms an area. The areas around the equator are hottest. That's because the Sun's path is directly overhead at midday. In those areas the Sun's rays hit Earth at their strongest.

The areas around the North and South Poles are coldest. That's because in those areas, the Sun is lower at midday. The Sun's rays hit Earth's surface at a low angle. The strength of the rays is much weaker at this angle.

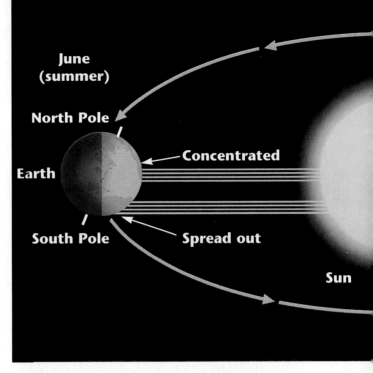

The Sun's rays strike the surface at different angles as the Earth travels around the Sun.

 **MONTHLY MEAN TEMPERATURE**

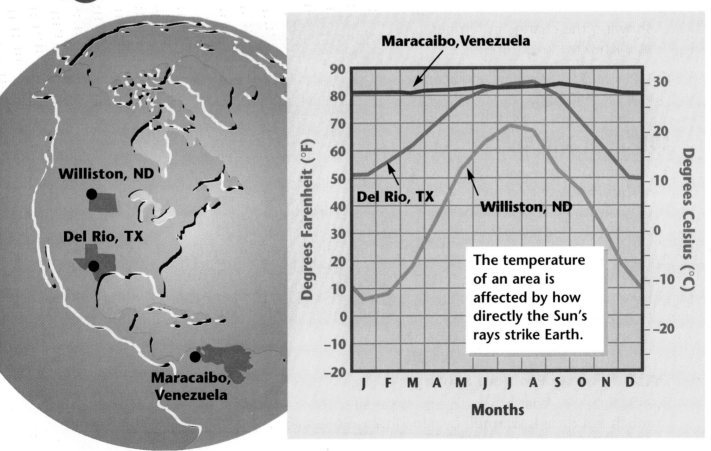

The temperature of an area is affected by how directly the Sun's rays strike Earth.

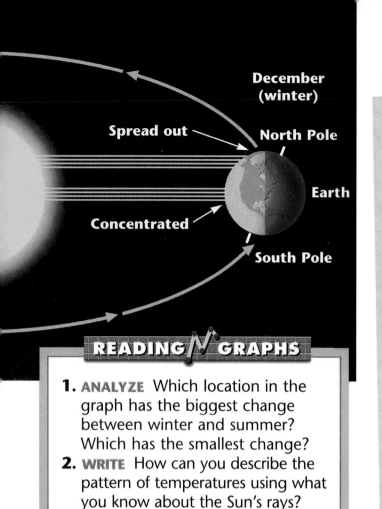

December
(winter)

Spread out

North Pole

Concentrated

Earth

South Pole

## READING GRAPHS

1. **ANALYZE** Which location in the graph has the biggest change between winter and summer? Which has the smallest change?
2. **WRITE** How can you describe the pattern of temperatures using what you know about the Sun's rays?

## Angles and Light

The angle at which sunlight strikes Earth's surface is so important, it is given a specific name. It is called the angle of **insolation**. *Insolation* is short for *in*coming *sol*ar rad*iation*. It means the amount of the Sun's energy that reaches Earth at a given place and time.

The diagram shows how sunlight warms Earth in summer and winter. The amount of warming depends on the angle of insolation. The greater the angle, the warmer it gets. The angle of insolation is always smaller near the poles than near the equator. That means while it's freezing cold in one part of the world, it's hot in another. How does Earth's position in its path around the Sun affect the angle of insolation where you live?

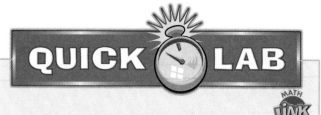

# QUICK LAB

# Investigating Angles

**HYPOTHESIZE** Why does the angle of insolation cause a difference in warming? Write a hypothesis in your *Science Journal.*

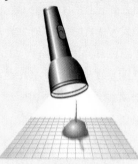

### MATERIALS

- flashlight
- sheet of graph paper
- modeling clay
- 3 toothpicks
- ruler
- *Science Journal*

## PROCEDURES

1. Fold a sheet of graph paper lengthwise in three equal parts. Put a small lump of clay in the middle of each part. Stand a toothpick straight up in each lump of clay.

2. Hold a flashlight directly over the first toothpick. Have a partner trace a line around the circle of light and trace the toothpick shadow.

3. **USE VARIABLES** Repeat step 2 for the other two toothpicks, changing only the angle of the flashlight.

4. **MEASURE** Count the number of boxes in each circle. Measure the lengths of the toothpick shadows. Record results in your *Science Journal.*

## CONCLUDE AND APPLY

1. **INFER** How is the length of the shadows related to the angle?

2. **INFER** How is the number of boxes in the circle related to the angle?

# What Has the Time Got to Do with It?

In the morning the Sun is close to the horizon. What happens as time goes by? By noon the Sun is high up in the sky, as high as it gets during the day. After noon the Sun is lower and lower in the sky.

How does this affect the angle of insolation? How do we measure it? In an earlier illustration, you saw that both location and time of year affect this angle. This illustration shows how the time of day affects the angle of insolation.

Measuring the angle of insolation is a challenge. It is not easy to see indi-vidual light rays. How can you tell if they are hitting a surface directly? Look at the shadows cast by objects they strike! The less direct the light rays, the longer the shadows. As you can see in the diagram, the angle of insolation is the same as the angle between the ground and the line from the tip of the shadow to the top of the wall.

## Brain Power

Why do many coolers have smooth, light-colored surfaces? What kinds of surfaces would you use to keep things warm?

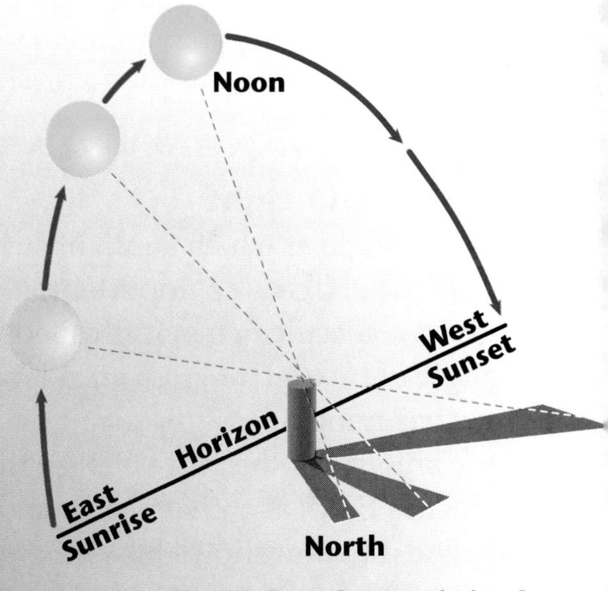

## MATH LINK ANGLE OF INSOLATION

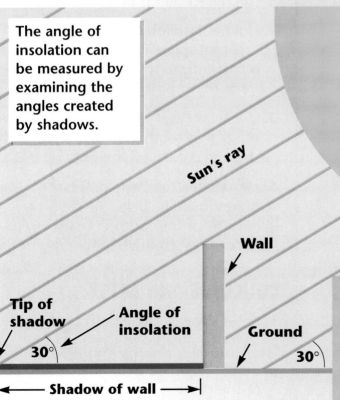

The angle of insolation can be measured by examining the angles created by shadows.

Sun's ray

Wall

Ground

Tip of shadow

Angle of insolation

30°

30°

|← Shadow of wall →|

Path of Sun

Noon

West Sunset

Horizon

East Sunrise

North

The higher the Sun is in the sky, the shorter the shadow.

## READING DIAGRAMS

1. **DISCUSS** How can you measure the angle of insolation without being able to see the Sun's rays individually?
2. **WRITE** What will happen to the angle as the Sun gets higher in the sky? How will this affect the temperature?

# Do Some Things Get Hotter than Others?

The Explore Activity showed that dark colors get hotter than light colors in the same light. This is why black asphalt roads get so hot in the sunlight. Dark soils and rocks also get very hot. White sand and light-colored soils do not get as hot in sunlight. Plants can also help keep an area cooler in sunlight than surrounding rocks and soil, or black asphalt.

*Texture* is how smooth or rough a surface is. Look at the drawing on the right. See how rough textures cause light to bounce around at many angles. Each time a little more energy is absorbed by the surface. Rough surfaces tend to get hotter in sunlight than smooth surfaces.

Why do you go swimming when it is hot and you want to cool off? Because the water is cooler than the air. The water and the land next to it are

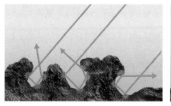
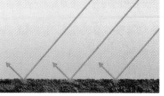

**Rough texture**      **Smooth texture**

**More impacts = more heat energy absorbed**
**Less impacts = less heat energy absorbed**

receiving identical Sun's rays. You would expect them to be the same temperature. Why is the water cooler? Water reacts differently to light energy. As you can see in the drawing below, the same amount of light energy will heat land to a higher temperature than it will heat water.

## READING DIAGRAMS

1. **DISCUSS** Which material is warmer after being placed near the light?
2. **DISCUSS** How can you use the graph to tell which substance heats faster?

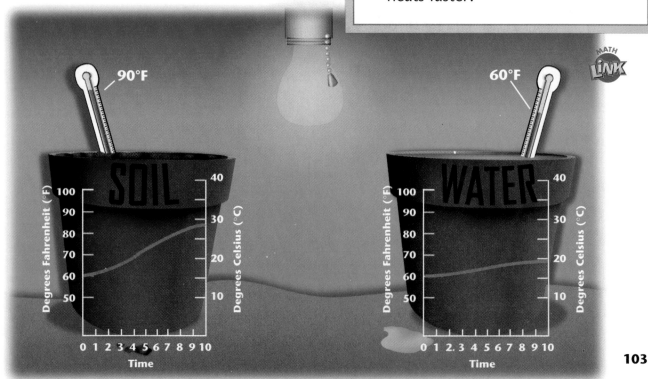

# Why Do You Cool Down as You Go Up?

Did you ever climb a high mountain? As you go higher and higher above sea level, air temperatures drop. The natural drop in air temperature with altitude is about 2°C (3.6°F) for every 305 meters (1,000 ft). On a recent day in June, the air temperature in Lewiston, Maine (elevation: 34 meters [110 ft]), was a pleasant 21°C (70°F). A two-hour drive away, the air temperature at Mount Washington, New Hampshire (elevation: 1,917 meters [6,288 ft]), was a frosty 1°C (34°F).

Driving up a mountain is really a journey up into the **atmosphere**, the air that surrounds Earth. The atmosphere reaches from Earth's surface to the edge of space. What if you could travel to the top part of the atmosphere? The diagram of the atmosphere shows what you would find.

You would find that the temperature does not fall steadily with altitude. It changes abruptly several times. These changes mark the boundaries of four main layers. These layers surround Earth like huge shells.

The layer closest to Earth's surface is the **troposphere** (trop′ə sfîr′). It's the narrowest layer—between 8 and 18 kilometers (5–11 miles) thick—but it contains most of the air in the atmosphere. All life on Earth exists here. In this layer all moisture is found and all clouds, rain, snow, and thunderstorms occur. Above this layer the air gradually thins out to the near-emptiness of space, with no exact upper boundary.

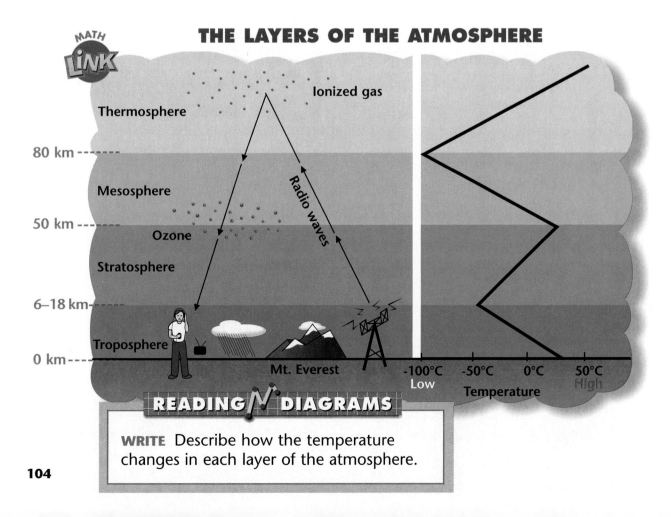

## THE LAYERS OF THE ATMOSPHERE

MATH LiNK

Thermosphere

Ionized gas

80 km

Mesosphere

Radio waves

50 km

Ozone

Stratosphere

6–18 km

Troposphere

0 km

Mt. Everest

-100°C Low    -50°C    0°C    50°C High

Temperature

## READING DIAGRAMS

**WRITE** Describe how the temperature changes in each layer of the atmosphere.

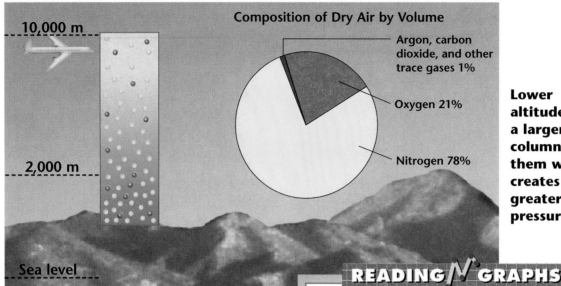

Composition of Dry Air by Volume

10,000 m

Argon, carbon dioxide, and other trace gases 1%

Oxygen 21%

2,000 m

Nitrogen 78%

Sea level

Lower altitudes have a larger air column above them which creates greater air pressure.

## READING / GRAPHS

1. **DISCUSS**  What is meant by *trace*?
2. **WRITE**  Which gas is the most abundant in the atmosphere?

# What Else Happens?

As you go higher in altitude, **air pressure** decreases steadily. Air pressure is the force put on a given area by the weight of the air above it. Air is a mixture of gases. It is made up mostly of *molecules* of nitrogen and oxygen. Molecules are the smallest pieces that a substance can be broken into without changing what the substance is.

The molecules have mass. They are attracted to Earth by gravity, so they have weight.

Normal air pressure is greatest at sea level. There the column of air extending above the surface to the top of the atmosphere is tallest. Sea level air pressure is about 1.04 kilograms per square centimeter (14.7 pounds per square inch). As you go higher in altitude, the height of the air column above you becomes shorter. Therefore the weight of that column—or air pressure—becomes less.

In the lower atmosphere, the composition of air varies very little. Up to an elevation of about 100 kilometers (62 miles), air consists of a mixture of gases, water vapor, and dust particles. The gases found in pure, dry air are shown in the circle graph. Nitrogen and oxygen make up 99 percent of the gases in dry air.

Water vapor is water in the gas phase. It should not be confused with clouds or fog, which are made of liquid or solid water. The amount of water vapor in air varies from $\frac{1}{10,000}$ of air in dry arctic regions to $\frac{1}{25}$ of air in moist equatorial regions.

The dust in air is made of particles so tiny that 100,000 lined up would only form a row 1 centimeter long. Some of it comes from Earth's surface, from fires and volcanic eruptions, or from tiny crystals of salt.

# What Is Weather?

When you say, "It sure is hot today!" the *it* is the air. You really mean that the air around you is hot. The same is true if you say, "It is windy, " or "It is cloudy," or give any other similar description of the **weather**. The weather is simply what the lower atmosphere, or troposphere, is like at any given place and time.

The conditions that make up weather are the characteristics that change. They are air temperature, air pressure, amount of moisture in the air, wind, clouds, and rain or snow.

## Measuring Temperature

You can measure temperature with a thermometer. Thermometers can use two different temperature scales. The Celsius scale is marked with the letter *C*. The Fahrenheit scale is shown by the letter *F*.

## Measuring Air Pressure

Air pressure is measured with a **barometer** (bə rom'i tər). Two common types of barometers are the mercury barometer and the aneroid barometer.

Mercury barometers use a glass tube with one closed end. The open end is submerged in liquid mercury. Air pressure on the mercury pushes it up into the tube. When the weight of the mercury column equals the air pressure, the mercury stops rising.

An *aneroid* (an'ə roid´) barometer is an accordion-like metal can with most of the air removed. Inside, a spring balances the outside air pressure. When outside air pressure increases, the can squeezes the spring. When air pressure decreases, the spring pushes outward. A needle inside indicates the changes in air pressure.

Room temperature

Freezing point

**Thermometer**

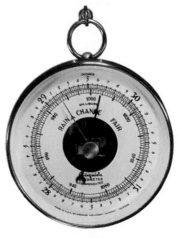

**Aneroid barometer**

These are two common types of barometers

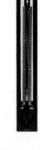

**Mercury barometer**

## How Can You Start a Weather Station?

You can monitor and record weather conditions for your own weather station. Measure and record the air temperature on both scales several times each day. If you have a barometer, you can measure and record the daily air pressure. You might also record the daily air pressure by listening to the weather reports. They often say, "The barometer reads . . . and is falling." They may say it "is rising." You will learn more about air pressure later in this chapter.

In the next few topics, you will add instruments to your weather station. Each instrument can be used to measure a different property of your local weather. By the end of the chapter, you will have a real working weather station.

Have you ever heard a day called a "scorcher"? That means a really hot day. On really hot days, your body can lose a lot of moisture. Your body gives off sweat gradually most of the time. On a hot day, your body tends to give off more and more. That's why you might consider having a bottle of water handy on a hot day.

On really cold days, many people have other problems—such as frostbite. You have to cover your face and hands to avoid contact with air at extremely low temperatures.

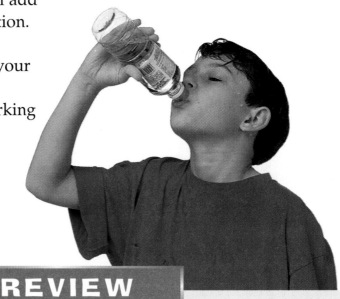

## REVIEW

**1.** How do temperatures on Earth depend on angles?

**2.** List factors that affect temperatures of places on Earth.

**3.** What is air pressure? How does it change in the atmosphere?

**4. COMPARE AND CONTRAST** How are the *troposphere* and *atmosphere* alike? Different?

**5. CRITICAL THINKING** *Analyze* Is the weather one or more than just one thing? Defend your answer.

**WHY IT MATTERS** THINK ABOUT IT
Why is the atmosphere so important for Earth?

**WHY IT MATTERS** WRITE ABOUT IT
How do you depend on the weather?

# NATIONAL GEOGRAPHIC

# World of SCIENCE

## What's UP?

### LAYERS OF THE ATMOSPHERE

**Thermosphere**
From 80–700 km (50–435 mi)

**Ionosphere**
From 60–400 km (36–240 mi)

**Mesosphere**
From 50–80 km (31–50 mi)

**Stratosphere**
From 11–50 km (5–31 mi)

**Troposphere**
From 0–11 km (0–7 mi)

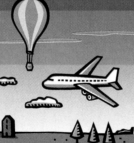
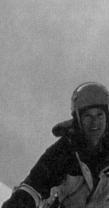

# Science, Technology, and Society

Take a deep breath. Chances are you can breathe easily. That's because Earth's atmosphere contains oxygen. At sea level breathing's easy. On a mountaintop, the breathing's more difficult. Why?

In the 1600s the newly invented barometer, a device for measuring air pressure, was taken high in the mountains. There the barometer registered a lower air pressure than at sea level. The lower the air pressure, the harder it is to breathe.

Over the centuries scientists have gone even higher to investigate the layers of Earth's atmosphere. The troposphere is the layer where all life and weather occur. The troposphere begins at sea level and rises 11 kilometers (7 miles).

In the late 1800s, a scientist launched a balloon carrying a thermometer and a barometer. He discovered a warm atmospheric layer we call the stratosphere. There sunlight changes oxygen into ozone, which is why we call it the ozone layer. Ozone absorbs the Sun's radiation and keeps it from reaching Earth.

In 1901 Guglielmo Marconi sent the first radio signal across the Atlantic Ocean. The radio waves couldn't bend to follow the curvature of the Earth. Instead they were reflected back by particles, or ions, in the ionosphere.

Scientists later identified the mesosphere and thermosphere. They also discovered that some chemicals used on Earth caused a thinning of the ozone layer. Because the ozone layer protects Earth from harmful radiation, the world's nations agreed to ban the chemicals.

**Air in the thermosphere is so thin that a special spacesuit is needed.**

## Discussion Starter

**1** TV signals bounce off satellites. What does this tell you about the waves that carry TV signals?

**2** When we protect the ozone layer, we protect ourselves. Why?

## interNET

To learn more about atmosphere, visit www.mhschool.com/science and enter the keyword **SKY.**

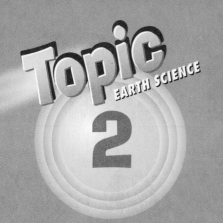

## Topic
### EARTH SCIENCE
### 2

## WHY IT MATTERS

**The amount of water in the air can affect how you feel.**

### SCIENCE WORDS

**water vapor** water in the form of a gas

**humidity** the amount of water vapor in the air

**evaporation** the changing of a liquid into a gas

**relative humidity** a comparison between condensation and evaporation

**condensation** the changing of a gas into a liquid

# Water in the Air

**W**hat if you were walking on this bridge? What would you see and feel all around you? Here's a hint. Put a cold glass of lemonade outside on a table on a hot, humid day. What do you see and feel on the outside of the glass?

What is a humid day like? You can feel a humid day. The word *humid* may make you think of moisture—fine droplets of water. Where is the moisture on a humid day?

## EXPLORE

**HYPOTHESIZE The lemonade glass has moisture on the side and in a puddle around the bottom. Where does the moisture come from? Is it from inside the glass? Write a hypothesis in your *Science Journal*. How might you design an experiment to test your ideas?**

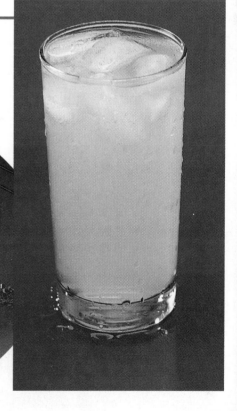

110

## Design Your Own Experiment

### WHERE DOES THE PUDDLE COME FROM?

### PROCEDURES

🥽 **SAFETY** Wear goggles.

1. **EXPERIMENT** Describe what you would do to test your idea about where the puddle came from. How would your test support or reject your idea?

2. **COMMUNICATE** Draw a diagram showing how you would use the materials. In your *Science Journal*, keep a record of your observations.

### CONCLUDE AND APPLY

1. **COMMUNICATE** Describe the results of your investigation.

2. **COMMUNICATE** What evidence did you gather? Explain what happened.

3. **INFER** How does this evidence support or reject your explanation?

### GOING FURTHER: Problem Solving

4. **USE VARIABLES** Do you get the same results on a cool day as on a warm day? How might you set up an investigation to show the difference?

5. **USE VARIABLES** Do you get the same results on a humid day as on a dry day? How might you set up an investigation to show the difference?

### MATERIALS

- plastic drinking glasses
- ice
- paper towels
- food coloring
- thermometer
- goggles
- *Science Journal*

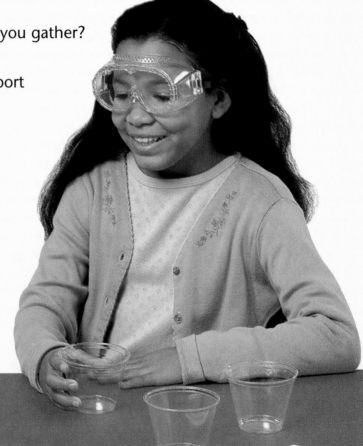

**111**

# Where Does the Puddle Come From?

The Explore Activity showed the water in the puddle on the table did not come from inside the glass! The water level in the glass did not drop as the puddle formed. The water in the puddle isn't lemonade. It didn't have the same color or smell.

The water in the puddle came from the air around the glass. When the warm air touched the cold glass, the air cooled. Droplets of water formed, ran down the side of the glass, and made a puddle on the table.

The water in the air is **water vapor**. Water vapor is water in the form of a gas. Water vapor is invisible, colorless, odorless, and tasteless. The amount of water vapor in the air is called **humidity**. Do not confuse humidity with droplets of liquid water you see in rain, fog, or clouds.

How does water vapor get into the air in the first place? Think about planet Earth. More than two-thirds of this planet is covered with liquid water—mostly oceans. Much of the rest—the land—has rivers, lakes, and water in the ground. The land is covered with plants. Plants also contain water. To get into the air, this liquid water must be changed into water vapor.

The changing of a liquid into a gas is called **evaporation**. This takes lots of energy. The main energy source for Earth is the Sun. Each day the Sun turns trillions of tons of ocean water into water vapor.

**GEOGRAPHY LINK**

## ESTIMATE THE FRACTION AMOUNT OF THE EARTH'S WATER

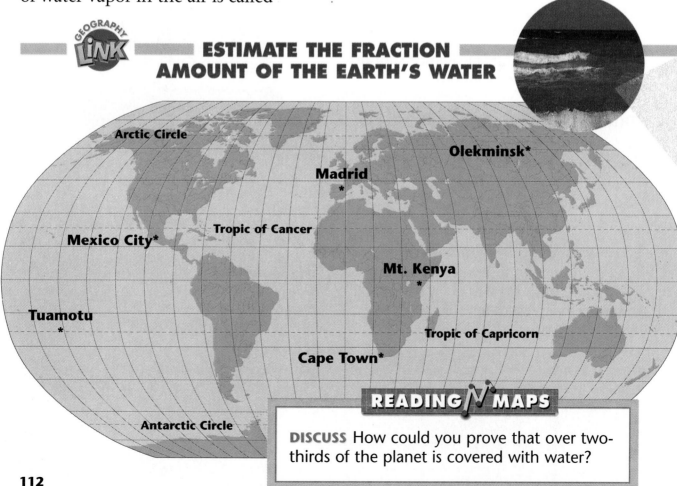

Arctic Circle

Olekminsk*

Madrid*

Tropic of Cancer

Mexico City*

Mt. Kenya*

Tuamotu*

Tropic of Capricorn

Cape Town*

Antarctic Circle

**READING MAPS**

**DISCUSS** How could you prove that over two-thirds of the planet is covered with water?

The Sun's energy gives molecules of water a "lift." Water molecules near the surface of the liquid "escape" into the atmosphere as water vapor. They move about in all directions. Some hit other molecules and return to the liquid. This is an example of **condensation**. Condensation is the changing of a gas into a liquid.

Plants' roots absorb water that has seeped into the ground. Plants transport the liquid water through their roots and stems to their leaves.

The leaves then give off water in the process called transpiration. This is the second-largest source of water vapor in the atmosphere.

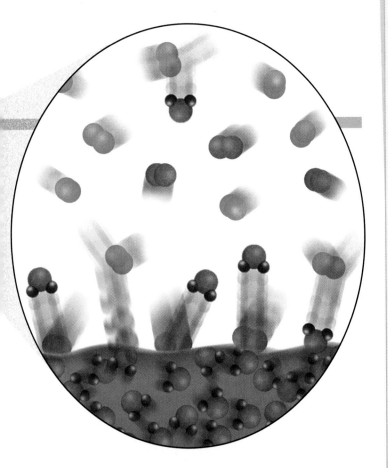

**Water molecules fit between moving molecules of gas in the air. Some water molecules are knocked back into the liquid water.**

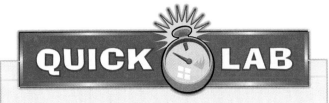

# QUICK LAB

# Transpiration

**HYPOTHESIZE** What evidence can you find for transpiration? Write a hypothesis in your *Science Journal.*

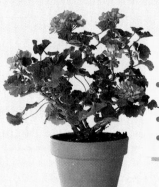

## MATERIALS
- potted houseplant (geraniums work well)
- transparent plastic bag
- *Science Journal*

## PROCEDURES

1. Place the plastic bag completely over the plant, and secure it tightly around the base of the stem. Do not put the soil-filled pot into the bag.

2. **OBSERVE** Place the plant in a sunny location, and observe it several times a day. Record your observations.

3. When you are done, remove the plastic bag from the plant.

## CONCLUDE AND APPLY

1. **COMMUNICATE** Describe what you see on the inside of the bag. Explain what happened.

2. **DRAW CONCLUSIONS** *Transpiration* sounds like *perspiration*—sweating. How might the two processes be alike?

3. **PREDICT** How would your results vary if you put the plant in the shade?

113

# How Much Water Is in Air?

Does water just keep evaporating from a puddle, a lake, or an ocean? Yes. Does this mean the amount of water vapor in the air increases without limit? No.

One reason is condensation. As Earth's water evaporates (water molecules leave the liquid water), water vapor in the atmosphere condenses (water molecules enter the liquid water). Evaporation and condensation are opposites, and they take place at the same time.

**Relative humidity** is a comparison of condensation and evaporation. It is expressed as a percentage. For example, 50% means one-half. Therefore, 50% relative humidity means that the number of water molecules condensing each second is half of the number of water molecules evaporating each second.

One hundred percent relative humidity means condensation equals evaporation. This means that as many water molecules condense each second as evaporate each second. The number of water molecules in each volume of air is as high as it can be at that temperature.

Think of the amount of water vapor in a given volume of air, such as in a cubic centimeter. This amount, at 100% humidity, depends on the temperature. The reason is that the warmer the water is, the greater the evaporation. This means that the air must have a greater amount of water in it for condensation to equal evaporation. The graph shows how, at 100% humidity, the amount of water vapor per cubic centimeter changes with temperature.

## READING GRAPHS

**DISCUSS** How does the amount of water vapor per cubic centimeter compare at 25°C and 40°C?

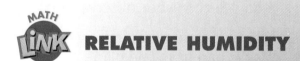

MATH **LINK** RELATIVE HUMIDITY

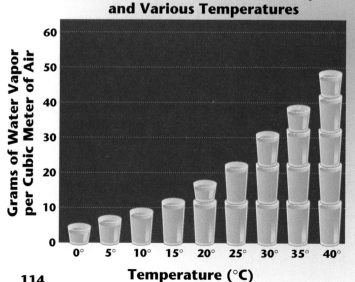

Water Vapor at 100% Humidity and Various Temperatures

Grams of Water Vapor per Cubic Meter of Air

Temperature (°C)

## Why Can Air Feel "Sticky"?

Relative humidity can be used to predict how the air will feel to a person. The higher the relative humidity, the less water can evaporate into the air. The less water, such as sweat, can evaporate from our skin, the wetter and "stickier" the air feels.

Relative humidity can also be used to predict when condensation will occur. Remember that condensation, like the drops of water on the lemonade glass, is the changing of a gas into a liquid. In the atmosphere condensation is usually the result of warm air being cooled. That is, when warm air is cooled, water vapor in it condenses.

Condensation explains what happened to the glass of lemonade. The cold glass cooled the air that touched it. Water vapor condensed, forming liquid droplets on the outside of the glass.

Can you see condensation happening? Have you ever seen frozen food held over hot water? What do you notice? You see a mist forming. When this happens in the air, a cloud forms. The greater the relative humidity, the more likely condensation will occur, and the greater the chance of clouds—and rain.

### Brain Power

You may have heard people complain on a hot day, "It's not the heat, it's the humidity!" Why do you think the humidity is so important, especially when the weather is hot? Why doesn't a cold day with 70 percent humidity feel as uncomfortable as a hot day with 70 percent humidity?

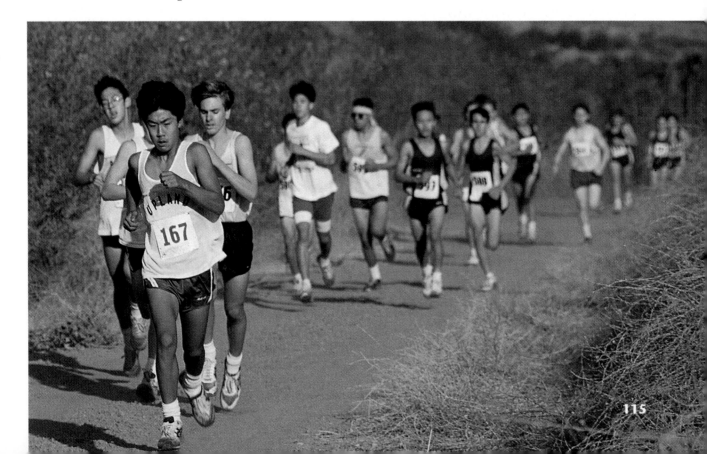

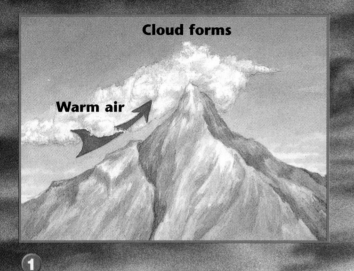

**Cloud forms**

**Warm air**

① 

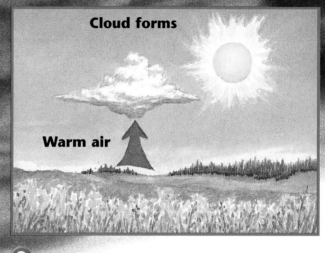

**Cloud forms**

**Warm air**

②

## What Happens Next?

How can warm, moist air cool off? You have learned that in the lower atmosphere, the air gets colder with increasing altitude.

- One way that air cools is by being pushed upward over mountains by winds.

- Heating of air also causes it to rise. When the ground is strongly heated by the Sun, air above the ground gets warmed and rises. It expands as it rises. As the air expands, it cools.

- Air can also be pushed upward when cooler air and warmer air meet. When the two meet, they don't mix. The lighter, warm air is pushed up over the heavier, cold air. The result is that the warm air is pushed up higher into the atmosphere, where it cools.

Whatever causes air to rise and cool, the end result is the same. As the air

**The process that forms droplets of water on the lemonade glass is also the process that forms clouds—condensation.**

rises and cools, the water vapor in it condenses into tiny water droplets, forming clouds.

If the temperature falls below the freezing point of water, its water vapor will form a cloud of tiny ice crystals.

In order for water vapor to condense, it must have a surface on which the liquid droplet or ice crystal will form. This surface is provided by the tiny dust particles that are part of the air. You will learn more about clouds in the next topic.

The glass of lemonade helped you see how several processes work. One process is evaporation. Evaporation occurs when liquid water from Earth's surface changes into a gas—water vapor. The water vapor rises and cools. Condensation takes place. Tiny droplets of water form on the glass— just as tiny droplets of water can form up in the sky and become a cloud.

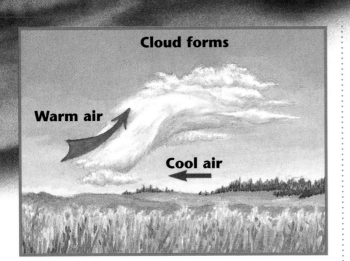

**Cloud forms**

**Warm air**

**Cool air**

③

## READING N DIAGRAMS

**1. DISCUSS** What can cause air to rise?

**2. WRITE** What happens to the air temperature as air rises?

Have you ever had sweat trickle down your face on a hot day? People sweat every day. Sweating is a way our bodies release wastes. We don't always feel the sweat because we sweat gradually and it evaporates.

As sweat evaporates, the water droplets absorb heat from the surface of the skin. This cools the skin. It is a way your body controls surface temperature.

On very hot days and when you are physically active, you may sweat a lot. The sweat builds up and does not evaporate fast enough to keep it from collecting.

On a low-humidity day, the sweat evaporates more quickly. You might think you're not sweating—but you are.

## REVIEW

**1.** Where does water vapor in the air come from? What produces it?

**2. COMPARE AND CONTRAST** How is relative humidity different from humidity? How are the two terms alike?

**3.** What causes water vapor to change into droplets of liquid water?

**4.** How does water vapor get cooled in the atmosphere?

**5. CRITICAL THINKING** *Apply* Would you say that the Sun is a cause of clouds? Defend your answer.

**WHY IT MATTERS** THINK ABOUT IT
How do the two processes evaporation and condensation depend on each other? Why can't there be one without the other?

**WHY IT MATTERS** WRITE ABOUT IT
Why are you more comfortable when the relative humidity is low than when it is high?

**117**

# SCIENCE MAGAZINE

# Comparing Quantities

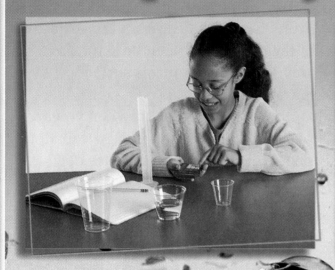

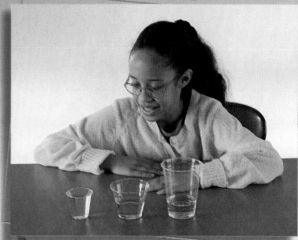

Weather forecasters express relative humidity as a percentage. Do this activity, and you'll get practice at calculating percentages.

## WHAT YOU NEED

- ▶ 3 plastic glasses (small, medium, large)
- ▶ graduated cylinder
- ▶ water

## WHAT TO DO

**1** Fill the small glass with water. Pour it in the cylinder to determine how much water the glass holds. Record this number. Repeat with the medium and large glasses.

**1** Fill the small glass with water again. What percent of its volume is filled? Record this percent.

**3** Pour the water from the small glass into the medium glass. Divide the amount of water in the medium glass by the amount of water it could hold. Multiply this number by 100. This is the percent of the medium glass that's filled with water. Record this percent.

**4** Refill the small glass. Now pour the water into the large glass. Find the percent of the large glass that's now filled with water. (Follow the procedure in step 3.) Record this percent.

**118**

# Math Link

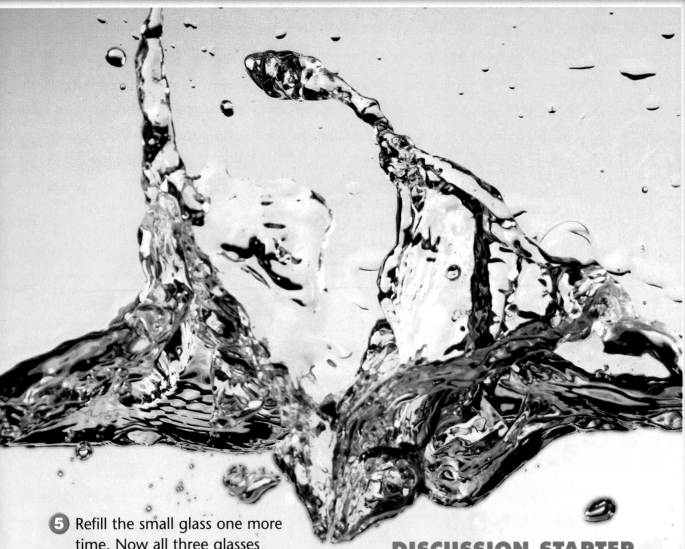

**5** Refill the small glass one more time. Now all three glasses should have the same amount of water in them.

**6** Apply the concept of percentages to relative humidity. Divide the rate of condensation by the rate of evaporation. Multiply by 100. The result is the relative humidity. For example, what if the rate of condensation is one-quarter the rate of evaporation? This means that the relative humidity is one divided by four ($\frac{1}{4}$) times 100, or 25%.

## DISCUSSION STARTER

1. If the rate of condensation equals the rate of evaporation, then what is the relative humidity?

2. If the rate of condensaton is half the rate of evaporation, then what is the relative humidity?

To learn more about humidity, visit *www.mhschool.com/science* and enter the keyword HUMIDITY.

*inter***NET**
**CONNECTION**

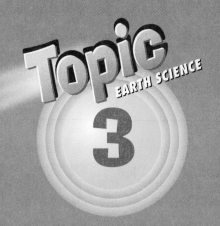

## WHY IT MATTERS

**Clouds, rain, snow, and hail can have great impact on crops and on us.**

### SCIENCE WORDS

**stratus cloud** a cloud that forms in a blanketlike layer

**cumulus cloud** a puffy cloud that appears to rise up from a flat bottom

**cirrus cloud** a high-altitude cloud with a featherlike shape, made of ice crystals

**fog** a cloud that forms at ground level

**precipitation** any form of water particles that falls from the atmosphere and reaches the ground

**water cycle** the continuous movement of water between Earth's surface and the air, changing from liquid to gas to liquid

# Clouds of Water and Ice

**H**ow can you predict the weather without using the instruments weather forecasters use? Look at the sky. There are clues up there. They're called clouds. Different kinds of clouds bring different kinds of weather. What is a cloud?

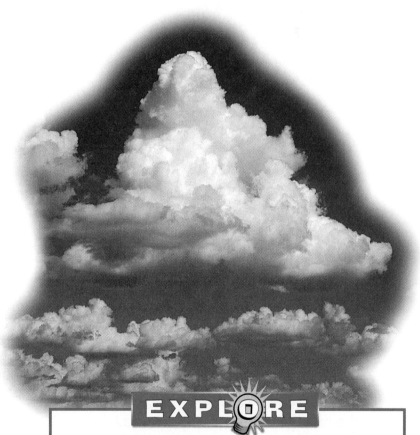

# EXPLORE

**HYPOTHESIZE** Sometimes the sky is full of clouds. Sometimes there are no clouds at all. Why? What makes a cloud form? What do evaporation and condensation have to do with it? Write a hypothesis in your *Science Journal*. How might you make a model to test your ideas?

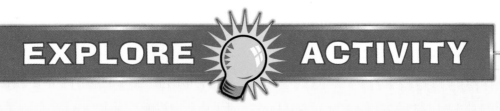

# EXPLORE ACTIVITY

## Investigate Why Clouds Form

Watch what can happen when you cool off some air.

### PROCEDURES

**SAFETY** Be careful handling the hot water. Use the handle to hold the mug. Do not burn yourself.

1. Chill container 1 by putting it in a refrigerator or on ice for about ten minutes.

2. Fill a mug with hot tap water.

3. **MAKE A MODEL** Fill container 2 with hot water. Place empty cold container 1 upside down on top of container 2 with the water. Fit the mouths together carefully. Place the ice cubes on top of container 1.

4. **OBSERVE** Write your observations in your *Science Journal*.

### MATERIALS
- hot tap water
- 2 identical clear containers
- mug
- 3 ice cubes
- food coloring
- refrigerator or freezer
- *Science Journal*

### CONCLUDE AND APPLY

1. **COMMUNICATE** What did you observe?

2. **COMMUNICATE** Where did this take place?

3. **COMMUNICATE** Where did the water come from?

4. **INFER** Explain what made it happen.

### GO FURTHER: Apply

5. **DRAW CONCLUSIONS** Where would you expect to find more clouds— over the ocean or over a desert? Why?

6. **INFER** Why don't all clouds look the same?

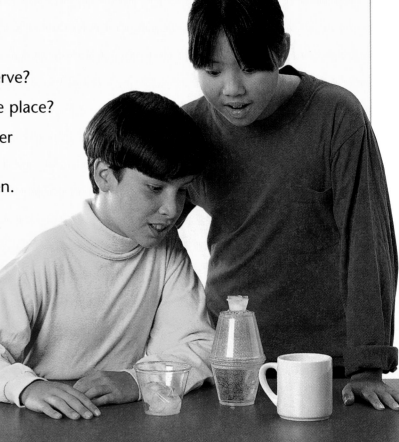

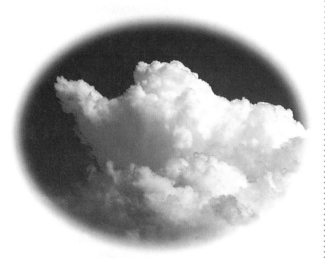

**Stratus clouds**

**Cumulus clouds**

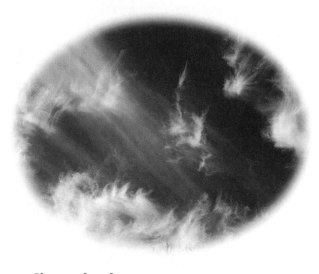

**Cirrus clouds**

# Why Do Clouds Form?

What has to happen for a cloud to form? The Explore Activity was a model of how clouds form. Clouds are made up of tiny water droplets or ice crystals. The air is filled with water vapor. When the air is cooled, the water vapor condenses. That is, the water molecules clump together around dust and other particles in the air. They form droplets of water.

Clouds look different depending on what they are made of. Water-droplet clouds tend to have sharp, well-defined edges. If the cloud is very thick, it may look gray, or even black. That's because sunlight is unable to pass through. Ice-crystal clouds tend to have fuzzy, less distinct edges. They also look whiter.

Clouds are found only in the troposphere. There are three basic cloud forms. **Stratus clouds** form in blanketlike layers. **Cumulus clouds** are puffy clouds that appear to rise up from a flat bottom. **Cirrus clouds** form at very high altitudes out of ice crystals and have a wispy, featherlike shape. If rain or snow falls from a cloud, the term *nimbo*—for "rain"—is added to the cloud's name.

Clouds are further grouped into families by height and form. They are low clouds, middle clouds, high clouds, and clouds that develop upward–clouds of vertical development. Cumulonimbus clouds develop upward. These clouds bring thunderstorms. They can start as low clouds and reach up to the highest clouds.

If moist air at ground level cools, a cloud can form right there. A cloud at ground level is called **fog**.

# TYPES OF CLOUDS

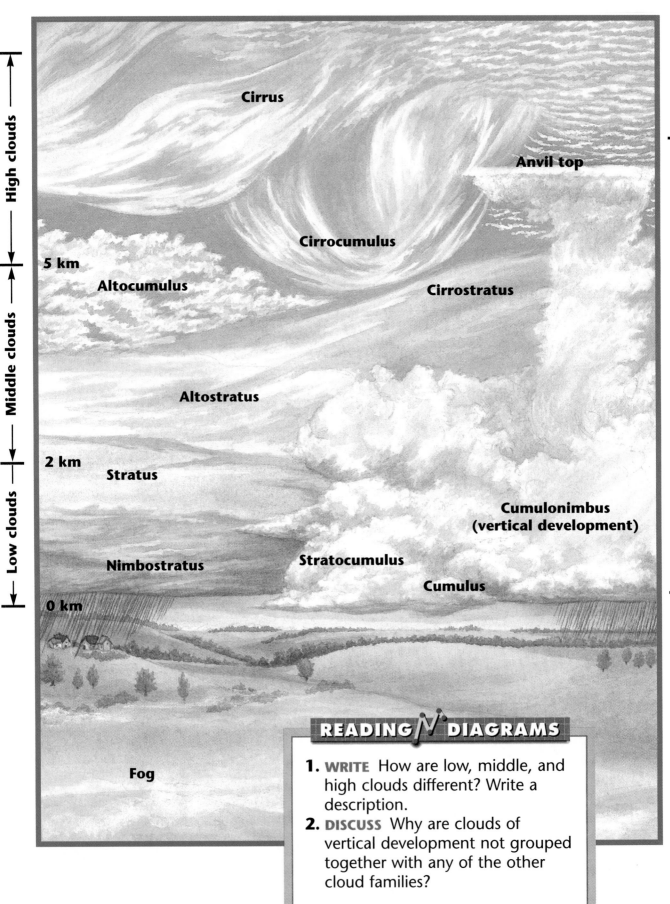

High clouds

Middle clouds

Low clouds

Cirrus

Anvil top

5 km

Altocumulus

Cirrocumulus

Cirrostratus

Altostratus

2 km

Stratus

Cumulonimbus
(vertical development)

Nimbostratus

Stratocumulus

Cumulus

Clouds of vertical development

0 km

Fog

## READING /\/ DIAGRAMS

1. **WRITE** How are low, middle, and high clouds different? Write a description.
2. **DISCUSS** Why are clouds of vertical development not grouped together with any of the other cloud families?

# How Do Rain and Snow Happen?

How do rain and snow form and fall? **Precipitation** is any form of water particles that falls from the atmosphere and reaches the ground. Precipitation can be liquid (rain) or solid (such as snow).

Clouds are made up of tiny water droplets or ice crystals. They are only about $\frac{1}{50}$ of a millimeter. These tiny particles are so light that they remain "hanging" in the air. This is why many clouds do not form precipitation.

Precipitation occurs when cloud droplets or ice crystals join together and become heavy enough to fall. They clump around particles of dust in the air. Each particle is like a *nucleus* that the water molecules condense around. The chart shows the different types of precipitation and how they form.

## READING IN CHARTS

1. **DISCUSS** Classify the types of precipitation into two groups—solids and liquids. Explain.
2. **WRITE** Which types of precipitation form in similar ways? Explain.

## TYPES OF PRECIPITATION

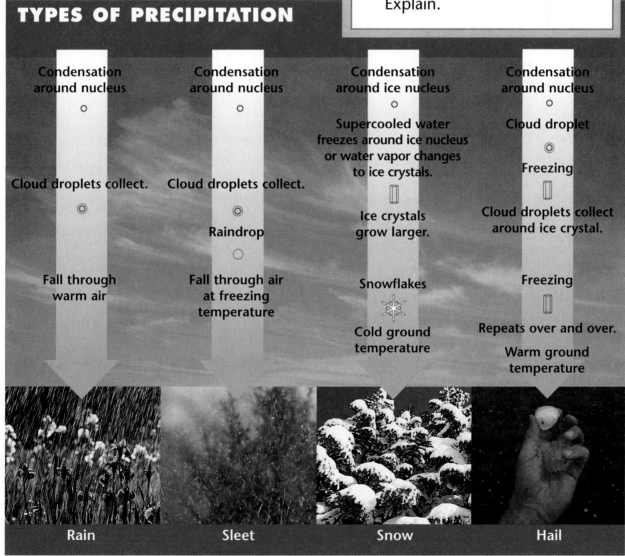

Condensation around nucleus

Cloud droplets collect.

Fall through warm air

**Rain**

Condensation around nucleus

Cloud droplets collect.

Raindrop

Fall through air at freezing temperature

**Sleet**

Condensation around ice nucleus

Supercooled water freezes around ice nucleus or water vapor changes to ice crystals.

Ice crystals grow larger.

Snowflakes

Cold ground temperature

**Snow**

Condensation around nucleus

Cloud droplet

Freezing

Cloud droplets collect around ice crystal.

Freezing

Repeats over and over.

Warm ground temperature

**Hail**

## How Are Cloud Type and Precipitation Related?

Do certain kinds of clouds give certain kinds of precipitation? Yes.

- In tall clouds there is more chance for droplets to run into one another and combine, making larger raindrops.

- Precipitation from large cumulus clouds is often heavy rain or snow showers. However, it usually doesn't last too long.

- Precipitation from stratus clouds is usually long lasting, with smaller drops of rain or snowflakes.

- Clouds with great vertical development hold a lot of water. These clouds are very *turbulent*, or violent. Their tops often reach heights where it is below freezing. They often produce great downpours. They also sometimes produce *hail*. Hail is pellets made of ice and snow.

These clouds have updrafts—strong winds move up inside. Hail forms when updrafts in these huge clouds hurl ice crystals upward again and again. As the crystals fall, they become coated with water. As they rise the water freezes into an icy outer shell. This process usually happens over and over, adding more and more layers to the hailstones. The more violent the updrafts, the bigger the hailstone can get before it falls to the ground.

**Path of Growing Hailstone**

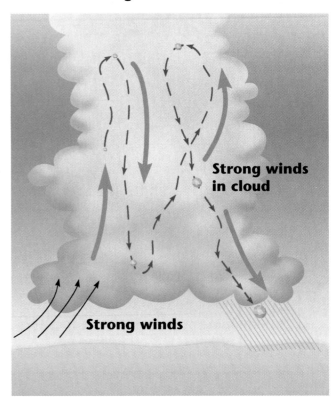

Strong winds in cloud

Strong winds

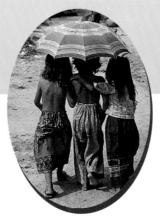

MATH LINK

# How Does Water Go Around and Around?

When precipitation reaches Earth's surface, it doesn't just disappear. Some of it evaporates right back into the atmosphere. Some of it runs off the surface into rivers and streams. We call this water *runoff*.

Much of it seeps into the ground. We call this water *groundwater*.

Groundwater collects in tiny holes, or pores, in soil and rocks. Groundwater can often seep down through soil and rocks when the pores are interconnected. It can fill up all the pores in a layer of rock below the surface. Much of this water eventually moves back to the rivers and then to lakes or oceans.

## Brain Power

What kind of precipitation is most common in your area? Where does the run off go?

## THE WATER CYCLE

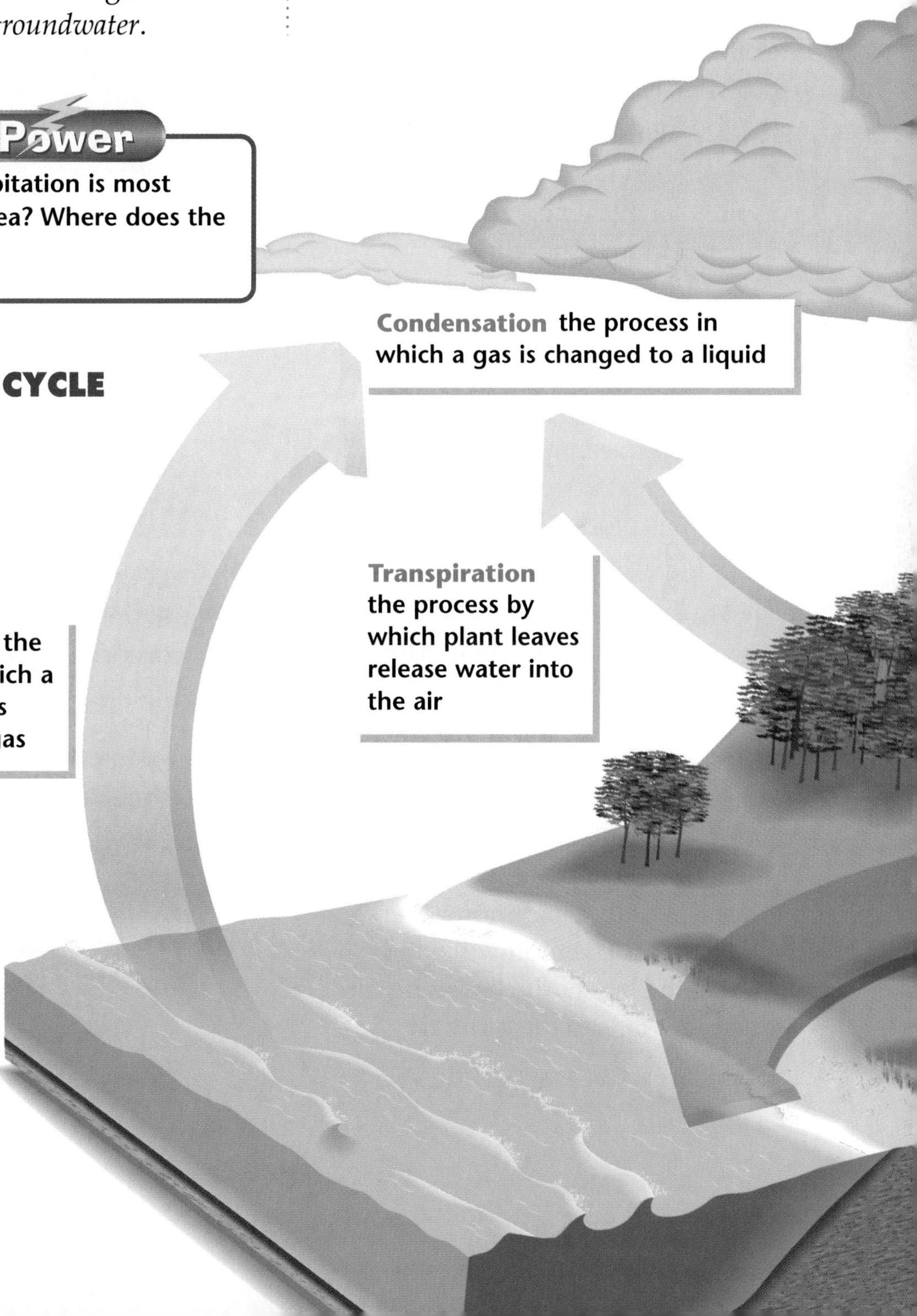

**Condensation** the process in which a gas is changed to a liquid

**Transpiration** the process by which plant leaves release water into the air

**Evaporation** the process in which a liquid changes directly to a gas

Earth's water moves from place to place through the processes of evaporation, condensation, and precipitation. Condensation and precipitation take water out of Earth's atmosphere. Evaporation puts water back into the atmosphere. This complex web of changes is called the **water cycle**.

The water cycle is the continuous movement of water between Earth's surface and the air, changing from liquid to gas to liquid. The diagram shows the many different paths water can take into and out of the atmosphere in the water cycle.

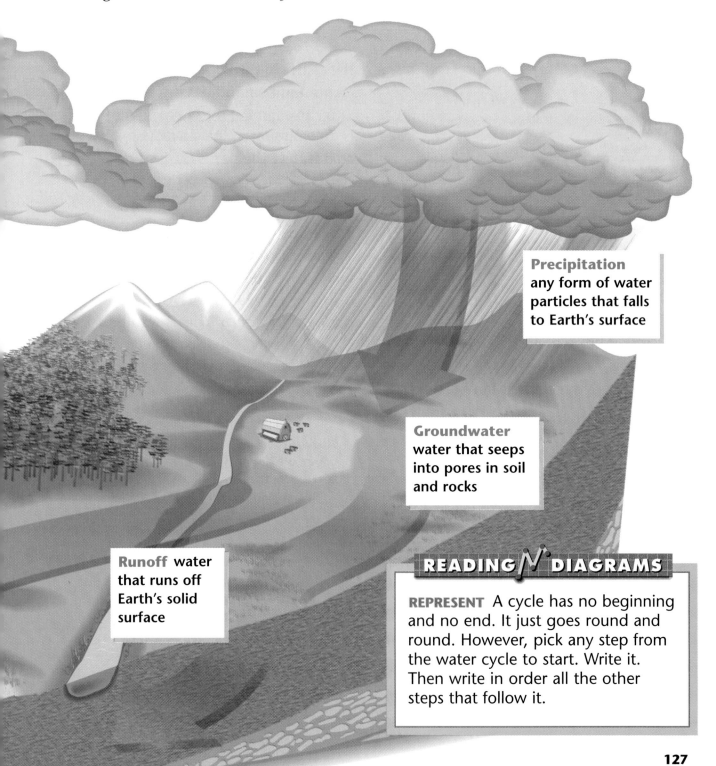

**Precipitation**
any form of water particles that falls to Earth's surface

**Groundwater**
water that seeps into pores in soil and rocks

**Runoff** water that runs off Earth's solid surface

## READING N DIAGRAMS

**REPRESENT** A cycle has no beginning and no end. It just goes round and round. However, pick any step from the water cycle to start. Write it. Then write in order all the other steps that follow it.

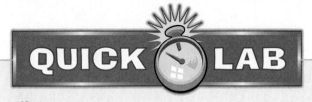

# QUICK LAB

## Feel the Humidity

**HYPOTHESIZE** Why do you feel warmer on a high humidity day? Write a hypothesis in your *Science Journal.*

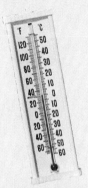

### MATERIALS
- 2-in.-square piece of old cotton cloth
- rubber band
- thermometer
- $\frac{1}{2}$ c of cold water
- 1 c of warm water
- Science Journal

## PROCEDURES

**SAFETY** Be careful handling warm water.

1. **OBSERVE** Record the air temperature in your *Science Journal.*

2. Put thermometer in cold water. Add warm water slowly until water temperature matches air temperature.

3. Wrap cloth around bulb of thermometer. Gently hold it with a rubber band. Dampen cloth in the water.

4. **OBSERVE** Wave thermometer gently in air. Record temperatures every 30 seconds for three minutes.

## CONCLUDE AND APPLY

1. **INFER** What happened to temperature of wet cloth? How does cloth feel? Explain.

2. **INFER** Suppose you try this experiment on a day that is humid and on a day that is dry. Will you get the same results? Explain.

# How Do You Record How Cloudy It Is?

In Topic 1 you started your weather station. Now that you have learned about humidity and precipitation, let's add observations of these weather conditions to your weather station.

As you record weather information each day, you might record the types of clouds you see in the sky. You can use the charts in this lesson to indicate the cloud family and the types of clouds.

Try to estimate the cloud cover—that is, the amount of the sky covered by clouds. Use the terms *clear, scattered clouds, partly cloudy, mostly cloudy,* or *overcast* to describe cloud cover.

## A Weather Station Model

One way to record cloud cover is to make a weather station model. Start by drawing a circle for each day. An empty circle means "clear skies." A fully shaded circle means "completely overcast." Portions of a circle are shaded to show different amounts of cloud cover.

**Showing cloud cover on a weather station model.**

○ Clear

● Overcast

◔ Scattered clouds

◑ Partly cloudy

◕ Mostly cloudy

# How Do You Measure Rainfall?

Precipitation is measured with a rain gauge. You can make a simple rain gauge from an empty coffee can. Just place it outside, open end up. Keep it out in the open, away from buildings or trees. When the precipitation stops, measure its depth in the can. You may measure in inches with a standard ruler. If you have a metric ruler, use millimeters (the smallest unit). Keep track of the type of precipitation and how much falls.

You should also record the relative humidity. Listen to weather reports or refer to your local newspaper to obtain the relative humidity.

If you ever had a baseball game rained out, you know how rain can ruin your day.

Rain may ruin your plans for a day, but rain is vital for life on Earth. Rain helps crops grow. That means food for you and others! Rain helps build the amount of water in wells and water-collecting areas, such as reservoirs. If you ever had a drought in your area, a time when there was little or no precipitation, you know how scarce water can be.

Hail on the other hand, can ruin entire crops. It can also damage cars and buildings.

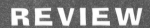

# REVIEW

1. How do clouds form?

2. What are some different types of precipitation? Why are there different types?

3. **SEQUENCE OF EVENTS** What are the main processes that show how liquid water changes in the water cycle? List the parts in order to show the changes.

4. How can you measure and describe the amount of precipitation and cloud cover on a given day?

5. **CRITICAL THINKING** *Apply* "Sun showers" are sudden rainfalls on a sunny day. How can a sun shower happen?

**WHY IT MATTERS** THINK ABOUT IT
What are some things you do that need a sunny day—or at least a day without precipitation? What do you do if it rains or snows?

**WHY IT MATTERS** WRITE ABOUT IT
If there was a drought in your area, what would you do to cut back on using water?

# Flood: Good News or Bad?

Can you imagine a flood being good news? It was to many ancient Egyptians living near the Nile River. They looked forward to its annual summer flood. Land that was flooded was better for crops!

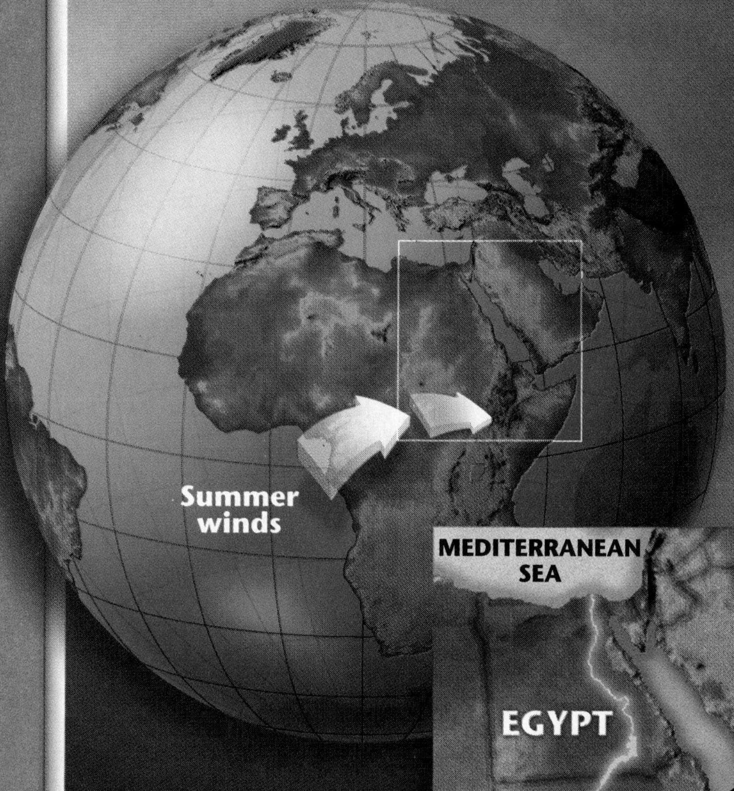

The flood wasn't all good news. Buildings and fences were swept away. Landowners had to hire "rope stretchers" to mark their property lines again.

No one knew for sure why the flood came. People believed that great rains fell near the source of the Nile to start the flood. It actually started in the mountains of Ethiopia!

Ethiopia has many mountains over 4,000 meters (13,000 feet) tall. In June the monsoons blow from the South Atlantic over the rain forests of Africa. When the winds reach the mountains of Ethiopia, giant rain clouds let loose their water in great thunderstorms. Rain-filled mountain streams join to form a great river. It carries the water to the Nile. By July the water reaches Egypt and produces the flood.

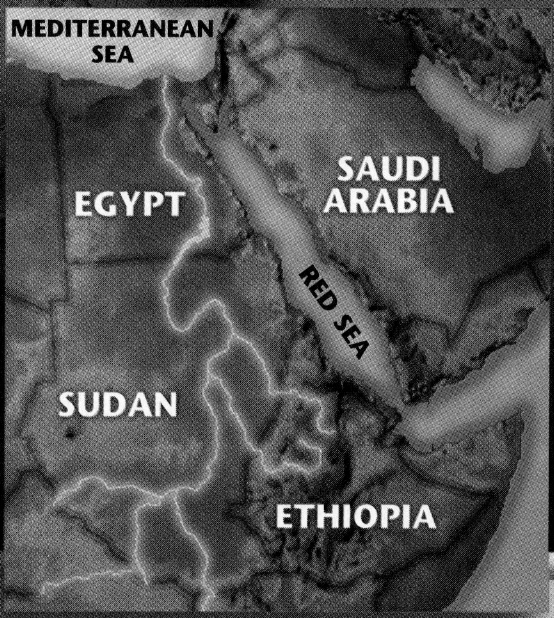

**Summer winds**

MEDITERRANEAN SEA

EGYPT

SAUDI ARABIA

RED SEA

SUDAN

ETHIOPIA

# Science, Technology, and Society

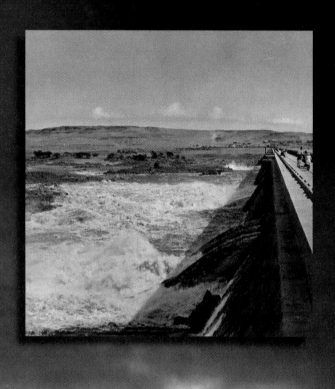

Today the flood waters are stopped soon after they reach Egypt. A high dam holds back the water to form a great lake. The good news is that buildings on the shore are no longer swept away. Fences mark boundaries, and instead of one crop a year, farmers plant two.

Stopping the flood has changed the environment, and that's bad news. The flood kept the fields fertile; but now farmers must use fertilizer. The Mediterranean was nourished by mud from the Nile. Now fish that were common are gone, and a serious disease is spread by snails thriving in the Nile's slow waters.

## DISCUSSION STARTER

1. A dry canyon has a FLOOD DANGER sign. How could the canyon flood when no rain is falling near the sign?

2. Straightening a river can stop flooding. Why? What are the disadvantages of doing it?

To learn more about floods, visit *www.mhschool.com/science* and enter the keyword OVERFLOW.

*inter*NET
CONNECTION

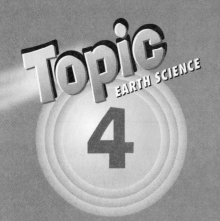

# Topic 4
## EARTH SCIENCE

## Why it matters

Wind results from differences in air pressure. Wind can be destructive but is often quite useful.

### SCIENCE WORDS

**wind** air that moves horizontally

**convection cell** a circular pattern of air rising, air sinking, and wind

**sea breeze** wind that blows from sea to land

**land breeze** wind that blows from land to sea

**Coriolis effect** the curving of the path of a moving object caused by Earth's rotating

**isobar** a line on a weather map connecting places with equal air pressure

**wind vane** a device that indicates wind direction

**anemometer** a device that measures wind speed

# Air Pressure and Wind

**W**hat makes the air move? Air is almost always on the move. Sometimes it's huge country-sized masses of air that are moving. Sometimes it's small patches. You've felt moving air. It's called wind. Some winds move so fast and powerfully, they can knock down trees or even lift trucks into the air. Winds move these balloons. Winds can be so gentle, they hardly ruffle your hair. Strong or weak, what makes winds blow?

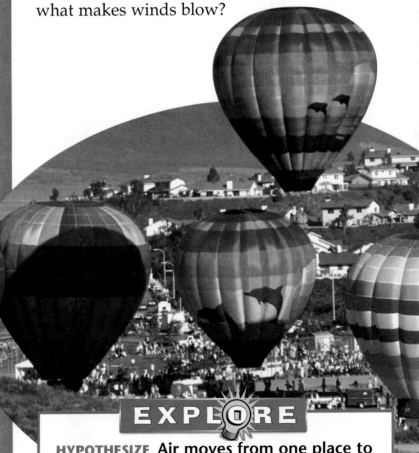

## EXPLORE

**HYPOTHESIZE** Air moves from one place to another because of differences in air pressure. What causes these differences? Write a hypothesis in your *Science Journal*. Make a model to test your ideas.

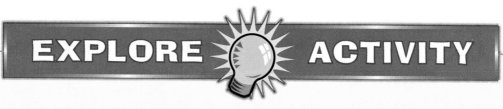

# EXPLORE ACTIVITY

# Investigate What Can Change Air Pressure

Put the atmosphere in a jar to explore air pressure.

## PROCEDURES

**1. MAKE A MODEL** Set up a jar-and-bag system as shown. Make sure the masking tape covers the hole in the jar. Have a partner place both hands on the jar and hold it firmly. Reach in and slowly pull up on the bottom of the bag. In your *Science Journal,* describe what happens.

**2. EXPERIMENT** Pull the small piece of tape off the hole in the bottom of the jar. Repeat step 1. Push in on the bag. Record results in your *Science Journal.*

**3. OBSERVE** Place some small bits of paper on the table. Hold the jar close to the table. Point the hole toward the bits of paper. Pull up on the bag, and observe and record what happens.

**4. EXPERIMENT** Do just the opposite. Push the bag back into the jar, and observe. What happened?

## CONCLUDE AND APPLY

**1. COMPARE AND CONTRAST** What differences did you observe with the hole taped and with the tape removed?

**2. INFER** Explain what happened each time you pushed the bag back into the jar. Why did it happen?

**3. DRAW CONCLUSIONS** How does this model show air pressure changes?

## GOING FURTHER: Problem Solving

**4. USE VARIABLES** Will the model work the same with paper clips? Bits of cotton? Rubber pads? Make a prediction, and test it.

### MATERIALS

- plastic jar with hole in bottom
- plastic sandwich bag
- rubber band
- masking tape
- *Science Journal*

**Step 1**

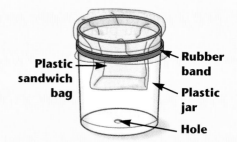

Plastic sandwich bag

Rubber band

Plastic jar

Hole

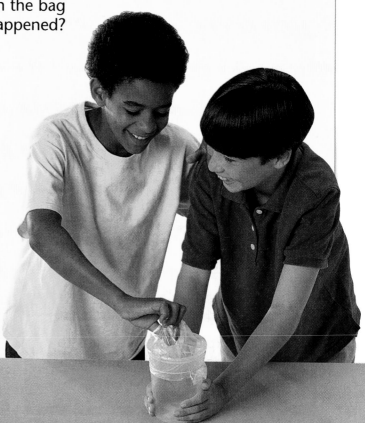

**133**

# How Do We Determine Wind Direction and Speed?

What do the roofs on the right have in common? Each has a curious-looking device on the roof. Did you know that each of these is a **wind vane**? A wind vane is used to tell wind direction. A wind vane has a pointer that blows around in the wind. The pointer is mounted so it can point to the different compass markings.

The tail of the pointer has a larger surface area than the tip. When a wind blows, it exerts more pressure on the tail than the tip. This causes the tail to swing around so that the tip points in the direction the wind is blowing from.

By looking at the compass markings, you can tell which direction the wind is blowing from. Can you tell the tip from the tail in each of the wind vanes shown?

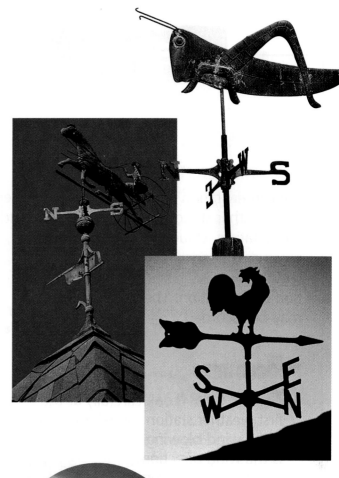

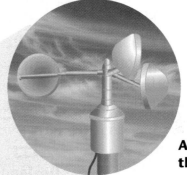

An anemometer gives the speed of a wind.

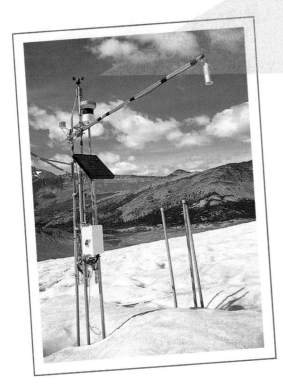

Wind speed is measured with a device called an **anemometer** (an'ə mom'i tər). An anemometer is a series of cups mounted on a shaft that can spin freely. When the wind blows against the cups, they spin like a pinwheel. The faster the wind blows, the faster the cups spin the shaft. A speedometer is attached to the shaft and calibrated to measure wind speed. Can you pick out the anemometer in the array of instruments at this weather station?

## What Is the Beaufort Scale?

In 1805 Sir Francis Beaufort of the British Navy devised a system for measuring wind speed by observing its effect on the surface of the sea. He assigned a number from 0 to 12 to each effect. This is the Beaufort scale.

Wind can be very useful. It is often used as a source of power. Winds turn special machinery—windmills—that produce electricity. It runs the machinery that grinds grain. It is still used today to pump water.

Wind also carries pollen to flowers. Seeds form as a result. Many kinds of seeds, in turn, are carried by wind to new places.

MATH LINK

## BEAUFORT WIND SCALE

| Type of Wind | Kilometers per Hour | Miles per Hour | Observations |
|---|---|---|---|
| 0 Calm | less than 1 | less than 0.6 | Calm; smoke rises straight up |
| 1 Light air | 1–5 | 0.6–3 | Weather vanes don't move |
| 2 Light breeze | 6–11 | 4–7 | Weather vanes move slightly |
| 3 Gentle breeze | 12–19 | 6–12 | Leaves move; flags stretch out |
| 4 Moderate breeze | 20–29 | 9–18 | Small branches sway |
| 5 Fresh breeze | 30–38 | 19–24 | Trees sway; white caps on ponds |
| 6 Strong breeze | 39–50 | 25–31 | Large branches sway |
| 7 Moderate gale | 51–61 | 32–38 | Hard to walk into the wind |
| 8 Fresh gale | 62–74 | 39–46 | Branches break off trees |
| 9 Strong gale | 75–87 | 47–54 | Shingles blow off roofs |
| 10 Whole gale | 88–101 | 55–63 | Trees are uprooted |
| 11 Storm | 102–117 | 64–73 | Extensive damage |
| 12 Hurricane | 118+ | 74+ | Violent destruction |

## REVIEW

1. What makes air pressure change?

2. What causes wind to blow in a particular direction?

3. Why are there zones of winds around the world?

4. **USE NUMBERS/INTERPRET DATA** On a weather map, how can you compare the speed and direction of winds?

5. **CRITICAL THINKING** *Apply* How might you make a simple device to tell wind direction?

**WHY IT MATTERS** THINK ABOUT IT
How would you use simple observation to get an idea of how fast the wind is moving?

**WHY IT MATTERS** WRITE ABOUT IT
What are some ways people can actually make use of the wind?

**READING SKILL**
Write a paragraph describing the main idea and supporting details of this lesson.

# In Tune with the Monsoon

Who's in tune with the monsoon winds? Nearly half of Earth's population! The word *monsoon* is Arabic for "season." Aptly named, monsoons change direction with the seasons. Winds blow in one direction for about six months, then in the opposite direction for about six months.

We often hear about monsoons in India and Pakistan, but did you know that other places also have them? Places include Africa, South America, Australia, and even the southern United States!

Why do monsoons change direction? In summer the Sun heats dry air over tropical land, while nearby oceans stay cooler. The warm air rises above the land, and cooler air from the ocean blows in to take its place. The wind blowing from the ocean brings heavy rain from June to October.

In winter the land cools off. Then as warm air rises over the ocean, cool air from the land rushes in to take its place. From November until May, a dry wind blows from the land out to the ocean.

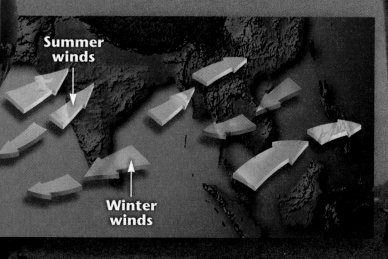

Summer winds

Winter winds

# Geography Link

In one part of India, the average winter rainfall is 2.54 centimeters (1 inch) a month. During the summer it gets up to 2.54 meters (100 inches) of rain a month!

Farmers depend on the monsoons. When the rain starts, farmers plant rice and other crops. If monsoons come late, nothing grows on the dusty land. However, really heavy rains can wash away the crops!

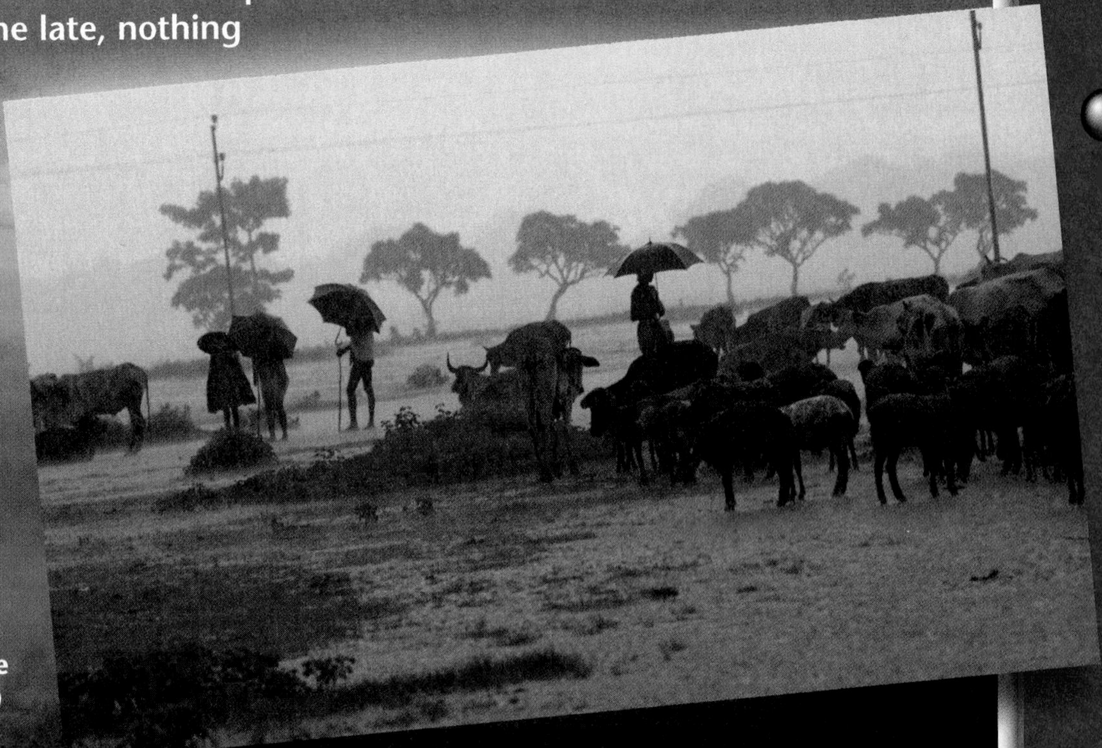

**In 1998 monsoons killed more than 1,000 people in India and Bangladesh and left millions homeless.**

## DISCUSSION STARTER

How do you think the monsoons affect people in monsoon regions who aren't farmers?

To learn more about the monsoons, visit *www.mhschool.com/science* and enter the keyword MONSOON.

*inter*NET
CONNECTION

## SCIENCE WORDS

air pressure p.105    evaporation p.112

cirrus cloud p.122    humidity p.112

condensation p.113    precipitation p.124

Coriolis effect p.138    stratus cloud p.122

cumulus cloud p.122    water vapor p.112

## USING SCIENCE WORDS

**Number a paper from 1 to 10. Fill in 1 to 5 with words from the list above.**

**1.** Rain, snow, and sleet are kinds of ___?___.

**2.** The ___?___ causes winds to follow a curved path over Earth's surface.

**3.** A(n) ___?___ forms in blanketlike layers.

**4.** Liquid changes directly to a gas by the process called ___?___.

**5.** The amount of water vapor in the air is called ___?___.

**6–10.** Pick five words from the list above that were not used in 1 to 5, and use each in a sentence.

## UNDERSTANDING SCIENCE IDEAS

**11.** Describe three kinds of clouds.

**12.** Where does weather take place?

**13.** How do water droplets form on the outside of a cold glass on a warm, humid day?

**14.** What are isobars?

**15.** What determines the amount of sunlight a region gets during the summer?

## USING IDEAS AND SKILLS

**16.** **READING SKILL: MAIN IDEA AND SUPPORTING DETAILS** Explain why north winds blow to the southwest.

**17.** Explain why hot days when the relative humidity is high are more uncomfortable than hot days when the relative humidity is low.

**18.** Why must both evaporation and condensation occur to have rain?

**19.** **USE NUMBERS/INTERPRET DATA** What kind of weather is city A having? City B?

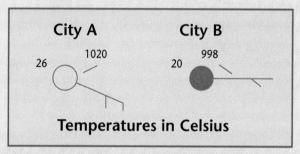

City A      City B

26   1020      20   998

**Temperatures in Celsius**

**20.** **THINKING LIKE A SCIENTIST** What if there were no plants? Do you think Earth would still get as much rain as it does now? State and explain a hypothesis. Describe how you might test your ideas.

## PROBLEMS and PUZZLES

**Draft Drift** Observe updrafts and downdrafts in your classroom. Make a sketch of the room. Use a compass to determine north, south, east, and west. Drop a feather, and watch its drift. Mark the "wind direction" on your map. Repeat in many parts of the room. Explain your results.

# CHAPTER 4

# WEATHER PATTERNS AND CLIMATE

Changes in the weather help scientists predict the weather. They can help you plan activities over a few days.

You may also plan activities over a year. When does your area have the highest temperatures? The lowest? Do you get tornadoes? Hurricanes? Heavy rainfall? When? Temperatures and rainfall are part of a weather pattern in an area that repeats year after year.

In Chapter 4 you'll learn about how weather is predicted. You learn more about patterns that repeat each year.

In Chapter 4 you will read for sequence of events. You will read the events that lead up to a thunderstorm and tornado.

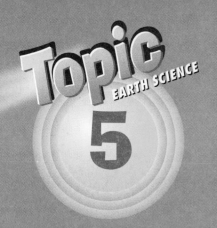

# Topic
### EARTH SCIENCE
## 5

## WHY IT MATTERS

**By studying air masses and fronts, we can predict changes in the weather.**

## SCIENCE WORDS

**air mass** a large region of the atmosphere where the air has similar properties throughout

**front** a boundary between air masses with different temperatures

**cold front** a boundary where cold air moves in under a mass of warm air

**warm front** a boundary where warm air moves in over a mass of cold air

**occluded front** a front formed where a cold front moves in under a warm front

**stationary front** an unmoving front where a cold air mass and a warm air mass meet

# Air Masses and Fronts

Should you plan a trip to the beach tomorrow? Or would it be wiser to locate your umbrella? The answer depends on knowing what kind of weather is on the way. To predict this, both you and weather forecasters can turn to weather maps. The maps show conditions at different weather stations across the country. They also show how weather is changing. This map is a simple kind of weather map you might see in a newspaper.

## EXPLORE

**HYPOTHESIZE** How can you tell where the weather may change? Write a hypothesis in your *Science Journal*. Test your ideas. How would you use a weather map to give a weather report of the country?

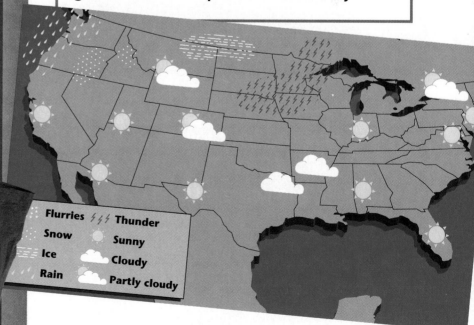

| Flurries | ⚡⚡⚡ Thunder |
| Snow | Sunny |
| Ice | Cloudy |
| Rain | Partly cloudy |

# EXPLORE ⚡ ACTIVITY

## Investigate How to Compare Weather

Use a map and key to predict the weather.

### PROCEDURES

**COMMUNICATE** Think of the country in large regions—the Northeast, the Southwest, and so on. Think of regions like the Pacific Coast, the Atlantic Coast, and the Gulf Coast. In your *Science Journal,* write a report for the weather in each region based on the map you see here.

### CONCLUDE AND APPLY

**1. INFER** Which areas are having warm, rainy weather?

**2. INFER** Where is the weather cool and dry?

### GOING FURTHER: Problem Solving

**3. INFER** How do you think weather in any part of the country may change, based on the data in this map? Give reasons for your answer. How would you check your predictions?

**4. INTERPRET DATA** Using weather maps in a newspaper, or the one on page 148, describe the weather.

> **MATERIALS**
> - station model key
> - newspaper weather map (optional)
> - pencil
> - crayons
> - newspaper
> - *Science Journal*

> W    E
>
> ◯━━━
>
> San Francisco
>
> Lines are drawn to show wind direction, not speed. This is a wind coming from the east, going west—an eastwind.

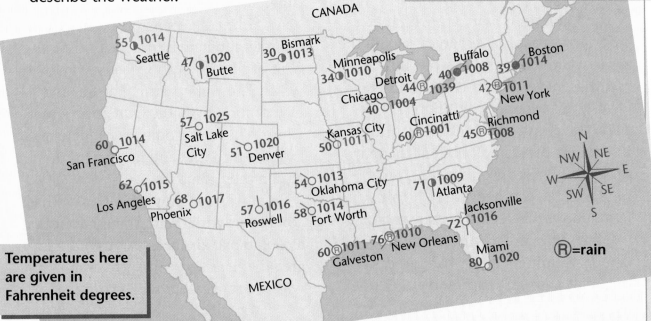

Temperatures here are given in Fahrenheit degrees.

149

# AIR MASSES

Continental
polar (cP)
cold, dry air

Maritime
polar (mP)
cool, moist air

Maritime
polar (mP)
cool, moist air

Pacific
Ocean

Atlantic
Ocean

Maritime
tropical (mT)
warm, moist air

Continental
tropical (cT)
hot, dry air

Maritime
tropical (mT)
warm, moist air

# How Can We Compare Weather?

The Explore Activity showed that cities across a large region can share the same weather. It also showed how the weather in different areas can differ.

Why are weather conditions in one part of a country different from those in another part? Look back at the map on page 149. Some of the cities are having clear, cool weather. The air throughout this region is cool and dry.

Other cities are having warmer, cloudy weather. The air throughout this region is warm and moist. A large region of the atmosphere where the air has similar properties throughout is called an **air mass**.

An air mass gets its properties from the region where it forms. Air over the Gulf of Mexico is above very warm water. The water warms the air, and evaporation from the Gulf adds water vapor. The air becomes warm and moist. Air masses are named for the region they come from.

As air masses move, they bring these conditions with them. What happens if a cool, moist air mass moves over an area that has warm, dry weather? The warm, dry weather will change.

Once an air mass is formed, it is moved by global winds. In the United States, global winds tend to move air masses from west to east.

Air masses with different conditions can "meet." That is, one runs into another. What happens when air masses with different temperatures meet? They don't mix together. Instead, a narrow boundary forms between them. This boundary is called a **front**. It marks the leading edge, or front, of an air mass that is moving into an area where another air mass is moving out. Weather changes rapidly at fronts. That's because you pass from one kind of air mass into another. Fronts often cause rainy, unsettled weather. There are several types of fronts that can form.

**Brain Power**

When air masses meet, they form fronts. What do you think happens when two fronts meet?

## A WEATHER FRONT

A front forms along the boundary between a warm air mass and a cold air mass.

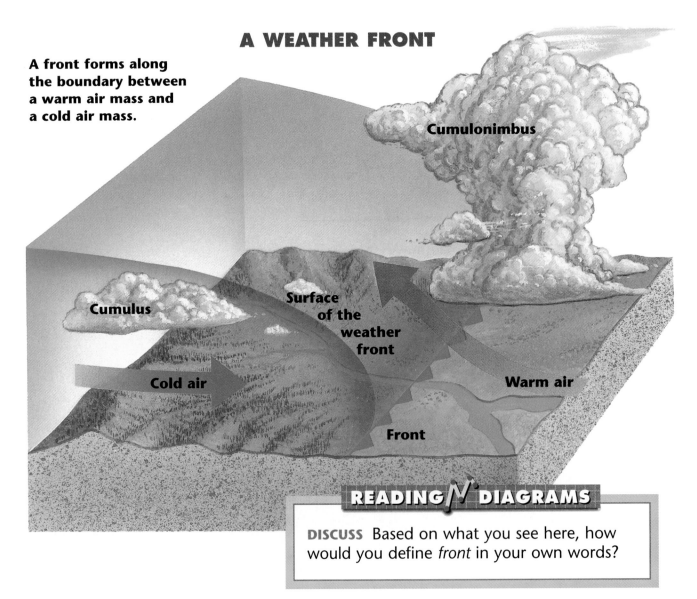

Cumulonimbus

Cumulus

Surface of the weather front

Cold air

Warm air

Front

**READING DIAGRAMS**

**DISCUSS** Based on what you see here, how would you define *front* in your own words?

151

## What Kinds of Fronts Are There?

There are several kinds of fronts. How do fronts make the weather change?

- In a **cold front**, cold air moves in under a warm air mass. Cold fronts often bring brief, heavy storms. There may be thunderstorms and strong winds. After the storm the skies are usually clearer, and the weather is usually cooler and drier.

- In a **warm front**, warm air moves in over a cold air mass. Warm fronts often bring light, steady rain or snow. The precipitation may last for days. Winds are usually light. Warm fronts may also bring fog—stratus clouds that form near the ground. Afterward the weather is usually warmer and more humid.

- An **occluded** (ə klüd′əd) **front** occurs when a cold front and a warm front meet. A fast-moving cold front

## WEATHER PRODUCED BY FRONTS

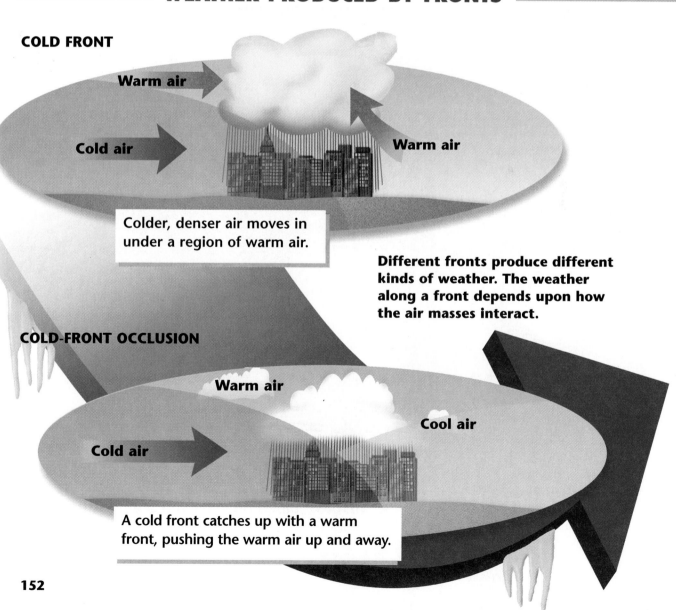

**COLD FRONT**

Warm air

Cold air

Warm air

Colder, denser air moves in under a region of warm air.

Different fronts produce different kinds of weather. The weather along a front depends upon how the air masses interact.

**COLD-FRONT OCCLUSION**

Warm air

Cool air

Cold air

A cold front catches up with a warm front, pushing the warm air up and away.

moves in on a warm front. There are two ways this can happen:

In a cold-front occlusion, the air behind the front is cold. The air ahead of the warm front is cool. What is happening is that cold air is moving in on cool air and warm air is pushed up between them. The weather along this front will be like that produced by a cold front.

In a warm-front occlusion, the air behind the incoming cold front is just cool, not cold. The air in front of the warm front, however, might be cold. Then the weather will be more like that produced by a warm front.

- A cold air mass and a warm air mass may meet and remain over an area for days without moving. This is called a **stationary front**. Stationary fronts usually have calm weather.

## READING /\/ DIAGRAMS

1. **WRITE** Write a paragraph comparing a warm front with a cold front.
2. **DISCUSS** Write an explanation of what an occluded front is.

**WARM FRONT**

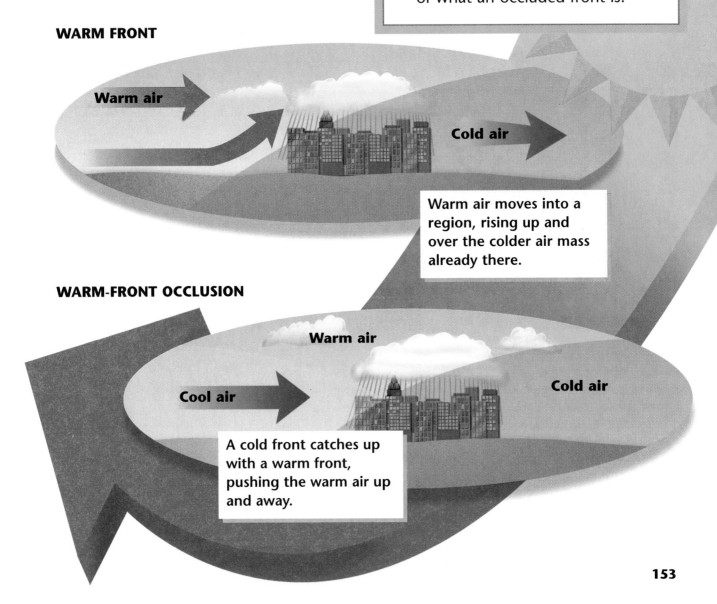

Warm air

Cold air

Warm air moves into a region, rising up and over the colder air mass already there.

**WARM-FRONT OCCLUSION**

Warm air

Cool air

Cold air

A cold front catches up with a warm front, pushing the warm air up and away.

153

## What Do Fronts Look Like from Space?

Pictures taken from space are great tools for seeing large weather patterns, such as fronts and storms. Scientists send up satellites in orbit around Earth. Some of these satellites are equipped to take pictures of weather patterns. These satellites move in orbit in a way that allows them to follow a weather pattern as it moves slowly across Earth's surface.

To find fronts on a satellite map, look for swirling lines of clouds. The curved lines often mark the movement of fronts.

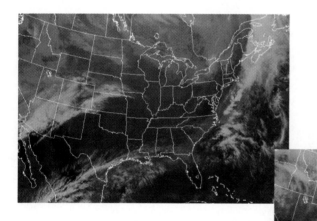

**Weather satellites are located above the equator. They are more than 36,000 km (22,000 miles) above Earth's surface. Several of these satellites work together to produce a nearly complete picture of the globe every half-hour.**

## Why Are Fronts Important?

Fronts are an important clue to how weather will change. As a front moves, areas just ahead of the front are about to have a change in weather. The weather may be cool and dry before a front approaches. The weather then becomes rainy and hot as the front passes by.

When fronts collide, scientists can locate places where the weather may change quickly, even dangerously. Sudden storms may break out. Knowing about fronts helps scientists to stay on the alert!

### READING MAPS

1. **DISCUSS** Where do you see low pressure systems in the satellite picture? What do the clouds appear to be doing?
2. **WRITE** What kind of weather is happening in different parts of the country in each map? Explain.

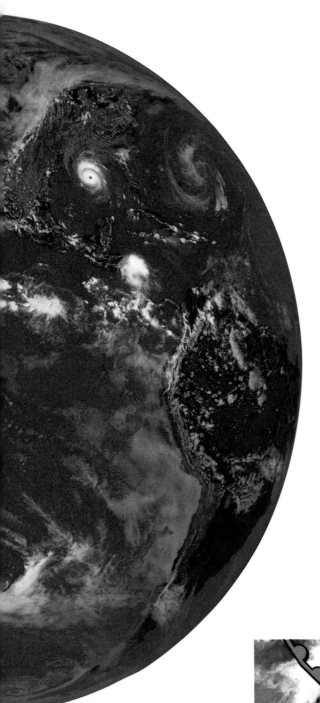

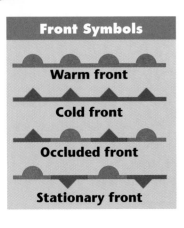

**Front Symbols**

Warm front

Cold front

Occluded front

Stationary front

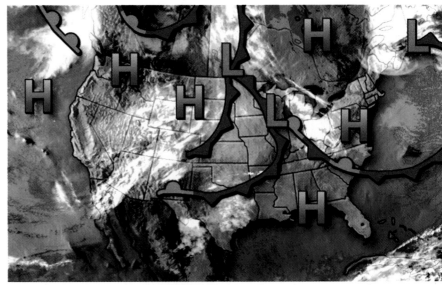

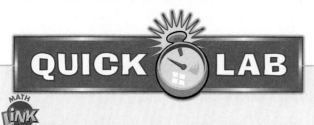

# QUICK LAB

*MATH LINK*

# Weather Prediction

**HYPOTHESIZE** How can you use a weather map to predict the weather? Write a hypothesis in your *Science Journal.*

## MATERIALS

• *Science Journal*

## PROCEDURES

**1. ANALYZE** The map shows weather in the United States at 6 P.M. on October 29. In your *Science Journal*, describe the weather in Washington, D.C. The temperatures are in degrees Celsius.

**2. ANALYZE** In your *Science Journal*, describe the weather in the northwest part of the country and the southeast.

## CONCLUDE AND APPLY

**INFER** Weather patterns move from west to east across the United States. How do you think the weather in Washington, D.C., will change in the next day or so? Explain your answer.

## How Is Weather Forecasting Done?

Scientists usually forecast the weather using a *synoptic weather map.* This type of map shows a summary of the weather using station models. By comparing maps made every six hours, scientists can tell how weather systems are moving. They then use this information to predict what the weather will be like hours later.

If you look at weather records to see what happened in the past, you can find patterns. *Statistical forecasting* is based on finding patterns.

For example, suppose you notice that the wind has just started blowing from the west. Past records show that 75 out of the last 100 times the wind blew from the west, your weather became clearer and colder. What weather prediction would you make?

*GEOGRAPHY LINK*

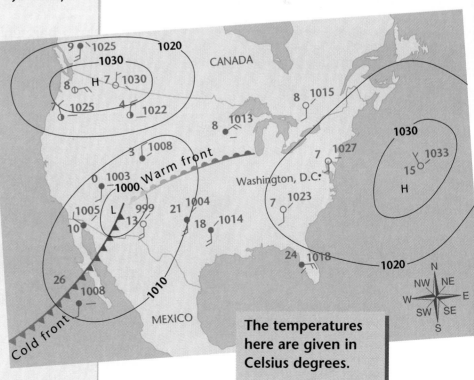

The temperatures here are given in Celsius degrees.

# How Else Is Forecasting Done?

Spaceships going to the Moon aren't aimed directly at the Moon. The Moon is always moving. The spaceship aims at where the Moon will be when the ship arrives. Scientists use the spaceship's speed and direction to calculate where this spot is. In the same way, knowing how the atmosphere is moving lets you predict the weather.

The problem is that the atmosphere is huge and complex. Even simple predictions require millions of calculations. This couldn't be done without computers. Computers do high-speed calculations to predict the atmosphere's motion. Predictions are compared with forecasts to account for any differences. Two-day forecasts are calculated every 12 hours. A five-day forecast is calculated daily.

No one can be sure about how the weather will change. A weather forecaster might give a clear prediction of tomorrow's weather. However, another air mass might move in. Everything can change.

Still many people and industries rely on accurate forecasts. Farmers need to know if heavy rains or frosts are coming. Ski slopes must be aware of how much snow is expected. Vacationers use forecasts to plan trips.

## REVIEW

1. What are four different kinds of air masses? How are they different?

2. **CAUSE AND EFFECT** What kind of weather is produced by a cold front? A warm front?

3. How can satellites help predict the weather?

4. How can weather maps help predict the weather?

5. **CRITICAL THINKING** *Apply* How can you tell what kind of front is passing by just by observing the weather?

**WHY IT MATTERS THINK ABOUT IT**
Why do you think people listen to the weather report?

**WHY IT MATTERS WRITE ABOUT IT**
How can changes in the weather affect how you spend your day?

# Weather Watch: Then and Now

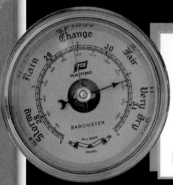

The barometer is invented. Changes in air pressure help modern scientists predict the weather.

The telegraph is invented. Forecasters begin talking to one another and sharing information.

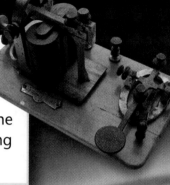

| 400 B.C. | A.D. 1643 | 1732 | 1840 | 1870 |
|---|---|---|---|---|

Aristotle writes one of the first books about weather. He tries to explain rain, snow, and other "meteors" from the sky!

Benjamin Franklin writes *Poor Richard's Almanac,* in which he predicts the next year's weather. He bases his forecasts on what he sees and a few measurements.

A telegraph system is set up across the nation. The system is used to collect weather data and warn people about storms.

Poor Richard, 1733.

AN

Almanack

For the Year of Christ

1733,

Being the First after LEAP YEAR.

And makes since the Creation   Years
By the Account of the Eastern Greeks   7241
By the Latin Church, when ☉ ent. ♈   6932
By the Computation of W.W.   5742
By the Roman Chronology   5682
   3494

# History of Science

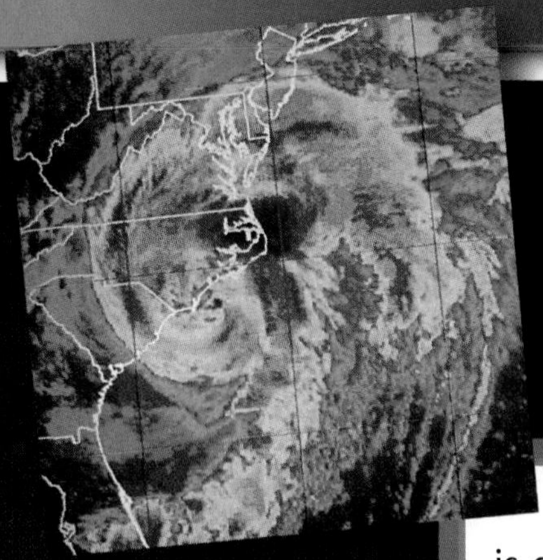

Four scientists in Norway use math and physics to explain weather and identify weather patterns.

Doppler radar is developed. It compares radio waves sent out with those that bounce back. The greater the difference, the faster a storm is moving.

Two kinds of satellites track weather patterns. One orbits about 36,000 kilometers (22,000 miles) above Earth, monitoring changes in storm systems. The other orbits only 850 kilometers (530 miles) above Earth to provide details about cloud systems.

**1918**      **1940**      **1954**      **1960**      **Today**

During World War II, radar is used to locate storms by bouncing radio waves off raindrops in clouds.

NASA sends up its first weather satellite.

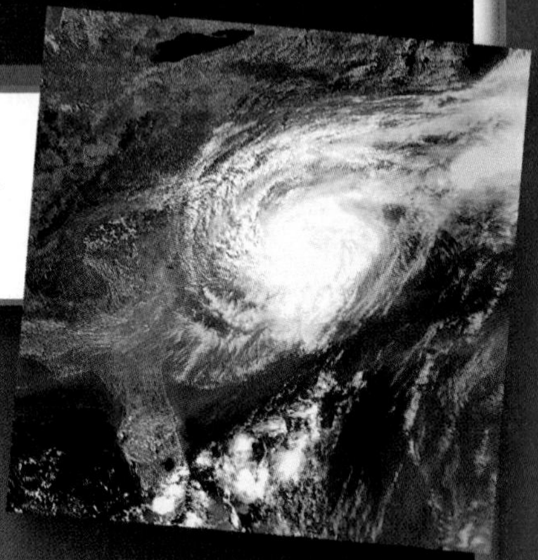

## DISCUSSION STARTER

How do you think computers have helped make weather predictions more accurate?

To learn more about weather watching, visit *www.mhschool.com/science* and enter the keyword WATCH.

*inter*NET
CONNECTION

159

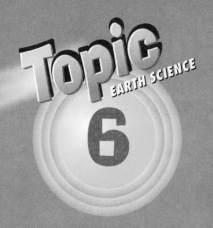

# Topic
## EARTH SCIENCE
## 6

## WHY IT MATTERS

Knowing about severe
storms can save lives.

## SCIENCE WORDS

**thunderstorm**  the most
common severe storm, formed
in cumulonimbus clouds

**tornado**  a violent whirling wind
that moves across the ground in a
narrow path

**hurricane**  a very large, swirling
storm with very low pressure at
the center

**storm surge**  a great rise of
the sea along a shore caused by
low pressure

# Severe Storms

**W**hat's it like to be in the path of a tornado?
People have reported a sound like the rumble
of an approaching freight train. A tornado
packs a windy wallop far more powerful than
any train, however. Tornadoes are the most
powerful storms on Earth. Although most
tornadoes are not very wide and they don't
last too long, when they touch down *watch out!*
Like deadly whirling brooms, they can sweep
away anything in their paths.

## EXPLORE

**HYPOTHESIZE**  Tornadoes strike all parts of
the United States. However, they are more
frequent in some regions than in others.
Where in the U.S. is "tornado country"?
Write a hypothesis in your *Science Journal.*
How might you test your hypothesis?

160

# Investigate What Severe Storms Are

To investigate what severe storms are, begin by plotting tornadoes on a map to tell where they are most likely to happen.

## MATERIALS
- map of U.S., including Alaska and Hawaii
- blue marker
- red marker
- *Science Journal*

## PROCEDURES

1. **INFER** The table shown here lists how many tornadoes occurred in each state over a 30-year period. It also shows about how many tornadoes occur in each state each year. Look at the data in the table for two minutes. Now write in your *Science Journal* what part of the country you think gets the most tornadoes.

2. **COLLECT DATA** Use the red marker to record the number of tornadoes that occurred in each state over the 30-year period. Use the blue marker to record the average number of tornadoes that occurred in a year in each state.

## CONCLUDE AND APPLY

1. **USE NUMBERS** Which states had fewer than 10 tornadoes a year? Which states had more than 20 tornadoes a year?

2. **INTERPRET DATA** Which six states had the most tornadoes during the 30-year period?

3. **INTERPRET DATA** Which part of the country had the most tornadoes?

### GOING FURTHER: Problem Solving

4. **DRAW CONCLUSIONS** Many people refer to a certain part of the country as "Tornado Alley." Which part of the country do you think that is? Why do you think people call it that? What else might these states have in common? Describe how you would go about finding the answer to that question.

| State | Total | Average per year |
|---|---|---|
| AL | 668 | 22 |
| AK | 0 | 0 |
| AZ | 106 | 4 |
| AR | 596 | 20 |
| CA | 148 | 5 |
| CO | 781 | 26 |
| CT | 37 | 1 |
| DE | 31 | 1 |
| FL | 1,590 | 53 |
| GA | 615 | 21 |
| HI | 25 | 1 |
| ID | 80 | 3 |
| IL | 798 | 27 |
| IN | 604 | 20 |
| IA | 1,079 | 36 |
| KS | 1,198 | 40 |
| KY | 296 | 10 |
| LA | 831 | 28 |
| ME | 50 | 2 |
| MD | 86 | 3 |
| MA | 89 | 3 |
| MI | 567 | 19 |
| MN | 607 | 20 |
| MS | 775 | 26 |
| MO | 781 | 26 |
| MT | 175 | 6 |
| NE | 1,118 | 37 |
| NV | 41 | 1 |
| NH | 56 | 2 |
| NJ | 78 | 3 |
| NM | 276 | 9 |
| NY | 169 | 6 |
| NC | 435 | 15 |
| ND | 621 | 21 |
| OH | 463 | 15 |
| OK | 1,412 | 47 |
| OR | 34 | 1 |
| PA | 310 | 10 |
| RI | 7 | 0 |
| SC | 307 | 10 |
| SD | 864 | 29 |
| TN | 360 | 12 |
| TX | 4,174 | 139 |
| UT | 58 | 2 |
| VT | 21 | 1 |
| VA | 188 | 6 |
| WA | 45 | 2 |
| WV | 69 | 2 |
| WI | 625 | 21 |
| WY | 356 | 12 |

# What Are Severe Storms?

The Explore Activity was about a violent kind of storm. It does not happen all the time. It forms under special conditions. Often this storm grows out of another, more common kind of storm—a **thunderstorm**.

Thunderstorms are the most common kind of severe storm. They form in clouds called *thunderheads*—cumulonimbus clouds. The storms cause huge electric sparks called *lightning*. The lightning heats the air and causes the noise called *thunder*. Thunderstorms usually have heavy rains and strong winds. Some thunderstorms also produce hail.

## First Stage

A thunderstorm starts when intense heating causes air to rise very quickly. A cloud forms where there is an upward rush of heated air, an *updraft*. As more and more warm, moist air is carried upward, the cloud grows larger and larger. Strong updrafts keep droplets of water and ice crystals in the cloud, so they grow in size, too. When the updrafts can't support them anymore, they fall as heavy rain or even hail. Look at the downpour falling from this thunderstorm.

## Second Stage

Once the rain falls, it causes downdrafts in the cloud. That is, air moves downward. When the air going up rubs against air going down, static electricity builds up. When enough builds up, there's a huge spark—lightning.

Lightning is unpredictable. It may jump from the cloud to the ground or from the ground to the cloud. It may jump between two thunderclouds. It may also jump from one spot to

## HOW A THUNDERSTORM FORMS

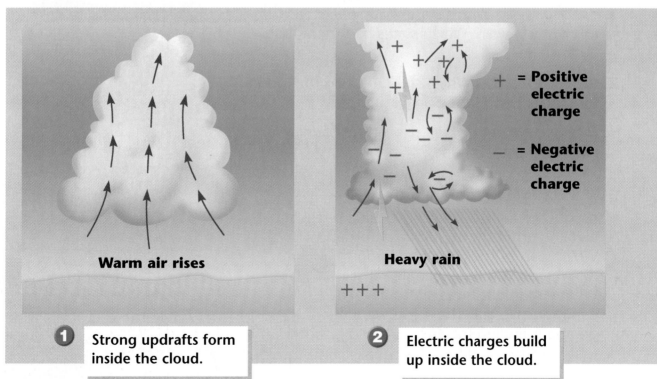

**Warm air rises**

**Heavy rain**

+ = Positive electric charge

− = Negative electric charge

**1** Strong updrafts form inside the cloud.

**2** Electric charges build up inside the cloud.

another within the cloud. Lightning superheats the air so the air suddenly expands. It slams into the air around it with such force that it makes a mighty sound—thunder.

### Third Stage

The storm dies when a downdraft becomes stronger than the updraft. Heavy rain lightens up and stops.

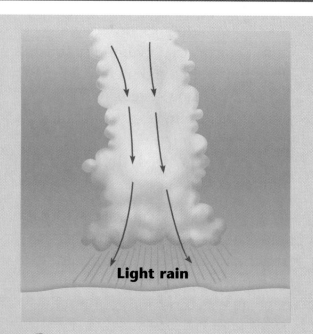

**Light rain**

3. A thunderstorm dies when a downdraft becomes stronger than the updraft. Heavy rain lightens up and stops.

**Brain Power**

In some parts of the country, people worry more about thunderstorms than they do in other regions. Why do you think this is so?

Thunderstorms usually form in the warm air just ahead of a cold front. The cold, dense air wedges under the warm, moist air and causes the warm air to rise rapidly. Be on the lookout for thunderstorms. They are likely when the weather is hot and humid and a cold front is approaching.

**READING DIAGRAMS**

**WRITE** Write a description of how a thunderstorm forms. Identify what happens during each stage of formation.

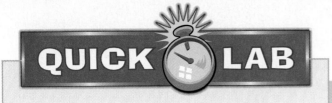

## Tornado in a Bottle

**HYPOTHESIZE**  How does a tornado form? Write a hypothesis in your *Science Journal*.

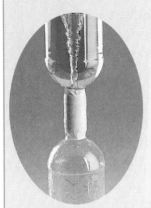

### MATERIALS
- two 2-L plastic bottles
- duct tape
- water
- paper towel
- pencil
- *Science Journal*

## PROCEDURES

**1. MAKE A MODEL**  Fill one bottle one-third full of water. Dry the neck of the bottle, and tape over the top. Use the pencil to poke a hole in the tape.

**2.** Place the other bottle upside down over the mouth of the first bottle. Tape the two bottles together.

**3. OBSERVE**  Hold the bottles by the necks so the one with the water is on top. Swirl them around while your partner gently squeezes on the empty bottle. Then place the bottles on a desk with the water bottle on top. Describe in your *Science Journal* what you see.

## CONCLUDE AND APPLY

**INFER**  How is this like what happens when a tornado forms? Explain.

# How and Where Do Tornadoes Happen?

The most violent thunderstorms often spin off even more dangerous storms—**tornadoes**. A tornado is a violent whirling wind that moves across the ground in a narrow path.

**How They Happen**

Late in the day, when Earth's surface is very warm, convection can get very strong. This can lead to a tornado. A tornado is sort of a runaway convection cell.

- When the updraft in a convection cell is really strong, the air rushes in from all sides at high speeds.

- The air curves into a spin. This lowers the pressure even more. Air rushes in even faster, and the pressure gets even lower, and so on. Like a spinning skater who pulls her arms in close to her sides, the spinning tornado gets faster and faster.

- As the tornado gets stronger, a funnel forms that eventually touches the ground. In the center of a tornado, winds can reach speeds of 500 kilometers per hour (about 300 miles per hour) or more. At such high speeds, winds can destroy anything in their path.

The speed of the wind in the tornado is not the speed with which the tornado moves across the ground. It moves across the ground very fast but can change its direction continually.

## Where They Happen

As the Explore Activity shows, most tornadoes in the United States seem to occur in the Midwest and in the South.

Tornadoes form where dry, cold air masses mix with warm, moist air masses. In the United States, this is most likely to happen in the Great Plains region and the Mississippi Valley. Florida also gets lots of tornadoes.

Tornadoes are most likely to occur when there are big differences in the air masses. This happens most often in early spring and summer. Tornadoes can also form over water. Such tornadoes are called *waterspouts*.

More tornadoes occur in the United States than in any other country, especially in the area known as Tornado Alley.

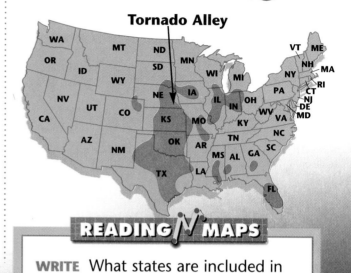

Tornado Alley

## READING MAPS

**WRITE** What states are included in Tornado Alley?

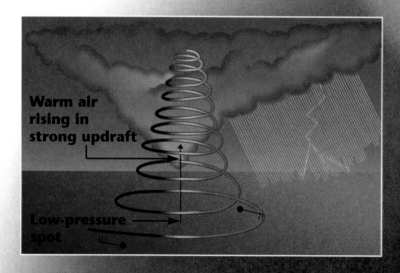

A tornado has a characteristic funnel-shaped cloud.

Warm air rising in strong updraft

Low-pressure spot

## READING DIAGRAMS

1. **DISCUSS** Where is the pressure lowest in the tornado?
2. **DISCUSS** In what direction is the wind spinning—clockwise (like the hands of a clock) or counterclockwise (the opposite)?

# How Do Hurricanes Form?

If you live near an ocean or the Gulf Coast, you may have experienced a **hurricane**. Hurricanes are very large, swirling storms with very low pressure at their center. They form over tropical oceans—near the equator.

Air masses near the equator tend to be very much alike. They don't form the fronts that you learned about in Topic 5. Instead, they form lots of thunderstorms.

- As global winds push these thunderstorms along, they line up in rows. Strong heating and lots of evaporation over the ocean can cause a large low-pressure center to form. If this happens winds begin to blow in toward the low.

- The Coriolis effect causes winds to spiral counterclockwise in the Northern Hemisphere. Clusters of thunderstorms are pulled into the spiral. The thunderstorms merge, forming a single large storm.

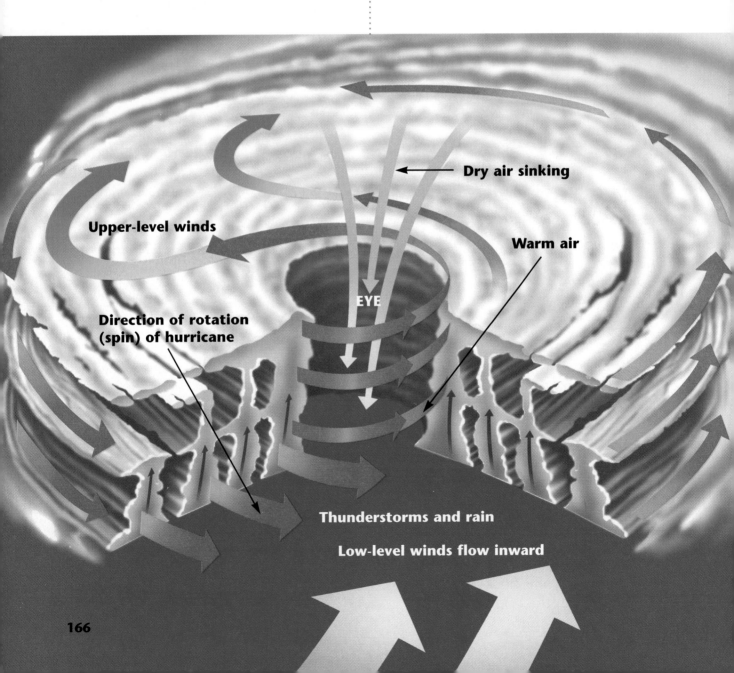

Dry air sinking

Upper-level winds

Warm air

EYE

Direction of rotation (spin) of hurricane

Thunderstorms and rain

Low-level winds flow inward

- As water vapor in the storms condenses, heat is released. The air is warmed. This decreases the air's density and pressure. Moisture evaporating into the air decreases the air's density and pressure even more. Low air pressure favors more evaporation. This lowers the pressure even more.

- The lower the air pressure, the faster are the winds that blow in toward the center of the storm. When the winds reach speeds of 120 kilometers per hour (about 75 miles per hour) or higher, the storm is a hurricane.

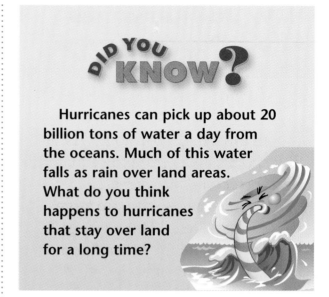

**DID YOU KNOW?**

Hurricanes can pick up about 20 billion tons of water a day from the oceans. Much of this water falls as rain over land areas. What do you think happens to hurricanes that stay over land for a long time?

- As the moist air in the storm rises and cools, condensation takes place. The clouds thicken. Heavy rains fall through the high winds. When fully formed a hurricane has an eye at its center. The eye is an area of light winds and skies that are nearly clear.

Hurricanes can easily grow to more than 700 kilometers (about 400 miles) in diameter. As you can see from the drawing, the image of Hurricane Fran shows it to be almost as large as the entire state of Florida!

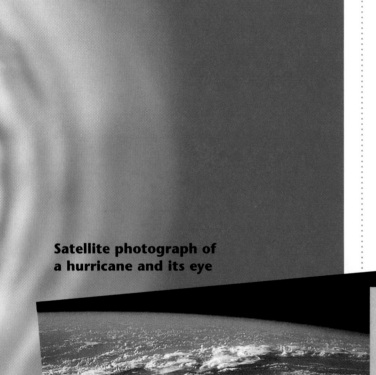

**Satellite photograph of a hurricane and its eye**

Direction of wind

Eye

**READING DIAGRAMS**

1. **DISCUSS** In which direction do winds turn in a hurricane—clockwise (the direction of the hands of a clock) or counter clockwise (the opposite)?
2. **DISCUSS** Where is the pressure the lowest?
3. **DISCUSS** Where is rain happening?

# How Do Hurricanes Affect Ocean Waves?

Just north of the equator, gentle global winds move hurricanes west to northwest at 10 to 20 kilometers per hour (6 to 12 miles per hour). As they move north, away from the equator, their speed tends to increase.

Hurricane winds whip up large waves in the ocean. These waves move outward from the storm and pound against a shore for days before the storm arrives. However, it is the **storm surge** that causes the most destruction. Storm surge is a great rise of the sea along a shore. Its main cause is low air pressure!

Air pressure normally presses down on the surface of the sea like a giant hand. When the pressure drops in a hurricane, it is like lifting the hand slightly. The surface of the sea rises, forming a bulge beneath a hurricane.

When the hurricane moves over a coast, the bulge can cause water levels to suddenly rise several feet, or surge.

Hurricane winds also push water ahead of the storm, forcing water onshore and adding to the storm surge. If the storm surge comes at high tide, it is even worse. Great storms have surges that raise the water level by 7 meters (about 20 feet) or more.

During a great storm, the surge, large waves, high winds, and torrential rain of the storm all happen at the same time. Low-lying coastal areas are flooded. Beachfront homes are destroyed. Beaches can get worn away.

### A Real Hurricane—Fran

On August 22, 1996, a storm formed off the coast of Africa and began moving west-northwest at about 10 miles per hour. By August 29 it had become more concentrated. Winds reached hurricane strength. Hurricane Fran was born. Fran continued moving west and was even stronger by the time it skirted the Bahamas. By September 5, 1996, Fran had 105-knot winds and was 400 km (250 miles) off the Florida coast.

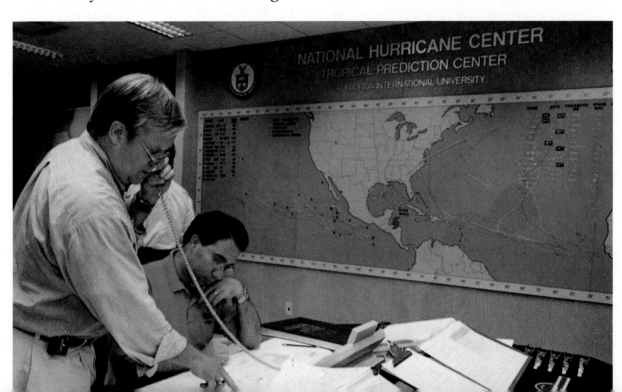

A large low-pressure system over Tennessee steered it westward, and it struck North Carolina and Virginia on September 6. Winds of 120 knots were clocked off Cape Fear as Fran came ashore. Sea level surged to 3.6 m (12 feet) above normal. As much as 40 cm (16 inches) of rain fell in parts of North Carolina. Thirty-four people died. Flash flooding caused most deaths. A storm surge on the North Carolina coast destroyed many beachfront houses.

High winds damaged trees and roofs. They also downed power lines, leaving 4.5 million people without power. Nearly half a million people were ordered to evacuate the coast. Altogether it is estimated that Fran caused 3.2 billion dollars of damage.

Hurricanes begin to die out when they move over land. Cut off from the warm ocean, the hurricane has no water to replace what falls as rain. Friction between the winds and the land decreases wind speed. When it has been over land long enough, it will completely die out.

Once Hurricane Fran moved ashore, it steadily weakened. By the time it reached central North Carolina, it was no longer a hurricane. By the time it reached the Great Lakes on September 9, it was no longer even a storm. The remains of Fran disappeared on September 10.

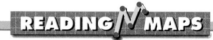

## READING MAPS

**1. WRITE** What ocean does a hurricane have to cross as it approaches North America from Africa?

**2. WRITE** What part of North America did Hurricane Fran reach?

GEOGRAPHY LINK

North America

Atlantic Ocean

Bahamas

Africa

South America

Severe storms can cause damage.

## What Can You Do to Be Safe in a Storm?

Hurricanes, tornadoes, and thunderstorms can be very dangerous. In order to stay safe in these storms, you need to follow certain safety rules.

**IF YOU HEAR STORM WATCHES OR WARNINGS ON TV OR RADIO, FOLLOW THEIR DIRECTIONS CAREFULLY!**

A storm watch means that conditions are right for a storm to form. A storm warning means that a storm has been spotted and is heading your way.

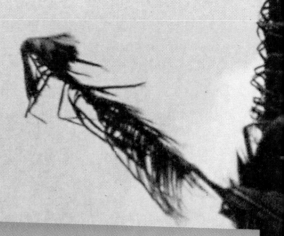

## Thunderstorm Safety Rules

1. Go inside a house or large building, but don't go into a small building that stands off by itself. It is also safe to stay inside a closed car or truck (not a convertible!). Be sure the doors and windows are closed. Do not touch any metal inside the car.

2. Stay away from pipes, faucets, electrical outlets, and open windows.

3. Don't use the telephone, except in an emergency. Electricity can travel through phone lines.

4. Stay away from the water. If you are in the water, GET OUT. Do not go out in a boat. Lightning is attracted to water.

5. If you are outside, be sure you are not the tallest thing around. Be sure, also, that you are not standing near or under the tallest thing around. Do not stand up on a beach, in an open field, or on a hilltop. Do not stand under a tree. Do not stand under an object that is standing alone in an open area.

6. If you are stuck in an open area, crouch down. Stay away from metal objects, including bicycles, motorcycles, farm equipment, golf clubs, and golf carts.

7. If your hair feels like it's standing on end, lightning may be about to strike. Crouch down. Lean forward, and put your hands on your knees. Try to make yourself as low to the ground as possible while touching as little of the ground as you can.

# Tornado Safety Rules

The National Weather Service issues a tornado watch when conditions for a tornado exist. Be on the alert. If a tornado is spotted, a tornado warning is given. Take action immediately.

1. At home open the windows slightly, then seek shelter. Stay away from windows and doors.

2. The safest place is in a storm cellar. The next safest is a basement. Stay under a table, staircase, or mattress. If you have no storm cellar or basement, seek shelter in a strong building. Stay on the ground floor. Stay under a table or bed, or in a closet.

3. Do not stay in a mobile home.

4. Outdoors lie facedown in a ditch. Cover your head to protect yourself from flying debris.

5. At school go to an inside hallway on the lowest floor. If your school has a tornado shelter, go there. Follow your teacher's or principal's directions.

# Hurricane Safety Rules

1. People living in coastal areas may be warned to board up their homes and head for safer, inland areas. If you live in an area connected to the mainland by a bridge, be sure you allow plenty of time to leave. Traffic on the bridge may be very heavy. People who live in low-lying areas that flood in heavy rains may also be warned to go to shelters.

2. Board or tape up windows and glass doors. Bring outdoor objects—such as furniture, bikes, potted plants—indoors.

3. Be sure you stock up on bottled water, canned and packaged foods, and first-aid supplies and medicines for the family and pets. Don't forget flashlights and fresh batteries. Test the flashlights ahead of time to be sure the bulbs are working. You may be without power for several days. Be sure the food you have can be eaten without cooking.

4. If your home is on sturdy, high ground, stay there. Otherwise go to a shelter.

5. Don't be fooled by the eye of the hurricane. Everything may be calm. Skies may be fair for a short time, but the rest of the hurricane's fury is right behind the eye.

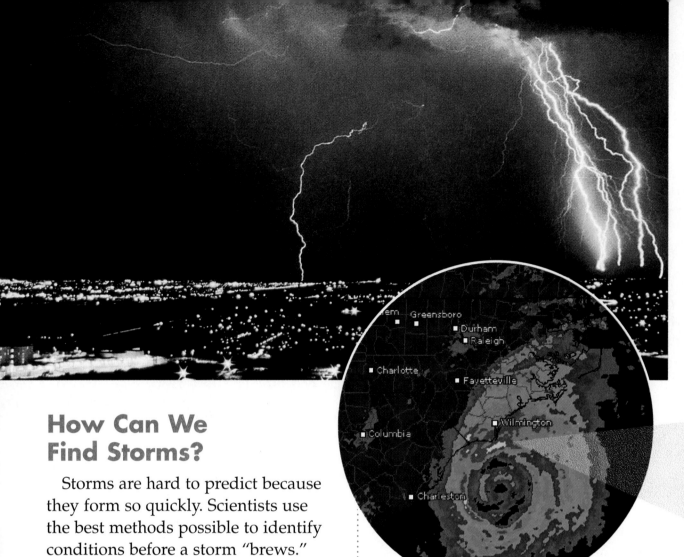

## How Can We Find Storms?

Storms are hard to predict because they form so quickly. Scientists use the best methods possible to identify conditions before a storm "brews." They look for clues, like the movement of fronts and the formation of very low pressure areas. Once these conditions are located, scientists keep a "weather eye" on them to see how they develop.

Special methods are used to find storms as they form. One such method is Doppler radar. The word *radar* stands for *ra*dio *d*etection *a*nd *r*anging. Radar works by sending out radio waves and recording their echo. The change in the radio signal from the original to the echo tells us something about where it reflected.

Doppler radar looks at how the echoes have changed in frequency from the original signals. This information gives clues about the movement of the reflective surface. Doppler radar is a very good tool for scientists to track storms. The radio waves reflect off storm clouds and are picked back up again at the radar stations.

With Doppler radar scientists can tell if raindrops are moving toward or away from them. Doppler radar can also spot spinning motions of clouds. These motions help warn scientists that tornadoes or hurricanes may be forming. Scientists use Doppler radar to find and track thunderstorms, tornadoes, and hurricanes. Doppler radar helps forecasters predict which way the storms will travel.

Scientists have used radar systems to track storms since the 1950s. More recently they have begun to use NEXRAD. *NEXRAD* stands for "*NEXt generation of weather RADar.*" NEXRAD is a new form of Doppler radar that is replacing older radar systems. NEXRAD can spot small particles such as blowing dust, very light snow, and even drizzle. NEXRAD is also more accurate than conventional radar at predicting floods and flash floods. It can show the exact locations of different fronts. It also shows changes in wind speed and direction. All of this information helps scientists make more and more accurate weather predictions.

**Forecasters can warn people when dangerous storms are headed their way.**

The more you know about severe storms, the more you can be safe. The dangers of a thunderstorm can be avoided by following simple rules. When a thunderstorm approaches, think "safety first." Even if you are playing an important ball game, the game has to stop, and you have to take cover. Hurricanes may mean that you and your family may have to leave your home until the storm passes.

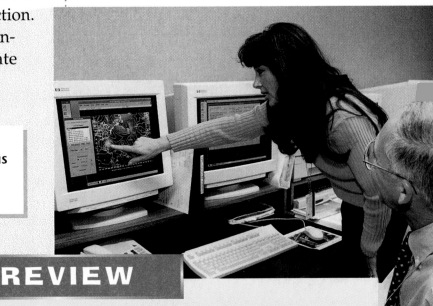

## REVIEW

1. **SEQUENCE OF EVENTS** How does a thunderstorm form?

2. How is a tornado related to a thunderstorm?

3. What causes a hurricane to form? What moves it in a certain direction?

4. Why can hurricanes cause so much damage?

5. **CRITICAL THINKING** *Analyze* Why do you think predicting a severe storm is so difficult?

**WHY IT MATTERS THINK ABOUT IT**
What would you have to do to prepare for a severe storm that might hit your area?

**WHY IT MATTERS WRITE ABOUT IT**
What are the two or three most important rules for staying safe in a severe storm? Explain your answer.

**READING SKILL**
Write a paragraph to explain the sequence of events involved when a tornado forms.

# Storm Tracking

It's easy for meteorologists to predict a storm that's part of a giant weather system; it's been reported by people experiencing it! Wind direction and changes in air pressure also signal a storm is near.

Smaller storm systems are harder to predict, but computers help. They are fed data about a storm's present location; current wind direction, air pressure, and rainfall; and how similar storms have behaved. The computer plots the path the storm will likely follow.

The use of radar has advanced hurricane prediction. Radar bounces radio waves off raindrops to discover where the storm is heading. Today, thanks to radar tracking, damage from hurricanes has been greatly reduced.

Tornadoes, or twisters, are the most violent windstorms. Because the right conditions for developing tornadoes occur quite often, they're hard to predict. The United States had more "killer tornadoes" during the first half of 1998 than in all of 1996 or 1997!

Doppler radar helps meteorologists predict tornadoes. It doesn't just spot a tornado's heavy rains, it tells the speed and direction of the funnel. With Doppler, people can be warned to seek cover before a twister hits!

There will be heavy rain all up the West Coast. Ships in the Pacific report storm conditions.

A tornado warning is in effect for Mills County. A tornado watch covers the rest of the region.

# Science, Technology, and Society

## DISCUSSION STARTER

**1.** How did people predict storms before the inventions of radio, computers, and radar?

**2.** Why does Doppler radar track storms better?

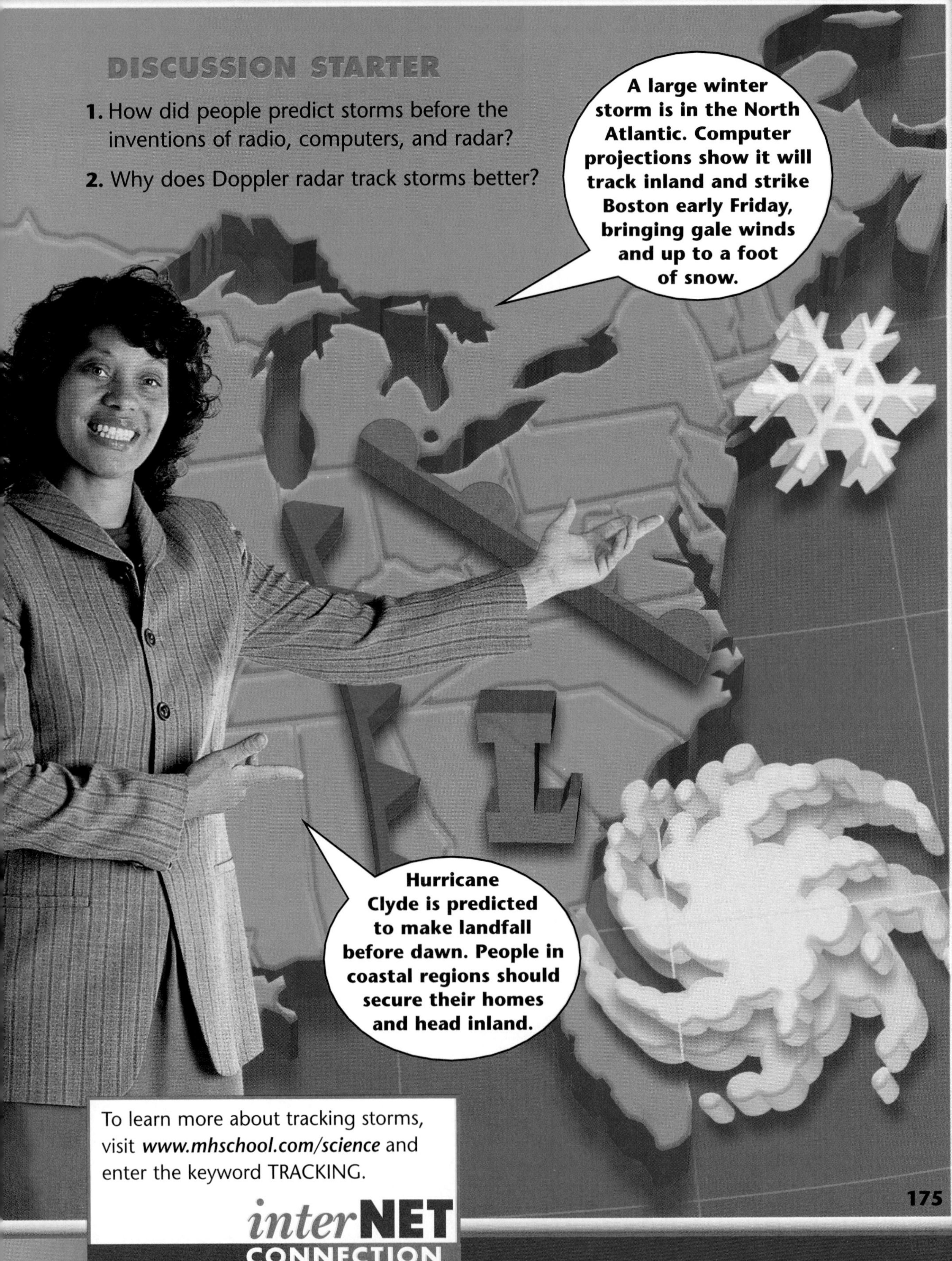

A large winter storm is in the North Atlantic. Computer projections show it will track inland and strike Boston early Friday, bringing gale winds and up to a foot of snow.

Hurricane Clyde is predicted to make landfall before dawn. People in coastal regions should secure their homes and head inland.

To learn more about tracking storms, visit *www.mhschool.com/science* and enter the keyword TRACKING.

*inter*NET CONNECTION

175

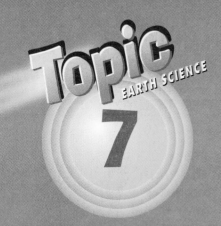

# Topic
## EARTH SCIENCE
### 7

## WHY IT MATTERS

**All places on Earth have patterns of changes in weather that repeat over time.**

## SCIENCE WORDS

**climate** the average weather pattern of a region

**radiative balance** a balance between energy lost and energy gained

**greenhouse effect** the ability of the atmosphere to let in sunlight but to not let heat escape

# Climate

**W**hat if you could live in each of these places? What would summers be like? What would winters be like? Which place do you think is wet and warm? Which is dry and cold? Which is hot and dry? Which place do you think has year-round weather most like yours? What evidence in the pictures did you use to answer these questions?

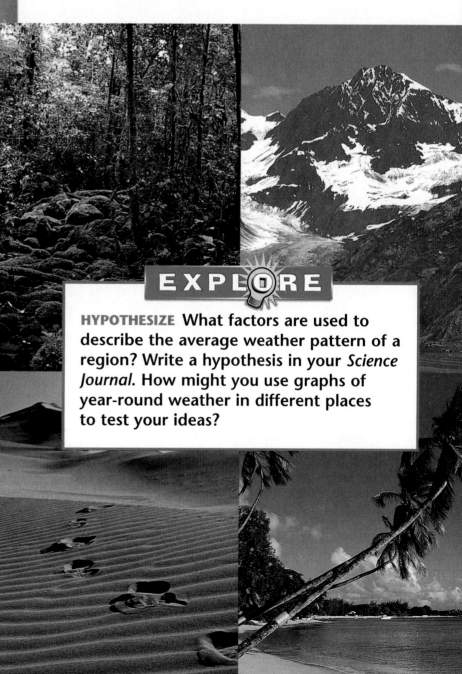

## EXPLORE

**HYPOTHESIZE** What factors are used to describe the average weather pattern of a region? Write a hypothesis in your *Science Journal*. How might you use graphs of year-round weather in different places to test your ideas?

# EXPLORE ACTIVITY

## Investigate What Weather Patterns Tell You

Compare weather patterns in two cities.

### MATERIALS

- *Science Journal*

### PROCEDURES

**1. USE NUMBERS** Look at the graph for city 1. The bottom is labeled with the months of the year. The left side is labeled with the temperature in degrees Celsius. Use this scale to read the temperature line. What is the average temperature in city 1 during July?

**2. USE NUMBERS** The right side of the graph is labeled with millimeters of precipitation. Use this scale when reading the precipitation bars. What is the average precipitation in city 1 during July?

**3.** Repeat steps 1 and 2 for city 2.

### CONCLUDE AND APPLY

**1. COMPARE AND CONTRAST** How do the annual amounts of precipitation compare for the two cities? Record your answer in your *Science Journal*.

**2. INTERPRET DATA** When is the average temperature highest for each city? Lowest?

**3. INTERPRET DATA** Describe the average weather pattern for each city. Be sure to include temperature and precipitation, and their relationship to the seasons.

### GOING FURTHER: Problem Solving

**4. ANALYZE** How would you go about making a graph of the weather patterns for your town?

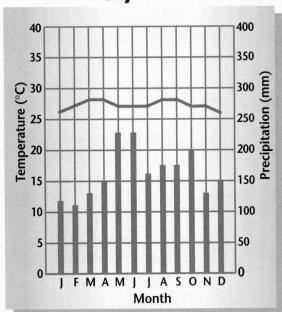

City 1

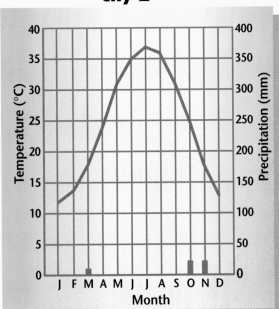

City 2

— Temperature (in Celsius)
■ Precipitation (in millimeters)

177

# What Do Weather Patterns Tell You?

Weather changes from day to day. However, the weather in any area tends to follow a pattern throughout the year. For example, Fairbanks, Alaska, tends to have long, cold winters and short, cool summers. Miami, Florida, tends to have long, hot summers and short, cool winters.

When you make descriptions such as these, you are describing the **climate** (klī′mit) of a region. Climate is the average weather pattern of a region. One way to describe a region's climate is with a temperature-precipitation graph, as in the Explore Activity.

The climate of a region can also be described by some other factors, such as winds, distance from a coast, mountain ranges, and ocean currents. The *climatic zones* shown here take all these factors into account.

Another way to describe the climate of a region is by the plants that grow there, such as, grasslands or coniferous forests. Each kind of plant requires its own conditions for growth, such as amount of sunlight, precipitation and temperature.

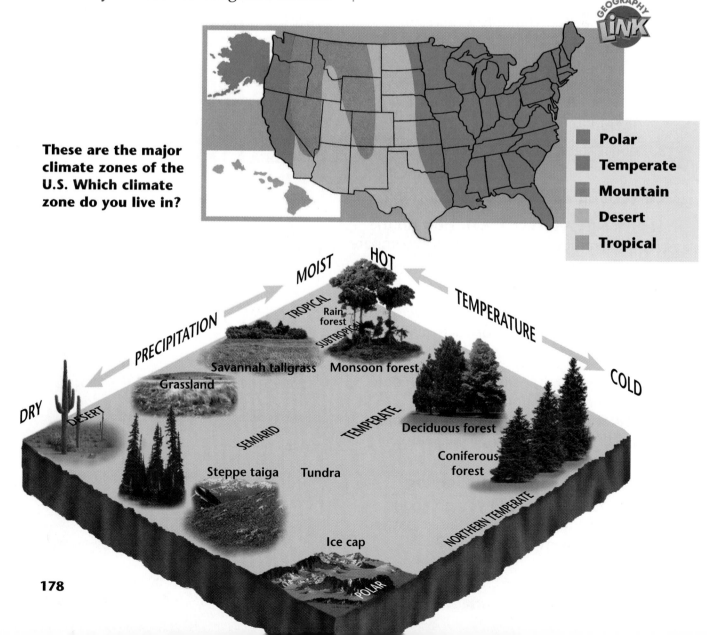

**These are the major climate zones of the U.S. Which climate zone do you live in?**

GEOGRAPHY
LINK

- Polar
- Temperate
- Mountain
- Desert
- Tropical

MOIST  HOT
PRECIPITATION
TROPICAL
Rain forest
SUBTROPICS
TEMPERATURE
Savannah tallgrass  Monsoon forest
Grassland
COLD
DRY
DESERT
SEMIARID
TEMPERATE
Deciduous forest
Steppe taiga  Tundra
Coniferous forest
NORTHERN TEMPERATE
Ice cap
POLAR

## Skill: Making a Model

### CLIMATES IN TWO AREAS

In this activity you will make a model of the soil conditions in the two cities on page 177. Use the information in the graph from the Explore Activity on page 177. The soil conditions you set up will model—or represent—the climates of the two cities.

on page 177

**MATERIALS**

- stick-on notepaper
- marking pencil or pen
- 2 trays of dry soil
- spray bottle of water (like a plant mister)
- lamp
- thermometer
- *Science Journal*

### PROCEDURES

**1. MAKE A MODEL** Put 3 cm of dry soil into each tray. Label one tray City 1 and the other tray City 2.

**2. USE NUMBERS** What do the bars on each graph in the Explore Activity represent? Make a list of the amounts given by the bars for each month for each city.

**3. USE VARIABLES** Model the yearly precipitation and temperature like this: Let 5 minutes equal 1 month. One squeeze of water sprayed on the tray equals 10 millimeters of precipitation. Every minute the lamp is on equals 20 degrees of temperature. That means that from 0 to 5 minutes is January. During January the City 2 tray gets no water and the lamp shines on it for $\frac{3}{4}$ minute. The City 1 tray gets 12 squeezes of water and the lamp shines on it for $1\frac{1}{4}$ minutes.

**4.** Model the two cities for all 12 months. Record your observations in your *Science Journal*.

### CONCLUDE AND APPLY

**1. COMPARE AND CONTRAST** Examine the soil in the trays. Compare them at the same points in each year, for example, June and December. How do they differ?

**2. EVALUATE** How does your model show climates?

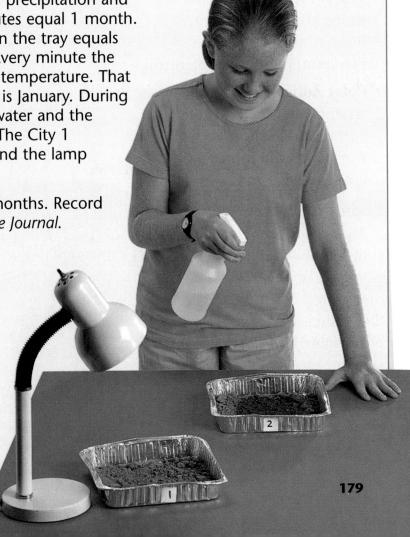

# What Affects Climate?

Several things affect temperature and precipitation over a long period of time.

## Latitude

One way to describe location is to tell the latitude of a place. Latitude is a measure of how far north or south a place is from the equator. The angle of insolation is different at different latitudes. As a result the temperatures are different at different latitudes.

- **Tropical Zone** Near the equator, temperatures are high all year. Rainfall is plentiful. At about 30° latitude in each hemisphere are deserts, areas of high temperatures and low precipitation.

- **Temperate Zones** In the middle latitudes, summers are warm and winters are cool or cold. Precipitation may be plentiful.

- **Polar Zones** At high latitudes, winters are long and cold. Summers are short and warm. Precipitation all year is low.

## Bodies of Water

A glance at any globe shows that land and water are not evenly distributed. Most of the globe is covered with water. However, some places on a continent can be more than 1,000 miles from any large body of water.

Land and water heat and cool at different rates. Land heats up faster in the sunlight than water does. Land also cools off faster than water. As a result air temperatures over land are warmer in summer and cooler in winter than they are over oceans at the same latitude.

## Winds and Ocean Currents

In Topic 4 you learned that wind patterns circle the globe. These patterns are not the day-to-day winds. Instead they are winds that blow continually above Earth's surface.

- **Wind Patterns** For example, just above and below the equator, the trade winds blow continually. In the middle latitudes are the westerlies. In the polar areas are the easterlies. Westerlies blow across the continental United States from west (the Pacific) to east. They bring warm, moist air to the west coast. They push air masses and fronts across the country.

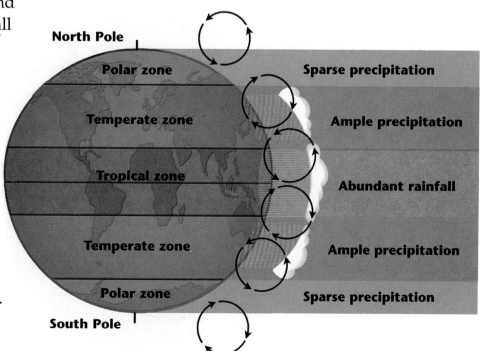

North Pole

Polar zone — Sparse precipitation

Temperate zone — Ample precipitation

Tropical zone — Abundant rainfall

Temperate zone — Ample precipitation

Polar zone — Sparse precipitation

South Pole

# HOW ALTITUDE AFFECTS CLIMATE

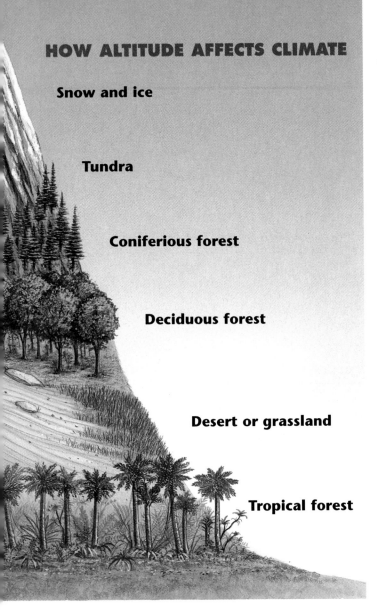

Snow and ice

Tundra

Coniferious forest

Deciduous forest

Desert or grassland

Tropical forest

- **Mountains** Along the base of a high mountain, you may find tropical plants growing. Halfway up you may find pine forests. At the mountain peaks, you will find permanent ice and snow. Mountain ranges affect climate, too. The Alps protect the Mediterranean coast from cold polar air. The Himalayas protect the lowlands of India from cold Siberian air. Mountain ranges also affect rain patterns. Often one side of the mountain gets lots of rain while the other side gets very little. Can you explain why?

- **Winds and Mountains** Global wind patterns can force air up along the side of a mountain. For example, warm moist air from the Pacific Ocean is blown up the side of the Sierra Nevada and the Cascades. As the air moves up, there is precipitation on the windward side. Having lost the moisture, dry air descends down the leeward side of the mountain.

- **Currents** These winds also move water across the surface of the ocean. As ocean water moves, it brings along warm or cool air from where it comes from to where it goes. A warm current, the Gulf Stream, flows up along the east coast. The California Current, a cool current, moves down along the west coast.

## Altitude

Altitude is a measure of how high above sea level a place is. The higher a place is above sea level, the cooler its climate is.

**Air passing over a mountain cools. Rain clouds may form and drop their moisture on that side of the mountain. Air reaching the other side is often dry.**

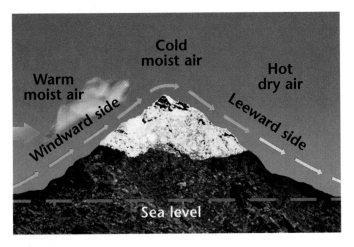

Warm moist air

Cold moist air

Hot dry air

Windward side

Leeward side

Sea level

# How Does Earth Gain and Lose Energy?

Earth's climates depend a great deal on the Sun's energy. Earth absorbs heat from sunlight. It also gives out, or *radiates*, heat into space. Earth gains and loses.

If the amount of energy gained balances the energy lost, Earth is in **radiative** (rā′dē ā′tiv) **balance**. Then Earth's average temperature remains about the same. Earth's average temperature is about 14°C (59°F). A tip of the balance will cause Earth's average temperature to rise or fall.

The atmosphere plays an important role in Earth's radiative balance. If Earth had no atmosphere, it would be a lot like the Moon, which has no atmosphere. Daytime temperatures on the Moon soar to more than 100°C (212°F). Nighttime temperatures drop to 115°C (240°F) below zero.

Earth's atmosphere acts as a protective blanket. Clouds and dust in the atmosphere reflect about 30 percent of incoming sunlight back out into space. The atmosphere absorbs another 15–20 percent. Only about half of incoming sunlight reaches Earth's surface. This keeps surface temperatures from rising too high during the day.

At night Earth's surface and the atmosphere radiate heat. The atmosphere absorbs most of this heat. The atmosphere, in turn, radiates this heat, together with its own heat. Earth absorbs back almost half of what it lost. This keeps Earth from getting too cold at night.

## EARTH'S ENERGY BUDGET

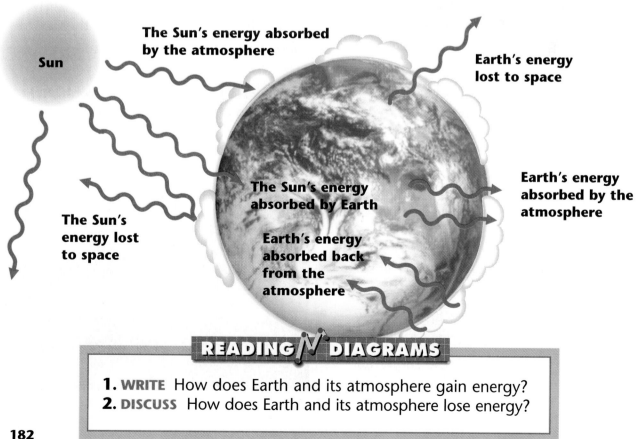

Sun

The Sun's energy absorbed by the atmosphere

Earth's energy lost to space

The Sun's energy lost to space

The Sun's energy absorbed by Earth

Earth's energy absorbed by the atmosphere

Earth's energy absorbed back from the atmosphere

## READING DIAGRAMS

**1. WRITE** How does Earth and its atmosphere gain energy?
**2. DISCUSS** How does Earth and its atmosphere lose energy?

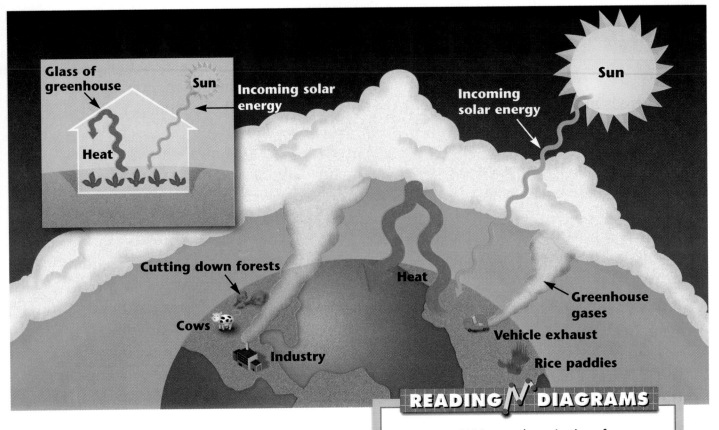

Glass of greenhouse

Sun

Incoming solar energy

Heat

Incoming solar energy

Sun

Cutting down forests

Heat

Greenhouse gases

Cows

Vehicle exhaust

Industry

Rice paddies

READING N DIAGRAMS

**DISCUSS** Write a description from this diagram of what causes the greenhouse effect.

## How Is Earth Like a Greenhouse?

Why doesn't all of Earth's heat just go out into space? The atmosphere keeps Earth warmer than it would otherwise be. This is called the **greenhouse effect**. Earth's atmosphere acts somewhat like the glass in a greenhouse. In a greenhouse the glass lets sunlight in but does not let heat escape. This helps create a warm environment in which plants can flourish.

Earth's greenhouse effect is caused by just a few gases. These greenhouse gases make up only a tiny part of the air. The main greenhouse gases are *water vapor and carbon dioxide*. Other gases also have less of an effect. These gases are *methane, nitrous oxide, and chlorofluorocarbons (CFCs)*.

Human activities are putting more and more greenhouse gases into the atmosphere. Many scientists are worried that these gases may change Earth's climate. Even a small increase in these gases adds to the greenhouse effect, making our planet warmer.

Scientists are still examining and interpreting data in order to understand the greenhouse effect better.

### Brain Power

Cans of items under pressure (hair sprays, paint sprays) indicate that they do not contain chlorofluorocarbons. Why is this an important statement to list on a label?

# Does Climate Change with Time?

There is much evidence that over long periods of time, Earth goes through warming and cooling trends. Warming and cooling are signs that Earth's radiative balance has shifted. What causes such shifts?

The shifts are caused by changes in sunlight. They are also caused by changes in the movements of air, water, landmasses, and Earth itself.

## The Sun's Output

The amount of energy the Sun sends out changes. One clue to how the Sun's output may be changing comes from sunspots. Sunspots are dark areas that appear on the surface of the Sun. They appear dark because they are cooler than the surrounding regions. They appear to be "storms" on the Sun.

Sunspots have been observed for centuries. However, they are not permanent. They appear and disappear over several days time, or over several months.

Also there are times when there are many large sunspots. Such a high count is called a sunspot maximum. The last sunspot maximum was in 1989.

A sunspot maximum appears to happen about every 11 years. Scientists also date changes in Earth's temperatures about the same times. Around the time of a sunspot maximum, Earth's average temperatures have gone up. The pattern is not exact or complete. However, it has led some scientists to suggest droughts, rainfalls, and very cold winters might be related to times when sunspots are very numerous or very few.

**The Sun's surface**

## Brain Power

When might the next sunspot maximum occur?

**Sunspot**

**When they appear sunspots can affect radio and TV broadcasts on Earth. Can they also affect temperatures?**

## Ocean Currents

How do the oceans help move Earth's heat around? Ocean currents act like huge conveyor belts, carrying heat from the equator to the poles. Changes in the speed and direction of these currents could explain sudden and long-term climate changes.

The continents have changed their positions over time. In fact the continents and ocean bottoms are still moving very gradually. Their climates are likely to change with their locations.

## Volcanoes

When volcanoes erupt they send dust and gases into the atmosphere. Atmospheric dust can block sunlight, causing cooling. In the past, eruptions were more frequent. The dust from all of those eruptions may have caused enough cooling to trigger ice ages. Volcanic eruptions are not as common today as they were in the past. While eruptions still cause cooling, they probably don't affect long-term climate as much as in the past.

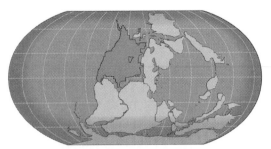

**300 Million Years Ago**

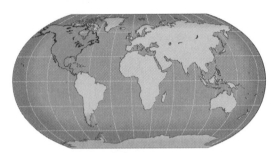

**Present**

**Do you think the ocean currents were the same 300 million years ago as they are today? Changes in ocean currents would profoundly affect climates.**

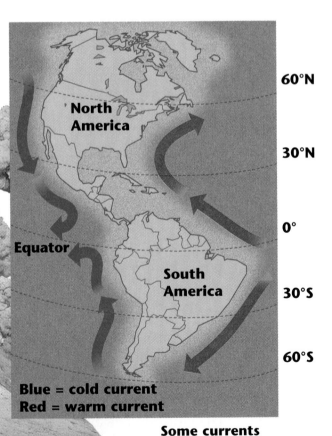

60°N

North America

30°N

0°

Equator

South America

30°S

60°S

**Blue = cold current**
**Red = warm current**

**Some currents affecting the Western Hemisphere today**

**Brain Power**

What difference does it make if Earth's climate gets just a couple of degrees warmer or cooler than it is today?

185

# How Can Climate Affect You?

How do you deal with cold weather? Cold weather cools the surface of the body. The body responds by circulating warm blood faster to counteract the cooling. The heart pumps faster. Blood pressure increases and puts a strain on the heart.

## Cold Climates

How can you stay warm in cold weather? Use proper clothing and shelter. Clothing traps body heat to warm the air close to your body. Cold-weather clothes are often made with materials that trap air between loose fibers. Your body heats the trapped air, and soon a thin, warm layer of air surrounds you.

## Hot Climates

In hot, dry climates, the main health problem is water loss. Heating the body triggers sweating. When sweat evaporates it cools the skin. However, if you don't drink enough water, your body eventually stops sweating. No sweat, no cooling. Body temperature rises. This can cause *hyperthermia* (overheating), which can be fatal.

Clothing can help you deal with the heat. Leaving your skin bare can make you feel hotter. That's because your skin absorbs the full energy of sunlight. It also increases your risk of getting skin cancer. Light-colored fabric protects the skin and reflects a lot of the sunlight. Loose clothing lets air circulate so sweat can evaporate and cool the body.

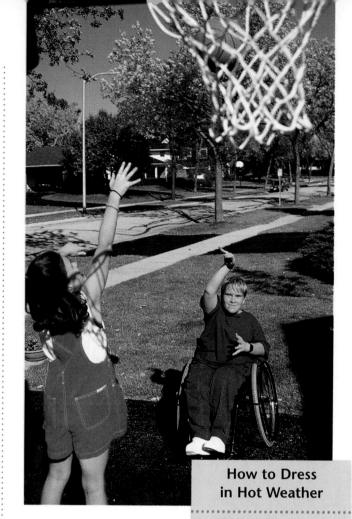

### How to Dress in Hot Weather

Light-colored, loose clothing that protects you from the Sun and lets your skin breathe

●

Sun hat

●

Sunscreen

### How to Dress in Cold Weather

Protect nose and ears on blustery, cold days

●

Keep hands, head, and feet warm

●

Dress in layers to trap body heat

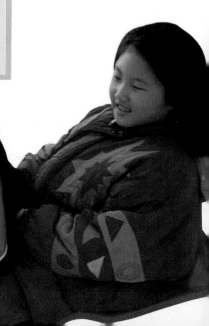

## Crops in the Past

Climate has been affecting how food is produced, since farming began, about 6,000 years ago. At that time average temperatures were about 2°C (4°F) warmer than today. There was also more rainfall. Crops thrived in the warm, moist climate. About A.D. 200 the climate started to cool. Crops failed.

By A.D. 900–1100, temperatures had warmed up again. However, by 1300 the climate had started to cool again. Between 1450 and 1850, there was a cold period called the Little Ice Age. There were many harsh winters. Stretches of cold, wet summers in the 1590s, the 1690s, and the 1810s caused crops to fail and led to famines.

## Crops Since 1900

Since 1900 the average temperature has increased by about 0.5°C (1°F). A drought during the 1920s–1940s led to the Dust Bowl days. Millions of acres of United States farmland dried out. Crops failed. Farmers went broke trying to pay their bills.

## WHY IT MATTERS

You may experience several climates in your lifetime. You may travel to faraway places with climates different from your own. In large states like Texas or California, you can experience many climates in different parts of the state.

When you become an adult, your job may bring you to climates different from your present climate. You may enjoy one climate more than another. You may choose to live in a climate different from the one you are used to.

**Winter fairs were held on the Thames River in London during the Little Ice Age.**

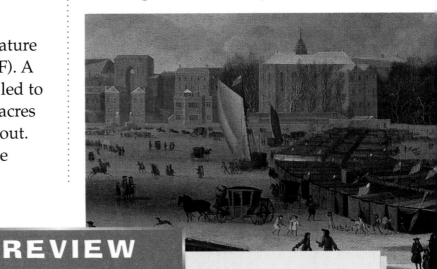

## REVIEW

1. What is climate? What are the main factors that are used to describe the climate of an area?

2. **MAKE A MODEL** How can you make models to show a dry climate and a moist climate?

3. Why are climates different at different places on Earth?

4. What is the greenhouse effect?

5. **CRITICAL THINKING** *Analyze* Do you think people can live in all climates? Explain your answer.

**WHY IT MATTERS** **THINK ABOUT IT**
What is the climate like in your area?

**WHY IT MATTERS** **WRITE ABOUT IT**
Choose a climate that is different from your own. How do people in that climate live differently from you?

# A WARMER WORLD?

"Our climate is definitely warming up," says Tom Karl, Senior Scientist at the National Climatic Data Center in North Carolina. It's the world's largest collector of weather data—its computers have more than 150 years of information. Every day 18 million more pages of weather data come in!

Karl and his team studied worldwide temperatures between 1900 and 1997. They discovered that 1997 was the warmest year since 1900 and that 9 of the past 11 years have been warmer than average!

Karl believes the cause is probably an increase in greenhouse gases. Not everyone agrees. In 1997 most state climate experts said global warming is natural, caused by changes in the Sun and in Earth's orbit. They added that Earth's climate would change even if no one lived on the planet!

## DISCUSSION STARTER

How do you think we can identify the cause of global warming?

To learn more about global warming, visit **www.mhschool.com/science** and enter the keyword WARM.

*inter*NET
**CONNECTION**

## SCIENCE WORDS

air mass p.150

climate p.178

cold front p.152

front p.151

greenhouse
  effect p.183

hurricane p.166

radiative
  balance p.182

storm surge p.168

tornado p.164

warm front p.152

## USING SCIENCE WORDS

Number a paper from 1 to 10. Fill in
1 to 5 with words from the list above.

1. The ___?___ may be making Earth
   warmer.

2. A great rise of sea level at a shore due
   to a hurricane is a(n)___?___.

3. A dangerous storm that forms over
   warm ocean waters is a(n) ___?___.

4. A(n) ___?___ forms when cold air
   moves in under a warm air mass.

5. The average weather pattern of a
   region is its ___?___.

6–10. Pick five words from the list
   above that were not used in 1 to 5,
   and use each in a sentence.

## UNDERSTANDING SCIENCE IDEAS

11. What is the difference between
    a cold front and a warm front?

12. How is the weather a warm front
    brings different from the weather
    a cold front brings?

13. What are two things that
    can affect climate?

14. What happens when a
    front stays over a region
    for a long time?

15. How are tornadoes and hurricanes
    different?

## USING IDEAS AND SKILLS

16. **READING SKILL: SEQUENCE OF
    EVENTS** Pick a severe storm.
    Describe how it forms.

17. Why is the severe storm you
    described in number 16 dangerous?

18. How are tornadoes often related to
    thunderstorms?

19. **MAKE A MODEL** What if your
    area was to get twice as much
    rain as usual for the next ten years?
    How would you make a model of
    your climate as it is now? How would
    you adjust it to study the effect of the
    extra rainfall?

20. **THINKING LIKE A SCIENTIST** Do you
    think that Earth is getting warmer?
    State and explain your hypothesis.
    Describe what you might do to test
    your ideas.

## PROBLEMS and PUZZLES

**Forecast Accuracy** Write down a
weather forecaster's five-day forecast.
Check the weather each day over the
five days. Determine a way to rate
how accurate the forecast turned out
to be. Repeat several times. Why
isn't it ever competely accurate?

# UNIT 2 REVIEW

## SCIENCE WORDS

air pressure p.105

atmosphere p.104

climate p.178

condensation p.115

convection
  cell p.136

Coriolis effect p.138

evaporation p.112

front p.151

greenhouse
  effect p.183

humidity p.112

hurricane p.166

precipitation p.124

thunderstorm
  p.162

tornado p.164

troposphere p.104

## USING SCIENCE WORDS

Number a paper from 1 to 10. Beside each number write the word or words that best complete the sentence.

1. The blanket of gases that surrounds Earth is the ___?___.

2. Evaporation increases the ___?___ in the air.

3. Evaporation is the opposite of ___?___.

4. Rain, sleet, and snow are all forms of ___?___.

5. Air rises and sinks in a(n) ___?___.

6. The curved paths of winds are caused by ___?___.

7. The boundary between two masses of air with different temperatures is called a(n) ___?___.

8. A violent spinning wind that moves in a narrow path is a ___?___.

9. The normal weather pattern of a place is called its ___?___.

10. Earth's atmosphere tends to trap heat because of the ___?___.

## UNDERSTANDING SCIENCE IDEAS

Write 11 to 15. For each number write the letter for the best answer. You may wish to use the hints provided.

11. On a hot day, a lake is likely to be
    a. cooler than nearby land
    b. hotter than nearby land
    c. the same temperature as the land
    d. the cause of the heat
    *(Hint: Read page 103.)*

12. Water drops that collect on a cold glass of lemonade come from
    a. the lemonade
    b. the air
    c. a puddle
    d. the glass itself
    *(Hint: Read page 112.)*

13. The water cycle describes how water
    a. flows upstream
    b. spins in a tornado
    c. changes form
    d. heats up the atmosphere
    *(Hint: Read pages 126–127.)*

14. Statistical weather forecasts are based on
    a. the kinds of fronts moving out of an area
    b. severe storms
    c. the chance of a weather pattern repeating itself
    d. weather station symbols
    *(Hint: Read pages 148–149.)*

15. Earth gets its heat from
    a. trees
    b. convection
    c. greenhouses
    d. the Sun
    *(Hint: Read page 182.)*

## USING IDEAS AND SKILLS

**16.** The troposphere is different from other layers of the atmosphere. What takes place there as a result of this difference?

**17.** Why does the air temperature usually increase between sunrise and noon?

**18.** How does water vapor get into the air?

**19.** What is fog, and how does it form?

**20.** How is air pressure related to air temperature?

**21. USE NUMBERS** What does a weather station model tell you?

**22.** What is the purpose of a weather station?

**23.** What causes thunderstorms?

## THINKING LIKE A SCIENTIST

**24. MAKE A MODEL** You use sand in a tray to model climates. Why would you build a model using simple things that do not seem to have anything to do with a topic?

**25.** What is the climate like where you live?

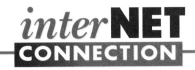

**interNET CONNECTION**

For more help in reviewing this unit, visit **www.mhschool.com/science**

## WRITING IN YOUR JOURNAL

**SCIENCE IN YOUR LIFE**
How does the weather affect your daily activities? Is there a difference between what you do on rainy days and what you do on clear, sunny days?

**PRODUCT ADS**
What products are advertised to protect you from the weather in the winter? In the summer? What is each product supposed to do? Are the products as good as the ads say? Explain.

**HOW SCIENTISTS WORK**
In this unit you learned about how weather data is collected. How do you think scientists decide what is the best kind of data to collect?

### Design your own Experiment

How much does humidity change over the course of a day? To find out, design an experiment using a glass of cold water, a thermometer, and a timer. Check your experiment with your teacher before you perform it.

# PROBLEMS and PUZZLES

## Heat Index

When the temperature and the relative humidity are both high, the air temperature may "feel" greater than what the thermometer reads. The temperature that you feel is called the *heat index*.

**Find** 90°F on the graph. Move your finger across the 90°F line to where it meets the 70% relative humidity line. At the point where the two lines meet, the heat index is 105°F. As you move your finger right to higher relative humidities, the heat index gets higher.

Find the heat index for any temperatures 80°F and over at relative humidities over 40% on the graph. The greater the heat index, the darker the shaded portions of the graph, the greater the chance of the heat affecting your health. How can knowing the heat index help you?

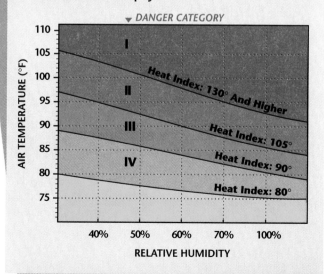

▼ DANGER CATEGORY

I

II

III

IV

Heat Index: 130° And Higher

Heat Index: 105°

Heat Index: 90°

Heat Index: 80°

AIR TEMPERATURE (°F): 110, 105, 100, 95, 90, 85, 80, 75

RELATIVE HUMIDITY: 40%, 50%, 60%, 70%, 100%

## Wind and Clouds

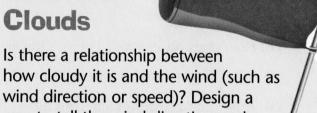

Is there a relationship between how cloudy it is and the wind (such as wind direction or speed)? Design a way to tell the wind direction each day. Keep a daily record of

• cloud cover

• wind direction

• wind speed (using the Beauford scale)

• fronts moving through your area (by listening to local weather reports)

**Put** this information together over a period of several weeks to try to find a relationship.

## Soggy Cereal Caper

Tanya left a box of Corn Roasties cereal open on an 80°F July day when the relative humidity was 80%. The cereal got soggy overnight. In December Tanya did the same thing when the temperature was 20°F and the relative humidity was also 80%. This time the cereal did not get soggy. Can you explain what made the cereal soggy in July but not in December? How could you test your answer?

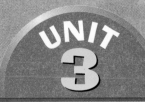

# UNIT 3

## MATTER

# CHAPTER 5

# PROPERTIES OF MATTER

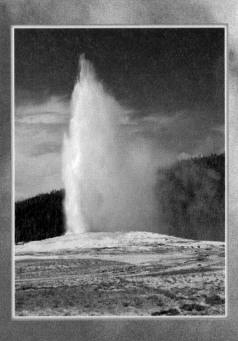

About every 65 minutes, Old Faithful erupts. It's just water . . . but what a sight! It is caused by a complicated series of events, but it all "boils" down to heat. The rocks beneath Old Faithful are very hot. They heat water in the ground. Think of what can happen to water heated in a pot over the stove. Water boils!

Any substance can boil, given the right temperature—even lead. At what temperature does lead boil? Read all about it in Chapter 5.

In Chapter 5 you will get many chances to read for the main idea of pages that have lots of details and facts.

193

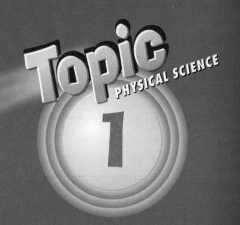

## WHY IT MATTERS

**There are many ways to measure matter.**

### SCIENCE WORDS

**mass** the amount of matter in an object

**volume** the amount of space an object takes up

**weight** (on Earth) a measure of the force of gravity between Earth and an object

**density** a measure of how tightly packed matter is; the amount of mass contained in a given volume

**buoyancy** the upward push on an object by the liquid (or gas) the object is placed in

**conduct** allow heat or electricity to flow through readily

**insulate** not allow heat or electricity to flow through readily

# What Matter Is

**W**hen you say something is "bigger" than something else, what does "bigger" mean? What is bigger than a circus tent? What is smaller? Is a car from the circus train bigger than the tent?

If the circus tent is taken down and folded up, are the same things bigger or smaller?

Bigger or smaller. More or less. In what ways can things be "more" or "less" than other things? How might a circus tent, folded or not, always be less than an elephant? Than a train car?

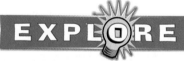

**HYPOTHESIZE** What properties do you use to compare things? Are there different ways something can be "more" than other things? Write a hypothesis in your *Science Journal*. Test your ideas.

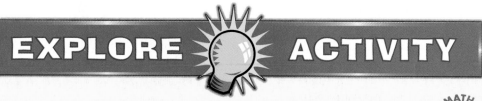
## Design Your Own Experiment

**WHICH IS MORE?**

### PROCEDURES

**MATERIALS**
- golf ball or wooden block
- blown-up balloon
- equal-pan balance
- ruler
- string
- box, such as a shoe box, big enough for the balloon to fit in
- pail of water
- *Science Journal*

**1. OBSERVE** Look at the golf ball (or wooden block) and blown-up balloon. Which is "more"? Think of how one object could be "more":
  - more when you use a balance
  - more when you put it in water and see how much the water level goes up, and so on
Record your observations in your *Science Journal*.

**2. PLAN** Use the equipment to verify one way that one object is more than another. Decide which of the three objects is "more" and which one is "less."

**3.** Repeat your measurements to verify your answer.

**4. COMPARE AND CONTRAST** Now use different equipment to compare the two objects. Is the same object still "more"? Explain.

**5.** Repeat your measurements to verify your answer.

### CONCLUDE AND APPLY

**1. COMMUNICATE** Identify the equipment you used. Report your results.

**2. COMPARE AND CONTRAST** For each test, which object was more? In what way was it more than the other object?

### GOING FURTHER: Problem Solving

**3. EXPERIMENT** What if you were given a large box of puffed oats and a small box of oatmeal? Which do you think would be more? Design an experiment to test your hypothesis. Tell what equipment you would use.

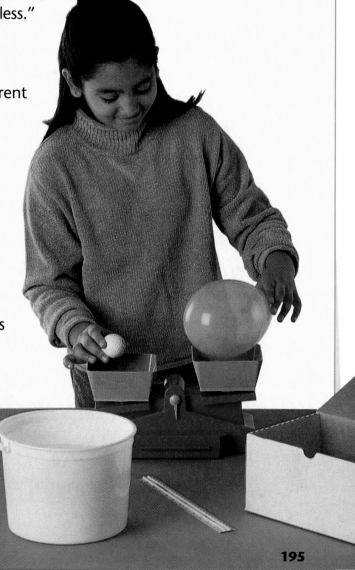

# Which Is More?

What is matter? All of the gases, liquids, and solids in the world around you—the air you breathe, the water you drink, and the chair you sit on—are made of matter. Testing to see whether a golf ball or a balloon was "more" in the Explore Activity measured *properties* of the matter in these objects.

The golf ball had more **mass** because it tipped the balance more. However, the balloon had more volume because it filled up a greater portion of a box.

Mass is a measure of the amount of matter in an object. Diagram 1 shows how a balance is used to measure mass. Known masses are placed on one side until they balance the unknown mass.

Mass is often reported in kilograms. The camera in the diagram has a mass of 1 kilogram because it comes into balance with this much known mass.

**Volume** measures how much space a sample of matter takes up. Volumes are often reported in cubic centimeters ($cm^3$). As diagram 2 shows, the volume of a sample of matter can be measured by seeing how many cubes of a chosen size it can fill.

The cough medicine in the dropper has a volume of 2 $cm^3$ because it can just fill two cubes that are 1 centimeter on a side.

Matter is defined using the properties of mass and volume. *Matter is anything that has mass and takes up space.*

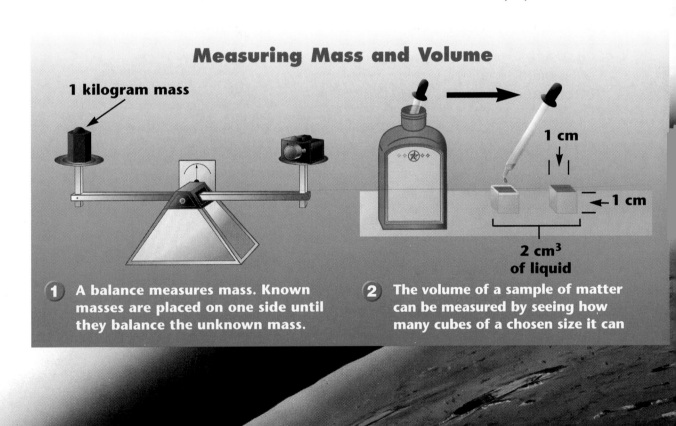

## Measuring Mass and Volume

**1 kilogram mass**

**1 cm**

**1 cm**

**2 cm³ of liquid**

1. A balance measures mass. Known masses are placed on one side until they balance the unknown mass.

2. The volume of a sample of matter can be measured by seeing how many cubes of a chosen size it can

# How Are Mass and Weight Different?

Suppose you find the mass of a certain book to be 1 kilogram. You might be tempted to say, "This book weighs 1 kilogram." However, this is incorrect. The book's **weight** is actually the force of gravity between Earth and the book. The book's mass, on the other hand, is a measure of the amount of matter in the book compared to known masses.

As you know, we can use kilograms to measure an object's mass. Yet to measure weight, we must use a quantity that describes the force of gravity between two masses. Scientists prefer to use a quantity called the *newton* (N) to measure force. One newton is the same as 0.22 pound. (Or 1 pound is 4.45 newtons.) Newtons and pounds both describe the amount of pull or push a force produces. In this case the force is the pull of gravity.

An object's weight depends on its location in the universe. If you were to travel to the Moon, for example, you would have less weight. The Moon has less mass than Earth, so the force of gravity between your body and the Moon would be less. However, your mass would remain unchanged, as in the diagram.

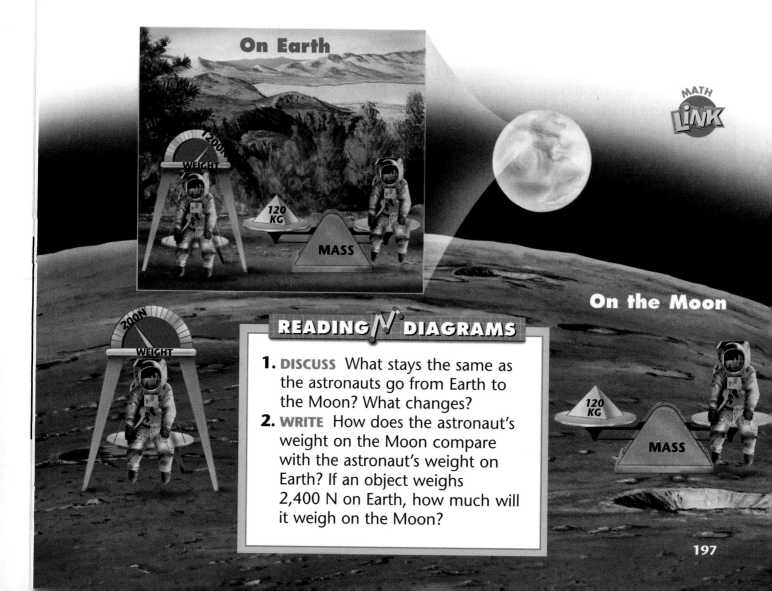

On Earth

On the Moon

## READING N DIAGRAMS

1. **DISCUSS** What stays the same as the astronauts go from Earth to the Moon? What changes?
2. **WRITE** How does the astronaut's weight on the Moon compare with the astronaut's weight on Earth? If an object weighs 2,400 N on Earth, how much will it weigh on the Moon?

197

# How Can Properties of Little Things Have Such Big Effects?

When the tiny particles that make up matter are more tightly packed together, the density is greater. This shows how properties of tiny things can combine to affect the properties of an entire material.

Like density, magnetism results from the combined effect of the properties of tiny particles. In iron metal, for example, each tiny particle of iron is itself a magnet.

Scientists have discovered that some materials become perfect conductors of electricity when they are very cold. The diagram shows a ceramic, glasslike material that conducts perfectly when cooled to 196° below 0°C (that is, –196°C).

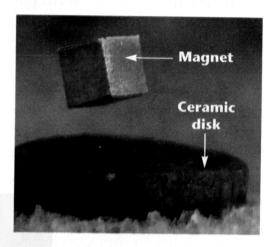

Magnet

Ceramic disk

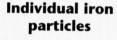

Individual iron particles

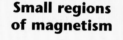

Small regions of magnetism

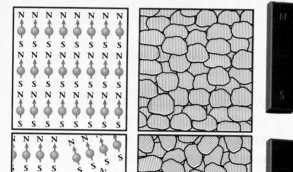

Magnetized iron bar

Demagnetized iron bar

The magnet causes electricity to flow in the ceramic. This causes a magnetic push that holds the magnet up. This effect can lift trains above the rails, so that they can travel faster.

**When iron particles in small areas of the metal line up, a permanent magnet is formed.**

# How Do We Use Properties of Matter?

Engineers and scientists use properties of matter when they design and build things. Aerogels are new materials with very low density and relatively great strength. Made of tiny pockets of air surrounded by thin walls of silica, aerogels are nearly transparent. Aerogels are very good insulators against heat. Insulated windows containing aerogel would be from 10 to 20 times better at holding in heat than ordinary glass windows!

You use many different properties of matter every day. Matter that conducts electricity lets you read at night or listen to your favorite CDs. Buoyancy allows you to float boats on a lake or helps you in swimming class. Magnets help you pick up metals or find your way home with the help of a compass.

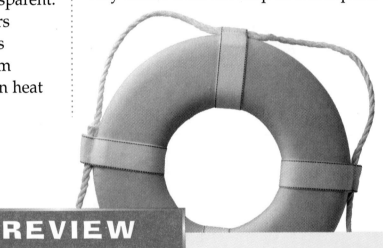

## REVIEW

1. List four properties of matter.

2. If a rock were taken from Earth to the Moon, how would its mass and weight be affected? Why?

3. What if you had paper clips, rubber bands, wood chips, straight pins, strips of aluminum foil, and glass beads? Using a property of matter you've learned, classify these objects. Show your results in a table.

4. **MAKE A MODEL** How does the density of warm water compare with the density of cold water? How would you design a model to test your ideas?

5. **CRITICAL THINKING** *Analyze* The density of corn oil is 0.92 g/cm³. What happens when corn oil is poured into water? Why does this happen?

**WHY IT MATTERS** THINK ABOUT IT
Think of the properties of matter you use every day. In what ways are they important to you?

**WHY IT MATTERS** WRITE ABOUT IT
Write a paragraph about a typical school day from the time you wake up until the time you go to sleep. What properties of matter do you rely on to get to school, do your homework, play with your friends?

**READING SKILL**
Reread pages 204–205. Look at the pictures and list facts. Write the main idea of these pages.

# FISH: Sink or Swim

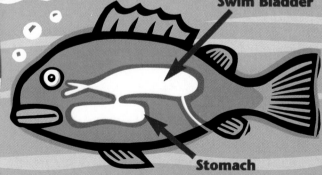

Swim Bladder

Stomach

Location of a fish's swim bladder

This diver has to add weights to sink; fish just deflate their swim bladders.

# Life Sciences Link

If you've ever tried to swim underwater, you know how difficult it is to stay down. Why is it so easy for fish? The answer is built-in— a swim bladder. A fish controls its swim bladder. To dive, the fish lets air out. The fish becomes less buoyant and sinks. Then the fish adds air to its swim bladder. The bladder makes the fish buoyant and it rises!

Ocean fish may have smaller swim bladders than fresh-water fish. Why? Salt water is denser than fresh water so less air is needed to float. Sharks don't have swim bladders. Instead they have large, oily livers. Oil is lighter than water, so the livers keep sharks afloat.

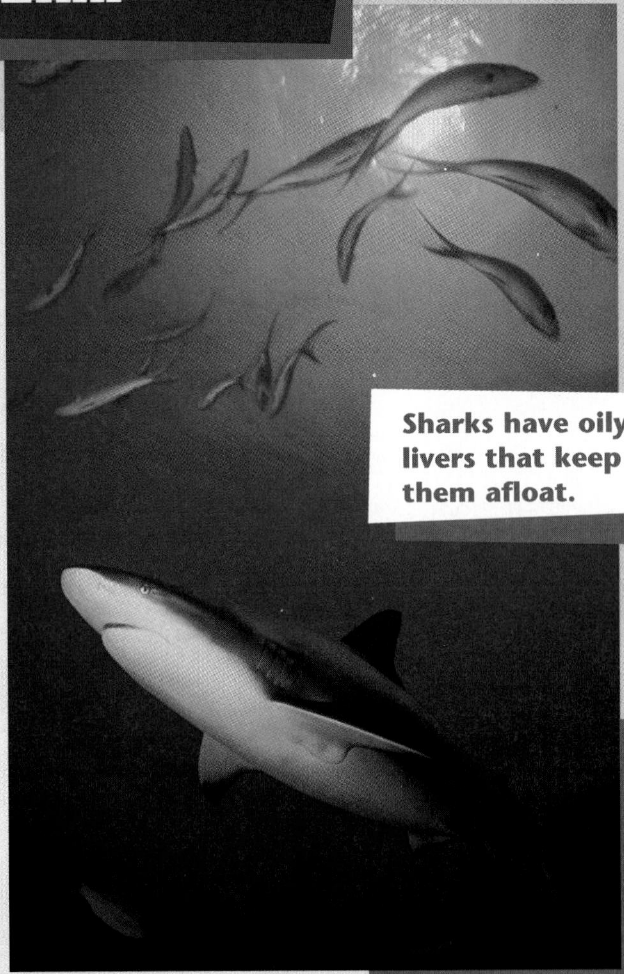

Sharks have oily livers that keep them afloat.

A fish's swim bladder works like the ballast tanks inside a submarine, which allow it to surface or dive. When the ballast tanks are full of air, the submarine floats in the water. To make the sub dive, water is pumped into the ballast tanks. To resurface, air is used to push the water out of the tanks.

A fish's sleek body also helps it dive. Sailfish move at about 109 kilometers per hour (68 miles per hour)! Compare that with the cheetah, the fastest land animal. It runs 96 kilometers per hour (60 miles per hour).

## Discussion
### Starter

1 How does a fish's swim bladder work?

2 What do sharks have instead of swim bladders?

inter**NET**
**CONNECTION** To learn more about swim bladders, visit www.mhschool.com/science and enter the keyword **SWIM.**

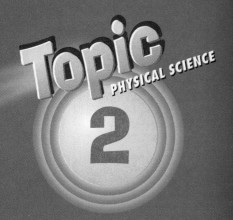

# Topic
## PHYSICAL SCIENCE
# 2

## WHY IT MATTERS

**All substances are made of tiny building blocks of matter.**

### SCIENCE WORDS

**element** a basic building block of matter; a pure substance that cannot be broken down into anything simpler

**compound** a chemical combination of two or more elements into a single substance

**atom** the smallest unit of an element that still has the properties of the element

**proton** a particle with a positive charge in the nucleus of an atom

**neutron** an uncharged particle in the nucleus of an atom

**electron** a particle with a negative charge moving around the nucleus of an atom

**nucleus** the dense center part of an atom

**molecule** a group of more than one atom joined together that acts like a single particle

# What Matter Is Made Of

How is Jupiter like Earth? How are they alike on the outside?

Both planets have atmospheres. What are the atmospheres made of? Are they similar? What are the planets made of "beneath" the atmospheres?

Here's a similar question. What is matter made of? If you cannot "look inside" something—a planet or a piece of matter—how can scientists tell what a planet or any piece of matter is made of?

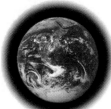

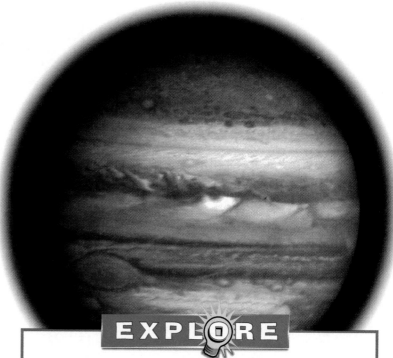

### EXPLORE

**HYPOTHESIZE** How can you tell what is inside a sealed opaque box—without opening it? What sorts of tests would you perform to try to identify its contents? Write a hypothesis in your *Science Journal.* Test your ideas.

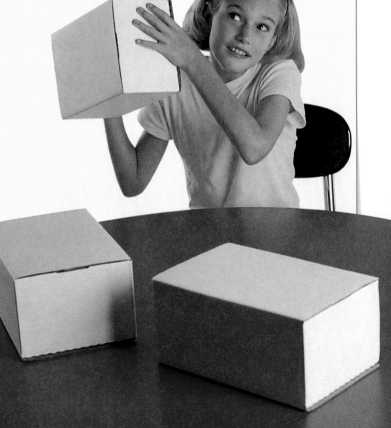
# Investigate How We Know What's "Inside" Matter

You will examine three boxes to tell how one box has something in common with each of the other two.

## PROCEDURES

**1. OBSERVE** Examine the three boxes, but do not open them. You can lift them, shake them, listen to the noises they make, feel the way their contents shift as you move them, and so on. Record your observations in your *Science Journal*.

**2. INFER** Try to determine what is in each box.

### MATERIALS

- 3 identical, sealed, opaque boxes
- *Science Journal*

## CONCLUDE AND APPLY

**1. COMMUNICATE** Describe in your *Science Journal* what you think is in each box.

**2.** How did you make your decision?

**3. COMPARE AND CONTRAST** Do these boxes have anything in common? In what ways are they similar? In what ways are they different?

### GOING FURTHER: Problem Solving

**4. EXPERIMENT** What if you had a can of peanuts and a can of stewed tomatoes? The cans looked the same except for the labels. Now what if your baby brother took the labels off? You wanted the peanuts, but you didn't want to open the tomatoes by mistake. What experiments could you do to find out what was inside— before you opened a can?

# How Do We Know What's "Inside" Matter?

In the Explore Activity, the boxes were sealed. Tests had to be done from the outside to infer what each box contained. In studying matter scientists face the same kind of challenge. The basic particles that make up matter are too small to be seen directly. In the past the tests scientists performed on matter gave only hints about how matter is put together. That's because particles of matter cannot be observed.

People have experimented with matter for thousands of years. In ancient times the goal was often a practical product like a colorful dye, a metal sword, or a plow. In recent centuries matter has also been studied with carefully planned scientific experiments.

The ancient Greek philosopher Aristotle believed that all matter was composed of four elements—earth, air, fire, and water. However, during the last three centuries, scientists have identified the true chemical elements. These substances are the basic building blocks of all matter. One of the most interesting elements is shown in the photograph at the bottom of the page. It expands very evenly when warmed and makes a good liquid for thermometers. What is it?

**1** This bronze coin was made about 2,500 years ago. Bronze is made by mixing the metals copper and tin.

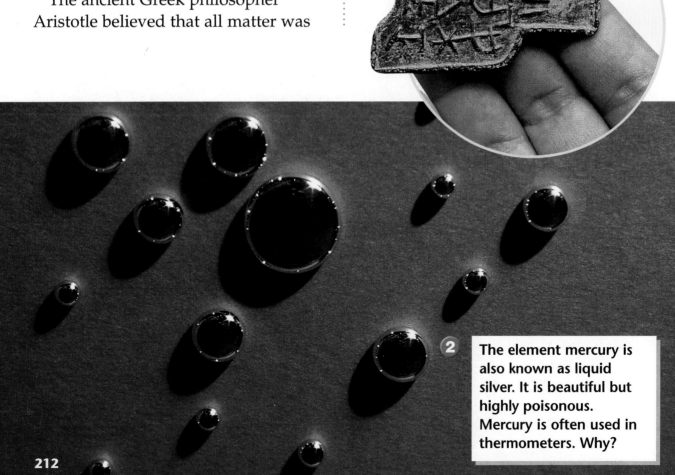

**2** The element mercury is also known as liquid silver. It is beautiful but highly poisonous. Mercury is often used in thermometers. Why?

## What Are the Elements?

Elements are pure substances that cannot be broken down into any simpler substances. You are probably familiar with many of them. Several are shown in the photographs. How many do you recognize?

Many elements have been known since ancient times but were not truly recognized as elements until the last few centuries. Other elements were found for the first time only recently. For example, germanium was not discovered until 1885. Also, some elements are not even found in nature. They have been made by scientists in nuclear reactors and huge machines called particle accelerators. Yet, even though there are many different elements, living organisms and most materials are made up of just a few elements.

Each element is given a special symbol of one or two letters. The first letter is always a capital. The second letter, if there is one, is never a capital. Sometimes the letters match the English name, such as Ni for nickel or Zn for zinc. In other cases the symbol comes from an ancient name. Gold, for instance, is given the symbol Au from its Latin name, *aurum*.

**A few elements are pictured here. How many other elements can you name?**

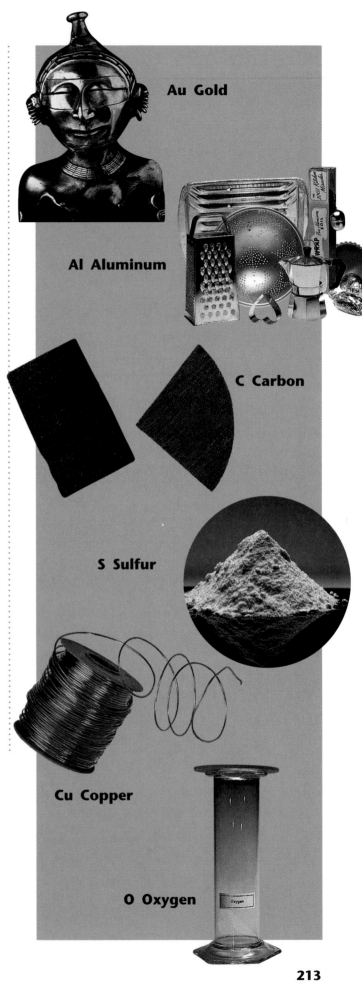

Au Gold

Al Aluminum

C Carbon

S Sulfur

Cu Copper

O Oxygen

# What Are Compounds?

Imagine looking at pure water through a microscope. It would look the same everywhere. Water has this appearance because it is a single substance. Yet the photograph below shows how passing electricity through water breaks it apart into two elements, hydrogen and oxygen. If water is a single substance, how could it contain the elements hydrogen and oxygen?

Actually, the hydrogen and oxygen in water are *chemically* combined. This makes them act like a single substance. Any substance that is formed by the chemical combination of two or more elements is called a **compound**.

All compounds are single substances that can only be broken apart into simpler substances by chemical reactions. Compounds have different *properties* than the elements that make them up, as the lower photographs show.

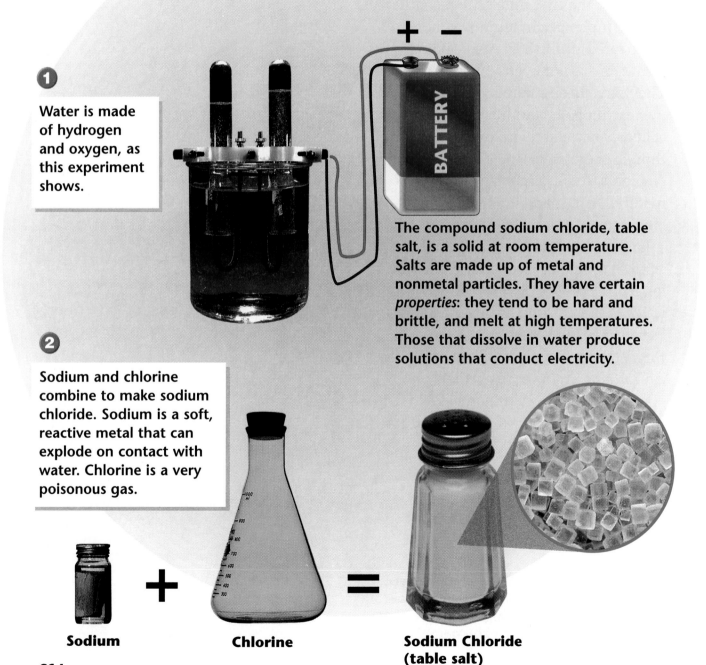

**1** Water is made of hydrogen and oxygen, as this experiment shows.

The compound sodium chloride, table salt, is a solid at room temperature. Salts are made up of metal and nonmetal particles. They have certain *properties*: they tend to be hard and brittle, and melt at high temperatures. Those that dissolve in water produce solutions that conduct electricity.

**2** Sodium and chlorine combine to make sodium chloride. Sodium is a soft, reactive metal that can explode on contact with water. Chlorine is a very poisonous gas.

**Sodium** + **Chlorine** = **Sodium Chloride (table salt)**

## How Do You Write a Compound's Name?

As you know, each element has a one- or two-letter symbol. Scientists also write symbols for compounds called *chemical formulas*. A compound's chemical formula contains the symbols for the elements that make it up.

The formula also contains numbers below the element symbols called *subscripts*. The table shows chemical formulas for some familiar compounds.

The subscripts in a chemical formula tell us the number of particles that combine together in a compound. For example, water is made up of two elements—hydrogen and oxygen. For every oxygen particle, there are two hydrogen particles. The formula for water is written $H_2O$.

Table sugar is made up of the elements carbon, hydrogen, and

### TABLE OF COMPOUNDS

| Compound | Chemical Formula |
| --- | --- |
| Water | $H_2O$ |
| Carbon dioxide | $CO_2$ |
| Baking soda (bicarbonate of soda) | $NaHCO_3$ |
| Table salt | $NaCl$ |
| Table sugar | $C_{12}H_{22}O_{11}$ |
| Glucose (a sugar) | $C_6H_{12}O_6$ |

oxygen. For every 12 carbon particles, there are 22 hydrogen particles and 11 oxygen particles. We write $C_{12}H_{22}O_{11}$ for table sugar's chemical formula. The photo shows what happens to table sugar when it is treated with strong sulfuric acid. (**Warning: Sulfuric acid is a dangerous substance.**) The acid takes out all the hydrogen and oxygen, leaving a black mass.

### Brain Power

What is this black mass made of? How could it have been in the sugar without turning the sugar black? Write out your ideas.

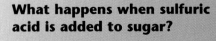
**What happens when sulfuric acid is added to sugar?**

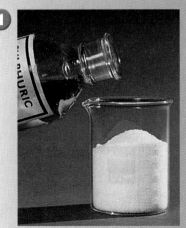
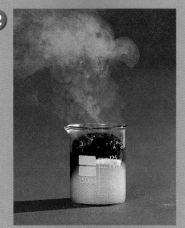
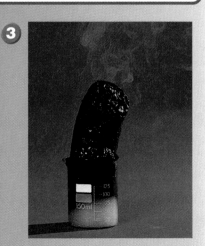

# What Are Elements Made Of?

In 1803 an English scientist named John Dalton stated an important theory: Matter is made up of tiny particles that cannot be cut apart into smaller pieces. Today we call Dalton's tiny particles **atoms**.

According to Dalton, the atoms of one element were all alike. Each element is made up of one kind of atom. However, the atoms of one element were different from the atoms of any other element. While many parts of Dalton's theory have been improved since 1803, the basic idea of atoms is correct. *An atom is the smallest unit of an element that retains the properties of the element.*

Many experiments since Dalton's day have shown us what atoms are like. Yet atoms are so small that we cannot see them directly, even through a microscope. Scientists have had to observe atoms indirectly, in much the same way as you would observe matter inside "mystery" boxes. A special microscope called a *scanning tunneling microscope* uses a very sharp needle that can trace the bumps in a surface made by individual atoms. The photograph below shows some of what such special microscopes can "see."

Images made by these microscopes show that atoms are discrete and often occur in well-ordered arrays.

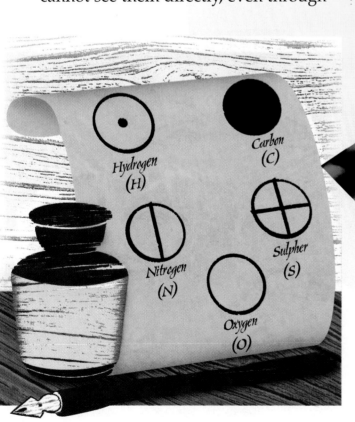

**Individual carbon atoms**

Dalton drew the symbols (left) for atoms. He believed that each element's atoms weighed a different amount from the atoms of other elements.

# What's Inside Atoms?

John Dalton imagined that atoms were like tiny steel marbles—solid and unbreakable. Yet we now know that atoms are made of still smaller particles. Atoms are far from being solid—they are mostly empty space!

Atoms contain three kinds of particles called **protons** (prō'tonz), **neutrons** (nü'tronz), and **electrons** (i lek'tronz). The protons and neutrons are located in a tiny, very dense body in the atom's center, called the atomic **nucleus** (nü'klē əs). The electrons are in the space outside the nucleus.

Protons and neutrons have nearly the same mass, but electrons are about 2,000 times less massive than protons and neutrons. Protons carry one unit of positive electric charge, while electrons carry one unit of negative electric charge.

Neutrons have no electric charge. All atoms have equal numbers of electrons and protons, so they have no overall electric charge.

The number of protons in an atom determines what element it is. For example, any atom with six protons is a carbon atom. Any atom with eight protons is an oxygen atom.

Look carefully at the diagrams on this page to see how atoms are put together.

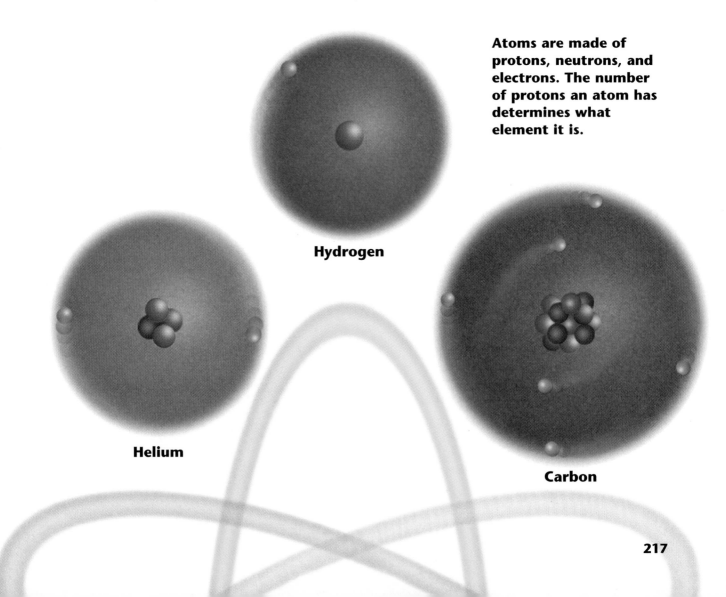

**Atoms are made of protons, neutrons, and electrons. The number of protons an atom has determines what element it is.**

Hydrogen

Helium

Carbon

# What Properties Do Elements Have?

We now know of 112 elements. These substances have many different properties. Yet there are patterns in the properties of the elements. Study the photographs on this page to learn about properties that can demonstrate these patterns.

## Chemical Reactivity

Some elements take part in chemical reactions much more easily than others. The magnesium reacts rapidly with the acid. Yet the copper hardly reacts at all. Reactive elements, like magnesium, are usually combined with other elements when found in nature.

## Melting and Boiling Temperatures

The elements shown are all at room temperature, about 22°C. Lead does not melt until it reaches 328°C, so it is a solid at 22°C. Bromine, though, melts at −7.2°C (7.2° below 0°C), and it is a liquid at 22°C. Fluorine is a gas at 22°C because it boils at −188°C (188° below 0°C).

## Metal Versus Nonmetal

About three-fourths of the elements are metallic, like copper, gold, silver, aluminum, iron, and nickel. Metals conduct electricity and heat well. Metals are also shiny when freshly polished, and many can be worked into thin sheets or different shapes. In contrast nonmetals, like iodine, phosphorus, and carbon, are often poor conductors of heat and electricity. They are not reflective like metals and are brittle.

**1** Property: **Chemical Reactivity** Magnesium takes part in chemical reactions much more easily than copper. Here the magnesium reacts rapidly with the acid. Yet the copper hardly reacts at all.

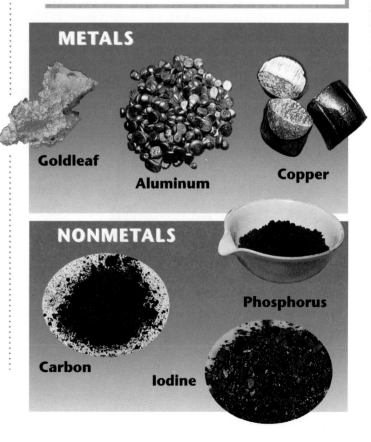

Magnesium

Copper

Hydrochloric acid

**2** Property: **Metal Versus Nonmetal** Metals, like copper, gold, silver, aluminum, iron, and nickel, are good conductors of electricity and heat. Nonmetals, like iodine, phosphorus, and carbon, are often poor conductors of heat and electricity.

**METALS**

Goldleaf

Aluminum

Copper

**NONMETALS**

Phosphorus

Carbon

Iodine

# How Can the Elements Be Grouped?

In 1869 a Russian scientist named Dmitri Mendeleyev found that the properties of the elements went through repeating cycles. Mendeleyev created a table of elements based on these cycles. To Mendeleyev's surprise, groups in his table contained elements with similar chemical properties. For example, one group contained lithium (Li), sodium (Na), potassium (K), rubidium (Rb), and cesium (Cs).

All of these elements combine with chlorine in the same way. The formulas for their chlorine compounds are LiCl, NaCl, KCl, RbCl, and CsCl.

We call Mendeleyev's table the periodic table after the "periodic" changes he found in the elements' properties. The elements are arranged in the periodic table by their chemical properties.

1. The metals lie on the left, and the nonmetals lie mainly on the right, with elements called metalloids in between.

2. Most of the elements are solids at room temperature, and all metals are solids except mercury.

3. The most reactive metals are at the lower left, and the most reactive nonmetals are in the second column from the right.

## THE MODERN PERIODIC TABLE

The number in each box is the number of protons an atom of that element has.

| H 1 | | | | | | | | | | | | | | | | | He 2 |
|---|---|---|---|---|---|---|---|---|---|---|---|---|---|---|---|---|---|
| Li 3 | Be 4 | | | | | | | | | | | B 5 | C 6 | N 7 | O 8 | F 9 | Ne 10 |
| Na 11 | Mg 12 | | | | | | | | | | | Al 13 | Si 14 | P 15 | S 16 | Cl 17 | Ar 18 |
| K 19 | Ca 20 | Sc 21 | Ti 22 | V 23 | Cr 24 | Mn 25 | Fe 26 | Co 27 | Ni 28 | Cu 29 | Zn 30 | Ga 31 | Ge 32 | As 33 | Se 34 | Br 35 | Kr 36 |
| Rb 37 | Sr 38 | Y 39 | Zr 40 | Nb 41 | Mo 42 | Tc 43 | Ru 44 | Rh 45 | Pd 46 | Ag 47 | Cd 48 | In 49 | Sn 50 | Sb 51 | Te 52 | I 53 | Xe 54 |
| Cs 55 | Ba 56 | La 57 | Hf 72 | Ta 73 | W 74 | Re 75 | Os 76 | Ir 77 | Pt 78 | Au 79 | Hg 80 | Tl 81 | Pb 82 | Bi 83 | Po 84 | At 85 | Rn 86 |
| Fr 87 | Ra 88 | Ac 89 | Rf 104 | Ha 105 | Sg 106 | Ns 107 | Hs 108 | Mt 109 | Uun 110 | Uuu 111 | Uub 112 | | | | | | |

Metals ▢
Metalloids ▢
Nonmetals ▢

| Ce 58 | Pr 59 | Nd 60 | Pm 61 | Sm 62 | Eu 63 | Gd 64 | Tb 65 | Dy 66 | Ho 67 | Er 68 | Tm 69 | Yb 70 | Lu 71 |
|---|---|---|---|---|---|---|---|---|---|---|---|---|---|
| Th 90 | Pa 91 | U 92 | Np 93 | Pu 94 | Am 95 | Cm 96 | Bk 97 | Cf 98 | Es 99 | Fm 100 | Md 101 | No 102 | Lr 103 |

## READING ⚡ CHARTS

1. **WRITE** Is sodium a metal or a nonmetal? Is chlorine a metal or a nonmetal?
2. **DISCUSS** Give an example of a substance that forms when a reactive metal and a reactive nonmetal combine.

# Can Atoms Join?

Some elements, such as neon, are made up of single atoms that do not attach to any partners. Yet other elements have atoms that attach to one or more additional atoms. Particles that contain more than one atom joined together are called **molecules**. All matter is made of atoms which may combine to form molecules.

Nitrogen is an example of an element that is made up of molecules. Its molecules have two atoms joined together. Some elements even exist in more than one form, such as oxygen.

Oxygen is usually made up of two-atom molecules, much like nitrogen. Yet oxygen can also exist as three-atom molecules. The three-atom form of oxygen is known as ozone. The three-atom ozone has properties different from the two-atom oxygen.

Molecules of elements always contain only one kind of atom. Yet compounds are made up of molecules that have different kinds of atoms joined together, as the lower diagram shows.

Note how the chemical formulas in both diagrams tell you the number of atoms in the molecules.

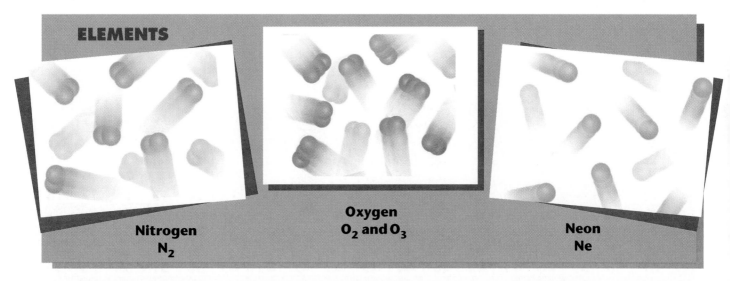

**ELEMENTS**

Nitrogen
$N_2$

Oxygen
$O_2$ and $O_3$

Neon
Ne

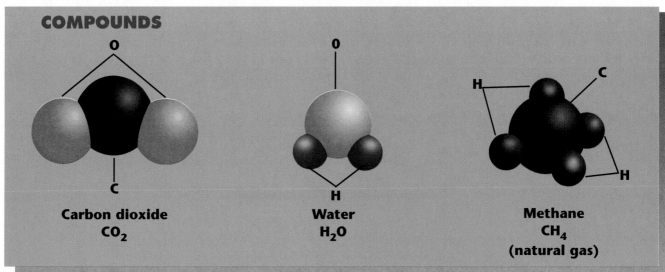

**COMPOUNDS**

Carbon dioxide
$CO_2$

Water
$H_2O$

Methane
$CH_4$
(natural gas)

When a compound forms from elements, changes occur in the way that atoms are linked together. This causes the compound to have properties different from the elements. For example, water is a liquid, yet it is formed from two gases, hydrogen and oxygen. The diagram shows why water has properties different from hydrogen and oxygen gas—the atoms are linked in a new way when water forms.

## Hydrogen Plus Oxygen Makes Water

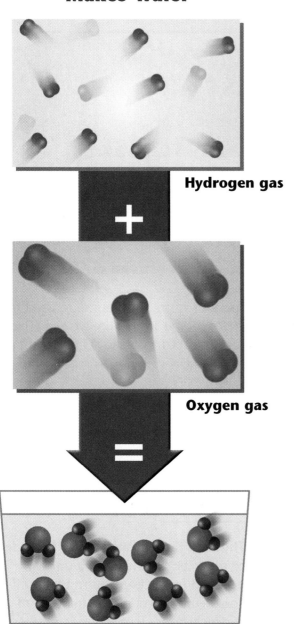

**Hydrogen gas**

**+**

**Oxygen gas**

**=**

**Liquid water**

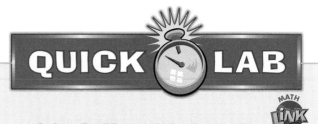

# QUICK LAB

MATH LINK

## Modeling Molecules

**HYPOTHESIZE** How do different elements combine to form molecules? Write a hypothesis in your *Science Journal.* Then try building your own molecules.

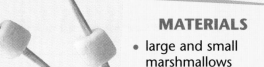

### MATERIALS
- large and small marshmallows
- toothpicks
- *Science Journal*

## PROCEDURES

**1.** Using small marshmallows for hydrogen atoms and large marshmallows for oxygen atoms, make two $H_2$ molecules and one $O_2$ molecule. Join the "atoms" with toothpicks.

**2.** Count the number of "atoms" of each type you have in your molecules. Record these numbers in your *Science Journal.* Take this many more marshmallows and make as many water molecules as you can, using toothpicks to join the atoms.

## CONCLUDE AND APPLY

**1. OBSERVE** How many water molecules did you make?

**2. INFER** Why would real water molecules have properties different from real hydrogen and oxygen molecules?

# How Do We Use Compounds?

By studying matter scientists have learned how to prepare compounds that are very useful. Many things are made from the atoms of just a small number of elements. The photographs on this page show several compounds that we depend on a great deal in modern life.

Take petroleum, for example. Petroleum is a complex mixture of *hydrocarbons*—compounds made of hydrogen and carbon atoms. Gasoline comes from petroleum. Its molecules usually have from 5 to 12 carbon atoms in chains. Gasoline gives off a lot of energy when it is burned, so we use it as a fuel in cars.

Many kinds of plastics are also made from hydrocarbons in petroleum or natural gas. Because they are made of molecules that have very long chains of atoms, plastics are called *polymers*.

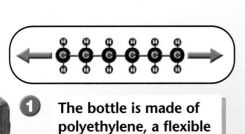

**1** The bottle is made of polyethylene, a flexible plastic made from hydrocarbons.

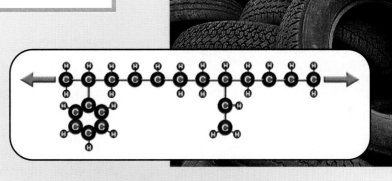

**2** Compounds from petroleum are used to make the rubber in this tire's tread. The rubber is treated to make it hard and durable.

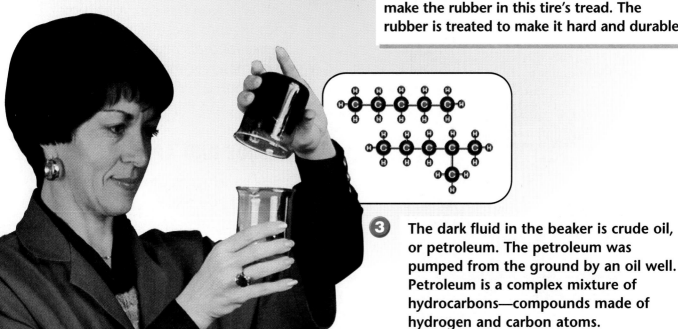

**3** The dark fluid in the beaker is crude oil, or petroleum. The petroleum was pumped from the ground by an oil well. Petroleum is a complex mixture of hydrocarbons—compounds made of hydrogen and carbon atoms.

Imagine what the world would be like if there were no compounds. You wouldn't be here! Your body is made of compounds containing the elements carbon, hydrogen, oxygen, and nitrogen. Neither would most of the things around you. There would be oxygen, but no carbon dioxide that plants need for survival. Of course, there wouldn't be any plants anyway. There wouldn't be any water or food or animals or things people build. There would be only the elements of the periodic table, floating around separately in space.

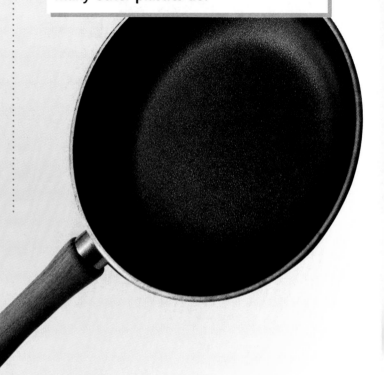

This pan is coated with Teflon, a special polymer made of carbon and fluorine atoms. Teflon is very slippery and makes a good, tough, nonstick coating. Teflon doesn't melt at high temperatures as many other plastics do.

## REVIEW

1. Why must some element symbols have two letters instead of just one?

2. A beryllium atom is made of four protons, five neutrons, and four electrons. Draw a model of this type of atom. Label each part.

3. Give an example of a compound whose properties are much different from the elements it is made of. Describe how it is different.

4. **INFER** Gold is often found in nature as pure nuggets. How does gold's location in the periodic table explain why it can be found in this way?

5. **CRITICAL THINKING** *Analyze* Look at the periodic table. List some other elements, besides neon, that are made up of single atoms that do not attach to any partners. Explain why you listed the elements you did.

**WHY IT MATTERS** THINK ABOUT IT
Think of ways elements and compounds are important in your life.

**WHY IT MATTERS** WRITE ABOUT IT
Write a paragraph about the compounds you use every day. Go to the library and find out more about some of these compounds. Then write another paragraph telling about what you learned from your research.

# It's ELEMENT-ary!

If you were in charge, how would you organize the world? In the fifth century B.C., a Greek named Empedocles came up with an idea that the world followed for centuries.

He decided that everything was made up of four elements—earth, air, fire, and water. Some things had more of one element than another. People thought bones were four parts fire, two parts water, and two parts earth!

Empedocles did, however, make one discovery that moved science forward. People had always thought that air was nothing. He showed that air could keep water out of a container. If water could only get in when the air got out, then air must be something!

Love and hate were the two forces Empedocles thought acted on the four elements. Love united the elements, then hate separated them into different forms. That's how everything, from aardvarks to zithers, was created!

Empedocles's theories were accepted for hundreds of years. People believed that they became ill because their bodies were out of balance. To cure people, doctors had to bring the elements back into harmony.

# History of Science

Muslim scientist Al-Kimya Jabir ben Haiyan has been called the "Father of Chemistry." He established chemistry as an experimental science in the eighth century A.D.

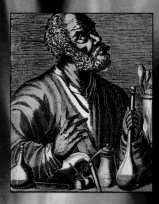

The first element—as we know the term—was discovered by Hennig Brand. He extracted phosphorus in 1669. Before the 18th century, there were only about ten known elements. During the next two centuries, most elements that occur in nature were discovered. Scientists also created about 20 synthetic elements.

Physicist Luis W. Alvarez was awarded a Nobel prize in 1968. He was a world leader in elementary particle physics and was known for his work on subatomic particles.

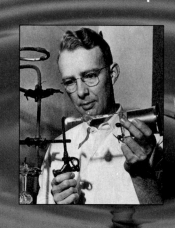

## DISCUSSION STARTER

1. Explain Empedocles's theory of the elements.

2. How did belief in the elements affect how people were treated for illnesses?

To learn more about the elements, visit **www.mhschool.com/science** and enter the keyword ELEMENTS.

*inter*NET CONNECTION

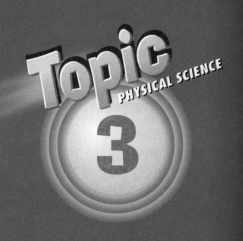

# Topic
## PHYSICAL SCIENCE
### 3

## WHY IT MATTERS

**Matter comes in three basic forms—solid, liquid, and gas.**

### SCIENCE WORDS

**state of matter** any of the forms matter can exist in

**melting point** the temperature at which a solid changes state into a liquid

**boiling point** the temperature at which a liquid changes state into a gas

**freezing point** the temperature at which a liquid changes state into a solid

# Solids, Liquids, and Gases

**W**hat is happening here? How many different kinds of matter do you see here? How are they changing?

Glaciers are huge sheets of moving ice and snow. At a shoreline, chunks of ice fall off and float away as icebergs.

Ice is solid water. You are looking at solid and liquid water. What does it take for solid ice to become liquid—to melt, that is. If all the ice trapped in glaciers melted, what would happen to sea levels around the world?

## EXPLORE

**HYPOTHESIZE** How does the temperature change as a block of ice melts? Does it increase? Write a hypothesis in your *Science Journal.* Test your ideas.

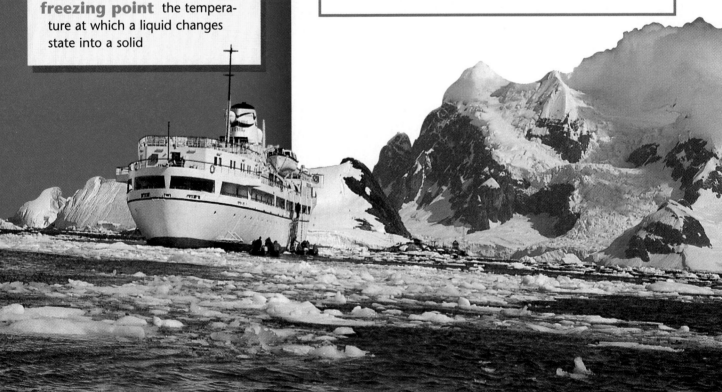

MATH LINK

# Investigate What Happens When Ice Melts

Take temperature readings to see what happens as ice melts.

## MATERIALS

- ice cubes
- water
- graduated cylinder
- plastic or paper cup
- thermometer
- heat source (lamp or sunlight)
- watch or clock
- *Science Journal*

## PROCEDURES

**1. MEASURE** Put ice cubes in the cup. Add 50 mL of water to the cup. Swirl the ice-and-water mixture together for 15 seconds.

**2. MEASURE** Place the thermometer in the cup. Wait 15 seconds. Then read the temperature. Record your observation in your *Science Journal*.

**3. MEASURE** Put the cup under a heat source (lamp or sunlight). Take temperature readings every 3 minutes as the ice melts.

**4. MEASURE** After all the ice has melted, continue taking temperature readings every 3 minutes for another 15 minutes.

## CONCLUDE AND APPLY

**1. OBSERVE** What happened to the temperature as the ice melted?

**2. HYPOTHESIZE** Why do you think you got the results described in question 1?

**3. INFER** What does ice become when it melts?

### GOING FURTHER: Problem Solving

**4. PREDICT** What do you think would happen if you didn't add any water to the ice? What do you think will happen if you add more water to the ice? Design an experiment to test each of your predictions. What do you think happens as you freeze water? How would you design an experiment to test your prediction?

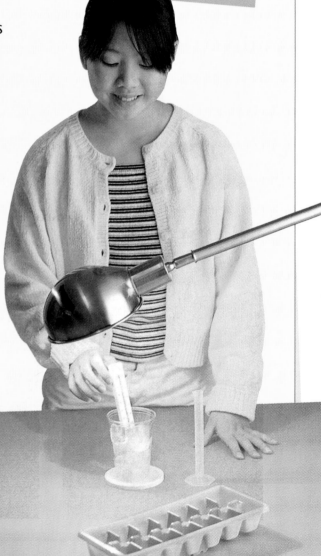

# ANIMALS: icy SURVIVAL

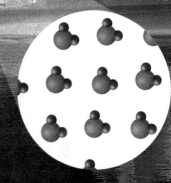

imagine a world where water's like most other substances—it becomes denser as it freezes. Ice, now heavier than water, sinks to the bottoms of ponds. The water quickly freezes from the bottom up into solid blocks of ice. Fish in the ponds freeze, too. That's the end of most freshwater fish.

In summer the ice near the top of the ponds melts, but not the ice at the bottom. That ice never melts. Each summer things get worse. Before long there's no liquid water left on Earth!

Luckily that scenario is science fiction, but real water is stranger than science fiction! Why doesn't it become denser when it turns solid? The answer lies in what happens when water molecules get cold enough to freeze.

As you know, water molecules are made of two hydrogen atoms and one oxygen atom. When water freezes, the molecules are kept farther apart than they are in liquid water.

Ice is only nine-tenths as dense as liquid water, so when water freezes, it expands. A given volume of ice weighs less than the same volume of water. That's why ice floats in your lemonade!

# Life/Earth Science Link

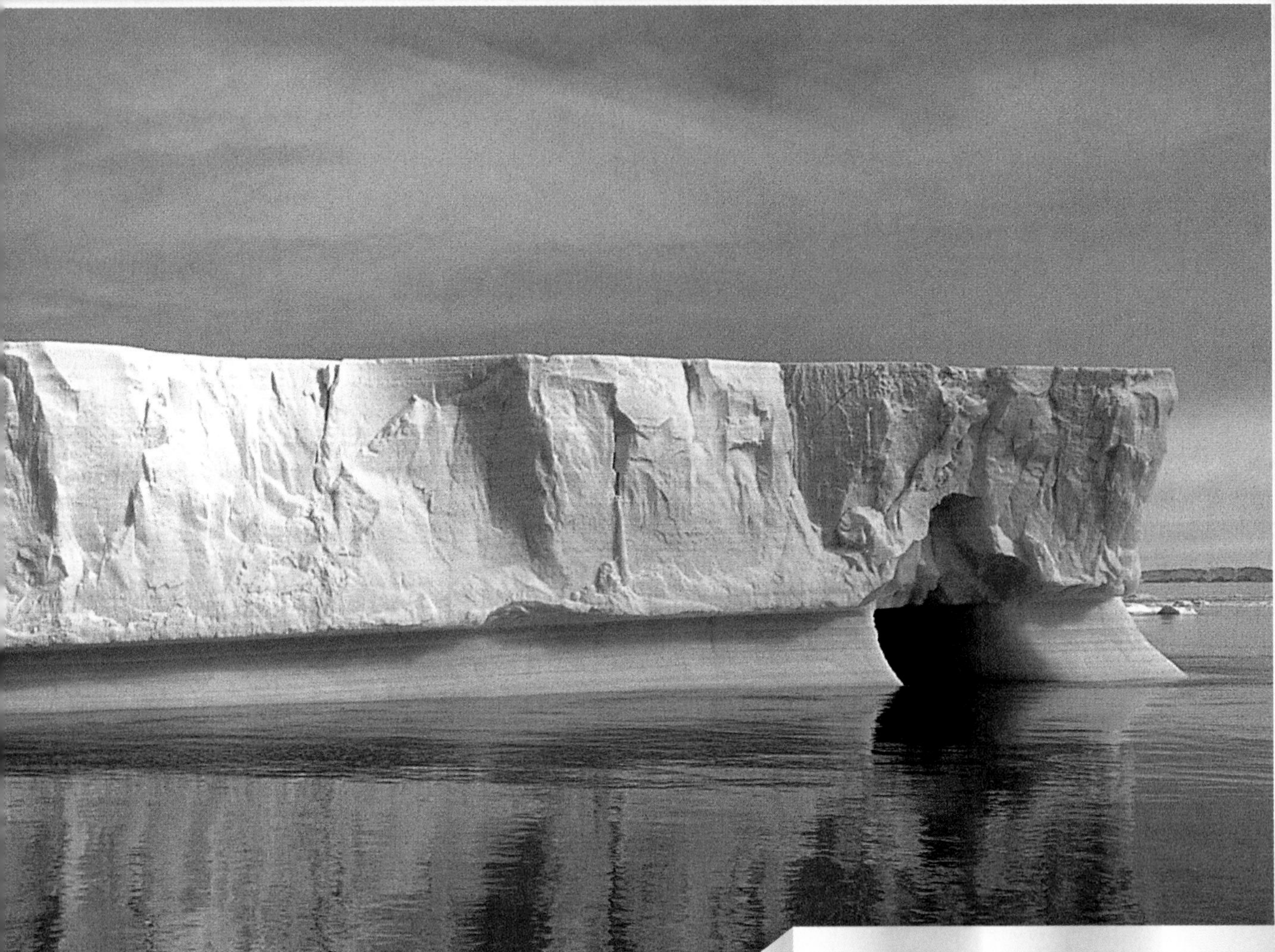

Ice forms a protective covering for ponds. Under the ice the water stays liquid, allowing plants and animals to survive the winter. Because ice floats, oceans have icebergs. They can mean trouble for ships, because most of an iceberg is underwater. Look at the ice cube in your lemonade. How much of it is under the surface?

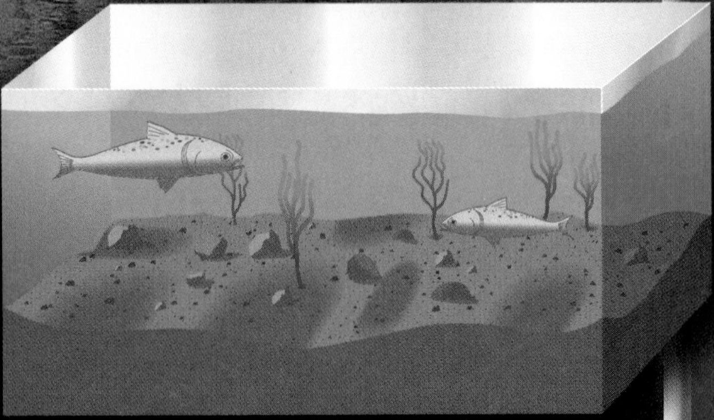

## DISCUSSION STARTER

1. How is the solid form of water different from most other solids?

2. Why don't ponds freeze from the bottom up in winter?

To learn more about survival in cold, visit *www.mhschool.com/science* and enter the keyword COLD.

*inter*NET
CONNECTION

## SCIENCE WORDS

atom p.216
compound p.214
electron p.217
element p.212
evaporation p.229
insulate p.204

mass p.196
molecule p.220
proton p.217
state of
matter p.228
weight p.197

## USING SCIENCE WORDS

**Number a paper from 1 to 10. Fill in 1 to 5 with words from the list above.**

1. Particles in atoms that have a positive charge are called __?__.

2. Particles made of more than one atom linked together are called __?__.

3. The force of gravity between a planet and an object is measured as __?__.

4. The process of going from a liquid to a gas is __?__.

5. Solid is one __?__.

6–10. **Pick five words from the list above that were not used in 1 to 5, and use each in a sentence.**

## UNDERSTANDING SCIENCE IDEAS

11. Describe two different ways water can turn from liquid to gas.

12. What is the difference between an object's mass and an object's weight?

13. What does an object's buoyancy depend on?

14. What are molecules made of?

15. Are all molecules compounds? Explain your answer.

## USING IDEAS AND SKILLS

16. Will a cube of aluminum metal will sink in any liquid? Explain your answer.

17. **READING SKILL: MAIN IDEA/ SUPPORTING DETAILS** What is the main difference between mass and weight? Support your answer with any facts or details necessary.

18. If you leave a pan of water on a warm stove for too long, you might find that the water is gone. Where would the water go? Why would the temperature of the stove burner matter?

19. **MAKE A MODEL** A boat is on a canal. It is going from a region of lower water to a region of higher water. The captain wants to know if throwing the cargo overboard will raise the water level. Explain how you could use a model to answer his question.

20. **THINKING LIKE A SCIENTIST** Which do you think would evaporate faster— pure water or salt water? Why? Describe an experiment that would test your idea.

## PROBLEMS and PUZZLES

**Chill Out** Why do people sprinkle salt on ice to melt it? Fill two glasses with ice, and add a thermo– meter to each. Pour a small amount of water in each. Wait for the thermometers to reach the melting point (0°C). Then add a table- spoon of salt to one glass, and shake gently. What hap- pens? How does this help you answer the first question?

# CHAPTER 6
# PUTTING
# IT ALL
# TOGETHER

What does it take to launch a space shuttle. It takes a lot of people knowing what to do, for one thing. It also takes a lot of fuel.

The fuel is burned. Burning is a kind of change. After the change happens, the fuel is not fuel anymore. What's left is a waste. Think of what happens when logs are burned in a campfire. What's left after the logs are burned?

In Chapter 6 you will look at many ways that matter can change.

In Chapter 6 you will read about many examples of cause and effect. One event

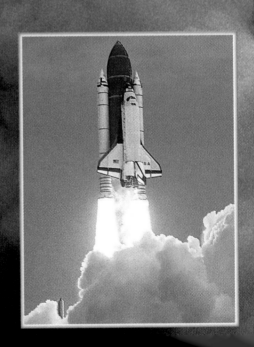

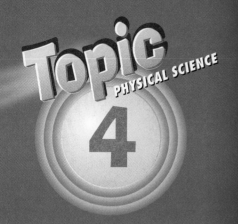

## WHY IT MATTERS

**Mixtures can be separated, but it isn't always easy to do.**

### SCIENCE WORDS

**mixture** two or more parts blended together yet keeping their own properties and not turning into a new substance

**solution** a mixture in which substances are completely blended so that the properties are the same throughout and the substances stay blended

**suspension** a mixture of substances that separate upon standing

**colloid** particles (or droplets) large enough to block out light spread throughout another substance

**emulsion** a liquid spread through another liquid

**aerosol** liquid drops or solid particles spread through a gas

**gel** a solid spread through a liquid

**foam** a gas spread through a liquid or solid

# Mixtures and Solutions

**W**hy do people call the Mississippi River the "muddy Mississippi"? What happens when the muddy Mississippi flows into the Gulf of Mexico?

The flowing water of the river meets up with standing water in the gulf. The river drops out much of what it is carrying. The "dropped out" materials build up in the Mississippi Delta.

The Mississippi is made of things mixed together. How many other examples can you give of things that are mixed together?

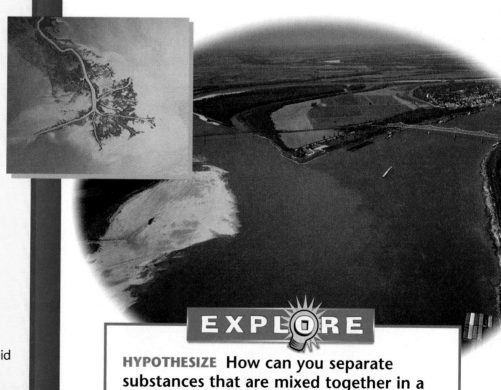

## EXPLORE

**HYPOTHESIZE** How can you separate substances that are mixed together in a way that they keep their properties? Write a hypothesis in your *Science Journal.* Design an experiment to test it.

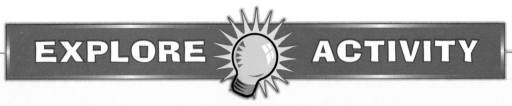

# Design Your Own Experiment

## HOW CAN YOU TAKE APART THINGS THAT ARE MIXED TOGETHER?

## PROCEDURES

**SAFETY** Wear goggles. Do not taste your sample.

1. **OBSERVE** Examine the sample your teacher gives you. It is made of different substances. One of the substances is table salt. What else does it seem to be made of? Record your observations in your *Science Journal*.

2. Design an experiment to separate the various ingredients in your sample.

3. Carry out your experiment.

### MATERIALS

- sample of substances mixed together
- hand lens
- toothpicks
- magnet
- paper (coffee) filters
- 2 cups or beakers
- water
- goggles
- *Science Journal*

## CONCLUDE AND APPLY

1. **INFER** How many parts or substances were mixed into your sample? How did you reach that conclusion?

2. **EXPLAIN** You knew one substance was salt. What properties of salt might help you separate it from the rest? Could you separate salt first? Why or why not?

3. **EXPLAIN** How did you separate out the substances? How did you use the properties of these substances to separate them?

### GOING FURTHER: Problem Solving

4. **EXPERIMENT** What if you were given white sand and sugar mixed together? How would you separate the two ingredients?

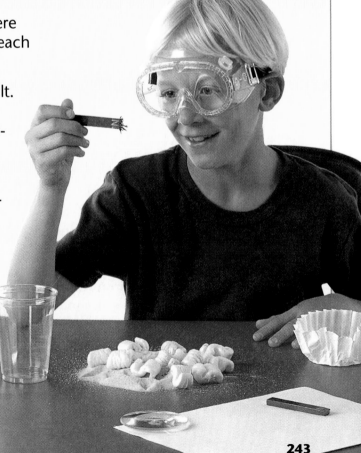

# How Can You Take Mixtures Apart?

The Explore Activity dealt with separating sand, salt, and iron filings that had been stirred together. The sand, salt, and iron filings were *physically* combined, so the material you started with was a **mixture**. The first photograph shows another such mixture—iron filings and yellow sulfur powder that have been stirred together.

The substance shown in the second photograph, iron disulfide, also contains both iron and sulfur. However, now the iron and sulfur are *chemically* combined and a new substance is formed.

How do mixtures and compounds differ? Compounds are produced by chemically combining substances. Yet mixtures are created by a physical combination of substances. In mixtures the parts simply blend together without forming new substances. Differences in chemical and physical properties of substances are used to separate mixtures and identify compounds.

A compound has different properties from the substances it contains. For example, iron disulfide is not magnetic, while pure iron is. In contrast, the parts of a mixture keep their original properties. Even though the iron has been mixed with sulfur in the first picture, it remains magnetic. You could pull a magnet through the mixture to remove the iron filings.

**Iron filings**   **Sulfur powder**

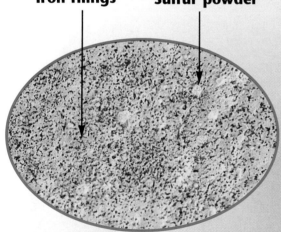

**Iron disulfide ("fool's gold")**

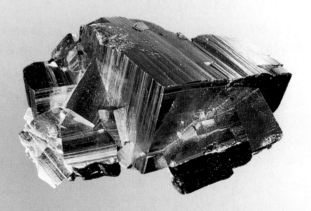

**1** When iron filings and yellow sulfur powder are stirred together to make a *mixture*, the substances keep their original properties. The iron remains magnetic. You could use a magnet to remove the iron filings.

**2** A magnet won't work here. This is *iron disulfide*, a mineral known as iron pyrite, or "fool's gold." Iron disulfide is a compound of iron and sulfur. When a *compound* forms, it has different properties from the substances it contains. Unlike iron, iron disulfide is not magnetic.

## Are All Mixtures Put Together the Same Way?

What if you stir one spoonful of sugar into a glass of water to make a sugar-water mixture? A friend could stir two spoonfuls of sugar into the same amount of water. You would both have the same kind of mixture. However, your friend's drink would have a much sweeter taste.

Like the sugar water, any type of mixture can contain varying amounts of the parts that make it up. Salt water could be barely salty or very salty. Granola cereal could have many or few raisins. Tea could be strong or weak, and so on.

On the other hand, compounds are *always* made up in the same way. For example, about two-fifths of the mass of *any* sample of table salt is sodium, and three-fifths is chlorine.

### Brain Power

Here are a number of household materials. Which are mixtures? Which are either elements or compounds? Write out why you placed each material in a particular group. Can you name additional household materials that are examples of elements, compounds, or mixtures?

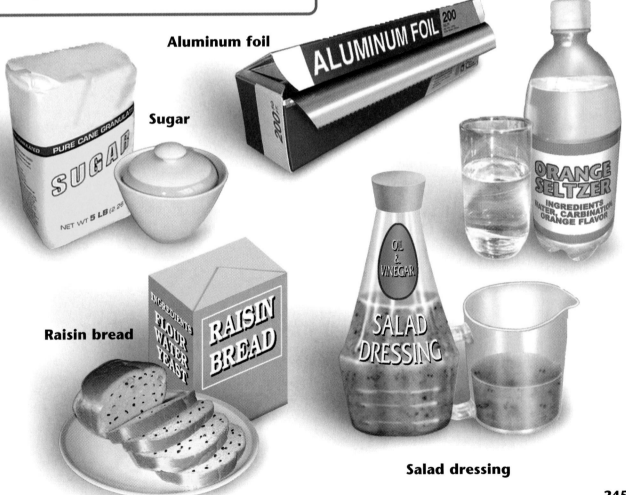

**Orange seltzer**

**Aluminum foil**

**Sugar**

**Raisin bread**

**Salad dressing**

245

# How Can Mixtures Be Separated?

We can separate the parts of mixtures using methods called physical separations. A physical separation gets the parts of a mixture away from one another without changing their identities.

Compounds can also be broken down into simpler parts, but not by physical separations. Chemical reactions are needed to separate compounds into their components.

The illustrations on these pages show examples of physical separation methods. Study them to see the steps and equipment needed.

The mud particles cannot pass through the pores in the paper, but the water molecules can. The mud collects in the paper, while the water drips through.

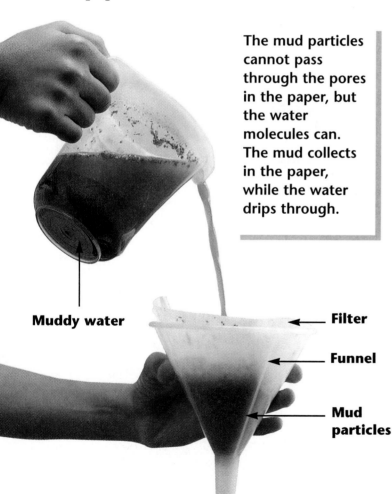

Muddy water

Filter

Funnel

Mud particles

Water

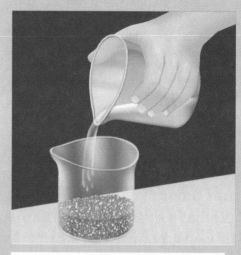

**1** To separate a mixture of sand and salt, pour in water and stir. The salt dissolves, but the sand doesn't.

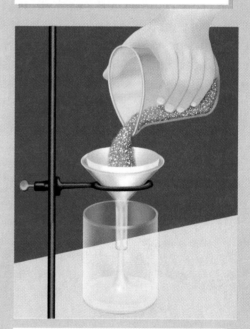

**2** Use a filter to separate the sand from the salt water.

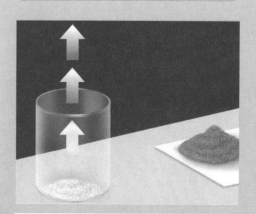

**3** Then let the water evaporate to get back the salt.

246

# SEPARATING SAND AND WOOD CHIPS

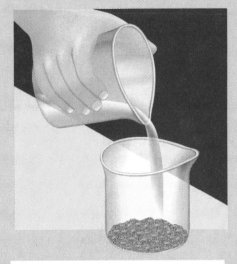

To separate sand and wood chips, first pour in water. Stir briefly.

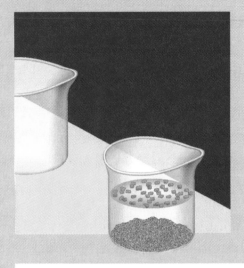

The wood chips float to the top, while the sand settles to the bottom. The wood chips can be skimmed off and dried. The water can be poured off, and the sand dried.

# SEPARATING ALCOHOL AND WATER

You could separate alcohol and water by heating them in this apparatus.

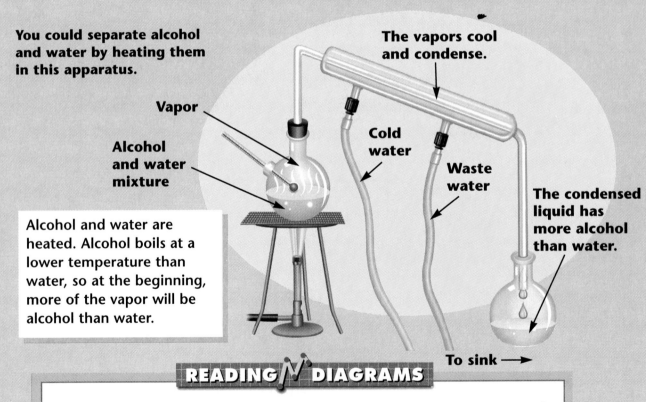

**Vapor**

**Alcohol and water mixture**

**The vapors cool and condense.**

**Cold water**

**Waste water**

**The condensed liquid has more alcohol than water.**

Alcohol and water are heated. Alcohol boils at a lower temperature than water, so at the beginning, more of the vapor will be alcohol than water.

**To sink →**

## READING *N* DIAGRAMS

1. **DISCUSS** What is one way to separate two substances in a mixture?
2. **DISCUSS** Could you separate sand and wood chips the same way you separate sand and salt? Explain.
3. **WRITE** Make a list of three ways to separate parts of a mixture.

247

# How Can Mixtures Be Classified?

Mixtures are not pure because they contain more than one element or compound. If the substances in a mixture are blended completely, the mixture looks the same everywhere, even under a microscope. We call such mixtures **solutions**.

On the other hand, the parts of a mixture may be only partly blended. The mixture may look "speckled," either to your eye or through a microscope. This type of mixture is said to be *heterogeneous* (het´ər ə jē'nē əs).

Solutions are usually transparent, or are evenly colored. They never settle into layers. Heterogeneous mixtures do settle into layers in a fluid.

Heterogeneous mixtures are either cloudy or opaque. The photographs on these pages show examples of solutions and heterogeneous mixtures.

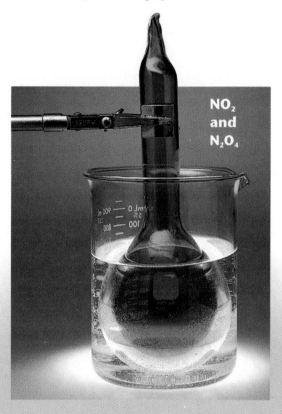

**Not all solutions are liquid. The tube contains a solution of two gaseous compounds, $NO_2$ and $N_2O_4$. $NO_2$ is red-brown, while $N_2O_4$ is colorless.**

$NO_2$ and $N_2O_4$

**These glasses contain salt water, tea, and a cherry drink. All of these liquids are solutions of different substances in water.**

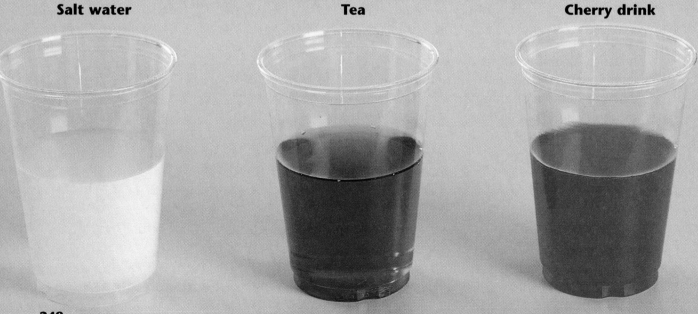

**Salt water**          **Tea**          **Cherry drink**

## Heterogeneous Mixtures Can Settle Into Layers

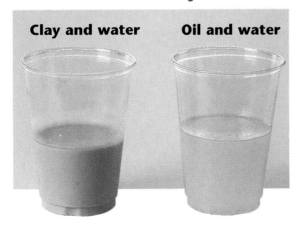

Clay and water    Oil and water

**1** Freshly shaken mixtures of clay and water, and oil and water

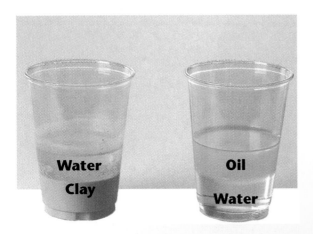

Water
Clay

Oil
Water

**2** The mixtures after they were allowed to stand for a length of time. Mixtures like clay and water, with suspended particles that are easily seen, are called suspensions.

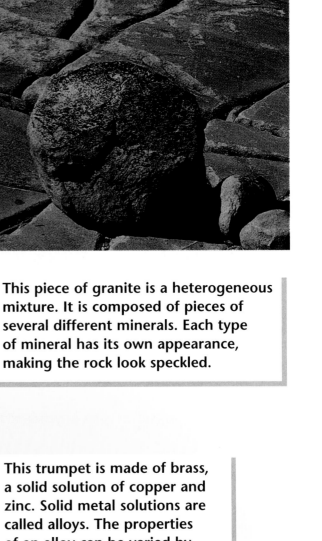

This piece of granite is a heterogeneous mixture. It is composed of pieces of several different minerals. Each type of mineral has its own appearance, making the rock look speckled.

This trumpet is made of brass, a solid solution of copper and zinc. Solid metal solutions are called alloys. The properties of an alloy can be varied by changing the amounts of the pure metals it contains.

## READING ∿ DIAGRAMS

1. **DISCUSS** What is the difference between a solution and a heterogeneous mixture?
2. **WRITE** Are solutions always liquids? Give two examples to justify your answer.

249

# Are There Other Kinds of Mixtures?

Milk is not transparent, so it cannot be a solution. Yet it does not settle out into layers, so it is not a heterogeneous mixture. Actually, milk is a special type of mixture called a **colloid**. Like milk, all colloids have properties between those of solutions and heterogeneous mixtures.

The first photograph shows what milk looks like under a micro-scope—droplets of fat spread throughout water. Other colloids are similar. They have particles of one material scattered through another. The particles are big enough to block or cloud light but not big enough to settle out.

There are many types of colloids. Milk is an example of an **emulsion**, a liquid (fat) spread through another liquid (water). The photographs show examples of other types of colloids.

Fat

Water

MILK

EARTH
LINK
SCIENCE

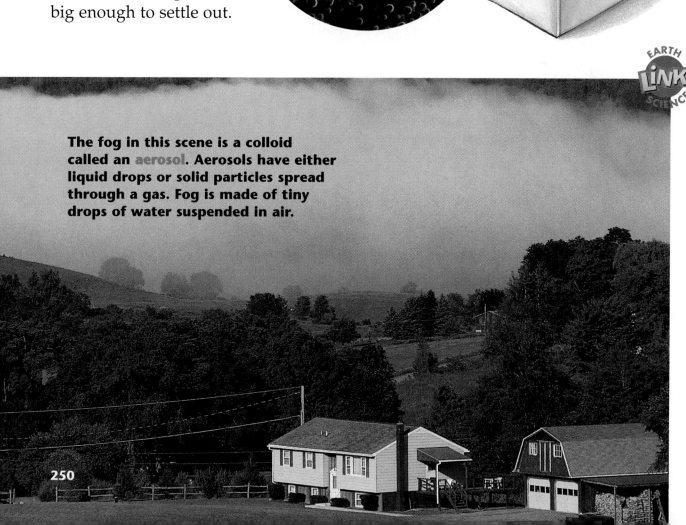

The fog in this scene is a colloid called an aerosol. Aerosols have either liquid drops or solid particles spread through a gas. Fog is made of tiny drops of water suspended in air.

Many food products are colloids. Gelatin dessert is a **gel**. A gel is a solid spread through a liquid. The solid in the gelatin is protein. The liquid in the gelatin is water. Whipped cream is a **foam**. A foam is a gas spread through a liquid. The gas in the whipped cream is air. The liquid in the whipped cream is water and fat. Marshmallows are a solid foam—a gas spread through a solid. The gas in the marshmallows is air. The solid in the marshmallows is a sweetened gelatin.

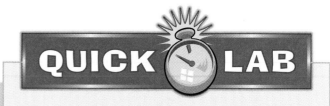

# QUICK LAB

## Kitchen Colloids

**HYPOTHESIZE** What happens to cream when you whip it? Write a hypothesis in your *Science Journal*. Test your ideas.

### PROCEDURE

**MATERIALS**
- whipping cream
- 2 bowls
- wire whisk
- ice
- *Science Journal*

**1.** Pour some whipping cream into a bowl. Set this bowl in a bed of ice in another bowl. Let the cream and bowl chill.

**2. EXPERIMENT** Use the whisk to whip the cream until it becomes a fluffy texture.

**3. OBSERVE** Let the cream warm and continue beating it. Observe how it changes. Record your observations in your *Science Journal*.

### CONCLUDE AND APPLY

**1. DEFINE** What kind of colloid is the whipped cream from step 2?

**2. INTERPRET DATA** What is it made of?

**3. INFER** In step 3 you made a colloid called a solid emulsion. What is this colloid commonly known as? What do you think it is made of?

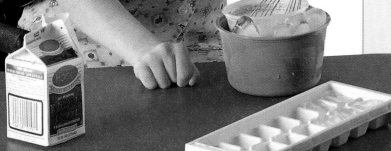

# How Else Can You Separate Important Mixtures?

The photograph below shows a tower that uses a process called *distillation*. It uses this process to separate important chemicals out of crude oil.

First, the crude oil is heated until it becomes a gas. Then, the vapors are sent to the tower. There they rise and cool. As they cool they condense to form liquids.

The substances with large molecules and high boiling points quickly cool into a liquid. The substances with small molecules and low boiling points rise higher in the tower before condensing. The condensed liquids are drawn off as shown.

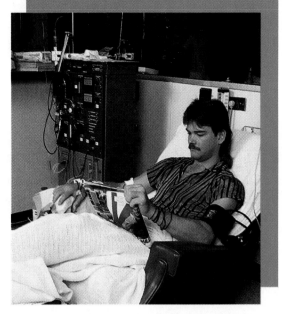

**This patient's kidneys can no longer clean waste products from his blood. Doctors pass his blood through a *dialysis* (dīal'ə sis) machine. The blood flows past a material that allows the waste products to leave but not the blood cells. After being filtered the blood is returned to the patient's body.**

## How Crude Oil Is Turned into Many Useful Products

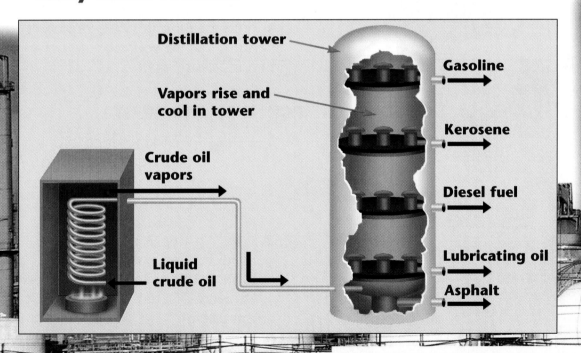

Distillation tower

Vapors rise and cool in tower

Crude oil vapors

Liquid crude oil

Gasoline

Kerosene

Diesel fuel

Lubricating oil

Asphalt

Crude oil is heated until it becomes a gas. The vapors are sent to the tower. There they rise, cool, and condense to form liquids. Substances with smaller molecules and lower boiling points rise higher in the tower before condensing.

Many things you use every day—from the air you breathe to the milk you drink to the steel in your bicycle—are mixtures. Some mixtures need to have just the right amounts of their ingredients each time. For example, you need a certain amount of oxygen in the air you breathe. The amount of iron, carbon, and other metals in steel determines its properties, such as hardness and resistance to rusting. For example, the steel in your bicycle is specially made to resist rusting. The steel expansion joints in the photograph on page 237 are made to expand on hot days and contract on cold days. As you go through your day, think of all the mixtures you use and why they are important to you.

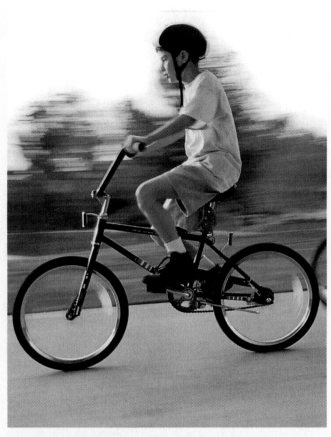

## REVIEW

1. How do the properties of sugar and water alone compare to the properties of a sugar-water solution?

2. How are mixtures different from compounds?

3. Air is a mixture of oxygen and nitrogen gas. What type of mixture is air? Why?

4. **INFER** Oil paints are made of colored particles suspended in oil. Are oil paints solutions, heterogeneous mixtures, or colloids? How do you know?

5. **CRITICAL THINKING** *Apply* Describe the steps you could follow to separate a mixture of sawdust and salt.

**WHY IT MATTERS** THINK ABOUT IT
Many of the mixtures you are familiar with are mixtures of water and another substance. What are some of these mixtures?

**WHY IT MATTERS** WRITE ABOUT IT
List the mixtures you think should always be blended the same way—with just the right amount of water and other substances. Explain why. List the mixtures you think are still okay if they are blended slightly differently each time. Explain why.

**READING SKILL**
What are some examples of cause and effect on pages 246–247? Write about them. Identify the cause and the effect.

# Got Milk?
# Got Butter?

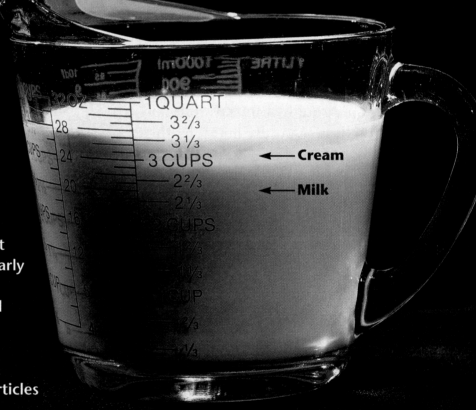

Cream ←

Milk ←

The success of mammals on Earth is helped by what they feed their newborns: milk produced by their mothers. Humans also raise other large mammals to produce milk for them.

A mammal's milk is seven-eighths water, but the other eighth has nearly everything needed for good health! Some food value comes from the lactose, or milk sugar, dissolved in it.

Part of milk is tiny particles suspended as colloids.

Milk has a lot of fat globs. Because they're lighter than water, the globs rise to the top of a container. Gravity pulls the heavier liquid down. The fat globs merge to become cream. Milk with little or no fat is skim milk.

Many people prefer skim or low-fat milk. The fat in milk contributes to weight problems, heart disease, and possibly other diseases.

Milk you buy has vitamins D and A added to make it more nutritious. It's been pasteurized—heated to kill disease-causing bacteria. The heating also makes some milk proteins inactive and slows down the spoiling.

Milk is homogenized by putting it through a fine screen to break fat

globs into tiny specks. They're so small that the movement of the other molecules in milk keeps them from rising. For that reason cream doesn't form at the top of homogenized milk.

By constantly moving cream in a closed container, you cause the fat globs to merge. Drain off the thin, watery stuff and you've got . . . butter!

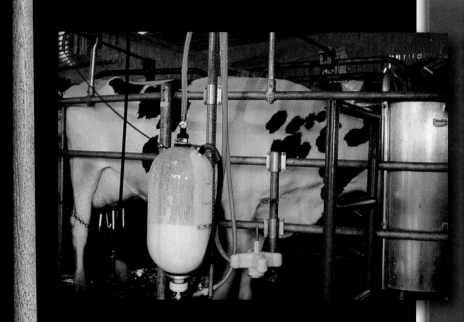

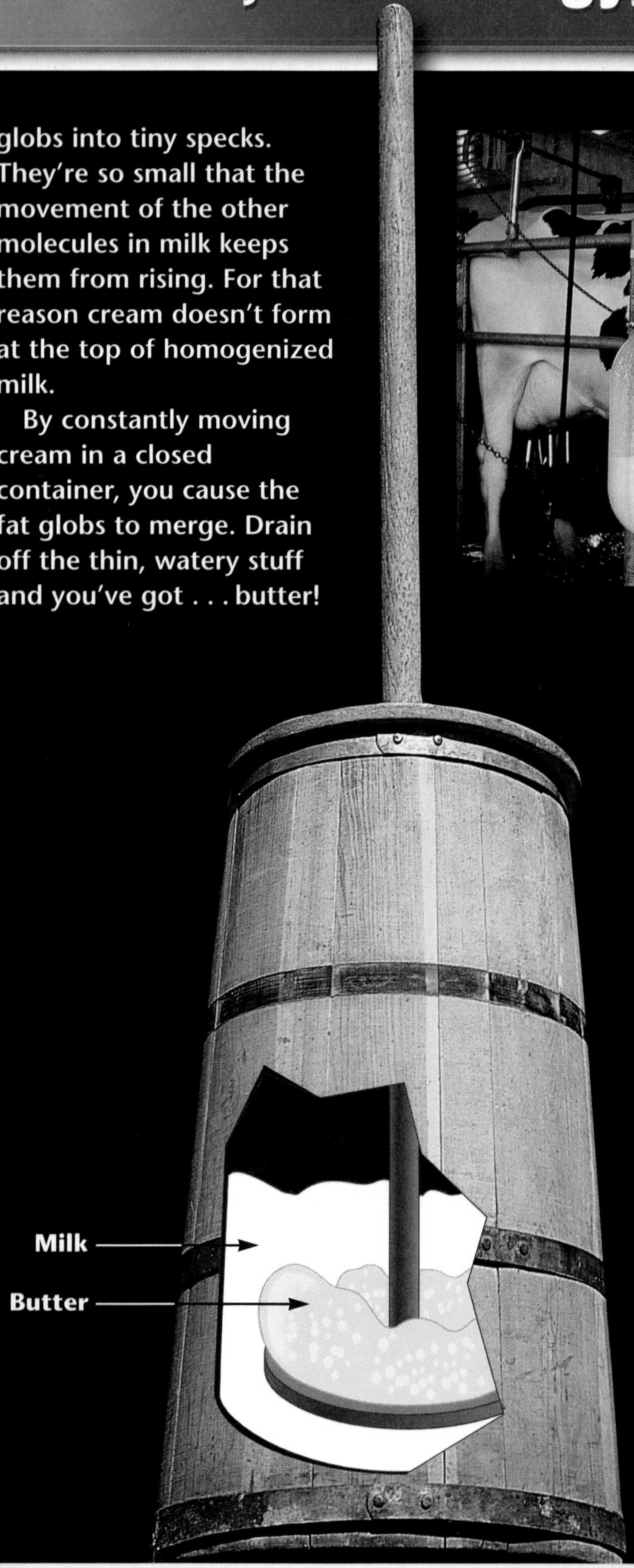

## DISCUSSION STARTER

1. What other foods are vitamins added to? Why do you think that is done?

2. Fat is used to make cells' outer membranes. How does this explain why mammals' milk is high in fat?

Milk

Butter

To learn more about milk products, visit *www.mhschool.com/science* and enter the keyword DAIRY.

*inter*NET
CONNECTION

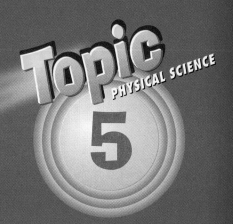

# Topic
## PHYSICAL SCIENCE
# 5

## WHY IT MATTERS

**Changes in matter can be useful to you.**

### SCIENCE WORDS

**physical change** a change in size, shape, or state, without forming a new substance

**chemical change** a change in matter that produces a new substance with different properties from the original

**chemical reaction** a chemical change of original substances into one or more new substances

**reactant** one of the original substances before a chemical reaction takes place

**product** one of the new substances produced when a chemical reaction takes place

# Chemical Changes

**W**hat does it take for the space shuttle to blast off and travel into space? One thing is fuel. What happens to the fuel?

When any fuel is used, it is changed. What are the signs that a fuel, like logs, is changing when it is burned? What is left of the fuel after it is burned?

How can you tell changes occur? Milk sours. Bread dough rises when baking powder is mixed into it. A runny egg hardens when it is cooked. What are other changes going on around you?

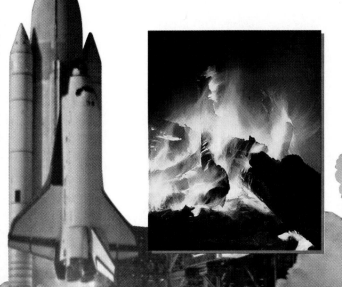

## EXPLORE

**HYPOTHESIZE How can you tell if a substance changes into something else? What signs would you look for? Write a hypothesis in your *Science Journal*. Test your ideas.**

256

# EXPLORE ⚡ ACTIVITY

# Investigate How You Can Recognize a Change

Experiment to find signs that a substance has changed.

## PROCEDURES

 **SAFETY** Wear goggles.

1. Make this grid on wax paper with a marking pen. Copy it into your *Science Journal*. Using a spoon, put a pea-sized amount of cornstarch in each of the three boxes in the first row.

2. **OBSERVE** Use a dropper to add five drops of water to the cornstarch in the first column. Stir with a tooth-pick. Record your observations in your *Science Journal*.

3. **EXPERIMENT** Using a different dropper, add five drops of vinegar to the cornstarch in the second column. Stir with a new toothpick. Record your observations.

4. **OBSERVE** Use a third dropper to add five drops of iodine solution to the cornstarch in the third column. Record your observations. CAUTION: Iodine is poisonous and can stain.

5. **EXPERIMENT** Repeat steps 1–4 for baking powder, baking soda, and salt.

## CONCLUDE AND APPLY

1. **INFER** In which boxes of the grid do you think substances changed into new substances? Explain your answers.

2. **INFER** Your teacher will give you samples of two unknown powders. Use what you have learned to identify these powders. Report on your findings.

### GOING FURTHER: Problem Solving

3. **EXPERIMENT** What if you were given a mixture of two of the powders? How might you use your grid to identify them?

## MATERIALS

- baking soda
- baking powder
- cornstarch
- salt
- iodine solution
- vinegar
- water
- wax paper
- permanent marker
- 4 toothpicks
- 3 droppers
- 4 plastic spoons
- 7 small cups
- goggles
- *Science Journal*

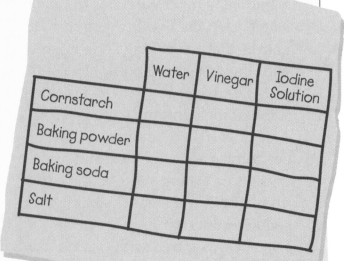

|  | Water | Vinegar | Iodine Solution |
|---|---|---|---|
| Cornstarch |  |  |  |
| Baking powder |  |  |  |
| Baking soda |  |  |  |
| Salt |  |  |  |

# How Can You Recognize a Change?

Different kinds of changes are going on all the time. In a **physical change**, matter changes in size, shape, or state without also changing identity. Physical changes include separating matter into different parts or mixing matter with new parts as long as no new substances are made.

The photograph below shows why a change of state is a physical change. The student is holding a small glass dish in the steam that is boiling out of a teakettle. When the steam—which is gaseous water—hits the dish, it cools and turns back into liquid water. When boiling water turns into steam, its state simply changes, not its chemical identity. We know that boiling is a physical change.

The photo above shows another example of a physical change. Here a student is mixing baking soda with water, as in the Explore Activity. He notices that the baking soda mixes with the water so thoroughly that it seems to disappear. However, when some of the liquid mixture is left in a shallow dish overnight, the water evaporates away. Left behind are crystals of baking soda, as the close-up view shows. Since the baking soda did not change in identity when it was mixed with water, the mixing was a physical change.

**1** When baking soda mixes with water, the baking soda seems to disappear. Yet when the water evaporates, baking soda is left behind. This is a physical change.

Baking soda

Baking soda and water mixture

**2** A change of state is a physical change. When the steam—gaseous water—hits the dish, it cools and turns back into liquid water.

Steam condenses to form liquid water

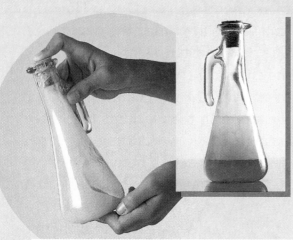

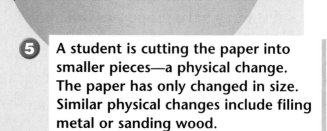

**5** A student is cutting the paper into smaller pieces—a physical change. The paper has only changed in size. Similar physical changes include filing metal or sanding wood.

**3** A student is shaking oil and vinegar to get them to mix thoroughly for her salad dressing. However, if the mixture stands too long, the oil and vinegar layer out. Since shaking oil and vinegar only temporarily mixes them, they have undergone a physical change.

**6** The craftsman is working the metal into a new shape—a physical change. The metal takes on a new form but is the same substance as before.

**4** A pharmacist is dissolving a few crystals of iodine in some alcohol mixed with water to make *tincture of iodine*. Tincture of iodine is used as an antiseptic to help protect cuts from germs. If the alcohol and water evaporate, iodine crystals remain. Making a tincture of iodine involves physical changes.

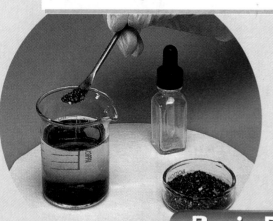

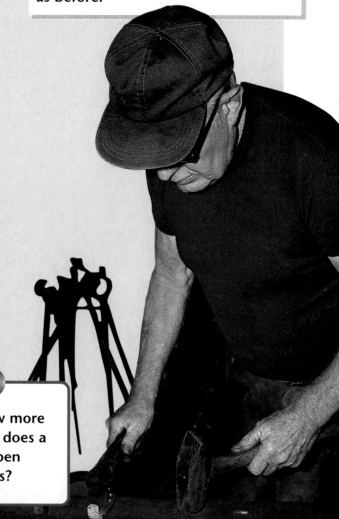

## Brain Power

The photographs on this page show more examples of physical changes. How does a change of size, shape, or state happen without making any new substances?

## How Else Can You Recognize a Change?

The Explore Activity on page 257 showed several **chemical changes**. Chemical changes occur when atoms link together in new ways. The changes in the linking patterns of the atoms create new substances. The new substances have properties different from the original substances from which they were formed.

The reaction between vinegar and baking soda is an example of a chemical change. When these two materials are mixed, gas bubbles form. A change in the linking pattern of the atoms in the vinegar and baking soda caused a new substance—carbon dioxide to form. Other new products formed, too. However, you could not see them because they remained in the liquid.

Chemical changes are often referred to as **chemical reactions**. The original substances are called the **reactants**. The new substances produced by the chemical change are called the **products**. During chemical reactions, the atoms in the reactants rearrange to form products with different properties. In the reaction between baking soda and vinegar, the baking soda and the vinegar are the reactants. The carbon dioxide, water, and a chemical called sodium acetate are the products.

### What Happens when Baking Soda and Vinegar Mix?

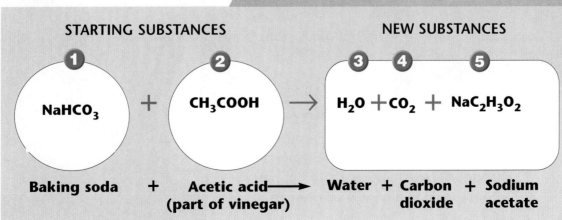

| STARTING SUBSTANCES | | NEW SUBSTANCES | | |
|---|---|---|---|---|
| ① | ② | ③ | ④ | ⑤ |
| $NaHCO_3$ | $+$ $CH_3COOH$ → | $H_2O$ | $+ CO_2 +$ | $NaC_2H_3O_2$ |
| Baking soda | + Acetic acid → (part of vinegar) | Water | + Carbon dioxide | + Sodium acetate |

## Which Are Easier to Reverse—Chemical or Physical Changes?

You'd probably agree that turning carbon dioxide gas, water, and sodium acetate back into baking soda and vinegar would be difficult. Simply stirring the three ingredients together wouldn't give you baking soda and vinegar. In general, chemical changes are difficult to reverse. Imagine trying to "unburn" toast or "unspoil" milk!

On the other hand, physical changes can sometimes be easily reversed. Yet this is not always true. For example, melting an ice cube can easily be reversed by cooling it until it freezes again. Stirring sugar into water can be reversed by letting the water evaporate. However, it would not be so easy to put pieces of paper back together after cutting them from a single page. Still, if a change seems very easy to reverse, it is more likely to be a physical change.

The photograph of a burning candle shows many changes are happening. Wax melts, runs down the side, and turns solid again. However, some of the wax turns into carbon dioxide gas and steam when it combines with oxygen in the air. This change releases enough heat to make the candle flame you see.

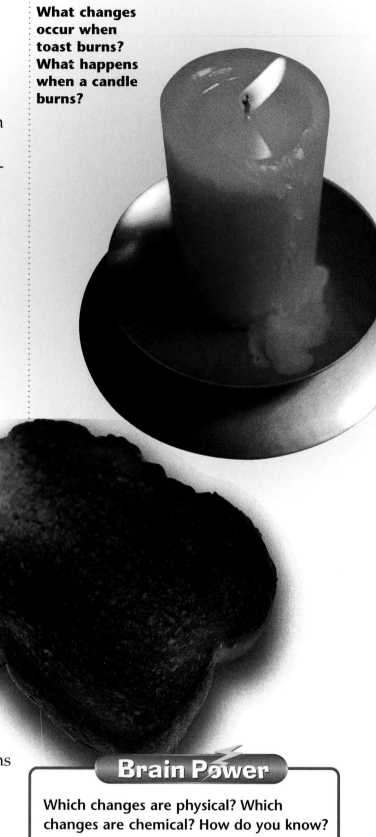

What changes occur when toast burns? What happens when a candle burns?

**Brain Power**

Which changes are physical? Which changes are chemical? How do you know?

# What Are the Signs of a Chemical Change?

Chemical reactions often show one or more signs that a chemical change has occurred. These signs include a color change, formation of a gas, and heat changes. The changes on these pages show some of these signs.

**①** When the reddish blueberry juice is mixed with a solution of baking soda, it turns to a greenish color. The green color results from a chemical change in the molecules of the blueberry juice. This reaction shows how a change of color indicates that a chemical change has occurred.

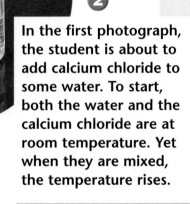

**②** In the first photograph, the student is about to add calcium chloride to some water. To start, both the water and the calcium chloride are at room temperature. Yet when they are mixed, the temperature rises.

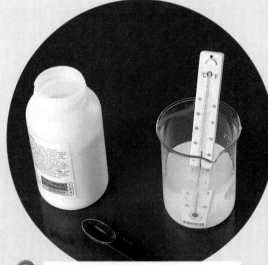

**③** The heat given off by mixing water and calcium chloride is a sign of a chemical change.

**④** Here lemon juice is being added to a solution containing dissolved baking soda. The bubbles you see are a sign of a chemical change. They are actually carbon dioxide gas formed by the reaction between acid in the lemon juice and the sodium bicarbonate in the baking soda.

# SIGNS OF CHEMICAL CHANGE

**5** Have you ever put hydrogen peroxide on a cut to kill germs? The bubbles tell you that a chemical change is occurring. The hydrogen peroxide is made of hydrogen and oxygen. When it comes into contact with bodily fluids, it reacts and gives off pure oxygen gas. The oxygen gas, in turn, kills germs in the cut and guards against infection.

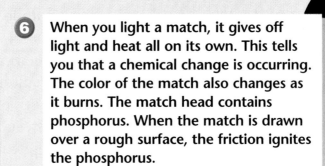

**6** When you light a match, it gives off light and heat all on its own. This tells you that a chemical change is occurring. The color of the match also changes as it burns. The match head contains phosphorus. When the match is drawn over a rough surface, the friction ignites the phosphorus.

**7** Eggs contain a lot of protein. Protein molecules are very long and threadlike. Normally protein molecules are folded into very specific shapes. However, when heated they unravel into random shapes. Egg protein begins to unravel at about 57°C. This chemical change causes it to turn white.

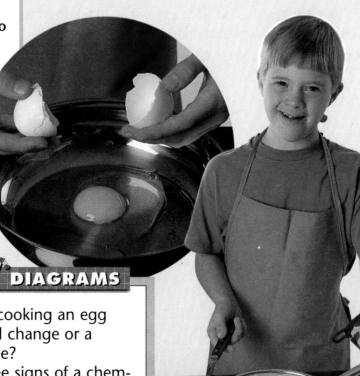

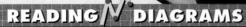

## READING DIAGRAMS

1. **DISCUSS** Does cooking an egg cause a physical change or a chemical change?
2. **WRITE** List three signs of a chemical change, and give an example of each.

# What Are Some Familiar Chemical Changes?

As a cake bakes, several chemical changes occur. Heat turns the baking soda (sodium bicarbonate) in the cake dough into sodium carbonate, steam, and carbon dioxide gas. The sodium carbonate is a harmless solid that remains in the cake. The steam helps make the cake moist. The bubbles of carbon dioxide help the dough expand and make the cake light and fluffy. The heat of the oven also triggers other chemical reactions in the cake batter. These strengthen the cake and keep it from collapsing after it is baked.

The red powder covering this wheelbarrow is iron oxide. Iron oxide is commonly known as rust. Rust forms when iron atoms in steel react with oxygen from the air. The reaction is very complex and needs moisture to occur. Steel objects are most likely to rust if they get wet and are not dried right away.

Rocket engines use chemical reactions that produce lots of heat. This space shuttle's main engines are powered by liquid hydrogen and liquid oxygen. When the two react together, they make water vapor and the energy the shuttle needs. The shuttle is also equipped with launch boosters that use a solid fuel. When the solid fuel burns, aluminum powder is converted to aluminum oxide.

This silver object is partly covered with a tarnish of silver sulfide. The silver sulfide forms when silver in the object reacts with sulfur or hydrogen sulfide in foods or the air. Several foods contain sulfur, particularly eggs. Mineral springs can produce small amounts of hydrogen sulfide, which smells like rotten eggs. You can even tarnish silver by wrapping it with a rubber band. Sulfur added to strengthen the rubber causes the tarnish to form. Polishes can be used to remove the tarnish and restore the silver's shiny appearance.

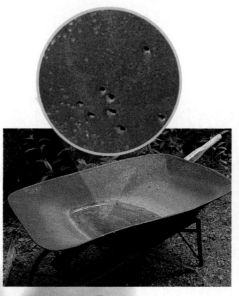

**Rust**

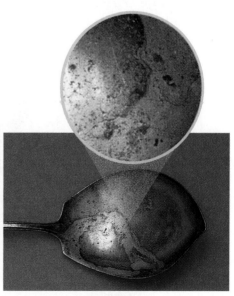

**Tarnish**

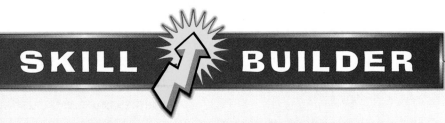

# SKILL BUILDER

# Skill: Experimenting

## PREVENTING RUST

You've learned steel forms rust when exposed to oxygen and moisture. Rusting can ruin metal objects. Can you find a way to stop or slow rusting? In this activity you will experiment to try to find the answer. In order to experiment, you need to do the following things. Form a hypothesis. Design a control. Carry out your experiment. Analyze and communicate your results.

## PROCEDURES  SAFETY Wear goggles.

1. **HYPOTHESIZE** The photograph shows a method for making a steel nail rust. Think of a way to protect a steel nail from rusting under such conditions. In your *Science Journal*, write down an explanation of why you think your method will work.

2. **EXPERIMENT** To test your method of rust protection, you need a control nail kept under normal conditions. Each experimental nail will have just one condition (variable) change. For example, suppose you wanted to make a nail rust. You might leave one nail in a clean, empty jar (the control). You might put another in water. You might put a third in lemon juice. The amount of rusting that occurs is called the *dependent variable.* Write out how you will set up the experimental and control nails for your experiment.

3. **EXPERIMENT** Carry out your experiment, and record your observations.

## CONCLUDE AND APPLY

1. **INFER** Write out a description of how well your hypothesis agreed with your results. Be sure to compare the experimental nail to the control nail.

2. **COMMUNICATE** Why did you need a control in this experiment?

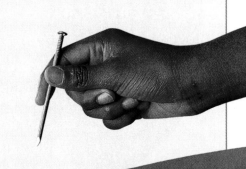

# How Do We Fight Rusting?

The car in the photo has been badly rusted. Since rusting continues to eat its way through iron-containing metals, it can weaken the metal. In some cases repairs are possible. In others the metal object is destroyed and must be discarded.

Scientists and engineers have worked very hard to find ways to prevent rusting. Painting or oiling steel surfaces can slow rusting, but more complex methods also exist.

Over the years a car's paint may get chipped. Rusting can start in these spots. Sometimes rust spots can be sanded and repainted to repair them. Other times the rusting may continue despite painting. This can be especially true if rusting starts from the inside out.

In galvanizing baths, steel objects are given a thin coating of zinc. In moist air zinc forms a self-protecting coating of zinc oxide. Zinc does not "rust" like steel. A coating of zinc on steel objects protects the steel underneath from rusting. Perhaps you have seen galvanized buckets or rain gutters.

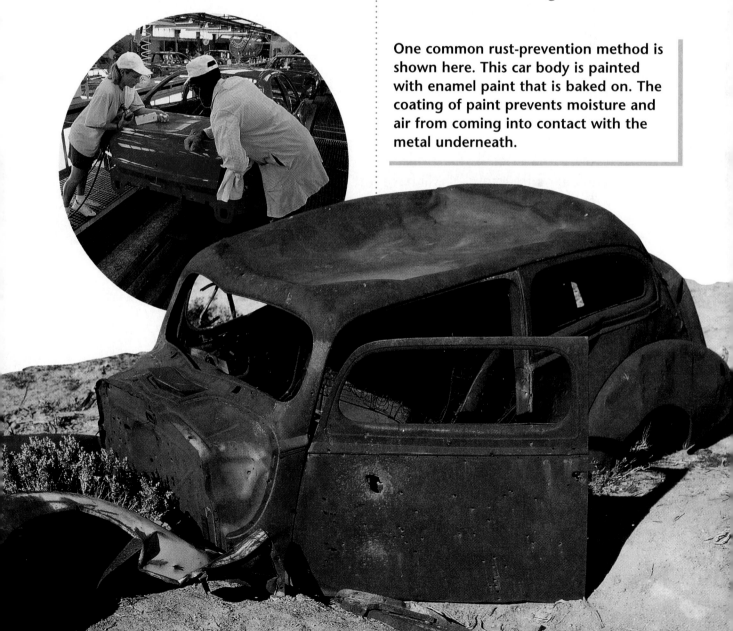

One common rust-prevention method is shown here. This car body is painted with enamel paint that is baked on. The coating of paint prevents moisture and air from coming into contact with the metal underneath.

# How Can Cookware Be Protected from Rusting?

Cookware in the kitchen is often exposed to moisture. If it were made of ordinary steel, it would rust fairly rapidly. Yet scientists have discovered a way to make a special type of steel that is rust resistant. Cooking pots are often made of a special alloy called stainless steel. In this type of steel, chromium and nickel are mixed with the iron, carbon, manganese, and silicon normally found in steel. The resulting alloy is very rust resistant.

## REVIEW

1. Is the rusting of a nail a chemical or a physical change? Why?

2. Is the melting of ice a chemical or a physical change? Why?

3. When a match burns, what evidence is there that a chemical change occurs?

4. 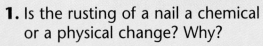 **EXPERIMENT** Suppose you wanted to find out if a cake bakes better with baking soda or baking powder. How do you think it would turn out? Design an experiment to test your ideas. Why might you want to use a *control*?

5. **CRITICAL THINKING** *Apply* What if a friend was just given a new bicycle? What advice could you give him or her about protecting the bike from rusting?

**WHY IT MATTERS** THINK ABOUT IT
In what other ways are chemical changes important in your everyday life?

**WHY IT MATTERS** WRITE ABOUT IT
Write a paragraph about an average school day. Describe all the chemical changes that you can think of that affect your day.

# SCIENCE MAGAZINE

# Checking Acids and Bases

**W**hat do you think of when you hear the word *acid?* Did you know that lots of things you eat are mild acids? It's true. Oranges and lemons have citric acid!

Many substances you use are *bases*. Bleach, soap, and ammonia are bases that break down grease and wash it away!

How can you tell an acid from a base? Not by tasting them, that could be very dangerous. You can scientifically check it out with litmus paper. Touch a substance with this special paper, and it tells if it's an acid, a base, or neutral—neither acid nor base. How? The paper turns red in an acid solution and blue in a base solution!

Juice from red cabbage or hydrangeas is a natural acid and base

indicator, or marker! Add acid to red cabbage juice, and the juice turns maroon. If there's a lot of acid, the juice turns pink. A neutral substance doesn't change the color. A base turns it green. A very basic substance turns it yellow.

If you mix an acid and a base, you get a salt and water! Lye (base) and hydrochloric acid mixed together produce table salt (sodium chloride) and water!

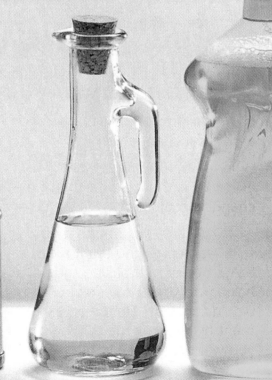

**Red cabbage juice indicates which things are acid and which are base.**

# A Closer Look

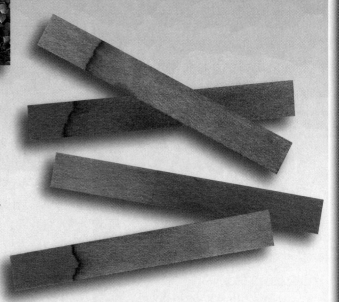

Hydrangeas turn blue in acid soil and pink in base soil.

A very strong acid that dissolves metal also helps you digest food! Your stomach produces the acid during digestion. If it makes too much, you get "heartburn" or "acid indigestion." You may take an antacid, or base, to make you feel better!

## DISCUSSION STARTER

1. Is water an acid or a base? How could you find out?

2. How might acid and base indicators be used to save lives?

To learn more about acids and bases, visit *www.mhschool.com/science* and enter the keyword PROPERTY.

**inter**NET
**CONNECTION**

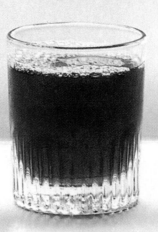

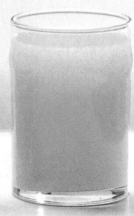

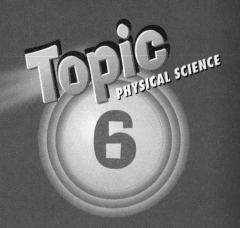

# Topic
## PHYSICAL SCIENCE
# 6

## WHY IT MATTERS

You depend on many kinds of energy from many different sources.

## SCIENCE WORDS

**kinetic energy** the energy of a moving object

**potential energy** energy stored in an object or material

**conduction** movement of energy from a hot object that comes into contact with a cooler object; the material remains in place

**convection** movement of energy by the flow of matter from place to place

**radiation** movement of energy in the form of waves that can travel through empty space

**wet cell battery** a battery containing liquid solution that produces the electric current

**dry cell battery** a battery that uses "dry chemicals" to produce an electric current

# Matter and Energy

If you were scuba diving off the coast of New England and saw this animal, what would you do? Swim the other way! It is an electric ray. It produces enough electricity to power a small motor. How does this feature help the animal survive?

Luckily you don't need an electric ray to run appliances for you. Batteries let you carry electricity with you wherever you go. A chemical reaction takes place inside a battery that produces electricity. Rays don't run out of electricity, however. Do batteries run out?

## EXPLORE

**HYPOTHESIZE** Is it better to buy heavy-duty batteries or less expensive ones? Which last longer? Which ones are really the least expensive to use? Write a hypothesis in your *Science Journal.* Test your ideas.

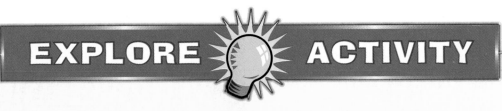

# EXPLORE ACTIVITY

# Investigate How Well Batteries Provide Energy

Test different batteries to see which is most economical.

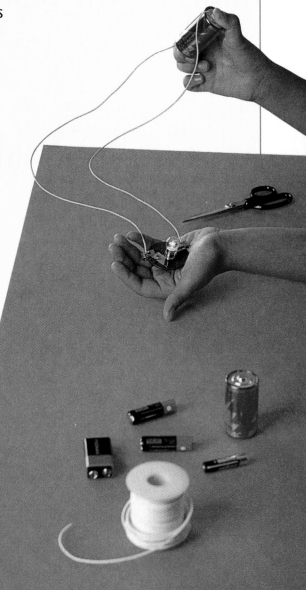

## MATERIALS

for each circuit to be tested:
- battery
- flashlight light bulb
- 2 wires
- *Science Journal*

## PROCEDURES

1. Connect one end of a wire to the light bulb. Connect the other end of the wire to the battery. Do the same for the other wire. Record in your *Science Journal* what time the light bulb went on. Record the type, size, and brand of battery you used.

2. **OBSERVE** Examine the light bulb every 15 minutes to see if it is still lit.

3. **COMMUNICATE** Record the time the light bulb goes off.

4. Repeat the experiment using another type or brand of battery.

## CONCLUDE AND APPLY

1. **USE NUMBERS** Divide the time each battery lasted by the cost of that type of battery.

2. **COMMUNICATE** Share your results with your class- mates. Were all the batteries you used made of the same chemicals?

3. **COMPARE** Make a graph of the class's results. Which batteries lasted the longest? Which batteries cost the least per hour of use? Were some brands longer lasting? Were some brands cheaper to use than others?

4. **INFER** Are the cheapest batteries the best buy? Are the longest lasting batteries the best buy?

## GOING FURTHER: Problem Solving

5. **APPLY** When might you choose the longest lasting batteries? The least expensive batteries? The batteries that cost the least per hour of use? Explain.

271

# How Well Do Batteries Provide Energy?

As the Explore Activity showed, a battery can produce heat and light when it is connected to a light bulb. Actually, the battery causes electricity to flow through the light bulb. The light bulb changes electrical energy into heat and light.

Chemical reactions are the source of the electrical energy a battery can provide. The reactions produce electrons, and each electron carries energy. When a closed circuit is available, the electrons will flow through the circuit from the battery's negative pole to its positive pole.

When electrons in a circuit pass through a light bulb, they give up some of their energy to a very thin wire in the bulb called the *filament* (fil'ə mənt). The filament gets hot enough to glow and give off light, as in the diagram.

After a time the chemical reactions that power a battery may use up the chemicals. This causes the battery to go dead. Sometimes the chemicals may even begin leaking out of old or dead

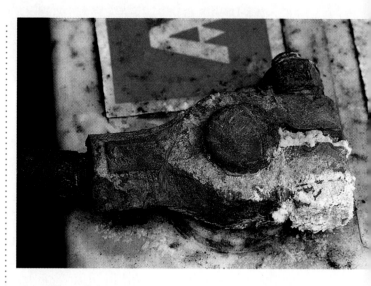

**Leaking battery**

batteries. Leaking batteries can be dangerous. Do not touch them. Find out from your community recycling office what you should do to get rid of them properly.

## READING DIAGRAMS

**DISCUSS** Describe the path electrons take in a closed circuit.

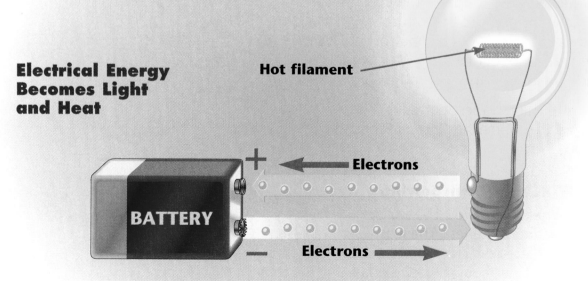

**Electrical Energy Becomes Light and Heat**

Hot filament

+

← Electrons

BATTERY

−

Electrons →

# What Are Two Main Kinds of Energy?

Look at the toy truck being driven. Its motion gives it a type of energy called **kinetic energy** (ki net′ik en′ər jē). Any object that is moving has kinetic energy.

When the toy truck is stopped, it appears to have no kinetic energy. Yet it has energy stored in its batteries waiting to be used. We refer to stored energy as **potential energy** (pə ten′shəl en′ər jē).

Forces between atoms create the potential energy in a battery. When a battery is used, chemical changes inside convert, or change, the potential energy into electrical energy. Electrical energy moves through a circuit and makes electrons move.

The electrical energy in a circuit can be converted into motion with motors like the one shown in the photograph. An electric motor changes electrical energy into useful kinetic energy, such as the kinetic energy of the toy truck below.

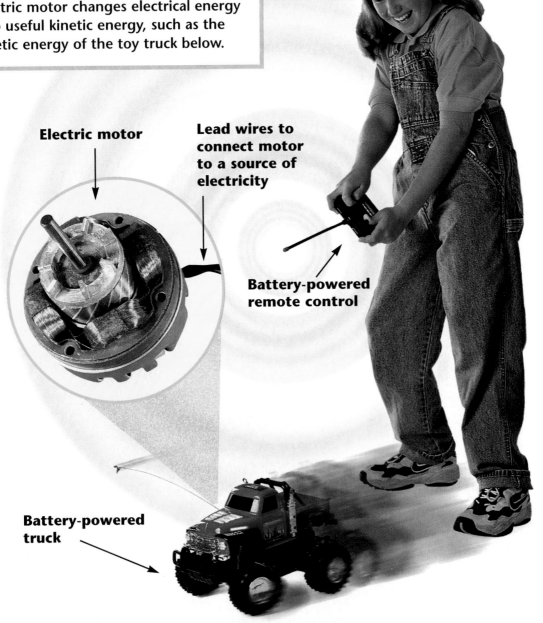

**Electric motor**

**Lead wires to connect motor to a source of electricity**

**Battery-powered remote control**

**Battery-powered truck**

273

# What Is Energy?

You've seen how chemical changes in a battery can produce electrical energy. You've also seen how that electrical energy can produce light, heat, or motion. All of these things are forms of energy. Yet what exactly is energy? We know energy has many forms. Yet defining energy can be a little difficult.

A good place to start in talking about energy is to look at what energy can do. Energy is a measure of how much work something can produce. To scientists work means moving matter around with forces. The energy something has is how much motion it can give to other matter.

Energy is not a type of matter. Matter is something you can often touch or see—solids, liquids, gases. Energy may be thought of as the ability to move matter around.

Battery-powered toys show us how electricity must have energy. The electricity can move them around. Light also has energy, as you have learned. Yet how could light move matter around? Think about what lasers can do.

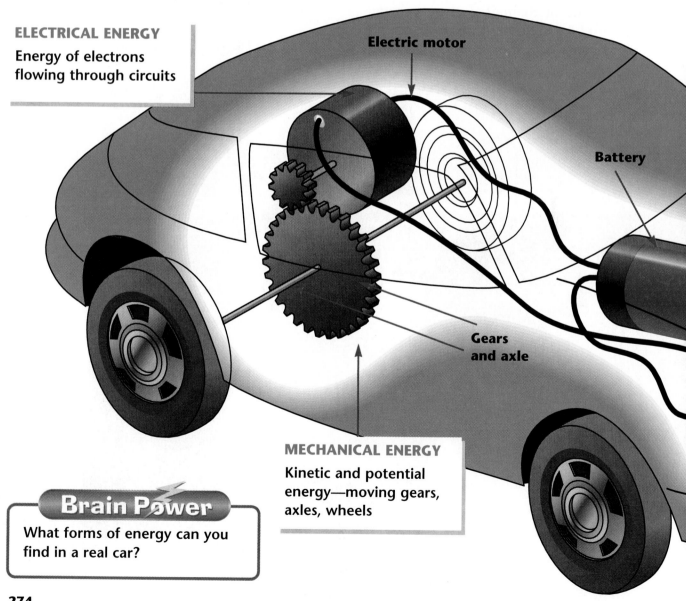

**ELECTRICAL ENERGY**

Energy of electrons flowing through circuits

**Electric motor**

**Battery**

**Gears and axle**

**MECHANICAL ENERGY**

Kinetic and potential energy—moving gears, axles, wheels

**Brain Power**

What forms of energy can you find in a real car?

# What Forms Does Energy Take?

Many forms of energy can be classified as kinetic or potential. Yet we also describe energy by its source or by how it is carried. For example, the energy produced by a chemical reaction is called chemical energy. Some typical forms of energy are shown in the table.

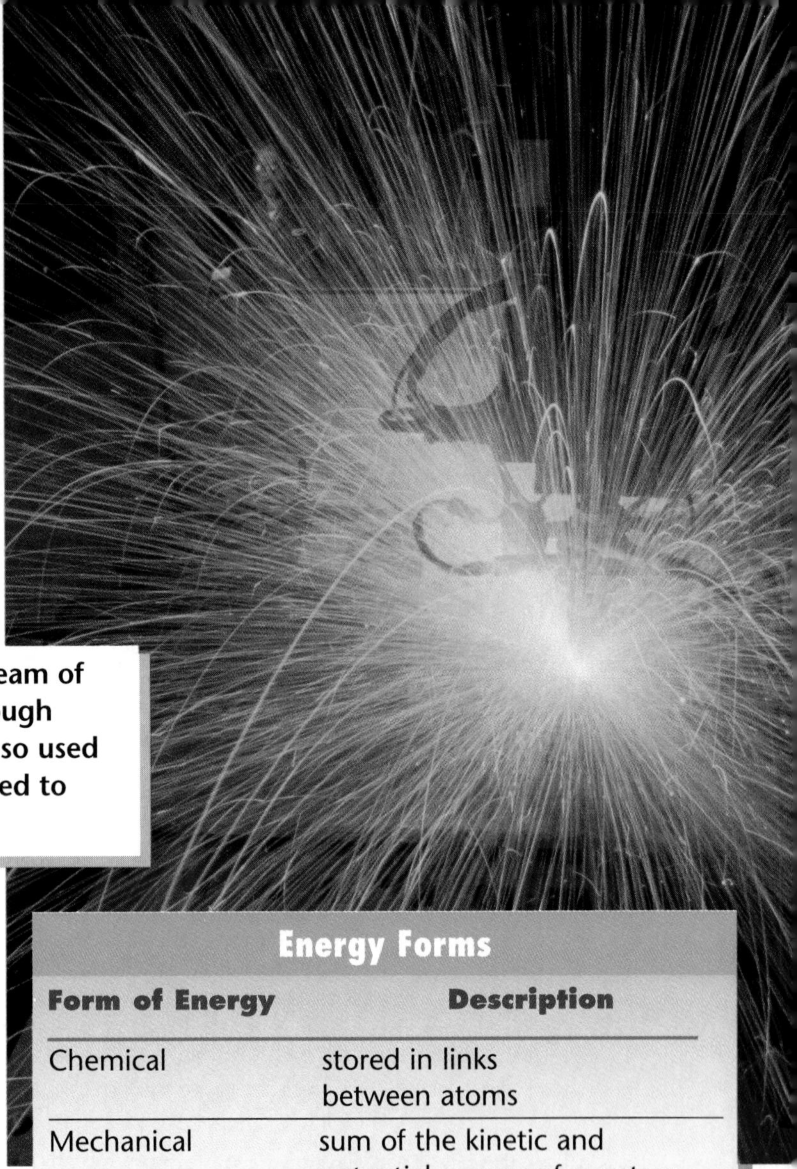

A laser—an intense, narrow beam of light—can cut like a knife through concrete or steel. Lasers are also used in surgery and can even be used to repair wounds.

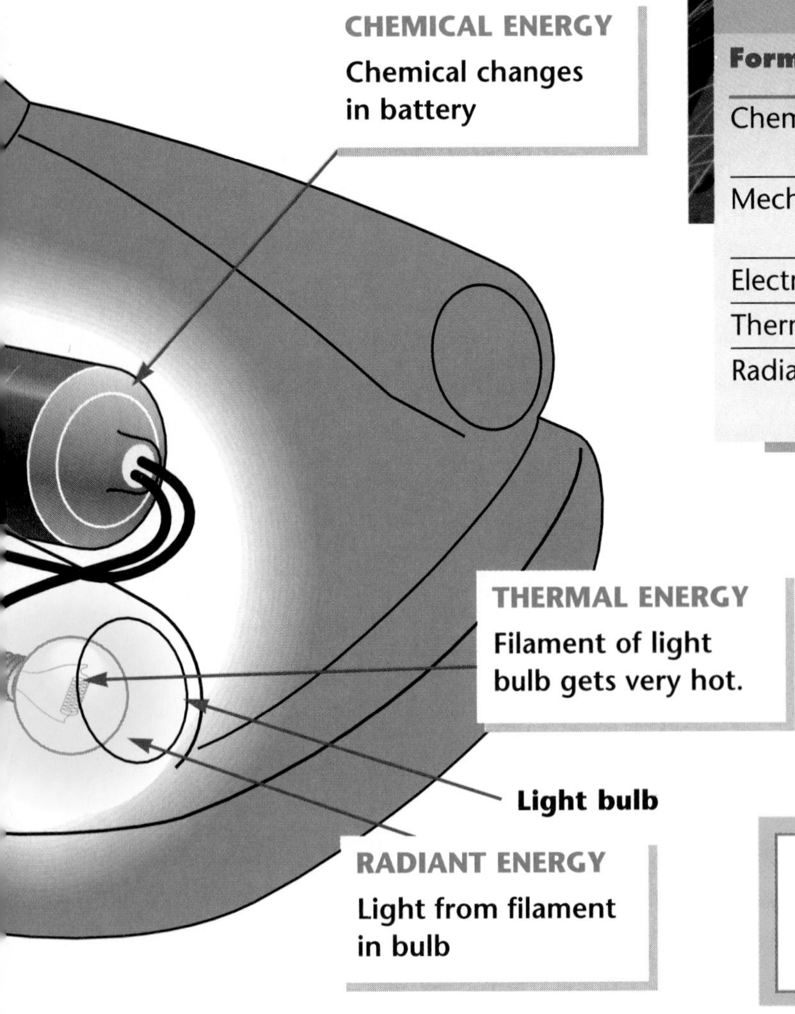

**CHEMICAL ENERGY**
Chemical changes in battery

## Energy Forms

| Form of Energy | Description |
| --- | --- |
| Chemical | stored in links between atoms |
| Mechanical | sum of the kinetic and potential energy of a system |
| Electrical | carried in circuits |
| Thermal | motion of atoms and molecules |
| Radiant | the energy of light |

**THERMAL ENERGY**
Filament of light bulb gets very hot.

**Light bulb**

**RADIANT ENERGY**
Light from filament in bulb

## READING IN DIAGRAMS

**WRITE** List the energy changes that take place in the toy car.

## How Can Electricity Be Measured?

When a battery is connected to a circuit, electrons are freed from some of the atoms in the battery's chemicals. Energy moves through the circuit, causing electrons to move.

Electricity can be measured in a number of ways. The circuit with two batteries has twice as many electrons flowing as the circuit with one battery. The bulb is also brighter when two batteries are present. This shows how the brightness of the bulb can measure the amount of electricity.

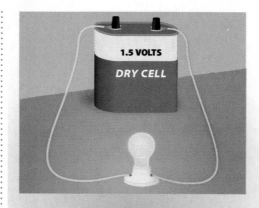

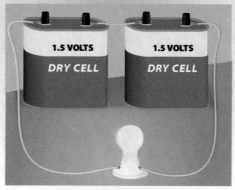

In some cases the amount of electrical energy in a circuit may not be great enough to light certain bulbs. For example, a flashlight battery could not light up a 60-watt light bulb from a lamp. Electrical energy can also be measured by the size of the bulb it can light.

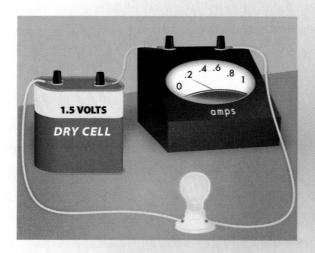

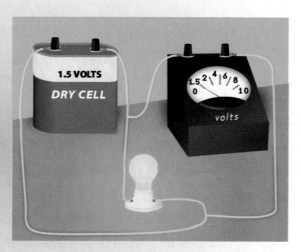

We can also use different kinds of meters to measure electricity. The *ammeter*, above, measures *amps*. It tells us how many electrons flow each second. The *voltmeter* measures *volts*.

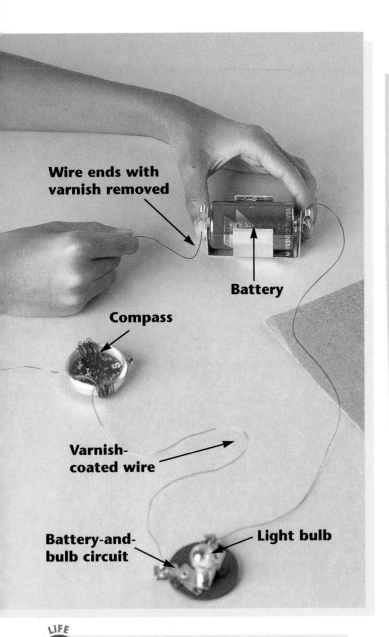

Wire ends with varnish removed

Battery

Compass

Varnish-coated wire

Battery-and-bulb circuit

Light bulb

Animals such as sharks, turtles, honeybees, homing pigeons, some migratory birds, tuna, and salmon are all able to detect Earth's magnetic field.

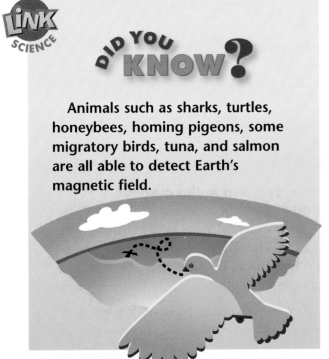

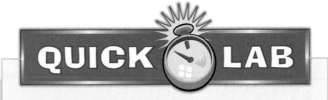

# QUICK LAB

## Measuring Electricity

**HYPOTHESIZE** Can electricity affect a magnet? Can a magnet be used to measure electricity? Write a hypothesis in your *Science Journal*. Test your ideas.

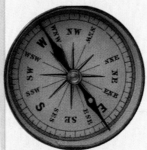

### MATERIALS

- compass
- 5 m of fine varnish-coated wire
- sandpaper
- 1.5-V battery and bulb circuit
- *Science Journal*

### PROCEDURES

1. Wrap fine varnished wire around a compass. Use sandpaper to remove the coating from the ends of the wire.

2. Turn the compass until the needle is lined up with the coils of wire.

3. Keeping the compass this way, connect the ends of the wire to a circuit of a battery and small light bulb. See the photograph.

4. **OBSERVE** What happens to the compass needle as you connect and disconnect the circuit? Record your observations in your *Science Journal*.

### CONCLUDE AND APPLY

1. **EXPLAIN** How did you know when electricity was flowing in the circuit?

2. **OBSERVE** When electricity was flowing, what did the compass needle do?

3. **INFER** How do you think the needle would move if you used a less powerful battery?

277

# What Are Sources of Heat?

When you cup your hands around a mug of hot chocolate, you feel warmth. This happens because heat flows from the warmer mug into your skin. Heat is the energy that flows out of objects because they are hotter than their surroundings. The photographs show several sources of heat.

Temperature is the quantity we use to measure how hot something is. Temperature really tells us how fast a material's molecules are moving. If one object has a higher temperature than another, heat will flow from the warmer object to the cooler one.

**The Sun is the most important source of heat for life on our planet. Nuclear reactions at the core of the Sun heat it to very high temperatures.**

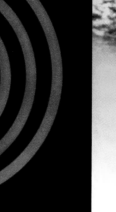

**The heating coils in this oven are warmed by an electric current. Electrons give up their energy to the coils. The space inside the oven is warmed by heat flowing from the hot coils.**

## How Does Heat Move?

Heat always flows from hotter materials to cooler materials, never the other way. In fact, the direction of heat flow between two objects tells us which one is hotter.

When heat flows, it can move through matter in two different ways—**conduction** (kən duk'shən) and **convection** (kən vek'shən). In conduction the heat passes through a material while the material itself stays in place. In convection hot parts of a material rise while cooler parts sink. In convection there is a flow of material and heat.

Heat can also flow by **radiation**, or electromagnetic waves. All objects we see around us give off radiation. Radiation carries energy and can travel through space. Radiation may warm objects. For example, radiation from the Sun warms Earth.

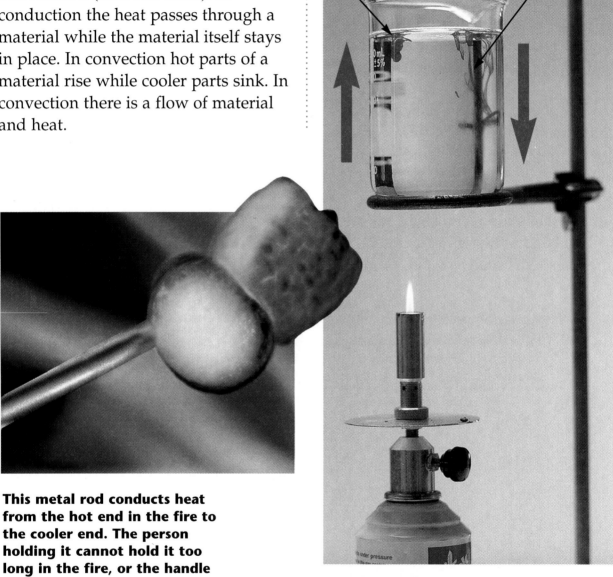

**Drop of dye**　　　**Drop of dye**

This metal rod conducts heat from the hot end in the fire to the cooler end. The person holding it cannot hold it too long in the fire, or the handle will get uncomfortably hot.

Drops of dye were placed at the spots indicated by the arrows. Convection in the water has moved the dye up on the heated side and down on the unheated side.

**279**

# What Materials Conduct Heat Well?

The photograph shows very hot tea in a foam cup. A metal spoon has been sitting in the tea for some time. The outside of the cup is slightly warm. Yet the spoon's handle is almost too hot to hold. Why has more heat flowed into the handle of the spoon than into the walls of the cup?

As you learned in Topic 1, some materials are better at conducting heat than others. The metal spoon is a good conductor of heat. However, the foam cup is a poor conductor of heat. As a result, heat flows quickly from the hot bowl of the spoon to its handle. Yet heat flows very slowly from the tea into the foam.

As the hot spoon shows, metals are the best conductors of heat. Other kinds of solids, such as wood or glass,

usually conduct much less heat than metals. Materials like wood and glass can be used to insulate heat.

Water, alcohol, and similar liquids also conduct heat more poorly than metals. Gases are the poorest thermal conductors of all. Look at the table to see how well common materials conduct heat.

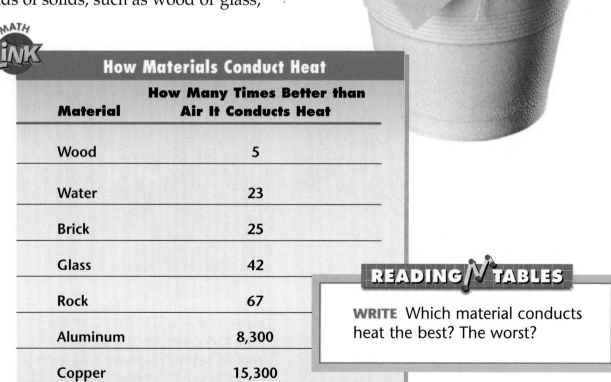

**MATH LINK**

## How Materials Conduct Heat

| Material | How Many Times Better than Air It Conducts Heat |
|----------|------------------------------------------------|
| Wood | 5 |
| Water | 23 |
| Brick | 25 |
| Glass | 42 |
| Rock | 67 |
| Aluminum | 8,300 |
| Copper | 15,300 |

**READING TABLES**

**WRITE** Which material conducts heat the best? The worst?

## Why Are Some Materials Better Conductors than Others?

As shown in the diagram, heat is carried through a material by the motion of molecules. At the hot end, the molecules move about rapidly. They collide with their neighbors, spreading the motion through the material. The spreading of the motion warms up other parts of the material.

In gases the molecules are widely separated. They cannot transfer heat between one another as easily as in liquids or solids. This explains why air is such a poor conductor of heat.

Why do metals conduct heat so well? Metals have electrons that are unusually free to move. When a metal is heated at one end, the free-moving electrons there can pick up kinetic energy. The electrons quickly carry the energy to other parts of the metal. That's what makes them warm up fast.

The free-moving electrons in metals also make them good conductors of electricity. In contrast, materials like glass or wood do not have free-moving electrons. So these materials are poorer conductors of heat and electricity.

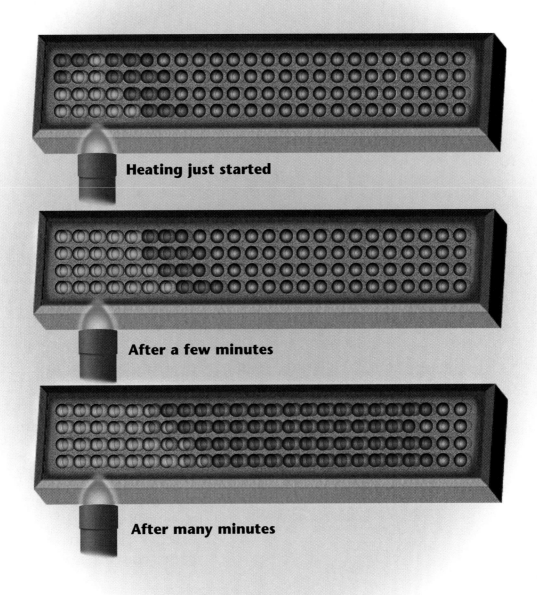

**Heating just started**

**After a few minutes**

**After many minutes**

# How Do Wet Cell Batteries Work?

All cars have a battery to provide electricity. The electricity is needed to operate things like the radio, head-lights, and tail lights. As the diagram shows, a car battery contains a sulfuric acid solution. For this reason it is called a **wet cell battery**. The chemical changes that produce electricity in a wet cell can be run backward. A running car can also supply electrons to its battery to recharge the battery for future use.

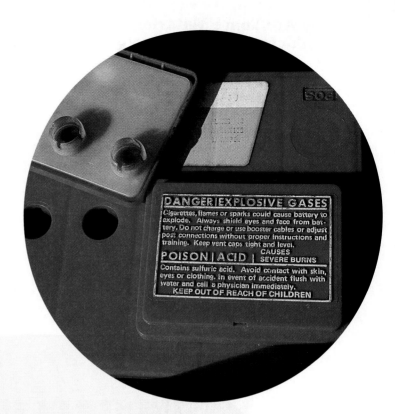

**Many batteries contain dangerous chemicals.**

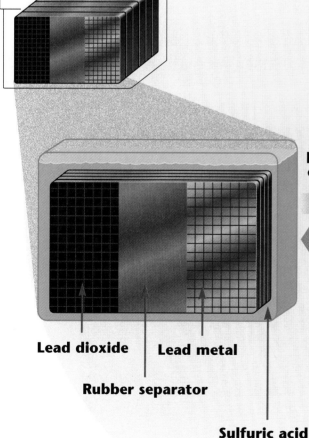

**+** **−**

**Lead dioxide**

**Lead metal**

**Rubber separator**

**Sulfuric acid**

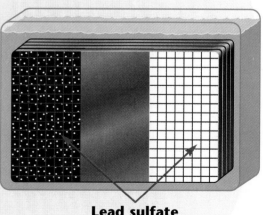

**Battery producing electricity**

**Battery being charged**

**Lead sulfate**

---

**READING IN DIAGRAMS**

1. **WRITE** Why is a car battery called a wet cell battery?
2. **DISCUSS** How can a wet cell car battery be recharged?

# How Do Dry Cell Batteries Work?

Flashlight batteries use chemical changes different from wet cell batteries. In fact, flashlight batteries do not have a liquid inside, so they are called **dry cell batteries**. Look at the diagram to see how dry cell batteries produce electricity.

Energy comes in many forms. The air in your home is warmed by heat convection. However, it may be that without electricity, your heat won't go on. There is energy stored in batteries and energy stored in the food you eat. The Sun gives us light and heat as well. You depend on various forms of energy to live, move, and have a comfortable life.

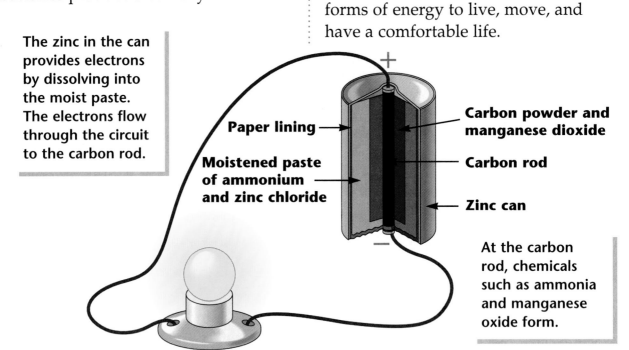

The zinc in the can provides electrons by dissolving into the moist paste. The electrons flow through the circuit to the carbon rod.

Paper lining

Moistened paste of ammonium and zinc chloride

Carbon powder and manganese dioxide

Carbon rod

Zinc can

At the carbon rod, chemicals such as ammonia and manganese oxide form.

## REVIEW

1. Describe how a battery makes a light bulb glow. Mention the different forms energy takes.

2. Why is energy not a form of matter?

3. How does heat energy get from place to place?

4. **INFER** Insulating windows have two layers of glass with air sealed in between. Why is the layer of air important?

5. **CRITICAL THINKING** *Analyze* Two flashlights have the same kind of bulb. Yet one glows more dimly than the other. Can you suggest why?

**WHY IT MATTERS** THINK ABOUT IT
What kinds of energy do you use every day?

**WHY IT MATTERS** WRITE ABOUT IT
Write a paragraph about the kinds of energy you use on a weekend. Explain why these kinds of energy are important to you.

# Cameras and Chemicals

Photography may seem like magic. You point a camera, click a shutter, and capture exactly how someone or something looks!

The science behind the magic is fairly simple. The film in a camera is sensitive to light. When exposed to light through a camera lens, the film reacts to the light. The film records what's dark and what's light.

Later the film is treated with chemicals. With black-and-white film, what's been exposed to lots of light turns dark, and what's been exposed to less light stays light. This film image is called a negative.

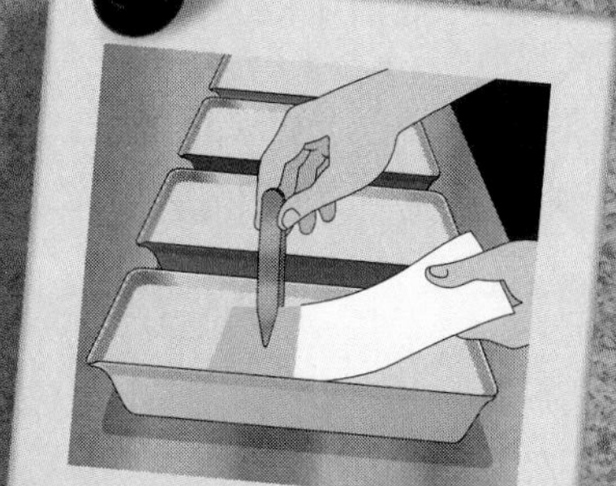

Next, light is shone through the negative onto light-sensitive paper. Then, the paper is treated with the same chemicals used to develop the film. This time the process is reversed, and a positive image appears on the paper. The click of the camera has frozen a moment in time.

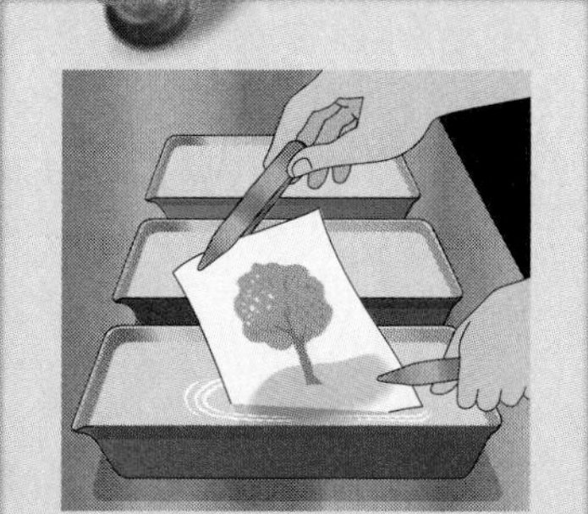

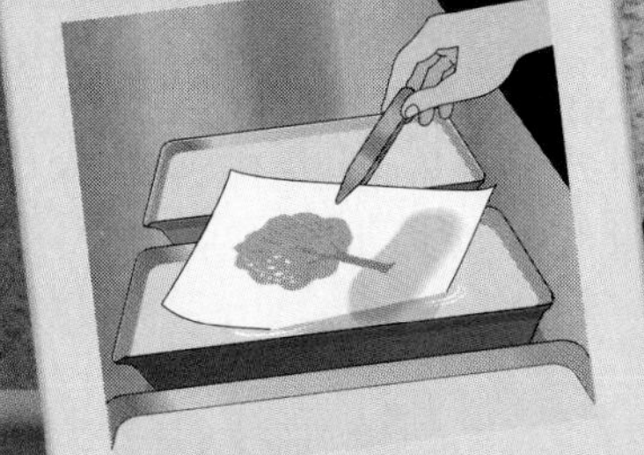

## DISCUSSION STARTER

1. What's a negative?

2. Describe how a photograph is developed.

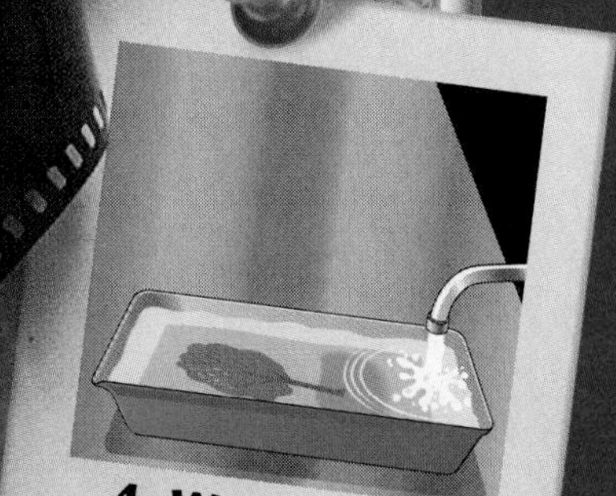

1. Developer

2. Stop

3. Fixer

4. Water rinse

To learn more about developing film, visit *www.mhschool.com/science* and enter the keyword DARKROOM.

*inter*NET
CONNECTION

284

## SCIENCE WORDS

chemical change
  p.260
chemical
  reaction  p.260
colloid  p.250
conduction  p.279
convection  p.279
emulsion  p.250

kinetic energy  p.273
mixture  p.244
physical
  change  p.258
potential
  energy  p.273
radiation  p.279
solution  p.248

## USING SCIENCE WORDS

**Number a paper from 1 to 10. Fill in 1 to 5 with words from the list above.**

1. A(n) __?__ looks the same everywhere, even under a microscope.

2. Tiny droplets of fat spread through water form a(n) __?__ .

3. In a(n) __?__ matter takes on a new form but not a new identity.

4. In a(n) __?__ two chemicals react to form a new substance.

5. Energy carried by light is __?__ .

**6–10.** Pick five words from the list above that were not used in 1 to 5, and use each word in a sentence.

## UNDERSTANDING SCIENCE IDEAS

11. Describe two ways heat energy can move from one place to another.

12. What is the difference between a mixture and a compound?

13. What is the difference between a physical change and a chemical change?

14. What is the difference between the energy of moving things and energy that is stored?

15. Describe two things that can happen during a chemical reaction.

## USING IDEAS AND SKILLS

16. A certain material can be separated by physical changes. Can it be a single compound? Why or why not?

17. **READING SKILL: CAUSE AND EFFECT** What signs are there that baking bread is a chemical change?

18. Invent a way for the energy from a burning candle to turn a wheel. Draw and explain your invention.

19. **EXPERIMENT** A friend says he removed tarnish from a silver spoon by putting it in the bottom of an aluminum pot containing a hot baking-soda solution. What really removed the tarnish? Describe how you would perform experiments to find out.

20. **THINKING LIKE A SCIENTIST** You want the walls of an outdoor doghouse to keep heat in on cold days. What would you use as insulation? Explain.

## PROBLEMS and PUZZLES

**Lemon Wonders** Work with a parent. Soak the tip of a toothpick in lemon juice. Use the soaked tip of the toothpick to write a word on paper. Let it dry. You can't see it. Have an adult place a hot electric iron on the paper and lift. Repeat until you see a change. What happens? Why?

# UNIT 3 REVIEW

## SCIENCE WORDS

atom p.216

chemical
  change p.260
density p.199
melting point p.229
molecule p.220
physical
  change p.258

potential
  energy p.273
solution p.248
state of
  matter p.228
suspension p.249

## USING SCIENCE WORDS

**Number a paper from 1 to 10. Beside each number write the word or words that best complete the sentence.**

1. If you know the mass and volume of an object, you can compute its __?__.

2. The smallest particle with the properties of an element is a(n) __?__.

3. The smallest particle with the properties of a compound is a(n) __?__.

4. The temperature at which a solid turns to liquid is its __?__.

5. Solid, liquid, and gas are three __?__.

6. Salt water is an example of a(n) __?__.

7. An example of a(n) __?__ is muddy water.

8. Raking a layer of leaves into a small pile is an example of a(n) __?__.

9. Burning the pile of leaves is an example of a(n) __?__.

10. Energy stored in a wound-up spring is an example of __?__.

## UNDERSTANDING SCIENCE IDEAS

**Write 11–15. For each number write the letter for the best answer. You may wish to use the hints provided.**

11. The density of a material may be measured in
    a. $kg^2$
    b. $g/cm^3$
    c. cm/s
    d. $m/g^3$
    *(Hint: Read page 200.)*

12. Which of the following is a liquid when at room temperature?
    a. oxygen
    b. butane
    c. mercury
    d. lead
    *(Hint: Read pages 232-233.)*

13. Which of the following is *not* a mixture?
    a. brass
    b. tea
    c. soap
    d. salt
    *(Hint: Read page 245.)*

14. Iron and oxygen can combine to form
    a. steel
    b. rust
    c. salt
    d. zinc
    *(Hint: Read page 264.)*

15. The energy produced by batteries comes from
    a. motion
    b. chemical reactions
    c. heat
    d. conduction
    *(Hint: Read page 272.)*

## USING IDEAS AND SKILLS

**16.** Vegetable oil floats on water. Explain what that tells you about their densities.

**17.** Use the chart on page 200 to decide if a block of aluminum would float or sink in a bowl of mercury.

**18.** 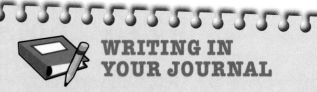 **MAKE A MODEL** Why do scientists use models to study atoms and molecules?

**19.** On a hot summer day, Mike the lineman strung a copper power line from one pole to the next. Tell why Mike made sure that the line sagged a little.

**20.** Describe two ways to separate mixtures.

**21.** Name three different kinds of mixtures, and give an example of each.

**22.** When water on your skin evaporates, it cools you off. Explain how this happens.

**23.** What happens when you mix baking soda and vinegar?

## THINKING LIKE A SCIENTIST

**24.** **EXPERIMENT** In the experiment on page 265, one nail was called the *control nail.* Explain the importance of using a control in scientific experiments.

**25.** Copy the chart on page 275. Add a third column giving an example of each type of energy.

## WRITING IN YOUR JOURNAL

### SCIENCE IN YOUR LIFE
Name and describe five different mixtures you can observe on your way from home to school.

### PRODUCT ADS
Whenever you use a cleaning material, you should always read the label carefully. Some kinds of cleaning materials should never be used together. Read the labels on several cleaning products, and identify warnings that refer to possible chemical reactions.

### HOW SCIENTISTS WORK
Scientists use a variety of models to understand and explain the natural world. A formula such as $H_2O$ is a model for water. Tell what the formula means. Give another example of a chemical formula, and tell what it means.

### Design your own Experiment
Describe a way to find out whether pure water or salt water has a greater density. Check with your teacher before carrying out the experiment.

**inter NET CONNECTION**

For help in reviewing this unit, visit *www.mhschool.com/science*

# PROBLEMS and PUZZLES

## The $1,000 Prize

Can all types of matter exist as a solid, a liquid, or a gas? A wealthy chemist had his doubts. He offered a $1,000 prize for someone who could prove

- that the element iron could exist as both a liquid and a gas
- that the element oxygen could exist as both a liquid and a solid

**Develop** a plan for how you could win the $1,000 prize. Show the steps you would take to prove each statement. What difficulties would you face in trying to win the prize?

**WIN $1,000!**

*if you can prove:*

| | |
|---|---|
| **Boiling temperature for iron** | 2,861 °C |
| **Melting temperature for iron** | 1,538°C |
| **Boiling temperature for oxygen** | -183°C |
| **Melting temperature for oxygen** | -219 °C |

## Fizz-ability

The makers of Fizzbery Super Fizz Soda are worried about bubble leakage—the tendency of bubbles to leak out of the bottle once it is open. How can bubble leakage be minimized? Should the soda be kept

- at warm temperatures?
- at cold temperatures?
- frozen? Or boiling?

**Devise** an experiment to test bubble leakage of Super Fizz Soda.

Predict your results. What would be the best way to prevent bubble leakage?

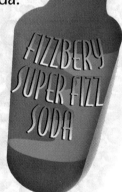

FIZZBERY SUPER FIZZ SODA

## The Big O

A chemist ran electric current through water to show that it was made of two gases, oxygen and hydrogen. The only problem was—she didn't know which gas was which.

- Both gases were invisible.
- Both gases exploded when they were exposed to a spark.
- From the picture you can tell that one gas had twice the volume of the other.

- The gas on the left actually weighed more than the gas on the right.

Which gas is oxygen? How do you know that it is oxygen? How could you prove that it was oxygen? Explain.

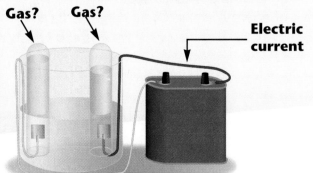

Gas?    Gas?    Electric current

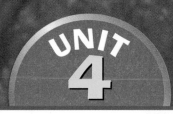

# EARTH AND ITS RESOURCES

## CHAPTER 7

# EARTH, YOUR HOME

Mountains give you a pretty good view of Earth, your home. Why are mountains as tall as they are? Will they always be as tall? What are they made of?

Mountains are only one kind of feature of your home, Earth. In Chapter 7 you'll read more about your home.

 In Chapter 7 you will read for sequence of events.

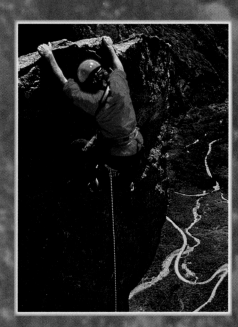

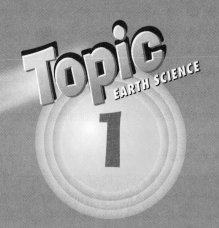

## WHY IT MATTERS

Earth provides the things needed to support life.

## SCIENCE WORDS

**solar system**  the Sun and the objects that are traveling around it

**planet**  any of the nine large bodies that travel around the Sun and shine by reflecting its light

**gravity**  a force of attraction, or pull, between any object and any other objects around it

**inertia**  the tendency of a moving object to keep moving in a straight line

**lithosphere**  the hard, outer layer of Earth, about 100 kilometers thick

**crust**  the rocky surface that makes up the top of the lithosphere

**resource**  any material that helps support life on Earth

**hydrosphere**  Earth's water

# Earth and Its Neighbors

If you could look at Earth from space, what would you see? The Sun, far in the distance, lights up Earth. Could you see Earth's clouds? How could you tell the water from the land?

Earth is not standing still in one spot. It is moving around the Sun in an almost circular path. A force holds Earth around the Sun. Why doesn't the force just pull Earth into the Sun?

## EXPLORE

**HYPOTHESIZE**  How does a force hold Earth around the Sun? What would happen if the force let go? Write a hypothesis in your *Science Journal.* Test your ideas.

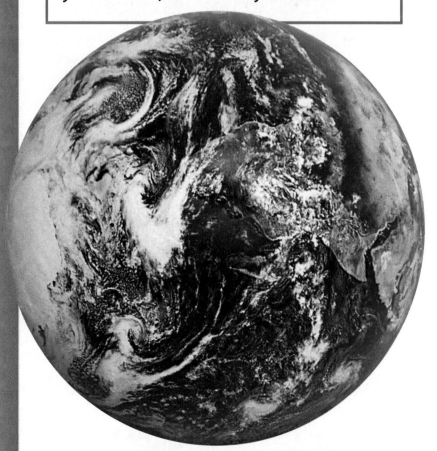

# Investigate How Earth and the Sun Are Held Together

Use a model to explore the force between the Sun and Earth.

**MATERIALS**

- clay
- 1 m of string
- scissors
- meterstick
- goggles
- *Science Journal*

## PROCEDURES

 **SAFETY** Wear goggles. Twirl the model close to the ground.

1. **MAKE A MODEL** Cut a 40-cm length of string. Wrap it around a small, round lump of clay in several directions. Tie the ends to make a tight knot. Measure 60 cm of string, and tie it to the string around the ball.

2. **OBSERVE** Spin the ball of clay slowly—just fast enough to keep the string tight and keep the ball off the ground. Keep the ball close to the ground. In your *Science Journal*, describe the path of the ball.

3. **EXPERIMENT** At one point while spinning, let the string go. What happens? In your *Science Journal*, describe the path of the ball of clay. Repeat until you get a clear picture of what happens.

## CONCLUDE AND APPLY

1. **IDENTIFY** How did your model represent Earth and the Sun? What represented Earth? Where was the Sun located? How did you represent the force between them?

2. **INFER** Explain what happened when you let the string go. Why do you think this happened?

### GOING FURTHER: Problem Solving

3. **USE VARIABLES** How would your results change if the mass of the clay was doubled? Tripled? How does the mass affect the pull on the string? Make a prediction. Try it.

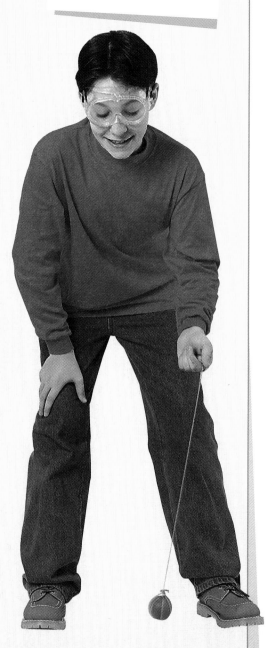

## How Are Earth and the Sun Held Together?

If you were traveling in a spaceship through space as fast as light, you would be passing stars. Perhaps in time you would approach one star in particular, the star you know as the Sun. If so you would be approaching your home address, the **solar system**. The solar system is the Sun and the objects that are traveling around it.

Our Sun is a star similar to other stars in the night sky. It appears so large and

bright to us because it is much closer to Earth. The Sun is composed mostly of hydrogen and helium. The formation of helium from hydrogen is what generates light and heat from the Sun.

The objects around the Sun include nine **planets**. Planets are objects that travel around a star in a path. That path is called an *orbit*. Like the clay ball in the Explore Activity, the planets are held in orbit around the Sun. The planets do not give off light, as stars do. They reflect light from their star. Earth and the other planets reflect sunlight.

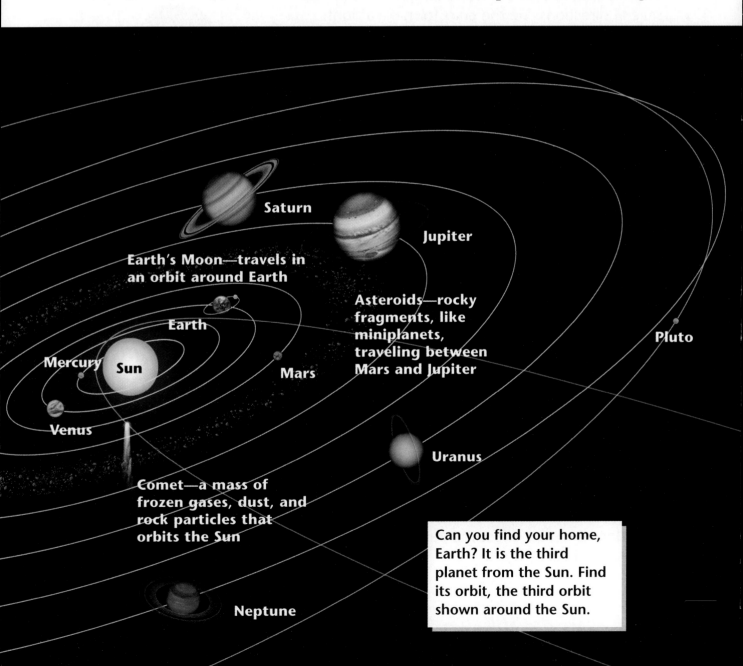

Saturn

Jupiter

Earth's Moon—travels in an orbit around Earth

Asteroids—rocky fragments, like miniplanets, traveling between Mars and Jupiter

Earth

Pluto

Mercury  Sun

Mars

Venus

Uranus

Comet—a mass of frozen gases, dust, and rock particles that orbits the Sun

Can you find your home, Earth? It is the third planet from the Sun. Find its orbit, the third orbit shown around the Sun.

Neptune

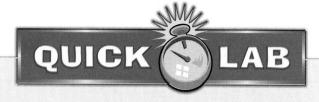

# QUICK LAB

## Orbit Times

**HYPOTHESIZE** What does the length of time for an orbit depend on? Write a hypothesis in your *Science Journal*. Test it.

### MATERIALS
- several sheets of graph paper
- *Science Journal*

| Planet | Average Distance to the Sun (million km) | Year Time for complete orbit around the Sun (in Earth days) |
|---|---|---|
| Mercury | 57.9 | 88 days |
| Venus | 108.2 | 224 days |
| Earth | 149.6 | 365 days |
| Mars | 227.9 | 687 days |
| Jupiter | 778.3 | 4,333 days |
| Saturn | 1,427 | 10,759 days |
| Uranus | 2,870 | 30,685 days |
| Neptune | 4,497 | 60,188 days |
| Pluto | 5,900 | 90,700 days |

## Brain Power

What is the farthest planet from the Sun? Is there only one answer? Explain.

### PROCEDURES

**COMMUNICATE** Use graph paper. Draw a bar graph to compare the revolution times for the planets. The vertical axis of the graph represents time. Decide how much time each square on the paper represents. The horizontal axis represents the planets. How many pieces of graph paper will you need? Write your description in your *Science Journal*.

### CONCLUDE AND APPLY

1. **DRAW CONCLUSIONS** Based on your graph and the data table, what relationship can you find between the length of the year (time) and the planet's location in the solar system?

2. **REVISE** How could you change your graph to show the relationship even better? What might your new graph reveal?

The orbit of each planet is almost a circle. Each orbit is slightly oval. What effect does an orbit of this shape have on the distance from a planet to the Sun?

One complete trip of an object in its orbit around the Sun takes one *year*. A year is different from planet to planet. For Earth one year is 365.25 days. The table shows how long a year takes for each planet. The time is given in days as days are timed on Earth.

293

# What Keeps the Planets in Orbit?

The clay ball in the Explore Activity was kept in orbit by holding the string. Earth travels around the Sun, but you won't find a string connecting them! What is it that holds Earth in its path around the Sun? What keeps Earth from flying off into space?

This question once puzzled scientists, too. They knew that everything in the solar system orbits the Sun. What holds it all together?

One scientist who lived about 300 years ago, Sir Isaac Newton, had some ideas to explain this. He described a "string" holding the Sun and a planet together. The string is an invisible force, which he called **gravity**. He described gravity as a property of all matter. It is a force of attraction, or pull, between any object and any other objects around it.

Gravity depends on two measurements—mass and distance. The more matter, or mass, in an object, the greater the pull in the object's direction. The closer two objects are, the stronger the pull of gravity between them.

When Newton's ideas are applied to the world around us, we find that they can explain how most objects behave. In fact Newton extended his ideas to include all objects on Earth, in the solar system, and beyond. His ideas are called the Law of Universal Gravitation.

**Sir Isaac Newton, 1642–1727, was an English mathematician and scientist. It is said that he thought of gravity when an apple dropped on his head.**

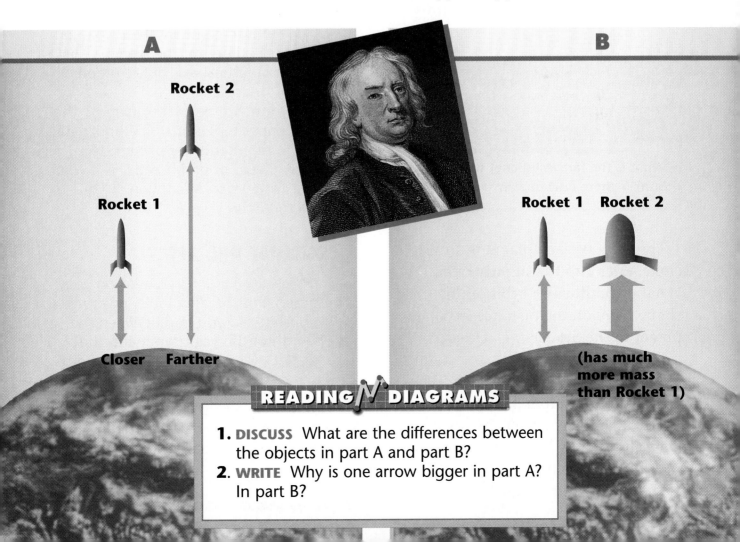

**A**

Rocket 2

Rocket 1

Closer    Farther

**B**

Rocket 1    Rocket 2

(has much more mass than Rocket 1)

## READING DIAGRAMS

1. **DISCUSS** What are the differences between the objects in part A and part B?
2. **WRITE** Why is one arrow bigger in part A? In part B?

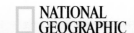

## FUNtastic Facts

The Sun makes up more than 99 percent of the mass of the entire solar system. The Sun's mass is more than 1,000 times greater than Jupiter's and about 330,000 times greater than Earth's. How might the Sun's mass compare with the mass of Mercury? Of Venus?

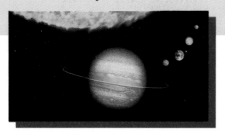

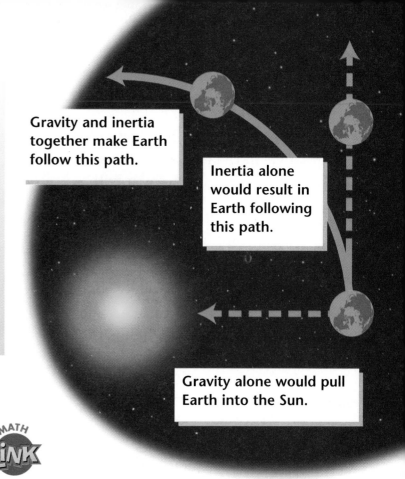

Gravity and inertia together make Earth follow this path.

Inertia alone would result in Earth following this path.

Gravity alone would pull Earth into the Sun.

**MATH LINK**

# Why Don't the Planets Fall into the Sun?

According to Newton's Law, there is a force of attraction between you and Earth. Earth pulls you. You pull Earth. When you stumble, why do you fall down? Why doesn't Earth fall up?

Compared to Earth you have a very small amount of mass. As a result your gravity is very weak. Earth's gravity, however, is very strong because Earth is so massive. Earth's pull is strong enough to make everything near it move in its direction, including you. That's why you fall "down" if you stumble.

The Sun has far more mass than Earth or any other planet. Since it is much more massive than Earth, its gravity is much stronger, too. The Sun's gravity holds all of the objects in

the solar system together. Without gravity Earth and all of the other objects orbiting the Sun would go flying off into space.

However, gravity alone is not the only reason why the planets stay in their orbits. Gravity alone would pull Earth into the Sun, because the Sun is so massive. That doesn't happen because the planets are moving. The planets, as do all objects, have a property called **inertia** (i nûr′shə). Inertia is the tendency of a moving object to keep moving in a straight line.

In the Explore Activity, the ball flew off in a straight line when the string was let go. The planets, too, because of their inertia would move in straight lines without gravity. Gravity "steers" the planets in their oval paths around the Sun. It is gravity and inertia that keep the planets in their orbits.

**295**

# How Does the Sun Light Up Earth?

The Sun does more than just hold the planets in their orbits in the solar system. It also provides them with light and warmth. The Sun is the reason for day and night. All planets spin, or *rotate*, like huge spinning tops. At any point in time, half of a planet is facing the Sun—it has daylight on that half. At the same time, half is facing away from the Sun—that half is in darkness, night.

As a planet rotates, places that are in darkness eventually turn to face the Sun and those in daylight eventually turn away. Each planet makes one complete spin in its day. Each planet has its own speed of turning. The length of a day (that is, one complete day-night cycle) is different for each planet.

How much light and warmth a planet receives depends on how far it is from the Sun. Light spreads out as it travels outward from the Sun. An area of 1 square meter on the planet Mercury receives much more energy than an area of 1 square meter on a farther planet— such as Pluto. That is why Mercury is much hotter than Pluto.

## MATH LINK

### LENGTH OF DAY

| Planet | Day = time for complete spin (in Earth hours or days) |
|---|---|
| Mercury | 59 days |
| Venus | 243 days |
| Earth | 24 hours |
| Mars | $24\frac{1}{2}$ hours |
| Jupiter | 9 hours 56 minutes |
| Saturn | 10 hours 40 minutes |
| Uranus | 17 hours 14 minutes |
| Neptune | 16 hours 6 minutes |
| Pluto | 6.39 days |

## READING CHARTS

1. **WRITE** Make a list of planets in order from the shortest day to the longest day.
2. **DISCUSS** Is there a relationship between the length of a planet's day and its distance from the Sun? Explain your answer.

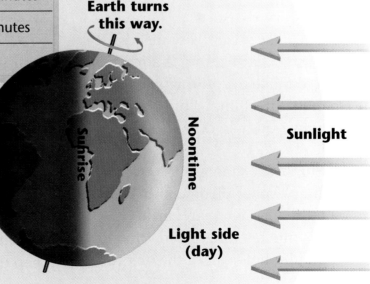

Earth turns this way.

Sunrise

Noontime

Sunlight

Dark side (night)

Light side (day)

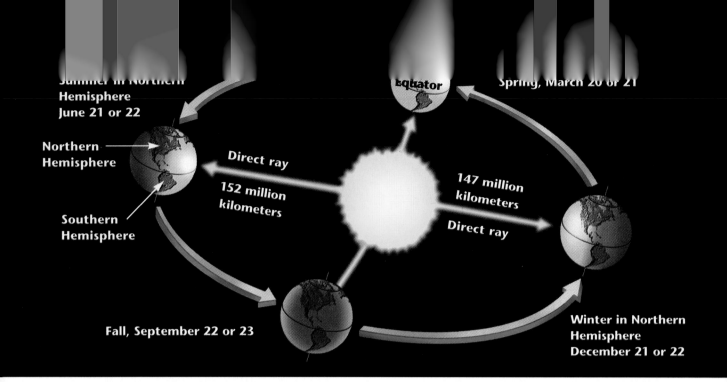

Summer in Northern
Hemisphere
June 21 or 22

Northern
Hemisphere

Southern
Hemisphere

Direct ray

152 million
kilometers

Fall, September 22 or 23

Equator

Spring, March 20 or 21

147 million
kilometers

Direct ray

Winter in Northern
Hemisphere
December 21 or 22

# Why Is Earth Special?

As the third planet from the Sun, Earth is at a location where it receives just the right amount of energy to provide living things with the warmth and light they need.

Different animals and plants live in different temperatures, in different climates, and at different heights above sea level on Earth.

Why are places generally cooler in winter than in summer?

Earth's orbit is like a slightly stretched circle—an oval. This shape brings Earth slightly closer to the Sun during part of the year and farther away during other parts of the year. In the Northern Hemisphere, Earth is actually slightly closer to the Sun during winter than during summer. Then what causes colder winters and warmer summers?

The answer is Earth's shape and tilt. Earth is tilted as it travels around the Sun. During the summer the Northern Hemisphere is tilted toward the Sun.

During the winter it is tilted away from the Sun. The sunlight reaching the Northern Hemisphere in the winter is more spread out. Temperatures are lower. In the Northern Hemisphere the midday summer Sun is higher in the sky. Temperatures are warmer.

The closer a place is to the equator, the less change there is in temperatures from season to season. Why? The midday Sun is high in the sky all year round.

Also, some surfaces warm up more than others when bathed in sunlight. Land heats up more than water. Dark soils heat up more than light-colored sands. As a result Earth ends up with a whole range of temperatures, which can support the many different kinds of life on Earth.

## Brain Power

How do plants or animals adapt to living through cold winters and hot summers? Give some examples.

297

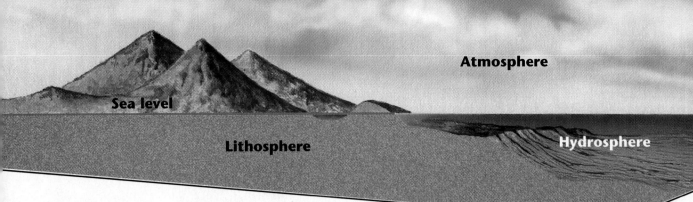

**Atmosphere**

**Sea level**

**Lithosphere**

**Hydrosphere**

**Earth**

# How Else Does the Sun Affect Earth?

Is Earth a solid planet? Liquid? Gas? Earth is all of these. It has a solid surface layer, mostly covered by a layer of water, all surrounded by layers of gases. The Sun interacts with all of these layers of Earth.

- The **lithosphere** (lith′ə sfîr′) is the hard, outer layer of Earth, about 100 kilometers thick. The rocky surface that makes up the top of the lithosphere is the **crust**. The crust includes the continents and the ocean floors.

The crust has the soil and many other **resources**. Earth's resources are materials that help support life on Earth. Earth has high mountains, like the Rockies. It also has low valleys, like those of the ocean bottoms.

- The **hydrosphere** (hī′drə sfîr′) is Earth's water—trillions of liters of water. Earth's waters are another valuable resource. There is so much water that it covers most of the lithosphere. Most of this water is called the ocean. It is salty because of minerals that have been washed into

it over the ages. The hydrosphere also includes all of Earth's lakes, rivers, streams, underground water, and ice. Most of this is fresh water, which we use for drinking, cooking, and bathing.

However, the hydrosphere is very thin compared to the diameter of Earth. Use a basketball to model Earth. If you dip the ball in water, the water wetting its surface would represent the hydrosphere.

The hydrosphere acts as a big heat absorber. Water changes temperature slowly compared to land. The oceans keep temperatures on Earth from changing too drastically.

The Sun is continually interacting with the lithosphere and hydrosphere. Plants and other producers on Earth's surface are trapping the Sun's energy and producing food. They also produce the gas oxygen in the process.

Also, water in and on the ground evaporates as it absorbs the Sun's energy. Water from the oceans evaporates. Evaporation is part of the water cycle. The Sun's energy is the driving force of this cycle.

# What Causes Weather?

Pictures of Earth taken from space show lots of white clouds swirling in the *atmosphere*. The atmosphere is not one, but many layers of gases that surround Earth. The atmosphere contains oxygen needed for living things on Earth. It also contains other gases that help protect Earth from forms of harmful energy from the Sun. These gases are more of Earth's precious resources.

Driven by the Sun's energy, the water cycle brings water into the atmosphere in the form of the gas water vapor. The water vapor condenses, or changes back into liquid. Clouds form as a result. Rain and snow fall from the clouds. The atmosphere carries the water all living things need far over the land as rain and snow. This process is part of what we call Earth's weather changes. It also distributes water over the surface as needed by living things.

The Sun's heating of Earth not only creates a water cycle, it also drives Earth's weather, the day-to-day changes in the atmosphere at each place on Earth. The Sun is also responsible for Earth's climates, the overall pattern of temperatures and rain or snow that each area has.

Part of Earth's weather are the winds that move across the surface. In addition to day-to-day winds, the Sun's energy drives the major wind systems of the atmosphere. Because of Earth's round shape, the surface is heated unequally. The result is the global wind patterns, such as the prevailing westerlies that blow across much of North America.

These winds, in turn, blow across Earth's oceans and drive surface ocean currents. These currents are movements of surface water in huge circular patterns. As ocean currents flow along the edges of continents, they affect the land's climate. The California Current carries cold water along the West Coast of our country, helping it stay cool there. On the East Coast, the Gulf Stream keeps the climate warm.

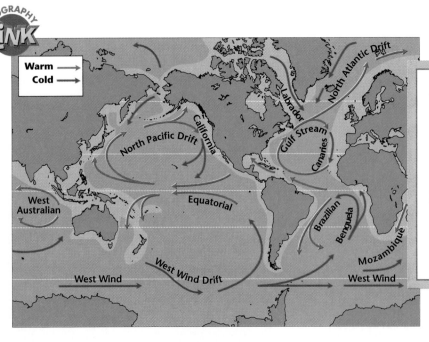

GEOGRAPHY LINK

Warm →
Cold →

North Atlantic Drift · Labrador · North Pacific Drift · California · Gulf Stream · Canaries · West Australian · Equatorial · Brazilian · Benguela · Mozambique · West Wind · West Wind Drift · West Wind

## READING MAPS

1. **WRITE** In what direction is the Gulf Stream flowing? How does this direction help keep the East Coast warm?
2. **DISCUSS** In what direction is the California Current flowing? How does it help keep the West Coast cool?

## What Is Earth's Closest Neighbor Like?

Earth is teeming with life and movement. You've seen how the Sun's energy helps produce seasons, day-to-day weather, and climates. You've seen the motion of Earth's surface currents.

With a telescope you can take a close look at Earth's nearest neighbor in the solar system. "Only" 400,000 kilometers from Earth, the Moon's surface does not look at all like Earth's surface. You won't see clouds or oceans. There are no hills covered with forests—in fact there are no signs of life at all.

The Moon has no hydrosphere. It has no atmosphere to speak of. There is no water to drink, no air to breathe. There is no weather. Without the atmosphere to trap heat and the hydrosphere to circulate it, temperatures change greatly during a Moon day. At midday on the Moon, the surface temperature climbs as high as 117°C, hotter than boiling water! During the lunar nighttime it drops to –193°C, cold enough to liquefy oxygen!

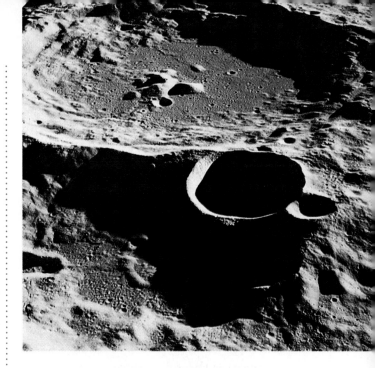

**Earth's nearest neighbor looks nothing much like Earth.**

The Moon has a lithosphere, a rocky surface. With a telescope you can see features of the surface—such as dark-colored regions called *maria* (mär'ē ə). *Maria* is Latin for "seas." In the past these areas were thought to be seas. They are really dry, flat land surrounded by mountains and ridges.

Much of the Moon's surface is covered with huge dents, called craters. Trails of rock and dust extend out from them. They reflect sunlight and look like rays coming out of the crater.

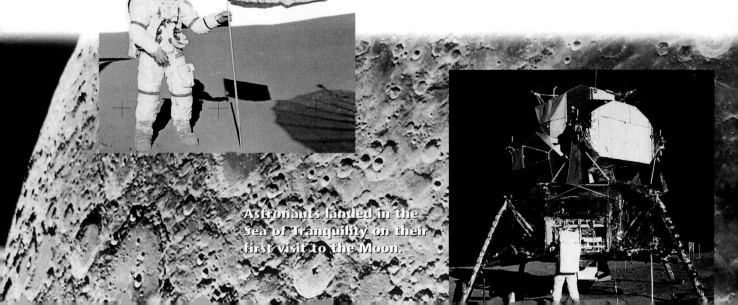

Astronauts landed in the Sea of Tranquility on their first visit to the Moon.

# How Does the Moon Affect Earth?

The Moon is not a planet. It travels in an orbit around Earth. "Moon" light is actually "Sun" light. Your part of Earth is not facing the Sun at night. However, the Sun's light reaches the Moon, and the Moon bounces it toward Earth.

The Moon can darken the sky during the day in an event called a solar eclipse. The Moon moves in its orbit directly between the Sun and Earth. For a short period, it casts a shadow on places on Earth.

If you live along a coast, you can see one way the Moon affects Earth. You can see the tides come in and go out. Tides are the rising and falling levels of water. Tides result from the gravity between Earth, the Sun, and the Moon. Living things along coasts depend on the tides.

## WHY IT MATTERS

When astronauts first visited the Moon in 1969, they faced a tough problem. How do you survive in such a place? They had to bring all of the things they needed to stay alive all the way from Earth. *Apollo 11* carried with it on its long journey through space everything needed to support life.

Earth is the only member of the solar system that supports life as we know it.

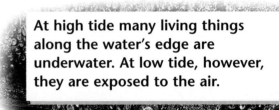

At high tide many living things along the water's edge are underwater. At low tide, however, they are exposed to the air.

## REVIEW

1. How would you state your address in space? Explain your answer.

2. How is gravity important for Earth?

3. How does the Sun affect life on Earth?

4. **DRAW CONCLUSIONS** Why is the Moon unlivable compared with Earth?

5. **CRITICAL THINKING** *Analyze* Would you weigh the same on all of the planets? Explain your answer.

**WHY IT MATTERS** THINK ABOUT IT
The Moon has only about one-sixth of the mass of Earth. That means it has one-sixth of Earth's gravity. What would it be like to carry out your daily activities on the Moon?

**WHY IT MATTERS** WRITE ABOUT IT
What would you need to bring along on a space mission to another planet? Explain your choices.

NATIONAL GEOGRAPHIC World of SCIENCE

# Searching FOR E.T.

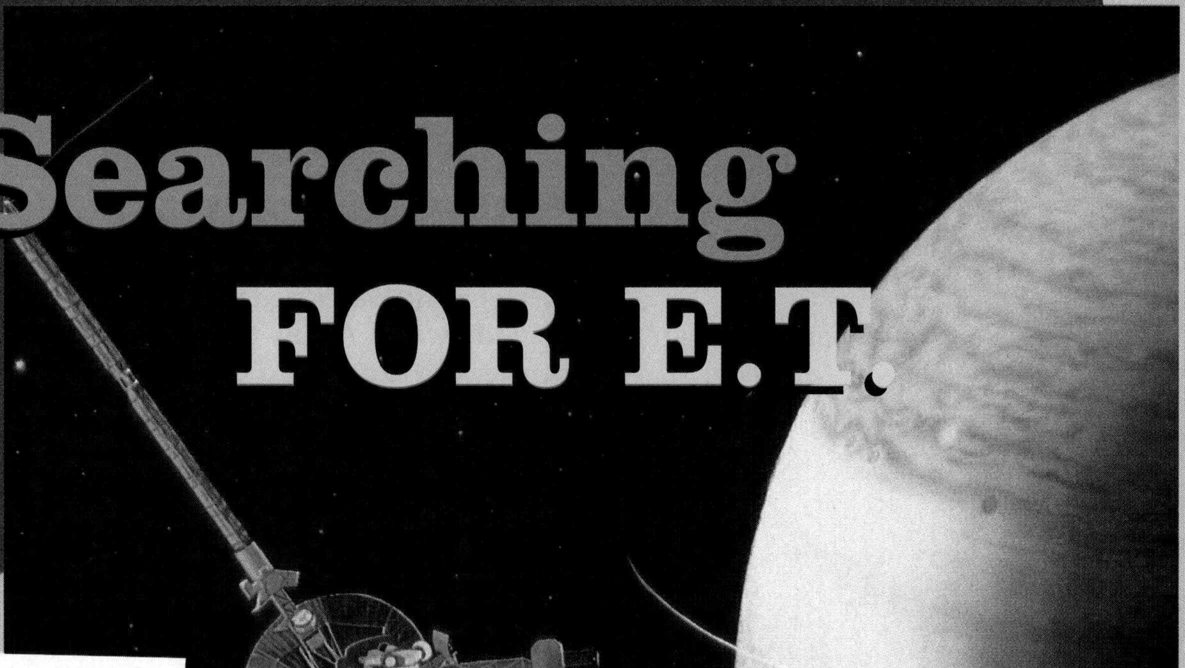

The space probe *Galileo* with Jupiter in the background

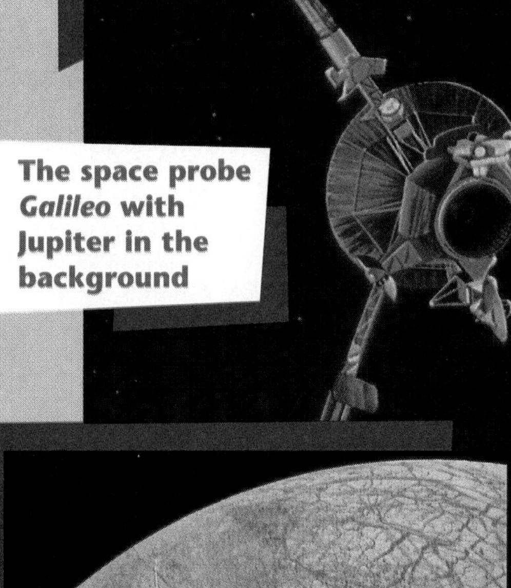

Europa, one of Jupiter's 16 moons, may have a liquid ocean that supports life.

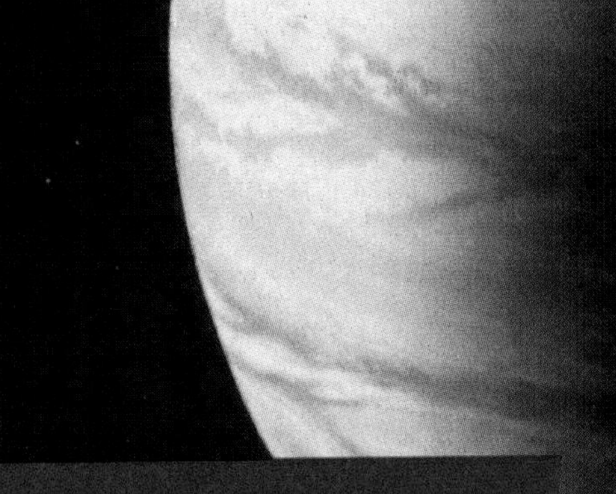

*Sojourner*, a 2-foot-tall rover, gathers data from Martian rocks during the 1997 Mars *Pathfinder* mission.

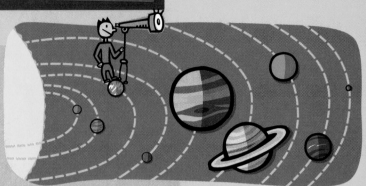

Could life exist anywhere else in our solar system? Life on Earth requires oxygen, water, sunlight, soil, gravity, and temperatures that are neither too hot nor too cold.

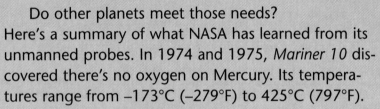

Do other planets meet those needs? Here's a summary of what NASA has learned from its unmanned probes. In 1974 and 1975, *Mariner 10* discovered there's no oxygen on Mercury. Its temperatures range from –173°C (–279°F) to 425°C (797°F).

In 1978 *Pioneer Venus 2* found that Venus's atmosphere of 97 percent carbon dioxide traps the Sun's heat. *Magellan* has orbited Venus since 1990, sending pictures of soil baked by temperatures that could melt lead!

*Pathfinder* found evidence in 1997 that Mars once had water. With temperatures between –21°C (–6°F) and –124°C (–191°F), could life exist there? On Earth algae live under Earth's polar ice caps, and tube worms live in very hot water near deep ocean vents.

The outer planets are made of gas, so they have no solid surface. However, in 1997 *Galileo* found that one of Jupiter's moons, Europa, was rocky, like Earth, and may have more water than Earth's oceans! The atmosphere on Titan, one of Saturn's moons, may be like Earth's was four billion years ago. In 2004 spacecraft will visit these moons.

*Voyager 2* has discovered that conditions on Uranus and Neptune probably won't support life. Probes haven't yet reached Pluto, a "snowball" smaller than Earth's moon.

## Discussion Starter

**1** What does finding life near ocean vents or under polar caps on Earth have to do with finding life on other planets?

**2** Do you think scientists will ever find human life on other planets in our solar system? Why or why not?

*inter*NET **CONNECTION** To learn more about space, visit *www.mhschool.com/science* and enter the keyword **CALLBACK**.

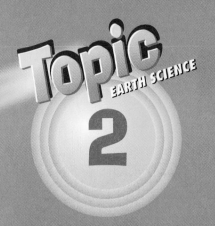

# Topic 2
EARTH SCIENCE

## WHY IT MATTERS

**Changes in Earth's crust affect the lives of many people.**

### SCIENCE WORDS

**fault** a crack in the crust, whose sides show evidence of motion

**geologist** a scientist who studies Earth

**magma** hot, molten rock deep below Earth's surface

**lava** magma that reaches Earth's surface

**weathering** the breaking down of rocks into smaller pieces

**erosion** the picking up and carrying away of pieces of rock

**deposition** the dropping off of bits of eroded rock

**meteorite** a chunk of rock from space that strikes a surface (such as Earth or the Moon)

# Earth's Changing Crust

**W**hat causes an earthquake? An earthquake seems to happen without warning. The ground shakes suddenly, often with enough power to damage objects on the surface.

Where do earthquakes happen? Earthquakes are common in places where the crust is "cracked." One such crack extends through much of the state of California. Why do you think earthquakes happen along this crack?

## EXPLORE

**HYPOTHESIZE What kind of motion causes an earthquake? Does it always cause destruction? Can it result in anything else? Write a hypothesis in your *Science Journal*. Test your ideas.**

304

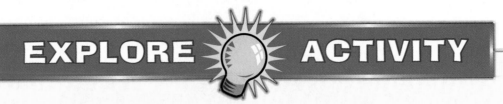

# Design Your Own Experiment

## WHAT MAKES THE CRUST MOVE?

## PROCEDURES

**1. MAKE A MODEL** Work with a partner to model layers of rock. You may use books, clay, or other materials to represent rock layers. Build your model on wax paper. Include a "crack" down through the layers. Stack cubes on the top of the model to represent buildings and other surface features.

**2. EXPERIMENT** Find as many ways of moving the model as you can to show how the crust may move during an earthquake. What happens to the surface features as you move the model each way? Draw and describe each way in your *Science Journal.*

**3. EXPERIMENT** How can you show movement without causing any visible effect on the surface features?

### MATERIALS

- 4–6 matching books (optional)
- layers of clay or modeling compound (optional)
- plastic knife (for use with clay)
- cubes
- wax paper
- *Science Journal*

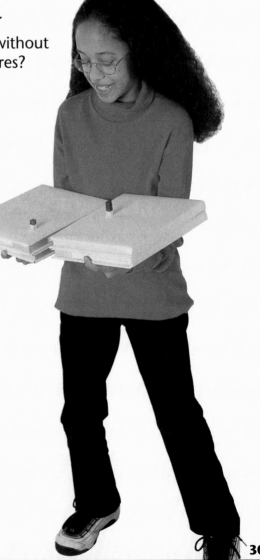

## CONCLUDE AND APPLY

**1. COMPARE AND CONTRAST** How many different ways could you move your model? How were they different?

**2. CAUSE AND EFFECT** How did each way you moved the model affect the surface features? How did each way change the positions of the layers? Explain.

**3. CAUSE AND EFFECT** How did you move the model without moving the surface features? Did the model change in any way? Explain.

## GOING FURTHER: Problem Solving

**4. EXPERIMENT** How can you use your model to show how a mountain might rise up high above sea level? Explain and demonstrate.

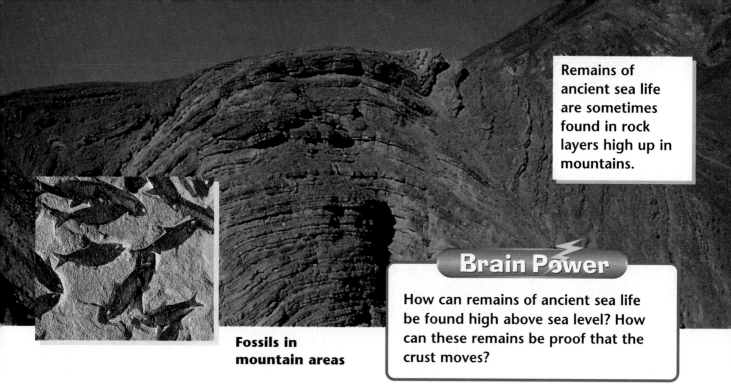

Remains of ancient sea life are sometimes found in rock layers high up in mountains.

**Fossils in mountain areas**

## Brain Power

How can remains of ancient sea life be found high above sea level? How can these remains be proof that the crust moves?

# What Makes the Crust Move?

Earth's crust is constantly moving, if not in one place then in another. Sometimes it moves quickly enough to be seen and felt. People who have been through an earthquake tell of seeing the ground heave up and down like an ocean wave.

As the Explore Activity showed, earthquakes are related to cracks in the crust called **faults**. These faults may have formed from earlier earthquakes. Sometimes they form while the earthquake happens. During an earthquake the crust on either side, or on both sides, of a fault is in motion.

During an earthquake vibrations travel through the crust. The farther away people are from the earthquake, the harder it is for them to feel the vibrations. However, delicate devices called *seismographs* (sīz'mə grafs') can record this motion at locations all around the crust.

Most of the time, however, the crust moves very slowly. Rocks can move slowly on either side of a fault over centuries. People only realize there is movement when something visibly changes position. Not all motion happens along faults, either. Often layers of the crust bend, such as you see here. Bending, like motion along a fault, may happen gradually over time.

To measure crust movement, *surveyors* (sər vā'ərz) measure *elevation*—how high a place is above sea level. They leave plaques called *bench marks* that tell the exact location and elevation of a place. When some bench marks are remeasured, they are found to have risen or sunk.

**Geologists** (jē ol'ə jists), scientists who study Earth, place sensitive devices all along faults, such as the San Andreas Fault in California. They hope that records of tiny movements can be used to predict an earthquake.

## Below the Crust

The crust is Earth's hard surface. Compared to the distance to Earth's center, it is very thin. It is only about one-thousandth of Earth's thickness.

Under the crust is the mantle, Earth's thickest layer. The rock material here is solid. Yet, it can flow like a liquid—as putty can "flow" when you squeeze it between your hands. Below the mantle is Earth's core. It is in two parts, a liquid outer core and a solid inner core.

The rock material in the mantle is in motion, something like heated water in a pot. It rises and pushes against the bottom of the crust. This movement causes the thin, brittle crust at the surface to break into pieces, or *plates*. The plates themselves can move along Earth's surface. Earthquakes and the slow motions of the crust all result from moving plates.

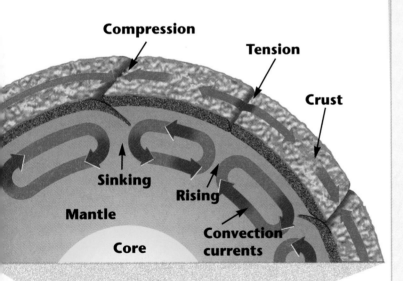

Compression

Tension

Crust

Sinking

Rising

Mantle

Convection currents

Core

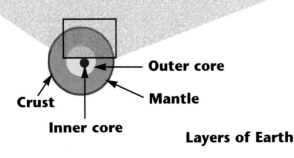

Crust

Outer core

Mantle

Inner core

**Layers of Earth**

# Model of Earth

**HYPOTHESIZE** Can materials with different properties be used to make a solid Earth? Write a hypothesis in your *Science Journal.*

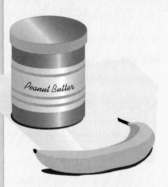

### MATERIALS
- mashed ripe banana (in a plastic bag)
- peanut butter
- hazelnut
- graham cracker crumbs (in a plastic bag)
- wax paper
- *Science Journal*

## PROCEDURES
### ⚠ SAFETY
Students who are allergic to peanuts should not do this activity!

1. **INFER** You will use four materials to make a model of Earth on wax paper. Each material is one of Earth's layers. Read step 2. Decide which material represents which layer. Decide how thick each layer needs to be.

2. **MAKE A MODEL** Wash your hands. Cover the nut with a layer of peanut butter. Put the covered nut in the bag of mashed banana so that banana covers it completely. Roll the result into the graham cracker crumbs on waxpaper.

## CONCLUDE AND APPLY

1. **DRAW CONCLUSIONS** Why does each material represent a different layer?

2. How thick did you decide to make each layer? Explain your reasoning.

# What Forces Act on the Crust?

What makes the crust move? As the plates of the crust move, they can collide. They can pull away from each other. They can also slide past each other. These movements cause three kinds of forces to act on the crust.

- *Tension* stretches or pulls apart the crust.

- *Compression* squeezes or pushes together the crust.

- *Shear* twists, tears, or pushes one part of the crust past another.

Each of these forces can cause a fault to form in the crust. Each can cause movement along a fault. These forces can also result in other kinds of motion in the crust.

As forces inside the Earth cause the crust to move upward, the land is built up. Compression can crumple rock layers into wavy folds. The mountains shown here formed when two pieces of crust crashed together.

The impact squeezed the crust, causing it to crumple into huge folds. Mountains made of crumpled and folded layers of rock are called *fold mountains*. The Appalachians, the Alps, and the Himalayas are all ranges of fold mountains.

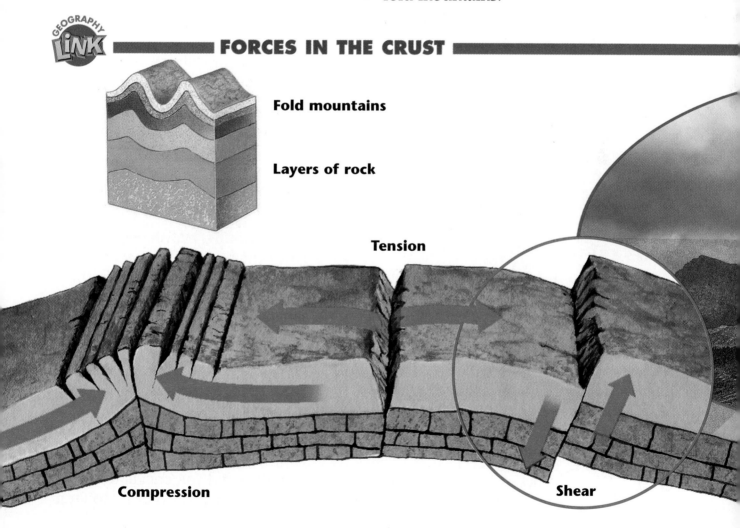

GEOGRAPHY LINK ■■■■ **FORCES IN THE CRUST** ■■■■

**Fold mountains**

**Layers of rock**

**Tension**

**Compression**

**Shear**

# What Else Can Constructive Forces Do?

Tension and shear can also build up the crust. Mountains can be formed as the crust is pulled apart. How? Hot molten rock deep below Earth's surface, called **magma**, rises upward. If magma reaches the surface, it may flow out as **lava**.

Lava flows out or is hurled out when a volcano erupts. This volcano is building a new island off the coast of Iceland. Its lava is gushing up through a crack between two pieces of crust that are being pulled apart.

**Surtsey, an island near Iceland, is forming from an undersea volcano.**

Tension and shear also cause great blocks of crust to break apart cleanly and move along faults. Blocks of crust moving along a fault can form *fault-block mountains*. A vast region of fault-block mountains known as the Basin and Range Province blankets several western states (see map).

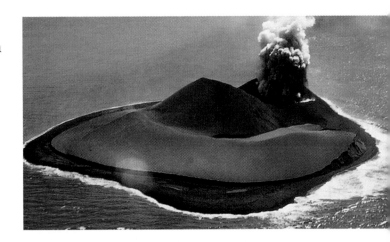

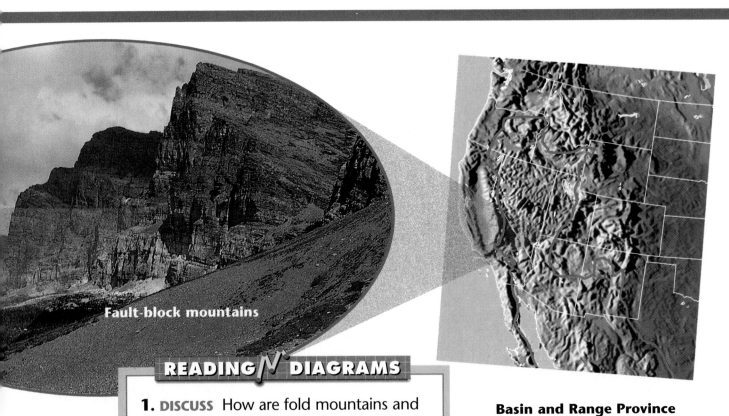

Fault-block mountains

**Basin and Range Province**

## READING ∧ DIAGRAMS

1. **DISCUSS** How are fold mountains and fault-block mountains the same? How are they different?
2. **WRITE** Write a paragraph about how a volcano can become a new island.

## What Other Forces Shape Earth's Surface?

While movements of the crust are building up Earth's surface, other forces are at work breaking it down. These processes are known as **weathering** (weth'ər ing) and **erosion** (i rō'zhən). Weathering is the breaking down of the materials of Earth's crust into smaller pieces. Erosion is the picking up and carrying away of the pieces. Weathering and erosion have been going on for billions of years! They both happen in many, many ways.

Weathering happens when the crust is exposed to water, air, and changes in temperature. How do these break down rocks?

Water can break down the crust in many ways. Water can dissolve some minerals right out of the crust. Moving water can make pieces of rock bang into each other. Small chips can break off the surface of the rock. This causes the rock to get smaller and rounder. The churning waters of a stream can wear down big pieces of rock into small rounded pebbles.

Wind is moving air. The wind blows sand and other broken bits of rock over Earth's surface. These particles also wear away rock.

Air also contains gases that react chemically to form new substances. Oxygen in air reacts with iron to form rust. Carbon dioxide and sulfur dioxide in air react with rain to form acids. These acids eat away at limestone rocks. The cavern seen here was once solid rock! Acid rainwater seeping through the rock dissolved part of it. It "ate away" a huge hole—the cavern!

**Rounded pebbles near a churning river**

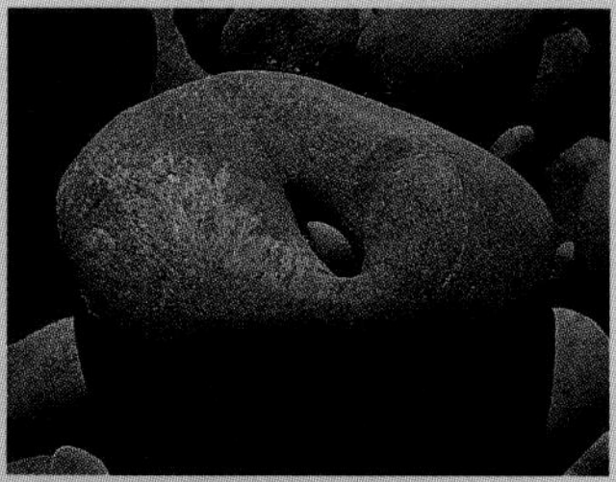

**This beautiful rock formation was carved by wind-blown sand.**

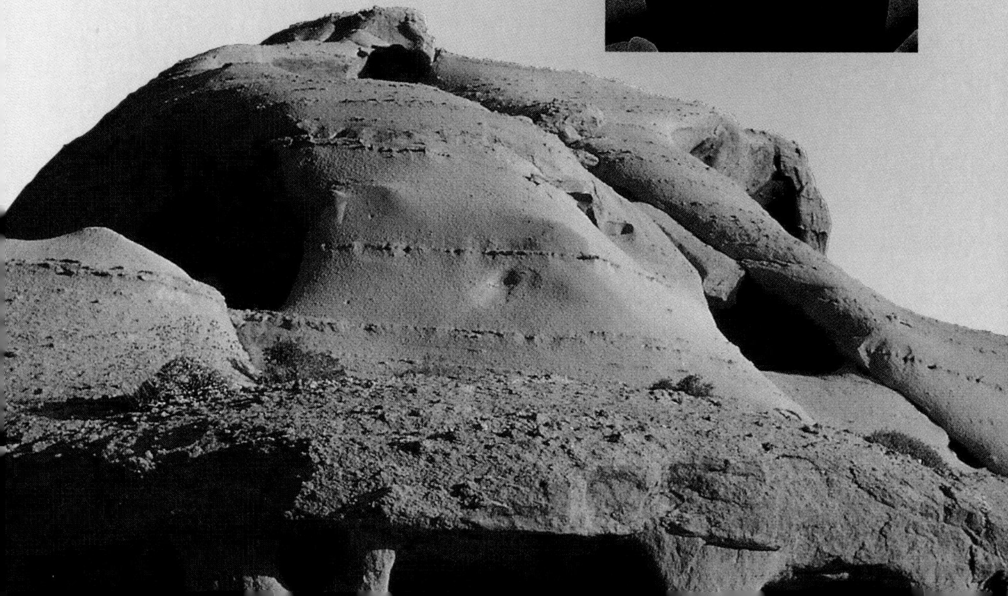

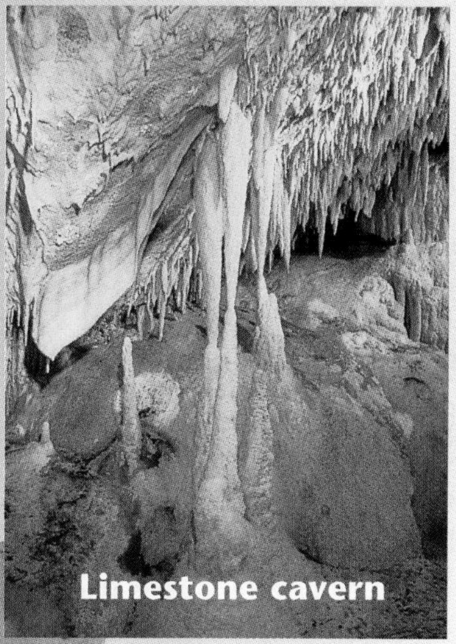

**Limestone cavern**

## What Does Temperature Do to Rocks?

If the temperature drops low enough, water can freeze. When water freezes it expands, or takes up more space. Water freezing in cracks in rocks expands against the rock. The force of the expanding water is so great that it can split the rock apart.

Changes in temperature also cause rock to expand and contract. A rock may be made of a number of different materials. Sometimes one part of a rock expands or contracts more than another part. This difference can cause one part of the rock to push or pull against another part of the rock. Some geologists think that this eventually can cause the rock to break.

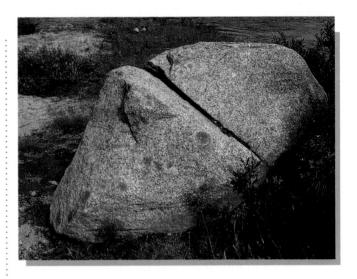

This huge boulder was eventually broken apart by small amounts of water that seeped into cracks and froze.

### Erosion

Erosion is the carrying away of pieces of weathered rock by gravity, water, wind, and ice. Piece by piece erosion can carry away a boulder, a hill, or even a whole mountain range!

The greatest agent of erosion is water. From the moment a drop of water falling from the sky first hits the ground, it erodes the land.

It may not seem like much, however, think of how many raindrops fall in a rainstorm. Altogether they can move a lot of soil.

Once water reaches the ground, it begins to flow downhill. Moving water can push and carry things along with it. Think of a raft full of people. How much do you think it weighs? What is moving all that weight along?

Water running downhill picks up pieces of rock and carries them down-hill. The faster the water is moving, the bigger the pieces of rock it can move.

### Brain Power

What if all of the topsoil in a region were washed away? How would the plants in the region be affected? How would this affect the animals in the region? The people living there?

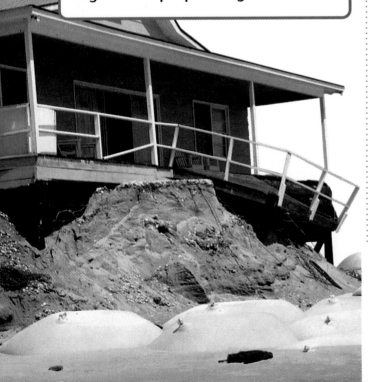

**What do you think happened to the ground under this house? Where do you think it went?**

311

# How Can Wind and Ice Erode Rock?

Wind is moving air. Wind can push things along with it, just like moving water. Yet air is less dense than water. Wind does not exert as hard a push as water moving at the same speed. Therefore, wind mostly erodes pieces of rock that are sand sized or smaller.

Ice also causes a lot of erosion. This glacier in Alaska is a moving river of ice. It may not move as quickly as water, but don't underestimate its power. When the ice of a glacier freezes onto rock and then the glacier moves downhill, the rock is torn right out of the ground. This glacier can carry chunks of rock bigger than your house with ease.

Glaciers also wear away the land as they flow over it. Place an ice cube in some sand for a minute or two. Then look at the bottom of the ice cube. What has become frozen into the bottom of the ice cube? Now rub the bottom of the ice cube on a bar of soap. What happens to the surface of the bar of soap?

Rocks of all sizes become frozen into the bottom of a glacier. As the glacier moves, the rock beneath it is scratched and worn down. Thousands of years ago, a glacier covered New York City. Can you guess how the scratches in these rocks in Central Park were made?

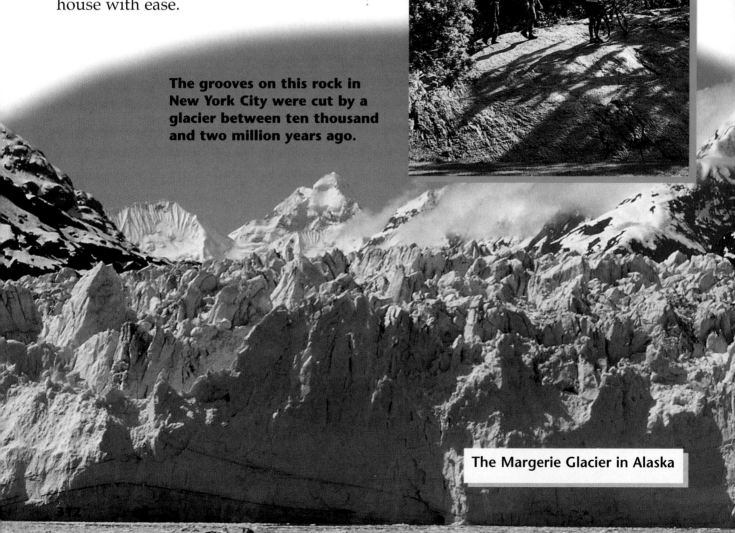

The grooves on this rock in New York City were cut by a glacier between ten thousand and two million years ago.

The Margerie Glacier in Alaska

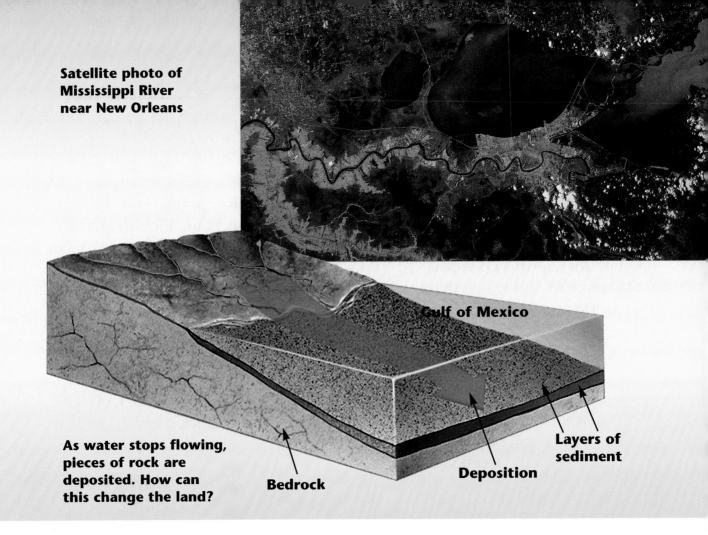

**Satellite photo of Mississippi River near New Orleans**

**Gulf of Mexico**

As water stops flowing, pieces of rock are deposited. How can this change the land?

**Bedrock**

**Deposition**

**Layers of sediment**

# Where Do Eroded Rocks Go?

What happens to pieces of rock that are carried along by wind, moving ice, or moving water? A fast wind eventually slows down. A glacier stops moving and eventually melts at its front end and sides. All streams eventually slow down and end when they flow into a large body of water, such as a lake or ocean.

When water stops moving, it also stops carrying along bits and pieces of rock. The pieces of rock are dropped to the bottom of the stream, lake, or ocean. The dropping off of bits of eroded rock is called **deposition** (dep′ə zish′ən).

Deposition also takes place when glaciers melt and winds stop blowing. Layer by layer, pile after pile, bits and pieces of rock deposited by water, wind, and ice build up Earth's surface.

Very slowly deposition may fill up depressions, or basins, in Earth's surface. It can build up land along shorelines and at the end of rivers. Deposition does not seem as dramatic as colliding continents. However, the slow, steady work of deposition is one of the greatest constructive actions on Earth.

## Brain Power

Look in your community for signs of change. Where do you see signs of weathering, erosion, or deposition?

313

# How Is the Moon Different from Earth?

Earth's Moon, our nearest neighbor in space, is a far different place from Earth. There is no evidence of earthquake faults as on Earth's crust. There are no erupting volcanoes. In fact there is no evidence of any of the kinds of motion that Earth's crust has.

Without air and water, there can be very little weathering or erosion. The Moon has almost no air or water. There are no streams, no glaciers, and no wind. The only weathering and erosion is due to the impact of rocks from space hitting the Moon's surface.

These rocks from space that strike a surface are called **meteorites**. Some craters formed by the impact of meteorites are big enough to be seen from Earth. Others are so tiny the entire crater is on a single mineral crystal.

**Meteorite impact has been recorded on the Moon's surface.**

Can meteorites also strike Earth's surface and produce craters? Yes! However, Earth's atmosphere protects its surface from many such impacts. Rocks from space "burn up" as they pass through Earth's atmosphere. The Moon has little atmosphere. How does that fact affect the Moon's surface?

Meteorite impacts shatter rocks on the Moon and also create a lot of heat. The heat melts the rock. Pieces of rock may melt together, and droplets and globs of molten rock can splatter outwards. Over time continual meteorite impacts break down the rock. The end result is a mixture of shattered pieces of rock, rock droplets, and melted-together bits of rock.

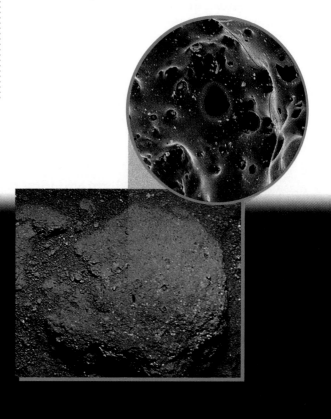

## Do Other Planets Change?

As the solar system has been explored, evidence of surface changes and erosion has been found on other worlds. There are perhaps thousands of volcanoes on Venus. The largest volcano in the solar system is Mars's Olympus Mons. It is 24 kilometers (15 miles) high and 550 kilometers (344 miles) across.

Some of Jupiter's moons also show evidence of constructive and destructive forces. The *Voyager* and *Galileo* spacecraft even sent back pictures showing some of Io's volcanoes erupting! The moons Ganymede, Callisto, and Europa have water ice. The presence of water, organic compounds, and internal heat mean life may be possible on Europa.

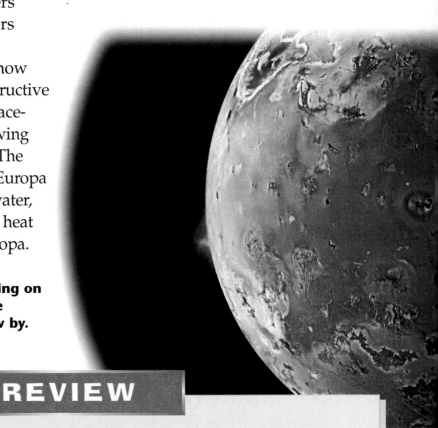

**This volcano was erupting on Jupiter's moon Io as the Voyager spacecraft flew by.**

## WHY IT MATTERS

Do any of Earth's forces threaten your community? Are you near a river that floods? Are you near a fault where earthquakes have been recorded in the past? What signs can you see in your community that Earth is changing? Are you prepared for Earth's next change?

## REVIEW

1. What are some types of evidence that show Earth's crust has moved?

2. What are three types of forces acting on Earth's crust?

3. How are earthquakes measured?

4. **COMPARE AND CONTRAST** What is the difference between weathering and erosion?

5. **CRITICAL THINKING** *Analyze* How do fault-block mountains compare to fold mountains?

**WHY IT MATTERS** THINK ABOUT IT
How do you think people can protect themselves if an earthquake happens?

**WHY IT MATTERS** WRITE ABOUT IT
How can people plan ahead to prepare for an earthquake or any other kind of force that can change the crust suddenly?

**READING SKILL**
Write a paragraph to explain the sequence of events involved when an earthquake occurs.

# Waves of Erosion

**H**ave you ever stood by the ocean and felt a wave pull the sand from under your feet? Waves constantly carry sand away from a beach, bit by bit. The sand is deposited elsewhere on the shoreline.

People who live by beaches can watch their "front yards" slowly disappear. Many beach homes are built on stilts. That puts the buildings above water during high tides and storms. However, if the sand supporting the stilts washes away, the houses fall!

If there are cliffs on a shoreline, the pounding waves can wear away the lowest parts. Eventually the cliffs collapse and fall into the water. Then waves slowly break the rocks into smaller pieces. In time the cliffs will become sand!

Stormy winter weather increases erosion. Fierce winds push the waves, giving them the strength to pick up and carry small stones. The stones pound cliffs along with the waves and help to break the rocks. The stronger

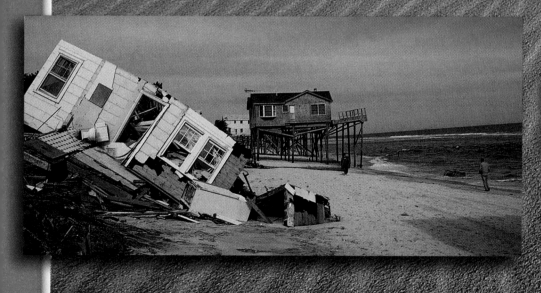

Waves can wear away the sand that supports a beachfront home.

# A Closer Look

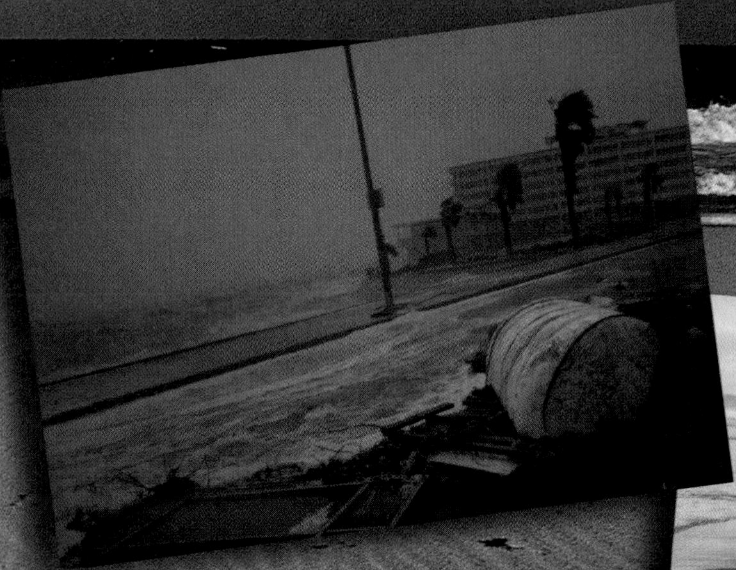

wind also pushes waves farther inland.
Some towns truck in sand to replace what's lost. Other towns build breakwaters close to shore. The stone and concrete breakwaters reduce the force of the waves before they reach shore. An island or a sandbar close to shore serves as a natural breakwater.

Nearly all sand and rock removed by wave erosion is deposited elsewhere. Only one percent is carried out to sea.

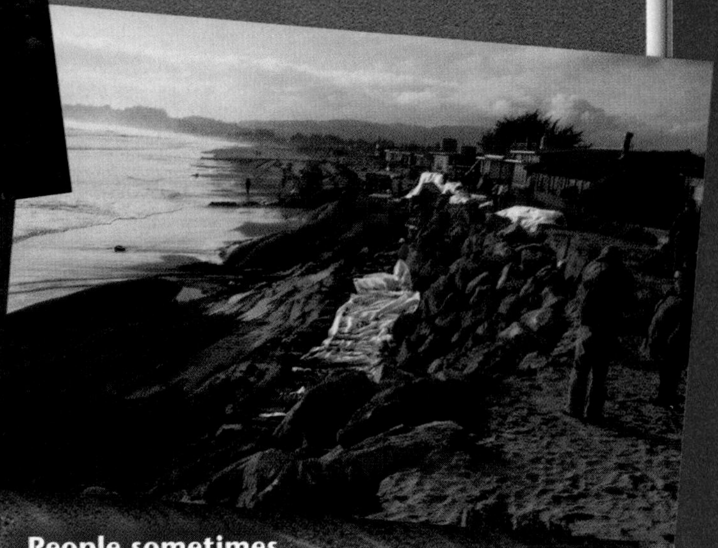

**People sometimes build sea walls to try to protect the beaches behind the walls from pounding waves.**

## DISCUSSION STARTER

1. How does erosion build beaches?

2. How do waves erode a cliff?

To learn more about erosion, visit *www.mhschool.com/science* and enter the keyword BREAKDOWN.

*inter*NET
CONNECTION

317

## WHY IT MATTERS

**Minerals are used in many different ways.**

### SCIENCE WORDS

**mineral** a solid material of Earth's crust with a definite composition

**luster** the way light bounces off a mineral's surface

**streak** the color of the powder left when a mineral is rubbed against a hard, rough surface

**hardness** how well a mineral resists scratching

**cleavage** the tendency of a mineral to break along flat surfaces

**ore** a mineral containing a useful substance

**gem** a mineral valued for being rare and beautiful

**nonrenewable resource** a resource that cannot be replaced within a short period of time or at all

# Minerals of Earth's Crust

**H**ow many substances do you think make up Earth's solid surface, the crust? Would you believe about 2,000?

The substances that make up Earth's crust are minerals. Here are two of them. One is gold. The other looks like gold, but isn't. It's nicknamed "fool's gold." Many of the miners who went to California in the 1800s could not tell real gold from fool's gold. Which of the two do you think is real gold?

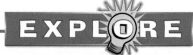
# EXPLORE

**HYPOTHESIZE How do you think people can tell minerals apart? Write a hypothesis in your *Science Journal*. Test your ideas.**

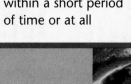

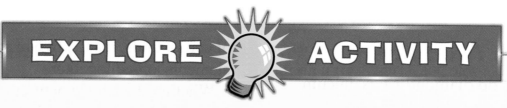

# EXPLORE ACTIVITY

# Investigate How You Can Identify a Mineral

Compare properties of minerals to tell minerals apart.

## PROCEDURES

**1. COMMUNICATE** Use tape and a marker to label each sample with a number. In your *Science Journal*, make a table with the column headings shown. Fill in numbers under "Mineral" to match your samples.

**2. OBSERVE** Use the table shown as a guide to collect data on each sample. Fill in the data in your table. Turn to the table on page 323 for more ideas to fill in "Other."

## CONCLUDE AND APPLY

**1. ANALYZE** Use your data and the table below to identify your samples. Were you sure of all your samples? Explain.

**2. MAKE DECISIONS** Which observations were most helpful? Explain.

### GOING FURTHER: Problem Solving

**3. DRAW CONCLUSIONS** How could you make a better Scratch (Hardness) test?

## MATERIALS

- mineral samples
- clear tape
- red marker
- copper penny or wire
- streak plate
- porcelain tile
- hand lens
- mineral property table (page 323, or see *Science Journal*)
- nail
- *Science Journal*

Color = color of surface

Porcelain Plate Test = the color you see when you rub the sample gently on porcelain

Shiny Like a Metal = reflects light like a metal, such as aluminium foil or metal coins

Scratch (Hardness): Does it scratch copper? A piece of glass?

Other: Is it very dense? (Is a small piece heavy?) Has it got flat surfaces?

| | Mineral | Color | Shiny Like a Metal (Yes/No) | Porcelain Plate Test | Scratch (Hardness) | Other |
|---|---|---|---|---|---|---|
| 1. | | | | | | |
| 2. | | | | | | |

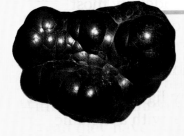

Hematite has a blackish color but a reddish streak.

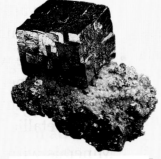

Galena has three cleavage planes. It breaks into cubes.

Mica has one cleavage plane. It breaks into sheets.

## MOHS' SCALE OF HARDNESS

| Hardness | Sample Mineral | Tool |
|---|---|---|
| 1 | Talc | |
| 2 | Gypsum | |
| | | Fingernail |
| 3 | Calcite | |
| | | Copper penny/wire |
| 4 | Fluorite | |
| | | Iron nail |
| 5 | Apatite | |
| | | Glass plate |
| 6 | Feldspar | |
| | | Steel file |
| 7 | Quartz | |
| | | Streak plate |
| 8 | Topaz | |
| 9 | Corundum | |
| 10 | Diamond | |

### READING CHARTS

1. **DISCUSS** Which mineral is the softest? The hardest?
2. **WRITE** Which minerals does a fingernail scratch? Which does a glass plate scratch?

## How Can Rubbing and Scratching Help?

Here are three other ways to identify a mineral.

- **Streak** is the color of the powder left when a mineral is rubbed against a hard, rough surface. Rub it against a porcelain streak plate. The streak is always the same for a given mineral, even if the mineral varies in color.

The streak may not be the color of the outer surface of the mineral. Fool's gold, pyrite, is brassy yellow, but it has a greenish black streak. Gold has a yellow streak. You would need a streak plate to tell that the real gold on page 318 is on the right.

- **Hardness** is a measure of how well a mineral resists scratching. Soft minerals are easily scratched. Mohs' scale of hardness is a numbered list of minerals. Talc, number 1, is the softest mineral. It can be scratched with your fingernail! Any item on the list, including the tools, can scratch something above it. You can use the tools to help find the hardness.

- The way a mineral breaks is also helpful. Some minerals have **cleavage**. This property is the tendency of a mineral to break along flat surfaces. Cleavage is described by the number of directions, or planes, the mineral breaks in.

322

Many minerals do not break smoothly. They are said to have *fracture*. Quartz, for example, shows jagged edges when it breaks.

Some minerals have special properties that help you identify them. Magnetite, for example, is attracted by a magnet. Some minerals are very dense—such as gold, silver, and galena. Even a small sample feels quite heavy.

## PROPERTIES OF MINERALS

| MINERAL | COLOR(S) | LUSTER (Shiny as metals) | PORCELAIN PLATE TEST (Streak) | CLEAVAGE (Number) | HARDNESS (Tools Scratched by) | DENSITY (Compared with water) |
|---|---|---|---|---|---|---|
| Gypsum | colorless, gray, white, brown | no | white | yes—1 | 2 (all five tools) | 2.3 |
| Quartz | colorless, various colors | no | none | no | 7 (none) | 2.6 |
| Pyrite | brassy, yellow | yes | greenish black | no | 6 (steel file, streak plate) | 5.0 |
| Calcite | colorless, white, pale blue | no | colorless, white | yes—3 (cubes) | 3 (all but fingernail) | 2.7 |
| Galena | steel gray | yes | gray to black | yes—3 (cubes) | 2.5 (all but fingernail) | 7.5 |
| Feldspar | gray, green, yellow, white | no | colorless | yes—2 | 6 (steel file, streak plate) | 2.5 |
| Mica | colorless, silvery, black | no | white | yes—1 (thin sheets) | 3 (all but fingernail) | 3.0 |
| Hornblende | green to black | no | gray to white | yes—2 | 5–6 (steel file, streak plate) | 3.4 |
| Bauxite | gray, red, brown, white | no | gray | no | 1–3 (all but fingernail) | 2.0–2.5 |
| Chalcopyrite | brassy to golden yellow | yes | greenish black | no | 3.5–4 (glass, steel file, streak plate) | 4.2 |
| Hematite | black or red-brown | yes | red or red-brown | no | 6 (steel file, streak plate) | 5.3 |

**A form of calcite shows double image because it refracts light twice as you look through it.**

## READING CHARTS

1. **WRITE** Which minerals would feel heaviest if you had equal-sized samples of all?
2. **DISCUSS** How is hornblende different from quartz? From feldspar? From mica?

# MONUMENTS TO MINERALS

The hotel's paint is peeling, but that doesn't matter. The last guest checked out years ago. Nobody lives in this town anymore. It's just one more ghost town in America's West.

Ghost towns were once busy places. Most were built soon after silver, copper, gold, or other minerals were discovered nearby. The towns were like a monument honoring the minerals!

In the late 1800s, hopeful miners and their families rushed to live in these new towns. They left just as quickly when the mines closed.

Jerome, Arizona, was built in 1882 on the steep sides of Cleopatra Hill. The town wasn't far from some new copper and gold mines. By the 1920s Jerome had a population of 15,000. Over time gravity and poor construction caused the town to slide down the hill. Its Sliding Jail moved 70 meters (230 feet)!

Soon Jerome faced bigger problems. By 1945 the copper and gold were gone, so the mines closed. By 1995 Jerome had a population of about 560.

Most ghost towns end up like Copper Hill, Arizona. Set up in 1908, the town had 500 residents, shops, a school, and a hospital by 1925. By 1933 Copper Hill was completely deserted. Can you guess why?

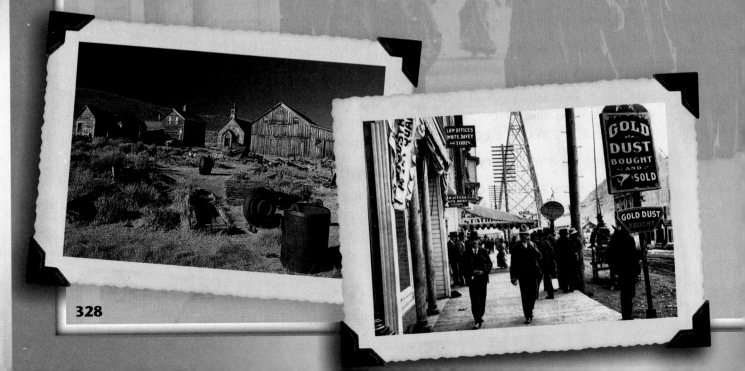

# History Link

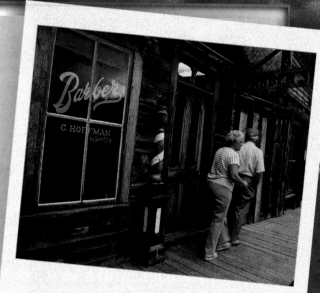

Some ghost towns have been preserved for others to enjoy.

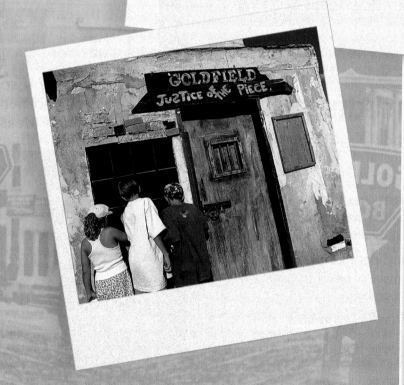

## DISCUSSION STARTER

1. What attracted people to places that later became ghost towns?

2. What caused people to leave Jerome and other ghost towns?

To learn more about mining, visit *www.mhschool.com/science* and enter the keyword MINES.

*inter*NET
CONNECTION

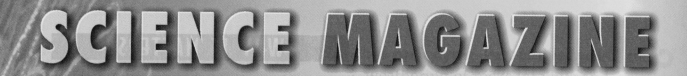

# What if There Were No Electricity?

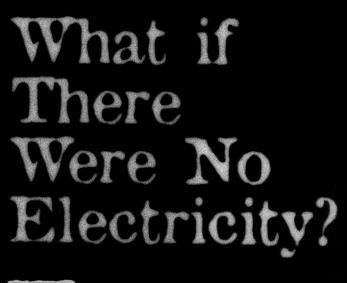

**W**hat if there were also no gas or oil deliveries? What would you do for energy? How would you get to school? Get the news of the day? Light your house? Cook your food? You'd probably learn to use different energy sources, like your ancestors did!

Electricity didn't come into use until the 1900s. What did people do before that? They burned wood or coal to make heat. They lit torches and candles to provide light. They cooked on wood-burning stoves or over logs in fireplaces. Town criers or newspapers told them the news of the day. People rode to town on horseback or in wagons.

# Science, Technology, and Society

In the 1970s America had an energy crisis. The country had become dependent on oil to provide its energy. Oil prices rose higher and higher, and then there was a shortage of oil. Americans had to cut down on their use of electricity. They did it by using some of the old sources their ancestors had used.

Stores couldn't keep coal- or wood-burning stoves in stock during the energy crisis. So many stoves were in use that in some places smoke hung over the town. This was in places that usually had very clean air, too!

Many people began carpooling or riding buses to save gas. Other people used human energy and walked or rode bikes to the store, school, or work. A few people even rode horses!

After a few years, the energy crisis was over. However, people still search for other energy sources because . . . what if it happens again!

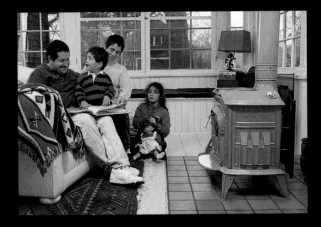

## DISCUSSION STARTER

1. If necessary how could your family use coal or wood instead of electricity?

2. What are some other ways you can save energy?

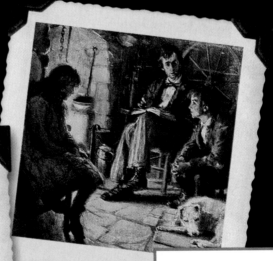

To learn more about alternate energy, visit *www.mhschool.com/science* and enter the keyword ALTERNATES.

*inter*NET
CONNECTION

# CHAPTER 7 REVIEW

## SCIENCE WORDS

| | |
|---|---|
| **erosion** p.310 | **mineral** p.320 |
| **fossil** p.335 | **ore** p.326 |
| **geologist** p.306 | **planet** p.292 |
| **hydrosphere** p.298 | **pollution** p.340 |
| **igneous** p.333 | **rock cycle** p.342 |
| **lithosphere** p.298 | **sedimentary** p.334 |
| **metamorphic** p.336 | **solar system** p.292 |

## USING SCIENCE WORDS

**Number a paper from 1 to 10. Fill in 1 to 5 with words from the list above.**

1. Rock that changes due to heat and pressure is __?__ rock.

2. The oceans are part of Earth's __?__.

3. The Sun and planets are part of the __?__.

4. A scientist who studies Earth is called a(n) __?__.

5. Earth is a(n) __?__ that orbits the Sun.

**6–10.** Pick five words from the list above that were not used in 1 to 5, and use each in a sentence.

## UNDERSTANDING SCIENCE IDEAS

11. Describe the difference in the way sedimentary and igneous rocks are formed.

12. Explain the difference between weathering and erosion.

13. Describe the rock cycle.

14. Describe two tests you can use to determine what minerals a rock is made of.

15. What is a fossil?

## USING IDEAS AND SKILLS

16. Why is it unlikely we will find life on other planets in our solar system?

17. Tension, compression, and shear affect rock differently. Is this true or false? Explain your answer.

18. **READING SKILL: SEQUENCE OF EVENTS** Explain the sequence of events that would happen if the force that keeps the planets orbiting the Sun did not exist.

19. **DEFINE** You find a rock that is made up of different-colored layers. It seems to be made of different-sized grains. Some of it looks as though it is made of tiny seashells glued together. What type of rock is it?

20. **THINKING LIKE A SCIENTIST** Do you think wet or dry sand warms up faster in sunlight? Why? State and explain your hypothesis. Describe how you might test your idea.

## PROBLEMS and PUZZLES

**Not Just Dirt** Where would you expect to find more living things, in soil from a desert or in soil from a forest? Explain your answer.

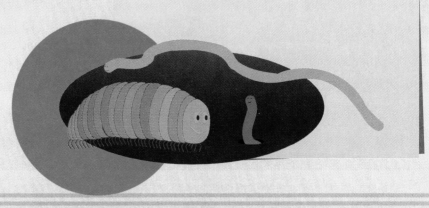

# CHAPTER 8
# EARTH'S AIR WATER, AND ENERGY

You can't drink ocean water. However, water from the oceans is part of a cycle that produces clouds, rain, and water for Earth's land—freshwater.

The oceans also provide food, and, in some places, energy. Drilling into the ocean bottom in the Gulf of Mexico off the coast of Texas provides a rich source of oil.

How else does planet Earth provide materials that make life possible?

In Chapter 8 you will read in order

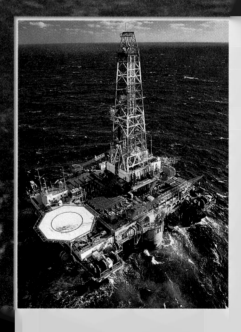

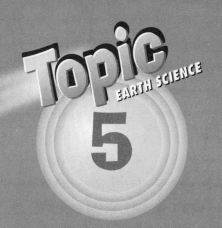

# Topic
## EARTH SCIENCE
# 5

## WHY IT MATTERS

**Air pollution affects everyone and everything.**

### SCIENCE WORDS

**renewable resource** a resource that can be replaced in a short period of time

**ozone layer** a layer of ozone gas in the atmosphere that screens out much of the Sun's UV rays

**fossil fuel** a fuel formed from the decay of ancient forms of life

**smog** a mixture of smoke and fog

**acid rain** moisture that falls to Earth after being mixed with wastes from burned fossil fuels

# Earth's Atmosphere

**E**very day American cars burn about 500 million gallons of gasoline. How do you think this affects the land, air, and water?

How can the air be different from day to day? The air may seem clear and clean on some days. If you live in or near a big city, you may have days when the air seems smoky, or "hazy." Why?

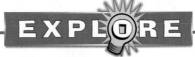

**EXPLORE**

**HYPOTHESIZE** What kinds of pollutants are in the air that can make it look as it does in the picture? Write a hypothesis in your *Science Journal*. Test your ideas.

348

## Investigate What Makes Air Dirty  MATH LINK

Try to collect pollutants to analyze them.

**MATERIALS**

- 12 cardboard strips, about 12 cm long
- petroleum jelly
- plastic knife
- transparent tape
- string
- hand lens
- metric ruler
- marker
- *Science Journal*

## PROCEDURES

**1.** Make square "frames" by taping together the corners of four cardboard strips. Make three frames, and label them A, B, and C. Tie a 30-cm string to a corner of each frame.

**2.** Stretch and attach three strips of tape across each frame, with all sticky sides facing the same way. Use a plastic knife to spread a thin coat of petroleum jelly across each sticky side.

**3. PREDICT** Hang the frames in different places to try to collect pollutants. Decide on places indoors or outdoors. Be sure to tell a parent or teacher where.

**4. OBSERVE** Observe each frame over four days. Note the weather and air condition each day in your *Science Journal*.

**5. USE NUMBERS** Then collect the frames. Observe the sticky sides with a hand lens and a metric ruler to compare particles.

## CONCLUDE AND APPLY

**1. INTERPRET DATA** How did the frames change over time? How did the hand lens and ruler help you describe any pollution?

**2. COMMUNICATE** Present your data in a graph to show differences in amounts.

### GOING FURTHER: Problem Solving

**3. PLAN** What kinds of pollutants would your frames not collect? How might you design a collector for them?

**4. PLAN** How might you extend this activity over different periods of time?

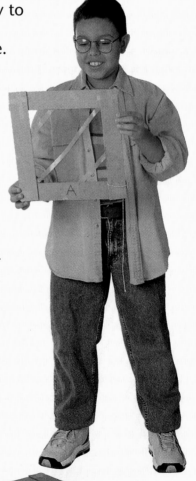

**349**

# How Do Living Things Use Air?

Why couldn't humans live on a planet that does not have an atmosphere as on Earth? Every minute of every day you need air.

Air is a mixture of nitrogen, oxygen, and a few traces of other gases, including water vapor. This mixture is a vital resource. It supports and protects life on Earth in many ways.

Almost all organisms need air to live. Actually, they need oxygen, one of the gases that is in air. On land living things have structures that enable them to get oxygen directly from the air. Living things in water habitats take in oxygen that is dissolved in the water.

What is oxygen for? Living things take in oxygen for respiration. In this process oxygen is used to break down food so that energy can be gotten from it. As a result of this process, living things give off wastes, including the gas carbon dioxide.

Why doesn't the atmosphere fill up with carbon dioxide? Plants and other producers, living things that have the green substance chlorophyll, take in carbon dioxide. They use it for making food. In the presence of light, these organisms carry on the process called photosynthesis. In this process they make food and give off oxygen.

Producers range in size from green plants to one-celled algae. They replace oxygen in the atmosphere. This makes oxygen a naturally **renewable resource.** A renewable resource is one that can be replaced. It can be replaced in a short enough period of time, such as a human lifetime, to support life on Earth.

## Brain Power

How do you take in oxygen? What are some structures that animals have to take in oxygen? How do plants take in oxygen?

## HOW EARTH'S ATMOSPHERE SUPPORTS LIFE

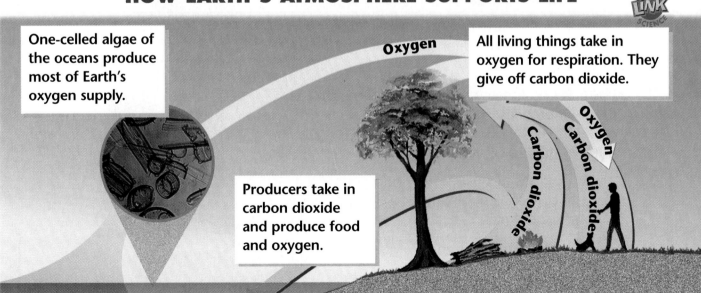

One-celled algae of the oceans produce most of Earth's oxygen supply.

Oxygen

All living things take in oxygen for respiration. They give off carbon dioxide.

Producers take in carbon dioxide and produce food and oxygen.

Oxygen

Carbon dioxide

# How Does Air Protect?

The atmosphere also acts as a protective shield. It shields Earth's surface from harmful energy that comes from the Sun. The atmosphere helps screen out harmful ultraviolet rays (UV rays) from the Sun. About 30 kilometers above your head is a layer of gas called ozone (ō′zōn). This **ozone layer** screens out from 95 to 99 percent of the Sun's UV rays.

The atmosphere also shields Earth from rocks from space. The "shooting stars" you see on a clear night are not stars. They are rocks from space that burn up due to friction with the air as they speed through the atmosphere.

The atmosphere also protects life from extremes of temperature. Clouds block sunlight during the day. At night they keep much of the heat from escaping into space, so that the planet does not "cool off." Whenever one part of the atmosphere gets hotter than another, the air moves or circulates in ways that spread the heat around.

Most of the air, about 78 percent, is nitrogen. Nitrogen is an important ingredient in food, namely proteins. How does it get into proteins? Nitrogen is taken from the air by certain kinds of bacteria. These bacteria change the nitrogen into a form that stays in the soil.

Plants use the changed form of nitrogen to make proteins. As living things eat the plants, nitrogen is passed along. It is returned to the air when living things die.

## READING DIAGRAMS

1. **DISCUSS** Do you see any cycles in this picture? Cycles are continuous processes, where one thing happens after another over and over in the same order.
2. **WRITE** Explain any cycles you see.

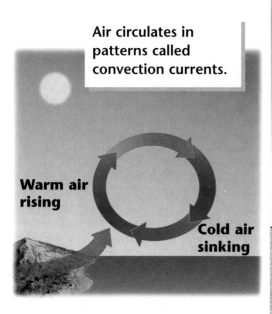

Air circulates in patterns called convection currents.

**Warm air rising**

**Cold air sinking**

Clouds at night prevent heat from escaping.

Nitrogen in air

Nitrogen goes from air to plants to all living things. When living things die, nitrogen is returned to the air.

# What Makes Air Dirty?

Many of the things we humans do add pollution to the air. The Explore Activity on page 349 showed a way to collect and observe solid pollutants. In addition to solids, there are harmful gases and liquids in the air. Where do they come from?

Many pollutants get into the air from burning **fossil fuels**. These fuels were formed from the decay of ancient forms of life. Fossil fuels include coal, oil, and natural gas. Cars, buses, trucks, and planes burn these fuels, as do many homes and power plants. The wastes from burning these fuels add pollution to the air.

Burning trash adds smoke to the air. Dust comes from plowed fields. It comes from construction sites and from mines. Factories add chemical wastes to the air.

Other events also add to air pollution. Volcanoes erupt and shoot gases and particles into the air. Forest fires and grass fires can spread smoke over great distances

All these pollutants can build up into thick clouds, called **smog**. Smog is a mixture of smoke and fog. It forms when smoke and fumes collect in moist, calm air. Smog irritates the eyes, nose, and throat. People with breathing problems have died from heavy smog.

Smog hangs like a brown cloud over many cities. Why do you think it is most common in big coastal cities like Los Angeles?

Sometimes ozone can form in smog. High up in the atmosphere, remember, ozone protects Earth from UV radiation. However, at ground level this gas can make people sick.

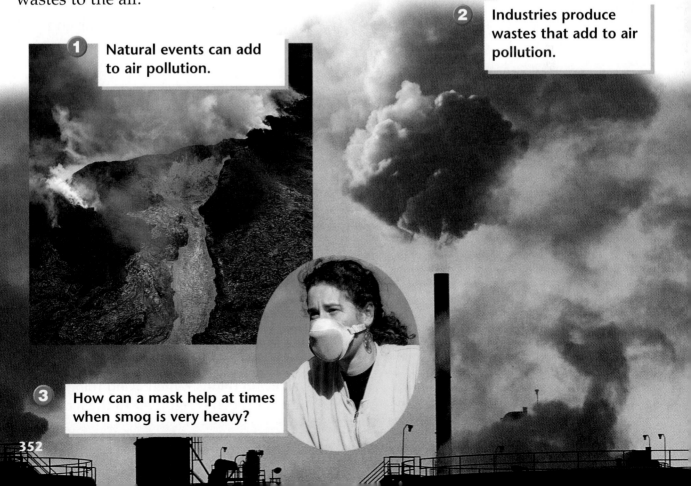

1 Natural events can add to air pollution.

2 Industries produce wastes that add to air pollution.

3 How can a mask help at times when smog is very heavy?

# How Can Rain Be Harmful?

What can destroy forests, kill animals and plants in lakes, and even eat away at buildings? Part of the answer comes from power plants that burn coal to produce energy. Another part comes from motor vehicles that burn gasoline.

Wastes that come from burning these fossil fuels travel into the air. In the air the wastes mix with moisture. They can form chemicals called acids in the moisture. The moisture with acids can eventually fall to Earth's surface as **acid rain**. This term includes all forms of precipitation—snow, hail, and sleet.

Acid rain can harm soil and water supplies. Some trees sicken and die if there is too much acid in the soil. Fish die in lakes whose waters contain too much acid. The acid weathers away statues and buildings. It can cause metal surfaces on cars to crumble.

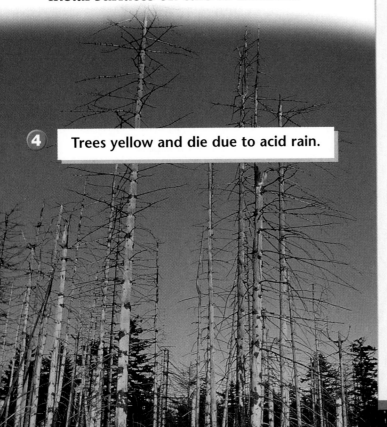

④ Trees yellow and die due to acid rain.

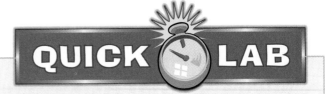 

# QUICK LAB

## Acids

PHYSICAL LINK SCIENCE

**HYPOTHESIZE** How can acid rain change a rock? Write a hypothesis in your *Science Journal*.

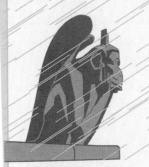

### MATERIALS
- chalk
- limestone and other rock samples
- vinegar (a mild acid)
- plastic cups
- goggles
- plastic wrap
- rubber bands
- plastic knife
- *Science Journal*

## PROCEDURES

 **SAFETY**
Wear goggles.

1. **USE VARIABLES** Break a stick of chalk into smaller pieces. Place some small pieces in a plastic cup. Place each rock sample in its own cup. Slowly pour vinegar in each cup to cover each object.

2. **OBSERVE** Watch for any changes in the chalk and the rocks. Watch for several minutes and then at later times in the day. Record your observations in your *Science Journal*.

3. Cover each cup using plastic wrap and a rubber band to help keep the vinegar from evaporating.

## CONCLUDE AND APPLY

1. **EXPLAIN** Vinegar is a mild acid. How did it change the chalk?

2. **COMPARE AND CONTRAST** Do all rocks change the same way? Explain based on your results.

# How Can We Clean Up the Air?

Cleaning up the air is a job that takes all nations to work on. That is why the Congress of the United States passed laws to protect the air. It passed the Clean Air Act in 1967 and added more parts in 1970, 1977, and 1990.

There are a few common pollutants found all over the United States. The Clean Air Act has many programs designed to decrease air pollution. This list from a booklet called "Plain English Guide to the Clean Air Act" gives you some idea of its scope. Do you see a part that might affect you or your family?

## Clean Air Resolutions

As a result of these laws, cars now have lowered the amounts of harmful wastes that are released. "Clean coal" methods were introduced to lower the amount of harmful wastes that result in acid rain. Power plants that burn coal can wash coal before burning it to remove sulfur. The sulfur can result in acid rain when the coal burns.

In 1970 the first Earth Day was celebrated. People were becoming very concerned about the health of planet Earth. That year the Environmental Protection Agency (EPA) was formed. The EPA is part of the United States government. It has the job of checking that laws are being followed. It investigates new dangers and offers solutions and guidelines.

## Stop Damage Before It's Too Late

These photographs show "holes" in the ozone layer. The ozone layer, remember, is a layer high up in the atmosphere that protects Earth from harmful UV radiation. However, it seems we humans have poked holes in this layer. The holes are letting UV radiation through.

How did the holes get there? Scientists are not totally sure. Much evidence points to substances that people have been using a lot. These substances are called CFCs, which is short for chlorofluorocarbons (klôr'ō flür'ō kär'bənz). They are gases used in such things as refrigerators, freezers, and air conditioners. When the CFCs leak out from these appliances, they rise into the atmosphere. There they can affect the ozone layer.

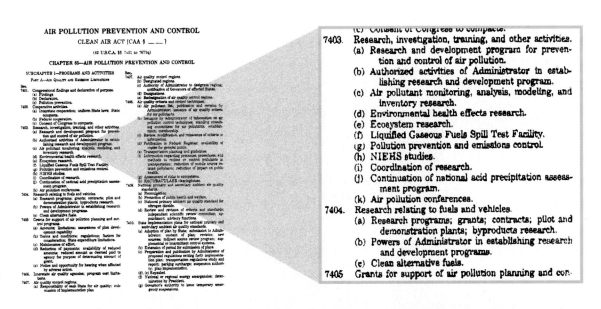

354

CFCs were also used in many aerosol spray cans. Spray paints, hair sprays, and even shaving foams released CFCs with each squeeze of the push button. Concern about the ozone layer changed that. In 1990 a group of representatives from around the world met in London. They signed an agreement to ban the use of CFCs worldwide in just ten years.

Aerosol spray cans now use substitutes. Just read the label on a spray can item and you can see for yourself.

**These photographs show holes developing in the ozone layer.**

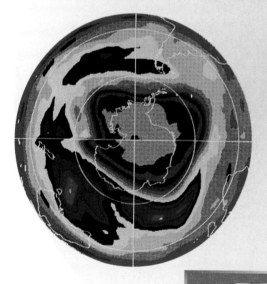
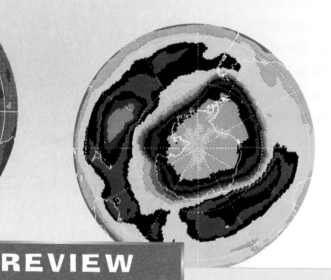

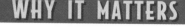

Air pollution harms trees, lakes, and buildings. It can also affect you directly. Air pollution can make people sick. It can make your eyes and nose feel like they are burning. It can make your throat feel itchy and irritated.

Laws help to protect the air. However, it takes people to save the air. The Clean Air Act can work only if people work together. For example, using less electricity can save fuel. Finding ways to cut down on using cars saves fuel, too. Cutting down on burning fuel lowers air pollution.

## REVIEW

**1.** Why is air important to living things?

**2.** How does the atmosphere protect Earth?

**3.** How do people pollute the air?

**4. CAUSE AND EFFECT** What causes acid rain? How does acid rain affect land and water?

**5. CRITICAL THINKING** *Apply* How can using less electricity cut down on use of fossil fuels?

**WHY IT MATTERS** THINK ABOUT IT
How do you know when air is polluted?

**WHY IT MATTERS** WRITE ABOUT IT
How can you cut down on using electricity and fuel? Be specific. Think about things you, your family, and your friends can do.

# PLANETARY WEATHER

What's the weather like on other planets, and should we care? Yes, knowing about the atmosphere on other planets tells us more about our whole solar system!

Over the years scientists have learned that Venus's atmosphere is 97 percent carbon dioxide. Venus is an example of the greenhouse effect. The layer of carbon dioxide traps the Sun's heat, making Venus's average temperature 460°C (860°F)!

Like Earth, Jupiter has storms. Ours begin when the Sun heats the atmosphere. On Jupiter, storms begin when bubbles of heat rise from its hot inner core. When it rains on Jupiter it rains liquid helium!

Venus has yellow clouds of sulfuric acid. Rain from these clouds is like acid rain on Earth, only worse.

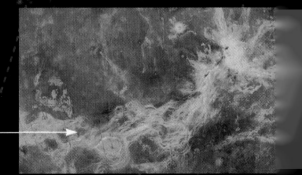

# A Closer Look

One of Jupiter's storms, the Great Red Spot, began long before telescopes were invented. It's two or three times the size of Earth.

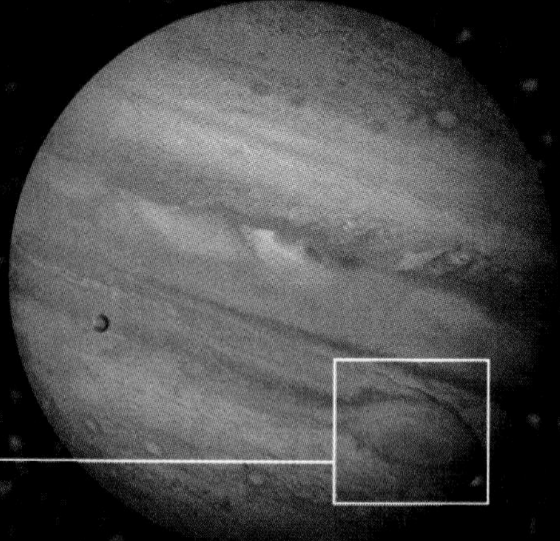

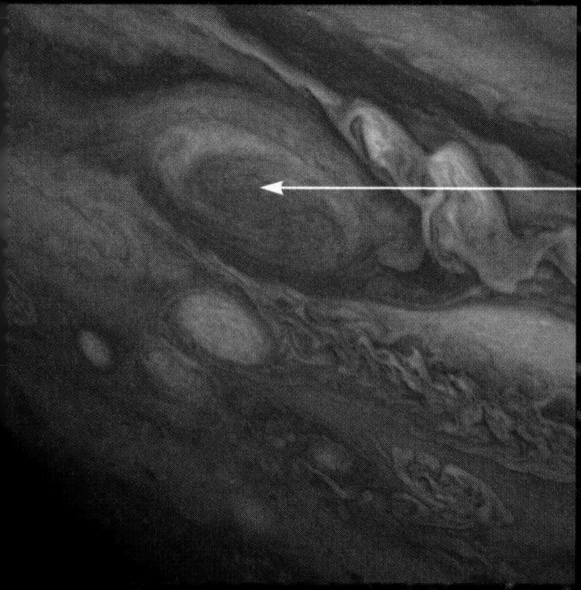

Saturn has three cloud layers—water clouds, ammonia clouds, and ammonia hydrosulfide clouds. Together they form . . . smog!

Venus, Jupiter, Saturn, Uranus, and Neptune have lightning, just as we do on Earth. The lightning is from electrical discharges.

Flashes on Jupiter may be 500 kilometers (310 miles) across!

Pluto has the greatest weather changes of all the planets. That's because its orbit is irregular. When Pluto's close to the Sun, the heat turns the frozen nitrogen on Pluto into a gas. This gives Pluto an atmosphere and weather to go with it. As Pluto moves farther from the Sun, the gas freezes.

## DISCUSSION STARTER

1. Why should the atmosphere on Venus be a warning to us on Earth?

2. What forms of weather do we share with other planets?

To learn more about weather on other planets, visit *www.mhschool.com/science* and enter the keyword CLIMATE.

*inter*NET CONNECTION

357

## WHY IT MATTERS

Everyone must help save water and keep it clean.

### SCIENCE WORDS

**desalination** getting fresh water from seawater

**water cycle** the continuous movement of water between Earth's surface and the air, changing from liquid to gas to liquid

**groundwater** water that seeps into the ground into spaces between bits of rock and soil

**water table** the top of the water-filled spaces in the ground

**aquifer** an underground layer of rock or soil filled with water

**spring** a place where groundwater seeps out of the ground

**well** a hole dug below the water table that water seeps into

**reservoir** a storage area for freshwater supplies

# Earth's Water Supply

On the average an American uses about 660 liters (178 gallons) of water a day. Where do we get all that water?

Over 70 percent of Earth's surface is covered with water. However, most of this is not fresh water but salt water in Earth's oceans. People don't use salt water for drinking or cleaning. Where does our fresh water come from then? How might we change salt water into fresh water?

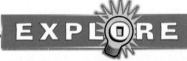

## EXPLORE

**HYPOTHESIZE** How can water with something dissolved in it be changed into fresh water? Write a hypothesis in your *Science Journal*. Test your ideas.

# Investigate How to Make Salt Water Usable

Decide how the water cycle can make salt water fresh.

## MATERIALS

- tea bag
- deep pan
- plastic cup
- saucer (or petri dish)
- large, clear bowl or container
- water
- *Science Journal*

## PROCEDURES

1. **MAKE A MODEL**  Keep a tea bag in a cup of water until the water is orange.

2. **MAKE A MODEL**  Place a pan where there is strong light (sunlight, if possible). Pour some tea water into the saucer. Put the saucer in the pan. Cover the saucer with a large bowl.

3. **OBSERVE**  Look at the bowl and pan several times during the day and the next day. Note any water you see on the bowl or in the pan. Write your observations in your *Science Journal*.

## CONCLUDE AND APPLY

1. **COMPARE AND CONTRAST** How was the water that collected in the bowl or pan different from the tea water?

2. **INFER**  What do you think caused the water to collect in the bowl and pan?

3. **DRAW CONCLUSIONS**  How does this model represent what might happen to salt water, the water of Earth's oceans?

### GOING FURTHER: Problem Solving

4. **USE VARIABLES**  How long did it take for water to collect in the bowl and pan? How might this process be speeded up?

5. **EVALUATE**  Do you think this model shows a useful way of turning ocean water into fresh water? Explain.

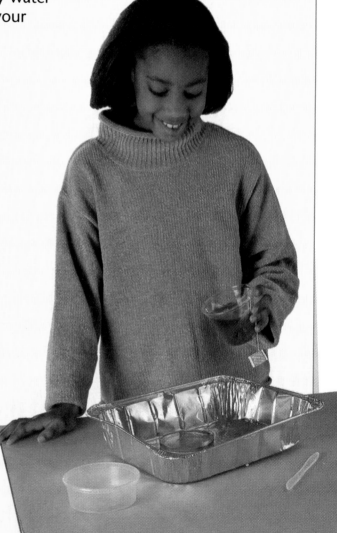

# How Do We Use Earth's Oceans?

If all the water in Earth's hydrosphere was represented by 100 cents, not even 3 cents would represent fresh water. Over 97 cents would be salt water. Salt water is water in the oceans as well as saltwater lakes and inland seas.

Much of the salt in salt water is halite, common rock salt. Salt water has seven times more salt than a person can stand. A person cannot survive drinking it. However, Earth's oceans and inland seas are still useful for the resources they contain.

- **Seafood** What kinds of seafood do you eat? Why are these foods healthful? The oceans support many forms of life. The water has dissolved gases, oxygen, and carbon dioxide, as well as minerals. Plants and other producers of the sea are able to get sunlight so that they can make food. They become food for other forms of sea life, which become food for us.

- **Minerals** Almost everything dissolves in water, at least a little. A pail of seawater contains almost every known element. It contains more minerals than just rock salt.

Hot water bubbling out of underwater volcanoes is especially mineral rich. It leaves rich deposits of minerals on the sea floor. Nodules, or lumps, of minerals can be picked up from the sea floor. They contain manganese and iron. Metals such as tin and gold are also found on the sea floor.

- **Fossil fuels** Offshore rigs pump oil and natural gas from beneath the ocean floor in many places around the globe. This fuel is worth more than all other resources taken from the oceans.

## WATER IN THE HYDROSPHERE

MATH LINK

Fresh water: 2.8%

Salt water: 97.2%

Lakes and streams: 0.01%

Surface water and groundwater: 0.6%

Ice caps and glaciers: 2.2%

Water vapor in atmosphere: 0.001%

## READING GRAPHS

1. **WRITE** Order the items in the bar graph from greatest to least.
2. **DISCUSS** Where is most of Earth's fresh water found?

## DESALINATION PLANT

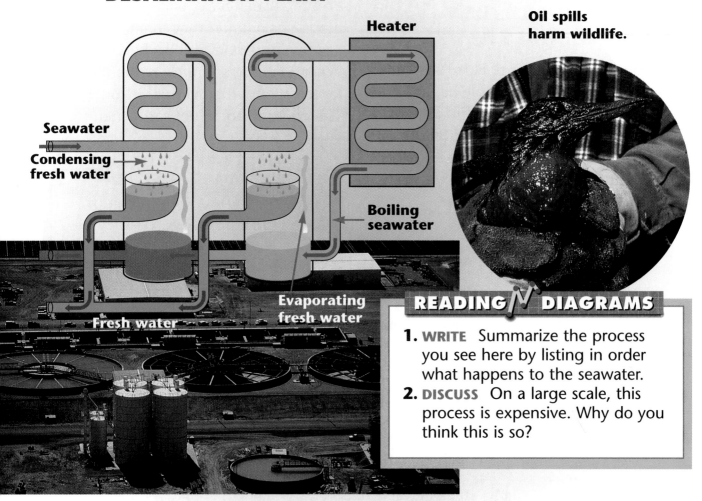

Heater

Oil spills harm wildlife.

Seawater

Condensing fresh water

Boiling seawater

Fresh water

Evaporating fresh water

### READING DIAGRAMS

1. **WRITE** Summarize the process you see here by listing in order what happens to the seawater.
2. **DISCUSS** On a large scale, this process is expensive. Why do you think this is so?

## How Can We Make Salt Water Usable?

You can't drink seawater or use it to water plants. You need fresh water. Your fresh water comes mostly from freshwater lakes and rivers.

Some areas have very little fresh water available. The islands of Malta, for example, are surrounded by the Mediterranean Sea. However, they have no permanent lakes or rivers. Over two-thirds of the water used by the people is gotten from seawater.

Getting fresh water from seawater takes a process called **desalination** (dē sal′ə nā′shən). The Explore Activity introduced this process.

Seawater contains dissolved rock salt and other materials. As water evaporates it leaves the dissolved materials behind. The liquid water that collects at the end of the process is free of dissolved materials.

What else is in seawater that can make it harmful? In the past barges loaded with garbage and poisonous wastes would sail out every day to dump their loads at sea. Sometimes accidents such as oil spills from tankers poured huge amounts of oil into the oceans.

Pollution in the ocean does not go away. It builds up. Eventually it can kill sea life. It ruins our seafood supplies in certain parts of the oceans.

# Where Does Fresh Water Come From?

Only a tiny fraction of Earth's water is usable fresh water. People use so much fresh water each day, you might wonder why it doesn't run out. Fresh water doesn't run out because it is constantly renewed by the **water cycle**.

In the water cycle, water is on the move—as a liquid that changes to a gas (water vapor) and back to liquid. When water evaporates, remember, it leaves behind the material it contained. The water vapor is not salt water.

## Brain Power

Do you think the water that falls to Earth's surface is always "clean"? Does this cycle provide water for every place on Earth? Explain your answers.

## WATER CYCLE

**1** The main source of water in the water cycle is the oceans. Every day trillions of liters of water evaporate from the oceans.

**2** Water also evaporates from rivers, lakes, and other sources on land. Plants give off water vapor as well.

**3** Water vapor in the air cools and condenses into tiny droplets. Bunches of tiny droplets collect into clouds.

**4** Water from clouds falls back to Earth's surface as precipitation. Rain and snow are the main sources of fresh water on land.

Water vapor in the atmosphere

Ice caps and glaciers

Lakes and streams

Drainage basins

**5** When water reaches the ground, three things happen to it. Some water seeps into the ground. Some runs downhill over the surface. Some evaporates back into the air.

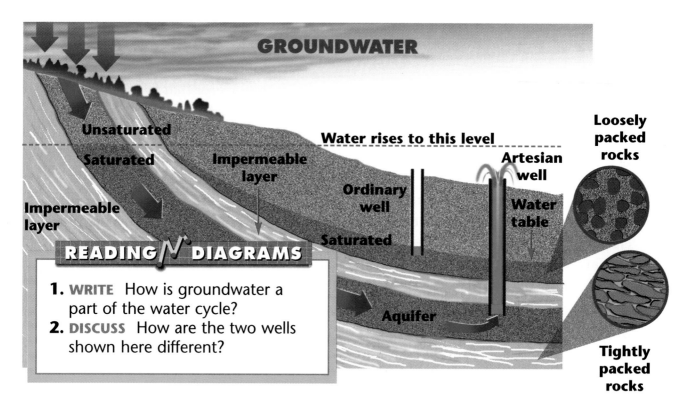

# GROUNDWATER

Unsaturated

Saturated

Impermeable layer

Impermeable layer

Water rises to this level

Ordinary well

Saturated

Artesian well

Water table

Loosely packed rocks

Aquifer

Tightly packed rocks

## READING IN DIAGRAMS

1. **WRITE** How is groundwater a part of the water cycle?
2. **DISCUSS** How are the two wells shown here different?

## Where Rain and Snow Go

When water falls back to Earth, where does it go? Some water seeps into the ground. It becomes **groundwater**. Groundwater seeps into the spaces between bits of rock and soil. It seeps downward until it is blocked by a kind of rock that is so tightly packed that it has few spaces.

Then the water starts to back up and fill the spaces in the soil and rocks above. The top of the water-filled spaces is called the **water table**. If the water table reaches above the surface, a pond, a lake, or a stream forms.

Ponds and lakes are still bodies of water. They form where water fills up low-lying places. Streams, however, flow downhill. As they flow they join with other streams, becoming larger, a river. Eventually rivers reach the oceans or other large bodies of water.

An underground layer of rock or soil that is filled with water is called an **aquifer** (ak′wə fər). Water can move through an aquifer for great distances.

Some groundwater seeps out of the ground in a **spring**. Springs occur where the water table meets the surface. They feed water into streams and lakes long after it stops raining.

Long ago people learned to tap into groundwater by digging **wells**. Wells are holes dug below the water table. The water seeps into the hole. In some wells people get the water out of the hole with pumps. Wells can also be dug deep into aquifers that are sandwiched between tightly packed layers of rock. Water spouts up in these wells because it is being squeezed by the rock layers.

Most supplies of fresh water for large towns and cities come from **reservoirs** (rez′ər vwärz′). Reservoirs are storage areas for freshwater supplies. They may be human-made or natural lakes or ponds. Pipelines transport the water from reservoirs.

## How Can Fresh Water Be Polluted?

Oceans are polluted by people dumping wastes and spilling chemicals. Fresh water can be polluted, too, in many ways.

- **Precipitation** Rain or snow may pick up pollutants from the air. Some chemicals in the air make the rain turn into an acid. Acid rain harms living things and property.

- **Runoff water** Fresh water also gets polluted as it runs off over the land. Water that runs over dumped garbage can end up in streams and lakes. In some cases garbage is dumped into rivers.

- **Groundwater** As water soaks down through the soil, it can pick up chemicals, such as pesticides.

- **Industry** Water used by industry gets polluted as it is used. For example, water that is used to help produce paper is filled with fibers and chemicals.

- You pollute water, too. Every time you flush the toilet, take a bath, brush your teeth, or wash dishes or clothes, water is polluted with wastes. Where do you think this water ends up?

Because of local pollution, many families use water-treatment devices in their faucets. Some families have to use bottled water for cooking and drinking.

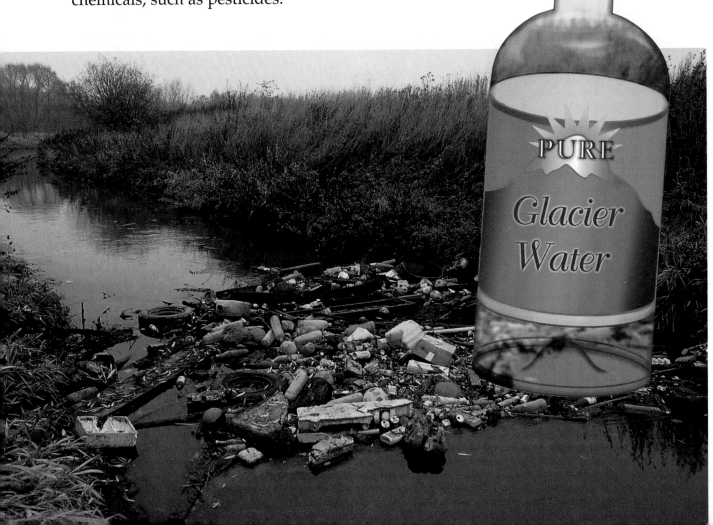

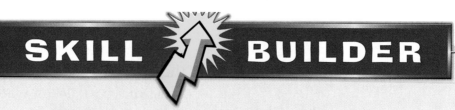
# Skill: Forming a Hypothesis

## HOW DO WASTES FROM LAND GET INTO LAKES AND RIVERS?

In seeking an answer to a question, the first thing you might do is find out as much as possible. You make observations. You might look up information.

Next, you would think of an explanation for these observations. That explanation is a hypothesis. It may be stated as an "If . . . then" sentence. "If water runs over land where garbage is dumped, then . . ." Sometimes you can test a hypothesis by making and observing a model.

### MATERIALS
- soil
- food color
- foam bits
- 2 deep pie pans
- 1 L (2 c) of water
- 2 textbooks
- *Science Journal*

## PROCEDURES

**1. FORM A HYPOTHESIS** Write a hypothesis to answer the question above.

**2. MAKE A MODEL** Pack moist soil to fill one-half (one side) of one pie pan. As you pack the soil, add 8–20 drops of food color to the soil just below the surface. Sprinkle crumbled bits of foam over the top.

**3. EXPERIMENT** Use two books to tilt the pan with the soil side up. Place the lower edge of the soil-filled pan in the other pan. Pour water over the uppermost edge of the pan. In your *Science Journal*, describe what happens. Let your model stand for some time and observe it again.

## CONCLUDE AND APPLY

**1. EXPLAIN** How does this model represent wastes on land?

**2. DRAW CONCLUSIONS** Based on the model, how do wastes from land get into water? Does the model support your hypothesis? Explain.

**3. FORM A HYPOTHESIS** How can some wastes be removed from water? Form a hypothesis, and test your ideas.

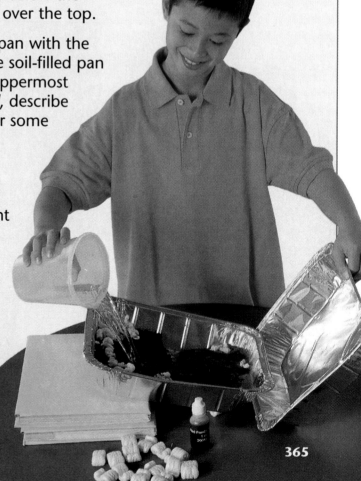

# How Can We Solve Water Problems?

Can polluted water be cleaned up? Yes, it can be—in many ways. For example, the water cycle helps clean water. Remember that when water evaporates, it leaves behind materials it contained. The water vapor and eventually the rain that forms no longer contain those materials.

When water seeps into the ground, the ground acts as a fine screen, or filter. Most dirt particles in water are trapped, or filtered out, as water seeps down through the ground. As a result a well that is dug down deep in the ground collects water that has been filtered.

Freshwater supplies for large areas can be cleaned on a large scale. Follow the steps in the process.

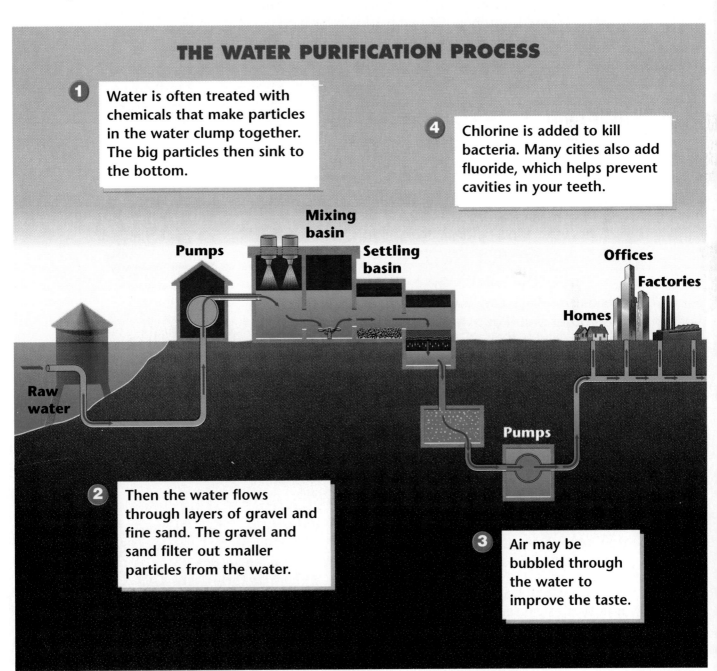

## THE WATER PURIFICATION PROCESS

**1** Water is often treated with chemicals that make particles in the water clump together. The big particles then sink to the bottom.

**4** Chlorine is added to kill bacteria. Many cities also add fluoride, which helps prevent cavities in your teeth.

Mixing basin

Pumps

Settling basin

Offices

Factories

Homes

Raw water

Pumps

**2** Then the water flows through layers of gravel and fine sand. The gravel and sand filter out smaller particles from the water.

**3** Air may be bubbled through the water to improve the taste.

# What Can You Do?

People waste fresh water more than they realize. Often water can be safely reused. At times when the rainfall is low, water supplies may be very low. You may live in a part of the country where water supplies are low much of the time. No matter where you live, saving and recycling water should be part of your daily routine.

## DAILY USES OF WATER

| Activity | Amount of Water Used |
|---|---|
| Flushing a toilet | 16–24 liters |
| Washing dishes | 32–80 liters |
| Taking a shower | 80–120 liters |
| Taking a bath | 120–160 liters |

### READING CHARTS

1. **REPRESENT** How could you make a graph to represent these numbers?
2. **WRITE** How does taking a shower help save water?

The United States Congress has passed laws such as the Safe Drinking Water Act and the Clean Water Act. These laws set standards for water purity. The Environmental Protection Agency (EPA) checks that these laws are being followed.

Laws are important. However, it takes people—like you—to help save water and keep it clean.

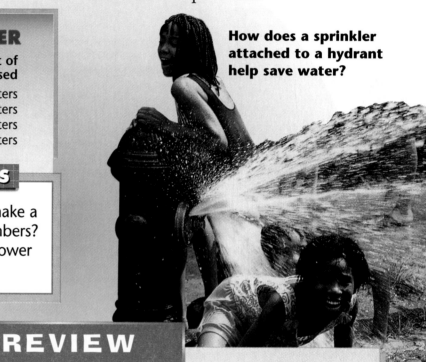

**How does a sprinkler attached to a hydrant help save water?**

## REVIEW

1. How do you depend on the oceans, even if you don't live near one?

2. **HYPOTHESIZE** How does the Sun help provide you with freshwater supplies?

3. How do wastes get into ocean water? Fresh water?

4. How can freshwater supplies be cleaned up?

5. **CRITICAL THINKING** *Evaluate* How can you tell the amount of water wasted in a day by a leaky faucet? Find a way to tell without wasting any.

**WHY IT MATTERS THINK ABOUT IT**
How would you add to the table above to include other ways you use water? To include other ways water is used in your neighborhood or town?

**WHY IT MATTERS WRITE ABOUT IT**
How can you help keep water clean? How can you save water?

# Water Works!

The people of San Antonio, Texas, get their water from one of Earth's great natural resources: the Edwards Aquifer. If too much water's taken from from the aquifer, however, the springs near San Antonio stop flowing. Then plants and animals that depend on the springs have no water source.

During dry periods very little water can be taken from the aquifer. "The city needs a water source that is reliable, even during droughts," says Ken Diehl of the San Antonio Water System (SAWS). He's a water recycling specialist in charge of treating sewer water so it can be used again!

**Air force bases near San Antonio use recycled water to wash planes and water lawns.**

First, mud and other solid material is removed from the water. Next, bacteria are used to kill harmful organisms. Then, the water is filtered. Chlorine is added to kill germs and is then removed. Finally, the cleaned water is pumped into the city's rivers.

In 1998 SAWS decided not to continue releasing all the recycled water into rivers. It began building a 125-kilometer (78-mile) pipeline to carry some recycled water to air force bases and businesses. Water for many activities, such as washing machinery, need not be as pure as drinking water.

# Making a Difference

Using recycled water will reduce SAWS's use of the aquifer by up to 20 percent. Diehl says, "For every drop of recycled water used, one drop of water from Edwards Aquifer is saved. SAWS is taking a leadership role in wisely using its water resources."

## DISCUSSION STARTER

1. What causes springs to stop flowing?

2. How does recycling water help the environment?

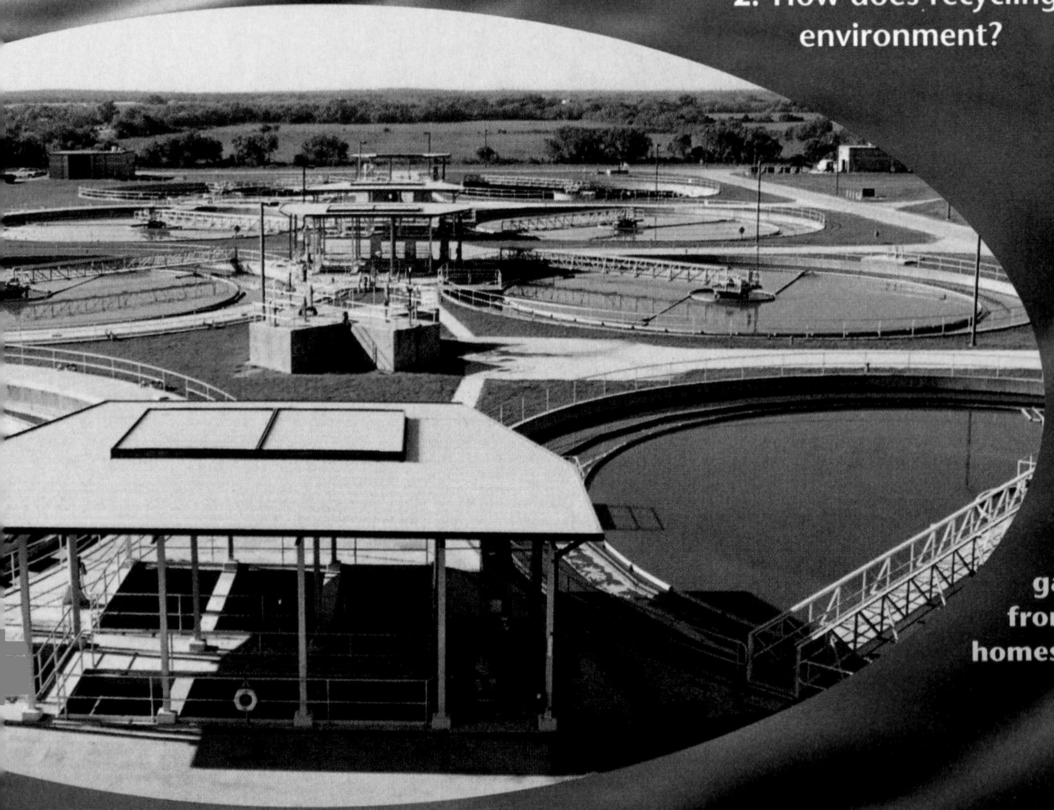

San Antonio has been recycling its water since the 1930s. SAWS cleans millions of gallons of water from San Antonio homes daily.

To learn more about waterworks, visit *www.mhschool.com/science* and enter the keyword WATERWORKS.

*inter*NET
CONNECTION

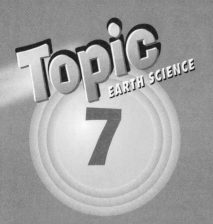

# Topic
### EARTH SCIENCE
# 7

## WHY IT MATTERS

Conserving energy is everyone's responsibility.

## SCIENCE WORDS

**alternative energy source** a source of energy other than the burning of a fossil fuel

**geothermal energy** Earth's internal energy

**biomass** plant matter or animal waste that can be used as a source of energy

# Energy Resources

**H**ow many hours a day do you use energy? What kinds do you use, and what do you use them for? Did you know that you are using energy all the time? How is that possible?

How many different ways are the people in this picture using energy?

## EXPLORE

**HYPOTHESIZE** How many different ways do you use energy each day? How can you use less energy? Write a hypothesis in your *Science Journal*. Test your ideas.

# EXPLORE ACTIVITY

## Investigate How People Use Energy

Record all the ways you use energy in a day.

## PROCEDURES

1. **COMMUNICATE** Make a list in your *Science Journal* of all the different *ways you use energy*. You might list cooking, heat or air conditioning, transportation, lighting, entertainment (TV, radio, CD player), computer, and so on.

2. **COMMUNICATE** Make a list of all the different *kinds of energy* you use in a day. Types of energy you might list include electricity (lights, TV), gasoline (riding in cars), gas (stove), wood (fireplace), oil (heat), solar energy.

3. **COLLECT DATA** Make a table listing all the kinds of energy you use in a day, how you use that energy, and how many hours you use each.

**MATERIALS**

• *Science Journal*

## CONCLUDE AND APPLY

1. **ANALYZE** How many different ways do you use electricity each day? How many hours a day do you use electricity? What other sources of energy do you use? How many hours a day do you use each?

2. **INFER** Make a log to keep track of your energy use at home and at school. How can you use that information to help you make a plan to save energy?

3. **USE NUMBERS** If it costs you an average of ten cents an hour for the energy you use, how much would the energy you use cost each week? About how much would it cost each month?

### GOING FURTHER: Apply

4. **HYPOTHESIZE** How can you use less electricity? How much money do you think you could save on energy use in a month? How would you go about testing your hypothesis?

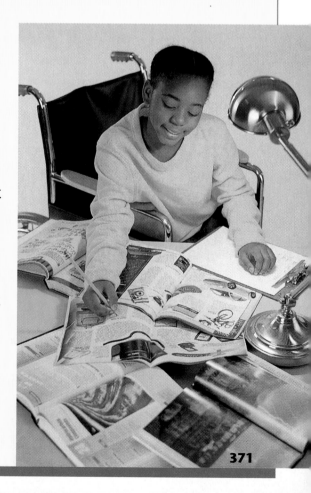

# How Do People Use Energy?

As the Explore Activity showed, you use a number of different energy sources each day. Where does the energy you use come from? Try tracing it back to its source. Many homes, schools, and businesses get heat by burning oil or natural gas. Some older buildings still burn coal for heat. Some homes burn wood for heat.

The heat in many other homes and businesses comes from electricity. So does the energy to run many common devices, such as lights, computers, radios, TVs, and washers. Some small devices such as flashlights and portable CD players get their electricity from batteries. Most of the other devices use electricity from a wall outlet. That electricity comes from a power plant. Electricity from that plant reaches your home through wires. However, the power plant makes electricity by using energy from burning fuels such as coal, oil, and natural gas.

It takes a lot of energy to move a car, bus, or train. Public and private transportation is one of the greatest uses of energy in today's world. Most vehicles get their energy from burning fuels such as gasoline or diesel oil. Others run on electricity, propane, or liquefied natural gas.

As you can see, most of the energy you use can be traced back to fossil fuels—coal, oil, or natural gas. These energy sources are burned in order to release energy.

## Brain Power

How did people solve their energy problems in the past? Find out what sources of energy they used and how.

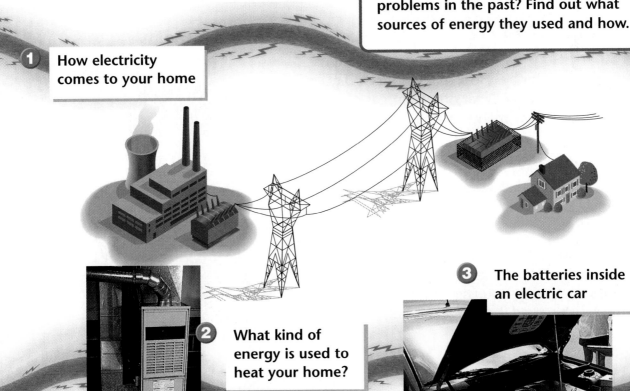

1. How electricity comes to your home

2. What kind of energy is used to heat your home?

3. The batteries inside an electric car

## How Are Fossil Fuels Turned into Energy?

Heat from burning fossil fuels can be used directly to heat homes, schools, businesses, and factories.

The heat can also be used to generate electricity. The heat is used to boil water and turn it into steam. The steam is trapped, and pressure builds up. Then the steam is released. The steam is directed at a big, pinwheel-like turbine. When the steam hits the turbine, it causes it to spin. The spinning turbine turns a generator to make electricity.

All fuels have advantages and disadvantages. The advantage of using fossil fuels is that they contain a lot of energy. However, fossil fuels take millions of years to form. Once used they cannot be replaced fast enough for future use. Therefore, they are nonrenewable.

Burning a fossil fuel also gives off smoke, gases, and other by-products. These pollute the environment. That is why the search is on for other, cleaner fuels.

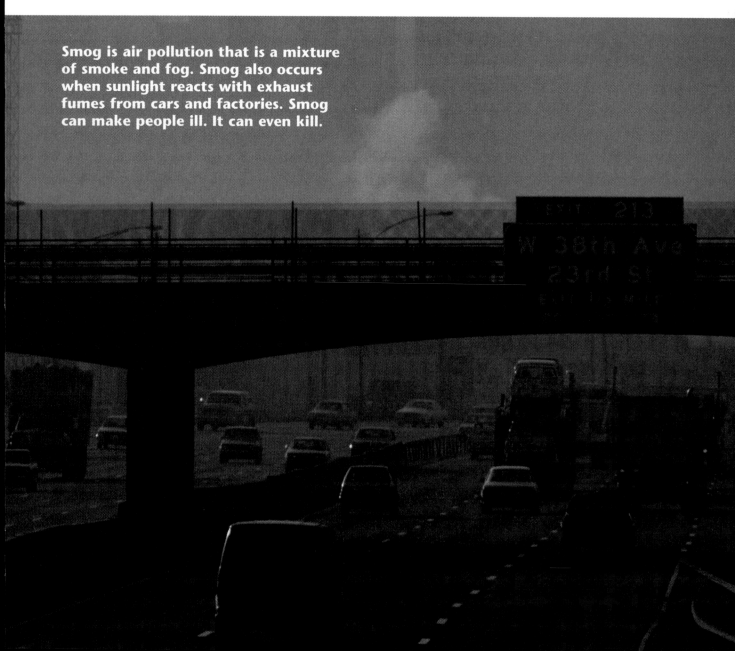

Smog is air pollution that is a mixture of smoke and fog. Smog also occurs when sunlight reacts with exhaust fumes from cars and factories. Smog can make people ill. It can even kill.

# Where Do Fossil Fuels Come From?

Fossil fuels are the remains of once-living things. Coal formed from the remains of dead plants buried in ancient swamps and forests. Natural gas and oil formed from the remains of tiny ocean plants and animals. These sea creatures died and fell to the bottom of the ocean. There their bodies were buried by layers of sand and mud. As more and more layers covered these remains, pressure on them built up. Eventually, the layers of sediments turned into sedimentary rock. Over millions of years, the plant and animal remains changed into oil and natural gas.

## Brain Power

To whom do Earth's energy resources belong? What should we do to try to conserve them?

## HOW FOSSIL FUELS ARE FORMED

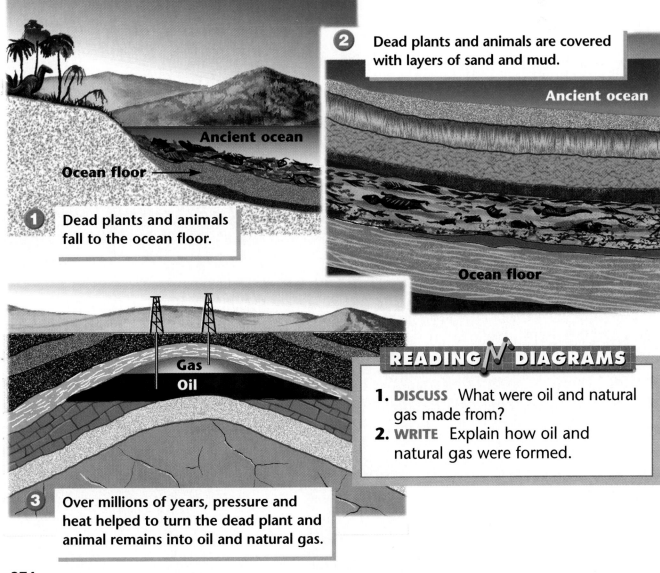

**Ancient ocean**

**Ocean floor** →

**1** Dead plants and animals fall to the ocean floor.

**2** Dead plants and animals are covered with layers of sand and mud.

**Ancient ocean**

**Ocean floor**

**Gas**

**Oil**

**3** Over millions of years, pressure and heat helped to turn the dead plant and animal remains into oil and natural gas.

## READING DIAGRAMS

1. **DISCUSS** What were oil and natural gas made from?
2. **WRITE** Explain how oil and natural gas were formed.

# How Much Energy Do We Have Left?

Our supplies of fossil fuels are limited, and fossil fuels are not a renewable energy source.

With the growth of industry, the demand for and use of energy also grows. The United States is the world's largest consumer of energy. The energy we use makes our lives easier. However, energy use pollutes the environment. It also speeds up the rate at which Earth's energy resources are used up.

If we continue to use fossil fuels at our present rate, we will run out of them. There are two possible solutions to this problem. One is to conserve our energy resources so that they will last longer. Another is to search for other sources of energy.

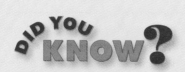

**The Sun is often called an inexhaustible source of energy. As far as you are concerned, it is. Yet even the Sun will run out of energy one day.**

**Astronomers estimate that the Sun will keep shining much the way it does today for "only" about another five billion years. What do you think will happen then?**

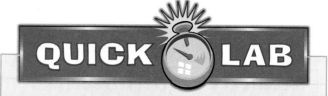

# Fuel Supply

**HYPOTHESIZE** We are using fossil fuels at the rates shown in the table. How long will Earth's fossil fuel supply last? Write a hypothesis in your *Science Journal.* Test your ideas.

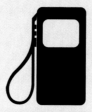

### MATERIALS
- *Science Journal*

This table shows how fast we are using up oil and natural gas.

| World Supply of Oil and Natural Gas (as of January 1, 1996) | |
|---|---|
| Oil | 1,007 billion barrels (1,007,000,000,000) |
| Natural gas | 4,900 trillion cubic feet |

| World Use of Oil and Natural Gas for 1995 | |
|---|---|
| Oil | about 70 million barrels a day (70,000,000) |
| Natural gas | about 78 trillion cubic feet |

## PROCEDURES

1. **OBSERVE** Examine the data in the table.

2. **COMMUNICATE** Draw a graph showing how long the fossil fuels we know about will last at our current rate of use.

## CONCLUDE AND APPLY

**INFER** Predict how long it will be until we run out of each type of fossil fuel.

# What Other Sources of Energy Are There?

Sources of energy other than the burning of fossil fuels are called **alternative energy sources**. Here are some alternative energy sources.

## Modern Waterwheels

Any whitewater rafter can tell you that running water has a lot of energy. That energy can be harnessed to do work using waterwheels. Running or falling water turns the wheel. The turning wheel spins an axle, which is attached to various machines to do work.

In a mill the axle turns a big stone that grinds up grain. In a sawmill it spins a blade to cut wood. In a *hydroelectric* (hī′drō i lek′trik) *plant*, running or falling water spins a gener-ator to make electricity.

## Harnessing the Wind

Have you ever watched a pinwheel spin in the wind? Wind, or moving air, can also spin a wheel. Holland is well known for its great windmills.

## Earth's Furnace

The Earth's interior is very hot. The most common evidence of that heat is simply hot water or steam coming out of the ground. The water is heated below the surface in places where magma collects. Earth's internal heat is called **geothermal** (jē′ō thûr′məl) **energy**. Geothermal energy can be used to heat homes and produce electricity.

- Homes in Boise, Idaho, have been heated by hot springs since the 1890s.
- At *The Geysers* in California, steam drives turbines that generate electricity. The steam comes from underground water heated by geothermal energy.

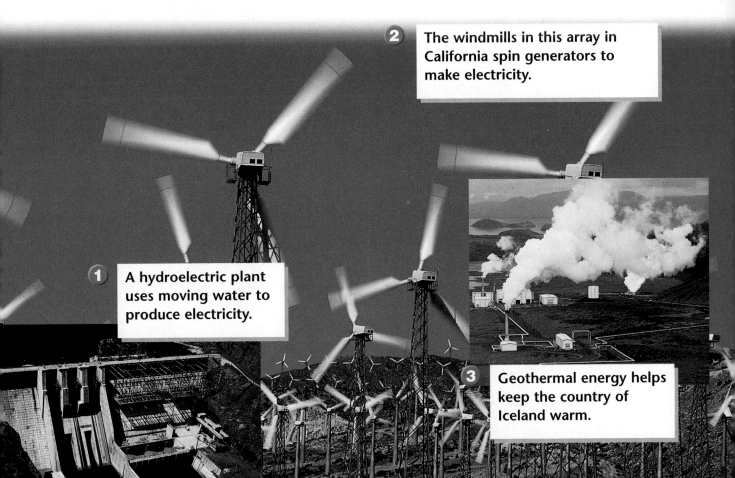

**2** The windmills in this array in California spin generators to make electricity.

**1** A hydroelectric plant uses moving water to produce electricity.

**3** Geothermal energy helps keep the country of Iceland warm.

# How Can We Use Solar Energy?

Every day the Sun bathes Earth in energy. We usually think of that solar energy simply as sunlight. Plants harness the Sun's energy through photosynthesis to make chemical compounds rich in energy. When you burn wood, you are releasing energy that a tree absorbed from the Sun.

Sunlight also gives water the energy to evaporate and rise into the atmosphere. In this way the energy of running water can also be traced back to sunlight.

Today people are using new ways to harness the power of sunlight. One way is to trap or concentrate sunlight with the use of solar panels, or collectors. The trapped sunlight can be used to heat water or entire homes. Another way to use it is with solar cells. Solar cells are devices that convert sunlight into electric energy.

## Tapping the Tide

Every day the tide causes the water level to rise and drop along the world's coastlines. Now imagine a big tank built just below the high-water level. The tide rises, and water fills the tank. When the tide drops, the water flows out of the tank. Add a water-wheel so the water flowing out of the tank spins the wheel. Now you have a spinning axle that can be used to do work. That's the idea behind this tidal power plant in Holland.

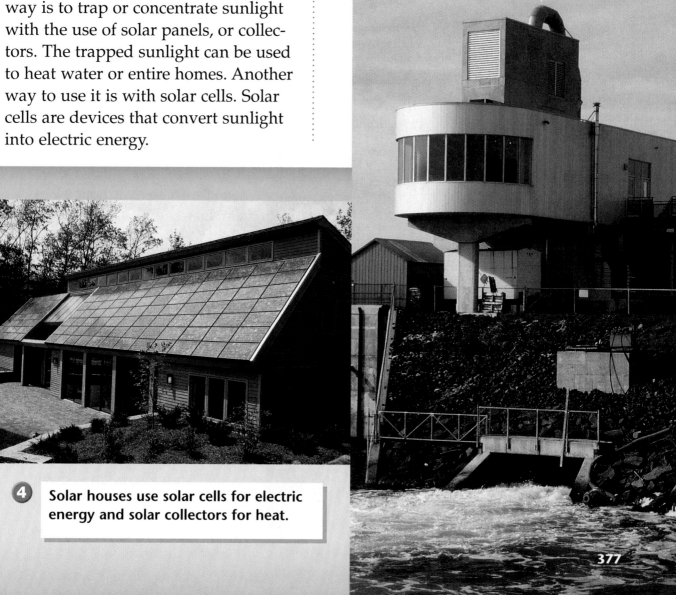

**5** **Tidal power plant in Holland**

**4** **Solar houses use solar cells for electric energy and solar collectors for heat.**

# How Can We Conserve Energy?

Unfortunately alternative energy sources are not fully replacing fossil fuels. Therefore, we need to conserve these nonrenewable resources.

What does it mean to conserve our resources? It means we don't waste what we have and we use as little of what we have as possible. Take a typical house as an example. Better insulation of homes has cut United States' consumption of fuel oil almost in half. Newly designed bodies and engines have doubled the gasoline mileage of most cars. If we could cut our present consumption in half, our oil reserves would last twice as long! How can we do that?

One way is to use alternative energy sources such as water, wind, and solar energy. Every watt of electricity we get from a solar cell is one less watt we have to get by burning oil or coal.

## How Else Stored Sunlight Is Used

You have learned that fossil fuels are the stored energy that came from once-living plants and animals. Fossil fuels are nonrenewable. However, plant matter and animal wastes or other remains—called **biomass**—can be used as a renewable energy source. Plant material and animal wastes that might wind up as garbage can be processed to form fuel. This is done in waste-treatment plants. The treated wastes can then be burned. Special devices called scrubbers help prevent pollutants from entering the air when these wastes are burned. Solid wastes can also be digested by bacteria. The bacteria produce methane gas in the process. Methane gas can be used as fuel.

Corn and other grains, and even sugarcane, can also be turned into fuel. This fuel can be used to heat foods. It can also be mixed with gasoline to help run cars while saving gasoline supplies.

**This car is powered by a special mixture that combines alcohol from biomass with gasoline.**

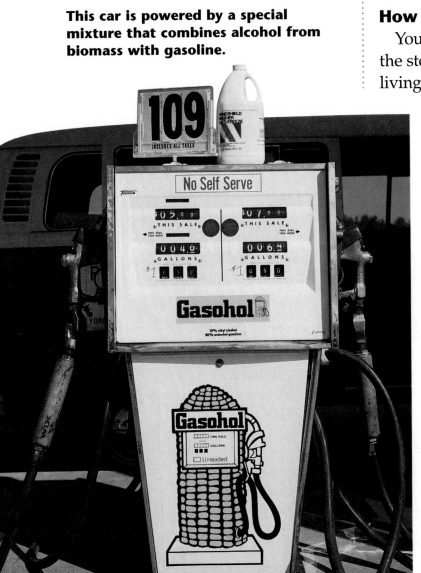

378

## Recycling

Another way to conserve energy is to recycle. Making things uses energy. If we can reuse a material, we save the energy needed to make it. For example, getting aluminum metal out of its ore takes a lot of electricity. If we recycled aluminum cans, some of the metal we needed would come from the cans rather than from ore. Can you think of other ways in which you could conserve energy?

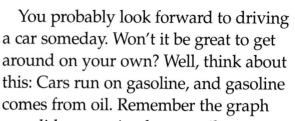

You probably look forward to driving a car someday. Won't it be great to get around on your own? Well, think about this: Cars run on gasoline, and gasoline comes from oil. Remember the graph you did comparing known oil reserves with our current rate of use? If we don't conserve, will there be enough gas for your car? Will there be enough gas for your children's cars? Will there be enough gas for their children?

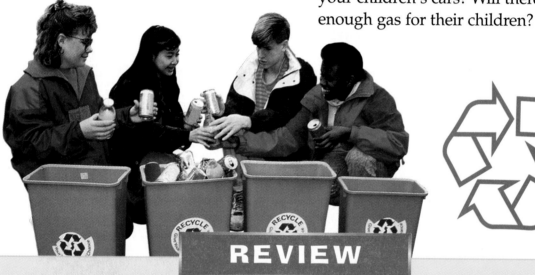

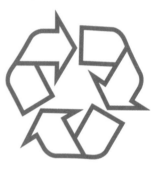

## REVIEW

1. How do you use energy each day?

2. Why are coal, oil, and natural gas called "fossil" fuels?

3. How does the burning of fossil fuels pollute the environment?

4. **COMPARE AND CONTRAST** List five ways people can help to conserve fossil fuels. Which of these suggestions do you think would conserve the most fuel? Which of these suggestions do you think more people would be willing to try?

5. **CRITICAL THINKING** *Analyze* What alternatives do we have to using fossil fuels for energy? What are some of the advantages and some of the disadvantages of using these energy sources?

**WHY IT MATTERS** THINK ABOUT IT
Alternative sources of energy help us to conserve fossil fuels. What if your house was close to a stream or bathed in strong sunlight every day, or there was a hot spring in your neighborhood? How could you use an alternative energy source to save energy in your home?

**WHY IT MATTERS** WRITE ABOUT IT
Describe how you might use an alternative energy source to supply some of the energy needs for your home.

**READING SKILL**
Write a paragraph to explain what conclusions you would draw about relying less on fossil fuels.

## Science, Technology, and Society

# Nuclear... or Not?

**N**uclear energy can be used to power a submarine, explode a bomb, or run a power plant. Today nuclear power costs about the same as coal power. Which is best to use?

Small amounts of uranium can run a nuclear power plant for years. Coal-fired plants use tons of coal daily, and someday we'll run out of coal.

Coal smoke adds to air pollution and global warming. Nuclear plants release only water vapor.

Both nuclear and coal plants can be damaged. In 1986 a nuclear plant in the Soviet Union burned. Radioactive fallout spread all over northern Europe.

Coal-fired plants have burned down, but damage was limited to the plant.

Both nuclear and coal wastes have leaked. Nuclear wastes can be radioactive for thousands of years. Coal ash can contaminate water supplies.

## DISCUSSION STARTER

1. What is a disadvantage of nuclear power? Of coal power?

2. Is nuclear or coal power better for the environment? Why?

The U.S. has more than 100 nuclear plants. They produce about one-tenth of our electricity.

Coal can pollute the air.

To learn more about nuclear energy, visit *www.mhschool.com/science* and enter the keyword NUCLEAR.

*inter*NET
CONNECTION

## SCIENCE WORDS

| | |
|---|---|
| acid rain p.353 | ozone layer p.351 |
| biomass p.378 | renewable p.350 |
| desalination p.361 | reservoir p.363 |
| fossil fuel p.352 | smog p.352 |
| groundwater p.363 | water table p.363 |

## USING SCIENCE WORDS

**Number a paper from 1 to 10. Fill in 1 to 5 with words from the list above.**

1. Oxygen is a(n) __?__ resource.

2. A renewable resource that gets energy from garbage is __?__.

3. A type of precipitation caused by air pollution is __?__.

4. Dangerous air pollution is called __?__.

5. Natural gas is a(n) __?__.

**6–10. Pick five words from the list above that were not used in 1 to 5, and use each in a sentence.**

## UNDERSTANDING SCIENCE IDEAS

11. What is the difference between renewable and nonrenewable energy sources?

12. How were fossil fuels formed?

13. Where does geothermal energy come from?

14. What is the difference between fossil fuels and biomass?

15. Explain how to turn salt water into fresh water.

## USING IDEAS AND SKILLS

16. How does smog form?

17. **READING SKILL: DRAW CONCLUSIONS** All electricity is made by burning fossil fuels. Is this true or false? Explain your answer.

18. Sunlight is free. However, solar energy is considered "too expensive" to use in the Northeast. How can something that is free be too expensive? Research the cost of various energy sources in your area.

19. **HYPOTHESIZE** Does rain remove pollutant particles from the air? Form a hypothesis. What could you do to test your hypothesis?

20. **THINKING LIKE A SCIENTIST** Does filtering water remove all impurities? Explain your answer. How would you prove your answer?

## PROBLEMS and PUZZLES

**Saving Soil** How do growing plants help conserve soil? Grow some grass seeds in a tray. In a second tray, lay down some soil. Tilt both trays, and use a watering can to produce "rain" over them. Which tray loses more soil?

# UNIT 4 REVIEW

biomass p.378

cleavage p.322

desalinization
    p.361

geothermal
    energy p.376

hydrosphere p.298

inertia p.295

lithosphere p.298

metamorphic
    rock p.336

mineral p.320

ozone layer p.351

renewable
    resource p.350

reservoir p.363

spring p.363

weathering p.310

## USING SCIENCE WORDS

**Number a paper from 1 to 10. Beside each number write the word or words that best complete the sentence.**

1. The tendency of an object to move continually in a straight line is called ___?___.

2. All of Earth's water is collectively called the ___?___.

3. The breakdown of rocks into small pieces is called ___?___.

4. Streak, luster, hardness, and cleavage are properties of ___?___.

5. Marble, formed by the action of heat and pressure on limestone, is a(n) ___?___.

6. Oxygen that is given off by plants is an example of a(n) ___?___.

7. The gas that screens out UV (ultraviolet) rays from the Sun is ___?___.

8. Groundwater seeps out of the ground at places called ___?___.

9. Fresh water can be produced from seawater by a process called ___?___.

10. Energy from geysers is an example of ___?___.

## UNDERSTANDING SCIENCE IDEAS

**Write 11 to 15. For each number write the letter for the best answer. You may wish to use the hints provided.**

11. The length of a day on a planet is always
    a. 24 hours
    b. one rotation of the planet
    c. dependent on its distance from the Sun
    d. the same for all planets
    *(Hint: Read page 296.)*

12. Which of the following can be scratched by glass?
    a. steel plate
    b. diamond
    c. chalk
    *(Hint: Read page 322.)*

13. Which of the following pollutes the air?
    a. sulfur
    b. calcium
    c. water
    d. oxygen
    *(Hint: Read page 354.)*

14. Most fresh water is found in
    a. groundwater
    b. ice caps and glaciers
    c. oceans
    d. lakes and streams
    *(Hint: Read page 360.)*

15. What fuel is used by most cars and trucks?
    a. natural gas
    b. electricity
    c. gasoline or diesel oil
    d. propane
    *(Hint: Read page 372.)*

## USING IDEAS AND SKILLS

**16.** Why doesn't Earth fly away from the Sun in a straight line?

**17.** In what way is the Moon's gravity important?

**18.** How do we know that Earth's surface can move?

**19.** **DEFINE** How is hardness defined for minerals?

**20.** What are the two types of coal? How are they related?

**21.** Explain what a renewable resource is. Give an example.

**22.** How does burning coal cause acid rain?

**23.** Where does the fresh water found in glaciers and rivers come from?

## THINKING LIKE A SCIENTIST

**24.** **HYPOTHESIZE** Explain why you might have to use a model to test a hypothesis.

**25.** Would a tidal power plant be able to produce electricity at all hours of the day? Explain.

## WRITING IN YOUR JOURNAL

**SCIENCE IN YOUR LIFE**
Describe two ways you use water each day and two ways businesses or farms use water. Explain how these uses might pollute water.

**PRODUCT ADS**
More and more ads are appearing for electric cars (EVs) that run on electricity rather than gasoline. Why do you think companies are starting to make such cars?

**HOW SCIENTISTS WORK**
Scientists routinely organize information in tables and graphs. Use two examples from this unit to tell why this is useful.

## Design your own Experiment

Form a hypothesis about how much garbage is produced in your school. Design an experiment to test your hypothesis. Think safety first. Review your experiment with your teacher before you attempt it.

## interNET CONNECTION

For help in reviewing this unit, visit *www.mhschool.com/science*

# PROBLEMS and PUZZLES

## Weathering Model

There are two types of weathering. Physical weathering is the grinding up of rocks into smaller pieces. Chemical weathering takes place when chemicals change or break down rocks.

Does physical weathering affect chemical weathering? Find out by filling two cups with water. Put a ground-up sugar cube in one cup and a whole cube in the other. Which type of sugar dissolves more quickly? Can you explain why?

**Ground-up sugar cube**     **Whole sugar cube**

## Garbage to the Moon

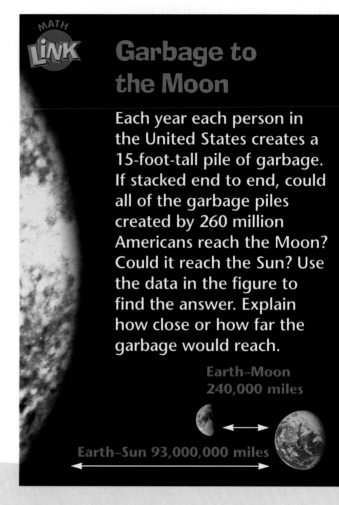

Each year each person in the United States creates a 15-foot-tall pile of garbage. If stacked end to end, could all of the garbage piles created by 260 million Americans reach the Moon? Could it reach the Sun? Use the data in the figure to find the answer. Explain how close or how far the garbage would reach.

**Earth–Moon 240,000 miles**

**Earth–Sun 93,000,000 miles**

## Soil: A Close-Up View

Fill a tall glass jar one-third full with soil. Add water to make the jar two-thirds full. Add a capful of water softener, if available. Then analyze your soil.

1. Shake the mixture well. Then let it settle for 15 to 20 minutes, until layers form.

2. Which layer settles first? Second? Third? Hold a sheet of paper next to the jar. Draw each layer that you see.

3. Compare your soil to the soil shown in the diagram. Is your soil sandy, silty, or high in clay?

4. Which kind of soil do you think is best for growing plants? Plant some seeds, and see if you are right.

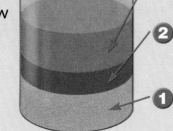

**3** **Clay:** The lightest, finest particles are clay. Some stay suspended in the water.

**2** **Silt:** The silt layer is made of the small, heavy particles. Silt settles after the sand.

**1** **Sand:** Sand settles first. The sand layer is made of the large, heavy particles.

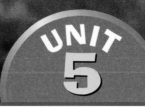

UNIT
5

# HUMAN BODY:PATHWAYS

## CHAPTER 9
# BLOOD
# AND AIR

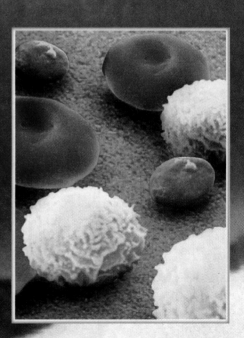

Do you ever receive mail? Think about how many people, buildings, and machines it takes to pick up and deliver mail to millions of homes and offices.

Your body is made up of more than 100 trillion living cells. To stay alive every cell needs nutrients and oxygen delivered to it all day, every day. Every cell also needs harmful wastes picked up and removed from your body.

No post office could do this much work. Do you know how your body does it?

In Chapter 9 locate details as you read.

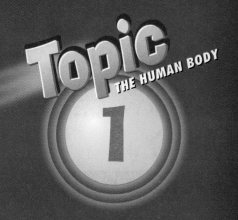
## WHY IT MATTERS

**Your body moves important materials to and from each of your cells.**

### SCIENCE WORDS

**plasma** the pale-yellow liquid part of blood that contains nutrients

**hemoglobin** a chemical that carries oxygen around in the body

**platelet** a cell fragment in blood that helps blood to form clots

**artery** a blood vessel that carries blood away from the heart

**vein** a blood vessel that carries blood toward the heart

**capillary** the smallest type of blood vessel, where materials are exchanged between blood and body cells

**transfusion** taking blood from one person and giving it to another person

**antibody** a protein in blood that helps the body find and destroy materials that may be harmful

# A Blood System

A 35-year-old man goes to an eye doctor. She uses a light to look into his eyes and asks, "Do you eat hamburgers with french fries at fast food restaurants?"

He answers, "Yes."

Looking in the other eye, she asks, "How about pizza, soy sauce, and sausage?" Again the answer is yes.

The doctor says, "Your eyes are fine, but I want you to see another doctor for your heart."

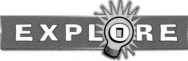

# EXPLORE

**HYPOTHESIZE** What do all the foods have in common? What do they have to do with his heart? Write a hypothesis in your *Science Journal*. Test your ideas.

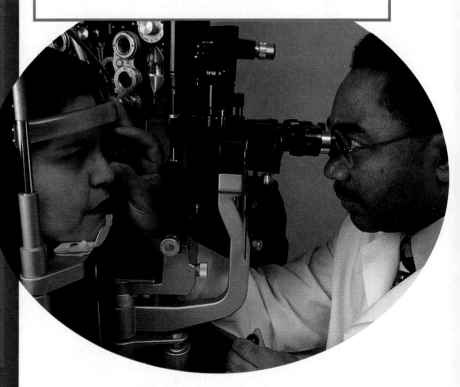

# EXPLORE ACTIVITY

# Investigate How Blood Travels

Examine the path blood takes through your heart.

## PROCEDURES

▨ **SAFETY** Use the scissors carefully!

1. **MAKE A MODEL** Draw an oval about the size of your fist on the paper. Cut it out. Cut the oval down the middle, and label it as shown.

2. Tape each piece of yarn to a white card. If *R* is the right side of the heart and *L* is the left side, trace the yarn and thread starting at *Out* on the *R* side. Sketch the model in your *Science Journal*.

3. **COMPARE** Tape the halves of the oval "heart" together. Does the path of the yarn and thread change?

## CONCLUDE AND APPLY

1. **SEQUENCE** Assume blood flows through the yarn and the thread. Where does blood that enters the right side of the heart come from? Where does it go?

2. **COMPARE AND CONTRAST** Where does blood come from to enter the left side of the heart? Where does it go? How is this different from the right side?

## GOING FURTHER: Problem Solving

3. **DRAW CONCLUSIONS** Why does the blood travel to the lungs? What do you think happens to the blood in the lungs?

## MATERIALS

- sheet of paper
- scissors
- tape
- 5 cm (2 in.) of red yarn
- 5 cm of blue yarn
- four 5-cm-square white cards
- 10 cm (4 in.) of red yarn
- 10 cm of blue yarn
- two 10-cm pieces of black thread
- *Science Journal*

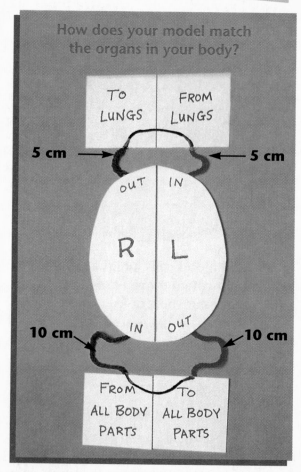

How does your model match the organs in your body?

**Tape the free ends of yarn to the proper parts of the model as shown. Label your oval as the above picture indicates.**

# How Does Blood Travel?

The Explore Activity showed that blood travels from all parts of your body to the heart. Then it is pumped to your lungs and back to the heart to be pumped out to the body again.

Blood is a mixture of liquid and cells. The pale-yellow liquid, called **plasma** (plaz′mə), is mostly water and contains nutrients. These nutrients include dissolved sugars, proteins, and gases.

Most cells in blood are red blood cells, which are shaped like a doughnut without the hole. They contain the chemical **hemoglobin** (hē′mə glō′bin), which carries oxygen around your body. Blood also contains germ-fighting white blood cells and **platelets** (plāt′lits). When you have a cut, platelets help stop the bleeding by forming clots.

Blood travels through three kinds of blood vessels—**arteries** (är′tə rēz), **veins** (vānz), and **capillaries** (kap′ə ler′ēz). Arteries are blood vessels that carry blood away from your heart. Veins are blood vessels that carry blood back to your heart. Capillaries are where materials are exchanged between the blood and body cells.

**Red blood cell**  **White blood cell**

Blood vessels can range in size from large to very tiny. The largest vessels connect directly to your heart. The smallest arteries and veins connect to the smallest type of blood vessel, called a capillary.

ARTERY

Red blood cells' unique shape helps them move easily to carry out their tasks.

CAPILLARY

## READING ⁄Ⅴ DIAGRAMS

**DISCUSS** How does blood flow change as blood moves from veins to capillaries?

Capillaries are too tiny to see without a microscope. Your red blood cells move through them in single file.

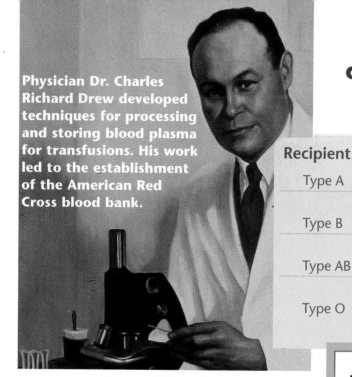

Physician Dr. Charles Richard Drew developed techniques for processing and storing blood plasma for transfusions. His work led to the establishment of the American Red Cross blood bank.

## GIVING BLOOD

| Recipient | Donor Type A | Type B | Type AB | Type O |
|---|---|---|---|---|
| Type A | YES | NO | NO | YES |
| Type B | NO | YES | NO | YES |
| Type AB | YES | YES | YES | YES |
| Type O | NO | NO | NO | YES |

## READING N CHARTS

1. **WRITE** Why do doctors need to know a patient's blood type before giving a transfusion?
2. **DISCUSS** If type O is the universal donor, which blood type would be the universal recipient?

# What's Your Blood Type?

Have you ever read about injured people who needed **transfusions** (trans fū′zhənz)? A transfusion is taking blood from a healthy person and giving it to another person who needs it. The person giving the blood is the *donor*. The person receiving the blood is the *recipient*.

People have been doing tranfusions for several hundred years. Some worked. Other times the transfused blood clumped, and the recipient died.

Scientists discovered two chemicals, called *antigens*, on the surface of red blood cells. They named the antigens A and B to distinguish between them.

People with only type A antigens in their blood have type A blood. People with only type B antigens have type B blood. AB blood contains both antigens. Blood without any A or B antigens is called type O blood.

Certain **antibodies** (an′ti bod′ēz) affect these chemical blood types. An antibody is a protein in blood that helps find and destroy harmful materials in the body.

Antibodies form clumps around unfamiliar antigens. For example, type A blood has antibodies to clump around blood cells with type B antigens.

Type O blood is special because it has no A or B antigens, so antibodies won't clump around it. This is why it is called the "universal donor" type.

Another chemical in blood cells is the Rh chemical. Blood with Rh chemical is called *Rh positive*. Blood without it is called *Rh negative*. Rh negative blood forms clumps around Rh positive blood. Doctors are very careful when mothers and babies have different blood types. They use special medicines to keep the two different blood types from clotting.

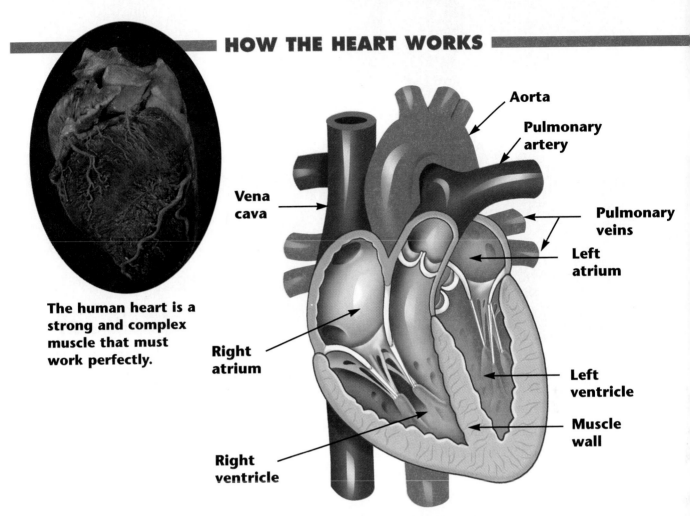

**The human heart is a strong and complex muscle that must work perfectly.**

Labels: Aorta, Pulmonary artery, Pulmonary veins, Left atrium, Left ventricle, Muscle wall, Right ventricle, Right atrium, Vena cava

## How Does the Heart Work?

Your heart constantly pumps blood to every part of your body. The Explore Activity showed how blood moves through the heart.

The heart is a muscle about the size of your fist, located in your rib cage.

The heart has two sides, a right side and a left side, separated by a thick muscular wall. Each side has two chambers for blood. The upper chamber is called the *atrium*. The lower chamber is called the *ventricle*. A one-way valve allows blood to move from the atrium to the ventricle.

Inside your heart special cells give off electrical signals without help from the brain or nerves. The signals make heart muscle cells contract and relax. First each atrium squeezes, then each ventricle. Each contraction and relaxation makes one heart beat. Your heart beats 70 to 80 times a minute. That's more than one beat every second. The most your heart muscle ever rests is a split second. No other muscle can work that hard without tiring.

On the heart's right side, blood from your body enters the atrium from the largest vein in your body, called the *vena cava*. This blood lacks oxygen and must get rid of wastes it collected from cells in the body. It travels through the atrium to the right ventricle and into the pulmonary artery.

**Blood travels through each chamber of your heart.**

## TO THE LUNGS

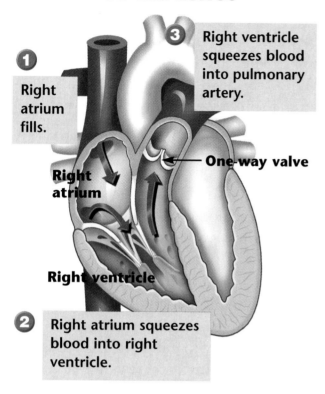

**1** Right atrium fills.

**3** Right ventricle squeezes blood into pulmonary artery.

One-way valve

Right atrium

Right ventricle

**2** Right atrium squeezes blood into right ventricle.

## FROM THE LUNGS

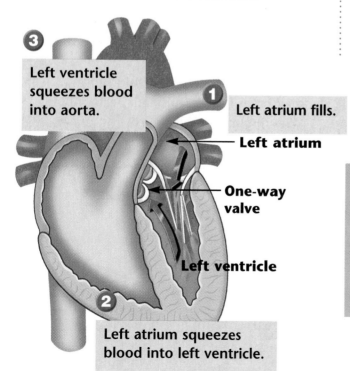

**3** Left ventricle squeezes blood into aorta.

**1** Left atrium fills.

Left atrium

One-way valve

Left ventricle

**2** Left atrium squeezes blood into left ventricle.

# How Do the Heart and Lungs Work Together?

The pulmonary artery carries blood into the lungs and branches into capillaries. Here the carbon dioxide leaves the blood to be exhaled by the lungs. Fresh oxygen from the lungs is attracted to the blood's hemoglobin. Hemoglobin carries oxygen around in the body, giving blood its bright red color.

The blood returns from the lungs to the heart through the pulmonary veins. The pulmonary veins conduct the blood into the left atrium. It flows to the left ventricle and out of the aorta.

The aorta is your largest artery. It carries blood full of oxygen into smaller and smaller arteries to reach every part of your body. As blood flows into the tiniest capillaries, it releases oxygen and other nutrients into the cells. Carbon dioxide and cell wastes enter the blood, giving it a blue-red color. Blood flows from the capillaries into larger and larger veins. Finally, the blood enters the vena cava again and flows into the right atrium.

## READING DIAGRAMS

**1. DISCUSS** What happens to the blood after it enters the right atrium? The left atrium?

**2. WRITE** When does blood flow to the lungs? From the lungs?

391

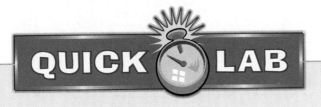

# QUICK LAB

## Squeeze Play

**HYPOTHESIZE** How easy is it for your heart to pump blood? What might it depend on? Write a hypothesis in your *Science Journal*.

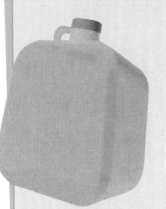

### MATERIALS
- empty plastic water bottle
- masking tape
- pushpin
- *Science Journal*

## PROCEDURES

1. **OBSERVE** Squeeze the bottle with one hand, and feel how much air flows out with the other.

2. **COMPARE** Cover the opening with tape. Make a small hole in the tape with the pushpin. Squeeze. Does more or less air flow out? Is the bottle easier or harder to squeeze?

## CONCLUDE AND APPLY

**DRAW CONCLUSIONS** If your arteries start to narrow, will your heart work harder or less hard?

# What Is Blood Pressure?

Every time your heart pumps, it squeezes blood out of your heart. The blood going to your lungs does not have far to go. The blood going through your aorta must travel to the top of your head and tips of your toes. To do that the left ventricle uses a strong force to push blood out. That force is your blood pressure.

The pushed blood presses on the artery walls from the inside. The elastic artery walls stretch and spring back to give your blood an extra push. You can feel an artery wall stretch by taking your pulse. To feel your pulse, place your fingers on the inside of your wrist. Count how many times it pulses in one minute.

Another way to gauge heart rate is by listening with a stethoscope. It sounds like "lub-dup, lub-dup, lub-dup." Can you guess what makes these sounds? It's not your blood or heart muscle. What's left?

## Brain Power

**MATH LINK**

A marathon runner's resting pulse may be as low as 40 beats per minute. Why might an athlete's resting pulse be so low?

**Athletes often use their pulse to measure how hard they are working.**

# How Do Blood Vessels Heal?

When you have a cut, blood pours out of the wound. Then the flow slows and soon stops. Bleeding stops because your blood clots.

Platelets help your blood to clot. They collect in a wound and stick to each other in a clump. Then proteins in your blood form a web of sticky threads. The threads and platelets trap red blood cells to form a clot that seals the wound. When the wound heals, the clot dissolves. If the clot does not dissolve, it can block the flow of blood in the blood vessels.

Germ-fighting white blood cells also rush to the wound. They attach to bacteria or viruses inside the wound. If the white cells in your blood don't destroy the germs, the white blood cells in your lymph vessels may.

Lymph vessels are similar to blood vessels. Instead of transporting blood, they collect *lymph*. Lymph is a straw-colored fluid surrounding the cells in your tissues. This fluid travels through lymph vessels that return the lymph to your blood.

Why don't the cells dry out as the lymph vessels collect fluid? More fluid leaks out of nearby capillaries to take its place.

Before returning to your blood, lymph passes through lymph nodes. Lymph nodes filter out harmful materials. They also produce white blood cells to fight infections. When you have a sore throat, you may feel swollen lymph nodes in your neck. They are a clue that your body is fighting germs that infected you.

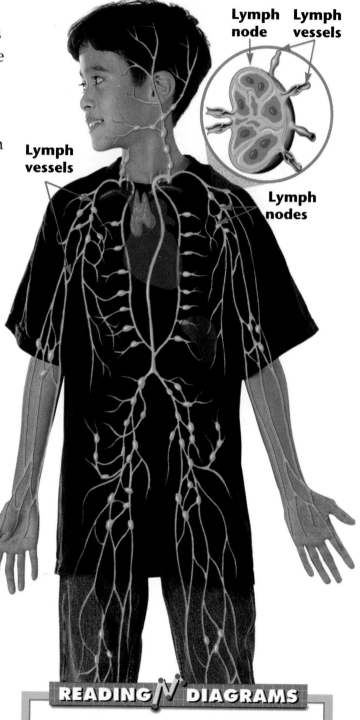

Lymph vessels run through your body to collect fluid and return it to the bloodstream.

Lymph node

Lymph vessels

Lymph vessels

Lymph nodes

## READING N DIAGRAMS

1. **DISCUSS** Why do you think the lymph vessels are located where they are in your body?
2. **WRITE** How are the lymph vessels like blood vessels? How are they different?

**Sickle cells do not move easily through blood vessels.**

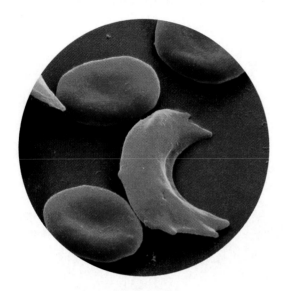

## How Can You Help Your Heart?

You can see some blood vessels indirectly through your skin. A doctor can see blood vessels clearly and directly inside your eyes.

At the beginning of this topic, the doctor looked into the man's eyes. She saw blood vessels starting to thicken and narrow. These are signs of high blood pressure that can weaken and damage the arteries.

In some people very salty foods cause high blood pressure. Those were the foods the doctor asked about. Unhealthy weight and smoking also affect blood pressure.

Fatty foods can damage your circulatory system. Fats collect in arteries, limiting your blood flow. The arteries narrow, harden, and clog.

Worst of all a clot may form in a narrowed artery. Clots can stop the normal flow of blood and cause a heart attack.

By eating the right foods, exercising, and taking medicines, the man in the story can lower his blood pressure.

Other diseases are inherited. *Sickle cell anemia* occurs when people inherit genes with the sickle cell trait.

People who get this trait from only one parent do not develop this disease but can pass it on.

If a person gets this gene from both parents, sickle cell anemia develops. The person's red blood cells curve into a C shape, called a sickle. Sickle cells cannot move or absorb oxygen easily.

Sometimes sickle cells pile up in the blood vessels. The person feels pain from these blocked blood vessels.

Sickle cell anemia occurs mostly in people whose ancestors lived in tropical areas. Scientists learned that people in these areas need one copy of the gene to protect them from malaria.

Doctors today can test for this gene and are doing research to cure the disease.

**Fatty foods damage arteries and make it hard for blood to pass.**

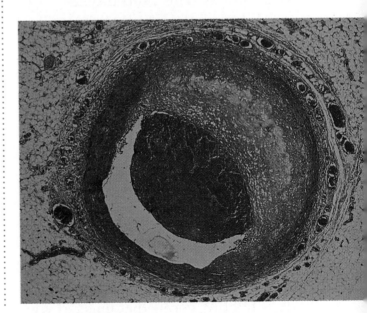

Understanding how blood travels through your body can help you take better care of your circulatory system. You now know that your cells need blood to provide essential oxygen and nutrients for them to use.

Knowing how blood travels helps you to understand how serious problems with your heart and blood vessels can be. If the circulatory system is not working well, it quickly affects every cell in your body. It is not enough to simply keep it from becoming damaged. You must be aware of how every part works together to make sure that it stays in top shape.

By eating right, exercising, and seeing your doctor regularly, you can strengthen and protect your circulatory system from harm.

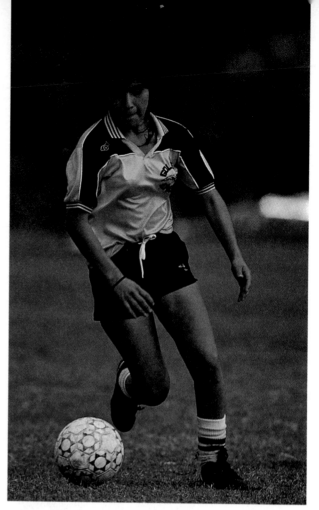

**Exercise encourages good blood flow in your body.**

# REVIEW

1. What are the three types of blood vessels your body uses to move blood in your body?

2. Name the four different blood types.

3. Describe the path blood takes through the heart.

4. **MEASURE** What is your resting pulse rate? How could you find out?

5. **CRITICAL THINKING** *Analyze* Why is the lymph system needed to keep your blood and cells healthy?

**WHY IT MATTERS** THINK ABOUT IT
Think about all of the places your blood travels to. What would happen to the rest of your body if part of your circulatory system were blocked?

**WHY IT MATTERS** WRITE ABOUT IT
What would make it easier for your blood to reach all of the cells in your body? What would make it more difficult? Write your ideas in your *Science Journal*.

**READING SKILL**
Look back at this topic. Locate the details you need, then write a paragraph to explain what the different parts of the blood do.

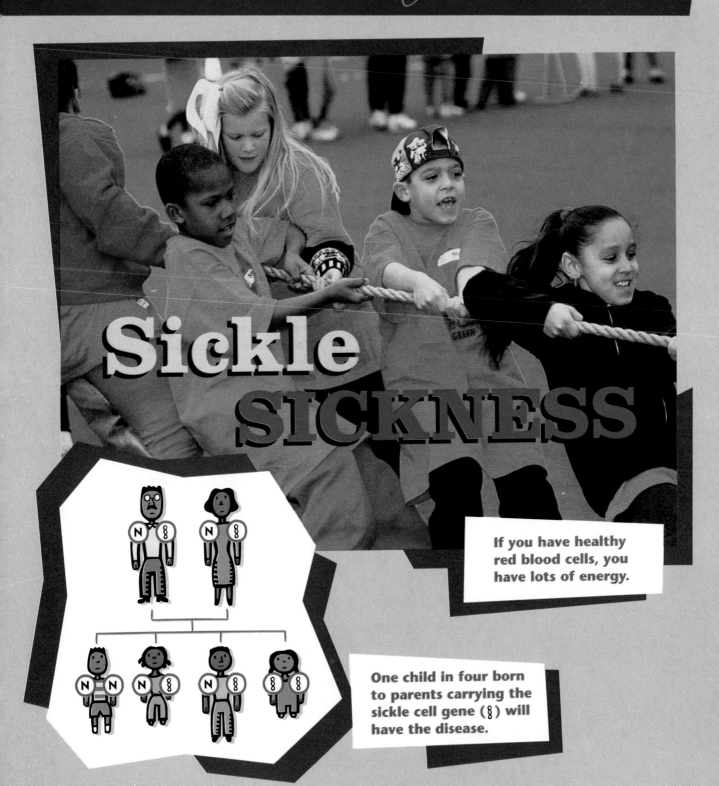

# Sickle SICKNESS

If you have healthy red blood cells, you have lots of energy.

One child in four born to parents carrying the sickle cell gene (§) will have the disease.

# Health Link

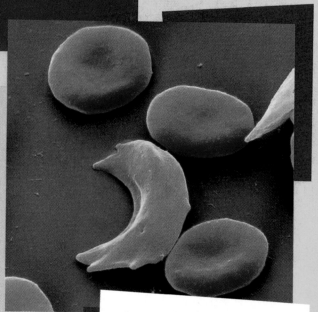

**H**ow do you feel today? If you're feeling energetic, you can probably thank your red blood cells. They're the cells that carry oxygen throughout your body. People who don't have enough red blood cells often feel tired and listless. Sickle cell anemia is a disease that affects the red blood cells. The disease makes the cells stiffen into hooklike, or sickle, shapes that can cause the cells to get stuck in small blood vessels. That blocks the flow of blood to parts of the body, causing pain. The affected red blood cells weaken and die. Without enough red blood cells, the person becomes anemic. That means he or she feels tired and weak.

Compare these normal red blood cells with the sickled cell.

Sickle cell anemia is inherited. To get the disease, a person must inherit a sickle cell gene from each parent. Many people carry one sickle cell gene. They're not affected by the disease. However, if two carriers have children, one in four of those children is likely to have the disease.

Sickle cell anemia is most common among people from Africa, the Mediterranean, the Caribbean, the Middle East, and India. More than 60,000 Americans now have the disease. About 2.5 million more carry the sickle cell gene.

People can take tests to find out whether they carry the sickle cell gene. This may help couples decide whether to have children. Tests can also identify newborns who have the disease.

## Discussion Starter

**1** Which body system does sickle cell anemia affect?

**2** Can you get sickle cell anemia by sharing a soda with a person who has it? Why or why not?

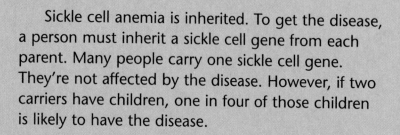

*inter*NET CONNECTION  To learn more about sickle cell anemia, visit www.mhschool.com/science and enter the keyword **SICKLE.**

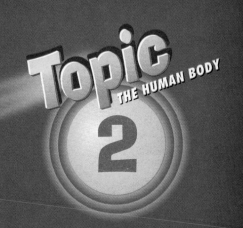

## WHY IT MATTERS

You need oxygen for all of your cells to use every day.

### SCIENCE WORDS

**respiration** the process of obtaining and using oxygen in the body

**diaphragm** a sheet of muscle below the chest cavity that helps control breathing

**trachea** a stiff tube lined with cartilage that transports air between the throat and lungs

**mucus** a sticky fluid that traps and prevents foreign particles from entering the body

**cilia** small hairlike structures that move small particles of dirt out of the respiratory system

**diffusion** the process by which a substance such as a gas moves from areas of high concentration to areas of low concentration

# A Breathing System

**W**hat do the following have in common: coughing, sneezing, wheezing, yawning, laughing, speaking, smelling, and hiccupping?

Why do climbers carry oxygen tanks to help them reach the tops of the world's highest mountains? Give up? Take a deep breath and try answering this: After you run as fast as you can for a short distance, why do you gasp for air when you stop running?

## EXPLORE

**HYPOTHESIZE** Many things can make it easier or harder for you to breathe. What might affect your breathing? Write a hypothesis in your *Science Journal*. Test your ideas.

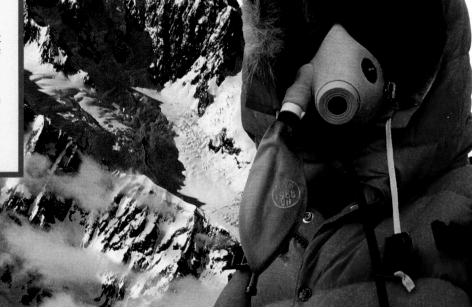

# EXPLORE ACTIVITY

# Investigate What Makes You Breathe

Use this experiment to learn what forces help
you to breathe.

## PROCEDURES

**SAFETY** Use the scissors carefully!

1. Attach the opening of the small balloon to the end
   of the straw with a rubber band.

2. Make a hole at the bottom of the cup with the
   scissors or pushpin. Hold the cup upside down. Pull
   the open end of the straw through the hole so the
   balloon hangs inside the cup. Seal the cup hole
   around the straw with clay.

3. Tie the "neck" of the large balloon. Cut off the wide
   end. Stretch the balloon over the cup's open end.
   Secure it with a rubber band.

4. **OBSERVE** Pull down slowly on the stretched balloon.
   What happens to the balloon inside the cup? Push
   up on the stretched balloon. What happens inside
   the cup? Record your answers in your *Science Journal*.

## CONCLUDE AND APPLY

1. **EVALUATE** Is there more or less space inside the cup
   when you pull down on the large balloon?

2. **IDENTIFY** When you pull the large balloon down,
   what fills the extra space in the cup?

## GOING FURTHER: Problem Solving

3. **COMPARE** How is the air pressure in the balloon
   similar to the air pressure in your lungs? Write down
   what you think happens when you breathe air into
   your lungs.

### MATERIALS

- clear-plastic cup
- flexible plastic straw
- scissors
- pushpin
- small balloon
- large balloon
- 2 rubber bands
- clay
- *Science Journal*

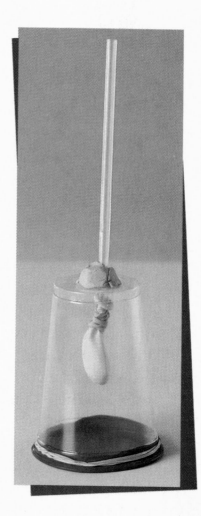

# HOW YOU BREATHE

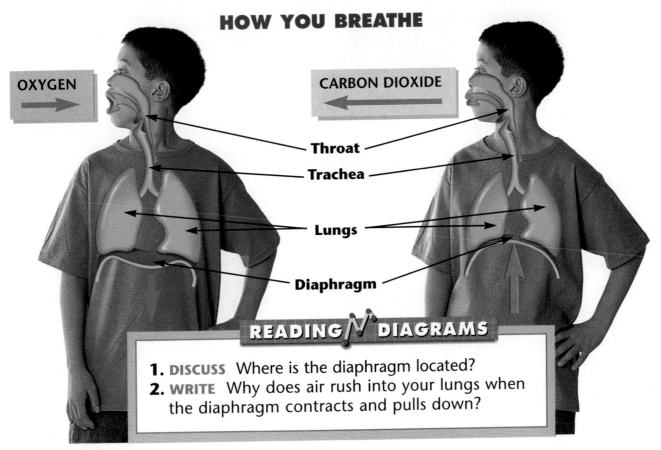

OXYGEN →

CARBON DIOXIDE ←

Throat
Trachea
Lungs
Diaphragm

## READING *N* DIAGRAMS

1. **DISCUSS** Where is the diaphragm located?
2. **WRITE** Why does air rush into your lungs when the diaphragm contracts and pulls down?

## What Makes You Breathe?

The Explore Activity showed that changing the amount of space in a closed space changes the air pressure. Air rushes into empty spaces and rushes out when a space becomes smaller. What if the air did not move in and out?

Your cells can't live more than a few minutes without oxygen. They use it to turn food into energy. The process of obtaining and using oxygen in the body is called **respiration** (res′pə rā′shən).

Oxygen comes from air you breathe into your lungs. There's just one catch: The lungs are soft, spongy tissues that can't pull in air on their own. They need muscles to do the work of breathing.

Two main muscles control breathing. One is located between your ribs. The other is a dome-shaped sheet of muscle called the **diaphragm** (dī′ə fram′). The diaphragm stretches below your chest cavity, under your lungs and above your abdomen.

To inhale, the diaphragm contracts and pulls down. Other muscles pull your ribs up and out. This creates more room in your chest. Air rushes into your lungs and fills the space.

To exhale, your diaphragm relaxes and returns to its dome shape. With less room inside your chest, the lungs get smaller and force air out.

Usually your diaphragm moves up and down smoothly. Sometimes the diaphragm jerks up and down causing hiccups. Laughing also makes your diaphragm move up and down more than usual.

The diaphragm causes you to inhale and exhale, but your respiratory system includes many other parts.

# What Happens When You Breathe?

When you inhale, air is pulled into your nose or mouth. Nose hairs trap large dirt and dust particles, and your body warms the air.

Air travels down into the **trachea** (trā′kē ə), a stiff tube lined with cartilage that transports air between the throat and lungs. The trachea's cartilage rings keep it open for air to enter. When you eat, your epiglottis keeps food out of your trachea. Your voice box, or larynx, is located at the top of the trachea.

Your nose, throat, and trachea are lined with **mucus** (mū′kəs) and **cilia** (sil′ē ə). Mucus is a moist, sticky fluid that traps small particles. Cilia (singular, *cilium*) are small hairlike structures that move particles and

mucus along your throat. The mucus is swallowed, and your stomach acids destroy the particles it has collected.

In your chest the trachea divides into two bronchial tubes. One tube enters each of your lungs. Each tube branches into smaller tubes called bronchioles.

At the end of each bronchiole are tiny air sacs called *alveoli*. Alveoli look like very tiny grapes organized in clusters. Capillaries carrying blood from the heart surround them.

Your alveoli exchange carbon dioxide for oxygen by **diffusion** (di fū′zhən). In diffusion a substance such as a gas moves from areas of high concentration to areas of low concentration.

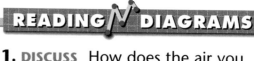

## READING DIAGRAMS

1. **DISCUSS** How does the air you breathe get to your lungs?
2. **WRITE** What do alveoli do?

The air you breathe is about 21 percent oxygen.

The blood in the capillaries of your lungs has very little oxygen.

The blood has a higher concentration of carbon dioxide than the air.

**Throat**

**Trachea**

**Lungs**

Carbon dioxide diffuses into the alveoli. From there it is exhaled.

**Air flow**

**Carbon dioxide**

**Oxygen**

**Capillary net**

**Alveoli**

Fresh oxygen diffuses from the alveoli to the blood.

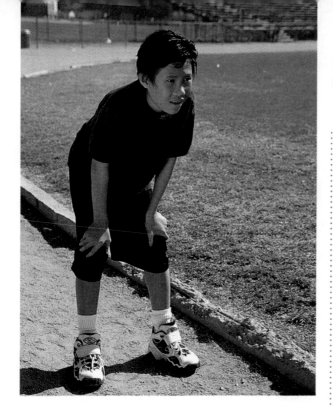

Breathing hard is your body's way of recovering from hard work.

## Can You Control Your Breathing?

Take a deep breath. Just now you controlled your breathing muscles by thinking about them. Even though you can control these muscles, you don't have to. Your brain controls breathing automatically by sensing carbon dioxide in your blood.

When you are tired, you may not breathe deeply enough. Carbon dioxide builds up in your blood. Your brain makes you take a deep breath, or yawn, to get rid of it.

When you run, your muscles need more oxygen to work hard. Your lungs can't take in oxygen quickly enough. When you stop running, you breathe hard to expel carbon dioxide and take in more oxygen.

If you visit mountainous places, you may feel tired, dizzy, or short of breath. The higher you go, the thinner the air gets. The gases in the air are more

spread out. You breathe in less oxygen with each breath. Mountain climbers carry oxygen tanks with them to avoid these symptoms. Over a long period of time at high altitudes, the body makes more red blood cells to gather enough oxygen without breathing hard.

With so many people breathing in oxygen and using it up, why doesn't the supply run out? Why doesn't the air turn poisonous from all of the carbon dioxide being exhaled?

The reason these things don't happen is because plants and algae use carbon dioxide in photosynthesis. During photosynthesis plants use carbon dioxide and release oxygen into the air. This process is the reverse of how we use oxygen and carbon dioxide. Plants put carbon dioxide to use and provide more oxygen for us to use.

### Brain Power

People sometimes yawn when they are not tired. Why do you think they do that?

What are some other ways plants help people?

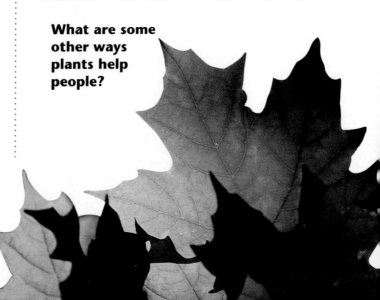

## Skill: Forming a Hypothesis and Measuring

**MATH LINK**

### HOW EXERCISE AFFECTS YOUR HEART AND LUNGS

A hypothesis is a reasonable, testable guess or statement about why something happens. It helps you design and learn from experiments. If the hypothesis is correct, the results will support it. If the hypothesis is wrong, you must rewrite it.

**MATERIALS**
- watch with a second hand
- *Science Journal*

1. **HYPOTHESIZE**  In your *Science Journal*, write a hypothesis about how exercise affects your pulse and breathing rates.

2. **MEASURE**  Place your index and middle fingers on the inside of your partner's wrist so you feel a pulse, or beat, on the artery. Count pulse rate for one minute. Have another student count how many times your partner breathes during the minute. Record the number of heartbeats as the resting pulse rate. Record the number of breaths as the resting breath rate.

3. **USE VARIABLES**  Have your partner do jumping jacks for two minutes, then measure pulse and breathing rates for one minute. Record results.

4. **COMPARE**  Wait two minutes, recount, and record both results.

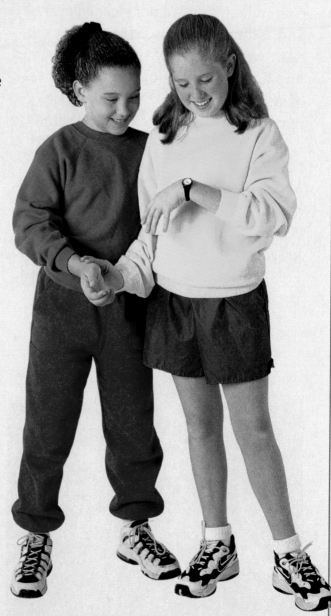

### CONCLUDE AND APPLY

1. **COMPARE**  How much faster was the pulse rate after exercising? How much faster was the breathing rate?

2. **DRAW CONCLUSIONS**  How does exercise affect the heart and the lungs?

3. **REVISE**  Does this prove your hypothesis? If not, how can you change and test it?

# What Can Harm Your Respiratory System?

Sometimes bacteria or viruses enter your respiratory system. Your nose may run as it makes excess mucus to trap germs. You cough and sneeze to expel germs. This is a normal process your body goes through to fight infection. Soon the immune system destroys the germs, and your system returns to normal.

Some people find breathing difficult even when they are not sick. Allergies and asthma can cause your airways to narrow. By spraying a mist of medicines into their lungs, people with asthma can breathe easier. People with allergies may take shots or pills to help them.

Respiratory problems can quickly become very serious. To keep your respiratory system healthy, exercise regularly and avoid smoking.

Exercise causes your heart and lungs to work hard for short periods of time. This work strengthens your heart and

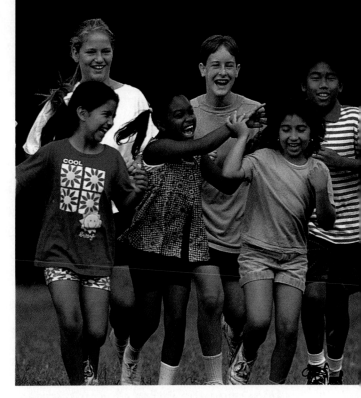

**Breathing hard during activity supplies your muscles with extra oxygen.**

breathing muscles. A stronger heart circulates more blood when it pumps. Stronger breathing muscles take in more oxygen and release more carbon dioxide.

Smoking damages your respiratory system. You inhale tobacco smoke and the chemicals used to prepare the tobacco. Chemicals in burning tobacco paralyze cilia. They cannot sweep dirt and germs out of the nose, throat, and breathing tubes. These particles enter your lungs and irritate the soft tissues there. Your lungs begin to form a thick lining, which can build up and block your bronchial tubes.

## Dangers of Smoking

Over time smoking destroys the air sacs in your lungs. Chemicals from smoke also cause cancers in the mouth, throat, and lungs. Many of these cancers are difficult to treat. Most cases of lung cancer cannot be cured.

**This athlete is using an inhaler for her asthma.**

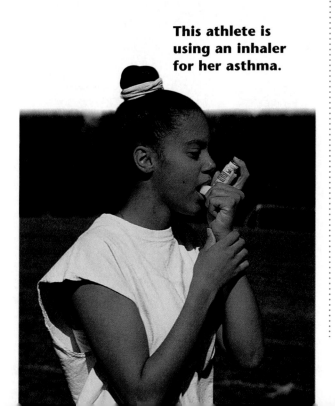

## WHY IT MATTERS

Understanding how your respiratory system works helps you keep it working at its best. You know how to strengthen and protect your lungs. By measuring your heart and breathing rates, you can learn how different activities affect your respiratory system. You will know when your respiratory system is working hard or being overworked.

By exercising and not smoking, you care for your throat, trachea, and lungs. Knowing about the complex actions of your respiratory system also helps you recognize problems with your breathing. If you ever have trouble breathing, tell an adult at once. You don't want anything to prevent your respiratory system from doing its job.

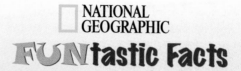
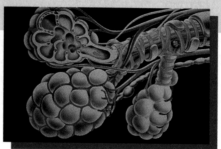
## REVIEW

1. What parts of the respiratory system take air from outside of your body into your lungs?

2. What two gases are exchanged in your lungs?

3. What does asthma do to the body that makes it difficult for people to breathe?

4. **HYPOTHESIZE/MEASURE** Create a hypothesis about what you can do to strengthen your respiratory system. What data would you need to collect to prove your hypothesis?

5. **CRITICAL THINKING** *Analyze* What are some ways that people can improve the quality of the air they breathe?

**WHY IT MATTERS** THINK ABOUT IT
What did you learn about your respiratory system that will help you to take better care of it?

**WHY IT MATTERS** WRITE ABOUT IT
Write down some additional things that you think would harm your respiratory system. Write down ways you can avoid or change these things.

# Asthma Attacks

Do you sneeze a lot when there's a lot of pollen or dust in the air? You may have an allergy. If you do your immune system will try to destroy the foreign substances you inhale.

In some people dust and pollen can trigger a serious asthma attack. Their bronchi and other airways swell up. The mucus that usually helps clean their lungs gets thicker and begins to block the airways. Muscles around their airways tighten until they're almost shut.

A mild asthma attack may cause only coughing, but a severe attack can trap air in the lungs. Air can't move in or out, making it impossible to take a deep breath. The person needs immediate medical help. Many asthma victims go to hospital emergency rooms for treatment.

Medicines can help to control asthma. Many people also carry bronchodilators. They contain medi-cine a person can

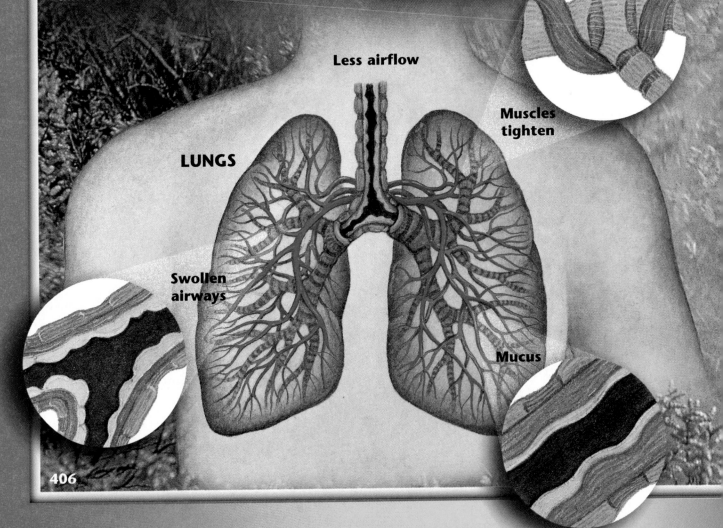

Less airflow

Muscles tighten

LUNGS

Swollen airways

Mucus

# Health Link

inhale if an attack starts. The medicine helps open airways and relax muscles.

Not all asthma attacks are caused by allergies. For some people exercising too much or getting upset can trigger an attack. On a winter day, breathing very cold air can start an attack.

About three million kids in the United States have asthma. It can't be cured, but it can be controlled. Asthma patients learn to watch for warning signs, such as feeling out of breath, coughing, or wheezing as they breathe. People with asthma also know the importance of taking their medication.

## DISCUSSION STARTER

1. How do allergies cause asthma?

2. How can people control asthma?

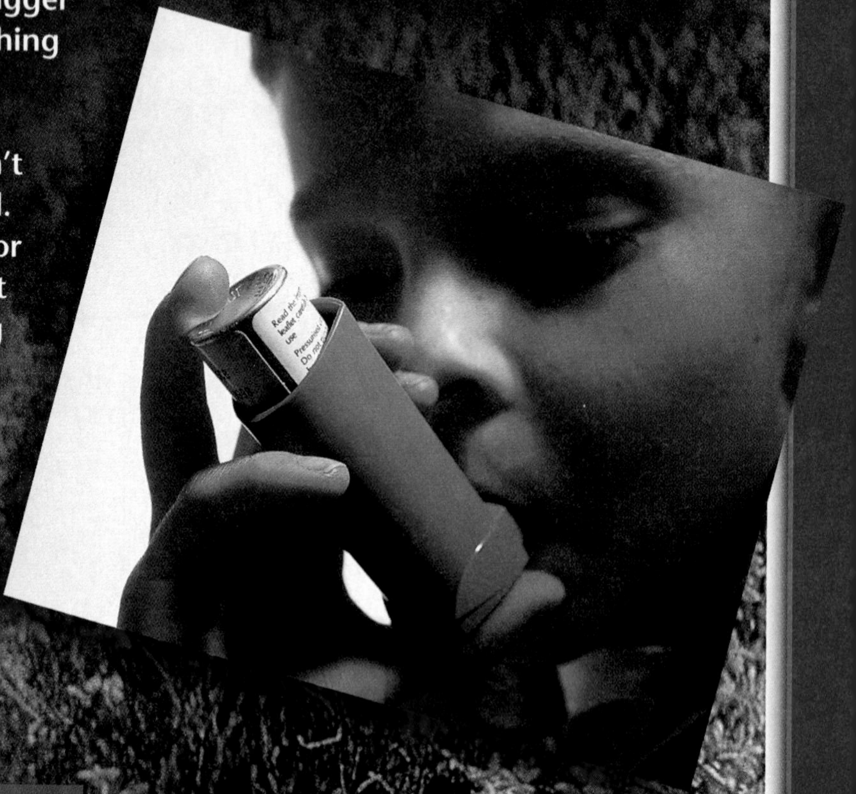

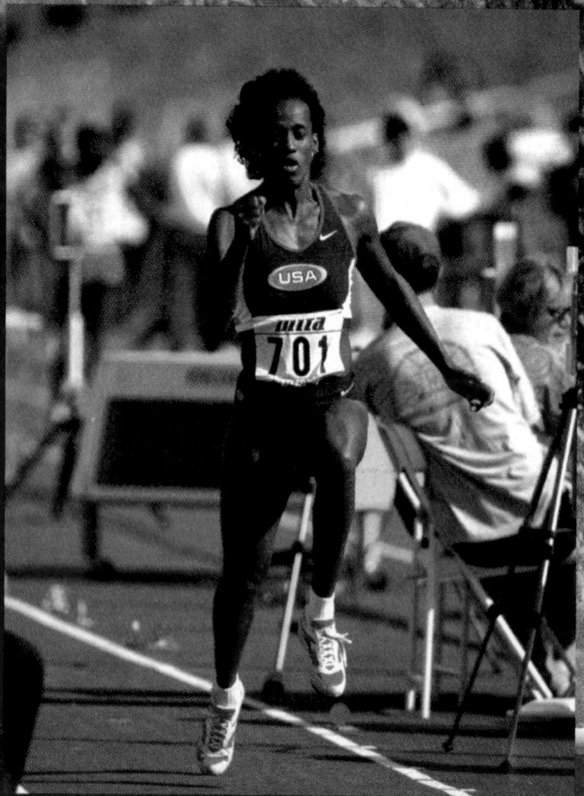

Having asthma doesn't rule out an active life. Jackie Joyner-Kersee won Olympic gold medals despite her asthma!

To learn more about asthma, visit *www.mhschool.com/science* and enter the keyword BREATHE.

*inter*NET CONNECTION

## SCIENCE WORDS

capillary  p.388

cilia  p.401

diaphragm  p.400

diffusion  p.401

hemoglobin  p.388

plasma  p.388

platelet  p.388

respiration  p.400

transfusion  p.389

vein  p.388

## USING SCIENCE WORDS

**Number a paper from 1 to 10. Fill in 1 to 5 with words from the list above.**

1. The body obtains oxygen by __?__.

2. Cell fragments that help to form clots are __?__.

3. The tiniest blood vessels in the body are called __?__.

4. A(n) __?__ transfers blood between two people.

5. Gases move from one location to another by __?__.

**6–10. Pick five words from the list above that were not used in 1 to 5, and use each in a sentence.**

## UNDERSTANDING SCIENCE IDEAS

11. How does blood travel through the heart?

12. Describe how the diaphragm changes shape when you breathe.

13. Explain what role lymph vessels play in your body.

14. What can cause high blood pressure?

15. What proteins help the body find and destroy harmful proteins?

## USING IDEAS AND SKILLS

16. At higher altitudes it becomes more difficult to breathe. Why does this happen, and how can your body adjust?

17. **READING SKILL: LOCATING DETAILS** The valves in the heart open in only one direction. Why is this important to your bloodstream?

18. The supply of oxygen in the air will run out because people are using it up. Is this true or false? Explain your answer.

19. **HYPOTHESIZE/MEASURE** What effect do you think high altitudes might have on athletes, such as runners or skiers? State your answer as a hypothesis, and suggest a way to test your idea.

20. **THINKING LIKE A SCIENTIST** Scientists try to learn if a disease is inherited or comes from behaviors, like smoking. What are some ways you could find this out? Write out your suggestions.

## PROBLEMS and PUZZLES

**Thump Thump** Is your heart the most active muscle in your body? To find out fill a bucket with 4 liters of water. Using a $\frac{1}{2}$-cup measuring cup, transfer all 4 liters of water to a second bucket in one minute. That is about the rate at which the heart pumps blood. At that rate how soon would your other muscles tire?

# CHAPTER 10
# USING
# FOOD AND
# STAYING
# FIT

Soon it will be time for another Olympics competition. Athletes from around the world will compete. Some will be only a few years older than you are.

Could you cross the finish line at the Olympics one day? That depends on how talented you are, how much you practice, and how much support you have. It also takes knowing how your body works so you can make it work at its best. When do you think your body works at its best?

In Chapter 10 you will read to find the main idea.

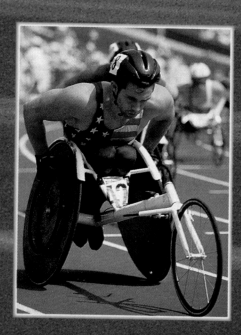

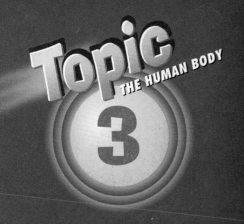
## WHY IT MATTERS

**Your body prepares food for your cells to use and eliminates the waste products left over.**

## SCIENCE WORDS

**digestion** the process of breaking food down into simpler substances for the body to use

**enzyme** a substance in a living thing that affects how fast chemical reactions take place

**bile** a greenish-yellow fluid produced by the liver to digest fats

**villus** a tiny fingerlike projection in the small intestine that absorbs digested food

**urea** a substance formed from waste material in the liver and excreted in urine

**excretion** the process of removing waste products from the body

**nephron** a structure in the kidney that filters blood

# A Food System

**E**very day people buy food to eat. A lot of what they buy and cook ends up in the trash.

Think about it. Foods come in boxes, bottles, trays, and bags. Some are recycled; the rest are tossed out.

Before cooking, fats, bones, seeds, peels, and other parts are removed from food. After the meal uneaten food is either saved or disposed of. Where do all of these wastes go?

## EXPLORE

**HYPOTHESIZE** Every day your body uses some of the food you eat and turns some of it into waste. What does your body keep? How does it get rid of wastes? Write a hypothesis in your *Science Journal.*

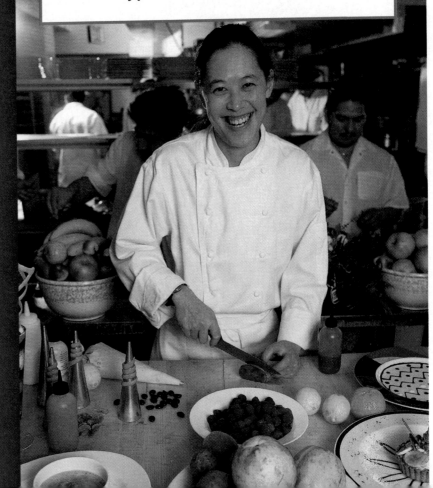

# EXPLORE ACTIVITY

## Design Your Own Experiment

### WHAT ARE SOME WAYS TO SORT MATERIALS?

### PROCEDURES

▨▨▨ **SAFETY** Use the scissors carefully!

1. Cut open the tea bag. Pour the tea leaves into the cup of water. Add pepper and cloves. Stir.

2. Open the coffee filter, and hold it over the bowl. Hold the tea strainer above the open filter.

3. Slowly pour the contents of the cup through the strainer and into the filter.

4. **OBSERVE** What is left in the strainer? What is left in the filter? Lift the filter. What is in the bowl? Record your observations in your *Science Journal*.

> **MATERIALS**
> - tea bag
> - cup half-filled with water
> - tea strainer or medium-sized strainer
> - ground pepper
> - cloves
> - coffee filter
> - plastic bowl
> - scissors
> - spoon
> - *Science Journal*

### CONCLUDE AND APPLY

1. **COMMUNICATE** What was in the strainer at the end of the activity? What was not present in the bowl at all?

2. **EXPLAIN** Why did the filtering system work? Why can some materials pass through while others cannot?

### GOING FURTHER: Problem Solving

3. **DRAW CONCLUSIONS** How could your body use a system like this to separate solids from a liquid? Would this remove wastes effectively? Why or why not?

4. **EXPERIMENT** Design your own filtering experiment. Try placing different materials in different liquids, then filtering them out. Try other materials as filters. Answer Conclude and Apply questions 1 and 2 for your experiment.

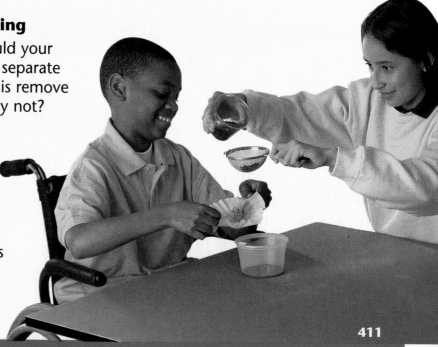

411

# What Are Some Ways to Sort Materials?

The Explore Activity showed that solid materials in a liquid can be sorted by size. Materials that are too large for the filter are trapped. Your body gets rid of some wastes in a similar way.

Many of these wastes come from the food you eat. Before getting rid of these wastes, the body separates out the useful nutrients. **Digestion** (di jes′chən) is the process of breaking down food into simple substances your body can use.

Digestion begins in the mouth when you chew your food. Chewing breaks the large pieces into smaller pieces. Chewing also moistens food with *saliva*, which contains **enzymes** (en′zīmz). An enzyme is a substance in a living thing that affects how fast chemical reactions take place. Saliva contains an enzyme that breaks food down into simple pieces that cells can use. Saliva is produced in the *salivary glands*.

When you swallow, the food travels down a tube called the *esophagus* to your stomach. In the stomach, food is mixed with gastric juice. Gastric juice contains acids and more enzymes to break down the proteins in your food.

The stomach walls contract to churn the food into a thick liquid. After a few hours, this liquid enters the *small intestine*.

In the small intestine, more digestive juices work on the food. Your *pancreas* makes a juice that breaks down proteins and changes starch to sugar. Other digestive juices come from your *liver*.

## THE DIGESTIVE SYSTEM

Teeth →

Salivary glands

← Esophagus

Liver

Stomach
Pancreas

Large intestine

Small intestine

← Anus

## READING ∥ DIAGRAMS

1. **DISCUSS** What happens to food after it leaves the stomach?
2. **WRITE** Describe what happens to the food you eat as it travels from your mouth to your stomach.

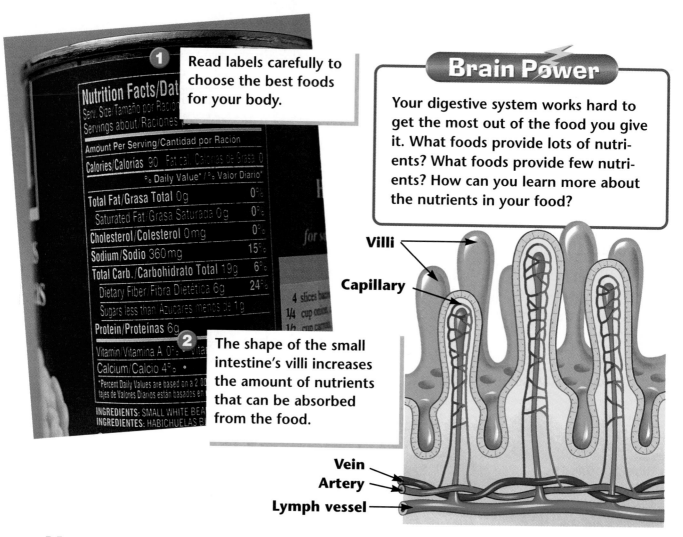

**1** Read labels carefully to choose the best foods for your body.

Your digestive system works hard to get the most out of the food you give it. What foods provide lots of nutrients? What foods provide few nutrients? How can you learn more about the nutrients in your food?

Villi

Capillary

**2** The shape of the small intestine's villi increases the amount of nutrients that can be absorbed from the food.

Vein
Artery
Lymph vessel

## How Are Nutrients Absorbed?

The liver is the largest organ inside your body and has many jobs to do. One job is to produce **bile** (bīl). Bile is a greenish-yellow fluid produced by the liver to digest fats. Bile helps with the digestion process in your small intestine.

Bile, pancreatic juices, and other intestinal juices break down most of the remaining foods. When all of the food is chemically broken into nutrients, digestion is complete.

Now the nutrients must be absorbed. The walls of the small intestine are lined with **villi** (vil′ī) (singular, *villus*). Villi are tiny fingerlike projections lining the small intestine that absorb digested food.

The villi are filled with capillaries. Digested food passes through the villi and capillaries to enter the bloodstream. The blood transports nutrients to every part of your body.

Not all food can be digested and changed into nutrients. Undigested food and excess water go from the small intestine to the *large intestine*.

Your body absorbs the water from the large intestine. The remaining solid, undigested food travels through the large intestine. Bacteria in the large intestine break down the solid wastes. At the end of the large intestine, these wastes exit your body through the *anus*.

**413**

# How Do Kidneys Work?

Your liver also purifies your blood. It filters out wastes, bacteria, drugs, and certain chemicals. Your liver converts these waste products into **urea** (yü rē′ə). As a pure substance, urea is a white powder, but in your body, urea is dissolved in urine. Urea is a substance formed from waste material that is carried by blood to the kidneys for **excretion** (ek skrē′shən). Excretion is the process of removing waste products from the body.

Put your hands around your back and feel your lowest ribs. Your bean-shaped kidneys are under them on each side of your spine.

Kidneys filter and clean blood of urea and other wastes. Each kidney contains more than one million **nephrons** (nef′ronz). Nephrons are structures in the kidneys that filter blood.

Blood enters your kidneys through arteries. It travels to capillaries to be cleaned by the nephrons. The cleaned blood leaves through veins. The wastes collect in your kidneys as liquid urine. The urine flows down *ureters* to a muscular bag called the *bladder*.

## HOW YOUR KIDNEYS WORK

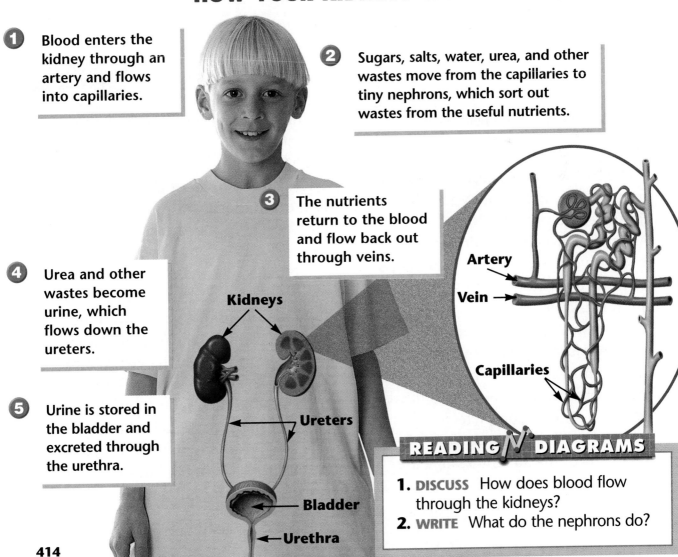

1. Blood enters the kidney through an artery and flows into capillaries.

2. Sugars, salts, water, urea, and other wastes move from the capillaries to tiny nephrons, which sort out wastes from the useful nutrients.

3. The nutrients return to the blood and flow back out through veins.

4. Urea and other wastes become urine, which flows down the ureters.

5. Urine is stored in the bladder and excreted through the urethra.

Kidneys

Ureters

Bladder

Urethra

Artery

Vein

Capillaries

### READING IN DIAGRAMS

1. **DISCUSS** How does blood flow through the kidneys?
2. **WRITE** What do the nephrons do?

414

## Skill: Making a Model

### HOW YOUR KIDNEYS WORK

A simple way to understand how kidneys and nephrons work is to make a model. Models can help us understand how things work. You can use very simple materials and familiar objects to represent complex systems. This model will show the sorting process of your excretory system.

**MATERIALS**
- plastic bag
- 5 red beans
- 5 white beans
- 5 rice grains
- 10 pennies
- *Science Journal*

### PROCEDURES

1. **MAKE A MODEL**  In this activity the bag stands for your blood, the red beans for urea, the white beans for sugars, the rice for salts, and the pennies for water. Place the beans, rice, and pennies in the bag. Record in your *Science Journal* what this represents.

2. Pour the contents of the bag on your desk to show materials moving from the blood to the nephrons.

3. Put all of the white beans back in the bag representing your blood. What does this illustrate?

4. Put four rice grains back in the bag to represent most of the salts.

5. Show that nearly all of the water returns to your blood by putting nine of the pennies back in the bag.

6. **OBSERVE**  Record what is left on your desk.

### CONCLUDE AND APPLY

1. **EXPLAIN**  What items were left in step 6? What happens to these items in your body? What would happen if none of the materials in step 2 moved back into your blood?

2. **PREDICT**  What would happen if none of the items ever left the blood? How could this harm your body?

### GOING FURTHER: Apply

3. **ANALYZE**  Many medicines are removed by your kidneys very quickly. How could you represent this in your model?

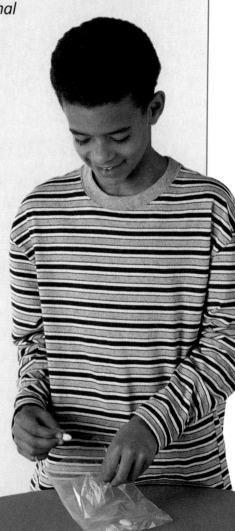

# HOW YOU SWEAT

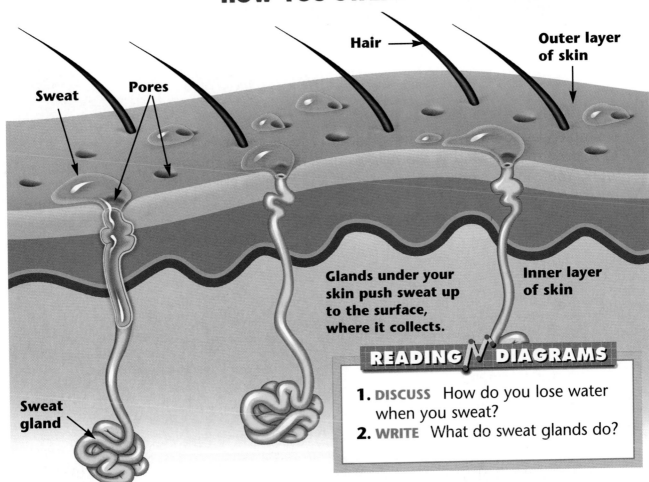

Sweat

Pores

Hair

Outer layer of skin

Sweat gland

Glands under your skin push sweat up to the surface, where it collects.

Inner layer of skin

## READING DIAGRAMS

1. **DISCUSS** How do you lose water when you sweat?
2. **WRITE** What do sweat glands do?

## What Is Sweat?

You already know how your body gets rid of carbon dioxide through exhaling. You also know how it gets rid of wastes from food. Your lungs, kidneys, and large intestine all take part in excretion.

Your skin also takes part in excretion when you sweat. Glands in the inner layer, or *dermis*, of your skin produce sweat.

Sweat is mostly water. If a drop of sweat has ever rolled onto your tongue, you know it contains more than water. Sweat tastes salty because it contains mineral salts the body doesn't need. There is also a tiny amount of urea in your sweat.

Sweat is excreted by your sweat glands onto the outer layer of your skin. On your skin's surface, it changes by evaporation from liquid water to gaseous water vapor. This change takes place in part because of your body heat. When you use body heat to evaporate the sweat, you feel cooler. On hot days or when you exercise, you sweat more to keep your body from overheating.

When the water in sweat evaporates, it leaves the mineral salts and urea behind on your skin. These salts can build up over time, causing body odor, blocking your pores, and irritating your skin. Washing the skin regularly removes the solid materials left behind by sweat.

**It is important to replace the water your body loses every day.**

## What Do You Need Water For?

Every time your heart beats, more blood flows into your kidneys. Over and over again, your kidneys filter and clean all of the blood in your body. Each time, water is used to transport the waste materials out.

Your kidneys perform a very difficult balancing act. Kidneys are responsible for balancing the amount of salt and water inside the body.

Your body is about two-thirds water. There is water inside and outside of your cells, in your blood, and in your lymph. Without water you could not cool down by sweating or remove wastes from your body.

You take in water every time you eat or drink. Cells make water during respiration. You lose water when you exhale and when you sweat. Water is also present in urine and solid food wastes.

It's up to your kidneys to balance the amount of water you lose with the amount you take in. When you sweat a lot on hot days, your body loses more water than usual. Your kidneys balance this by making less urine. If you drink more than usual, your kidneys will increase the amount of urine produced.

Drinking 6 to 8 glasses of water a day helps your kidneys do their job. With the right amount of water, kidneys can keep wastes moving out of your body. The water is also used by your blood, lymph, and cells. Without water your body struggles to carry out its work with limited resources. Make sure your body has enough water to do its work.

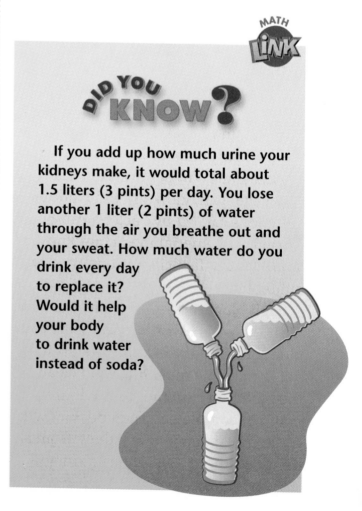

**MATH LINK**

**DID YOU KNOW?**

If you add up how much urine your kidneys make, it would total about 1.5 liters (3 pints) per day. You lose another 1 liter (2 pints) of water through the air you breathe out and your sweat. How much water do you drink every day to replace it? Would it help your body to drink water instead of soda?

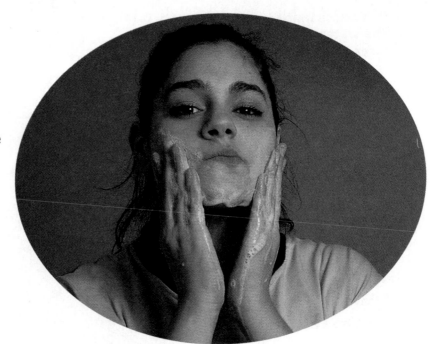

**Washing your face removes salt and urea left behind from sweat.**

## What Can You Do?

You depend on your excretory system. If the wastes are not removed or your body must remove too much waste, you become sick.

Too much food or the wrong foods cause your stomach to hurt. Certain conditions can also cause ulcers in your stomach.

Drugs and alcohol can damage your liver, which removes them from your bloodstream. Viruses and bacteria can infect the liver, kidneys, and bladder. Infections caused by bacteria can be treated with special medicines known as *antibiotics*. Penicillin is one type of antibiotic.

High blood pressure strains the kidneys, which work closely with your blood vessels. If the kidneys start to fail, a machine must filter and clean the blood. In extreme cases a kidney may fail completely. Then doctors will try to transplant a new kidney from a donor. Without at least one kidney, a person will die.

Many of these problems are preventable with proper nutrition. Foods with fiber help your large intestine excrete solid wastes. Drinking water makes your kidneys' job easier. Water and juices can keep your bladder healthy, too.

Washing your skin daily removes salts and other wastes left behind by sweat. It will keep your skin from becoming clogged and irritated.

### Why Body Wastes Are Important

Why is it important for doctors to know what wastes your body is getting rid of? The wastes your body excretes can also indicate if you are sick. For example, doctors can detect *diabetes* by examining your urine. Diabetes is a condition in which the body's sugar levels are too high. Too much sugar in the urine may mean that not enough is staying in the body. Doctors can also test for other nutrients, bacteria, and types of cells in your urine.

Knowing how your body separates useful materials from wasteful materials helps you to take care of it.

Even things you may not think about can help your body. Chewing food well helps your esophagus and stomach. Drinking liquids provides water for your kidneys to use. Avoiding drugs and alcohol keeps your liver from working harder to remove wastes from your blood.

Now you know how hard your body works to remove wastes. You can help it by watching what you eat and by drinking plenty of water. You also know more about how your doctor can help you if you have problems with your digestion or excretory system.

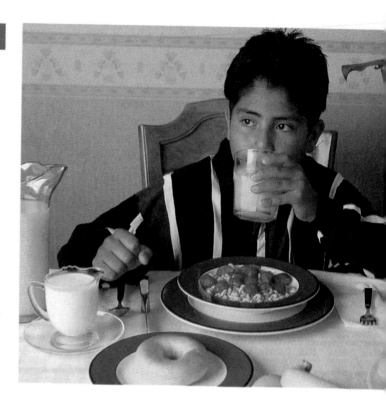

## REVIEW

1. Where are solid food wastes stored in your digestive system before they are excreted?

2. What is the waste material produced in your kidneys called?

3. Where is urine stored before leaving the body?

4. **MAKE A MODEL** How do exercise and weather affect how you feel when you sweat? How would you design a model to illustrate this?

5. **CRITICAL THINKING** *Apply* When your doctor prescribes medicines for you to take, what happens to the medicines in your body? How does your excretory system affect how often you must take more?

**WHY IT MATTERS** THINK ABOUT IT
What are some of the ways your diet affects your digestive and excretory systems? What would happen if you ate less food than normal? What if you ate too much?

**WHY IT MATTERS** WRITE ABOUT IT
Write down what you can do to take better care of your digestive system.

**READING SKILL**
Write a paragraph explaining the main idea of this topic.

# Your Chemical Factory

**D**id you ever think of your liver as a storage chest? It is . . . sort of. Every minute about 10 percent of your blood is traveling through your liver. The blood brings the energy, vitamins, and minerals it picked up from food you've digested. The liver stores the vitamins and minerals until you need them!

A human liver weighs 3 to 4 pounds. As the blood moves through, the liver changes the blood's chemistry. That's why a liver is called a chemical factory! This important organ has more than 500 vital functions.

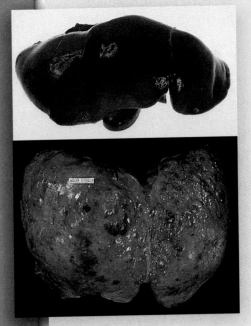

**Alcohol can damage the liver. That's why it's best to say no to drinking!**

**It treats alcohol, steroids, and other drugs as poisons.**

# A Closer Look

It makes $\frac{1}{2}$ to 1 liter (1 to 2 pints) of greenish-yellow bile per day to store in the gallbladder. Bile helps you digest fats.

It filters wastes, poisons, bacteria, and other foreign substances out of the blood.

It helps you fight disease.

It produces the protein that allows your blood to clot. Without it you could bleed to death from a small cut!

It changes sugar in the bloodstream into a starch-like substance called glycogen and stores it. When your body needs energy, the liver changes the glycogen back into sugar.

Humans can live only about five days without a liver. If it isn't too badly damaged, a liver repairs itself—if only 10 percent of the liver is left after an operation, it grows back to full size!

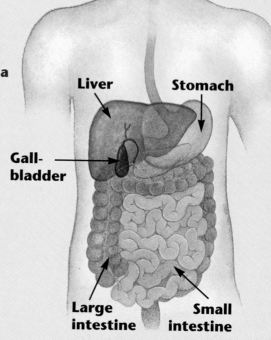

Liver

Stomach

Gall-bladder

Large intestine

Small intestine

## DISCUSSION STARTER

1. How does the liver help the body handle wastes?

2. How does the liver help you feel energetic?

To learn more about your liver, visit *www.mhschool.com/science* and enter the keyword LIVER.

*inter*NET
CONNECTION

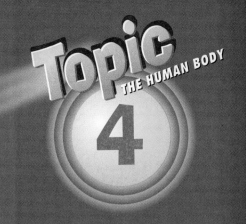

## WHY IT MATTERS

**Proper diet and exercise can help you to stay healthy.**

### SCIENCE WORDS

**physical fitness** the condition in which your body is healthy and works the best it can

**aerobic exercise** a brisk and constant physical activity that increases the supply of oxygen to the muscles

**balanced diet** a diet, maintained over time, that includes a variety of foods providing nutrition in moderate amounts

**food group** one of the groups made up of foods that contain similar amounts of important nutrients

# Fitness

The next time you watch a sport, keep your eye on the athletes. How long do they play without stopping? When they stop, how many athletes huff and puff to catch their breath?

Do any athletes look so tired you think they can't keep playing? Do any seem so full of energy that they could go on and on? Through exercise and practice, athletes can train their bodies to be physically fit.

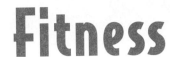

## EXPLORE

**HYPOTHESIZE** Being physically fit means your body is working at its best. Do you know what makes a body physically fit? How fit do you think your body is? Write your ideas in your *Science Journal*.

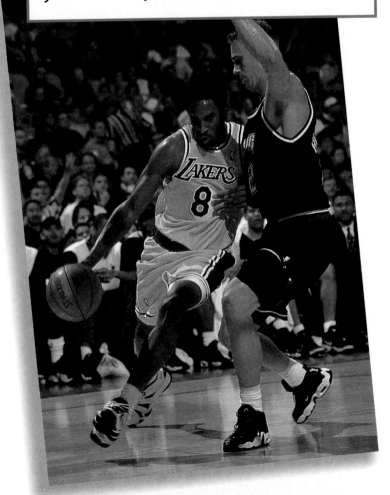

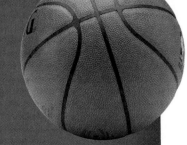

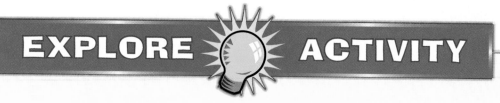
# Investigate What Fitness Is

Explore skills needed for fitness.

## MATERIALS
- *Science Journal*

## PROCEDURES

**1. OBSERVE** Look at the photographs of the athletes on this page.

**2. COMMUNICATE** In each picture identify which body parts are being exercised. In your *Science Journal*, describe what you think is the most important skill or ability needed to do each activity.

## CONCLUDE AND APPLY

**1. COMPARE** How are the skills you identified different from each other? Are the skills different for each activity? Do some skills and abilities usually go together?

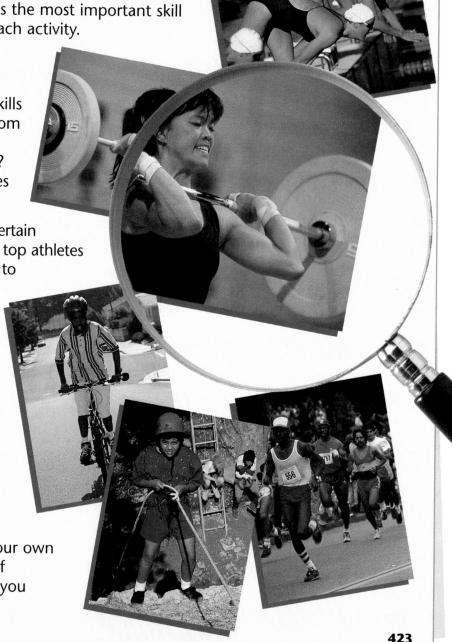

**2. EVALUATE** Everyone has certain skills and abilities. How do top athletes use their skills and abilities to succeed? What type of training is involved in different activities? How much time do you think top athletes spend each week practicing these skills? Why do you think most top athletes train for years in order to master their sports?

## GOING FURTHER: Apply

**3. ANALYZE** In your *Science Journal*, record some of your own skills and abilities. Think of activities that would help you use those skills.

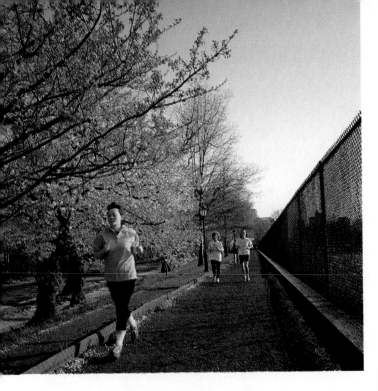

There are many different ways to get aerobic exercise.

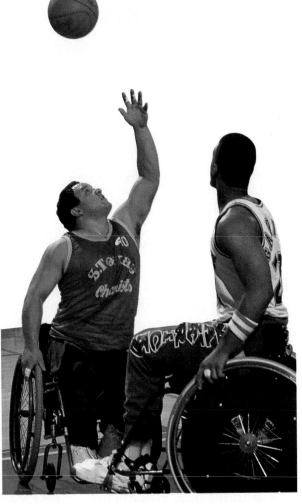

## What Is Fitness?

The Explore Activity showed that skills and abilities help people to do all kinds of activities. Some require athletes to be physically fit.

**Physical fitness** (fiz′i kəl fit′nəs) is the condition in which your body is healthy and works the best it can. It involves working your skeletal muscles, bones, joints, heart, and respiratory system.

You control your skeletal muscles by thinking. Your brain sends electrical messages along nerves to make your muscles contract. The muscles pull on the bones they are attached to. When the electrical messages stop, your muscles return to their original size and position.

The more you use a muscle, the stronger it becomes. Even when relaxed, toned muscles stay slightly contracted.

Your muscles need energy to work and grow. The energy comes mainly from food combined with oxygen.

Taking your pulse at rest lets you know how hard your heart works even before you exercise.

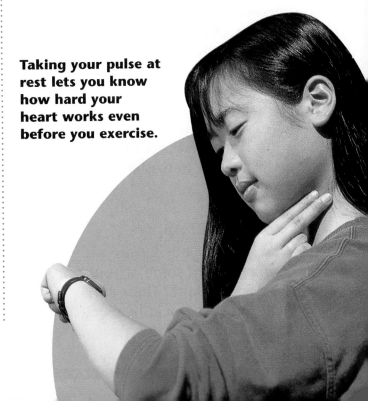

As you exercise or become more active, your breathing rate increases to provide this oxygen. Your heart pumps faster to speed oxygen to your muscles.

In time your lungs will take in more air with each breath. Your heart will pump more blood with each beat. They do more work with less effort.

Brisk and constant physical activity that increases the supply of oxygen to the muscles is called **aerobic exercise** (â rō′bik ek′sər sīz′). Aerobic exercises include swimming, jogging, and biking.

### Brain Power

How can you exercise your muscles, bones, joints, heart, and lungs? Would you need one activity or several?

### Improving Physical Fitness

Aerobic exercises improve your physical fitness if you do them three to five times a week for about half an hour without stopping.

Stretching your muscles helps you gain flexibility to bend and move more easily. As you exercise more, your endurance lets you stay active longer without tiring.

As your muscles become stronger, you lift, pull, and push with more force. Your bones grow thicker and stronger. The energy your muscles use also forces your body to store less fat.

You can move and change position quickly without losing your balance. You can also react faster. Your body parts will work together to be coordinated and responsive.

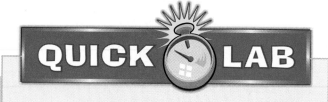

# QUICK LAB

## Hit the Target

**HYPOTHESIZE** Your heart rate indicates if you are exercising hard enough. How can you monitor your heart during exercise? Write a hypothesis in your *Science Journal*.

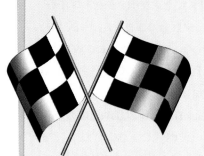

**MATERIALS**
• watch with a second hand
• *Science Journal*

**1.** To improve your heart and lungs, you must reach your target rate during exercise. To find your target rate, subtract your age from 220.

**2.** Multiply the result first by 0.7 and then by 0.8. Write the numbers down. Your target rate is between those two numbers.

**3.** **COMPARE** Take your pulse for one minute. Record the number. Take your pulse again after exercising for one minute. Record the new number.

**4.** **DRAW CONCLUSIONS** How close is your heart rate after exercising to your target rate? Were you exercising hard enough to help your heart? Were you exercising long enough? How can your resting pulse tell you if your heart is getting stronger over time?

# Can Food Help You Stay Fit?

There is more to fitness than exercise. Without a healthy diet, your body cannot work at its best.

One of the best sources of energy is in the sugars and starches of fruits, vegetables, and whole grains.

Your muscles are made of proteins. To keep them strong, you need food rich in proteins, such as meat, beans, and nuts. Your body breaks down food proteins into building blocks used for growth and repair.

Your body also needs some stored fat for energy. However, too much fat can harm your heart and blood vessels.

Most people get enough fat in the food they eat every day.

Muscles and bones also need vitamins and minerals to stay strong and do their jobs.

To make sure your body has these ingredients, eat a **balanced diet** (bal'ənsd di'it). This means a diet, maintained over time, that includes a variety of foods providing nutrition in moderate amounts.

A balanced diet includes all major **food groups** (füd grüps). Each group contains foods with similar amounts of important nutrients. The Food Guide Pyramid indicates how many servings of each group you need each day.

## THE FOOD GUIDE PYRAMID

HEALTH LINK

The Food Guide Pyramid makes it easy to remember to eat a balanced diet. Remember that you also need to drink enough water—about eight large glasses a day.

**READING CHARTS**

1. **DISCUSS** Is your diet balanced?
2. **WRITE** Describe healthful menus for a breakfast, a lunch, and a dinner.

**Fats, Oils, and Sweets**
Use sparingly

**Milk, Yogurt, and Cheese Group**
2–3 Servings

**Meat, Poultry, Fish, Dry Beans, Eggs, and Nuts Group**
2–3 Servings

**Vegetable Group**
3–5 Servings

**Fruit Group**
2–4 Servings

**Bread, Cereal, Rice, and Pasta Group**
6–11 Servings

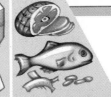
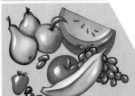

# How Can You Stay Safe?

To help prevent sports injuries, you should always warm up by bending and stretching. After your workout, bend and stretch to cool down. Your heart and breathing rates will slowly return to normal as you cool off.

You can also reduce injuries by learning the right way to perform exercises and sports moves. Ask your teacher or a coach. Find out if you need safety equipment, such as a helmet, kneepads, elbow pads, wrist guards, or goggles. Knowing sports safety can also prevent you from harming someone else.

Never ignore your body's signals. If you feel pain or can't breathe, your body is telling you to slow down and stop exercising.

## WHY IT MATTERS

Proper diet and exercise are part of a healthy lifestyle. They ensure that your body can do all of the activities you want it to do.

A stronger, healthier body will be able to do more for you now. As you grow older, proper diet and exercise will help your body stay strong, toned, and in shape.

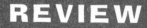

## REVIEW

1. What type of exercise strengthens your heart and lungs?

2. How can you determine your target heart rate for exercising?

3. How can you find out how much food from each group should be eaten every day?

4. **DRAW CONCLUSIONS** If you exercise regularly, your heart and lungs will get stronger. How will this affect your resting heart rate?

5. **CRITICAL THINKING** *Apply* What might happen if you don't get a balanced diet? How can people who can't eat certain foods make sure they still get enough nutrients?

**WHY IT MATTERS** THINK ABOUT IT
Why would athletes need to understand how their bodies work? Would this information help them to form good habits?

**WHY IT MATTERS** WRITE ABOUT IT
Write some practical ways you can use this information. How can your diet more closely match the Food Guide Pyramid? How can you get enough exercise each week?

# SCIENCE MAGAZINE

# Summer Sports Safety

**W**ant to enjoy the summer without getting hurt? Follow these tips!

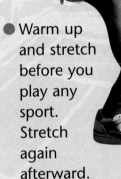

- Warm up and stretch before you play any sport. Stretch again afterward.

- Swim with a partner. The buddy system helps to save lives.

- Drink lots of fluids, especially when it's hot and humid.

- Wear protective padding, a helmet, or shoes required in the sport.

- Exercise and work out regularly. When you're fit and flexible, you're less likely to be injured.

- Eat balanced meals. Calcium, phosphorus, and vitamin D help build strong bones. Muscles need protein, carbohydrates, magnesium, and other minerals and vitamins.

- Take some time to just kick back and relax!

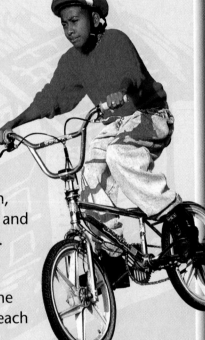

- Follow the rules of each sport.

## DISCUSSION STARTER

1. Which tip is most likely to keep you safe? Why?

2. Which tip do you think most kids ignore? Why?

To learn more about safety, visit *www.mhschool.com/science* and enter the keyword SAFE.

*inter*NET
CONNECTION

## SCIENCE WORDS

aerobic
   exercise p.425
balanced
   diet p.426
bile p.413
digestion p.412

enzyme p.412
excretion p.414
food group p.426
nephron p.414
urea p.414
villus p.413

## USING SCIENCE WORDS

**Number a paper from 1 to 10. Fill in 1 to 5 with words from the list above.**

1. Brisk activity is ___?___.

2. A diet that includes a variety of nutritious foods is a(n) ___?___.

3. Substances in living things that control the speed of chemical reactions are called ___?___.

4. Digested food is absorbed in the small intestine by ___?___.

5. The liver forms ___?___.

**6–10. Pick five words from the list above that were not used in 1 to 5, and use each in a sentence.**

## UNDERSTANDING SCIENCE IDEAS

11. Where does digestion start in the body?

12. How does exercise affect the amount of water your body needs?

13. How can you be sure to get a balanced diet every day?

14. Explain how the liver participates in both your digestive and excretory systems.

15. Describe the role your kidneys play in excretion.

## USING IDEAS AND SKILLS

16. Regular exercise improves your physical fitness. What parts of the body might be involved in exercise?

17. People can survive without food longer than they can survive without water. Is this true or false? Explain your answer.

18. **READING SKILL: FIND THE MAIN IDEA** Digested food is changed physically by the teeth and chemically by enzymes. Explain why both changes must happen.

19. **MAKE A MODEL** How could you build a model to show the effects of exercise on different parts of the body?

20. **THINKING LIKE A SCIENTIST** Many people do not eat enough nutritious food every day. Suggest some reasons for this. Suggest ways to encourage people to eat healthier foods. How can you find out if your suggestions will work?

## PROBLEMS and PUZZLES

**Break Down** How does bile break down fat? To find out pour some olive oil into a test tube. Then, add an equal amount of water. Next, use a clean medicine dropper to add five drops of liquid detergent to one of the test tubes. The olive oil represents fat, so which substance represents bile? How does it act on the olive oil?

# UNIT 5 REVIEW

## USING SCIENCE WORDS

aerobic
  exercise p.425
artery p.388
balanced diet p.426
bile p.413
cilia p.401
food group p.426

mucus p.401
nephron p.414
plasma p.388
trachea p.401
vein p.388
villus p.413

## USING SCIENCE WORDS

**Number a paper from 1 to 10. Beside each number write the word or words that best complete the sentence.**

1. The liquid part of blood that contains nutrients is the ___?___.

2. Blood vessels that carry blood away from the heart are ___?___.

3. Air travels to the lungs through the ___?___.

4. The hairlike structures that push dust and mucus along the throat are ___?___.

5. Dust entering your nose when you breathe is trapped by a liquid called ___?___.

6. A fluid produced by the liver to digest fats is called ___?___.

7. The structures in the kidney that filter blood are ___?___.

8. Jogging is a kind of ___?___.

9. Good nutrition is the result of a(n) ___?___.

10. Dairy products make up a(n) ___?___.

## UNDERSTANDING SCIENCE IDEAS

**Write 11 to 15. For each number write the letter for the best answer. You may wish to use the hints provided.**

11. The function of lymph nodes is to
    a. filter blood
    b. filter lymph
    c. make blood clot
    d. add oxygen to lymph
    *(Hint: Read page 393.)*

12. The blood vessels that exchange materials with cells are
    a. villi
    b. veins
    c. capillaries
    d. arteries
    *(Hint: Read page 388.)*

13. Why might you feel dizzy on a mountaintop?
    a. There isn't enough oxygen.
    b. There aren't enough plants.
    c. The Sun is bright.
    d. It is cold.
    *(Hint: Read page 402.)*

14. The functions of the liver include
    a. digesting food
    b. pumping blood
    c. making vitamins
    d. making urea
    *(Hint: Read page 414.)*

15. How many daily servings of vegetables are recommended in a healthy diet?
    a. 2–3
    b. 2–4
    c. 3–5
    d. 6–11
    *(Hint: Read page 426.)*

## USING IDEAS AND SKILLS

**16.** Sketch a red blood cell. Tell why the shape is important.

**17.** Since there are four blood types and two Rh types, how many combined types are there in all? List them.

**18.** 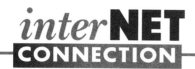 **COMMUNICATE** Explain what happens in the alveoli of the lungs.

**19.** What is the purpose of a yawn?

**20.** What is the purpose of a sneeze?

**21.** Where does bile come from, and what does it do?

**22.** How do nutrients absorbed in the small intestine get into blood?

**23.** Why is aerobic exercise generally good for people?

## THINKING LIKE A SCIENTIST

**24.** **PREDICT** Imagine that a person from a city located on a mountain travels down to a city in a valley. How might the person's breathing be affected? Why?

**25.** When and why do you sweat?

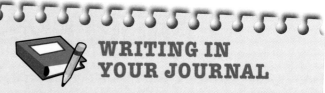

## WRITING IN YOUR JOURNAL

**SCIENCE IN YOUR LIFE**
Tell why it is important for you to drink six to eight glasses of water every day.

**PRODUCT ADS**
Describe two or three TV ads for fast foods. Do any of them explain why these foods are nutritious? If so, give examples.

**HOW SCIENTISTS WORK**
In this unit you learned that with the discovery of different blood types, scientists were able to answer the question of why some blood transfusions don't work. What other questions about the human body do you think scientists might be asking today?

### Design your own Experiment

Does holding your breath affect your heart rate? Determine a way to see if your heart rate is changed by holding your breath for short periods of time, such as 15 seconds, 30 seconds, and 45 seconds. Check with your teacher before carrying out the experiment.

*inter*NET **CONNECTION**

For help in reviewing this unit, visit *www.mhschool.com/science*

# PROBLEMS and PUZZLES

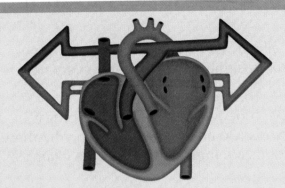

## The Heart Is a Lonely Road

Imagine the circulatory system is a highway and you are a blood cell traveling through it. What kinds of road signs do you see in the heart? Trace the picture shown, and provide road signs for it. Your signs might include such words as *One Way, To the Lungs, Body, Entering Left Atrium, Turn Ahead, Left Turn Only,* and so on. Explain why you chose each sign.

## Storing Oxygen

Your body is able to store food for the future. For example, you can go hours, even days, without eating. Does your body have the same ability to store oxygen? Explain.

How would your oxygen-storing ability compare with that of a whale? Imagine that you could increase the human body's ability to store oxygen. What kind of body structure can you imagine that could accomplish this? Make a design for an oxygen-storing structure in the body.

## The Great Kidney Debate

People with damaged kidneys can live better lives with a kidney transplant. Where should kidneys come from? Organize a debate to address the following questions.

- Should kidneys be taken from animals such as baboons to help people?

- Most kidneys come from healthy people who are killed in road accidents. Should all drivers be required to carry a kidney donor card?

- Kidney transplants are expensive. Should wealthy people be able to spend extra money to get the kidney that they need?

- Who should get kidneys? Should the young be favored over the old, or should kidneys be distributed on a first come, first served basis?

- People have two kidneys. Should they be allowed to sell one kidney? Should selling kidneys be against the law?

# REFERENCE SECTION

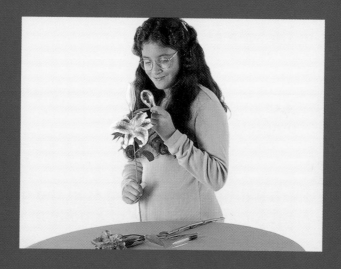

# DIAGRAM BUILDERS

## Building the Water Cycle

A cycle is a number of events or processes that happen in a given order over and over again. For example, Monday follows Sunday, Tuesday follows Monday, and so on, over and over again. Every drop of water is part of the water cycle. The water cycle is the continuous movement of water between Earth's surface and the air. **What happens to water in this cycle?**

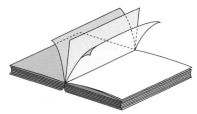

### BASE

To find out, look at the diagram on the facing page. You can see many processes all happening at the same time. You can study this cycle one process at a time by lifting up all the plastic overlays (1, 2, 3). Look at the page beneath, the base. **What sources of water do you see? What source of energy do you see?**

### OVERLAY 1

**1** Now drop overlay 1 onto the base.
**What happens to liquid water? Why?**

### OVERLAY 2

**2** Now drop overlay 2 onto overlay 1.
**What process follows those shown on the first overlay? What happens to the water?**

### OVERLAY 3

**3** Now drop overlay 3 onto overlay 2.
**What processes complete the cycle?**

### SUMMARIZE

**What can happen to a drop of water that is in the ground, in the leaf of a plant, or at the surface of a body of water?**

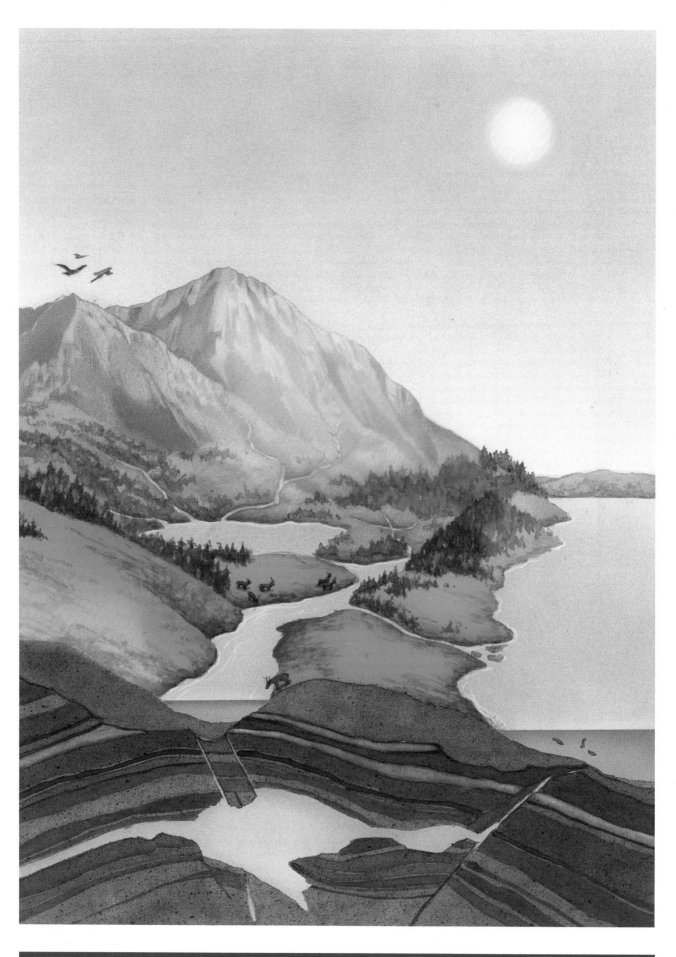

**BASE: Start with water on and in the ground.**

# DIAGRAM BUILDERS
## Activities

## 1 Make a Diagram

What cycles can you describe that take place over a week, a month, or a year? Make a diagram to show how the parts of the cycles are arranged.

## 2 Write About a Main Idea

Does a cycle have a beginning? An end? Write out your idea. Use the Water Cycle diagram to support your idea.

## 3 Make a Model

Use art materials, natural materials, and any other supplies to make a model of the water cycle. How might you make a working model that shows at least some of the processes of the cycle?

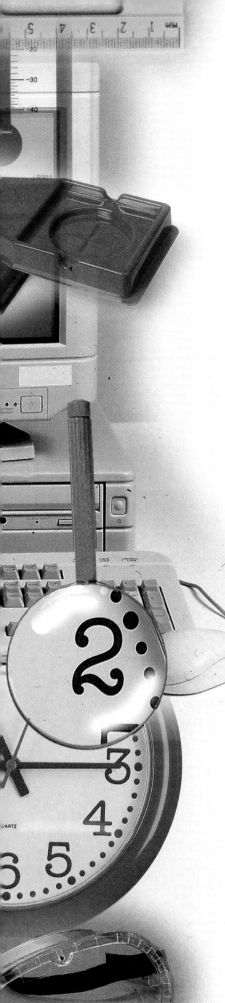

# REFERENCE SECTION

# HANDBOOK

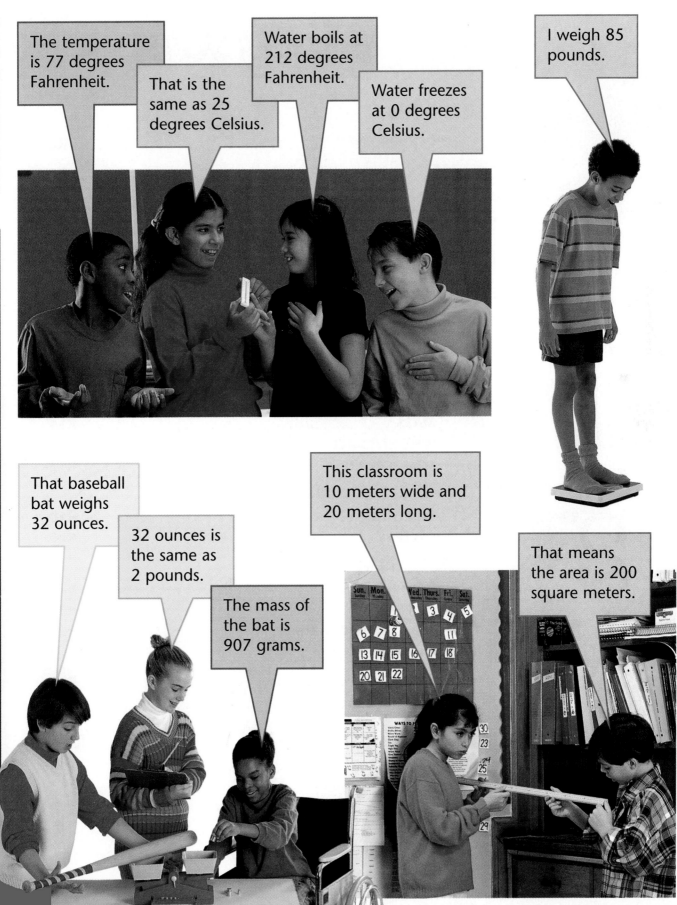

The temperature is 77 degrees Fahrenheit.

That is the same as 25 degrees Celsius.

Water boils at 212 degrees Fahrenheit.

Water freezes at 0 degrees Celsius.

I weigh 85 pounds.

That baseball bat weighs 32 ounces.

32 ounces is the same as 2 pounds.

The mass of the bat is 907 grams.

This classroom is 10 meters wide and 20 meters long.

That means the area is 200 square meters.

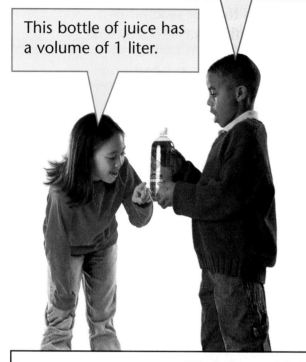

This bottle of juice has a volume of 1 liter.

That is a little more than 1 quart.

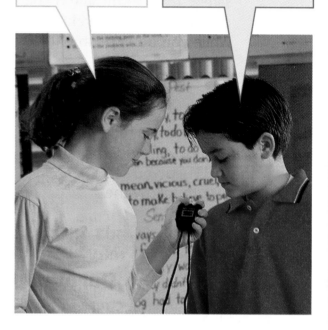

She can walk 20 meters in 5 seconds.

That means her speed is 4 meters per second.

# Table of Measurements

## SI (INTERNATIONAL SYSTEM) OF UNITS

**Temperature**

Water freezes at 0°C and boils at 100°C.

**Length and Distance**

1,000 meters = 1 kilometer
100 centimeters = 1 meter
10 millimeters = 1 centimeter

**Volume**

1,000 milliliters = 1 liter
1 cubic centimeter = 1 milliliter

**Mass**

1,000 grams = 1 kilogram

## ENGLISH SYSTEM OF UNITS

**Temperature**

Water freezes at 32°F and boils at 212°F.

**Length and Distance**

5,280 feet = 1 mile
3 feet = 1 yard
12 inches = 1 foot

**Volume of Fluids**

4 quarts = 1 gallon
2 pints = 1 quart
2 cups = 1 pint
8 fluid ounces = 1 cup

**Weight**

2,000 pounds = 1 ton
16 ounces = 1 pound

# Weight/Force

You use a spring scale to measure weight. An object has weight because the force of gravity pulls down on the object. Therefore, weight is a force. Weight is measured in newtons (N) like all forces.

## Measure the Weight of an Object

1. Look at your spring scale to see how many newtons it measures. See how the measurements are divided. The spring scale shown here measures up to 5 N. It has a mark for every 0.1 N.
2. Hold the spring scale by the top loop. Put the object to be measured on the bottom hook. If the object will not stay on the hook, place it in a net bag. Then hang the bag from the hook.
3. Let go of the object slowly. It will pull down on a spring inside the scale. The spring is connected to a pointer. The pointer on the spring scale shown here is a small bar.
4. Wait for the pointer to stop moving. Read the number of newtons next to the pointer. This is the object's weight. The mug in the picture weighs 4 N.

## More About Spring Scales

You probably weigh yourself by standing on a bathroom scale. This is a spring scale. The force of your body stretches a spring inside the scale. The dial on the scale is probably marked in pounds—the English unit of weight. One pound is equal to about 4.5 newtons.

*Here are some other spring scales you may have seen.*

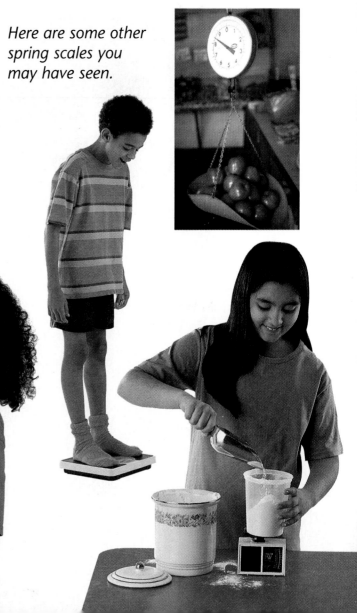

# Temperature

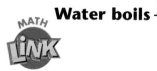

You use a thermometer to measure temperature—how hot or cold something is. A thermometer is made of a thin tube with colored liquid inside. When the liquid gets warmer, it expands and moves up the tube. When the liquid gets cooler, it contracts and moves down the tube. You may have seen most temperatures measured in degrees Fahrenheit (°F). Scientists measure temperature in degrees Celsius (°C).

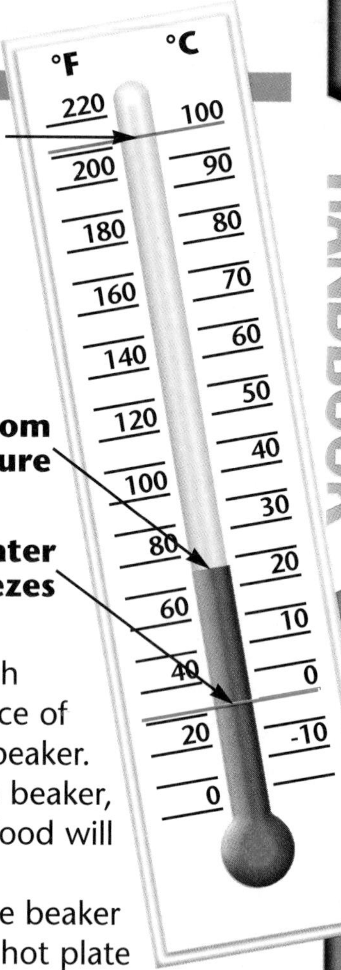

Water boils →

Room temperature

Water freezes

°F | °C
220 | 100
200 | 90
180 | 80
160 | 70
140 | 60
120 | 50
100 | 40
80 | 30
60 | 20
40 | 10
20 | 0
0 | -10

## Read a Thermometer

1. Look at the thermometer shown here. It has two scales—a Fahrenheit scale and a Celsius scale. Every 20 degrees on the Fahrenheit scale has a number. Every 10 degrees on the Celsius scale has a number.
2. What is the temperature shown on the thermometer? At what temperature does water freeze? Give your answers in °F and in °C.

## What Is Convection?

1. Fill a large beaker about two-thirds full of cool water. Find the temperature of the water by holding a thermometer in the water. Do not let the bulb at the bottom of the thermometer touch the sides or bottom of the beaker.
2. Keep the thermometer in the water until the liquid in the tube stops moving—about a minute. Read and record the temperature in °C.

3. Sprinkle a little fish food on the surface of the water in the beaker. Do not knock the beaker, and most of the food will stay on top.
4. Carefully place the beaker on a hot plate. A hot plate is a small electric stove. Plug in the hot plate, and turn the control knob to a middle setting.
5. After a minute measure the temperature of water near the bottom of the beaker. At the same time, a classmate should measure the temperature of water near the top of the beaker. Record these temperatures. Is water near the bottom of the beaker heating up faster than near the top?
6. As the water heats up, notice what happens to the fish food. How do you know that warmer water at the bottom of the beaker rises and cooler water at the top sinks?

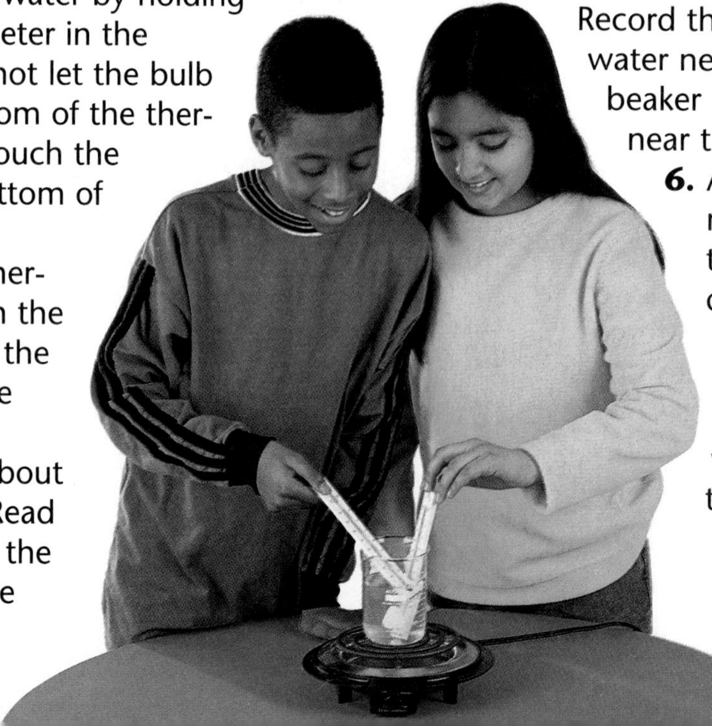

# Weather

What information is included in a weather report? You might think of temperature, cloud cover, wind speed, amount of rainfall, and so on. Various instruments are used to measure these parts of the weather. Some of them are shown here.

## Barometer

A barometer measures air pressure. Most barometers are like the one shown here. It contains a flat metal can with most of the air removed. When air pressure increases (rises), the air pushes more on the can. A pointer that is attached to the can moves toward a higher number on the scale. When air pressure decreases (falls), the air pushes less on the can. The pointer moves toward a lower number on the scale.

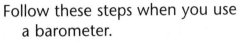

**29.73 inches** ⟶

Notice that the barometer above measures air pressure in inches and in centimeters. The long arrow points to the current air pressure, which is 29.73 inches of mercury. That means the air pushing down on liquid mercury in a dish would force the mercury 29.73 inches up a tube, as the drawing shows. What is the air pressure in centimeters?

Follow these steps when you use a barometer.

1. Look at the current air pressure reading marked by the long arrow.
2. Turn the knob on the front of the barometer so the short arrow points to the current pressure reading.
3. Check the barometer several times a day to see if the pressure is rising, falling, or staying the same.

## Rain Gauge

A rain gauge measures how much rain falls. This instrument is simply a container that collects water. It has one or more scales for measuring the amount of rain.

The rain gauge shown here has been collecting rain throughout the day. How much rain fell in inches? In centimeters?

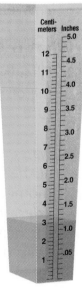

## Weather Vane

A weather vane indicates wind direction. A weather vane is basically an arrow that is free to spin on a pole. Wind pushes on the widest part of the arrow—the tail—so that the arrow points to the direction that the wind is coming from. Letters on the weather vane show directions. If the vane doesn't have letters, you can tell direction with a compass. What direction is the wind coming from in the picture?

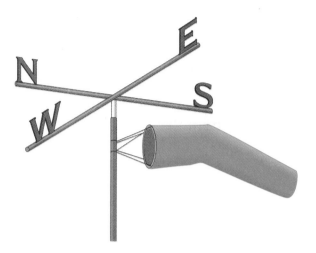

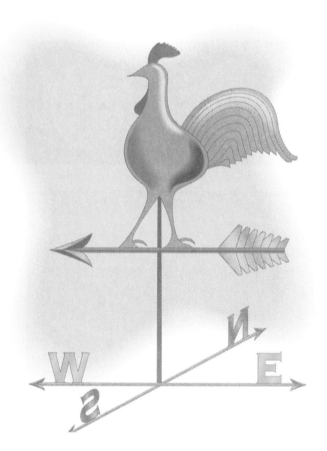

## Windsock

A windsock also indicates wind direction. You may have seen windsocks at airports. Windsocks are usually large and bright orange so that pilots can easily see which way the wind is blowing. The large opening of the windsock faces the wind. The narrow part of the windsock points in the direction that the wind is blowing. Which way is the wind blowing in the picture?

## Anemometer

An anemometer measures wind speed. It is usually made of three shallow cones, or cups, that spin on an axle. The wind makes the cups and axle spin. The axle is attached to a dial that indicates wind speed. The faster the wind blows, the faster the cups turn.

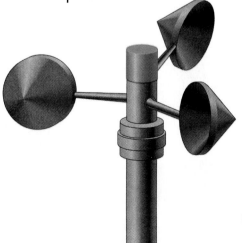

# Cycles

Much of what happens in nature happens in cycles. A cycle is a process that keeps repeating itself. For example, the movement of water through the environment is a cycle. Water evaporates from the ground, rises into the air, condenses into clouds, and falls back to Earth as rain or snow. Once on the ground, it might evaporate again, and the cycle continues.

The drawings below illustrate other natural cycles. See if you can describe each cycle shown.

Think about some cycles in your own life—things that you do over and over again on a regular basis. Describe a daily cycle from your experience. Describe a weekly cycle from your experience.

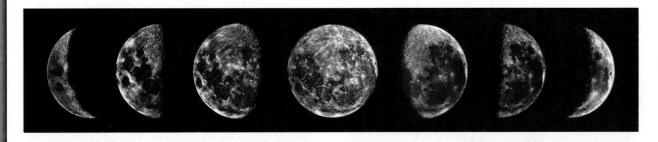

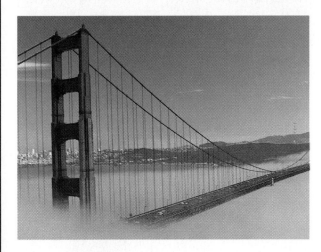
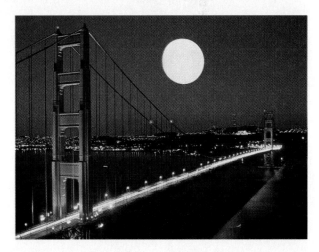

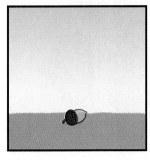
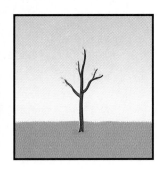
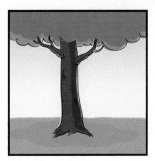
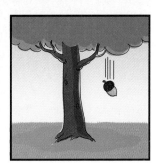

# Make Graphs to Organize Data

When you do an experiment in science, you collect information. To find out what your information means, you can organize it into graphs. There are many kinds of graphs.

## Circle Graphs

A circle graph is helpful to show how a complete set of data is divided into parts. The circle graph here shows how water is used in the United States. What is the single largest use of water?

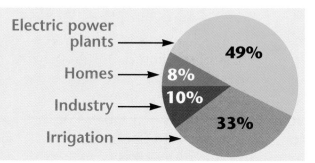

Electric power plants ⟶ 49%
Homes ⟶ 8%
Industry ⟶ 10%
Irrigation ⟶ 33%

## Bar Graphs

A bar graph uses bars to show information. For example, what if you do an experiment by wrapping wire around a nail and connecting the ends of the wire to a battery? The nail then becomes a magnet that can pick up paper clips. The graph shows that the more you wrap the wire around the nail, the more paper clips it picks up.

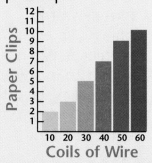

How many paper clips did the nail with 20 coils pick up? With 50 coils?

## Line Graphs

A line graph shows information by connecting dots plotted on the graph. For example, what if you are growing a plant? Every week you measure how high the plant has grown. The line graph below organizes the measurements you collected so that you can easily compare them.

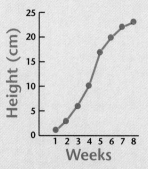

1. Between which two weeks did the plant grow most?
2. When did plant growth begin to level off?

## Make a Graph

What if you collect information about how much water your family uses each day?

| Activity | Water Used (L) |
|---|---|
| Drinking | 10 |
| Showering | 180 |
| Bathing | 240 |
| Brushing teeth | 80 |
| Washing dishes | 140 |
| Washing hands | 30 |
| Washing clothes | 280 |
| Flushing toilet | 90 |

Decide what type of graph would best organize such data. Collect the information and make your graph. Compare it with those of classmates.

# Make Maps to Show Information

## Locate Places

A map is a drawing that shows an area from above. Most maps have coordinates—numbers and letters along the top and side. Coordinates help you find places easily. For example, what if you wanted to find the library on the map? It is located at B4. Place a finger on the letter B along the side of the map, and another finger on the number 4 at the top. Then move your fingers straight across and down the map until they meet. The library is located where the coordinates B and 4 meet, or very nearby.

1. What color building is located at F6?
2. The hospital is located three blocks north and two blocks east of the library. What are its coordinates?
3. Make a map of an area in your community. It might be a park, or the area between your home and school. Include coordinates. Use a compass to find north, and mark north on your map. Exchange maps with classmates, and answer each other's questions.

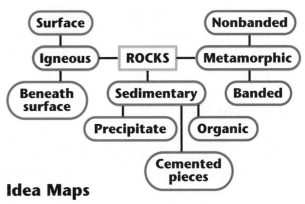

## Idea Maps

The map shows how places are connected to each other. Idea maps, on the other hand, show how ideas are connected to each other. Idea maps help you organize information about a topic.

The idea map above connects ideas about rocks. This map shows that there are three major types of rock—igneous, sedimentary, and metamorphic. Connections to each rock type provide further information. For example, this map reminds you that igneous rocks are classified into those that form at Earth's surface and far beneath it.

Make an idea map about a topic you are learning in science. Your map can include words, phrases, or even sentences. Arrange your map in a way that makes sense to you and helps you understand the ideas.

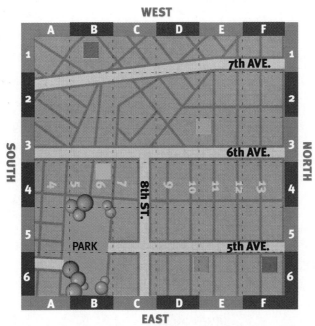

# Make Tables and Charts to Organize Information

Tables help you organize data during experiments. Most tables have columns that run up and down, and rows that run across. The columns and rows have headings that tell you what kind of data goes in each part of the table.

## A Sample Table

What if you are going to do an experiment to find out how long different kinds of seeds take to sprout? Before you begin the experiment, you should set up your table. Follow these steps.

1. In this experiment you will plant 20 radish seeds, 20 bean seeds, and 20 corn seeds. Your table must show how many radish seeds, bean seeds, and corn seeds sprouted on days 1, 2, 3, 4, and 5.

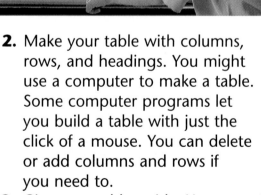

2. Make your table with columns, rows, and headings. You might use a computer to make a table. Some computer programs let you build a table with just the click of a mouse. You can delete or add columns and rows if you need to.
3. Give your table a title. Your table could look like the one here.

## Make a Table

Now what if you are going to do an experiment to find out how temperature affects the sprouting of seeds? You will plant 20 bean seeds in each of two trays. You will keep each tray at a different temperature, as shown below, and observe the trays for seven days. Make a table you can use for this experiment.

## Make a Chart

A chart is simply a table with pictures as well as words to label the rows or columns.

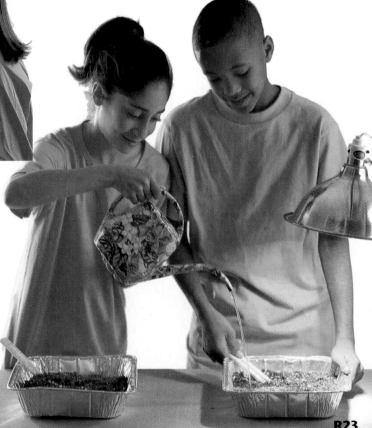

# Computer

A computer has many uses. The Internet connects your computer to many other computers around the world, so you can collect all kinds of information. You can use a computer to show this information and write reports. Best of all you can use a computer to explore, discover, and learn.

You can also get information from CD-ROMs. They are computer disks that can hold large amounts of information. You can fit a whole encyclopedia on one CD-ROM.

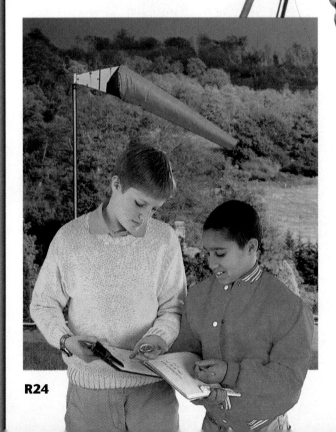

## Use Computers for a Project

Here is how one group of students uses computers as they work on a weather project.

**1.** The students use instruments to measure temperature, wind speed, wind direction, and other parts of the weather. They input this information, or data, into the computer. The students keep the data in a table. This helps them compare the data from one day to the next.

2. The teacher finds out that another group of students in a town 200 kilometers to the west is also doing a weather project. The two groups use the Internet to talk to each other and share data. When a storm happens in the town to the west, that group tells the other group that it's coming their way.

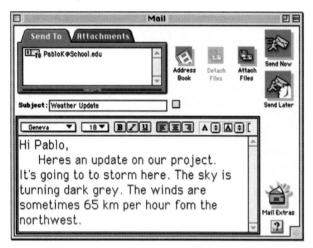

3. The students want to find out more. They decide to stay on the Internet and send questions to a local TV weather forecaster. She has a Web site and answers questions from students every day.

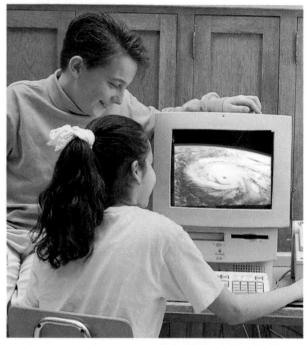

4. Meanwhile some students go to the library to gather more information from a CD-ROM disk. The CD-ROM has an encyclopedia that includes movie clips with sound. The clips give examples of different kinds of storms.

5. The students have kept all their information in a folder called Weather Project. Now they use that information to write a report about the weather. On the computer they can move around paragraphs, add words, take out words, put in diagrams, and draw their own weather maps. Then they print the report in color.

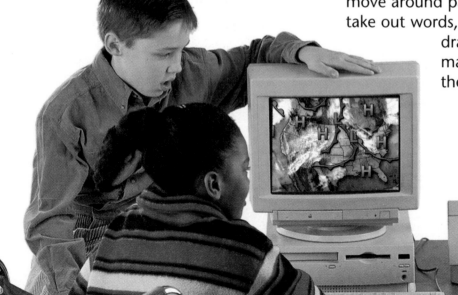

# Calculator

Sometimes after you make measurements, you have to analyze your data to see what it means. This might involve doing calculations with your data. A calculator helps you do time-consuming calculations.

## Find an Average

The table shows the lengths of a group of unshelled peanuts. What is the average length of the peanuts? You can use a calculator to help you find out.

| Peanut | Length (mm) |
|--------|-------------|
| 1 | 32 |
| 2 | 29 |
| 3 | 30 |
| 4 | 31 |
| 5 | 33 |
| 6 | 26 |
| 7 | 28 |
| 8 | 27 |
| 9 | 29 |
| 10 | 29 |
| 11 | 32 |
| 12 | 31 |
| 13 | 23 |
| 14 | 36 |
| 15 | 31 |

1. Make sure the calculator is on. Press the [ON] key.
2. Add the numbers. To add a series of numbers, enter the first number and press [+]. Repeat until you enter the last number. Then press [=]. Your total should be 447.
3. While entering so many numbers, it's easy to make a mistake and hit the wrong key. If you make a mistake, you can correct it by pressing the clear entry key, [CE]. Then continue entering the rest of the numbers.
4. Look at the list of lengths, and estimate what you think the average length is. Find the average length of the peanuts by dividing your total by the number of peanuts. If 447 is displayed, press [÷] [1] [5] [=]. How close was your estimate to the actual average?

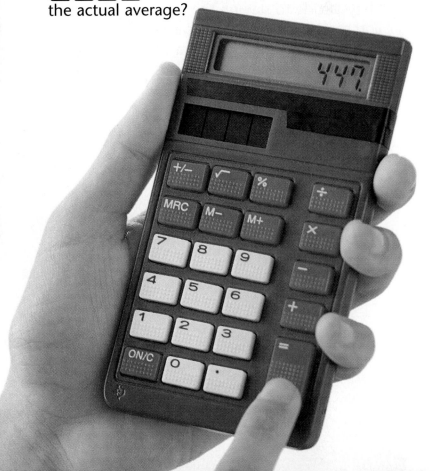

# GLOSSARY

This Glossary will help you to pronounce and understand the meanings of the Science Words introduced in this book. The page number at the end of the definition tells where the word appears.

## A

**acid rain** (as'id rān) Moisture that falls to Earth after being mixed with wastes from burned fossil fuels. (p. 353)

**adaptation** (ad'əp tā'shən) A characteristic that enables a living thing to survive in its environment. (p. 86)

**aerial root** (âr'ē əl rüt) A root that never touches the ground but can take in moisture from the air. (p. 20)

**aerobic exercise** (â rō'bik ek'sər sīz') A brisk and constant physical activity that increases the supply of oxygen to the muscles. (p. 424)

**aerosol** (âr'ə sôl') A type of colloid in which liquid drops or solid particles are spread throughout a gas. (p. 250)

**air mass** (âr mas) A large region of the atmosphere where the air has similar properties throughout. (p. 150)

**air pressure** (âr presh'ər) The force put on a given area by the weight of the air above it. (p. 105)

**alternation of generations** (ôl'tər nā'shən uv jen'ə rā'shənz) The process in which offspring are reproduced sexually, their offspring are reproduced asexually, and so on. (p. 49)

**alternative energy source** (ôl tûr'nə tiv en'ər jē sôrs) A source of energy other than the burning of a fossil fuel. (p. 376)

**alveoli** (al vē'ə lī') n. pl., sing. **alveolus** (-ləs) Clusters of air sacs at the end of each bronchiole. (p. 401)

**anemometer** (an'ə mom'i tər) A device that measures wind speed. (p. 142)

**angiosperm** (an'jē ə spûrm') A seed plant that produces flowers. See **gymnosperm**. (p. 58)

**antibody** (an'ti bod'ē) A protein in blood that helps the body find and destroy materials that may be harmful. (p. 389)

**antigen** (an'ti jən) Either of two chemicals on the surfaces of type A or type B blood cells that limit their usefulness in providing blood transfusions. (p. 389)

**aquifer** (ak'wə fər) An underground layer of rock or soil filled with water. (p. 363)

**artery** (är'tə rē) A blood vessel that carries blood away from the heart. (p. 388)

**asexual reproduction** (a sek'shü əl rē'prō duk'shən) The production of a new organism from only one cell. (p. 50)

**atmosphere** (at'məs fîr') The blanket of gases that surrounds Earth. (pp. 104, 299)

**atom** (at'əm) The smallest unit of an element that retains the properties of that element. See **molecule**. (p. 216)

## B

**bacterium** (bak tîr'ē əm) sing., n., pl. **bacteria** (-ē ə) A member of either of two kingdoms of one-celled living things that have no nucleus, or center, in their cell body. (p. 13)

---

## PRONUNCIATION KEY

The following symbols are used throughout the McGraw-Hill Science 2001 Glossaries.

| | | | | | | | | | |
|---|---|---|---|---|---|---|---|---|---|
| a | at | e | end | o | hot | u | up | hw | white | ə | about |
| ā | ape | ē | me | ō | old | ū | use | ng | song | | taken |
| ä | far | i | it | ô | fork | ü | rule | th | thin | | pencil |
| âr | care | ī | ice | oi | oil | ù | pull | th | this | | lemon |
| | | îr | pierce | ou | out | ûr | turn | zh | measure | | circus |

′ = *primary accent; shows which syllable takes the main stress, such as* **kil** *in* **kilogram** (kil'ə gram')

′ = *secondary accent; shows which syllables take the lighter stresses, such as* **gram** *in* **kilogram**

**balanced diet** (bal′ənst dī′it) A diet, maintained over time, that includes a variety of foods providing nutrition in moderate amounts. (p. 426)

**barometer** (bə rom′i tər) A device for measuring air pressure. (p. 106)

**Beaufort scale** (bō′fərt skāl) A system for measuring wind speed by observing its effect on the surface of the sea, using a scale of 0 (low) to 12 (high) for each effect. (p. 143)

**bench mark** (bench märk) A plaque telling the exact location and elevation of a place. (p. 307)

**bile** (bīl) A greenish-yellow fluid produced by the liver to digest fats. (p. 413)

**biomass** (bī′ō mas′) Energy from plant matter or animal waste. (p. 378)

**bladder** (blad′ər) A muscular bag that collects urine produced by the kidneys. (p. 414)

**boiling point** (boil′ing point) The particular temperature for each substance at which it changes state from a liquid to a gas. (p. 229)

**bronchial tubes** (brong′kē əl tübz) The two tubes that connect the trachea to each of your lungs. (p. 401)

**bronchioles** (brong′kē olz) Smaller passages of the bronchial tubes that branch throughout the lungs. (p. 401)

**buoyancy** (boi′ən sē) The upward push of a liquid on an object placed in it. (p. 202)

**C**

**cambium** (kam′bē əm) The layer in plants that separates the xylem from the phloem. (p. 20)

**camouflage** (kam′ə fläzh′) An animal's use of its appearance to protect itself against predators. (p. 89)

**capillary** (kap′ə ler′ē) The smallest type of blood vessel, where materials are exchanged between blood and body cells. (p. 388)

**chemical change** (kem′i kəl chānj) A change of matter that occurs when atoms link together in a new way, creating a new substance different from the original substances. (p. 260)

**chemical reaction** (kem′i kəl rē ak′shən) Another name for chemical change. (p. 260)

**chlorofluorocarbons (CFCs)** (klôr′ō flur′ō kär′bənz) Gases used in such things as refrigerators, freezers, and air conditioners. CFCs may make "holes" in the ozone layer. (p. 355)

**chlorophyll** (klôr′ə fil′) A green chemical in plant cells that allows plants to use the Sun's energy for making food. (p. 4)

**chloroplast** (klôr′ə plast′) The part of a plant cell containing chlorophyll, the green substance that enables the plant to produce food. (p. 32)

**cilia** (sil′ē ə) Small hairlike structures that move small particles of dirt out of the respiratory system. (p. 401)

**cirrus cloud** (sir′əs kloud) A high-altitude cloud with a featherlike shape, made of ice crystals. (p. 122)

**classification** (klas′ə fi kā′shən) The science of finding patterns among living things. (p. 5)

**classify** (klas′ə fī′) To place materials that share properties together in groups. (p. 205)

**cleavage** (klē′vij) The tendency of a mineral to break along flat surfaces. (p. 322)

**climate** (klī′mit) The average weather pattern of a region. (p. 178)

**climatic zone** (klī mat′ik zōn) A region that has similar weather patterns based on temperature, precipitation, wind, distance from a coast, mountain ranges, ocean currents, and vegetation. (p. 178)

**cold front** (kōld frunt) A front where cold air moves in under a warm front. (p. 152)

**colloid** (kol′oid) A special type of mixture in which the particles of one material are scattered through another and block the passage of light without settling out. (p. 250)

**complete flower** (kəm plēt′ flou′ər) A flower that has petals, stamens, and pistils. (p. 70)

**compound** (kom′pound) Any substance that is formed by the chemical combination of two or more elements and acts like a single substance. (p. 214)

**compression** (kəm presh′ən) A movement of plates that presses together or squeezes Earth's crust. (p. 308)

**condensation** (kon′den sā′shən) The changing of a gas into a liquid. (p. 115)

**conduct** (v., kən dukt') To allow heat to pass through easily. (p. 204)

**conduction** (kən duk'shən) The passing of heat through a material while the material itself stays in place. (p. 279)

**conifer** (kon'ə fər) Any of a group of gymnosperms that produce seeds in cones and have needlelike leaves. (p. 59)

**contour plowing** (kon'tür plou'ing) Preventing erosion by plowing across rather than up and down a slope. (p. 341)

**contract** (v., kən trakt') To shrink, as when a material gets cooler. (p. 235)

**convection** (kən vek'shən) The flow of heat through a material, causing hot parts to rise and cooler parts to sink. (p. 279)

**convection cell** (kən vek'shən sel) A circular pattern of air rising, air sinking, and wind. (p. 136)

**core** (kôr) The center of Earth, lying below the mantle. (p. 307)

**Coriolis effect** (kôr'ē ō'lis i fekt') The curving of the path of a moving object caused by Earth's rotation. (p. 138)

**cortex** (kôr'teks) The layer of tissue just inside the epidermis of a plant's roots and stems. (p. 20)

**cotyledon** (ko'tə lē'dən) A tiny leaflike structure inside the seed of an angiosperm. (p. 62)

**crop rotation** (krop rō tā'shən) Growing different crops each year so that the soil does not use up the same kinds of minerals year after year. (p. 341)

**cross-pollination** (krôs'pol'ə nā'shən) The transfer of pollen from one flower to another. (p. 72)

**crust** (krust) The rocky surface that makes up the top of the lithosphere and includes the continents and the ocean floor. (p. 298)

**crystal** (kris'təl) The geometric shape a mineral forms when its atoms and molecules get into fixed patterns. (p. 320)

**cumulus cloud** (kū'myə ləs kloud) A puffy cloud that appears to rise up from a flat bottom. (p. 122)

**cycad** (sī'kad) One of the evergreen gymnosperms that resemble palms and have seed-bearing cones. (p. 59)

**D**

**deciduous** (di sij'ü əs) Said of a plant that loses its leaves each fall. *See* **evergreen**. (p. 59)

**density** (den'si tē) A measure of how tightly packed the matter in an object is. (p. 199)

**deposition** (dep'ə zish'ən) The dropping off of bits of eroded rock. (p. 313)

**desalination** (dē sal'ə nā'shən) Getting fresh water from seawater. (p. 361)

**diaphragm** (dī'ə fram') A sheet of muscle below the chest cavity that controls breathing. (p. 400)

**dicot** (dī'kot') An angiosperm with two cotyledons in each seed. *See* **monocot**. (p. 62)

**diffusion** (di fū'zhən) The process by which a substance such as a gas moves from areas of high concentration to areas of low concentration. (p. 401)

**digestion** (di jes'chən) The process of breaking food down into simpler substances for the body to use. (p. 412)

**downdraft** (doun'draft') A downward rush of air caused by the falling of rain during a thunderstorm. (p. 162)

**dry cell battery** (drī sel bat'ər ē) A battery that produces electricity but has no liquid inside it. (p. 283)

**E**

**electron** (i lek'tron) A particle in the space outside the nucleus of an atom that carries one unit of negative electric charge. (p. 217)

**element** (el'ə mənt) Pure substances that cannot be broken down into any simpler substances. (p. 212)

---

**PRONUNCIATION KEY**

a **at**; ā **ape**; ä **far**; âr **care**; e **end**; ē **me**; i **it**; ī **ice**; îr **pierce**; o **hot**; ō **old**; ô **fork**; oi **oil**; ou **out**; u **up**; ū **use**; ü **rule**; u̇ **pull**; ûr **turn**; hw **white**; ng **song**; th **thin**; <u>th</u> **this**; zh **measure**; ə **about, taken, pencil, lemon, circus**

GLOSSARY

**elevation** (el'ə vā'shən) How high a place is above sea level. (p. 307)

**embryo** (em'brē ō') The immature plant inside a seed. (p. 74)

**emulsion** (i mul'shən) A type of colloid in which one liquid is spread through another. (p. 250)

**enzyme** (en'zīm) A chemical that breaks down food into simple pieces that cells can use. (p. 412)

**epidermis** (ep'i dûr'mis) An outermost layer of such plant parts as roots and leaves. (p. 20)

**epiglottis** (ep'i glot'is) A cartilage flap above the trachea that keeps food from entering the lungs. (p. 401)

**erosion** (i rō'zhən) Picking up and carrying away pieces of rocks. (p. 311)

**esophagus** (i sof'ə gəs) The tube that connects the mouth to the stomach. (p. 412)

**evaporation** (i vap'ə rā'shən) The changing of a liquid into a gas. (pp. 112, 229)

**evergreen** (ev'ər grēn') Seed of a gymnosperm that keeps its leaves for at least a few years. *See* **deciduous**. (p. 59)

**excretion** (ek skrē'shən) The process of removing waste products from the body. (p. 414)

**expand** (ek spand') To spread out, as when a material gets hotter. (p. 235)

**F**

**fault** (fôlt) A crack in the crust whose sides show evidence of motion. (p. 306)

**fault-block mountain** (fôlt blok moun'tən) A mountain formed by blocks of Earth's crust moving along a fault. (p. 309)

**fertilization** (fûr'tə lə zā'shən) The joining of a female sex cell and a male sex cell into one cell, a fertilized egg. (pp. 50, 73)

**fibrous root** (fī'brəs rüt) One of the many hairy branching roots that some plants have. (p. 20)

**foam** (fōm) A type of colloid in which a gas is spread throughout a liquid. (p. 251)

**fog** (fôg) A cloud that forms at ground level. (p. 123)

**food group** (füd grüp) One of the groups made up of foods that contain similar amounts of important nutrients. (p. 426)

**fossil** (fos'əl) Any remains or imprint of living things of the past. (p. 335)

**fossil fuel** (fos'əl fū'əl) A fuel formed from the decay of ancient forms of life. (p. 352)

**freezing point** (frēz'ing point) Another name for melting point when a substance changes state from a liquid to a solid. (p. 229)

**frond** (frond) The leaf of a fern. (p. 49)

**front** (frunt) A boundary between air masses with different temperatures. (p. 151)

**fruit** (früt) The ripened ovary of a flowering seed plant. (p. 75)

**fungi** (fun'jī) *pl. n., sing.* **fungus** (fung'gəs) Members of a kingdom that contains one-celled and many-celled living things that absorb food from their environment. (p. 11)

**G**

**gel** (jel) A type of colloid in which a solid is spread throughout a liquid. (p. 251)

**gem** (jem) A mineral valued for being rare and beautiful. (p. 326)

**geologist** (jē ol'ə jist) A scientist who studies Earth. (p. 307)

**geothermal energy** (jē'ō thûr'məl en'ər jē) Earth's internal energy. (p. 376)

**germination** (jûr'mə nā'shən) The sprouting of a seed into a new plant. (p. 75)

**ginkgo** (ging'kō) *n., pl.* **ginkgoes** A large gymnosperm with fan-shaped leaves. (p. 59)

**gnetophyte** (ne'tō fīt') One of the gymnosperms that are closely related to flowering plants and live in both deserts and the tropics. (p. 59)

**gravitropism** (grav'i trō'pi'zəm) The response of a plant to gravity. (p. 84)

**gravity** (grav'i tē) A force of attraction, or pull, between any object and any other objects around it. Gravity is a property of all matter. (p. 294)

**greenhouse effect** (grēn'hous' i fekt') The ability of the atmosphere to let in sunlight but not to let heat escape. (p. 183)

**groundwater** (ground wô′tər) Water that seeps into the ground into spaces between bits of rock and soil. (pp. 126, 363)

**gymnosperm** (jim′nə spûrm′) A seed plant that does not produce flowers. *See* **angiosperm**. (p. 58)

## H

**hail** (hāl) Pellets made of ice and snow. (p. 125)

**hardness** (härd′nis) How well a mineral resists scratching. (p. 322)

**hemoglobin** (hē′mə glō′bin) A chemical that carries oxygen around in the body. (p. 388)

**high-pressure system** (hī′ presh′ər sis′təm) A pattern surrounding a high-pressure center, from which winds blow outward. In the Northern Hemisphere, these winds curve to the right in a clockwise pattern. (p. 140)

**humidity** (hū mid′i tē) The amount of water vapor in the air. (p. 112)

**humus** (hū′məs) Decayed plant or animal material in soil. (p. 339)

**hurricane** (hûr′i kān′) A very large, swirling storm with very low pressure at the center. (p. 166)

**hydrocarbon** (hī′drə kär′bən) Any of the large group of compounds made solely from hydrogen and carbon atoms. (p. 222)

**hydroelectric plant** (hī′drō i lek′trik plant) A factory where running or falling water spins a generator to make electricity. (p. 376)

**hydrosphere** (hī′drə sfîr′) Earth's water, whether found in continents and oceans, and includes the fresh water in ice, lakes, rivers, and underground water. (p. 298)

**hydrotropism** (hī drot′rə piz′əm) The response of a plant to a nearby source of water. (p. 85)

**hyperthermia** (hī′pər thûr′mē ə) The overheating of the body that can be caused by overexposure in a hot, dry climate. (p. 186)

**hypothesis** (hī poth′ə sis) A guess or *if . . . then* statement that can be answered clearly in an experiment. (p. 35)

## I-K

**igneous rock** (ig′nē əs rok) A rock formed when melted rock material cools and hardens. (p. 332)

**imperfect flower** (im pûr′fikt flou′ər) A flower with either a stamen or a pistil, but not both. (p. 70)

**incomplete flower** (in′kəm plēt′ flou′ər) A flower that lacks petals or stamens or pistils. (p. 70)

**inertia** (i nûr′shə) The tendency of a moving object to keep moving in a straight line. (p. 295)

**insolation** (in′sə lā′shən) The amount of the Sun's energy that reaches Earth at a given time and place. *Insolation* is short for *in*coming *sol*ar *r*adi*ation*. (p. 100)

**insulate** (in′sə lāt′) To prevent heat from passing through. (p. 204)

**isobar** (i′sə bär′) A line on a weather map connecting places with equal air pressure. (p. 140)

**kinetic energy** (ki net′ik en′ər jē) The energy of any moving object. (p. 273)

## L

**land breeze** (land brēz) Wind that blows from land to sea. (p. 137)

**larynx** (lar′ingks) The voice box, located at the upper end of the trachea. (p. 401)

**lava** (lä′və) Magma that reaches Earth's surface. (p. 309)

**lightning** (līt′ning) One of the huge electric sparks that leap from clouds to the ground in thunderstorms. (p. 162)

**lithosphere** (lith′ə sfîr′) The hard, outer layer of Earth, about 100 kilometers thick. (p. 298)

**long-day plant** (lông′dā plant) Plants that bloom when there is much more daylight than darkness. (p. 86)

**low-pressure system** (lō′presh′ər sis′təm) A pattern surrounding a low-pressure center, in which winds blow in toward the center. In the

---

### PRONUNCIATION KEY

a **at**; ā **ape**; ä **far**; âr **care**; e **end**; ē **me**; i **it**; ī **ice**; îr **pierce**; o **hot**; ō **old**; ô **fork**; oi **oil**; ou **out**; u **up**; ū **use**; ü **rule**; u̇ **pull**; ûr **turn**; hw **white**; ng **song**; th **thin**; <u>th</u> **this**; zh **measure**; ə **about, taken, pencil, lemon, circus**

Northern Hemisphere, these winds blow to the right in a counterclockwise pattern. (p. 140)

**luster** (lus′tər) The way light bounces off a mineral's surface. (p. 321)

## M

**magma** (mag′mə) Hot, molten rock deep below Earth's surface. (p. 309)

**mantle** (man′təl) The thickest layer of Earth, lying just under the crust. (p. 307)

**mass** (mas) A measure of the amount of matter in an object. (p. 196)

**melting point** (melt′ing point) The particular temperature for each substance at which it changes state from a solid to a liquid. (p. 229)

**membrane** (mem′brān) A thin envelope surrounding the nucleus of a cell. (p. 12)

**metamorphic rock** (met′ə môr′fik rok) A rock formed under heat and pressure from another kind of rock. (p. 336)

**meteorite** (mē′tē ə rīt′) A chunk of rock from space that strikes a surface (such as Earth or the Moon). (p. 314)

**mimicry** (mim′i krē) An animal's use of its appearance to look like a different, unpleasant animal as a protection against predators. (p. 89)

**mineral** (min′ər əl) A solid material of Earth's crust with a definite composition. (p. 320)

**mixture** (miks′chər) A physical combination of two or more substances that are blended together without forming new substances. (p. 244)

**molecule** (mol′ə kūl′) The smallest piece that matter can be broken into without changing the kind of matter; a group of more than one atom joined together that acts like a single particle. *See* **atom**. (p. 220)

**monocot** (mon′ə kot′) An angiosperm with one cotyledon in each seed. *See* **dicot**. (p. 62)

**mountain breeze** (moun′tən brēz) A cool night wind that blows down a mountain slope to replace the warmer air in the valley. (p. 137)

**mucus** (mū′kəs) A clear fluid that traps and pre-vents foreign particles from entering the body. (p. 401)

## N

**nephron** (nef′ron) A structure in the kidney that filters blood. (p. 414)

**neutron** (nü′tron) A particle in the nucleus of an atom that has no net electric charge. (p. 217)

**NEXRAD** (neks′rad′) A new form of Doppler radar that is used to track storms. The word stands for *NEXt generation of weather RADar.* (p. 173)

**nonrenewable resource** (non′ri nü′ə bəl rē′sôrs′) A resource that cannot be replaced within a short period of time or at all. (p. 327)

**nonvascular** (non vas′kyə lər) Containing no plant tissue through which water and food move. (p. 7)

**nucleus** (nü′klē əs) **1.** A dense, dark structure inside the cell. (p. 12) **2.** One of the airborne dust particles around which water molecules condense as droplets or ice crystals before falling as precipitation. (p. 123)

## O

**occluded front** (ə klüd′id frunt) A front formed where a warm front and cold front meet. (p. 152)

**orbit** (ôr′bit) The path of a planet traveling around a star. (p. 292)

**ore** (ôr) A mineral containing a useful substance. (p. 326)

**ovary** (ō′və rē) A structure containing egg cells. (p. 72)

**ozone layer** (ō′zōn lā′ər) A layer of ozone gas in the atmosphere that screens out much of the Sun's UV (ultraviolet) rays. (p. 351)

## P

**parasite** (par′ə sīt′) An angiosperm that lives off other plants. It cannot live on its own because it has little or no chlorophyll. (p. 60)

**perfect flower** (pûr′fikt flou′ər) A flower with both male and female parts, that is, both a stamen and a pistil. (p. 70)

**periodic table** (pîr′ē od′ik tā′bəl) A table in which the elements are arranged in groups with similar properties. (p. 219)

**phloem** (flō′em) The tissue through which food

from the leaves moves down through the rest of a plant. (p. 20)

**photoperiodism** (fō′tō pîr′ē ə diz′əm) The flowering response of a plant to changing periods of daylight and darkness. (p. 86)

**photosynthesis** (fō′tə sin′thə sis) The food-making process in green plants that uses sunlight. (p. 32)

**phototropism** (fō tot′rə piz′əm) The response of a plant to changes in light. (p. 84)

**phylum** (fī′ləm) *sing. n., pl.* **phyla** (-lə) One of the large groups in the animal kingdom. (p. 10)

**physical change** (fiz′i kəl chānj) A change of matter in size, shape, or state without any change in identity. (p. 258)

**physical fitness** (fiz′i kəl fit′nis) The condition in which your body is healthy and works the best it can. (p. 424)

**planet** (plan′it) Any of the nine objects that travel around the Sun and shine by reflecting its light. (p. 292)

**plant behavior** (plant bi hāv′yər) The response of plants to conditions in their environments. (p. 82)

**plasma** (plaz′mə) The pale-yellow liquid part of blood that contains nutrients. (p. 388)

**plate** (plāt) One of the pieces of Earth's crust that has been broken by upward pressure from the mantle. (p. 307)

**platelet** (plāt′lit) A cell fragment in blood that helps blood to form clots. (p. 388)

**pollen** (pol′ən) Dustlike grains in the flower of a plant that contain its male sex cells. (p. 64)

**pollination** (pol′ə nā′shən) The transfer of a pollen grain to the egg-producing part of a plant. (p. 72)

**pollutant** (pə lü′tənt) An unnatural substance added to Earth's land, water, or air. (p. 340)

**pollution** (pə lü′shən) Adding any unnatural substances to Earth's land, water, or air. (p. 340)

**polymer** (pol′ə mər) Any plastic, such as polyethylene, that is made of hydrocarbon molecules with very long chains of atoms. (p. 222)

**potential energy** (pə ten′shəl en′ər jē) Stored energy. (p. 273)

**precipitation** (pri sip′i tā′shən) Any form of water particles that falls from the atmosphere and reaches the ground. (p. 124)

**product** (prod′ukt) A new substance produced by a chemical change. (p. 260)

**property** (prop′ər tē) A characteristic of matter. (p. 196)

**prop root** (prop rüt) One of the roots that grow out of a plant's stemlike main roots and helps prop up the plant. (p. 20)

**protective coloration** (prə tek′tiv kul′ə rā′shən) An animal's blending in with its background to protect itself against predators. (p. 89)

**protist** (prō′tist) A member of a kingdom that contains one-celled and many-celled living things, some that make food and some that hunt for food. (p. 12)

**proton** (prō′ton) A particle in the nucleus of an atom that carries one unit of positive electric charge. (p. 217)

## Q-R

**radiation** (rā′dē a′shən) The giving off of infrared rays through space. (p. 279)

**radiative balance** (rā′dē ā′tiv bal′əns) A balance between energy lost and energy gained. (p. 182)

**reactant** (rē ak′tənt) An original substance at the beginning of a chemical reaction. (p. 260)

**relative humidity** (rel′ə tiv hū mid′i tē) A comparison between the actual amount of water vapor in the air and the amount the air can hold at a given temperature. (p. 114)

**renewable resource** (ri nü′ə bəl rē′sôrs′) A resource that can be replaced in a short period of time. (p. 350)

---

**PRONUNCIATION KEY**

a **at**; ā **ape**; ä **far**; âr **care**; e **end**; ē **me**; i **it**; ī **ice**; îr **pierce**; o **hot**; ō **old**; ô **fork**; oi **oil**; ou **out**; u **up**; ū **use**; ü **rule**; u **pull**; ûr **turn**; hw **white**; ng **song**; th **thin**; th **this**; zh **measure**; ə **about, taken, pencil, lemon, circus**

**reservoir** (rez'ər vwär') A storage area for fresh-water supplies. (p. 363)

**resource** (rē'sôrs') Any material that helps support life on Earth. (p. 290)

**respiration** (res'pə rā'shən) 1. The process of obtaining and using oxygen in the body. (p. 400) 2. The release of energy in plants from food (sugar). (p. 33)

**response** (ri spons') What a living thing does as a result of a stimulus. (p. 84)

**rhizoid** (rī'zoid) One of the hairlike fibers that anchors a moss to the soil and takes in water from the soil. (p. 46)

**rhizome** (rī'zōm) The underground stem of a fern. (p. 49)

**rock** (rok) A naturally formed solid in the crust made up of one or more minerals. (p. 332)

**rock cycle** (rok sī'kəl) Rocks changing from one form into another in a never-ending series of processes. (p. 342)

**root cap** (rüt kap) A thin covering made up of cells that protect the root tip of a plant as it grows into the soil. (p. 20)

**runoff** (run'ôf) Precipitation that falls into rivers and streams. (p. 126)

**S**

**sea breeze** (sē brēz) Wind that blows from sea to land. (p. 137)

**sedimentary rock** (sed'ə men'tə rē rok) A rock made of bits of matter joined together. (p. 334)

**seed** (sēd) An undeveloped plant with stored food sealed in a protective covering. (p. 58)

**seed coat** (sēd kōt) The outer covering of a seed. (p. 74)

**seed dispersal** (sēd di spûr'səl) The movement of a seed from the flower to a place where it can sprout. (p. 75)

**self-pollination** (self'pol'ə nā'shən) The transfer of pollen from an anther to a stigma in the same plant. (p. 72)

**sexual reproduction** (sek'shü əl rē'prō duk'shən) The production of a new organism from a female sex cell and a male sex cell. (p. 50)

**shear** (shîr) A movement of plates that twists, tears, or pushes one part of Earth's crust past another. (p. 308)

**short-day plant** (shôrt'dā plant) Plants that bloom when there is more darkness and less daylight. (p. 86)

**sickle cell anemia** (sik'əl sel ə nē'mē ə) An inherited blood disease in which the red blood cells curve into a C shape and cannot move or absorb oxygen easily. (p. 394)

**smog** (smog) A mixture of smoke and fog. (p. 352)

**solar system** (sō'lər sis'təm) The Sun and the objects that are traveling around it. (p. 292)

**solution** (sə lü'shən) A mixture of substances that are blended so completely that the mixture looks the same everywhere, even under a microscope. (p. 248)

**spore** (spôr) Cells in seedless plants that grow into new organisms. (p. 46)

**spring** (spring) A place where groundwater seeps out of the ground. (p. 363)

**states of matter** (stāts uv mat'ər) One of the three forms that matter can take—solid, liquid, or gas. (p. 228)

**stationary front** (stā'shə ner ē frunt) An unmoving front where a cold air mass and a warm air mass meet. (p. 153)

**statistical forecasting** (stə tis'ti kəl fôr'kas'ting) Predicting weather by using past weather records, based on the chances of a pattern repeating itself. (p. 156)

**stimulus** (stim'yə ləs), *sing.*, *pl.* **stimuli** (-lī) Something in the environment that causes a living thing to react. (p. 84)

**stomata** (stō'mə tə) *pl. n.*, *sing.* **stoma** Pores in the bottom of leaves that open and close to let in air or give off water vapor. (p. 25)

**storm surge** (stôrm sûrj) A great rise of the sea along a shore caused by low-pressure clouds. (p. 168)

**stratus cloud** (strā'təs kloud) A cloud that forms in a blanketlike layer. (p. 122)

**streak** (strēk) The color of the powder left when a mineral is rubbed against a hard, rough surface. (p. 322)

**strip farming** (strip fär′ming) Trapping runoff by alternating tightly growing grasses with more widely spaced plants. (p. 341)

**surveyor** (sər vā′ər) A specialist who makes accurate measurements of Earth's crust. (p. 307)

**suspension** (sə spen′shən) Mixtures in which suspended particles can easily be seen. (p. 249)

**synoptic weather map** (si nop′tik we<u>th</u>′ər map) A type of map showing a summary of the weather using station models. (p. 156)

### T

**taproot** (tap′rüt′) A root that has few hairy branches and grows deep into the ground. (p. 20)

**tension** (ten′shən) A movement of plates that stretches or pulls apart Earth's crust. (p. 308)

**terracing** (ter′is ing) Shaping hillsides into steps so that runoff and eroded soil get trapped on the steps. (p. 341)

**thunder** (thun′dər) The noise caused by lightning-heated air during a thunderstorm. (p. 162)

**thunderhead** (thun′dər hed′) A cumulonimbus cloud in which a thunderstorm forms. (p. 162)

**thunderstorm** (thun′dər stôrm′) The most common severe storm, formed in cumulonimbus clouds. (p. 162)

**tidal power plant** (tī′dəl pou′ər plant) A factory where the flow of tidewater is used to make electricity. (p. 377)

**tissue** (tish′ü) A group of similar cells that work together at the same job. (p. 5)

**tornado** (tôr nā′dō) A violent whirling wind that moves across the ground in a narrow path. (p. 164)

**trachea** (trā′kē ə) A stiff tube lined with cartilage that transports air between the throat and lungs. (p. 401)

**trade winds** (trād windz) A belt of winds around Earth moving from high pressure zones toward the low pressure at the equator. (p. 139)

**transfusion** (trans fü′zhən) Taking blood from one person and giving it to another person. (p. 389)

**transpiration** (tran′spə rā′shən) The loss of water through a plant's leaves, which draws water up through the plant to replace it. (pp. 25, 113)

**tropism** (trō′piz′əm) A growth response of a plant toward or away from a stimulus. (p. 84)

**troposphere** (trop′ə sfîr′) The layer of the atmosphere closest to Earth's surface. (p. 104)

### U

**updraft** (up′draft′) An upward rush of heated air during a thunderstorm. (p. 162)

**urea** (yu̇ rē′ə) A substance formed from waste material in the liver and excreted in urine. (p. 414)

**ureter** (yu̇ rē′tər) One of two long, narrow tubes that carry urine from the kidneys to the bladder. (p. 414)

**urethra** (yu̇ rē′thrə) The tube through which urine passes from the body. (p. 414)

### V

**valley breeze** (val′ē brēz) A cool wind that blows up a mountain slope and replaces the slope's rising Sun-warmed air. (p. 137)

**variable** (vâr′ē ə bəl) One of the changes in a situation that may affect the outcome of an experiment. (p. 35)

**vascular** (vas′kyə lər) Containing plant tissue through which water moves up and food moves down. (p. 7)

**vein** (vān) A blood vessel that carries blood toward the heart. (p. 388)

**villus** (vil′əs) *n., pl.* **villi** (vil′ī) One of many tiny fingerlike projections in the small intestine that absorb digested food. (p. 413)

**volume** (vol′ūm) A measure of how much space an object takes up. (p. 196)

---

### PRONUNCIATION KEY

a **at**; ā **ape**; ä **far**; âr **care**; e **end**; ē **me**; i **it**; ī **ice**; îr **pierce**; o **hot**; ō **old**; ô **fork**; oi **oil**; ou **out**; u **up**; ū **use**; ü **rule**; u̇ **pull**; ûr **turn**; hw **white**; ng **song**; th **thin**; <u>th</u> **this**; zh **measure**; ə **about, taken, pencil, lemon, circus**

# W-X

**warm front** (wôrm frunt) A front where warm air moves in over a cold front. (p. 152)

**water cycle** (wô'tər sī'kəl) The continuous movement of water between Earth's surface and the air, changing from liquid to gas to liquid. (pp. 127, 362)

**waterspout** (wô'tər spout') A tornado that forms over water. (p. 165)

**water table** (wô'tər tā'bəl) The top of the water-filled spaces in the ground. (p. 363)

**water vapor** (wô'tər vā'pər) Water in the form of a gas. (p. 112)

**weather** (we<u>th</u>'ər) What the lower atmosphere is like at any given place and time. (p. 106)

**weathering** (we<u>th</u>'ər ing) Breaking down rocks into smaller pieces. (p. 311)

**weight** (wāt) The force of gravity between Earth and an object. (p. 197)

**well** (wel) A hole dug below the water table that water seeps into. (p. 363)

**wet cell battery** (wet sel bat'ə rē) A battery that uses a chemical solution to produce electricity. (p. 282)

**wind** (wind) Air that moves horizontally. (p. 136)

**wind vane** (wind vān) A device that indicates wind direction. (p. 142)

**xylem** (zī'ləm) The tissue through which water and minerals move up through a plant. (p. 20)

GLOSSARY

# INDEX

*Indicates an activity related to this topic.

**INDEX**

    *Indicates an activity related to this topic.

**INDEX**

*Indicates an activity related to this topic.

**INDEX**

# CREDITS

**Maps:** Geosystems

**Transvision:** Richard Hutchings (photography, TP1); Guy Porfirio (illustration)

**Illustrations:** Denny Bond: pp. 33; Ka Botzis: pp. 406, 420-421; Barbara Cousins: pp. 203, 388, 390-391, 413, 416, 426; Marie Dauenheimer: pp. 4, 5; Drew-Brook-Cormack: pp. 116, 123; John Edwards: pp. 197, 200, 203, 292; Peter Fasolino: pp. 237, 250; Thomas Gagliano: pp. 134-135, 137; Greg Harris: pp. 151, 181; Virge Kask: pp. 10, 70, 72-74, 76-77; George Kelvin: pp. 24, 32, 35, 50-52, 83, 85-86, 93, 298, 307-308, 313, 337, 339, 350-351, 362-363, 374; Katie Lee: pp. 32, 54; Rebecca Merrilees: pp. 20-23, 37-38, 49; Dave Merrill: pp. 299, 309; Mowry Graphics: pp. 126, 150, 185; Steve Oh: pp. 393, 400, 401, 412, 414; Saul Rosenbaum: pp. 96, 102-103, 114, 125, 136, 152, 162-163, 165, 183; Wendy Smith: pp. 6, 8-9, 60, 62; Steve Stankiewicz: pp. 114, 138, 148-149, 156, 161, 165, 169, 174, 185, 230, 236, 238, 246, 254, 272, 275, 277, 282-284, 320-321, 342, 361, 366, 372, R13, R15, R18-R20; Art Thompson: pp. 100, 140, 166, 178, 180, 188, 199, 203, 245-247, 252, 296-297.

**Photography Credits:** All photographs are by Richard Hutchings Photography except as noted below:

TOC: iii: images copyright ©1998 PhotoDisc, Inc. iv: NASA/Digital Stock. v: Digital Stock. vi: ©Cabisco/VU. vii: NASA/Digital Stock. viii: ©John D. Cunningham/VU. ix: Ken Eward/Science Source/Photo Researchers, Inc. S2, S3: ©David M. Sanders; S4: *t.r.* J.A. Kraulis/Masterfile; *b.r.* Antman/The Image Works; *bkmk.* Tom & Pat Leeson/Photo Researchers, Inc. S5: David Mager. S6: *t.l., t.m.* Michael P. Gadomski/Photo Researchers, Inc.; *t.r.* Gregory K. Scott/Photo Researchers, Inc.; *b.l.* Michael Quintonings/National Geographic Society; *b.m.* Richard Megna/Fundamental Photographs; *b.r.* Paul Silverman/Fundamental Photographs. S7: Culver Pictures. S9: Gary Braasch/Woodfin Camp & Assoc. S10: *b.l.* Michael Quintonings/National Geographic Society; S11: Linde Waidhofer/Liaison International. S12: *l.* Jan Halaska/Photo Researchers, Inc. S14: *t.m.* Richard Hutchings/PhotoEdit; *b.m.* Polecat. S15: Joyce Photographics/Photo Researchers, Inc. S16: *t.r.* Ken N. Johns/Photo Researchers, Inc.; *b.* Sandra Baker/Liaison International. S17: Courtesy Tree Musketeers. **Unit 1** 1: *bkgnd.* Zig Leszcynski/Animals Animals; *inset* Bryan Reinhart/Masterfile. 2: *l.* Allsport/Rick Stewart; *r.* Jerry Wachter/Photo Researchers, Inc. 4: Peter Miller/Photo Researchers, Inc. 5: ©Dick Thomas/VU. 7: ©Jeff J. Daly/VU. 11: *l.* ©Veronika Burmeister/VU; *m.* ©Doug Sokell/VU; *r.* R.M. Meadows/Peter Arnold, Inc. 12: *t.l.* Patrick W. Grace/Science Source/Photo Researchers, Inc.; *b.l.* Gilbert S. Grant/Photo Researchers, Inc.; *l.m.* ©Veronika Burmeister/VU; *r.* ©R. Kessel-G. Shih/VU; *r.m.* ©Cabisco/VU. 13: *t.l.* Phil Degginger/Color-Pic; *b.l.* ©R. Robinson/VU; *t.r.* Blair Seitz/Photo Researchers, Inc.; *b.r.* ©VU. 14: *l.* ©Arthur R. Hill/VU; *r.* ©R.F. Ashley/VU. 16: *l.* Dr. Dennis Kunkel/PhotoTake; r. Gregory Ochocki/Photo Researchers, Inc. 17: D.P. Wilson/Eric & David Hosking/Photo Researchers, Inc. 18: *m.l.* ©George Herben/VU; *m.r.* ©Ken Lucas/VU; *b.r.* ©Arthur Morris/VU. 25: G. Buttner/OKAPIA/Photo Researchers, Inc. 26: *l.* ©David S. Addison/VU; *r.* ©Tim Hauf/VU. 27: James R. Holland/National Geographic Society. 28: *bkgnd.* J.C. Teyssier/Publiphoto/Photo Researchers, Inc.; *b.* Tom & Pat Leeson/Photo Researchers, Inc. 30: *l., r.* images copyright ©1998 PhotoDisc, Inc.; *m.* Michael P. Gadomski/Photo Researchers, Inc. 34: ©John Gerlach/VU. 36: ©Jack M. Bostrack/VU. 39: Gerry Ellis/ENP Photography. 40: *bkgnd.* ©Doug Sokell/VU; *b.* Michael P. Gadomski/Photo Researchers, Inc. 41: *t.* ©Ned Therrien/VU; *b.* ©David M. Philips/VU. 42: images copyright ©1998 PhotoDisc, Inc. 43: *bkgnd.* ©TSM/David D. Keaton; *inset* ©TSM/Charles Krebs. 44: ©Tim Hauf/VU. 46: *l.* ©Doug Sokell/VU; *m.* ©John Trager/VU. 47: *l.* ©Bill Beatty/VU; *r.* ©David Sieren/VU; *t.r.* ©Fritz Polking/VU; *b.r.* ©E.F. Anderson/VU. 48: *l.* Dan Suzio/Photo Researchers, Inc. 49: ©David Sieren/VU. 52: ©Dick Keen/VU. 53: George Haling/Photo Researchers, Inc. 56: *l.* Bonnie Sue/Photo Researchers, Inc.; *r.* Peter Skinner/Photo Researchers, Inc. 58: *l.* ©Jim Hughes/VU; *m.* ©VU; *r.* ©Gerald & Buff Corsi/VU. 59: *t.* ©E. Webber/VU; *b.l.* ©John N. Trager/VU; *b.r.* V.P. Weinland/Photo Researchers, Inc. 60: *t.* ©V. McMillan/VU; *b.* ©TSM/Dick Keen. 61: *t.* ©E.F. Anderson/VU; *b.* ©Bud Nielsen/VU. 63: *t.* ©Mark S. Skalny/VU; *b.* ©Arthur R. Hill/VU. 64: *l.* ©John Gerlach/VU; *r.* Jerome Wexler/Photo Researchers, Inc. 65: Alan & Linda Detrick/Photo Researchers, Inc. 66: *bkgnd.* Richard R. Hansen/Photo Researchers, Inc.; Dennis Fagan/Lady Bird Johnson Wildflower Center. 68: *t.* Dr. Jeremy Burgess/Photo Researchers, Inc.; *b.* Gunter Ziesler/Peter Arnold, Inc. 71: *t.* ©Derrick Ditchburn/VU; *m.* ©Doug Sokell/VU; *b.* Adam Jones/Photo Researchers, Inc. 74: R.C. Carpenter/Photo Researchers, Inc. 75: *l.* ©Inga Spence/VU; *m.* ©Ken Wagner/VU; *r.* ©Stephen J. Lang/VU. 79: Kenneth W. Fink/Photo Researchers, Inc. 80: *bkgnd.* Runk/Schoenberger/Grant Heilman Photography, Inc; *t.* Bill Gillette/Stock, Boston; *b.* Jeff Greenberg/PhotoEdit. 81: Emil Muench/Photo Researchers, Inc. 82: *l.* George & Judy Manna/Photo Researchers, Inc.; *r.* ©Mack Henley/VU. 84: ©David Newman/VU. 85: ©R. Calentine/VU. 87: ©Dick Keen/VU. 88: *t.* ©Parke H. John, Jr./VU; *b.* ©Bill Beatty/VU. 89: *b.l.* Steve Kaufman/Peter Arnold, Inc.; *t, b.r.* ©Stan W. Elems/VU. 90: *l.* ©Joe McDonald/VU; *m.* ©Arthur Morris/VU; *r.* ©Barbara Gerlach/VU. 91: Richard T. Nowitz/Corbis. 92: *bkgnd.* Brock May/Photo Researchers, Inc.; *t.* Joel Sartore/Grant Heilman Photography, Inc. **Unit 2** 97: *bkgnd.* ©Paul Chesley/TSI; *inset* images copyright ©1998 PhotoDisc, Inc. 98: *t.* ©Francis/Donna Caldwell/VU; *b.* ©Joe McDonald/VU. 106: *l., m.* Runk/Schoenberger/Grant Heilman Photography, Inc; *r.* Yoav Levy/Photo Researchers, Inc. 107: David Waitz. 108: Jay Smith/High and Wild Mt. Guides. 109: NASA/Corbis. 110: SuperStock. 112: Amy C. Etra/PhotoEdit. 115: Tony Freeman/PhotoEdit. 120: ©John Cunningham/VU. 122: *t.* ©A.J. Copley/VU; *m.* ©Henry W. Robison/VU; *b.* ©Mark A. Schneider/VU. 124: *l.* ©D. Cavagnaro/VU; *m.l.* ©W. Banaszewski/VU; *m.r.* ©Mark E. Gibson/VU; *r.* Layne Kennedy/Corbis. 125: Peter Turnley/Corbis. 128: Runk/Schoenberger/Grant Heilman Photography, Inc. 129: ©TSM/Aaron Rezney. 130: *bkgnd.* Digital Stock. 131: Sean Sexton Collection/Corbis. 132: David G. Houser/Corbis. 136: Superstock. 137: ©TSM/Torleif Svensson. 139: NASA. 142: *t.l.* ©Deneve Feigh Bunde/VU; *t.r.* ©Tom Edwards/VU; *b.l.* ©Mark E. Gibson/VU; *b.r.* ©Science VU. 144: *bkgnd.* Carl Purcell/Photo Researchers, Inc. 145: Tiziana and Gianni Baldizzone/Corbis. 147: *bkgnd.* ©Ed Degginger/Bruce Coleman, Inc./PNI; *inset* ©Gene Moore/PhotoTake/PNI. 148: images copyright ©1998 PhotoDisc, Inc. 154: *m.* NASA; *b.l., b.r.* ©1998 AccuWeather, Inc. 155: ©1998 AccuWeather, Inc. 157: ©TSM/David Stoecklei. 158: *b. bkgnd.* NASA; *t.l.* Paul Seheult/Eye Ubiquitous/Corbis; *t.r.* images copyright ©1998 PhotoDisc, Inc.; *b.r.* Corbis-Bettmann. 159: *t.l.* National Weather Service/AP/Wide World; *t.r.* NASA/AP/Wide World. 160: ©VU. 163: ©Nada Pencik/VU. 165: ©Gene Moore/PhotoTake. 167: ©Science VU. 168: Carlos Guerrero. 169: *bkgnd.* ©Marc Epstein/VU; *inset* ©Mark A. Schneider/VU. 170: *bkgnd.* ©R.F. Meyers/VU. 172: *t.* Keith Kent/Peter Arnold, Inc. 173: Carlos Guerrero. 176: *t.l.* ©TSM/Carlos Humberto; *t.r.* ©Martin G. Miller/VU; *b.l.* ©TSM/Strauss/Curtis; *b.r.* ©TSM/Torleif Svensson. 184: *l.* ©Science VU; *r.* ©VU. 185: Steve Kaufman/Peter Arnold, Inc. 186: *t.* ©Don Smetzer/TSI; *b.* Jeff Greenberg/PhotoEdit. 187: Abraham Hondius/Bridgeman Art Library Intl. Ltd. **Unit 3** 193: *bkgnd.* ©Yoav Levy/PhotoTake; *inset* images copyright ©1998 PhotoDisc. 194: Jonathon Blair/Corbis. 201: *t.l.* Klaus Guldbrandsen/Science Photo Library/Photo Researchers, Inc.; *t.r.* George Bernard/Photo Researchers, Inc.; *m.l.* The Purcell Team/Corbis; *m.r.* Vaughan Fleming/Science Photo Library/Photo Researchers, Inc.; *b.l.* Buddy Mays/Corbis; *b.r.* Wolfgang Kaehler/Corbis. 203: Walter Meayers Edwards. 204: *t.* Ed Degginger/Color-Pic, Inc.; *m., b.* Phil Degginger/Color-Pic, Inc. 206: *t.* IBM Research/Peter Arnold, Inc.; *b.* ©National Railway of Japan/PhotoTake. 207: images copyright ©1998 PhotoDisc, Inc. 208, 209: Stephen Frink/Southern Stock/PNI. 210: NASA. 212: *t.* Lowell Georgia/Photo Researchers, Inc.; *b.* Rich Treptow/Photo Researchers, Inc. 213: *t.l.* ©Science/VU; *t.r., m., b.l., b.r.,* Charles D. Winters/Photo Researchers, Inc.; *m.l.* Russ Lappa/Science Source/Photo Researchers, Inc. 214: *t.l.* Runk/Schoenberger/Grant Heilman Photography, Inc.; *f.b.r.* ©Bill Beatty/VU; *b.m.* ©Yoav Levy/PhotoTake; *b.l. & b.r.* images copyright ©1998 PhotoDisc, Inc. 215: David Taylor/Photo Researchers, Inc. 216: *t.* IBM Research/Peter Arnold, Inc.; *b.* ©Science VU/BMRL. 218: *f.t.l., f.t.r.* E.R. Degginger/Color-Pic, Inc.; *t.l.* George Bernard/Photo Researchers, Inc.; *t.m., t.r.* Klaus Guldbrandsen/Photo Researchers, Inc.; *m.* Rich Treptow/Photo Researchers, Inc.; *b.l.* Charles D. Winters/Photo Researchers, Inc.; *b.r.* Russ Lappa/Photo Researchers, Inc. 222: *t.l.* Christine Coscioni/CO2, Inc; *t.r.* Leonard Lessin/Peter Arnold, Inc.; *b.l.* ©API/VU. 223: Christine Coscioni/CO2, Inc. 224: *l.* ©Gilbert L. Twiest/VU; *r.* Joe Sohm/Chromosohm/Stock, Boston. 225: images copyright ©1998 PhotoDisc, Inc. 226: ©Javier Domingo/PhotoTake. 228: *l.* Gordon Wiltsie/Peter Arnold, Inc.; *m.* Clyde H. Smith/Peter Arnold, Inc.; *r.* Jeff & Alexa Henry/Peter Arnold, Inc. 229: Cesar Llacuna. 232: *t.* ©Jakub Jasinski/VU; *b.l.* ©Kjell B. Sandved/VU; *b.r.* Darrell Gulin/Corbis. 234: *t.l.* ©Carolina Biological Supply/PhotoTake; *t.r.* Cesar Llacuna; *m.* Christine L. Coscioni/CO2, Inc; *b.* Charles D. Winters/Photo Researchers, Inc. 236: *t.* ©TSM/Mugshots; *b.* ©TSM/Chris Rogers. 237: Richard Choy/Peter Arnold, Inc. 238: Rod Plack/Photo Researchers, Inc. 241: ©TSM/Mark M. Lawrence. 242: *l.* Mark Marten/Science Source/Photo Researchers, Inc.; *r.* Alex S. MacLean/Peter Arnold, Inc. 244: *r.* Jacana/Photo Researchers, Inc. 248: *t.* Charles D. Winters/Photo Researchers, Inc. 249: *t.r.* Gordon Wiltsie/Peter Arnold, Inc.; *b.* ©Artville LLC 1997. 250: *t.* M.I. Walker/Photo Researchers, Inc.; *b.* ©S. Strickland/Naturescapes/VU. 252: *t.* ©SIU/VU; *b.* ©Mark E. Gibson/VU. 253: Michael Newman/Poto Edit. 254: Larry Lefever/Grant Heilman Photography, Inc. 255: *t.* ©David S. Addison/VU; *b.* David R. Frazier /Photo Researchers, Inc. 256: *l.* NASA; *r.* ©Doug Sokell/VU. 259: *b.l.* Phil Degginger/Color-Pic, Inc.; *b.r.* ©A.J. Copley/VU. 261: *t.* Christine Coscioni/CO2, Inc; *b.* Cesar Llacuna. 263: Lee Snyder/Photo Researchers, Inc. 264: *l.* NASA; *m.* Christine L. Coscioni/CO2, Inc.; *inset* ©Science/VU; *r., inset* Leonard Lessin/Peter Arnold, Inc. 266: *t.* ©TSM/Roger Ball; *b.* ©Science/VU. 267: Craig Lovell/Corbis. 269: *l.* ©John D. Cunningham/VU; *r.* Geoff Bryant/Photo Researchers, Inc. 270: Jeff Rotman. 272: E.R. Degginger/Color-Pic, Inc. 273: *l.* Leonard Lessin/Peter Arnold, Inc. 275: Ed Young/Corbis. 277: *r.* images copyright ©1998 PhotoDisc, Inc. 278: *l.* Andrew McClenaghan/Photo Researchers, Inc.; *r.* ©Science/VU. 279: *l.* Richard Hamilton Smith/Corbis. 282: Runk/Schoenberger/Grant Heilman Photography, Inc. **Unit 4** 289: © Nathan Bilow/TSI. 290: © NASA/PhotoTake. 294: *t.* Blocker Collections/UT Medical Branch. 295: Mehau Kulyk/Photo Researchers, Inc. 300: *t.* World Perspectives/Explorer/Photo Researchers, Inc.; *b.l., b.r. bkgnd.* NASA; *b.* ©Science/VU. 301: Jim Zipp/Photo Researchers, Inc. 302: *t.l, t.r.* NASA/JPL/Caltech; *b.l.* NASA; *b.r.* NASA/JPL. 304: *l.* ©Science/VU; *r.* David Parker/Science Photo Library/Photo Researchers, Inc. 306: *l.* Sinclair Stammers/Science Photo Library/Photo Researchers, Inc.; *r.* ©John D. Cunningham/VU. 309: *l.* Dr. E.R. Degginger/Color-Pic, Inc.; *r.* ©Stella Snead/Bruce Coleman, Inc. 310: *l.* Jerry Schad/Photo Researchers, Inc.; *m.* Robert Godwin/National Audubon Society/Photo Researchers, Inc.; *r.* Jim Steinberg/Photo Researchers, Inc. 311: *t.* ©Steve McCutcheon/VU; *b.* Gilbert Grant/Photo Researchers, Inc. 312: *l.* Renee Lynn/Photo Researchers, Inc.; *r.* ©Albert J. Copley/VU. 313: Terranova International/Photo Researchers, Inc. 314: *t.* David Scharf/Peter Arnold, Inc.; *m.* Bruce Coleman, Inc.; *b.* ©NASA/PhotoTake. 315: NASA/Science Photo Library/Photo Researchers, Inc. 316: *bkgnd.* Dave Bartruff/Stock, Boston; *b.* ©Mark Mellett/Stock, Boston. 317: *l.* Annie Griffiths Belt/Corbis; *r.* Morton Beebe-S.F./Corbis. 318: *l.* Joyce Photographics/Photo Researchers, Inc.; *r.* Tom McHugh/Photo Researchers, Inc. 320: *t.l.* Joyce Photographics/Photo Researchers, Inc.; *m.l.* E.R. Degginger/Photo Researchers, Inc.; *b.l.* Cesar Llacuna; *m.* Charles D. Winters/Timeframe Photography Inc./Photo Researchers, Inc.; *r.* George Whiteley/Photo Researchers, Inc. 321: *t.l.* Roberto De Gugliemo/Science Photo

# PERIODIC TABLE OF THE ELEMENTS

Atomic Number (number of protons) — 1
Symbol — **H**
Element — Hydrogen
State of Matter

**1**

| 1 | 2 | 3 | 4 | 5 | 6 | 7 | 8 | 9 |
|---|---|---|---|---|---|---|---|---|

**1** 1 **H** Hydrogen

**2** 3 **Li** Lithium | 4 **Be** Beryllium

**3** 11 **Na** Sodium | 12 **Mg** Magnesium

**4** 19 **K** Potassium | 20 **Ca** Calcium | 21 **Sc** Scandium | 22 **Ti** Titanium | 23 **V** Vanadium | 24 **Cr** Chromium | 25 **Mn** Manganese | 26 **Fe** Iron | 27 **Co** Cobalt

**5** 37 **Rb** Rubidium | 38 **Sr** Strontium | 39 **Y** Yttrium | 40 **Zr** Zirconium | 41 **Nb** Niobium | 42 **Mo** Molybdenum | 43 **Tc** Technetium | 44 **Ru** Ruthenium | 45 **Rh** Rhodium

**6** 55 **Cs** Cesium | 56 **Ba** Barium | 57 **La** Lanthanum | 72 **Hf** Hafnium | 73 **Ta** Tantalum | 74 **W** Tungsten | 75 **Re** Rhenium | 76 **Os** Osmium | 77 **Ir** Iridium

**7** 87 **Fr** Francium | 88 **Ra** Radium | 89 **Ac** Actinium | 104 **Rf** Rutherfordium | 105 **Db** Dubnium | 106 **Sg** Seaborgium | 107 **Bh** Bohrium | 108 **Hs** Hassium | 109 **Mt** Meitnerium

**The Most Reactive Metals**

**Lanthanide Series**

58 **Ce** Cerium | 59 **Pr** Praseodymium | 60 **Nd** Neodymium | 61 **Pm** Promethium | 62 **Sm** Samarium | 63 **Eu** Europium

**Actinide Series**

90 **Th** Thorium | 91 **Pa** Protactinium | 92 **U** Uranium | 93 **Np** Neptunium | 94 **Pu** Plutonium | 95 **Am** Americium

## In the Classroom

- Read all of the directions. Make sure you understand them. When you see ▨, be sure to follow the safety rule.

- Listen to your teacher for special safety directions. If you don't under-stand something, ask for help.

- Wash your hands with soap and water before an activity.

- Wear safety goggles when your teacher tells you to wear them and whenever you see 🥽. Wear them when working with anything that can fly into your eyes.

- Wear splash-proof goggles when working with liquids.

- Wear a safety apron if you work with anything messy or anything that might spill.

- If you spill something, wipe it up right away or ask your teacher for help.

- Tell your teacher if something breaks. If glass breaks do not clean it up yourself.

- Keep your hair and clothes away from open flames. Tie back long hair and roll up long sleeves.

- Be careful around a hot plate. Know when it is on and when it is off. Remember that the plate stays hot for a few minutes after you turn it off.

- Keep your hands dry around electrical equipment.

- Don't eat or drink anything during an experiment.

- Put equipment back the way your teacher tells you.

- Dispose of things the way your teacher tells you.

- Clean up your work area, and wash your hands with soap and water.

## In the Field

- Always be accompanied by a trusted adult—like your teacher or a parent or guardian.

- Never touch animals or plants without the adult's approval. The animal might bite. The plant might be poison ivy or another dangerous plant.

## Responsibility

- Treat living things, the environment, and each other with respect.